Lecture Notes in Artificial Intelligence   7080

Subseries of Lecture Notes in

LNAI Series Editors

Randy Goebel
  University of Alberta, Edmonton, Canada
Yuzuru Tanaka
  Hokkaido University, Sapporo, Japan
Wolfgang Wahlster
  DFKI and Saarland University, Saarbrücken, Germany

LNAI Founding Series Editor

Joerg Siekmann
  DFKI and Saarland University, Saarbrücken, Germany

Chattrakul Sombattheera   Arun Agarwal
Siba K. Udgata   Kittichai Lavangnananda (Eds.)

Multi-disciplinary Trends
in Artificial Intelligence

5th International Workshop, MIWAI 2011
Hyderabad, India, December 7-9, 2011
Proceedings

 Springer

Series Editors

Randy Goebel, University of Alberta, Edmonton, Canada
Jörg Siekmann, University of Saarland, Saarbrücken, Germany
Wolfgang Wahlster, DFKI and University of Saarland, Saarbrücken, Germany

Volume Editors

Chattrakul Sombattheera
Mahasarakham University
Khamreang, Kantarawichai, Mahasarakham, Thailand
E-mail: chattrakul.s@msu.ac.th

Arun Agarwal
University of Hyderabad
Hyderabad, Andhra Pradesh, India
E-mail: aruncs@uohyd.ernet.in

Siba K. Udgata
University of Hyderabad
Hyderabad, Andhra Pradesh, India
E-mail: udgatacs@uohyd.ernet.in

Kittichai Lavangnananda
King Mongkut's University of Technology
Thonburi, Bangkok, Thailand
E-mail: kitt@sit.kmutt.ac.th

ISSN 0302-9743   e-ISSN 1611-3349
ISBN 978-3-642-25724-7   e-ISBN 978-3-642-25725-4
DOI 10.1007/978-3-642-25725-4
Springer Heidelberg Dordrecht London New York

Library of Congress Control Number: Applied for

CR Subject Classification (1998): I.2, H.3, H.4, F.1, C.2, I.4

LNCS Sublibrary: SL 7 – Artificial Intelligence

Typesetting: Camera-ready by author, data conversion by Scientific Publishing Services, Chennai, India

Printed on acid-free paper

Springer is part of Springer Science+Business Media (www.springer.com)

Preface

This LNCS/LNAI volume contains papers presented at the 5th Multi-Disciplinary International Workshop on Artificial Intelligence, MIWAI-2011 (http://khamreang. msu.ac.th/miwai11/) held during December 7–9, 2011, at the University of Hyderabad, India. The earlier four versions of MIWAI (known as Mahasarakham International Workshop on Artificial Intelligence (http://khamreang.msu.ac.th/ miwai10/)) were organized at the Faculty of Informatics, Mahasarakham University, Thailand. It was decided that MIWAI ought to reach out beyond Thailand to mutually benefit contributions from the Asia-Pacific Region and the rest of the world.

This workshop aimed to be a meeting place where excellence in AI research meets the needs for solving dynamic and complex problems in the real world. The academic researchers, developers, and industrial practitioners had extensive opportunities to present their original work, technological advances and practical problems. Participants were able to learn from each other and exchange their experiences in order to finetune their activities and provide help to each other. The main purposes of the MIWAI series of workshops are as follows:

- To provide a meeting place for AI researchers and practitioners to meet in a friendly and non-competitive atmosphere
- To inform research participants about cutting-edge AI research via the presence of outstanding international invited speakers
- To raise the standards of practice of AI research by providing participants with feedback from an internationally renowned Program Committee

MIWAI-2011 received around 71 full papers from 14 different countries spreading across 4 continents. The review process involved 163 reviews by as many as 77 reviewers, and was carried out with no specific target to what the number of accepted papers was to be. In the end, 38 papers were accepted as full-length papers for publication and oral presentation. We accepted only full length papers to enable detailed and fruitful discussions on these papers during the presentation. The acceptance rate was around 50%. Although this may seem high, judging by the quality of submissions this is justified. Some of the rejected papers indeed had potential, but were finally excluded in order to maintain the quality of the workshop. The accepted papers which are included in this volume cover the multifarious nature of the artificial intelligence research domain, ranging from theoretical to real-world applications.

The thrust areas of this workshop were agent-based simulation, agent-oriented software engineering, agents and Web services, agent-based electronic commerce, auctions and markets, AI in video games, computer vision, constraint satisfaction, data mining, decision theory, distributed AI, e-commerce and AI, game theory, Internet/WWW intelligence, industrial applications of AI, intelligent tutoring, knowledge representation and reasoning, machine learning, multi-agent planning and learning, multi-agent systems and their applications, multi-agent systems and evolving intelligence, natural language processing, neural networks, planning and scheduling, robotics, uncertainty in AI, and Web services

The workshop featured a keynote talk by B. Chandrasekaran, Professor Emeritus, Laboratory for Artificial Intelligence Research, Ohio State University, which focused on diagrammatic reasoning and imagination. The various invited talks by James F. Peters, from the Computational Intelligence Laboratory, University of Manitoba, Canada, Sheela Ramanna, Professor and Chair, Department of Applied Computer Science, University of Winnipeg, Canada, Ronald R. Yager, Director, Machine Intelligence, Iona College, USA, and Manish Gupta, Department of IBM Research, India enhanced the significance and contributions of MIWAI even more.

MIWAI-2011 also included two tutorials for the benefit of students and researchers. B. Yegnanarayana, Professor and Microsoft Chair, Speech and Vision Laboratory, IIIT Hyderabad, India, gave a tutorial on 'Introduction to Neural Networks' and Prof. M. N. Murty Dept. of CSA, IISc, Bangalore, India gave a tutorial on 'Knowledge-Based Information Retrieval'.

We gratefully acknowledge our sponsors IBM India, Locuz Enterprise Solutions Ltd, IDRBT and Winzest without whose support this workshop would have been impossible to organize. Their support was used to (a) plan and organize the meeting (b) ensure the participation of keynote and invited speakers, (c) facilitate student participation (by reducing their accommodation costs and, for some, travel costs), (d) publish this proceedings book, and (e) institute a best paper award.

We are grateful for the support of the Local Organizing Team and the army of volunteers to run the events in a coordinated way. We also wish to acknowledge our sincere appreciation for all the support extended by University of Hyderabad administration and staff members. The workshop website was developed, hosted and supported by Mahasarakham University and we record our appreciation for the developer team.

Last but not least, we wish to take this opportunity to thank all the authors of submitted papers for their interest in AI research and MIWAI 2011, adherence to the deadlines and patience with the review process. The quality of any refereed volume depends on the expertise and dedication of the reviewers. We are indebted to the Program Committee members and the external reviewers who not only produced excellent reviews but also completed it within the short time-frame.

Finally, all efforts and hard work would be rewarding and worthwhile if the readers find the papers in these proceedings inspiring and academically fruitful. The editorial board sincerely hopes that the previous statement is true.

December 2011

Chattrakul Sombattheera
Arun Agarwal
Siba K. Udgata
Kittichai Lavangnananda

Organization

Steering Committee

Members

Rajkumar Buyya	University of Melbourne, Australia
Jerome Lang	CNRS, Universite Paris-Dauphine, France
James Peters	University of Manitoba, Canada
Wirat Ponngsiri	Mahasarakham University, Thailand
Srinivasan Ramani	IIIT Bangalore, India
C. Raghavendra Rao	University of Hyderabad, India
Leon Van Der Torre	University of Luxembourg, Luxembourg

Conveners

Richard Booth	University of Luxembourg, Luxembourg
Chattrakul Sombattheera	Mahasarakham University, Thailand

General Co-chairs

Arun Agarwal	University of Hyderabad, India
Chattrakul Sombattheera	Mahasarakham University, Thailand

Program Co-chairs

Siba Udgata	University of Hyderabad, India
Kittichai Lavangnananda	KMUTT, Thailand

Publicity Committee

Tho Quan	Hochiminh City University of Technology, Vietnam
Alok Singh	University of Hyderabad, India
Rajeev Wanker	Univerisity of Hyderabad, India

Local Organizing Committee (University of Hyderabad)

H. Mohanty	S. Bapiraju	T. Shoba Rani
C.R. Rao	Atul Negi	K. Swarupa Rani
P.N. Girija	Rajeev Wankar	Y.V. Subba Rao
K.N. Murthy	S. Durga Bhavani	B. Wilson Naik
Chakravarthi	Alok Singh	P. Anupama

M. Nagamani   R.P. Lal   Vineet Nair
P.S.V.S. Sai Prasad   Rukma Rekha   Anjeneya Swami K.

Program Committee

Samir Aknine	Paris 6, France
S. Bapiraju	University of Hyderabad, India
Arun Agarwal	University of Hyderabad, India
Raj Bhatnagar	University of Cincinnati, USA
Laor Boongasame	Bangkok University, Thailand
Veera Boonjing	KMITL, Bangkok
Richard Booth	University of Luxembourg, Luxembourg
Roger Boyle	University of Leeds, UK
B. Chakravarthy	University of Hyderabad, India
Matthew Dailey	Asian Institute of Technology, Thailand
Chattrakul Sombattheera	Mahasarakham University, Thailand
Kittichai Lavangnananda	KMUTT, Thailand
B.L. Deekshatulu	Univerity of Hyderabad, India
Juergen Dix	Clausthal University of Technology, Germany
Patrick Doherty	Linköping University, Sweden
Andreas Herzig	Université Paul Sabatier, France
Sachio Hirokawa	University of Kyushu, Japan
Sarun Intakosum	KMITL, Thailand
Jerome Lang	CNRS, Université Paris-Dauphine, France
Fangzhen Lin	Hong Kong University of Science and Technology, Hong Kong
Chidchanok Lursinsap	Chulalongkorn University, Thailand
Jerome Mengin	Université Paul Sabatier, France
Sheila Miller	United States Military Academy, USA
K.N. Murthy	University of Hyderabad, India
P. Nagabhushan	Mysore University, India
Ekawit Nantajeewarawat	SIIT, Thailand
Vineet Padmanabhan	University of Hyderabad, India
James F. Peters	University of Manitoba, Canada
Guilin Qi	Southeast University, Nanjing, China
Tho Quan	Hochiminh City University of Technology, Vietnam
C. Raghavendra Rao	University of Hyderabad, India
Siba Udgata	University of Hyderabad, India
Sheela Ramanna	University of Winnipeg, Canada
V. Ravi	IDRBT, India
Andre Rossi	Université de Bretagne-Sud, France

Samrat Sabat	University of Hyderabad, India
Lethanh Sach	Hochiminh City University of Technology, Vietnam
V.N. Sastry	IDRBT, India
Jun Shen	University of Wollongong, Australia
Alok Singh	University of Hyderabad, India
Virach Sornlertlamvanich	NECTEC, Thailand
Siriwan Suebnukarn	Thammasat University, Thailand
Boontawee Suntisrivaraporn	SIIT, Thailand
Leon van der Torre	University of Luxembourg, Luxembourg
Paul Weng	Université Paris 6, France

Reviewers

Alisa Kongthon
Andre Rossi
Arun Agarwal
B.N.B. Ray
Boontawee
    Suntisrivaraporn
Chidchanok Lursinsap
Ekawit Nantajeewarawat
Jakub Peksinski
Jun Shen
Laor Boongasame
Manas Ranjan Patra
Moumita Patra
Rajeev Wankar
Richard Booth
Samrat Sabat
Sateesh Pradhan
Shirshu Varma
Siriwan Suebnukarn
Suresh Chandra
    Satapathy
V. Ravi
Virach
    Sornlertlamvanich

Alok Singh
Andreas Herzig
Atul Negi
Bapi Raju S.
Chakravarthy Bhagvati
C. Raghavendra Rao
Guilin Qi
James Peters
K.N. Murthy
Layak Ali
Matthew Dailey
Panduranga
    Nagabhushan
Ramakanta Mohanty
S. Mini
Sarun Intakosum
Sheela Ramanna
Shivashankar S.
Sobha Rani T.
Tho Quan
Vasavi Janupudi
Vivek Singh
Amer Farea
Anurag Baghel

B.L. Deekshatulu
Bijay Panigrahi
Chattrakul
    Sombattheera
Durga Bhavani S.
Hrushikesha Mohanty
Jérôme Lang
Kittichai
    Lavangnananda
Leon Van Der Torre
Meghyn Bienvenu
Raj Bhatnagar
Ramanaiah O.B.V.
Sai Prasad P.S.V.S.
Sastry V.N.
Sheila Miller
Siba K. Udgata
Srinivas Sethi
Ujjwal Maulik
Vineet Padmanabhan
    Nair
Yannick Chevalier

Table of Contents

Associated Near Sets of Distance Functions in Pattern Analysis*

James F. Peters

Computational Intelligence Laboratory,
Department of Electrical & Computer Engineering, Univ. of Manitoba,
E1-526, 75A Chancellor's Circle, Winnipeg, MB R3T 5V6
jfpeters@ee.umanitoba.ca

Abstract. This paper introduces description-based associated sets of distance functions, where members are topological structures helpful in pattern analysis and machine intelligence. An associated set of a function is a collection containing members with one or more common properties. This study has important implications in discerning patterns shared by members of an associated set. The focus in this paper is on defining and characterising distance functions relative to structures that are collections of sufficiently near (far) neighbourhoods, filters, grills and clusters. Naimpally-Peters-Tiwari distance functions themselves define approach spaces that generalise the traditional notion of a metric space. An important side-effect of this work is the discovery of various patterns that arise from the descriptions (perceptions) of associated set members. An application of the proposed approach is given in the context of camouflaged objects.

Keywords: Apartness, approach space, associated set, Čech distance, cluster, collection, near sets, pattern analysis, topological structure.

1 Introduction

The focus of this paper is on associated sets of distance functions that provide a basis for pattern analysis and machine intelligence. New forms of near sets (see, e.g., [1–7]) are a direct byproduct of the proposed approach to associated sets. Briefly, an *associated set of a function* is a collection containing members with at least one common property such as nearness or apartness (see, *e.g.*, [8–11]). In an associated set with members with the nearness property, the members are similar to each other. By contrast, in an associated set with the apartness property, the members are dissimilar (not near). By experimenting with different

---
* Many thanks to S. Tiwari, S. Naimpally, C.J. Henry & S. Ramanna for their insights concerning topics in this paper. I also want to offer a special tribute to Prof. Dr. M. Khare for her work on grill-determined spaces, *L*-merotopies, and *L*-contiguities. This research has been supported by the Natural Sciences and Engineering Research Council of Canada (NSERC) grant 185986, Manitoba NCE MCEF grant, Canadian Arthritis Network grant SRI-BIO-05.

C. Sombattheera et al. (Eds.): MIWAI 2011, LNAI 7080, pp. 1–13, 2011.

distance functions D, for example, we can learn which distance function yields the largest associated set of D and facilitate discovery of patterns.

Traditionally, a distance function is classified in terms of the properties of a Frechét metric space [12]. A distance function $d : X \times X \to \mathbb{R}$ satisfying all of the properties of a Frechét space is called a **metric**, i.e., for all $x, y \in \mathbb{R}$, d satisfies metric space properties, namely, *non-negativity* $(d(x, y) \geq 0)$, *separateness* $(d(x, y) = 0 \Leftrightarrow x = y)$, *symmetry* $(d(x, y) = d(y, x))$, and *triangle inequality* $(d(x, y) \leq d(x, z) + d(z, y))$ [12, 13]. The notion of a metric space gives rise to the notion of nearness of points and sets [7, §1.2]. This paper considers associated sets of distance functions that define approach spaces [14] and provide generalisations of Frechét metric spaces (this will be explained in the sequel).

Members of associated sets of a distance function provide a means of defining and characterising approach distance functions. Pairs of topological structures such as filters, grills and clusters form an associated set, provided the structures are *sufficiently near* to (or *sufficiently apart* from) each other. Patterns among members of an associated set are discovered by considering the distance between feature vectors that provide descriptions of associated set members. On a higher level, one can look across distinct associated sets and consider patterns that arise from descriptions of members of the associated sets. Obviously, associated sets $\mathcal{E}_1, \mathcal{E}_2$ are near, provided $\mathcal{E}_1, \mathcal{E}_2$ are not disjoint, i.e., $\mathcal{E}_1, \mathcal{E}_2$ have one or more members in common so that $\mathcal{E}_1 \cap \mathcal{E}_2 \neq \varnothing$. By the same token, associated sets will be far from each other, provided the descriptions of pairs of members of $A \in \mathcal{E}_1, B \in \mathcal{E}_2$ are sufficiently apart, i.e., for a distance function $\rho : \mathcal{P}(X) \times \mathcal{P}(X) \to (0, \infty]$ such that $\rho(\{A\}, \{B\}) > \varepsilon$ for $\varepsilon \in (0, \infty]$.

The notions of sufficiently near and sufficiently apart leads to the introduction of associated near sets of a distance function (see Sect. 2). Let $E_\varepsilon(\rho), E'_\varepsilon(\rho)$ denote a pair of associated sets of distance function ρ. Next, let $E_\varepsilon(D_d)$ be an associated set of distance function D_d. Then $E_\varepsilon(\rho), E'_\varepsilon(\rho) \in E_\varepsilon(D_d)$, provided $D_d(A, B) < \varepsilon$, i.e., $A \in E_\varepsilon(\rho), B \in E'_\varepsilon(\rho)$ are sufficiently near. The function D_d is the Čech distance between nonempty sets [15], i.e.,

$$D_d(A, B) = \inf \{d(a, b) : a \in A, b \in B\},$$

where $d(a, b) = |a - b|$ is the standard distance between points a, b. This, in turn, means that $E_\varepsilon(\rho), E'_\varepsilon(\rho)$ are near, provided its members are near. This leads to a new associated set, namely,

$$E_\varepsilon(D_d) = \{E_\varepsilon(\rho), E'_\varepsilon(\rho)\}.$$

where a pair of associated sets $E_\varepsilon(\rho), E'_\varepsilon(\rho)$ are members of the new associated set $E_\varepsilon(D_d)$. Such an associated can include two or more near sets.

An important part of this paper on associated sets is a consideration of the work by M. Katětov [16] and S. Tiwari [17] on merotopic spaces. M. Katětov observed that merotopic spaces are obtained by topologising certain parts of a nonempty set. The term *mero* comes from the Greek word *meros* (part). Historically, a consideration of merotopic distance starts with a study of approach spaces (see, e.g., [14, 17, 18]). Usually, an approach space distance function $\delta : X \times \mathcal{P}(X) \longrightarrow [0, \infty]$ maps a member of a set and a subset (part) of a set to a number in $[0, \infty]$. Recently, a generalised approach space X has been introduced [4, 5] such that a structure on X is determined by a distance function $\rho : \mathcal{P}(X) \times \mathcal{P}(X) \longrightarrow [0, \infty]$ that maps a pair of nonempty sets to a number in $[0, \infty]$.

In its most basic form, an approach merotopy is a measure of the nearness of members of a collection. For collections $\mathcal{A}, \mathcal{B} \in \mathcal{P}^2(X)$, a function $\nu : \mathcal{P}^2(X) \times \mathcal{P}^2(X) \longrightarrow [0, \infty]$ satisfying a number of properties is a called an ε-approach merotopy. A pair of collections are near, provided $\nu(\mathcal{A}, \mathcal{B}) = 0$. For $\varepsilon \in (0, \infty]$, the pair $\mathcal{A}, \mathcal{B}$ are *sufficiently near*, provided $\nu(\mathcal{A}, \mathcal{B}) < \varepsilon$. In this work, a determination of nearness and sufficient nearness results from considering the distance between descriptions of sets of objects to determine the *perceived* similarity or dissimilarity of the sets. A consideration of descriptive forms of *sufficient nearness* has considerable practical significance, since the distance between most collections of sets in science, engineering, and the arts is usually not zero (the descriptions of such collections of subsets are seldom identical). In addition, the search for patterns among objects of interest leads to associated sets of approach merotopies. The main contribution of this paper is the study of patterns found in near sets such as near clusters that are members of associated sets of distance functions, *e.g.*, near sets that are camouflaged objects or digital images from remote sensors.

2   Preliminaries

This section introduces lower and upper associated sets. Let X be a nonempty ordinary set. The collection of all subsets of X is denoted by $\mathcal{P}(X)$ and collections of subsets of $\mathcal{P}(X)$ is denoted by $\mathcal{P}^2(X)$. In keeping with an interest in the distance between nonempty sets, start with subsets $A, B \in \mathcal{P}(X)$. Let $\rho(a, b)$ be the standard distance between $a \in A, b \in B$ and let $D_\rho : \mathcal{P}(X) \times \mathcal{P}(X) \longrightarrow [0, \infty]$ be the Čech distance [15] between A and B defined by

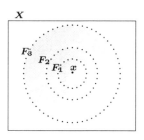

Fig. 1. Sample $E_\varepsilon(D_\rho)$

$$D_\rho(A, B) \doteq \begin{cases} \inf \{\rho(a, b) : a \in A, b \in B\}, & \text{if } A, B \neq \varnothing, \\ \infty, & \text{if } A \text{ or } B = \varnothing. \end{cases}$$

In the proposed approach to associated sets of a function, let X denote a nonempty set of objects (*e.g.*, digital images) of interest with subsets $A, B \in \mathcal{P}(X)$ and let $D(A, B)$. Then define the lower and upper associated sets of the Čech distance function D_ρ, where

$$E_\varepsilon(D_\rho) \doteq \{B \in \mathcal{P}(X) : D(A, B) < \varepsilon\} \text{ (\textbf{Lower Associated Set (LAS)}),}$$
$$E^\varepsilon(D_\rho) \doteq \{B \in \mathcal{P}(X) : D(A, B) \geq \varepsilon\} \text{ (\textbf{Upper Associated Set (UAS)}).}$$

Remark 1. **Sufficiently Near Sets**. The notion of *sufficiently near* appears in N. Bourbaki [19, §2, p. 19] in defining an open set, *i.e.*, a set A is open if, and only if, for each $x \in A$, all points *sufficiently near* x belong to A. Moreover, a property holds for all points sufficiently near $x \in A$, provided the property holds for all points in the neighbourhood of x. Set F_1 in Fig. 1 is an example of an open set represented by a dotted boundary. In fact, sets F_2, F_3 are also examples of open sets.

Bourbaki's original view of *sufficiently near* is now extended to members of a lower associated set (LAS), where, for example, the property *associated* holds for all members of a LAS, provided, for each $A \in E_\varepsilon(D_d)$, all members $B \in E_\varepsilon(D_\rho)$ are sufficiently near A. For example, the properties *similar shape* and *similar colour* also hold for the members of the LAS in Fig. 1 if, and only if, the descriptions of the members of X are sufficiently near (this is explained in Example 3).

Nonempty sets A, B that are considered *sufficiently near* each other if, and only if, $D(A, B) < \varepsilon$ for $\varepsilon \in (0, \infty]$. Otherwise, sets A, B are far, *i.e.*, *sufficiently apart*, provided $D_\rho(A, B) \geq \varepsilon$. In a more general setting, nearness and apartness are considered relative to the gap between collections $\mathcal{A}, \mathcal{B} \in \mathcal{P}^2(X)$ in an approach space [20] (see Sect. 5). The choice of a particular value of ε is application dependent and is typically determined by a domain expert.

Example 1. **Sample Lower Associated Set**. For small ε, the ascending subsets $F_1, F_2, F_3 \subset X$ in Fig. 1 are sufficiently near each other (*e.g.*, $D_\rho(F1, F2) < \varepsilon$, since $F_1 \subset F_2$). Hence, $E_\varepsilon(D_\rho) = \{F_1, F_2, F_3\}$.

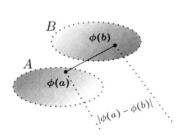

Fig. 2. $\rho(\phi(a), \phi(b))$

Pattern analysis is aided by considering the descriptions of members of associated sets. To see this, let $\Phi = \{\phi_1, \dots, \phi_i, \dots, \phi_n\}$ denote a set of probe functions, where $\phi_i : X :\to \mathbb{R}$. Feature vectors (vectors of probe function feature extracted from objects) provide a basis for set descriptions, *e.g.*, for pixels $a \in A, b \in B$ in Fig. 2, the standard distance between pixel descriptions is computed using $|\phi(a) - \phi(b)|$ for a single pixel feature represented by the probe ϕ. Then $|\Phi|$ equals the number probe functions in Φ. Let $\Phi_x = \{\phi_1(x), \dots, \phi_{|\Phi|}(x)\}, \Phi_y = \{\phi_1(y), \dots, \phi_{|\Phi|}(y)\}$ for the description of $x \in X, y \in Y$ and let $\Phi_X = \{\Phi_x : x \in X\}$ and $\Phi_Y = \{\Phi_y : y \in Y\}$ for the descriptions of sets X, Y, respectively. Then a description-based gap functional $D_{\rho_{\|\cdot\|}}$ is defined in terms of the Čech distance between set descriptions, where

$$D_{\rho_{\|\cdot\|}}(\Phi_X, \Phi_Y) = \begin{cases} \inf\{\rho_{\|\cdot\|}(\Phi_x, \Phi_y)\}, & \text{if } \Phi_X \text{ and } \Phi_Y \text{ are not empty,} \\ \infty, & \text{if } \Phi_X \text{ or } \Phi_Y \text{ is empty.} \end{cases}$$

The function $\rho_{\|\cdot\|} : \Phi_X \times \Phi_Y :\mapsto [0, \infty]$ is defined by

$$\rho_{\|\cdot\|}(\Phi_x, \Phi_y) = \sum_{i=1,n} |\phi_i(x) - \phi_i(y)| \text{ for } x \in X, y \in Y.$$

For $|\Phi| = 1$, put $\rho_{\|\cdot\|}(\phi(x), \phi(y)) = |\phi(x) - \phi(y)|$ for probe $\phi \in \Phi$.

Example 2. **Sample Distance Between Pixel Descriptions**. In Fig. 2, sets A, B represents parts of a digital image and $a \in A, b \in B$ represent pixels in A and B, respectively. Let ϕ denote a probe used to extract a feature value from a pixel. Then $\phi(a), \phi(b)$ represent the descriptions of pixels a, b, which each description contains only one feature value. Then $\rho_{\|\cdot\|}(\phi(a), \phi(b))$ gives the Čech distance between A and B.

This line of reasoning leads to descriptive associated sets of a function. For descriptive Čech distance $D_{\rho_{\|\cdot\|}}$, define descriptive lower and upper associated sets.

$$E_\varepsilon(D_{\rho_{\|\cdot\|}}) = \left\{ B \in \mathcal{P}(X) : D_{\rho_{\|\cdot\|}}(A, B) < \varepsilon \right\} \text{ (\textbf{Lower Associated Set} (DLAS))},$$

$$E^\varepsilon(D_{\rho_{\|\cdot\|}}) = \left\{ B \in \mathcal{P}(X) : D_{\rho_{\|\cdot\|}}(A, B) \geq \varepsilon \right\} \text{ (\textbf{Upper Associated Set} (DUAS))}$$

Example 3. **Sample Descriptive Lower Associated Set**. In Fig. 1, sets

$$F_1, F_2, F_3 \subset X$$

represent ascending subsets of a digital image X. Let $\Phi = \{\phi_R, \phi_G, \phi_B\}$ be a set of probes used to extract colour feature values (amount of red, green and blue) from pixels in an image. Notice, for example, for a small ε,

$$D_{\rho_{\|\cdot\|}}(\Phi_{F_1}, \Phi_{F_2}) = \inf \{\rho_{\|\cdot\|}(\Phi_{F_1}, \Phi_{F_2})\} < \varepsilon,$$

since the pixel colours in F_1, F_2, F_3 are uniformly close to each other. This gives an example of a DLAS with three members, namely, $E_\varepsilon(D_{\rho_{\|\cdot\|}}) = \{F_1, F_2, F_3\}$. In addition, $E_\varepsilon(D_{\rho_{\|\cdot\|}})$ in Fig. 1 is an example of a filter (ascending subsets). Each of the sets in Fig. 1 is an example of what is known as a descriptive spherical neighbourhood, each with a different radius. A **descriptive spherical neighbourhood** with centre x and radius r is a set N_x defined by

$$N_x = \left\{ y \in X : \rho_{\|\cdot\|}(\Phi_x, \Phi_y) < r \right\}.$$

Since sets F_1, F_2, F_3 have a common center pixel x, $E_\varepsilon(D_{\rho_{\|\cdot\|}})$ is also an example of what is known as a point cluster.

3 Topological Structures: Filters, Grills, Cluster Points

Several topological structures useful in pattern analysis are introduced in this section. For collections $\mathcal{A}, \mathcal{B} \in \mathcal{P}^2(X)$, we define

$$\mathcal{A} \vee \mathcal{B} \equiv \{A \cup B : A \in \mathcal{A}, B \in \mathcal{B}\},$$
$$\mathcal{A} \wedge \mathcal{B} \equiv \{A \cap B : A \in \mathcal{A}, B \in \mathcal{B}\},$$
$$\mathcal{A} \prec \mathcal{B} \Leftrightarrow \forall A \in \mathcal{A}, \exists B \in \mathcal{B} : B \subseteq A \ \ (i.e., \ \mathcal{A} \ \text{corefines} \ \mathcal{B}),$$
$$sec(\mathcal{A}) = \{B \subseteq X : A \cap B \neq \varnothing, \text{ for all } A \in \mathcal{A}\}.$$

A **filter** on X is a nonempty subset $\mathcal{F}$ of $\mathcal{P}(X)$ satisfying: $\varnothing \notin \mathcal{F}$; if $A \in \mathcal{F}$ and $A \subseteq B$, then $B \in \mathcal{F}$; and if $A \in \mathcal{F}$ and $B \in \mathcal{F}$, then $A \cap B \in \mathcal{F}$. A maximal filter on X is called an *ultrafilter* on X. A subcollection $\mathcal{B}$ in a filter $\mathcal{F}$ is a **filter base**, provided every member of $\mathcal{F}$ contains some element of $\mathcal{B}$. For example, in Fig. 1, F_1 is a filter base for the filter $\mathcal{F} = \{F_1, F_2, F_3\}$. A point $x \in X$ is a **cluster point of a filter** $\mathcal{F}$, provided every neighbourhood of x intersects every set of the filter base. Pixel $x \in F_1$ in Fig. 1 is an example of a cluster point (see, also, Example 5). In the sequel, the notion of a cluster point will be extended to collections of subsets called clusters. An example of a cluster is the collection $\mathcal{F}$ in Fig. 1. A detailed discussion about clusters is given in Sect. 6.

A **grill** on X is a subset $\mathcal{G}$ of $\mathcal{P}(X)$ satisfying: $\varnothing \notin \mathcal{G}$; if $A \in \mathcal{G}$ and $A \subseteq B$, then $B \in \mathcal{G}$; and if $A \cup B \in \mathcal{G}$, then $A \in \mathcal{G}$ or $B \in \mathcal{G}$. It has been observed that grill-related concepts have great importance in the study of nearness-like structures [21]. Notice that, for any $x \in X$, $[x] = \{A \subseteq X : x \in A\}$ is an ultrafilter on X, which is also a grill on X. There is one-to-one correspondence between the set of all filters and the set of all grills on X by the relation: $\mathcal{F}$ is a filter on X if and only if $sec(\mathcal{F})$ is a grill on X; and $\mathcal{G}$ is a grill on X if and only if, $sec(\mathcal{G})$ is a filter on X.

4 Distance and Approach Spaces

A brief introduction to approach spaces is given in this section.

Definition 1. Lowen Distance. *A function $\delta : X \times \mathcal{P}(X) \longrightarrow [0, \infty]$ is called a* Lowen distance *on X, if, for any $A, B \subseteq X$ and $x \in X$, the following conditions are satisfied:*

(D.1) $\delta(x, \{x\}) = 0$,
(D.2) $\delta(x, \varnothing) = \infty$,
(D.3) $\delta(x, A \cup B) = \min\{\delta(x, A), \delta(x, B)\}$,
(D.4) $\delta(x, A) \leq \delta(x, A^{(\alpha)}) + \alpha$, for $\alpha \in [0, \infty]$, where $A^{(\alpha)} \doteq \{x \in X : \delta(x, A) \leq \alpha\}$.
The pair (X, δ) is called an approach space [14, 18].

Definition 2. Generalised Approach Space. *A generalized approach space (X, ρ) [4, 5, 22] is a nonempty set X equipped with a distance function $\rho : \mathcal{P}(X) \times \mathcal{P}(X) \longrightarrow [0, \infty]$ if, and only if, for all nonempty subsets $A, B, C \in \mathcal{P}(X)$, ρ satisfies properties (A.1)-(A.5), i.e.,*

(A.1) $\rho(A,A) = 0$,

(A.2) $\rho(A,\varnothing) = \infty$,

(A.3) $\rho(A,B \cup C) = \min\{\rho(A,B),\rho(A,C)\}$,

(A.4) $\rho(A,B) = \rho(B,A)$,

(A.5) $\rho(A,B) \leq \rho(A,B^{(\alpha)}) + \alpha$, for every $\alpha \in [0,\infty]$, where $B^{(\alpha)} \doteq \{x \in X : \rho(\{x\},B) \leq \alpha\}$.

Remark 2. **Distance and Descriptive Approach Spaces.** It has been observed that the notion of distance in an approach space is closely related to the notion of nearness [17, 23]. The Lowen distance [14] δ (from Def. 1) is generalised [4] to distance ρ in Def. 2 by replacing the first argument in δ with a set instead of a single element x. Then $\delta(x,A)$ is rewritten as $\rho(\{x\},A)$ for $\{x\}, A \in \mathcal{P}(X)$.

This is an important change in the notion of approach distance introduced to satisfy the need to consider the distance between sets such as sets of points in pairs of digital images. This change is both significant as well as useful in the study of near sets [1, 2], especially in the context of approach spaces [6, 24] and topology [7] and the discovery of patterns in associated sets [10, 11]. This observation led to the introduction of the descriptive distance between sets [3].

The pair (X, D_ρ) is a generalised approach space defined with the Čech distance. The distance $D(A,B)$ was introduced by E. Čech in his 1936–1939 seminar on topology [15] (see, also, [25–27]). Using the descriptive Čech distance $D_{\rho_{\|\cdot\|}}$, the pair $(X, D_{\rho_{\|\cdot\|}})$ is a *descriptive approach space*.

5 Approach Nearness Spaces

Let $\mathcal{A}, \mathcal{B} \in \mathcal{P}^2(X)$. In an approach mero-topic space (X,ν), a collection $\mathcal{A}$ is said to be near (similar) to a collection $\mathcal{B}$ if and only if there exists subsets $A \in \mathcal{A}$ and $B \in \mathcal{B}$ such that $\nu(\{A\},\{B\}) = 0$ (*cf.* [18]). In practice, this seldom occurs. Instead, consider when sets A and B are close enough relative to a threshold c.

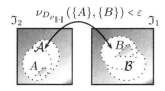

Fig. 3. Near Images

This mainly motivates the introduction of an ε-approach merotopy on X [5]. In this section, we axiomatize ε-approach nearness spaces, where $\varepsilon \in (0,\infty]$, to study the topological properties of ε-approach merotopic spaces.

Definition 3. *Let $\varepsilon \in (0,\infty]$. Then, in a manner similar to [17], a function $\nu : \mathcal{P}^2(X) \times \mathcal{P}^2(X) \longrightarrow [0,\infty]$ is an ε-approach merotopy on X if, and only if, for any collections $\mathcal{A}, \mathcal{B}, \mathcal{C} \in \mathcal{P}^2(X)$, the properties (AN.1)-(AN.5) are satisfied:*

AN.1 $\mathcal{A} \prec \mathcal{B} \Longrightarrow \nu(\mathcal{C},\mathcal{A}) \leq \nu(\mathcal{C},\mathcal{B})$,

AN.2 $(\cap \mathcal{A}) \cap (\cap \mathcal{B}) \neq \varnothing \Longrightarrow \nu(\mathcal{A},\mathcal{B}) < \varepsilon$,

AN.3 $\nu(\mathcal{A},\mathcal{B}) = \nu(\mathcal{B},\mathcal{A})$ and $\nu(\mathcal{A},\mathcal{A}) = 0$,

AN.4 $\varnothing \in \mathcal{A} \Longrightarrow \nu(\mathcal{C}, \mathcal{A}) = \infty$,
AN.5 $\nu(\mathcal{C}, \mathcal{A} \vee \mathcal{B}) \geq \nu(\mathcal{C}, \mathcal{A}) \wedge \nu(\mathcal{C}, \mathcal{B})$.

The pair (X, ν) *is called an* ε-**approach merotopic space.**

For an ε-approach merotopic space (X, ν), we define the **closure operator** cl_ν by $cl_\nu(A) = \{x \in X : \nu(\{\{x\}\}, \{A\}) < \varepsilon\}$, for all $A \subseteq X$, i.e., $cl_\nu(A)$ is the set of interior points plus the boundary points of A. Let $cl_\nu(\mathcal{A}) = \{cl_\nu(A) : A \in \mathcal{A}\}$. Then an ε-approach merotopy ν on X is called an ε-*approach nearness* on X and (X, ν) is called an ε-**approach nearness space**, if the following condition is satisfied:

(AN.6) $\nu(cl_\nu(\mathcal{A}), cl_\nu(\mathcal{B})) \geq \nu(\mathcal{A}, \mathcal{B})$.

In this case, cl_ν is a Kuratowski closure operator on X.

Example 4. ε-**Approach Nearness Space.** Let D_ρ be the Čech distance. Then the function $\nu_{D_\rho} : \mathcal{P}^2(X) \times \mathcal{P}^2(X) \longrightarrow [0, \infty]$ defined by

$$\nu_{D_\rho}(\mathcal{A}, \mathcal{B}) := \sup_{A \in \mathcal{A}, B \in \mathcal{B}} D_\rho(A, B) \text{ and } \nu_{D_\rho}(\mathcal{A}, \mathcal{A}) := \sup_{A \in \mathcal{A}} D_\rho(A, A) = 0,$$

is an ε-approach merotopy on X. The **Čech closure operator** $cl_{\nu_{D_\rho}}$ on X is defined by

$$cl_{\nu_{D_\rho}}(A) = \{x \in X : \nu_{D_\rho}(\{x\}, A) < \varepsilon\}, A \subseteq X.$$

Further, if

$$\nu_{D_\rho}(cl_{D_\rho}(A), cl_{D_\rho}(B)) \geq D_\rho(A, B), \text{ for all } A, B \subseteq X,$$

then cl_{D_ρ} is a Kuratowski closure operator on X. In this case, ν_{D_ρ} is an ε-approach nearness on X and (X, D_ρ) is an ε-approach nearness space.

Remark 3. **Sufficiently Near Sets.** Nonempty sets A and B that are considered *sufficiently near* each other if, and only if, $D(A, B) < \varepsilon$ for $\varepsilon \in (0, \infty]$. Otherwise, sets A, B are far, *i.e.*, *sufficiently apart*, provided $D_\rho(A, B) \geq \varepsilon$.

Example 5. **Descriptive ε-Approach Nearness Space.** A argument similar to the one given in Example 4 leads to $(X, D_{\rho_{\|\cdot\|}})$, a *descriptive ε-approach nearness space*. From what has already observed, this means that the descriptive associated set $E_\varepsilon(D_{\rho_{\|\cdot\|}})$ from Example 3 is also an example of a cluster point in the descriptive ε-approach nearness space $(X, \nu_{D_{\rho_{\|\cdot\|}}})$ for the set X in Fig. 1. Again, for example, the pair of digital images in Fig. 3 belong to a descriptive ε-approach nearness space $(X, \nu_{D_{\rho_{\|\cdot\|}}})$ for the set $X = \mathfrak{I}_1 \cup \mathfrak{I}_2$.

6 Clusters in Approach Nearness Spaces

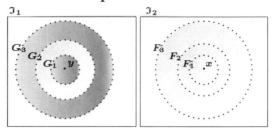

Fig. 4. Sample Near Clusters

In this section, topological structures called clusters are introduced in the context of ε-approach nearness spaces. A collection called a cluster can be found by gathering together subsets C, D in a collection $\mathcal{C} \in \mathcal{P}^2(X)$ such that each pair of subsets $C, D \in \mathcal{C}$ are sufficiently near. More precisely, the sufficient nearness of subsets C, D in a cluster $\mathcal{C}$ defined in terms of an ε-approach nearness ν on X so that $\nu(\{C\}, \{D\}) < \varepsilon$.

Definition 4. (cf. [28]). **ν-Cluster.** Let $\mathcal{C} \in \mathcal{P}^2(X)$ and (X, ν) be an ε-approach nearness ν on X. Then $\mathcal{C}$ is a ν-cluster, if the following conditions are satisfied.

(Cluster.1) $C, D \in \mathcal{C} \Longrightarrow \nu(\{C\}, \{D\}) < \varepsilon$,
(Cluster.2) $\nu(\{A\}, \{C\}) < \varepsilon$, for all $C \in \mathcal{C} \Longrightarrow A \in \mathcal{C}$,
(Cluster.3) $C \cup D \in \mathcal{C} \Longrightarrow C \in \mathcal{C}$ or $D \in \mathcal{C}$.

Example 6 **Cluster from Digital Images.** For $\mathfrak{I}_1, \mathfrak{I}_2$ in Fig. 4, let $X = \mathfrak{I}_1 \cup \mathfrak{I}_2$. Also, let the probes ϕ_R, ϕ_G, ϕ_B used to extract pixel colour values and let $\nu_{D_{\rho_{\|\cdot\|}}}$ denote an ε-approach nearness defined in terms of $D_{\rho_{\|\cdot\|}}$ that returns the gap between pixel color descriptions. Hence, we obtain a pair of descriptive lower associated sets $\mathcal{E}_{\mathfrak{I}_1} = \{G_1, G_2, G_3\}$ and $\mathcal{E}_{\mathfrak{I}_2} = \{F_1, F_2, F_3\}$. Then $\mathcal{C} = \mathcal{E}_{\mathfrak{I}_1} \cup \mathcal{E}_{\mathfrak{I}_2}$ is a cluster.

Proof
(Cluster.1): From Fig. 4, observe that, for each pair $C, D \in \mathcal{C}$, it is the case that $\nu_{D_{\rho_{\|\cdot\|}}}(\{C\}, \{D\}) < \varepsilon$ for arbitrarily small ε, since some of the pixels in each member of the pair C, D contain the same colour (*i.e.*, there are pixels in subset $C \in \mathcal{C}$ and $D \in \mathcal{C}$ that have matching colours), leading to a zero or near zero value of the ε-approach nearness $\nu_{D_{\rho_{\|\cdot\|}}}$.
(Cluster.2): Assume $\nu_{D_{\rho_{\|\cdot\|}}}(\{A\}, \{C\}) < \varepsilon$ for each $C \in \mathcal{C}$. This means that there are pixels in A that are close in colour to pixels in each C. Hence, $A \in \mathcal{C}$, since membership of a set in $\mathcal{C}$ is determined by the fact that the gap between colour descriptions of pixels in members of $\mathcal{C}$ is sufficiently near.
(Cluster.3): Immediate.

Example 7. (From [17]). Let (X, ν) be an ε-approach nearness space. Denote $\mathfrak{e}(x) = \{A \subseteq X : x \in cl_\nu(A)\}$, $x \in X$. Then $\mathfrak{e}(x)$ is a ν-cluster, for all $x \in X$.

Example 8. Let $(X, \nu_{D_{\rho_{\|\cdot\|}}})$ be a descriptive ε-approach nearness space. Denote $\mathfrak{e}(x) = \{A \subseteq X : x \in cl_{\nu_{D_{\rho_{\|\cdot\|}}}}(A)\}$, $x \in X$. This means the description of x is sufficiently near the descriptions of the members of each $A \in \mathfrak{e}(x)$. Then $\mathfrak{e}(x)$ is a $\nu_{D_{\rho_{\|\cdot\|}}}$-cluster, for all $x \in X$.

Proposition 1. [17, *cf.* Proposition 4.2]
Let (X,ν) be an ε-approach nearness space. Then every ν-cluster is a grill on X.

Definition 5. *An ε-approach nearness space (X,ν) is called an AN_1-space, if*
$$\nu(\{\{x\},\{y\}\}) < \varepsilon \Longrightarrow x = y.$$

The above property of an ε-approach nearness space results that its underlying topological space (X, cl_ν) is T_1. A topological space is type T_1 if, and only if, distinct points are not near each other. In the context of an ε-approach nearness space (X,ν), for distinct points $x, y \in X, x \neq y, \nu(\{x\},\{y\}) > \varepsilon$.

Definition 6. *An ε-approach nearness space (X,ν) is said to be* complete *if $\bigcap cl_\nu(\mathcal{A}) \neq \varnothing$, for all ν-clusters $\mathcal{A}$ of X.*

In a metric space, this definition of completion reduces to the usual definition of completion, i.e. a metric space is complete if and only if each Cauchy sequence[1] is convergent. Let (X,ν) be an ε-approach nearness space, X^* be the set of all ν-clusters and $f : X \longrightarrow X^*$ be defined as $f(x) = \mathfrak{e}(x)$. Define $\nu^* : \mathcal{P}^2(X^*) \times \mathcal{P}^2(X^*) \longrightarrow [0,\infty]$ as follows. Let

$$\Omega, \mathfrak{I} \in \mathcal{P}^2(X^*), \nu^*(\Omega,\mathfrak{I}) = \nu(\bigcup\{\bigcap \omega : \omega \in \Omega\}, \bigcup\{\bigcap \tau : \tau \in \mathfrak{I}\}).$$

Then

Lemma 1. (X^*,ν^*) *is a complete AN_1-space.*

Proof. See [17, Theorem 5.6].   □

Let $\mathcal{A}_\varepsilon^*$ denote the set of all lower associated sets of $\nu_{D_{\rho_{\|\cdot\|}}}^*$-clusters in a descriptive ε-approach nearness space $(X, \nu_{D_{\rho_{\|\cdot\|}}}^*)$. Let $\mathcal{L} \in \mathcal{A}_\varepsilon^*$. Then, for each pair of clusters $\mathcal{C}, \mathcal{D} \in \mathcal{L}, \nu_{D_{\rho_{\|\cdot\|}}}^*(\mathcal{C},\mathcal{D}) < \varepsilon$. From Lemma 1, obtain

Theorem 1. *The following are equivalent:*
  (*i*) $(\mathcal{A}_\varepsilon^*, \nu_{D_{\rho_{\|\cdot\|}}}^*)$ *is complete.*
  (*ii*) *The members of $\mathcal{A}_\varepsilon^*$ are sufficiently near each other.*

Proof. (i) $\Rightarrow \bigcap cl_{\nu_{D_{\rho_{\|\cdot\|}}}}(\mathcal{A}) \neq \varnothing$, for all $\nu_{D_{\rho_{\|\cdot\|}}}^*$-clusters $\mathcal{A}$ of $\mathcal{A}_\varepsilon^* \Leftrightarrow$ (ii).   □

Example 9. In Example 6, $\mathcal{A}_\varepsilon^* = \mathcal{C}$ is a complete space, since $\bigcap cl_{\nu_{D_{\rho_{\|\cdot\|}}}^*}(\mathcal{A}) \neq \varnothing$ for all the lower associated sets $\mathcal{A} \in \mathcal{A}_\varepsilon^*$.

---

[1] A Cauchy sequence is a sequence of elements that are sufficiently near each other as the sequence progresses.

Fig. 5. Camouflaged Man in Lower Associated Cluster Space

7 Cluster Space Patterns

Fig. 6. $E_\varepsilon(\nu_{D_{\rho_{\|\cdot\|}}}) = \mathfrak{I}$

From a pattern analysis perspective, Theorem 1 is important. The completeness of a descriptive lower associated cluster space $(\mathcal{A}_\varepsilon^*, \nu_{D_{\rho_{\|\cdot\|}}})$ means that the each pair members $\mathfrak{I}, \mathfrak{I}' \in \mathcal{A}_\varepsilon^*$ will contain at least one pair of clusters $\mathcal{C} \in \mathfrak{I}, \mathcal{C}' \in \mathfrak{I}'$ that are sufficiently near each other, *i.e.*, clusters $\mathcal{C}, \mathcal{C}'$ are descriptively similar. In pattern language, clusters $\mathcal{C}, \mathcal{C}'$ have least one pattern in common. This idea is illustrated in terms of clusters found in camouflaged objects by Liu Bolin[2] in Fig. 5.

For simplicity, each lower associated set in $\mathcal{A}_\varepsilon^*$ will contain only one cluster. The space $\mathcal{A}_\varepsilon^*$ contains lower associated sets of clusters $\mathfrak{I}, \mathfrak{I}'$. For example[3], $E_\varepsilon(\nu_{D_{\rho_{\|\cdot\|}}}) = \mathfrak{I} = \{\mathcal{C} : \mathcal{C} = \{C_1, C_2, C_3\}\}$ shown in Fig. 6, where $\nu_{D_{\rho_{\|\cdot\|}}}(A, B) < \varepsilon$ for all $A, B \in \mathfrak{I}$. In addition, lower associated set $\mathfrak{I}' = \{\mathcal{C}' : \mathcal{C}' = \{G_1, G_2, G_2\}\}$ and $\mathcal{A}_\varepsilon^* = \{\mathfrak{I}, \mathfrak{I}'\}$ is complete for a particular choice of a set Φ of pixel features, *e.g.*, choose Φ to have ϕ_R, ϕ_G, ϕ_B from Ex 6 and, ϕ_e, ϕ_l, ϕ_c (edge orientation, edge length, edges present, respec-

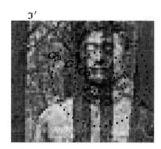

Fig. 7. $E_\varepsilon(\nu_{D_{\rho_{\|\cdot\|}}}) = \mathfrak{I}'$

tively). The red colour in the clusters in Figs. 6 and 7 contain pixels with similar descriptions and reveal patterns in the camouflaged man.

---

[2] See, *e.g.*, http://www.moillusions.com/tag/liu-bolin
[3] Choose the **Nbd** option in the NEAR system, http://wren.ece.umanitoba.ca to verify that $\mathfrak{I}, \mathfrak{I}'$ are sufficiently near clusters.

8   Conclusion

This article considers the completion of cluster spaces $\mathcal{A}_\varepsilon^*$ and lower associated sets of sufficiently near clusters for a particular class of distance functions. This leads to a new approach to pattern analysis in digital images.

References

1. Peters, J.: Near sets. Special theory about nearness of objects. Fund. Inform. 75(1-4), 407–433 (2007)
2. Peters, J., Wasilewski, P.: Foundations of near sets. Info. Sci. 179, 3091–3109 (2009)
3. Peters, J.: Metric spaces for near sets. Ap. Math. Sci. 5(2), 73–78 (2011)
4. Peters, J., Naimpally, S.: Approach spaces for near families. Gen. Math. Notes 2(1), 159–164 (2011)
5. Peters, J., Tiwari, S.: Approach merotopies and near filters. Gen. Math. Notes 3(1), 1–15 (2011)
6. Peters, J.: How near are Zdzisław Pawlak's paintings? Merotopic distance between regions of interest. In: Skowron, A., Suraj, S. (eds.) Intelligent Systems Reference Library volume dedicated to Prof. Zdzisław Pawlak, pp. 1–19. Springer, Berlin (2011)
7. Naimpally, S., Peters, J.: Topology with Applications. World Scientific, Singapore (to appear, 2012)
8. Coble, A.: Associated sets of points. Trans. Amer. Math. Soc. 24(1), 1–20 (1922)
9. Bruckner, A.: On characterizing classes of functions in terms of associated sets. Canad. Math. Bull. 10(2), 227–231 (1967)
10. Peters, J., Tiwari, S.: Associated near sets. Theory and application. Demo. Math. (2011), communicated
11. Ramanna, S., Peters, J.: Nearness of associated rough sets: Case study in image analysis. In: Peters, G., Lingras, P., Yao, Y., Slezak, D. (eds.) Selected Methods and Applications of Rough Sets in Management and Engineering, pp. 62–73. Springer, Heidelberg (2011)
12. Fréchet, M.: Sur quelques points du calcul fonctionnel. Rend. Circ. Mat. Palermo 22, 1–74 (1906)
13. Sutherland, W.: Introduction to Metric & Topological Spaces. Oxford University Press, Oxford (1974,2009); 2nd ed. (2008)
14. Lowen, R.: Approach Spaces: The Missing Link in the Topology-Uniformity-Metric Triad. Oxford Mathematical Monographs, pp. viii + 253. Oxford University Press, Oxford (1997)
15. Čech, E.: Topological Spaces, revised Ed. by Z. Frolik and M. Katǎtov. John Wiley & Sons, NY (1966)
16. Katětov, M.: On continuity structures and spaces of mappings. Comment. Math. Univ. Carolinae 6, 257–278 (1965)
17. Tiwari, S.: Some Aspects of General Topology and Applications. Approach Merotopic Structures and Applications, supervisor: M. Khare. PhD thesis, Department of Mathematics, Allahabad (U.P.), India (January 2010)
18. Lowen, R., Vaughan, D., Sioen, M.: Completing quasi metric spaces: an alternative approach. Houstan J. Math. 29(1), 113–136 (2003)
19. Bourbaki, N.: Elements of Mathematics. In: General Topology, Part 1, pp. i-vii, 437. Hermann & Addison-Wesley, Paris & Reading, MA, U.S.A (1966)

20. Peters, J.: ε-Near Collections. In: Yao, J.-T., Ramanna, S., Wang, G., Suraj, Z. (eds.) RSKT 2011. LNCS, vol. 6954, pp. 533–542. Springer, Heidelberg (2011)
21. Khare, M., Tiwari, S.: Grill determined L-approach merotopological spaces. Fund. Inform. 48, 1–12 (2010)
22. Peters, J., Tiwari, S.: Completing extended metric spaces: An alternative approach (2011), communicated
23. Khare, M., Tiwari, S.: L-approach merotopies and their categorical perspective. Demonstratio Math. 48 (to appear, 2012)
24. Ramanna, S., Peters, J.: Approach Space Framework for Image Database Classification. In: Hruschka Jr., E.R., Watada, J., do Carmo Nicoletti, M. (eds.) INTECH 2011. CCIS, vol. 165, pp. 75–89. Springer, Heidelberg (2011)
25. Beer, G., Lechnicki, A., Levi, S., Naimpally, S.: Distance functionals and suprema of hyperspace topologies. Annali di Matematica pura ed applicata CLXII(IV), 367–381 (1992)
26. Hausdorff, F.: Grundzüge der Mengenlehre, pp. viii + 476. Veit and Company, Leipzig (1914)
27. Leader, S.: On clusters in proximity spaces. Fundamenta Mathematicae 47, 205–213 (1959)
28. Naimpally, S.: Proximity Spaces, pp. x+128. Cambridge University Press, Cambridge (1970) ISBN 978-0-521-09183-1

Enhancing Cooperation in Distributed Information Systems Using Conviviality and Multi-Context Systems

Patrice Caire[1] and Antonis Bikakis[2]

[1] University of Namur, PReCISE Research Center, Computer Science Department, Belgium
[2] Department of Information Studies, University College London

Abstract. Modern information systems are characterized by the distribution of information and services among several autonomous heterogeneous entities. A major requirement for the success of such systems is that participating entities cooperate by sharing parts of their local knowledge. This paper presents a novel approach for modeling and enhancing cooperation in distributed information systems, which combines two formal models from the field of Knowledge Representation and Reasoning: a conviviality model and Multi-Context Systems. Our aim is two-fold. First, we develop a combined model for context-based representation and cooperation. Second, we provide the means for measuring cooperation leading to the design and evaluation of more convivial systems.

Keywords: Distributed Artificial Intelligence, Knowledge Representation and Reasoning, Conviviality, Multi-Context Systems, Social Dependence Networks.

1 Introduction

Facilitating cooperation is a major challenge for distributed information systems. However, when cooperation is achieved among human and /or artificial entities, e.g. by enabling information exchange between them, such systems allow participating entities to enrich their local knowledge both in terms of quality and quantity. Moreover, for environments where the communication between entities cannot be guaranteed, e.g. Ambient Intelligence environments, it is also important for an entity to maintain multiple connections, so that it has more than one alternative choice to cooperate.

Systems that can be classified as distributed information systems, may include distributed databases, peer-to-peer systems, web social networks, mobile computing systems, the Semantic Web and many others. Despite their major differences with respect to their architectures, their aims and the nature of participating entities, all these systems are characterized by some common features, namely: (a) the available knowledge is distributed among several, possibly heterogeneous, human or artificial entities; (b) there is an available means of communication through which participating entities communicate and cooperate by sharing parts of their local knowledge; (c) each entity remains autonomous in the sense that it may take decisions independently, e.g. regarding which entities to communicate with, share knowledge or, more generally cooperate with, which parts of its knowledge should remain private, etc.; and (d) the system is open and dynamic in the sense that various entities may join or leave the system at

C. Sombattheera et al. (Eds.): MIWAI 2011, LNAI 7080, pp. 14–25, 2011.
© Springer-Verlag Berlin Heidelberg 2011

random times and without prior notice. As a result, the structure of the system and the available system knowledge typically vary over time.

Taking into account the aim and special features of distributed information systems, a major requirement for the success of such systems is that participating entities cooperate by sharing local knowledge. We hereby address this issue and formulate it with the following research question:

How to enhance cooperative Distributed Information Systems (DIS)?

This breaks down into the following subquestions:

1. How to model local knowledge and information exchange in DIS?
2. How to model cooperation in DIS?
3. How to enhance cooperation in such systems?

To address these questions we combine two different formal models from the field of Knowledge Representation and Reasoning: a *conviviality model* [1,2] and *Multi-Context Systems* [3,4].

The concept of *conviviality*, issued from social science, has many ambiguous and non-technical definitions; it has been associated with concepts including empathy, trust, solidarity, and security [5]. Here we use Illich's definition of conviviality as "individual freedom realized in personal interdependence" [6]. In distributed information systems, individual freedom is linked with the choice to keep personal knowledge and beliefs at the local level, while interdependence is understood as reciprocity, i.e. cooperation. Participating entities depend on each other to achieve the enrichment of their local knowledge.

On the other hand, *Multi-Context Systems* (MCS) are logical formalizations of distributed context theories connected through a set of mapping rules, which enable information flow between contexts. A *context* can be thought of as a logical theory - a set of axioms and inference rules - that models local knowledge. In distributed information systems, a context may formally describe the local knowledge and beliefs of an entity, while mappings represent the information exchange between different entities.

In this work we introduce the groundings for convivial information exchanges among the entities of Multi-Context Systems. We believe that the work, although still in its infancy, is advanced enough to provide a solid ground for further research in fields such as artificial social systems, distributed artificial intelligence and DIS.

The layout of this paper is structured as follows. In section 2, we introduce a motivating example from the field of Social Networks. In section 3, we provide the necessary background information on Multi-Context Systems and tools for conviviality. In section 4, we present our model using the running example. In section 5, we summarize and describe the next steps of this work.

2 Motivating Scenario

In [7], the authors used a scenario from Social Networks to illustrate a representation model for distributed peer theories and an algorithm for distributed query evaluation in Multi-Context Systems. In this paper, we extend the scenario to illustrate how to model and enhance convivial information systems.

2.1 A Use Case from Social Networks

Consider the following use case from the domain of social networks. It involves a university social network, called *"uni.scholar.space"*. People studying or working for the university can become members of the network and form groups through which they can discuss their common interests, arrange meetings, share information and other resources, such as electronic books, journals, papers or reports. We first present a simple use case of the system. Then, we extend this use case, and show how we can enhance cooperation between the system's users.

Simple Case. Alice, Bob, Charlie and Dan are members of uni.scholar.space. They have created a group, which they use to share information about articles that are relevant to their research interests. Alice, who is the head of the group, has configured a software agent to crawl the Web and seek articles that are relevant to the group's interests. For each article, the agent collects specific information, e.g. the name of the journal that the article was published in, and its keywords. If the article matches Alice's preferences, the agent recommends the article to Alice. The other members of the group (Bob, Charlie and Dan) use their own software agents, which recommend articles to their users based on Alice's recommendations, but also encode and share their personal research knowledge.

Consider that Alice's agent finds a new article on the Web, which has been recently published in the "Ambient Intelligence" journal (an imaginary journal) and has two keywords: "Multi-Agent Systems" and "Semantic Web". Alice is interested in articles that combine the fields of "Computer Applications", "Artificial Intelligence" and "Distributed Computing". Alice's agent cannot match the article with Alice's preferences, and therefore cannot determine how to recommend the article. The agent, then, attempts to contact the agents of the other members of the group so that they can collectively decide whether the article may be interesting for the group.

Bob is an expert in distributed computing. In this case, he knows that Multi-Agent Systems is a distributed computing model and shares this information with Alice. Charlie specializes in the field of Knowledge Representation and Reasoning (KRR), which is a subfield of Artificial Intelligence. His agent identifies Semantic Web as a subfield of Knowledge Representation and Reasoning, and shares this knowledge with Alice's agent. Dan's main research field is Mobile Applications, a specific type of computer applications. He is not aware, though, whether the paper title ("Ambient Intelligence") or any of the two keywords ("Multi-Agent Systems" and "Semantic Web") may be linked to this field. Based on the available information, Alice's agent cannot determine whether the paper matches Alice's preferences. Figure 1(*a*) illustrates this simple case. A circle represents an agent acting on behalf of one of the users involved in the scenario, i.e., "A" for Alice, "B" for Bob and so on. Arrows indicate information exchanges among the agents.

Extended Case. Consider now, that the system accesses the public profile of another registered user, Emma, who is an expert in "Pervasive Computing", a type of mobile applications. The system recommends Emma as a contact to Dan, based on their common research interests. Emma knows that "Ambient Intelligence" is a journal specializing

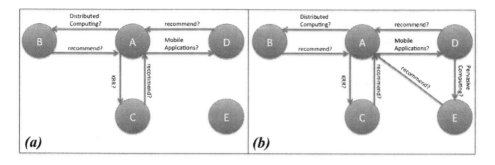

Fig. 1. Running example

in pervasive computing, and shares this knowledge with Dan. Using this information, Alice's agent may now determine that the article should be recommended to Alice. It shares this recommendation with the agents of the other group members, and also with Emma's agent in counter-part for the information she provided to the group (Figure 1(*b*)).

2.2 Assumptions and Requirements

The implementation of the scenarios described above requires the combination of technologies from various fields including Software Engineering, Human-Computer Interaction, Computer Networks and Knowledge Representation and Reasoning (KRR). Our focus is on issues related to KRR. We implicitly make the follow simplifying assumptions for issues that are out of the scope of this paper.

- There is an available infrastructure for communication between the users' devices - the university network. The network is assumed to support various types of communications, both wired and wireless, and various types of devices, ranging from desktop computers to mobile phones.
- Each agent is aware of parts of the knowledge that the other agents possess. This feature is provided by uni.scholar.space to its registered members. Typically, as in all social networks today, each user has her own public profile, and may share more information with her contacts, or members of common groups.
- Each device has the required computing capabilities to conduct some simple reasoning tasks.

The specific problems that we try to address are:

- How to develop a common model not only for the representation of the agents' local knowledge, but also for the sharing of knowledge through information exchange.
- How to extend the system so that it can facilitate and enhance cooperation among its members, whereby providing them with more opportunities for information exchanges.

3   Background

3.1   Multi-Context Systems

Multi-Context Systems (*MCS* [3,4]) are logical formalizations of distributed context theories connected through a set of mapping rules, which enable information flow between contexts. A *context* can be thought of as a logical theory - a set of axioms and inference rules - that models local knowledge. Together with the *Propositional Logic of Context(PLC* [8,9]) they are considered as the most prominent approaches in the field of contextual reasoning, which was introduced in AI by McCarthy [10] as an approach for the problem of *generality*. MCS have been argued to be most adequate with respect to the three dimensions of contextual reasoning (*partiality, approximation, proximity*) and shown to be technically more general than PLC [11].

Several distributed systems and applications have been developed on top of formal models of context, including (*a*) the CYC common sense knowledge base [12]; (*b*) contextualized ontology languages, such as Distributed Description Logics [13] and C-OWL [14]; (*c*) context-based agent architectures [15,16]; and (*d*) distributed reasoning algorithms for Mobile Social Networks [17] and Ambient Intelligence systems [18].

Recently, nonmonotonic extensions of MCS have been proposed to deal with context imperfections. *Contextual Default Logic* [19] extends MCS with default mapping rules to handle missing information and conflicts caused by mapping rules, while *Contextual Defeasible Logic* (*CDL* [20,21]) uses preferences to resolve potential inconsistencies caused by mapping rules. For the rest of the paper, we will use the representation model of CDL, though similar results may also be obtained for other MCS.

In CDL, the original Multi-Context Systems model is extended with defeasible rules, and a preference relation reflecting the trust each context assigns to other contexts. Specifically, CDL defines a MCS C as a collection of distributed context theories C_i: A context C_i is defined as a tuple of the form (V_i, R_i, T_i), where V_i is the vocabulary used by C_i (a finite set of positive and negative literals), R_i is a set of rules, and T_i is a preference ordering on C.

R_i consists of two sets of rules: the set of local rules and the set of mapping rules. The body of a local rule is a conjunction of *local* literals (literals that are contained in V_i), while its head contains a local literal. There are two types of local rules: (a) *Strict rules*, of the form

$$r_i^l : a_i^1, a_i^2, ...a_i^{n-1} \rightarrow a_i^n$$

They express sound local knowledge and are interpreted in the classical sense: whenever the literals in the body of the rule ($a_i^1, a_i^2, ...a_i^{n-1}$) are strict consequences of the local theory, then so is the conclusion of the rule (a_i^n). Strict rules with empty body denote factual knowledge; (b) *Defeasible rules*, of the form

$$r_i^d : b_i^1, b_i^2, ...b_i^{n-1} \Rightarrow b_i^n$$

They are used to express uncertainty, in the sense that a defeasible rule (r_i^d) cannot be applied to support its conclusion (b_i^n) if there is adequate contrary evidence.

Mapping rules associate literals from the local vocabulary V_i (*local literals*) with literals from the vocabularies of other contexts (*foreign literals*). The body of each such rule is a conjunction of local and foreign literals, while its head is labeled by a single local literal. A mapping rule is modeled as a defeasible rule of the form:

$$r_i^m : a_i^1, a_j^2, ...a_k^{n-1} \Rightarrow a_i^n$$

Finally, each context C_i defines a partial preference ordering T_i on C to express its confidence in the knowledge it imports from other contexts. T_i is modeled as a directed acyclic graph, in which vertices represent system contexts and arcs represent preference relations between the contexts that label the connected vertices. A context C_j is preferred by C_i to context C_k, denoted as $C_j >^i C_k$, if there is a path from vertex labeled by C_k to vertex labeled by C_j in T_i.

3.2 Conviviality

Computer systems have to be user friendly and convivial [22], a concept from the social sciences defined by Illich as "individual freedom realized in personal interdependence" [6]. Multiagent systems technology can be used to realize tools for conviviality when we interpret "freedom" as choice [2]. For example, if your research fields are rapidly evolving, and there is only one colleague who can provide you with updates, then you depend on this colleague for your updates, but if there several colleagues who can do so, then you do not depend on a single one. We say that there is more choice, and thus it is more convivial.

Tools for conviviality are concerned in particular with dynamic aspects of conviviality, such as the emergence of conviviality from the sharing of properties or behaviors whereby each member's perception is that their personal needs are taken care of [23,24].

We measure conviviality by counting the possible ways agents have to cooperate, indicating degree of choice or freedom for these agents to engage in coalitions. Our coalitional theory is based on dependence networks [25,26], labeled directed graphs where the nodes are agents, and each labeled edge represents that the former agent depends on the latter one to achieve some goal. According to [1], conviviality may be measured by the number of reciprocity based coalitions that can be formed. Some coalitions, however, provide more opportunities for their participants to cooperate with each other than others, being thereby more convivial. To represent the interdependencies among agents in the coalitions, we use dependence networks. Abstracting from tasks and plans we define a dependence network as in definition 1 [1,2]:

Definition 1 (Dependence networks). *A dependence network is a tuple $\langle A, G, dep, \geq \rangle$ where: A is a set of agents, G is a set of goals, dep : $A \times A \to 2^G$ is a function that relates with each pair of agents, the sets of goals on which the first agent depends on the second, and $\geq: A \to 2^G \times 2^G$ is for each agent a total pre-order on sets of goals occurring in his dependencies: $G_1 >_{(a)} G_2$.*

We now recall the assumptions and requirements for conviviality measures introduced in [2]. Our assumptions are first, that cycles identified in a dependence network are considered as coalitions, and second, that the conviviality of a dependence network is evaluated in a bounded domain. When referring to cycles, we are implicitly signifying simple cycles (as defined in [27]), also discarding self-loops. Moreover, when referring to conviviality, we always refer to potential interaction not actual interaction.

Our requirements are first, that larger coalitions are more convivial than smaller ones, and second, that the more coalitions in the dependence network, the higher the conviviality measure, *ceteris paribus*.

Conviviality classification. We further recall from [1,2] the conviviality classification proposed to allow an intuitive grasp of conviviality measures through a ranking of the dependence networks. Following are the five definitions of conviviality classes, from the absolute best to the absolute worst convivial networks. Figure 2, illustrates the different types of dependence networks that correspond to each conviviality class. The arrow on the top of the figure depicts the direction of increasing conviviality. The scale goes from the worst case (no conviviality) to the best case (maximal conviviality).

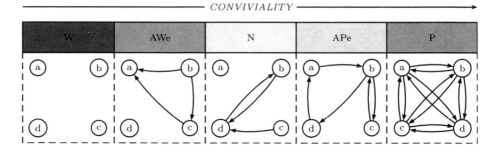

Fig. 2. Conviviality classes

Definition 2 (P). *A dependence network DN is P convivial (most convivial), iff all agents in DN belong to all cycles, i.e., $\forall a_i \in A$ and $\forall c_k \in C, a_i$ is s.t. $a_i \in c_k$, where $C = \{c_1, \ldots, c_l\}$ is the set of all cycles.*

Definition 3 (APE). *A dependence network DN is APE convivial, iff all agents in DN belong to at least one cycle, i.e., $\forall a_i \in A, \exists c_k \notin C, s.t. a_i \in c_k$, where $C = \{c_1, \ldots, c_l\}$ is the set of all cycles.*

Definition 4 (N). *A dependence network DN is N convivial, iff there exists at least one cycle in DN, and there is at least one agent not in a cycle, i.e., $\exists a, b \in A$ s.t. $a, b \in c_k$, where $c_k \notin C$, and $\exists d \in A$ s.t. $d \notin c_i, \forall c_i \in C$, where $C = \{c_1, \ldots, c_l\}$ is the set of all cycles.*

Definition 5 (AWE). *A dependence network DN is AWE convivial, iff there is no cycle in DN, i.e., $C = \{\emptyset\}$, and s.t. $\exists dep(a, b) = \{g_i\}$, where $a, b \in A$ and $g_i \in G$.*

Definition 6 (W). *A dependence network DN is W convivial (worst convivial), iff there is no dependency between the agents in DN, i.e., $\nexists dep(a, b) = \{g_i\}$, where $a, b \in A$ and $g_i \in G$.*

4   Model

In this section, we first apply our Multi-Context System formalism to our motivating example. Then, building on our model, we apply our conviviality formalism. Finally, we discuss the resulting model.

4.1   Formalization of the Use Case Scenario as a Multi-Context System

The use case scenario described in Section 2 can be formalized as follows using the language of Contextual Defeasible Logic. The group of agents can be defined as a Multi-Context System consisting of five context theories. Each context theory encodes the local knowledge of an agent in terms of local rules, and the association between the local knowledge and the knowledge of the other agents in terms of mapping rules.

Simple Case. All agents share some common local knowledge, which refers to the information about the journal article:

$$\rightarrow ambient\_intelligence$$
$$\rightarrow semantic\_web$$
$$\rightarrow mas$$

Alice's local knowledge also includes her preferences, based on which the agent decides whether an article should be recommended:

$$r_{A1}^d : computer\_applications_A, artificial\_intelligence_A,$$
$$distributed\_computing_A \Rightarrow recommend_A$$

Alice's agent also uses the following mapping rules to import information from the other agents:

$$r_{A2}^m : distributed\_computing_B \Rightarrow distributed\_computing_A$$
$$r_{A3}^m : krr_C \Rightarrow artificial\_intelligence_A$$
$$r_{A4}^m : mobile\_applications_D \Rightarrow computer\_applications_A$$

Bob's agent uses one local strict rule to encode Bob's knowledge that "Multi Agent Systems" is a distributed computing model (r_{B1}^l). It also uses a mapping rule (r_{B2}^m) to import the recommendation of an article from Alice's agent:

$$r_{B1}^l : mas \rightarrow distributed\_computing_B$$
$$r_{B2}^m : recommend_A \Rightarrow recommend_B$$

Charlie's knowledge that "Semantic Web" is a subfield of "Knowledge Representation and Reasoning" is encoded as a local strict rule (r_{C1}^l), while his agent also uses a similar mapping rule to import recommendations from Alice's agent (r_{C2}^m).

$$r_{C1}^l : semantic\_web \rightarrow krr_C$$
$$r_{B2}^m : recommend_A \Rightarrow recommend_C$$

Dan's agent uses one mapping rule that imports recommendations for articles from Alice's agent (r_{D2}^m).

$$r_{D1}^m : recommend_A \Rightarrow recommend_D$$

Extended Case. In the extended case, Dan's agent uses another one mapping rule ($r_{D2.}^m$), which is suggested by the system and associates "pervasive computing" used by Emma with "mobile computing":

$$r_{D2}^m : pervasive\_computing_E \Rightarrow mobile\_computing_D$$

Emma's agent uses a local strict rule that associates the "Ambient Intelligence" journal with "pervasive computing" (r_{E1}^l), and a mapping rule that imports recommendations for articles from Alice's agent (r_{E2}^m).

$$r_{E1}^m : ambient\_intelligence \rightarrow pervasive\_computing_E$$
$$r_{E2}^m : recommend_A \Rightarrow recommend_E$$

4.2 Conviviality in Multi-Context Systems

In this subsection, we build on the Multi-context model proposed in subsection 4.1, and apply our conviviality formalism to the motivating example.

Simple case. Let DN_1, visualized in Figure 3 (a) be a dependence network corresponding to the coalition C_1, where: $C_1 : \{(A, g_1, B, g_2), (A, g_1, C, g_2), (A, g_1, D, g_2)\}$, and where:

- Agents $Ag = \{A, B, C, D, E\}$, respectively represent Alice, Bob, Charlie, Dan and Emma;

- Goals $G = \{g_1, g_2\}$, where the two main goals are the following: $\{g_1\}$ is to find the relevance of articles, and $\{g_2\}$ is to get recommended articles. (For easier reading, goals have been simplified to the two generic goals g_1 and g_2.)

- Dependencies are built from the Multi-context System rules, that is: $dep(A, B) = \{g_1\}$, $dep(A, C) = \{g_1\}$, $dep(A, D) = \{g_1\}$: agent A depends on agents B, C and D to achieve its goal g1: to find the relevance of articles; and $dep(B, A) = \{g_2\}$, $dep(C, A) = \{g_2\}$, $dep(D, A) = \{g_2\}$: agent B, C and D depend on agent A to achieve their goals g2: to get recommended articles.

- Agents' preferences are inferred from the agents local knowledge as indicated in the Multi-Context System model.

Extended case. Now, let DN_2, visualized in Figure 3 (b), be the dependence network corresponding to the coalition C_2, where:

$C_2 : \{(A, g_1, B, g_2), (A, g_1, C, g_2), (A, g_1, D, g_2), (A, g_1, D, g_1, E, g_2)\}$, and where:

- Agents $Ag = \{A, B, C, D, E\}$ are as previously;

- Goals $G = \{g_1, g_2\}$, where the two main goals are the following: $\{g_1\}$ is to find the relevance of articles, and $\{g_2\}$ is to get recommended articles, as previously;

- Dependencies are built from the Multi-context System rules, that is:
  $dep(A, B) = \{g_1\}$, $dep(A, C) = \{g_1\}$, $dep(A, D) = \{g_1\}$: agent A depends on agents B, C and D to achieve its goal g1: to find the relevance of articles, but so does also agent D from E as $dep(D, E) = \{g_1\}$;
  $dep(B, A) = \{g_2\}$, $dep(C, A) = \{g_2\}$, $dep(D, A) = \{g_2\}$, $dep(E, A) = \{g_2\}$: agent B, C, D and E depend on agent A to achieve their goals g2: to get recommended articles;

- Agents' preferences are inferred from the agents local knowledge as indicated in the Multi-Context System model.

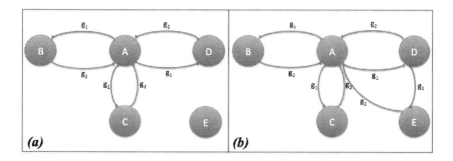

Fig. 3. Dependence networks DN_1 and DN_2

4.3 Discussion

Consider the two dependence networks DN_1 and DN_2, respectively corresponding to the agents coalitions C_1 and C_2, illustrated in Figure 3. In C_1, some agents are in a cycle while one, namely E, is isolated and does not depend on any other agents. Hence, from Definition 4, C_1 belongs to the N conviviality class. In contrast, all agents in coalition C_2 belong to at least one cycle. Hence, from Definition 3, C_2 belongs to the APe conviviality class. It is said to be *Almost Perfectly* convivial. All agents are engaged in reciprocal dependence relations: each one gives to the coalition and receives from it. All agents are pursuing goals and cooperate with at least one other agent to achieve the recommendations.

By recommending Emma to Dan, the system facilitates the information exchange among the agents and enhances the conviviality, making the system more effective and enjoyable to use. Moreover, by providing more choices for the agents to choose from, the system allows more possibilities for agents to reach their goals of gathering relevant information for their group members. We note that in the simple case, agent A is a central point and there a bottleneck and a weakness for C_1, as if it leaves the coalition all cycles disappear. In the extended case, however, the choice, provided by involvement of agent E, contributes to more robust system.

5 Summary

In this paper we proposed a model for knowledge representation, information exchange and cooperation in distributed information systems. Using a use case scenario from the field of Social Networks we highlighted how cooperation can be enhanced in such systems using two formal models: a conviviality model and a context representation model called Multi-Context Systems. The proposed approach may be applied to various types of distributed information systems, such as mobile computing systems, Ambient Intelligence systems, social networks and the Semantic Web.

There are many different directions towards which this work may be extended. As we already argued in Section 3, the conviviality model may also be combined with other Multi-Context Systems, such as Contextual Default Logic [19] and managed Multi-Context Systems [28]. The latter approach extends the definition of mappings to support more types of operations on contexts, such as revision and updates. Moreover, it is more general than CDL, since it allows contexts to use different representation models (e.g. relational databases, ontologies and logic programs).

Another interesting direction is to extend the proposed model with temporal aspects so that we are able to handle the dynamics of distributed information systems. To this direction, we will study the adoption of temporal dependence networks and temporal reciprocity measures introduced in [2].

Finally, considering the privacy requirements of users of Social Networks, Ambient Intelligence systems and other types of distributed information systems, we plan to study the tradeoff between privacy and conviviality in such systems. Both privacy protection and cooperation are essential for the adoption and success of such systems, therefore a tradeoff analysis will contribute to finding the right balance between the two properties in future information systems.

References

1. Caire, P.: New Tools for Conviviality: Masks, Norms, Ontology, Requirements and Measures. PhD thesis, Luxembourg University, Luxembourg (2010)
2. Caire, P., Alcade, B., van der Torre, L., Sombattheera, C.: Conviviality measures. In: 10th International Joint Conference on Autonomous Agents and Multiagent Systems (AAMAS 2011), Taipei, Taiwan, May 2-6 (2011)
3. Giunchiglia, F., Serafini, L.: Multilanguage hierarchical logics, or: how we can do without modal logics. Artificial Intelligence 65(1) (1994)
4. Ghidini, C., Giunchiglia, F.: Local Models Semantics, or contextual reasoning=locality+compatibility. Artificial Intelligence 127(2), 221–259 (2001)
5. Caire, P.: How to import the concept of conviviality to web communities. International Journal of Web Based Communities (IJWBC) 6(1), 99–113 (2009)
6. Illich, I.: Tools for Conviviality. Marion Boyars Publishers, London (1974)

7. Bikakis, A., Antoniou, G.: Local and Distributed Defeasible Reasoning in Multi-Context Systems. In: Bassiliades, N., Governatori, G., Paschke, A. (eds.) RuleML 2008. LNCS, vol. 5321, pp. 135–149. Springer, Heidelberg (2008)

8. Buvac, S., Mason, I.A.: Propositional Logic of Context. In: AAAI, pp. 412–419 (1993)

9. McCarthy, J., Buvač, S.: Formalizing Context (Expanded Notes). In: Aliseda, A., van Glabbeek, R., Westerståhl, D. (eds.) Computing Natural Language, pp. 13–50. CSLI Publications, Stanford (1998)

10. McCarthy, J.: Generality in Artificial Intelligence. Communications of the ACM 30(12), 1030–1035 (1987)

11. Serafini, L., Bouquet, P.: Comparing formal theories of context in AI. Artificial Intelligence 155(1-2), 41–67 (2004)

12. Lenat, D.B., Guha, R.V.: Building Large Knowledge-Based Systems; Representation and Inference in the Cyc Project. Addison-Wesley Longman Publishing Co., Inc., Boston (1989)

13. Borgida, A., Serafini, L.: Distributed Description Logics: Assimilating Information from Peer Sources. Journal of Data Semantics 1, 153–184 (2003)

14. Bouquet, P., Giunchiglia, F., van Harmelen, F., Serafini, L., Stuckenschmidt, H.: C-OWL: Contextualizing Ontologies. In: Fensel, D., Sycara, K., Mylopoulos, J. (eds.) ISWC 2003. LNCS, vol. 2870, pp. 164–179. Springer, Heidelberg (2003)

15. Parsons, S., Sierra, C., Jennings, N.R.: Agents that reason and negotiate by arguing. Journal of Logic and Computation 8(3), 261–292 (1998)

16. Sabater, J., Sierra, C., Parsons, S., Jennings, N.R.: Engineering Executable Agents using Multi-context Systems. Journal of Logic and Computation 12(3), 413–442 (2002)

17. Antoniou, G., Papatheodorou, C., Bikakis, A.: Reasoning about Context in Ambient Intelligence Environments: A Report from the Field. In: KR, pp. 557–559. AAAI Press (2010)

18. Bikakis, A., Antoniou, G., Hassapis, P.: Strategies for contextual reasoning with conflicts in Ambient Intelligence. Knowledge and Information Systems 27(1), 45–84 (2011)

19. Brewka, G., Roelofsen, F., Serafini, L.: Contextual Default Reasoning. In: IJCAI, pp. 268–273 (2007)

20. Bikakis, A., Antoniou, G.: Defeasible Contextual Reasoning with Arguments in Ambient Intelligence. IEEE Trans. on Knowledge and Data Engineering 22(11), 1492–1506 (2010)

21. Bikakis, A., Antoniou, G.: Partial Preferences and Ambiguity Resolution in Contextual Defeasible Logic. In: Delgrande, J.P., Faber, W. (eds.) LPNMR 2011. LNCS, vol. 6645, pp. 193–198. Springer, Heidelberg (2011)

22. Caire, P., Villata, S., Boella, G., van der Torre, L.: Conviviality masks in multiagent systems. In: 7th International Joint Conference on Autonomous Agents and Multiagent Systems (AAMAS 2008), Estoril, Portugal, May 12-16, vol. 3, pp. 1265–1268 (2008)

23. Caire, P., van der Torre, L.: Convivial ambient technologies: Requirements, ontology and design. The Computer Journal 3 (2009)

24. Caire, P.: Designing convivial digital cities: a social intelligence design approach. AI and Society 24(1), 97–114 (2009)

25. Castelfranchi, C.: The micro-macro constitution of power. Protosociology 18, 208–269 (2003)

26. Sichman, J.S., Conte, R.: Multi-agent dependence by dependence graphs. In: Procs. of The First International Joint Conference on Autonomous Agents & Multiagent Systems, AAMAS 2002, pp. 483–490. ACM (2002)

27. Cormen, T.H., Leiserson, C.E., Rivest, R.L., Stein, C.: Introduction to Algorithms, 2nd edn. The MIT Press (2001)

28. Brewka, G., Eiter, T., Fink, M., Weinziel, A.: Managed Multi-Context Systems. In: IJCAI (2011)

A Rule Based Approach to Group Recommender Systems

Vineet Padmanabhan, Siva Krishna Seemala, and Wilson Naik Bhukya

Department of Computer and Information Sciences,
University of Hyderabad, Hyderabad - 500046, India
{vineetcs,naikcs}@uohyd.ernet.in

Abstract. The problem of building Recommender Systems has attracted considerable attention in recent years, but most recommender systems are designed for recommending items for individuals. In this paper we develop a content based group recommender system that can recommend TV shows to a group of users. We propose a method that uses decision list rule learner (**DLRL**) based on **Ripper** to learn the rule base from user viewing history and a method called RTL strategy based on social choice theory strategies to generate group ratings. We compare our learning algorithm with the existing C4.5 rule learner and the experimental results show that the performance of our rule learner is better in terms of literals learned (size of the rule set) and our rule learner takes time that is linear to the number of training examples.

Keywords: Rule Based Systems, Recommender Systems, Machine Learning.

1 Introduction

There is lot of data available in the Internet in the form of books, articles, movies, music, web sites etc. and therefore, selecting particular items that are of our own interest is very difficult. In a similar manner we can see Television viewing largely as a family or social activity. Children most often watch with their siblings and young people would like to watch television with friends. For these reasons, we believe that adaptive television should be able to adapt to groups of people watching together. So we need systems for recommending items (e.g. books, movies, web sites) that takes into consideration our own as well as a groups interest. These systems are generally known as Personalised Recommender Systems/Group Recommender Systems (GRS) [6,3,10].

Recommender Systems are usually of two types: *collaborative recommender systems* and *content based recommender systems*. In collaborative recommender systems, a database consisting of many user's ratings of a variety of items is maintained. To recommend items for an active user, it simply searches the database to find similar users as the active user. Based on those similar users, it will recommend the items. But there are problems like *cold start, first rater, popularity bias* etc. with collaborative recommender systems. Cold-start occurs when there

C. Sombattheera et al. (Eds.): MIWAI 2011, LNAI 7080, pp. 26–37, 2011.

is not enough similar users in the database. First rater problem occurs when the item is new or it hasn't been rated earlier by any user. Popularity bias occurs when an item is recommended based on the opinion of other similar users. In recent years, a few group recommender systems have been designed. Most of these systems have been developed based on collaborative filtering techinique [1,17] and hence, they suffer from the above mentioned problems. Our approach uses content based recommendation [13]. A content-based system selects items based on the correlation between the content of the items and the user's preferences as opposed to a collaborative system that chooses items based on the correlation between people with similar preferences. Recommendations are made by comparing a user profile with the content of each document in a collection. To learn user profile, machine learning algorithms are used, the popular ones being decision tree rule learners and Naive Bayes classifier. In this work we adopt rule learners.

Though decision tree rule learners have previously been used to develop recommender systems it has been shown that there are some drawbacks with decision trees. For instance in [5] it has been noted that even a pruned decision tree may be too cumbersome, complex, and inscrutable to provide insight into the domain at hand. Also there is a replicated subtree problem with decision trees in the sense that it often happens that identical subtrees have to be learned at various places in a decision tree. Another important observation pointed out by Mitchell [11] is that Sequential Covering algorithms (Decision List Learners) are better than Simultaneous covering algorithms (Decision Tree rule learners) when plenty of data is available. One more point to be noted is that of [15] in which he proved that decision list (ordered rule sets) with at most k-conditions per rule is strictly more expressive than decision tree of depth k.

Taking into consideration the above observations, we outline in this paper a content based group recommender system (GRS) which is based on a decision list rule learner (DLRL). DLRL is a multi-class rule learner and is used to learn user profiles. It works well for single user as well as group. To generate group ratings we propose a combined strategy called RTL (not **recursive theory learner** as used in machine learning community) which is superior to the existing social choice theory strategies. We compared the performance of our learning algorithm with the C4.5 rule learner and experimental results show that the performance of our rule learner is better in terms of the literals learned (size of the rule set) (i.e., needs less number of literals (conditions) than the decision tree rule learner (C4.5)).

This paper is organized as follows: In Section 2 we briefly discuss about related approaches for group recommender systems. Section 3 explains our approach to TV group recommender systems. Here we provide the learning algorithm for our model and outline an example that shows the working of the proposed model. Further we outline a combined strategy called RTL and demonstrate with the help of an example its working. Section 4 shows the experimental results and Section 5 talks about related work. We conclude with Section 6.

2   Strategies for GRS

There are three common strategies to develop Group recommender systems. (1) **Group Agent:** In this approach, there is a common account for the group. Group agent learns the preferences for the group and based on that it will recommend the items. But the drawback here is that it works well for the whole group, but if some members in the group are not present then no recommendation is done. (2) **Merging recommendations:** In this approach, each user profile is learned initially. From each user profile separate recommendation list is generated for each user. Finally, all user recommendation lists will be merged to get a group recommendation list. (3) **Merging User profiles:** In this approach, each user profile is learned initially. All these user profiles are merged to get a common user profile. Finally, recommendations are generated using common user profile.

2.1   Social Choice Theory Strategies

Social choice (also called as group decision making)-is deciding what is best for a group, given the opinions of individuals. These strategies are as follows: `Plurality Voting` [8]: In this Strategy, each voter votes for his or her most preferred alternative. The alternative with the most votes win. For instance, consider Table 1. wherein A, B, C..., J are 10 TV programs. The corresponding rating of each TV program for three different users (John, Adam, Mary) are also given. From Table 1, it can be inferred that John prefers A, E, I. Adam prefers B, D, F, H. Mary prefers A. Clearly TV program A is the recommended program because it occurs twice in these three preferred lists. `Utilitarian Strategy`

Table 1. Example to demonstrate Social choice Strategies

Tv-Programs	A	B	C	D	E	F	G	H	I	J
John	10	4	3	6	10	9	6	8	10	8
Adam	1	9	8	9	7	9	6	9	3	8
Mary	10	5	2	7	9	8	5	6	7	6

[7]: In this strategy, instead of using ranking information, utility values are used. This can be done in multiple ways: additive or multiplicative. For example, the utility values for the 10 programs in Table 1. will be 21, 18, 13, 22, 26, 26, 17, 23, 20, 22 respectively. The TV program E and F are having highest utility values. So either E or F is the recommended program. `Least misery strategy` [12]: In this strategy, the item with large minimum individual rating will be recommended. The idea behind this strategy is that a group is as happy as its least happy member. For Example, the group rating for the 10 TV programs based on Least Misery Strategy will be 1, 4, 2, 6, 7, 8, 5, 6, 3, 6 respectively. From the above group ratings, F has the highest rating. So TV program F is recommended by Least misery strategy. `Most pleasure strategy` [8]: Making

new list with the maximum of individual ratings. For Example, from Table 1 the group rating for 10 TV programs based on this strategy will be 10, 9, 8, 9, 10, 9, 6, 9, 10, 8 respectively. From the above group ratings, A, E, I are having the highest rating values. So either A, E or I will be the recommended TV program. `Average without Misery strategy [9]`: In this strategy, a new list of ratings is made with the average of the individual ratings, but without items that score below a certain threshold for individuals. The item with maximum value will be recommended. For example, from Table 1. considering a threshold of 4 the average values for 10 TV programs will be -, 18, -, 22, 26, 26, 17, 23, -, 22 respectively. The TV program E and F are having highest utility values. So either E or F is the recommended program.

3   Proposed Method

As mentioned earlier, our method for TV group recommender is developed based on decision list rule learner and social choice theory strategies. In our approach, each training example is a collection of 12 attribute-value pair. Those attributes are: Date, Day, Time, Channel, ProgramName, Category, Genre, Classification, Starring, Language, Duration, Rating. Here, the rating is a 5-scaled one 0, 1, 2, 3, 4. 0 indicates bad program, 1 indicates average program, 2 indicates above average program, 3 indicates a good program, 4 indicates an excellent program. The proposed architecture is shown in Figure 2(d) which can be explained as follows; initially, the system has no idea to recommend any tv programs except if we add any external rules. For few weeks, it will collect ratings for each and every program the user has watched. These are the training examples to the learning algorithm. From these training examples the learning algorithm learns the set of rules that cover all training examples. This process will be done for every user i.e., for each user, we get a separate rule base (User profile). Now we know that any TV guide contains information regarding TV programs i.e., Day, Date, Time, Channel etc. By using the rule base of each user we generate predicted ratings of programs in the TV guide which is shown as TV Guide + Classification in Figure 2(d). These programs with predicted ratings are nothing but recommendation list for each individual user. Finally, social choice theory strategies are used to get a combined (group) recommendation list.

3.1   Our Learning Algorithm

Learning algorithm plays major role in content based recommendation approach. It is used to learn user profiles. Our learning algorithm is a decision list rule learner based on RIPPER [2] and FOIL [14] rule learners. It is a multi-class rule learner wherein there are five classes : bad, average, above average, good, excellent. Initially, all training examples are divided into two sets: training data and prune data. Training data is used to learn the set of rules. Prune data is used to prune the rules to avoid over-fitting. FOIL Information gain is given as $FOIL\ Gain(L, R) = t(\log_2(\frac{p_1}{p_1+n_1}) - \log_2(\frac{p_0}{p_0+n_0}))$ where L is the candidate literal to add to rule R, p_0 is the number of positive bindings of R, n_0 is the number of negative bindings of R, p_1 is the number of positive bindings of R + L, n_1 is the number of negative bindings of R + L, t is the number of positive bindings of R also covered by R + L. The formula used to prune the rule is defined as $v = \frac{(p-n)}{(p+n)}$ where p is the number of positive examples covered by the rule in prune data set and n is the number of negative examples covered by the rule in the prune data set. Pruning criteria is deleting the final sequence of conditions that maximizes v. The different steps involved in our learning algorithm is shown in Algorithm 1.

Algorithm 1. Learning Algorithm used in proposed method

Input: Train Data,Prune Data
Output: set of rules
Step 1: **foreach** *class* **do**
  | Find the number of training examples for that class;
end
Take the class with maximum number of examples, make that as Default class;
Step 2: Take an empty RuleSet;
while *No class has left* **do**
    take the next smallest class;
    Consider training examples for that class as positive, remaining as negative;
    while *All positive examples covered* **do**
        Take empty Rule;
        Add conjuncts to rule as soon as it improves FOIL Information gain;
        prune the rule by deleting any final sequence of conditions;
        Mark covered positive examples by this rule;
        Add this rule to RuleSet;
    end
end
Step 3:Add Default Rule to RuleSet;
Return RuleSet;

To understand the working of the proposed method, let us consider 12 TV programs (training examples) as shown in Figure 1 and five users namely User 1, User 2, User 3, User 4, User 5. User ratings for these TV programs are shown under the columns R(U1) to R(U5). As we described earlier, each training example is a collection of 11 attribute-value pair. Here the ratings 0, 1, 2, 3, 4 correspond to **bad(B)**, **average(A)**, **above average(AA)**, **good(G)**, **excellent(E)** classes respectively. To show the working of external rules, let us assume that User 1 and User 3 wants to watch programs only in Telugu and English. Other three users wants to watch the programs in Hindi also. These conditions can be added to the rule base as (1) **bad** if Language = ¬ Telugu OR ¬English for User1 and User3 and (2) **bad** if Language = ¬ Telugu OR ¬ English OR ¬ Hindi for Users 2, 4 and 5. DLRL (Decision List Rule Learner) orders the classes according to the class prevalence, i.e., the number of training examples for that class. For each user the number of examples for different classes are shown in Table 2. DLRL learns the rules from the training examples for each user. Learning starts from the least prevalence class to the highest prevalence class. For example, in Table 2, User1 has two **bad** class examples which is having least class prevalence as compared to other classes and therefore rules for that class will be learned first. After that good, average, above average, excellent

DATE	DAY	TIME	PROGRAM TITLE	CATEGORY	GENRE	LANGUAGE	CLASSIFICATION	CHANNEL	STARRING	DURATION	R(U1)	R(U2)	R(U3)	R(U4)	R(U5)
01/01/09	Thu	8a.m	MVNAME1	movie	action	English	U/A	HBO	Omald	2hours	4	3	4	3	4
01/01/09	Thu	12p.m	MVNAME2	movie	comedy	Telugu	U/A	Gemini	Rajendra	3hours	3	4	3	4	3
01/01/09	Thu	5p.m	MVNAME3	movie	cartoon	English	U/A	Cartoon Nw	unknown	2hours	0	0	4	0	4
01/01/09	Thu	9p.m	MVNAME4	movie	horror	English	A	StarWorld	asdf	2hours	1	1	4	1	3
02/01/09	Fri	9a.m	MVNAME5	movie	comedy	English	A	HBO	Naresh	3hours	3	4	3	4	3
02/01/09	Fri	12p.m	MVNAME6	movie	cartoon	Telugu	U/A	ETV	unknown	2ours	0	0	4	0	4
02/02/09	Fri	5p.m	MVNAME7	movie	action	English	U/A	StarMovies	Bond	2hours	4	3	4	3	4
02/02/09	Fri	9p.m	MVNAME8	movie	horror	Telugu	A	Teja	J.D.Chakra	3hours	1	1	4	1	3
03/03/09	Sat	9a.m	MVNAME10	movie	action	English	U/A	H.B.O	Omald	2hours	4	3	4	3	3
03/03/09	Sat	5p.m	MVNAME11	movie	action	Telugu	U/A	Teja	Hritik roshan	3hours	4	3	4	3	4
03/03/09	Sat	4p.m	MVNAME12	movie	comedy	English	U/A	StarMovies	das	2hours	3	4	3	4	3
03/03/09	Sat	9p.m	MVNAME13	movie	horror	English	A	H.B.O	k.p.Kar	2hours	1	1	4	1	3

Fig. 1. Example to Demonstrate the Proposed Method

Table 2. DLRL Class ordering

	B	A	AA	G	E
User 1	2	3	0	3	4
User 2	2	3	0	3	4
User 3	0	9	0	0	3
User 4	2	3	0	3	4
User 5	0	5	0	0	7

Table 3. Example Instances

D	Day	T	P	C	G	L	CL	Ch	S	D
04/04	Sat	5pm	M14	Mov	co	Eng	U/A	Z	Ab	2
04/04	Sat	5pm	M15	Mov	ac	Eng	U/A	G	Ch	2
04/04	Sat	9pm	M16	Mov	ac	H	U/A	H	Bo	2
04/04	Sat	9pm	M17	Mov	ho	T	A	G	Ch	3

class rules will be learned. The class with highest prevalence is taken as default class and it is added to the rule base as default rule meaning that if all the above rules fail to classify a particular TV program then it belongs to the default class. Each rule looks like : **Class :- List of conditions** meaning that **If (list of conditions) then Class**. The learned rules for all the users 1, 2 and 4 are as follows:

– **RULE BASE for User1:**
  External rules: Bad :- Language = ¬Telugu OR ¬English
  Learned Rules: Bad :- CATEGORY = movie AND GENRE = cartoon AND CLASSIFICA-TION = U/A. Good :- CATEGORY = movie AND GENRE = comedy. Average:- TIME = 9p.m AND CATEGORY = movie AND GENRE = horror. Default Rule: Excellent :- ()

– **RULE BASE for User2 and User 4:**
  External rules: Bad :- Language = ¬Telugu OR ¬English OR ¬Hindi
  Learned Rules: Bad :- CATEGORY = movie AND GENRE = cartoon AND CLASSIFICA-TION = U/A. Excellent: CATEGORY = movie AND GENRE = comedy. Average :- TIME = 9p.m AND CATEGORY = movie AND GENRE = horror. Default Rule: good :- ().

The rule base for User1 can be interpreted as follows: 1) Classify a program as bad if it is not in English or Telugu. 2) A program is also bad if it is a cartoon movie with classification U/A. 3) A program is good if it is a comedy movie. 4) A program is average if it is a horror movie being telecast at 9 PM in the night. 5) A program is excellent if it does not fall into any of the categories from 1 to 4. Other rule bases can be interpreted in a similar manner. Now let us consider four upcoming TV programs as shown in Table 3. These are the new instances which needs to be classified according to the learned rules. To reduce the Table size we have shortened the attribute names but they are the same as in Figure 1. For example, the first instance in Table 3 is a TV program having the following attributes and values (Date = 04/04/09,

Day = Saturday, Time = 5pm, Program-Title = Movie 14, Genre = Comedy, Category = Movie, Language = English, Classification = U/A, Channel = Zoom, Starring = Abhisek, Duration = 2hours). In a similar manner other instances can be interpreted. The classification for these new instances according to the learned rules is shown in the first five rows of Table 4 (for User 1 to User 5). For example, the first row of Table 4 shows the classification of the 4 new instances for User 1 in which instance 1 is classified as **good** (rating 3), instance 2 as **excellent** (rating 4), instance 3 as **bad** (rating 0) and instance 4 as **average** (rating 1). This rating is obtained from the Rule base of User1 which in turn is generated by our rule learner (DLRL). In a similar manner ratings for other users can be achieved.

Table 4. Classification based on Learned rules and Social choice strategies

Users	Instance 1	Instance 2	Instance 3	Instance 4
User 1	3	4	0	1
User 2	4	3	4	1
User 3	3	4	0	4
User 4	4	3	4	1
User 5	3	4	3	4
1. Utilitarian (Addition)	17	18*	11	11
2. Utilitarian (Multiplication)	432	576*	0	16
3. Least misery strategy	3*	3*	0	1
4. Most pleasure strategy	4*	4*	4*	4*
5. Average without misery	3.4	3.6*	-	-
6. RTL strategy(Our method)	20	21*	-	12

In the above sections we have seen how to generate/classify ratings for new instances for each individual user. Now we will extend the procedure to generate group ratings with the help of social choice theory strategies. Rows 6-11 of Table 4 shows the ratings given by the different strategies as well as the recommended instance for each of these strategies (* indicates the recommended instances by the respective strategies). In the case of Utilitarian strategy as discussed in Section 2.2 group ratings are generated based on the utility values. These utility values can be taken as sum or multiplication of all the ratings for the particular instance. These utility values are shown in rows 6 and 7 of Table 4 as Utilitarian (Addition) and Utilitarian (Multiplication). From these values, we can say that instance 2 is the recommended TV program by the utilitarian strategy because it has the highest utility value. In the case of Least misery strategy, group ratings are generated based on the least rating of a particular item. These least rating values are shown in row 8 of Table 4. From these values we take the largest minimum which is 3. Hence we can say that instance 1 and instance 2 are equally recommended TV programs because these instances have 3 as the maximum value. When we consider Most pleasure strategy it can be seen that group ratings are generated based on the highest rating of the particular item. These highest values are shown in row 9 of Table 4. From these values, we can say that all instances are equally recommended because these instances are having 4 as the maximum value. Coming to Average without misery strategy, group ratings are generated based on the Average of all the ratings for a particular item and items are only considered if all the ratings are

---

Algorithm 2. RTL strategy used in proposed method

Input: InstanceRatingVector(I), Number of users (N)
Output: Recommended Instances
Step 1: **if** *all Instances in I has an user rating "0"* **then**
   | countNoOfRepeat=0;
   | goto step 2;
end
else
   | Remove the instances in I which has an user rating 0 ;
   | countNoOfRepeat=0;
   | goto step 2;
end
Step 2: **foreach** *instance i in I* **do**
   | C_i = the sum of all user rating + minimum user rating for instance "i";
end
max = maximum value in C_i;
if *countNoofRepeat = N* **then**
   | **foreach** *Instance i in I* **do**
   | | **if** *max=C_i* **then**
   | | | **return** i;
   | | **end**
   | **end**
end
if *max appears multiple times in C_i and countNoofRepeat < N* **then**
   | **foreach** *instance i in I* **do**
   | | Remove the least rating entries for instance "i"
   | **end**
   | countNoOfRepeat++;
   | repeat step2;
end
else
   | **return** i
end

---

more than the given threshold. For example, if we take threshold = 1 then the average values for the four new instances are shown in row 9 of Table 4. Instances 3 and four are ignored because of having the ratings less than the assumed thresold. From these values, we can say that instance 2 is the recommended TV program by this strategy because it has highest average value.

From the above example we observed that no method alone is sufficient to recommend the best TV program. For instance, suppose we take five users and two TV programs with ratings{4, 3, 2, 4, 3},{4, 3, 3, 3, 3}. Then by utilitarian strategy these two programs are equally recommended because the sum of all ratings in both lists are equal. But out of these two TV programs, TV program2 is better, because for TV program2 group member's happiness is atleat 3, where as for TV program1 it is 2. Similarly in the case of least misery strategy, assume that we take two users and five TV programs with ratings {4, 3, 3, 4, 3}, {4, 3, 3, 3, 3}. These two TV programs are equally recommended by least misery strategy because in both cases least rating is 3. But we can say that first program is better if we consider whole group happiness. In the case of most pleasure strategy, we consider only the single user's happiness which is not a suggestable method. As far as Average without misery strategy is concerned, we ignore some TV programs based on a particular threshold value and thus end up having TV programs which are average programs for all users.

As we pointed out above a single strategy alone would not be sufficient to get the most accurate result as far as ruled based group recommenders are concerned. Therefore, we need a combined strategy that considers three factors: 1) Least group member happy (like least misery strategy) 2) Most group member happy (like most pleasure strategy) 3) Total group happy (like Utilitarian strategy). We name this strategy as RTL strategy (Repeat Total plus Least group happiness strategy). Here the idea is to calculate the sum of least happiness and total happiness for each instance and calculate the maximum of this summed values and then recommend that instance. If we have maximum value for multiple instances then, take only those instances, remove the minimum values (least happiness) from these instances and apply the same process for the new set of instances repeatedly. Hence the name Repeat Total plus Least group happiness strategy. The working of RTL strategy is shown in Algorithm 2. To give an example to show how the algorithm works, let us take five users and two TV programs with ratings, $I_1 = \{1, 2, 1, 1, 4\}$, $I_2 = \{1, 2, 2, 2, 2\}$. Here we go directly to Step 2 of Algorithm 2 as the first step is not applicable. Then $C_1 = 9 + 1 = 10$ (i.e., the sum of all user rating $(1 + 2 + 1 + 1 + 4 = 9)$ + minimum user rating (1) for instance i. Step 2 of Algorithm 2). Similarly, $C_2 = 9 + 1 = 10$, countNoOfRepeat $= 0$, max $= 10$. Since max $= 10$ appears multiple times in C, according to the second "if condition" in Step 2 of Algorithm 2, I_1 will be $\{2, 4\}$ and I_2 will be $\{2, 2, 2, 2\}$. Now countNoOfRepeat $= 1$, $C_1 = 6 + 2 = 8$ and $C_2 = 8 + 2 = 10$. Therefore, Instance 2 will be recommended. The ratings given by RTL strategy for the 4 new instances in Table 3 is shown in row 11 of Table 4. According to RTL strategy instance 2 will be recommended and the reader can verify that out of the 4 new instances, instance 2 is the best fit for the group. Another experimental analysis we did was to collect all the training examples and arrange them into a number of clusters, each belonging to different category (movies, news, sports, drama, business, etc.). Each different cluster can be further divided into five sub-clusters. Each sub-cluster belongs to different kind of class (bad, average, above-average, good and excellent). Cluster contains similar kind of examples. To measure similarity, Euclidean distance was used. To get the classification for the instances (upcoming TV programs), we calculated the similarity between the examples in the sub-cluster and the instance.

4   Experimental Results

Unfortunately, we were not able to get any existing datasets for the TV group recommender systems. Hence we collected different datasets containing 46, 74, 93, 106 and 119, 150 training examples for different TV programs from an indian online TV guide called burrptv (tv.burrp.com). We ran our DLRL and C4.5 rule learners on these datasets and we noted the number of literals learned for these datasets for Decision tree rule learner (C4.5), Cluster based approach and Decision list rule learner(DLRL: Our method). These are shown in Figure 2 (a). From Figure 2 (a) we can see that DLRL performance is better in terms of literals learned (size of the rule set) (i.e. needs less number of literals (conditions) than the decision tree rule learner(C4.5) and cluster based approach for recommending an item). Anyway, we know that cluster based approach requires to store all the examples in order to recommend the items. We noted the time required to learn the different datasets and this is shown in Figure 2 (b) (No. of training examples and Time in seconds). From these experimental results, we can say that the performance of DLRL is almost linear to the training examples. For a data set of size 76 the number of literals (conjuncts in the precondition

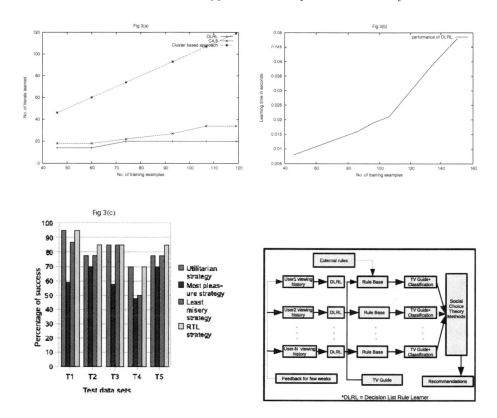

Fig. 2. (a) No. of Literals learned by different approaches (b) DLRL performance (c) Comparison of RTL and other social choice strategies (d) Proposed Architecture

of each rule) learned using our learner was 14 whereas using C4.5 it was 22. We did a second experiment to compare RTL strategy to other existing social choice theory strategies. For this purpose we created five different test datasets. Since we did not know the real group rating for the examples in the test datasets we defined an ideal instance for a group. An instance is said to be ideal if it fully satisfies every user in a group. Based on this ideal instance we created a factor called percentage of success to compare the strategies. This factor is defined as follows: let n be the number of users in a group, instance $I = \{i_1, i_2, \ldots, i_n\}$ and an ideal instance $I_{ideal} = \{j_1, j_2, \ldots, j_n\}$ be the rating vectors then, the Percentage of Success for instance $I = \frac{\sum_{k=1}^{n} \frac{i_k}{j_k}}{n} \times 100$. For example, let us take five users and two TV programs with ratings: $I_1 = 1, 2, 1, 1, 4$, $I_2 = 1, 2, 2, 2, 2$. Here the ideal instance will be $I_{ideal} = \{1, 2, 2, 2, 4\}$, the percentage of success for $I_1 = \frac{(1/1+2/2+1/2+1/2+4/4)}{5} \times 100 = 80\%$ and the percentage of success for $I_2 = \frac{(1/1+2/2+2/2+2/2+2/4)}{5} \times 100 = 90\%$. Here we note that Utilitarian strategy and least misery strategy recommends I_1 and I_2, Most pleasure strategy recommends I_1, RTL strategy recommends I_2 which has max percentage of success. In our experiment we calculated the percentage of success in the instances of five different test datasets and we obsereved that RTL strategy always recommends the instance which has best percentage of success. The percentage of success for these test datasets for utilitarian, least misery, most pleasure and RTL strategy are shown in Figure 2(c).

5   Related Work

In [1] a group recommendation approach based on collaborative filtering and genetic programming is proposed. In this work the authors assume that the input data already contains 'items' ratings given by individuals and then use genetic algorithm to get 'items' group ratings. In our approach both individual as well as group ratings are *learned*. The individual ratings are learned by the rule learner and the group ratings using social choice theory strategies. Moreover we use content based approach whereas in [1] the approach is that of collaborative filtering and hence suffers from cold-start, first-rater and popularity bias problems. [17] make use of content based approach and outlines a method to merge individual user profiles to get common user profile. Here the merging is based on individual user preferences on features (e.g. genre, actor and keyword about a program) whereas we combine individual user ratings on whole programs rather than features. The obvious disadvantage of this approach is that it increases the time and effort required to do the recommendation. [16] also uses content-based approach but the focus is more on developing an ontology language like OWL through which digital TV programs can be described and then to relate them through their semantic characteristics. There are no experimental results to show how this can be acheived. In [8] no mention is made on how to get user profiles. Social choice theory strategies are mentioned but again how to include a learning component to make use of those strategies is not shown. [4] proposes a group recommender system based on Bayesian Network. They do not discuss about how groups are formed but sums up by saying that *a group is a new entity where recommendations are made by considering the particular recommendations of its members in some way.* In our case we are more interested in combining individual user models to adapt to groups such as how humans select a sequence of television items to suit a group of viewers.

6   Conclusions

In this work, we developed a content based group recommender system for TV shows based on decision list rule learner (DLRL) and a method to generate group ratings (RTL) based on social choice theory strategies. We compared the performance of our learning algorithm with the existing C4.5 rule learner. Results show that the performance of our rule learner is better in terms of the literals learned (size of the rule set) and our rule learner takes time that is linear to the number of training examples. It is also shown that our combined strategy of RTL is better than the existing Social Choice theory strategies.

References

1. Chen, Y.L., Cheng, L.-C., Chuang, C.N.: A group recommendation system with consideration of interactions among group members. Expert Syst. Appl. 34(3), 2082–2090 (2008)
2. Cohen, W.W.: Fast effective rule induction. In: ICML, pp. 115–123 (1995)
3. Cole, J.J., Gray, M.J., Lloyd, J.W., Ng, K.S.: Personalisation for user agents. In: AAMAS 2005, Utrecht, The Netherlands, pp. 603–610 (2005)
4. de Campos, L.M., Luna, J.M., Huete, J.F., Morales, M.A.: Group recommending: A methodological approach based on bayesian networks. In: ICDE Workshops, pp. 835–844 (2007)
5. Fürnkranz, J.: Separate-and-conquer rule learning. Artificial Intelligence Review 13(1), 3–54 (1999)
6. Gutta, S., Kurapati, K., Lee, K.P., Martino, J., Milanski, J., Schaffer, J., Zimmerman, J.: Tv content recommender system. In: AAAI/IAAI, Austin, USA, July 30-August 3, pp. 1121–1122 (2000)
7. Hogg, L., Jennings, N.R.: Variable Sociability in Agent-Based Decision Making. In: Jennings, N.R. (ed.) ATAL 1999. LNCS, vol. 1757, pp. 305–318. Springer, Heidelberg (2000)
8. Masthoff, J.: Group modeling: Selecting a sequence of television items to suit a group of viewers. User Model. User-Adapt. Interact. 14(1), 37–85 (2004)
9. McCarthy, J.F., Anagnost, T.D.: Musicfx: An arbiter of group preferences for computer aupported collaborative workouts. In: CSCW, pp. 363–372 (1998)
10. McCarthy, K., Salamó, M., Coyle, L., McGinty, L., Smyth, B., Nixon, P.: Group recommender systems: a critiquing based approach. In: International Conference on Intelligent User Interfaces, Australia, January 29- February 1, pp. 267–269 (2006)
11. Mitchell, T.M.: Machine Learning. McGraw Hill, USA (1997)
12. O'Connor, M., Cosley, D., Konstan, J.A., Riedl, J.: Polylens: A recommender system for groups of user. In: ECSCW, Germany, pp. 199–218 (September 2001)
13. Pazzani, M.J., Billsus, D.: Content-Based Recommendation Systems. In: Brusilovsky, P., Kobsa, A., Nejdl, W. (eds.) Adaptive Web 2007. LNCS, vol. 4321, pp. 325–341. Springer, Heidelberg (2007)
14. Quinlan, J.R.: Learning logical definitions from relations. Machine Learning 5, 239–266 (1990)
15. Rivest, R.L.: Learning decision lists. Machine Learning 2(3), 229–246 (1987)
16. Tubio, R., Sotelo, R., Blanco, Y., Lopez, M., Gil, A., Pazos, J., Ramos, M.: A tv-anytime metadata approach to tv program recommendation for groups. In: Consumer Electronics, ISCE, pp. 1–3 (April 2008)
17. Yu, Z., Zhou, X., Hao, Y., Gu, J.: Tv program recommendation for multiple viewers based on user profile merging. User Model. User-Adapt. Interact. 16(1), 63–82 (2006)

Combining Collaborative Filtering and Sentiment Classification for Improved Movie Recommendations

Vivek Kumar Singh[1], Mousumi Mukherjee[2], and Ghanshyam Kumar Mehta[2]

[1] Departemnt of Computer Science, South Asian University,
New Delhi-110067, India
[2] Departemnt of Computer Science, Banaras Hindu University,
Varanasi-221005, India
{vivekks12,mou.sonai,ghanshyam4u2000}@gmail.com

Abstract. Recommender systems are traditionally of following three types: content-based, collaborative filtering and hybrid systems. Content-based methods are limited in their applicability to textual items only, whereas collaborative filtering due to its accuracy and its black box approach has been used widely for different kinds of item recommendations. Hybrid method, the third approach, tries to combine content and collaborative approaches to improve the recommendation results. In this paper, we present an alternative approach to a hybrid recommender system that improves the results of collaborative filtering by incorporating a sentiment classifier in the recommendation process. We have explored this idea through our experimental work in movie review domain, with collaborative filtering doing first level filtering and the sentiment classifier performing the second level of filtering. The final recommendation list is a more accurate and focused set.

Keywords: Collaborative Filtering, Movie Review Mining, Opinion Analysis, Recommender Systems, Sentiment Classification.

1 Introduction

The increased penetration of the Internet and the new more participative Web 2.0 has facilitated a large number of users to use & interact with web applications. The users are now able to interact with web applications in a more participative way by contributing in a variety of forms, such as rating, tagging, writing blogs, social networking and sharing items with friends. This increased interaction is generating huge amount of information that can be exploited in different ways. However, this information overload also becomes problematic for users when they try to search and locate a desired item on the web. A recommender system is a program that solves this problem by automatically filtering and presenting items of interest to a user. Recommender systems constitute a problem-rich and applied area with many practical applications that help users to deal with information overload and provide personalized services to them. Amazon, Netflix, Google News personalization and MovieLens are examples of some of the popular and powerful industry scale recommender systems.

C. Sombattheera et al. (Eds.): MIWAI 2011, LNAI 7080, pp. 38–50, 2011.
© Springer-Verlag Berlin Heidelberg 2011

During the past few years a good amount of research has been done on recommender systems with significant advances being made in all the approaches: content-based, collaborative filtering and the hybrid. Traditionally the hybrid systems try to combine the content-based and collaborative filtering approaches in various ways to produce results better than any of the individual methods. In this paper, we have proposed and experimented with a different kind of hybrid approach, where we combined the collaborative filtering with a sentiment classification phase instead of the traditional content similarity based analysis process. We collected a standard user-movie rating dataset and then obtained review data for the movies in the dataset. First phase of the experimental work involved applying the collaborative filtering method to obtain first level recommended list for a user. In the second phase, sentiment classifier was used to label each movie as 'positive' or 'negative'. The final list of movie recommendations included only those movies that are recommended by collaborative filtering phase and are also labeled 'positive' by sentiment classifier. The recommendations of our approach are much more focused and accurate.

To the best of our knowledge no experimental work on this kind of hybrid approach has been done in the past. This paper therefore presents a new approach to designing a hybrid recommender system for data items involving textual reviews. The rest of the paper is organized as follows. Section 2 describes the collaborative filtering approach of recommender system design and section 3 illustrates the sentiment classification problem and approaches. Section 4 describes the experimental setup and the results obtained. The paper concludes (section 5) with a brief summary of the results, followed by a short discussion of usefulness and relevance of this work.

2   Collaborative Filtering

The recommendation problem can be formally defined as follows: Let U be the set of all users and I be the set of all possible items that can be recommended. The items may include books, movies, products, restaurants, vacations etc. The set I of items can be very large, with possibly millions of items. And similarly the set U of users can also be very large with millions of users in some cases. Let r be a recommender utility function that measures the usefulness of an item i to a user u, i.e., $r : U \, X \, I \rightarrow R$, where R is a totally ordered set of non-negative integers or real numbers. Then the recommendation problem is to choose for each user $u \, \epsilon \, U$, such items $i \, \epsilon \, I$ that maximizes the users utility, i.e., $i_u = arg \, max_{\, i \, \epsilon \, I} \, r \, (\, u, \, i \,)$. The utility usually refers to some rating value associated with different items [1]. However, the central problem is that the recommender utility r is usually not defined on the whole of $U \, X \, I$ space, but only on some subset of it. Therefore, the recommender system needs to extrapolate from known to unknown ratings. Once the unknown ratings are estimated, actual recommendations of an item to a user are made by selecting the highest rating among all the estimated ratings for that user. This extrapolation can be done in a number of ways using machine learning, approximation theory and heuristics.

Recommender systems aim to show items of interest to a user. In order to do so a recommender system may exploit the following inputs: (a) *user's profile* – attributes like age, gender, geographical location, net worth etc., (b) *information about various items available* – content associated with item, (c) *interactions of users* – such as ratings, tagging, bookmarking, saving, emailing, browsing history etc., and (d) *the context of where the items will be shown* [2]. These inputs may be used by a recommender system to produce following kinds of results: (a) users who watched this video watched these other videos, (b) new items related to a particular item, (c) users similar to a particular user, and (d) the products a user may be interested in. Amazon's recommendation saying 'users who bought this also bought…', youtube's 'related videos' and Netflix's movie recommendations are all examples of recommender system in action. As stated earlier, traditionally there have been three approaches to recommender system design: *content-based, collaborative filtering*, and *hybrid*.

In *content-based approach* a user is recommended those items that are similar in content to the items liked by the user in the past. The items in the entire set are compared with the items liked by the user in the past and only the best matching items are recommended [2]. Usually content-based approaches are used with textual data such as news, web pages etc. Content-based recommendation is a good choice when the item is of textual nature (in fact content similarity can be computed only when text document vector representations are available) or if the user transaction history is not available. However, it suffers from the problems of non-applicability on non-textual data (such as videos), overspecialization and new user problem. Unlike content-based systems, *collaborative filtering* recommends an item to a user, either based on items previously rated by similar users (user-based-analysis) or based on the knowledge about items similar to the items rated by the user in the past (item-based-analysis) [2]. Collaborative filtering takes a black-box approach and hence has applicability on wider class of items ranging from movies to videos. It may, however, suffer from problems of new user, new item and sparsity of data. *Hybrid systems* try to combine content-based and collaborative filtering approaches in various ways, to exploit the benefits of both the approaches and minimizing their individual disadvantages.

2.1   Collaborative Filtering Process

Collaborative recommender systems can be of two types: *memory-based* and *model-based*. *Memory-based algorithms* essentially are heuristics that make predictions based on the entire collection of previously rated items by the users. The value of an unknown rating r (u,i) is computed as an aggregate of the ratings of some other (usually the N most similar) users for the same item i. A similar scheme with items can be adopted if related users are to be recommended. Various approaches to compute similarity between users or items in a collaborative recommender system have been used. The most prominent ones are: (a) cosine-based similarity, (b) correlation-based similarity, and (c) adjusted cosine-based similarity. The Cosine based similarity between two items x and y (represented as vectors) is computed as follows:

$$sim(x, y) = \cos(\vec{x}, \vec{y}) = \frac{\vec{x}.\vec{y}}{\|\vec{x}\|_2 \times \|\vec{y}\|_2} = \frac{\sum_{s \in S_{xy}} r_{x,s} r_{y,s}}{\sqrt{\sum_{s \in S_{xy}} r_{x,s}^2} \sqrt{\sum_{s \in S_{xy}} r_{y,s}^2}} \qquad (1)$$

To explain the notion of similarity let's consider an example scenario where there are three users who rate certain photos. The ratings done by these users are as shown in table 1 below.

Table 1. Example rating data by three users

	Anushka	Marisha	Vishakha	Average
Photo 1	3	2	1	2
Photo 2	4	2	3	3
Photo 3	2	4	5	11/3
Average	3	8/3	3	26/3

Given this data we can easily answer at least two questions: (a) what are the set of related photos for a given photo, and (b) for a user, who are the other users similar to her. We can satisfy these queries by generating item-to-item and user-to-user similarity tables, respectively. In order to obtain item-to-item similarity we first normalize the values in each row of the table 1 so as to obtain table 2. This is done by dividing each of the cell entries by the square root of the sum of squares of the entries in that row. For example, each value in the first row is divided by $\sqrt{3^2 + 2^2 + 1^2} = \sqrt{14} = 3.74$ to get the normalized values.

Table 2. Normalized ratings

	Anushka	Marisha	Vishakha
Photo 1	0.8018	0.5345	0.2673
Photo 2	0.7428	0.3714	0.557
Photo 3	0.2981	0.5963	0.7454

The similarity between two items can then be computed using any of the three similarity computations: cosine, correlation or adjusted cosine. For example, the cosine similarity between items can be computed by taking the dot product of normalized values of their row vectors. (Cosine similarity between photo 1 and photo 2 will be 0.8018*0.7428 + 0.5345*0.3714 + 0.2673*0.557 − 0.943). The cosine similarity values computed as above can thus be used to develop an item-to-item similarity matrix as in table 3. Then using table 3 we can answer the first question, i.e., photo 2 is more similar to photo 1 (value = 0.943). The closer to 1 value an i,j entry in the table is, the more similar are the items i and j.

Table 3. Item-to-Item similarity

	Photo 1	Photo 2	Photo 3
Photo 1	1	0.943	0.757
Photo 2	0.943	1	0.858
Photo 3	0.757	0.858	1

Similarly the rating data can be used to answer the second question (users similar to a particular user). In order to do so we first transpose the table 1 to result in table 4 and then normalize the entries in each row to obtain the normalized table as in table 5. The data in the table can then be used to develop user-to-user similarity matrix by computing dot product of the row vectors in a similar manner. The resultant user-to-user similarity matrix for the data in table 5 is shown in table 6. This can now be used to answer the second question, i.e., user 2 and 3 are very similar (value = 0.97).

Table 4. Example rating data by three users

	Photo 1	Photo 2	Photo 3	Average
Anushka	3	4	2	3
Marisha	2	2	4	8/3
Vishakha	1	3	5	3
Average	2	3	11/3	26/3

Table 5. Normalized ratings

	Photo 1	Photo 2	Photo 3
Anushka	0.5571	0.7428	0.3714
Marisha	0.4082	0.4082	0.8165
Vishakha	0.1690	0.5071	0.8452

Table 6. User-to-User similarity

	Anushka	Marisha	Vishakha
Anushka	1	0.83	0.78
Marisha	0.83	1	0.97
Vishakha	0.78	0.97	1

The second kind of collaborative filtering algorithms, *model-based collaborative filtering*, use the collection of ratings to first learn a model, which is then used to make rating predictions. Model-based algorithms typically use techniques like Latent Semantic Indexing (LSI), Bayesian Classification & Clustering, Probabilistic Latent Semantic Indexing (PLSI), Markov decision processes and Latent Dirichlet Allocation (LDA).

Collaborative filtering algorithms can be applied across any type of data (video, news, books, movies, user profiles in social network etc.) since they treat the data item as black-box and do not use information about content of the item. What it needs is a user-item matrix of past transactions to compute both user-to-user similarity and item-to-item similarity. If the data corresponding to which users have liked what items in the past, is available, collaborative filtering can be performed. It does not matter at all whether this data of 'likes' is for some movie or a book. However, collaborative filtering suffers from the problem of new users who have not rated sufficient number of items. Similarly, it is also a problem with items that are new and not yet rated by sufficient number of users, and hence are unlikely to be the candidates for recommendation to a user. The hybrid recommender systems try to combine features from both the methods to produce better and more useful results. However, the limitation of new users and new items still remains, unless only the content-based approach computes the final recommendation in that case.

3   Sentiment Classification

The sentiment classification problem can be formally defined as follows: Given a set of documents D, a sentiment classifier classifies each document $d \in D$ into one of the two classes, **positive** and **negative**. Positive means that d expresses a positive opinion and negative means that d expresses a negative opinion. Sometimes a neutral class is used as well. There have been numerous approaches of sentiment classification of texts such as movie reviews, product ratings and political campaigns in the past. Most of the experiments performed so far employed one of the two approaches: (a) using a text classifier -such as Naïve Bayes, SVM or kNN- that takes a machine learning approach to categorize the documents in positive and negative groups; and (b) using a semantic orientation approach- that computes orientation of documents towards 'positive' and 'negative' classes based on aggregated polarity of selected opinionated POS tags extracted from the document. A related approach is the SentiWordNet based scheme that uses a committee of ternary classifiers to compute positive, negative and objective scores for selected terms in the documents and then their aggregated score determines the class of the document. Unlike the other two approaches it can also compute the intensity of polarities. Some of the other past works on sentiment classification have also attempted to determine the strengths of positive and negative orientations. Few prominent research works on sentiment classification on above mentioned themes can be found in [3], [4], [5], [6], [7], [8], [9], [10] & [11].

In our reference to sentiment classification, we are confined to document-level classification of sentiments as described above and not to a feature-based opinion mining or comparative sentence & relation mining, which is another important area of research in sentiment classification. We have used two approaches for sentiment classification, namely (a) classifying sentiments through a semantic orientation scheme using POS tag extraction; and (b) by using a Naïve Bayes text classifier. The sentiment label 'positive' is assigned to a movie only if its review is labeled as 'positive' by both the approaches. This was done since the data collected had a bias towards the positive class.

3.1   Semantic Orientation Approach

The basic motivation behind semantic orientation approach is to classify documents based on the statistics of usage of positive and negative words in it. A document having more positive words is likely to be classified as positive. The use of more positive terms represents the positive (or happy/ favorable) aspect of the writer. The semantic orientation approach starts with extracting phrases that conform to a specific Part of Speech [12]. These selected POS tags are the ones that represent opinionated or subjective parts of the text. Adjectives and adverbs are often the best choices. Thereafter, the semantic orientation of extracted phrases is computed using the **Pointwise Mutual Information** (PMI) measure given in Eq. 2 below,

$$PMI(term_1, term_2) = \log_2\{Pr\ (term_1 \Delta term_2)/Pr(term_1) . Pr\ (term_2)\} \quad (2)$$

where, $Pr(term_1 \blacktriangle term_2)$ is the co-occurrence probability of $term_1$ and $term_2$ and $Pr(term_1).Pr(term_2)$ gives the probability that two terms co-occur if they are statistically independent. The ratio between $Pr(term_1 \blacktriangle term_2)$ and $Pr(term_1).Pr(term_2)$ measures the degree of statistical independence between them. The log of this ratio is the amount of information that we acquire about the presence of one word when we observe the other. The Semantic Orientation (SO) of a phrase can thus be computed by using the Eq. 3,

$$SO(phrase) = PMI(pharse, "excellent") - PMI(phrase, "poor") \quad (3)$$

where, PMI (phrase, "excellent") measures the association of the phrase with positive reference word "excellent" and PMI (phrase, "poor") measures the association of phrase with negative reference word "poor". These values are calculated by issuing search query of the form "phrase * excellent" and "phrase * poor" to a search engine. The number of hits obtained is used as a measure of PMI value.

The terms "excellent" and "poor" are used as reference words since they are often used to express the two extremes (positive and negative) of the polarities. Other reference words like "fantastic" and "terrible" may also be used. The selection of the reference words may be based on the domain of texts, though it does not affect the performance of the classifier substantially. The SO value for all the extracted phrases is hence computed using this scheme. To determine the semantic orientation of the entire document, the SO values of the opinionated phrases in it are aggregated. One simple scheme is to use '+1' value for every positive term and '-1' for every negative term. Then if the aggregate (sum) of SO values of all the selected terms in a review is positive (a higher threshold value of 4 or 5 may also be chosen to reduce positive bias often found in review data), the review is labeled as 'positive' and 'negative' otherwise. This algorithm is referred to as SO-PMI-IR.

There is however one important concern related to using this approach. The number of extracted terms in any real word situation is often very large. For every term at least three search queries are required to compute its SO value, thereby requiring a large number of search queries to be made. This is a time consuming task. A variation of this scheme is SO-PMI-LSA [4], which uses Latent Semantic Analysis. In this scheme, the term-document matrix is first reduced using Singular Value Decomposition (SVD) and then $LSA(word_1, word_2)$ is computed by measuring the cosine similarity (as described in Eq. 1) of the compressed row vectors corresponding to $word_1$ and $word_2$. Thereafter, the Semantic orientation of a word is computed by using Eq. 4,

$$SO(word) = LSA(word, \{positive\ terms\}) - LSA(word, \{negative\ terms\}) \quad (4)$$

where, positive terms refer to words like 'good', 'superior', 'excellent' etc. and negative terms refer to words like 'bad', 'poor', 'inferior' etc. The LSA of a word is computed with term vectors of positive and negative words occurring in the document set. Experimental results have shown that SO-PMI-IR and SO-LSA have approximately the same accuracy on large dataset.

3.2   Naïve Bayes Machine Learning Approach

The other approach to sentiment classification is to use a supervised machine learning classifier to classify the documents in two classes. Naïve Bayes and SVM are two frequently used techniques for this purpose. Naïve Bayes [13] is a probabilistic learning method which computes the probability of a document d being in class c as in eq. 5 below.

$$P\ (c|d)\ \alpha\ P(c)\prod_{1 \le k \le n_d} P(t_k|c) \quad (5)$$

where, P (t_k/c) is the conditional probability of a term t_k occurring in a document of class c. P(t_k/c) is thus a measure of how much evidence t_k contributes that c is correct class. P(c) is the prior probability of a document occurring in class c. The goal in text classification is to find the best class for a document. The key idea in this classification is thus to categorize documents based on statistical pattern of occurrence of terms. The selected terms are often called features. For categorizing documents into two categories of 'positive' and 'negative', extracting terms with specific tags such as adjectives could be a good choice. The class membership of a document can be computed as in eq. 6

$$c_{map} = arg \max_{c \in C} \hat{P}(c|d) = arg \max_{c \in C} \hat{P}(c) \prod_{1 \le k \le n_d} \hat{P}\ (t_k|c) \quad (6)$$

where, P` is an estimated value obtained from the training set. In order to reduce the computational complexity resulting from multiplication of large number of probability terms, the eq. 8 can be transformed to eq. 7.

$$C_{map} = arg \max_{c \in C} [\log \hat{P}(c) + \sum_{1 \le k \le n_d} \log \hat{P}(t_k|c)] \quad (7)$$

Each conditional parameter P(t_k/c) in eq. 7 is a weight that indicates how good an indicator the term t_k is for class c, and the prior log P`(c) indicates the relative frequency of class c. We have implemented Naïve Bayes algorithm by using terms with POS tag label of adjective. The term frequency of these terms is used rather than merely their presence. This is known as multinomial Naïve Bayes approach. This scheme however has the limitation that it requires prior training data. Usually some documents from the dataset for which actual classes must be known are supplied as training input to the classifier, which then uses this training set to identify term occurrence probabilities in the two classes: positive and negative.

4   Experimental Setup and Results

We have combined the collaborative filtering approach with sentiment classification for designing a new hybrid recommender system for recommending movies. We have obtained a user-movie rating dataset for a large number of users and movies from a standard movie dataset. Thereafter we collected one review each of almost every movie in the dataset. We first performed collaborative filtering to obtain first level recommendation of movies, based on user's past rating of movies. The result set of this first level filtering gives us the movie ids which are recommended to the user by collaborative filtering approach. This recommendation list is then refined by removing those movies whose review is labeled 'negative'. The sentiment classification has been done in parallel to the collaborative filtering task. The final recommendation list is obtained by combining results of both the tasks.

4.1   Collecting Film Rating and Review Data

We have used the film rating dataset collected by the movielens project [14]. The movielens project has three datasets for movie ratings. We have used the moderately sized dataset comprising of 3900 films rated by 6040 users with a total of 1000209 ratings. On an average every user rated at least 20 films. The dataset comprise of three different files *ratings.dat*, *movies.dat* and *users.dat*. Each data in ***ratings.dat*** file is in the format of *user id::movie id::rating::timestamp*. The ratings were on a 5 star scale. The file ***movie.dat*** contained data in the format of *movie id::title::genre*. The file ***users.dat*** contained data in the format of *user id::gender::age::occupation::zip code*. The title of the movie was similar to that used in IMDB [15]. This rating data was sufficient to perform collaborative filtering. However, in order to perform sentiment classification, review data is necessary. Therefore, we collected one review each (critic's summary review and not user review -as it can help in reducing the positive class bias as well) for all the movies in the rating data. We collected reviews for almost all the films (except a few not available in IMDB) to perform sentiment classification. This part of data collection was very time consuming and tiresome.

4.2   Performing Collaborative Filtering

The rating data was used to compute both user-to-user similarity and movie-to-movie similarity using the cosine-based similarity measure. In user-to-user similarity, we compute a 6040X6040 matrix containing normalized similarity values. Every i,j entry indicates how similar a user i is to user j in terms of movie rating preferences. In movie-to-movie similarity, we computed a 3900X3900 matrix indicating the similarity of movies. Once this similarity data is computed, we can generate list of movie recommendations for a user by finding the movies that have high similarity to the movies rated high by the user. An alternative strategy could be to use user similarity to suggest movies to a user. However, this is more computation intensive due to large number of users (6040) and that a user rated only a few movies. A snapshot of recommendation results of the collaborative filtering for a particular user is shown in Fig. 1.

4.3   Sentiment Classification of Film Reviews

Our experimental formulation involved applying sentiment classification to further refine the recommendation results of collaborative filtering. In order to do so we performed sentiment classification of film reviews using both the Naïve Bayes machine learning and unsupervised semantic orientation approaches. The Naïve Bayes classifier was trained by using another movie review dataset comprising of 1400 reviews, with 700 reviews labeled as positive and remaining 700 as negative [16]. The unsupervised semantic orientation approach was executed directly on the experimental data. We used the cached SO values collected for a previous experimental work on movie review sentiment classification [17] for computing semantic orientation of the reviews, after augmenting it with the SO values for the terms extracted from the present review data but not present in it. A movie is labeled 'positive' only if its review is classified as positive by both the Naïve Bayes and the semantic orientation approaches. The sentiment label result was stored in a table. These labels were then used to refine the first level recommendations generated by the collaborative filtering approach. We have verified the accuracy of sentiment labeling using manual sentiment labels assigned to reviews by a group of students. To cope up with some misclassifications we used two approaches (naïve Bayes and semantic orientation) and labeled a movie as 'positive' only if both the approaches classify its review as positive.

```
User ID: 424

You Rated:

 2987(3), 2555(2), 2629(2), 1682(4), 2484(3), 2701(2), 2568(1), 3004(3), 1269(4), 2713(2), 1911(3), 3516(3),
2643(3), 2572(4), 3016(2), 2720(1), 2722(2), 2732(2), 2724(4), 2581(4), 2805(3), 266(2), 2828(1), 2683(4),
2761(4), 2699(5), 2770(3), 2856(1), 2358(1), 2369(5), 3175(4), 2888(3), 2302(2), 2394(4), 2975(5)

Collaborative Filtering Based Recommendation for You (rec_threshold>=0.7):

11     25     32     39     46     260    288    289    292    293    296    342    356
357    360    368    412    428    435    440    441    456    457    465    471    492
587    588    608    866    902    903    910    911    915    916    930    953    969
1036   1046   1059   1063   1091   1092   1094   1097   1101   1124   1127   1136   1188
1210   1230   1242   1247   1270   1302   1307   1347   1387   1396   1415   1416   1639
1673   1678   1684   1821   1835   1879   2245   2266   2291   2300   2301   2311   2355
2369   2394   2396   2581   2671   2692   2699   2706   2716   2721   2770   2779   2841
2858   2863   2872   2890   2943   2947   2975   3044   3052   3088   3099   3114   3175
3213   3269   3358   3418   3548   3578   3668   3676   3698   3712   3784   3819
```

Fig. 1. A Sample result of the first level recommendations using collaborative filtering

4.4   Combining the Results for Final Recommendations

The final set of recommended film list for a user was obtained by taking an intersection of results of both the approaches of collaborative filtering and sentiment classification. The first level of recommendation obtained by the collaborative filtering was the broader list of movies recommended to the user based on his past rating transactions. Out of this list only those movies are finally included in the recommendation list that are labeled 'positive' during sentiment classification of the movie review data. A snapshot of the result of sentiment classification of certain movie reviews is shown in Fig. 2. The final recommended list thus contain only those movies that are related to movies rated high by the user in the past and are also appreciated (indicated by positive review as a measure of movie quality). This is therefore a much better and focused recommendation as compared to the recommendations produced only by collaborative filtering.

```
User ID: 424
**Final list of recommended movies(CF + SO labels '+ve')**

Result format- Movie_id::Movie Name:: Genre

32::Twelve Monkeys (1995)::Drama|Sci-Fi
260::Star Wars: Episode IV - A New Hope
293::Professional, The (a.k.a. Leon: The Professional)
296::Pulp Fiction (1994)::Crime|Drama
356::Forrest Gump (1994)::Comedy|Romance|War
357::Four Weddings and a Funeral (1994)::Comedy|Romance
428::Bronx Tale, A (1993)::Drama
440::Dave (1993)::Comedy|Romance
456::Fresh (1994)::Drama
457::Fugitive, The (1993)::Action|Thriller
588::Aladdin (1992)::Animation|Children's|Comedy|Musical
608::Fargo (1996)::Crime|Drama|Thriller
866::Bound (1996)::Crime|Drama|Romance|Thriller
903::Vertigo (1958)::Mystery|Thriller
911::Charade (1963)::Comedy|Mystery|Romance|Thriller
930::Notorious (1946)::Film-Noir|Romance|Thriller
969::African Queen, The (1951)::Action|Adventure|Romance|War
1136::Monty Python and the Holy Grail (1974)::Comedy
1247::Graduate, The (1967)::Drama|Romance
1270::Back to the Future (1985)::Comedy|Sci-Fi
2841::Stir of Echoes (1999)::Thriller
2947::Goldfinger (1964)::Action
3088::Harvey (1950)::Comedy
```

Fig. 2. A Sample result of the second level recommendations using sentiment classification

5   Conclusion

This paper describes our experimental work on designing a new kind of hybrid recommender system that combines collaborative filtering and sentiment classification. We applied the system on movie-ratings and review data. Collaborative filtering was performed on rating data comprising of about one million ratings of 3900 movies contributed by 6040 users. The sentiment classification involved one review each of 3900 movies included in the rating data. We performed sentiment classification using two approaches: Naïve Bayes and unsupervised SO-PMI-IR. A movie was labeled 'positive' only if its review was classified as positive by both the approaches. This was done to reduce the positive class bias found in most of the online review data and hence to improve the accuracy of the sentiment labeling process. The results obtained produce a more focused and better recommendation of movies. Out of all the movies that may be recommended to a user by collaborative filtering, the system recommends only those movies which score well on the measure of 'positive' sentiment expressed in review of that movie. Therefore, the chance of recommended movies being liked by the user is much higher.

This is a novel hybrid approach to recommender system that, to the best of our knowledge, has not been experimented in the past. This design has been verified to perform well in the movie recommendation domain, but it can also be used in any domain that involves user ratings and textual reviews. Though as with traditional content and collaborative hybrids, it also has the limitation of non-applicability on non-textual data. However, this method undoubtedly presents better recommendations than using collaborative filtering alone and hence is a better recommender system design. Any real world system that collects user ratings and reviews can be adapted to use this hybrid recommendation approach. The combined recommendations produced using the approach represents a more restricted and focused set of items recommended to a particular user.

References

1. Adomavicius, G., Tuzhilin, A.: Towards the Next Generation of Recommender Systems: A Survey of the State-of-the-Art and Possible Extensions. IEEE Transactions on Knowledge and Data Engineering 17(6), 734–749 (2006)
2. Alag, S.: Collective Intelligence in Action. Manning, New York (2009)
3. Dave, K., Lawerence, S., Pennock, D.: Mining the Peanut Gallery-Opinion Extraction and Semantic Classification of Product Reviews. In: Proceedings of the 12th International World Wide Web Conference, pp. 519–528 (2003)
4. Turney, P.: Thumbs up or thumbs down? Semantic orientation applied to unsupervised classification of reviews. In: Proceedings of ACL 2002, 40th Annual Meeting of the Association for Computational Linguistics, Philadelphia, US, pp. 417–424 (2002)
5. Esuli, A., Sebastiani, F.: Determining the Semantic Orientation of terms through gloss analysis. In: Proceedings of CIKM 2005, 14th ACM International Conference on Information and Knowledge Management, Bremen, DE, pp. 617–624 (2005)
6. Pang, B., Lee, L., Vaithyanathan, S.: Thumbs up? Sentiment classificationusing machine learning techniques. In: Proceedings of the Conference on Empirical Methods in Natural Language Processing, Philadelphia, US, pp. 79–86 (2002)
7. Kim., S.M., Hovy, E.: Determining sentiment of opinions. In: Proceedings of the COLING Conference, Geneva (2004)
8. Durant, K.T., Smith, M.D.: Mining Sentiment Classification from Political Web Logs. In: Proceedings of WEBKDD 2006. ACM (2006)
9. Liu, B.: Web Data Mining: Exploring Hyperlinks, Contents and Usage Data. Springer, Heidelberg (2002)

10. Turney, P., Littman, M.L.: Unsupervised Learning of Semantic Orientation from a Hundred-Billion-Word corpus. NRC Publications Archive (2002)
11. Esuli, A., Sebastiani, F.: SentiWordNet: A Publicly available lexical resource for opinion mining. In: Proceedings of the Fifth Conference on Language Resources and Evaluation (LREC 2006), Geneva (2006)
12. Penn Treebank Project, http://www.cis.upenn.edu/~treebank/home.html
13. Manning, C.D., Raghavan, P., Schutze, H.: Introduction to Information Retrieval, pp. 238–258. Cambridge University Press, New York (2008)
14. Movielens dataset, http://grouplens.org/node/73
15. Internet Movie Database, http://www.imdb.com
16. http://www.cs.cornell.edu/people/pabo/movie-review-data/
17. Singh, V.K., Mukherjee, M., Mehta, G.K.: Combining a Content Filtering Heuristic and Sentiment Analysis for Movie Recommendations. In: Venugopal, K.R., Patnaik, L.M. (eds.) ICIP 2011. CCIS, vol. 157, pp. 659–664. Springer, Heidelberg (2011)

Automatic Composition and Mediation
on Multiple-Language Semantic Web Services

Tho T. Quan[1], Cach N. Dang[1], Ngan D. Le[2],
Chattrakul Sombattheera[3], and Quan Vu Lam[1]

[1] Faculty of Computer Science and Engineering,
Hochiminh City University of Technology, Vietnam
qttho@cse.hcmut.edu.vn, tucach@hcmutrans.edu.vn,
vu_06_04@yahoo.com
[2] Data Mining Department, Institute for Infocomm Research (I2R),
A*STAR, Singapore
dnle@i2r.a-star.edu.sg
[3] Mahasarakham University, Thailand
chattrakul.s@msu.ac.th

Abstract. Web services have been attracting many attentions in both research and industry communities due to their potential of being invoked automatically based on users requests. In order to make this potential practical, there are two tasks needed to be fulfilled including (i) automatic discovery and composition of appropriate services and (ii) automatic invocation of sequenced services to achieve the desired goal. However, the lack of a mechanism of semantic representation in typical services descriptions has hindered this vision significantly. The recently introduced Semantic Web services are promising to overcome this obstacle by employing ontologies to describe the service operations, therefore the semantics of the provided services can be understood and reasoned automatically by computer programs. Nevertheless, since the standard for ontological knowledge representation over the Semantic Web services has not been completely established yet, there are many description languages have been introduced. Automatic composition and mediation of multiple-language Semantic Web services thus become a challenging issue.

In this paper we introduce an approach to tackle this problem. Based on extended plug-in technique for service discovery, we develop a framework for composition of multiple services and make use of concept similarity evaluated over ontological concepts to handle the problem of multiple service description languages. We also discuss automatic mediation of multiple services to have the involved services automatically invoked necessarily. To show the practical aspect of our approach, we have applied the composition framework on the most two popular description languages, namely OWL-S and WSMO. The initial results showed that our approach has achieved reasonable performance in terms of accuracy.

Keywords: Semantic Web services, ontology concept similarity, composition, service mediation, OWL-S, and WSMO.

C. Sombattheera et al. (Eds.): MIWAI 2011, LNAI 7080, pp. 51–62, 2011.
© Springer-Verlag Berlin Heidelberg 2011

1   Introduction

Currently, Web services have provided a mechanism for interoperability between applications. Recently, the rapid development of the Semantic Web has prompted the development of applications based on the Semantic Web environment. Thus, Semantic Web services [1], an enhancement of current Web services, have been introduced. Since the XML-based descriptions of the typical Web services are limited in terms of semantic representations, Semantic Web services overcome this problem by employing semantics to describe the service via the means of ontology. Basically, ontology is a formal conceptualization whose semantic meaning is well-defined, thus understandable and sharable by both humans and computer programs [2]. In Semantic Web services, ontological descriptions are represented by corresponding ontology description languages.

Today Semantic Web services have become an important technology in e-business due to its strength in supporting discovery, composition, and invocation. Therefore, users can have their requirements fulfilled in the Semantic Web environment in an automatic manner. To illustrate this, let us consider the following motivating scenario.

- Assume a customer is end-user who would like to travel from New York, USA to Hue, Vietnam to attend the second ACIIDS conference. He uses the proposed system to search for the most suitable composition of *travel service providers* for the traveling. He needs to key in information such as his personal information, credit card number, and so on via the Graphic User Interface (GUI) of the proposed system.
- Travel service providers are companies providing traveling services by using *airplane, train, and bus.* They advertise their service information through a recommendation system's repository. These services contain all information about the travelling including information about locations (start and destination) and price via Web services. An advertised Web services includes input, output, and operation of the service profile which were created based on ontologies.
- The recommendation system will receive the advertised information from the travel providers, it indexes and stores the information in its repository. Upon a request from a user, the system searches the most suitable composition of travel service providers. The service composition information will then be returned to the user.

Currently, the Web users must still rely on manual methods to find the services they request. With the recent advancement of the Semantic Web, researchers have developed several composition systems that can compose multiple Semantic Web services to automate the search. However, most of the reported systems only support a certain kind of service description, which do not reflect the trends of multiple semantic service description language that are currently co-existing today. To handle multiple-language Semantic Web service, a recommendation system as above described would need to tackle the following issues in a cross-language enviroment: (i) automatic discovery and composition of services; and (ii) automatic conversion of ontological data schema to allow the services exchange their input/output data once being invoked.

In this paper, we discuss a theoretical framework for a recommendation system that can fulfill the two abovementioned problems. In particular, of practical aspects, our system supports the two most popular Web services description languages of OWL-S and WSMO. Other languages such as METRO-S and WSDL-S will be considered as a part of future work. The rest of the paper is organized as follows. Section 2 introduces a brief background of OWL-S and WSMO. Section 3 gives the theoretical framework of discovery and composition on Semantic Web services, in which the problem of handling multiple description languages is also discussed. Section 4 presents a particular composition algorithm of composing services over OWL-S and WSMO. Section 5 discusses automatic schema conversion for services mediation. Experimental results are presented in Section 6. The related work is presented in Section 7, followed by the conclusion in Section 8.

2   Description Languages for Semantic Web Services

2.1   OWL-S: Semantic Markup for Web Services

Upper ontology for services. OWL-S defines a Semantic Web service via four basic classes, namely *Service, ServiceProfile, ServiceModel,* and *ServiceGrounding*. The class *Service* provides an organizational point for a Web service. It has *presents, describedBy,* and *supports* properties which have ranges are *ServiceProfile, ServiceModel,* and *ServiceGrounding*, respectively. Generally, *ServiceProfile* provides the information needed for discover, composition, and interoperation purpose, while the *ServiceModel* and *ServiceGrounding* are used together for the invocation purpose once the services are found. Therefore, in some aspects, *ServiceProfile* is the most important because the Web services are useless if they cannot be discovered. OWL-S based on a set of Ontology Web Language - OWL ontologies to declare these classes, and therefore, OWL becomes the core of the specification.

The OWL Web Ontology Language. The Web Ontology Language (OWL) [3] was designed by the W3C and is the standard for ontology description in the semantic Web. It is used when the information contained in documents needs to be processed by applications as opposed to situations where the content only needs to be presented to humans. An OWL ontology may include descriptions of *classes, instances of classes, properties*, as well as *range* and *domain constraints on properties*. It may also contain various types of *relationships* between classes or between properties. A class, which is also called concept in ontology, defines a group of individuals that belong together. Individuals are also called instances corresponding to actual entities that can be grouped into these classes. Properties are used to describe relationships between individuals or from individuals to data values.

2.2   WSMO: Web Service Modeling Ontology

WSMO Elements. The core elements of WSMO [4] are *Ontologies, Goals, Web Services,* and *Mediators*. The terminology used by every WSMO element is provided by ontologies, which consist of the following parts: *Non-Functional Properties,*

Imported Ontologies, Used Mediators, Axioms, Concepts, Relations, Functions and *Instances*. Just as OWL-S is based on OWL, WSMO is based on the Web Service Modeling Framework (WSMF) [5]. A *Goal* which is similar to requested Web service described in OWL-S, expresses what the user wants. It describes what the service provides. There are four different types of mediators, namely: *ooMediators*, *ggMediators*, *wgMediators* and *wwMediators*.

Web Service Modeling Framework (WSMF). The Web Service Modeling Language WSML is a language for the specification of ontologies and different aspects of Web services [6]. As an ontology language, WSML is similar to OWL which contains information about *classes, instances of classes, properties*, as well as *range* and *domain constraints on properties*. It may also contain various types of *relationships* between classes or between properties. One of the major difference between OWL and WSMF is OWL is XML-based while WSMF is not.

3   Discovery and Composition on Multiple-Language Semantic Web Services

3.1   Web Services Discovery and Matchmaking

Conventionally, the input of output of a Web service are respectively described in its *pre-condition* and *post-condition*. When embedded in an information system, the Web service will be then invoked accordingly if the system detects that the post-condition of the Web service matches with the given requirements. These requirements are referred to as the *goal*. When multiple Web services are available, the process of finding suitable Web services whose post-conditions perfectly match the goal becomes a complex task known as *Web service discovery*.

Recently, *Logic Programming* (LP) [7.8] has been considered as a suitable paradigm for automated reasoning over the web services. Thus, the required infrastructure for LP-based Web Service discovery has been introduced in WSML [9]. Reasoning in LP is performed by the means of answering *conjunctive query* which is defined as a predicate composed from one or other predicates rather than itself [8]. For example, a Web service describing transportation means searching can be represented as conjunctive query as follows.

-      F_{in}:- city(A), city(B), depart_from(A), goto(B)
-      F_{out}:- means(C), connected_by(C,A,B)
-      F_{share}:- A,B.

F_{in} implies the pre-condition of the service, which describes a problem of traveling from city A to city B. F_{out} implies the goal of searching for a transportation means C that connects A to B. F_{share} implies shared variables between the input and output of the service, which are A and B. We denote $pre(Q)$, $post(Q)$ and $shared(Q)$ as pre-condition, post-condition and shared variable of a query Q accordingly.

For discovery of suitable service, the notion of *query containment* is adopted in [8] as follows. A query Q_1 is containted in Q_2, or $Q_1 \subseteq Q_2$ if $s(Q_1) \subseteq s(Q_2)$ in which s

denotes the set of facts that the corresponding query holds. Accordingly, we denote a *containing mapping* h from Q_2 to Q_1 if h satisfies at least one of the followings:

- h is identity function
- h maps the head of Q_2 to that of Q_1
- for any subgoal $G(y_1,...,y_n)$ of Q_2, $G(h(y_1),...,h(y_n))$ is a fact in Q_1^* where Q_1^* is the set of all facts that can be deducted from Q_1.

One can easily observe that $Q_1 \subseteq Q_2$ iff there exists a containing mapping from Q_2 to Q_1. The containing mapping hence set a theoretical foundation for the *matchmaking* problem between concepts. When the system successfully matches concepts between the desired goal and pre/post conditions of a service, the service is considered discovered for the goal.

3.2   Web Services Composition

The technique of service discovery presented in Section 3.1 allows us to find a certain service that fulfills the requirements from users. However, in many practical situations, the system needs to compose a sequence of services in order to achieve a desired goal. That urges the necessity of composition of multiple discovered services. Formally, the composition problem is defined as follows.

Give a goal G and a set of services S_W which are presented as conjunctive queries, find a set of services $\{W_1,...,W_N\} \subseteq S_W$ fulfilling the following conditions:

- $\exists i: pre(G) \subseteq pre(W_i)$
- $\forall i, \exists i \neq j: post(W_i) \subseteq post(G) \vee post(W_i) \subseteq pre(W_j)$
- $\exists i: post(W_i) \subseteq pre(G)$.

3.3   Composition on Multiple-Language Semantic Web Services

Even though well-defined as discussed in Section 3.1 and Section 3.2, the automated composition on Web services is currently still far from being applied effectively in real applications, due to the lack of semantics captured in service description. With the introduction of Semantic Web services, whose descriptions are presented in form of ontologies, the solution for this problem is made possible.

However, up to now, there have still not had a standard defined for description language of Semantic Web services yet. As a consequence, Semantic Web services may be written in various languages, which hinder the system capability of inferring and reasoning on them. To adapt with this context, we revise the non-trivial condition of the containing mapping between Semantic Web services (i.e. the third condition) as follows. For any subgoal $G(y_1,...,y_n)$ of Q_2, $G(h(y_1),...,h(y_n))$ is a *similar* fact in Q_1^* where Q_1^* is the set of all facts that can be deducted from Q_1.

Here we stress in the significance of similar facts (or concepts) between two queries, since described in different languages, two ontologies concepts in two distinct services may not need to be exactly the same, but reasonably similar. To show how this idea can be applied in practical situation, in Section 4 we will discuss how to evaluate similarity between concepts presented in two most popular ontology-based descriptive languages for Web services, namely OWL-S and WSMO.

4   OWL-S and WSMO Composition Algorithm

As mentioned in section 1, composition system for OWL-S and OWL-S Web services and composition system for WSMO and WSMO Web services were introduced in [10] and [11], respectively. The focus of this paper is on composing OWL-S and WSMO Web services. The algorithm for this composition is an extension of the algorithm described in [10] which is for OWL-S and OWL-S Web services.

The composition algorithm introduced by Bao Duy *et al.* [10] is a progressive AI-planning-like algorithm which proceeds in a recursive depth-first manner. The algorithm composes the advertised Web services by connecting their inputs and outputs based on their similarity. The resultants are expressed in the form of directed multi-graphs of advertised Web services and inter-connecting edges. The similarity between input and output of Web services is the core of the algorithm. The 'best solution' is the one with the highest similarity between matching connections.

Concept similarity (CS), which is the core of the algorithm, measures the similarity between two concepts from the same ontology or different ontologies. The concept similarity algorithm includes four main components: *syntactic similarity, properties similarity, context similarity,* and *neighbourhood similarity*. The final similarity result is the average of the sum of the four components as the following formula:

$$ CS = \frac{w_s * synSim + w_p * proSim + w_c * conSim + w_n * neiSim}{w_s + w_p + w_c + w_n} $$

where w_s, w_p, w_c, and w_n are weights defined by users. Details of the concept similarity algorithm and how to define w_s, w_p, w_c, and w_n were introduced in [12]. This algorithm is applied to matching two concepts from the same or different OWL ontologies.

In order to employ [12] to measure concept similarity between OWL and WSML ontologies, we need to extract information from WSML which defines *concept name, concept description, properties, context* and *neighborhood relationship*. Figure 1

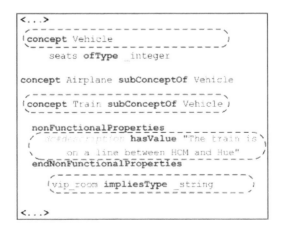

Fig. 1. A portion of WSML specification

presents a portion of an example of a WSML ontology example. The ontology has several concepts such as *Vehicle, Airplane,* and *Train. Airplane* and *Train* concepts have relationship 'subConcept' of *Vehicle* concept. The *Train* concept has properties.

Figure 2 presents a matching example between two concepts from OWL and WSML ontologies, respectively. Each component in OWL is matched against corresponding component in WSML which was described in figure 1. Figure 2 does not present a fully matching between two concepts but some components including *syntactic, property,* and *neighborhood* similarity since the *context* is not presented here.

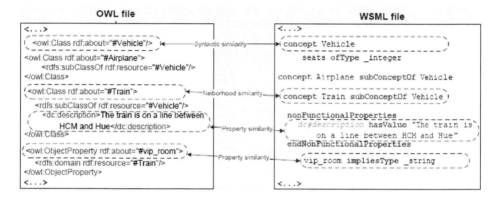

Fig. 2. OWL and WSML concept similarity measurement example

5   Web Services Mediation

In Section 4, we have discussed composition of ontological concepts described by different descriptive languages. This technique provides a theoretical mechanism to evaluate the similarities between ontological concepts. The composition algorithm mentioned in Section 4 has been proven working well on lab-scale scenarios. How, when implemented real systems, this approach suffers from the difficulties of schematic inconsistency between ontology concepts. For example, a real-life concept can be represented as a single concept in a certain ontology, but broken down into multiple concepts in another ontology. Thus, in a real system, we need to implement the operation of *service mediation* which consists of the following tasks *Schema mapping* and *Instance conversions.*

5.1   Schema Mapping

In order to implement the composition algorithm discussed in Section 4, it is needed to develop a so-called *discovery engine* that is able to discover and compose the suitable Web services based on their concept similarities. In a general context, there would be many Semantic Web services available in many ontology languages. Therefore, we need to map the schematic representations of all ontologies into a *common schema*, on which the discovery engine will operate. In our research, we adopt *XSLT* [15], an XML-based language, as the common schema, since XSLT is supported by all of ontology description languages. For example, the mapping between WSMO ontology concepts and XSLT concepts is given in Figure 3.

WSMO	XLST
concepts	elements
instances	nested elements
attributes	order of elements
relations	attributes
unordered sets	character data

Fig. 3. Mapping between WSMO and XSLT concepts

Fig. 4. Example of mapping ontology concept name into XML element name

There are two major mapping actions to be taken into consideration: *loweringSchema*, which maps ontology concepts into XLST schema; and *liftingSchema*, which maps XLST schema back to corresponding ontology concepts. These two mappings will be performed respectively before and after the discovery task carried out by the discovery engine. Figure 4 illustrates a case in which an ontology concept is mapped into XML schema in XLST.

5.2   Instance Conversion

After discovered and composed, the Semantic Web services will be invoked accordingly to achieve the desired goals. When service *A* is composed to service B, for example, the output of *A* will be regarded as the input of *B*. Since *A* is a Semantic Web service, the output of A should be a kind of some ontology instances. Correspondingly, service *B* also expects the input in the form of some ontology instances. Even though the discovery engine has beforehand discovered that there are considerable similarities occurring between the input of *A* and output of *B*, *B* probably could not work properly with the input being given from *A* due to different conceptual schema of the two corresponding ontologies. Therefore, the system needs to perform the instance conversion to fully convert instance schemas from ontology *A* to those of *B*.

6   Experiment and Results

As there is no standard test data or benchmark available for web service composition, especially for composition Web services based on different specifications, we developed 10 Web service profiles based on the scenario to validate the designed and developed algorithm. This section introduces the test data, the result, and discussion on the results.

6.1   Testing Data

Among 10 Web service profiles developed, there are five OWL-S Web services and five WSMO Web services. Four of the ten Web services are created based on the scenario given in Section 1, the other six services are from different domains (buy and sell computer). The purpose of creating such the testing data is to test the ability of the system to come out with a solution.

Web service profiles. Among four Web services were created based on the scenario, three of them are OWL-S Web services and the other one is WSMO Web services.

OWL-S Web services are presented as in table 1 including three services, namely, *Train_service_from_HCM_to_Hue*,   *Search_location*,   and   *Flight_service_from_NewYork_to_Sydney*. In the table, *owl_OA* is the shortcut of

   "http://localhost/WSComposition/Ontology/OWL-S/travel/TravelOntologyA.owl"
and *owl_OB* is the shortcut of
   "http://localhost/WSComposition/Ontology/OWL-S/travel/TravelOntologyB.owl"

Table 1. OWL-S Web service profiles

	Service profile	Input (name/type)	Output (name/type)
1	Train_service_from HCM_to_Hue.owl	HCM / *owl_OA#HCM*	Hue / *owl_OA#Hue* Train / *owl_OA#Train* Price / *owl_OB#Price*
2	Searching_location.owl	Person / *owl_OB#Person* PhoneNumber/*owl_OA#PhoneNumber*	Location/ *owl_OA#Location*
3	Flight_service_from NewYork_to_Sydney.owl	NewYork/ *owl_OA#NewYork*	Sedney/*owl_OA#Sedney* Airplane/ *owl_OA#Airplane*

Similarly, WSMO Web services are presented as in Table 2 including two services, namely, *Travel_Australia* and *Goal* which is a requested service or designed service. In the table, *wsml_OA* is the shortcut of

   "http://localhost/WSComposition/Ontology/WSML/travel/TravelOntologyA.wsml"
and *wsml_OB* is the shortcut of
   "http://localhost/WSComposition/Ontology/WSML/travel/TravelOntologyB.wsml"

Some different terms between WSMO and OWL-S:

- *Precondition* in WSMO is *input* in OWL-S
- *Post-condition* in WSMO is *output* in OWL-S
- *Goal* in WSMO is *requested Web service* in OWL-S.

Table 2. WSMO Web service profiles

	Service Description/Goal	Precondition (name/type)	Postcondition (name/type)
1	Flight_service_from_S ydney_to_HCM.wsml	Sedney/*wsml_OA#Sedney* Airplane/*wsml_OA#Airplane* Location/*wsml_OB#Location*	HCM/*wsml_OA#HCM*
2	Goal.wsml	Person/*wsml_OB#Person* PhoneNumber/*wsml_OB#* *PhoneNumber* NewYork/*wsml_OA#NewYork*	Hue/*wsml_OA#Hue* Train/*wsml_OA#Train* Price/*wsml_OB#Price*

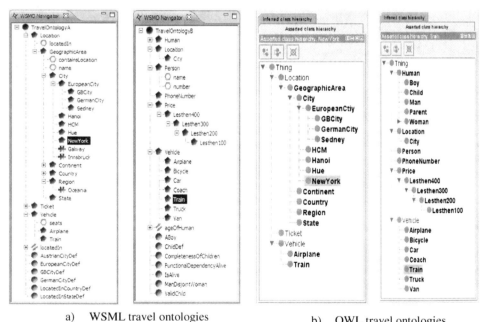

   a)   WSML travel ontologies   b)   OWL travel ontologies

Fig. 5. Travel ontologies

Ontologies created. The above Web services were developed based on ontologies. They are OWL and WSML ontologies for OWL-S and WSMO Web services, respectively. These ontologies are shown as in Figure 5.

6.2   Results

With the above test data, the results were obtained in the form of a composition graph, as shown in Figure 6. The graph represents that in order to travel to Hue, Vietnam, from New York, USA. Since there is no direct flight from New York to Hue, a composition of possible flights and other vehicles should be a good solution for the traveller. As shown in the result, the traveller must first flight from New York, USA to Sydney, Australia. Next, he/she must take another flight from Sydney to Ho Chi Minh City (HCM), Vietnam. Finally, he/she will take a train from Chi Minh City to Hue, Vietnam which is the destination.

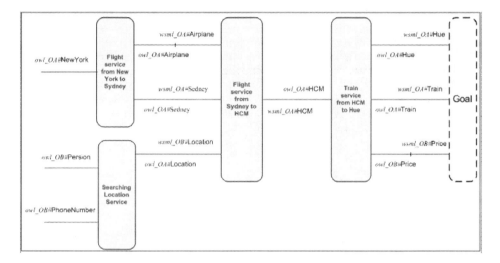

Fig. 6. Composition result

7   Conclusion

The paper has introduced a recommendation system to compose and mediate multiple advertised Web services to satisfy a request. The proposed system has overcome the language heterogeneity problem of current composition systems by supporting Web services based on OWL-S and WSMO which are the two most popular semantic Web service description languages. A composition scenario was introduced to illustrate how the system works. Test data were conducted based on the scenario and experiments were carried out to confirm the validity of the system. As a part of the future work, the system will be extended to support METRO-S and WSDL-S Web service specifications. The extended algorithm will be developed as the same manner with the system has been developed.

Acknowledgment. This work is part of the Higher Education Project 2 project (supported by World Bank and Hochiminh – Vietnam National University).

References

1. Honglei, Z., Son, T.C.: Semantic Web Services. IEEE Intelligent Systems 16, 46–53 (2001)
2. Gruber, T.: A Translation Approach to Portable Ontologies Specification. Journal Knowledge Acquisition - Special issue: Current issues in knowledge modeling 5(2) (1993)
3. W3C, OWL - Web Ontology Language Overview, Organization, Editor
4. Roman, D., Lausen, H., Keller, U.: Web Service Modeling Ontology - Standard (WSMO - Standard), WSMO deliverable D2 version 1.1
5. Fensel, D., Bussler, C.: The Web Service Modeling Framework WSMF. In: Electronic Commerce Research and Applications (2002)
6. Lausen, H., et al.: WSML - a Language Framework for Semantic Web Services. In: Position Paper for the W3C Rules Workshop, Washington DC, USA (2005)
7. Nilss, U., Maluszynski, J.: Logic, Programming and Prolog, 2nd edn. (2000)
8. Ullman, J.D.: Principles of Database and Knowledge-base Systems. The New Technologies, vol. II. Computer Science Press, Rockville (1989)
9. Roman, D., et al.: Web service modeling ontology. Applied Ontology 1(1), 77–106 (2005)
10. Tran, B.D., Tan, P.S., Goh, A.E.S.: Composing OWL-S Web Services. In: IEEE International Conference on Web Services (ICWS), Salt Lake City, Utah, USA (2007)
11. Sapkota, B., et al.: D21.v0.1 WSMX Triple-Space Computing, in WSMO Working Draft (2005)
12. Ngan, L.D., Hang, T.M., Goh, A.: Semantic Similarity between Concepts from Different OWL Ontologies. In: 2006 IEEE International Conference on Industrial Informatics, Singapore (2006)
13. Maximilien, E.M., Singh, M.P.: A Framework and Ontology for Dynamic Web Services Selection. IEEE Internet Computing 8(5), 84–93 (2004)
14. McIlraith, S., Son, T., Zeng, H.: Semantic Web Services. IEEE Intelligent Systems 16(2), 46–53 (2001)
15. XSL Transformation, http://www.w3.org/TR/xslt

Fibred BDI Logics: Completeness Preservation in the Presence of Interaction Axioms

Vineet Padmanabhan[1], Guido Governatori[2], and Abdul Sattar[2]

[1] Department of Computer and Information Sciences,
University of Hyderabad, Hyderabad - 500046, India
vineetcs@uohyd.ernet.in
[2] NICTA, Queensland Research Laboratory, Brisbane, Australia
guido.governatori@nicta.com.au,
A.Sattar@griffith.edu.au

Abstract. In [6,9] the authors have shown how to combine propositional BDI logics using Gabbay's *fibring* methodology and in [11,10] they outlined a tableaux proof procedure for the fibred BDI logic. In this paper we provide a proof related to completeness preservation of the combined BDI logic in the presence of interaction axioms of the form $\Box_1 \varphi \Rightarrow \Box_2 \varphi$ in terms of canonical models. To be more precise, let $\Lambda_a, \Lambda_b, \Lambda_c, \Lambda_d$ be canonical normal modal logics and $\Lambda_{abcd} = \Lambda_a \odot \Lambda_b \odot \Lambda_c \odot \Lambda_d$ be the logics obtained by fibring/dovetailing $\Lambda_a, \Lambda_b, \Lambda_c, \Lambda_d$. Then we show that $\Lambda_{abcd} \oplus \Diamond_a \Box_b \varphi \Rightarrow \Box_c \Diamond_d \varphi$ is characterised by the class of fibred models satisfying the condition $\forall \omega \in W$, $\forall \boldsymbol{f} \in \mathbf{F}$, $\mathfrak{R}^{ac}(\omega) \sqsubseteq_N \mathfrak{R}^{bd}(\omega)$.

Keywords: KRR, Logics for Multiagent Systems, Theorem Proving.

1 Introduction

BDI-logics [13,14,18] are normal[1] multi-modal logics for modelling belief, desire and intention with three families of modal operators $\mathrm{BEL}_i, \mathrm{DES}_i, \mathrm{INT}_i, i \in Agents$. The logic **KD45** of modal logic is used for the belief operator BEL and the logic **KD** for DES and INT respectively. The semantics is given through standard Kripke frames by defining three families of accessibility relations, (b_i, d_i, i_i) for belief, desire and intention. The binary relations b_i are Euclidean, transitive and serial whereas the relations for intention i_i and desires d_i are serial. Additionally, the BDI framework impose constraints between the different mental attitudes in the form of *interaction axioms*. For instance, interaction axioms of the form $\mathrm{INT}(\varphi) \to \mathrm{DES}(\varphi)$, $\mathrm{DES}(\varphi) \to \mathrm{BEL}(\varphi)$ denoting respectively intentions being stronger than desires and desires being stronger than beliefs. Hence the basic BDI logic $\mathbb{L}$ is the combination of different component logics plus the two interaction axioms as given below (we adopt the following symbols: $\oplus$ Addition of Axioms, $\otimes$ Combination of logics, $\odot$ Fibring of logics.)

$$\mathbb{L} \equiv (\otimes_{i=1}^n \mathbf{KD45}_{\mathrm{BEL}_i}) \otimes (\otimes_{i=1}^n \mathbf{KD}_{\mathrm{DES}_i}) \otimes (\otimes_{i=1}^n \mathbf{KD}_{\mathrm{INT}_i}) \tag{1}$$
$$\oplus \ \{\mathrm{INT}_i \varphi \to \mathrm{DES}_i \varphi\} + \{\mathrm{DES}_i \varphi \to \mathrm{BEL}_i \varphi\}$$

---

[1] General modal systems with an arbitrary set of normal modal operators all characterised by the axiom **K**: $\Box(\varphi \to \psi) \to (\Box\varphi \to \Box\psi)$ and the necessitation rule, i.e., $\vdash \varphi / \vdash \Box\varphi$.

C. Sombattheera et al. (Eds.): MIWAI 2011, LNAI 7080, pp. 63–74, 2011.

Any BDI theory, or for that matter any fully-fledged Multi-Agent-System (MAS) theory, modelling rational agents consists of a combined system of logic of beliefs, desires, goals and intentions as mentioned above. They are basically well understood standard modal logics *combined together* to model different facets of the agents. A number of researchers have provided such combined systems for different reasons and different applications. However, investigations into a general methodology for combining the different logics involved has been mainly neglected to a large extent. Some earlier works [6,9,10,11] have investigated a particular combining technique called *fibring* [5] and it has been shown how to reconstruct the logical account of BDI in terms of *dovetailing* (a special case of fibring) together with the multi-modal semantics of Catach [2]. Further, they have also identified conditions under which completeness transfers from the component logics (Λ_1 and Λ_2) to their fibred/dovetailed composition ($\Lambda_{1,2}^{\boldsymbol{f}}/\Lambda_{1,2}^{\mathfrak{D}}$), with the help of canonical model structures. *What the authors did not show was a proof related to completeness preservation in the case where interaction axiom of the form* $\Box_1\alpha \Rightarrow \Box_2\alpha$ *is added to the fibred/dovetailed composition, i.e.,* $\Lambda_{1,2}^{\boldsymbol{f},\mathfrak{D}} \oplus \Box_1\alpha \Rightarrow \Box_2\alpha$. In this paper we outline a result related to completeness preservation in such cases. Our study differs from that of other combining techniques like *fusion* in terms of the interaction axiom. For instance, normal bimodal and polymodal logics without any interaction axioms are well-studied as *fusions* of normal monomodal logics in [17] and property transfer for such logics has also been dealt with [7]. Moreover *fusions* of normal modal logics without interaction axioms is the same as *dovetailing*. But difficulty arises with the extra interaction axiom. Then we need a more general concept like *fibring*.

2   Fibring BDI Logics

The basic BDI logic $\mathbb{L}$ given in (1) is defined from three component logics, **KD45**$_n$ for belief, and **KD**$_n$ for desires and intentions. For sake of clarity, consider just two of the component logics, Λ_1(**KD45**) and Λ_2(**KD**) and their corresponding languages $\mathscr{L}_{\Lambda_1}, \mathscr{L}_{\Lambda_2}$ built from the respective sets $\mathfrak{Q}_1$ and $\mathfrak{Q}_2$ of atoms having classes of models $\mathfrak{M}_{\Lambda_1}, \mathfrak{M}_{\Lambda_2}$ and satisfaction relations $\models_1$ and $\models_2$. Hence we are dealing with two different systems S_1 and S_2 characterised, respectively, by the class of Kripke models $\mathscr{K}_1$ and $\mathscr{K}_2$. For instance, we know how to evaluate $\Box_1\varphi$ (BEL(φ)) in $\mathscr{K}_1$ (**KD45**) and $\Box_2\varphi$ (DES(φ)) in $\mathscr{K}_2$ (**KD**). We need a method for evaluating $\Box_1$ (resp. $\Box_2$) with respect to $\mathscr{K}_2$ (resp. $\mathscr{K}_1$). To do so, we link (fibre), via a *fibring* function the model for Λ_1 with a model for Λ_2 and build a fibred model of the combination. The fibring function evaluates (give yes/no) answers with respect to a modality in S_2, being in S_1 and vice versa. The interpretation of a formula φ of the combined language in the fibred model at a state w can be given as $\omega \models \varphi$ if and only if $\boldsymbol{f}(\omega) \models^* \varphi$, where $\boldsymbol{f}$ is a fibring function mapping a world to a model *suitable for interpreting* φ and $\models^*$ is the corresponding satisfaction relation ($\models_1$ for Λ_1 or $\models_2$ for Λ_2).

Example 1. Let Λ_1, Λ_2 be two modal logics as given above and $\varphi = \Box_1\Diamond_2\mathfrak{p}_0$ be a formula on a world ω_0 of the fibred semantics. φ belongs to the language $\mathscr{L}_{(1,2)}$ as the outer connective ($\Box_1$) belongs to the language $\mathscr{L}_1$ and the inner connective ($\Diamond_2$) belongs to the language $\mathscr{L}_2$. By the standard definition we start evaluating $\Box_1$ of $\Box_1\Diamond_2$ at

ω_0. According to the standard definition we have to check whether $\Diamond_2 \mathfrak{p}_0$ is true at every ω_1 accessible from ω_0 since from the point of view of $\mathscr{L}_1$ this formula has the form $\Box_1 p$ (where $p = \Diamond_2 \mathfrak{p}_0$ is atomic). But at ω_1 we cannot interpret the operator $\Diamond_2$, because we are in a model of Λ_1, not of Λ_2. To evaluate this we need the fibring function $\mathfrak{f}$ which at ω_1 points to a world v_0, a world in a model suitable to interpret formulae from Λ_2. Now all we have to check is whether $\Diamond_2 \mathfrak{p}_0$, is true at v_0 in this last model and this can be done in the usual way. Hence the fibred semantics for the combined language $\mathscr{L}_{(1,2)}$ has models of the form $(\mathscr{F}_1, \omega_1, v_1, \mathfrak{f}_1)$, where $\mathscr{F}_1 = (W_1, R_1)$ is a frame, and $\mathfrak{f}_1$ is the fibring function which associates a model $\mathfrak{M}_\omega^2$ from $\mathscr{L}_2$ with ω in $\mathscr{L}_1$ i.e. $\mathfrak{f}_1(\omega) = \mathfrak{M}_\omega^2$.

Now we will define a fibred structure for BDI logics. Let $\mathbf{I}$ be a set of labels representing the modal operators for the intentional states (belief, desire, intention) for a set of agents, and $\Lambda_i, i \in \mathbf{I}$ be modal logics whose respective modalities are $\Box_i, i \in \mathbf{I}$.

Definition 1. *[5] A fibred model is a structure* $(W, S, R, \mathbf{a}, v, \tau, \mathbf{F})$ *where*

- *W is a set of possible worlds;*
- *S is a function giving for each ω a set of possible worlds, $S^\omega \subseteq W$;*
- *R is a function giving for each ω, a relation $R^\omega \subseteq S^\omega \times S^\omega$;*
- *$\mathbf{a}$ is a function giving the actual world $\mathbf{a}^\omega$ of the model labelled by ω;*
- *v is an assignment function $v^\omega(\mathfrak{q}_0) \subseteq S^\omega$, for each atomic $\mathfrak{q}_0$;*
- *τ is the semantical identifying function $\tau : W \to \mathbf{I}$. $\tau(\omega) = i$ means that the model $(S^\omega, R^\omega, \mathbf{a}^\omega, v^\omega)$ is a model in $\mathscr{K}_i$, we use W_i to denote the set of worlds of type i;*
- *$\mathbf{F}$, is the set of fibring functions $\mathfrak{f} : \mathbf{I} \times W \mapsto W$. A fibring function $\mathfrak{f}$ is a function giving for each i and each $\omega \in W$ another point (actual world) in W as follows:*

$$\mathfrak{f}_i(\omega) = \begin{cases} \omega & \text{if } \omega \in S^{\mathfrak{M}} \text{ and } \mathfrak{M} \in \mathscr{K}_i \\ a \text{ value in } W_i, & \text{otherwise} \end{cases}$$

such that if $\omega \neq \omega'$ then $\mathfrak{f}_i(\omega) \neq \mathfrak{f}_i(\omega')$. It should be noted that fibring happens when $\tau(\omega) \neq i$. Satisfaction is defined as follows with the usual boolean connections:

$$\omega \models \mathfrak{q}_0 \text{ iff } v(\omega, \mathfrak{q}_0) = 1, \text{ where } \mathfrak{q}_0 \text{ is an atom}$$

$$\omega \models \Box_i \varphi \text{ iff } \begin{cases} \omega \in \mathfrak{M} \text{ and } \mathfrak{M} \in \mathscr{K}_i \text{ and } \forall \omega'(\omega R \omega' \to \omega' \models \varphi), \text{or} \\ \omega \in \mathfrak{M}, \text{ and } \mathfrak{M} \notin \mathscr{K}_i \text{ and } \forall \mathfrak{f} \in \mathbf{F}, \mathfrak{f}_i(\omega) \models \Box_i \varphi. \end{cases}$$

We say the model satisfies φ iff $\omega_0 \models \varphi$.

A fibred model for $\Lambda_{\mathbf{I}}^{\mathfrak{f}}$ can be generated from fibring the semantics for the modal logics $\Lambda_i, i \in \mathbf{I}$. The detailed construction runs as follows: Let $\mathscr{K}_i$ be a class of models $\{\mathfrak{M}_1^i, \mathfrak{M}_2^i, \ldots\}$ for which Λ_i is complete. Each model $\mathfrak{M}_n^i$ has the form $(S, R, \mathbf{a}, v)$ where, as given earlier, S is the set of possible worlds, $\mathbf{a} \in S$ is the actual world and $R \subseteq S \times S$ is the accessibility relation. v is the assignment function, a binary function, giving a value $v(\omega, \mathfrak{p}_0) \in \{0, 1\}$ for any $\omega \in S$ and atomic $\mathfrak{p}_0$. The actual world $\mathbf{a}$ plays a role in the semantic evaluation in the model, in so far as satisfaction in the model is defined as satisfaction at $\mathbf{a}$. We can assume that the models satisfy the condition $S = \{\omega \mid \exists n \, \mathbf{a} \, R^n \omega\}$. This assumption does not affect satisfaction in models because points not accessible from $\mathbf{a}$ by any power R^n of R do not affect truth values at $\mathbf{a}$. Moreover we assume that all sets of possible worlds in any $\mathcal{K}_i$ are all pairwise disjoint, and that there are infinitely many isomorphic (but disjoint) copies of each model in $\mathcal{K}_i$. We use the notation $\mathfrak{M}$ for a model and present it as $\mathfrak{M} = (S^{\mathfrak{M}}, R^{\mathfrak{M}}, \mathbf{a}^{\mathfrak{M}}, v^{\mathfrak{M}})$ and write $\mathfrak{M} \in \mathcal{K}_i$, when the model $\mathfrak{M}$ is in the semantics $\mathcal{K}_i$. Thus our assumption boils down to $\mathfrak{M} \neq \mathfrak{N} \Rightarrow S^{\mathfrak{M}} \cap S^{\mathfrak{N}} = \varnothing$. In fact a model can be identified by its actual world, i.e., $\mathfrak{M} = \mathfrak{N}$ iff $a^{\mathfrak{M}} = a^{\mathfrak{N}}$. Then the fibred semantics can be given as follows: (1) $W = \bigcup_{\mathfrak{M} \in \bigcup_i \mathcal{K}_i} S^{\mathfrak{M}}$; (2) $R = \bigcup_{\mathfrak{M} \in \bigcup_i \mathcal{K}_i} R^{\mathfrak{M}}$; (3) $v(\omega, \mathfrak{q}_0) = v^{\mathfrak{M}}(\omega, \mathfrak{q}_0)$, for the unique $\mathfrak{M}$ such that $\omega \in S^{\mathfrak{M}}$; (4) $\mathbf{a}^{\omega} = \mathbf{a}^{\mathfrak{M}}$ for the unique $\mathfrak{M}$ such that $\omega \in S^{\mathfrak{M}}$. For more details see [9]. Before going further we need to be aware of a variant of fibring called dovetailing.

Dovetailing is a special case of fibring in the sense that a dovetailed model is a fibred model that must agree with the current world on the values of atoms. For instance, in the above section we saw that the function $\mathbf{f}$ can be viewed as functions giving for each $\omega \in S^1 \cup S^2$, an element $\mathbf{f}(\omega) \in S^1 \cup S^2$ such that if $\omega \in S^i$ then $\mathbf{f}(\omega) \in S^j, i \neq j$. If $\mathscr{L}_1$ and $\mathscr{L}_2$ share the same set of atoms $\mathfrak{Q}$ then we can compare the values $v(\omega, \mathfrak{q}_0)$ and $v(\mathbf{f}(t), \mathfrak{q}_0)$ for an atom $\mathfrak{q}_0$ which need not be identical. If we require from the fibring functions that for each $\omega \in S^i$, $\mathbf{f}_j(t) \in S^j$ and each $\mathfrak{q}_0 \in \mathfrak{Q}$ we want $v(\omega, \mathfrak{q}_0) = v(\mathbf{f}_i(\omega), \mathfrak{q}_0)$, then this fibring case is referred to as *dovetailing*. This means that the actual world of the model fibred at ω, $\mathbf{f}_i(\omega)$, can be identified with ω. The set of fibring functions $\mathbf{F}$ is no longer needed, since we identified ω with $\mathbf{f}_i(\omega)$, for every fibring function $\mathbf{f}$. Two theorems are given below, the proof of which can be found in [5].

Theorem 1 (Dovetailing and Normal Modal Logic). *Assume Λ_i, $i \in I$ all are extensions of $\mathbf{K}$ formulated using traditional Hilbert axioms and the rule of necessitation, then $\Lambda_I^{\mathfrak{D}}$ can be axiomatized by taking the union of the axioms and the rules of necessitation for each modality $\square_i$ of each Λ_i*

Theorem 2 (Fibring = Dovetailing). *If Λ_i, $i \in I$ admit necessitation and satisfy the disjunction property, then $\Lambda_I^{\mathbf{f}} = \Lambda_I^{\mathfrak{D}}$.*

It is immediate to see that BDI logic without interaction axioms is nothing else but combinations of normal multi-modal logics Therefore, according to Theorem 1, dovetailing provides a general methodology for generating BDI-like systems.

3   Semantics for Mental States with Interaction Axioms

The technique of fibring/dovetailing as mentioned above does not take into account any interaction of modalities. However, in a BDI model mental states are very often connected to each other in the form of interaction axioms as shown in the introduction. Thus what is needed is a methodology to capture them. In this section we use Catach approach [2] to extend dovetailing in order to develop a general semantics that covers both the basic modalities and their interactions. Briefly Catach's approach runs as follows: Let I be a set of atomic labels; complex labels can be built from atomic ones using the neutral element "λ", the sequential operator ";", and the union operator "$\cup$". If i is an atomic label and α a well-formed formula, then the expression $[i]\alpha$ corresponds to the modal formula $\Box_i\alpha$, and $\langle i \rangle\alpha$ to $\Diamond_i\alpha$. Furthermore we assume that $[\lambda] = \langle \lambda \rangle$. The transformation of complex labels into modalities is governed by the following rules:

$$[\lambda]\alpha \Leftrightarrow \alpha; \qquad [a;b]\alpha \Leftrightarrow [a][b]\alpha; \qquad [a\cup b]\alpha \Leftrightarrow [a]\alpha \wedge [b]\alpha.$$

According to the above conditions we can identify, for example, the formula $\Box_1\Box_2 A \wedge \Box_3 A \wedge A$ with the expression $[(1;2) \cup 3 \cup \lambda]$. Let us consider now the expression $\langle a \rangle[b]\alpha \Rightarrow [c]\langle d \rangle\alpha$, known as the a,b,c,d-incestuality axiom [3,12] (we will use $G^{a,b,c,d}$ to refer to it). It can be used to generate, among others, the well known D, T, B, 4 and 5 axioms of modal logic. For example, when $a = b = \lambda$ and $c = d = 1$ we obtain the symmetry axiom B for $\Box_i$. It is then immediate to see that the above axiom schema covers many existing systems of multi-modal logic, including the BDI system and make the generation of a large class of new ones possible. As far as dovetailed models are concerned it is possible to define a mapping ρ between labels and the accessibility relations of dovetailed models.

Definition 2. *Let a and b be labels, i an atomic label, and $(\mathsf{W}, \mathsf{R}(i), \mathbf{a}, \mathsf{v})$ a dovetailed model. Then $\rho(i) = \mathsf{R}(i)$; $\rho(\lambda) = \Delta$; $\rho(a;b) = \rho(a)|\rho(b)$; $\rho(a\cup b) = \rho(a)\cup\rho(b)$; where the operators $\cup$ (union) and $|$ (composition) are defined for binary relations, and Δ is the diagonal relation over W (i.e., $\rho(\lambda) = \Delta$, where $\Delta = \{(\omega,\omega) \mid \omega \in \mathsf{W}\}$, the identity relation).*

Definition 3. *Let a, b, c, and d be labels. A dovetailed model $\mathfrak{D} = (\mathsf{W}, \mathsf{R}(i), \mathbf{a}, \mathsf{v})$ enjoys the a,b,c,d-incestuality property iff the following condition holds for $\mathfrak{D}$.*

$$\rho(a)^{-1}|\rho(c) \subseteq \rho(b)|\rho(d)^{-1}. \tag{2}$$

where $\rho(i)^{-1}$ is the *converse* relation of $\rho(i)$. The incestuality condition can be reformulated as follows: If $(\omega,\omega') \in \rho(a)$ and $(\omega,\omega'') \in \rho(c)$ then there exists ω^* such that $(\omega',\omega^*) \in \rho(b)$ and $(\omega'',\omega^*) \in \rho(d)$.

Theorem 3. *[2] Let $\mathscr{L}_{BDI}$ be a normal multi-modal system built from a finite set of axioms $G^{a,b,c,d}$. Then $\mathscr{L}_{BDI}$ is determined by the class of dovetailed models satisfying the a,b,c,d-incestuality properties.*

Catch originally proved the above theorem for what he calls multi-frames. Trivially multi-frames correspond to dovetailed models. In particular this result provides the characterization of a wide class of interaction axioms such as the relationships among mental attitudes of rational agents in terms of dovetailing.

4 Conditions on the Fibring Function

In the previous two sections we saw (1) how BDI-like systems (without interaction axioms) can be reconstructed using dovetailing and (2) how to generate a range of BDI-like interaction axioms through a general axiom schema like $G^{a,b,c,d}$. In this section we outline what conditions would be required on the fibring functions in order to cope with the a,b,c,d-incestuality schema. We assume that the combination of two complete logics need not be complete when we include interaction axioms. We want to identify conditions under which completeness can be preserved. But before identifying the specific conditions on the fibring functions we need to introduce certain notions and constructions related to completeness preservation in terms of canonical models and canonical logics. In the canonical model construction, a *world* is a maximal consistent sets of wff. Thus for any normal propositional modal system S, its canonical model $\langle W, R, v \rangle$ is defined as follows: $W = \{\omega : \omega$ is a maximal S-consistent set of wff $\}$; For any pair of worlds ω and any $\omega' \in W$, $\omega R \omega'$ iff $\{\varphi : \Box\varphi \in \omega\} \subseteq \omega'$; For any variable $\mathfrak{p}_0$ and any $\omega \in W$, $v(\mathfrak{p}_0, \omega) = 1$ iff $\mathfrak{p}_0 \in \omega$. But in the case of a fibred model the above construction needs to be modified accordingly as follows: Let $\Lambda_i, i \in \mathbf{I}$ be monomodal normal logic with languages $\mathcal{L}_i$. Let Σ_Λ be the set of all Λ-maximal consistent sets of formula. Given a set S of formulas, $\Lambda^{\Box_i}(S) = \{\varphi : \Box_i\varphi \in S\}$ and $\Lambda^{\mathcal{L}_i}(S) = \{\varphi : \varphi = \Box_i\psi$ or $\varphi = \Diamond_i\psi, \varphi \in S\}$. The canonical model for $\Lambda_i^{\boldsymbol{f}}, C_i^{\boldsymbol{f}}$, is the structure $\langle W, S, R, \mathbf{F}, a, \tau, v \rangle$, where

- $W = \Sigma_\Lambda \times \mathbf{I}$.
- S is a function $W \mapsto \wp W$ such that $S^\omega = \{(x,i) \in W : \tau(\omega) = i\}$. In other words the set of worlds of the same type as ω.
- $R^\omega \subseteq S^\omega \times S^\omega$ such that $xR^\omega y$ iff $\Lambda^{\Box_{\tau(\omega)}}(x) \subseteq y$.
- $\mathbf{F}$ is the set of functions $\boldsymbol{f} : \mathbf{I} \times W \mapsto W$ (fibring functions) such that

$$\boldsymbol{f}_i, (x,j) = \begin{cases} (x,j) & i = j \\ (x,i) & x = a^\omega \\ (y,i) & \text{otherwise} \end{cases}$$

  where $\Lambda^{\mathcal{L}_i(x)} \subseteq y$, and if $x \neq y$, then $\boldsymbol{f}_i(x) \neq \boldsymbol{f}_j(y)$.
- $a^\omega = \omega$, $\tau(x,i) = i$, $v(\mathfrak{p}_0, \omega) = 1$ iff $\mathfrak{p}_0 \in \omega$, for $\mathfrak{p}_0$ atomic.

Lemma 1. *For every formula φ and every world ω in the canonical model*

$$v(\omega, \varphi) = 1 \text{ iff } \varphi \in \omega.$$

Proof. The proof is by induction on the complexity of φ. The only difference with the proof of the monomodal case is when $\varphi = \Box_i\psi$ and $\tau(\omega) \neq i$. If $v(\omega, \Box_i\psi) = 1$, then for every $\boldsymbol{f} \in \mathbf{F}$ $v(\boldsymbol{f}_i(\omega), \Box_i\psi) = 1$, and we can apply the standard construction for modalities and we obtain that $\Box_i\psi \in \boldsymbol{f}_i(\omega)$. Let us now suppose that $\Box_i\psi$ is not in ω. Since ω is maximal $\neg\Box_i\psi \in \omega$; thus $\Diamond_i\neg\psi \in \omega$. $\Lambda^{\mathcal{L}_i} \subseteq \boldsymbol{f}_i(\omega)$, hence $\Diamond_i\neg\psi \in \boldsymbol{f}_i(\omega)$, from which we derive a contradiction. Thus $\Box_i\psi \in \omega$. The other direction is similar.

As an immediate consequence of the Lemma we have the following theorem.

Theorem 4. $\Lambda_i^{\boldsymbol{f}} \vdash \varphi$ iff $C_i^{\boldsymbol{f}} \models \varphi$.

Definition 4. *Let $\mathcal{F}_\Lambda$ be the frame of the canonical model for Λ. Λ is canonical iff for every valuation v, $(\mathcal{F}_\Lambda, v)$ is a model for Λ.*

Clearly the above definition is equivalent to the usual condition for a modal logic to be canonical (i.c., that the frame of the canonical model is a frame for Λ). However the fibring construction inherits the valuation functions from the underlying models, and we can obtain different logics imposing conditions on the fibring functions based on the assignments of the variables. The fibred frame for $\mathscr{L}_{1,2}$ is obtained in the same way as the fibred model, replacing the occurrences of models with frames.

Lemma 2. *Let* $\mathfrak{M}_{\zeta}^{\mathfrak{f}} = (W, S, R, F, a, \tau, v)$ *be the canonical model for* $\Lambda_I^{\mathfrak{f}}$. *Then for each* $\omega \in W$ $(S^{\omega}, \mathring{R}^{\omega}, v^{\omega})$ *is the canonical model for* $\tau(\omega)$.

Proof. By inspection on the construction of the canonical model for $\Lambda_I^{\mathfrak{f}}$.

From the above Lemma we obtain:

Theorem 5. *Let* $\Lambda_i, i \in I$ *be canonical monomodal logics. Then* $\Lambda_I^{\mathfrak{f}}$ *is canonical.*

For instance the inclusion axiom $\square_1 \varphi \Rightarrow \square_2 \varphi$ is characterized by the dovetailed models where $R_2 \subseteq R_1$. However, such a constraint would be meaningless for fibred models where each modality has its own set of possible worlds. So, what is the corresponding condition on fibred models? As we have already seen a fibring function is defined as

$$\mathfrak{f} : I \times W \to W$$

where I is the set of modalities involved and W is a set of possible worlds. It is worth noting that given a world we can identify the model it belongs to, and that there is a bijection $\mathfrak{M}$ between the actual worlds and their models. So to deal with the inclusion axiom the following constraint must be satisfied:

$$\forall \omega \in W \ \forall \ \mathfrak{f} \in \mathbf{F} : \mathfrak{M}(\mathfrak{f}_2(w)) \sqsubseteq_N \mathfrak{M}(\mathfrak{f}_1(\omega)) \tag{3}$$

where $\sqsubseteq_N$ is the inclusion morphism thus defined:

Definition 5. *Let* $\mathfrak{M}_1$ *and* $\mathfrak{M}_2$ *be two models. Then* $\mathfrak{M}_2 \sqsubseteq_N \mathfrak{M}_1$ *iff there is a morphism* $\mathbf{w} : W_2 \mapsto W_1$, *such that*

- *for each atom* $\mathfrak{p}_0$, $v_2(\omega, \mathfrak{p}_0) = v_1(\mathbf{w}(\omega), \mathfrak{p}_0)$;
- *if* $x R_2 y$ *then* $\mathbf{w}(x) R_1 \mathbf{w}(y)$.

The constraint on the fibring functions to support the *inclusion axiom*, is in alliance with the incestuality axiom $G^{a,b,c,d}$ as stated in the previous section, that is, $R_2 = \rho(c)$ and $R_1 = \rho(b)$. The incestuality axiom can be characterised by giving appropriate conditions that identify the (fibred) models $\mathfrak{M}_1$ and $\mathfrak{M}_2$ involved in the inclusion morphism. It is now possible to provide a characterisation of the fibring/dovetailing of normal modal logics with the incestuality axiom (i.e. $\Diamond_a \square_b \varphi \Rightarrow \square_c \Diamond_d \varphi$). But before giving the characterisation theorem we have to take care of some constructions with respect to the labels a, b, c, d of $G^{a,b,c,d}$. We have to define new cross-modality relations (Fig.1.) among the possible worlds in a fibred model. Firstly we explain the relation R^i where $i = a, b, c, d$ and this is done at two levels. The first level deals with the construction of labels (atomic as well as complex) without taking the operations of union and composition into consideration. This is given as follows:

1. When $i = a$ and a is atomic, $\mathfrak{R}^a(\omega) = \{\omega' : \tau(\omega) = a$ and $\omega R^\omega \omega'\}$
2. When $i = a$ and $\tau(\omega) \neq a$, $\mathfrak{f}_a(\omega) R^{\mathfrak{f}_a(\omega)} \omega'$ where $\mathfrak{f}_a(\omega)$ is the particular fibring function, belonging to the set of fibring functions $\mathbf{F}$, associating a model from ω' with the actual world ω.

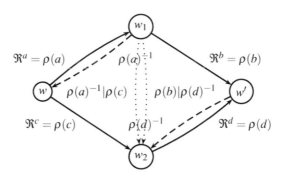

Fig. 1. Incestuality with respect to cross-modality relations

From this definition and keeping in line with the definition of canonical models as given in the previous section $\omega R^a \omega'$ iff $\{\varphi : [a]\varphi \in \omega\} \subseteq \omega'$. In a similar manner, at the second level, complex labels in terms of union and compostion could be given as follows

- $\mathfrak{R}^{b;c}(\omega) = \{\omega' : \exists \omega'' : \omega \mathfrak{R}^b \omega'' \wedge \omega'' \mathfrak{R}^c \omega'\}$
- $\mathfrak{R}^{b\cup c}(\omega) = \{\omega' : \omega \mathfrak{R}^b \omega'\} \cup \{\omega' : \omega \mathfrak{R}^c \omega'\}$

From this we can arrive at the following definition.

Definition 6. *Let a and b be labels, i an atomic label, and $\langle W, S, R, F, \mathbf{a}, \tau, v\rangle$ a fibred model. Then*

$$\rho(i) = \mathfrak{R}^i; \quad \rho(\lambda) = \Delta; \quad \rho(a;b) = \rho(a)|\rho(b); \quad \rho(a \cup b) = \rho(a) \cup \rho(b);$$

where the operators $\cup$ (union) and $|$ (composition) are defined for binary relations, and Δ is the diagonal relation over W

Definition 7. *Let $\mathfrak{M} = \langle W, S, R, F, \mathbf{a}, \tau, v\rangle$ be a fibred model, a be a label, and $\omega \in W$. With $\mathfrak{M}(\omega) \upharpoonright \mathfrak{R}^a$ we denote the fibred model $\langle W', S, R, F, \mathbf{a}, \tau, v\rangle$, where $W' = \{w' \in W : \omega \mathfrak{R}^a w'\}$.*

Theorem 6. *Let $\Lambda_a, \Lambda_b, \Lambda_c, \Lambda_d$ be canonical normal modal logics and $\Lambda_{abcd} = \Lambda_a \odot \Lambda_b \odot \Lambda_c \odot \Lambda_d$. Then $\Lambda = \Lambda_{abcd} \oplus \Diamond_a \Box_b \varphi \Rightarrow \Box_c \Diamond_d \varphi$ is characterised by the class of fibred models satisfying*

$$\forall \omega \in W , \forall \mathfrak{f} \in \mathbf{F} , \mathfrak{M}^{ac}(\omega) \sqsubseteq_N \mathfrak{M}^{bd}(\omega)$$

where (1) $\mathfrak{M}^{ac}(\omega) = \mathfrak{M}(\omega) \upharpoonright \rho(a)^{-1} | \rho(c)$ and (2) $\mathfrak{M}^{bd}(\omega) = \mathfrak{M}(\omega) \upharpoonright \rho(b) | \rho(d)^{-1}$ as shown in Fig.2.

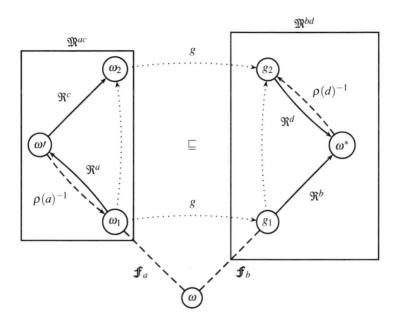

Fig. 2. Inclusion morphism, Fibring and Incestuality

Proof. For the proof we have to note that, thanks to the fact that Λ_i ($i \in \{a,b,c,d\}$) are canonical, for any pair of world ω and ω', the maximal consistent sets associated with them are the same, i.e., $S^\omega = S^{\omega'}$, they are the set of all the maximal consistent sets. Thus no matter of the fibring function we choose, we have that the structure of the models obtained from the $\boldsymbol{f}_i$'s are the same. Therefore we can use the identity over Σ_Λ as the morphism **g** in the inclusion morphism. Moreover by the definition of canonical models the relation $\omega_1 \mathfrak{R}^a \omega_2$ can be given as

$$\omega_1 \mathfrak{R}^a \omega_2 \text{ iff } \{\varphi : [a]\varphi\} \subseteq \omega_2 \tag{4}$$

It should be kept in mind that a world ω in the canonical fibred model is a pair, (Σ, t), where Σ is a maximal Λ-consistent set of formulas and t is a label for a modality (check our construction of canonical models). Also we have to be careful about $\mathfrak{R}^a$ as a could be a complex label and hence we need steps 1. and 2. as mentioned above. Accordingly if we examine the fibring of (Σ, t) with respect to the label a, i.e., $\boldsymbol{f}_a(\Sigma, t)$, we have two cases:

1. $\tau(\Sigma, t) = a$ $(t = a)$
2. $\tau(\Sigma, t) \neq a$ $(t \neq a)$

For (1)

$$(\Sigma, a) \mathfrak{R}^a (\Sigma', a) \text{ iff } \{\varphi : \Box_a \varphi \in \Sigma\} \subseteq \Sigma' \tag{5}$$

For (2) we have two subcases

1. if $\mathbf{a}^{(\Sigma,t)} = (\Sigma,t)$ then $\boldsymbol{f}_a(\Sigma,t) = (\Sigma,a)$ and then

$$(\Sigma,a)\Re^a(\Sigma',a) \text{ iff } \{\varphi : \Box_a\varphi \in \Sigma\} \subseteq \Sigma' \tag{6}$$

2. if $\mathbf{a}^{(\Sigma,t)} \neq (\Sigma,t)$, where $\mathbf{a}$ is a function giving the actual world $\mathbf{a}^\omega$ of the model labelled by ω, then $\boldsymbol{f}_a(\Sigma,t) = (\Sigma^*,a)$ such that

$$\Sigma^{\mathscr{L}_a} \subseteq \Sigma^* \text{ and } (\Sigma^*,a)\Re^a(\Sigma',a) \text{ iff } \{\varphi : \Box_a\varphi \in \Sigma^*\} \subseteq \Sigma'$$

and then

$$(\Sigma,t)\Re^a(\Sigma',a) \text{ iff } \{\varphi : \Box_a\varphi \in \Sigma^*\} \subseteq \Sigma' \tag{7}$$

In both cases one can find that

$$(\Sigma,t)\Re^a(\Sigma',a) \text{ iff } \{\varphi : \Box_a\varphi \in \Sigma\} \subseteq \Sigma'. \tag{8}$$

Hence by the above construction we obtain

$$\omega\Re^a\omega_1 \text{ iff } \{\varphi : \Box_a\varphi \in \omega\} \subseteq \omega_1 \tag{9}$$

or equivalently

$$\omega\Re^a\omega_1 \text{ iff } \{\Diamond_a\varphi : \varphi \in \omega_1\} \subseteq \omega \tag{10}$$

Now according to the definition of inclusion morphism we have to show that if $(\omega_1,\omega_2) \in \rho(a)^{-1} \mid \rho(c)$ then $(\mathbf{g}(\omega_1),\mathbf{g}(\omega_2)) \in \rho(b) \mid \rho(d)^{-1}$ where $\mathbf{g}$ is the morphism of the inclusion morphism. Now

$$\omega_1,\omega_2 \in \rho(a)^{-1} \mid \rho(c) \text{ iff } \exists z : (\omega_1,z) \in \rho(a)^{-1} \wedge (z,\omega_2 \in \rho(c)).$$

But this corresponds to

$$\exists z, z\Re^a\omega_1 \wedge z\Re^c\omega_2 \text{ (if } z = \omega \text{ then } \omega\Re^a\omega_1 \text{ and } \omega\Re^c\omega_2). \tag{11}$$

On the other hand

$$(\mathbf{g}(\omega_1),\mathbf{g}(\omega_2)) \in \rho(b) \mid \rho(d)^{-1} \text{ iff } \exists t : (\mathbf{g}(\omega_1^b,t)) \in \rho(b) \wedge (t,\mathbf{g}(\omega_2)) \in \rho(d)^{-1}$$

and therefore

$$\exists t : \mathbf{g}(\omega_1)\Re^b t \wedge \mathbf{g}(\omega_2)\Re^d t \text{ (if } t = \omega^* \text{ then } \omega_1\Re^b\omega^* \text{ and } \omega_2\Re^d\omega^*) \tag{12}$$

Since $\mathbf{g}$ is the identity over Σ_{max} (11) and (12) imply that for every maximal Λ-consistent sets of sentences ω, ω_1 and ω_2

if $\{\varphi : \Box_a\varphi \in \omega\} \subseteq \omega_1$ and $\{\varphi : \Box_c\varphi \in \omega\} \subseteq \omega_2$ then
$\{\varphi : \Box_b\varphi \in \omega_1\} \cup \{\varphi : \Box_d\varphi \in \omega_2\}$ is Λ-consistent

For suppose that this not the case. Then for some $\Box_b\varphi_1,\ldots,\Box_b\varphi_n \in \omega_1$ and some $\Box_d\psi_1,\ldots,\Box_d\psi_m \in \omega_2$ we have

$$\vdash_\Lambda \varphi_1 \wedge \cdots \wedge \varphi_n \Rightarrow \neg(\psi_1 \wedge \cdots \wedge \psi_m)$$

and by the rule $\vdash \alpha \Rightarrow \beta / \vdash \Diamond \alpha \Rightarrow \Diamond \beta$ we can get

$$\vdash_\Lambda \Diamond_d(\varphi_1 \wedge \cdots \wedge \varphi_i) \Rightarrow \Diamond_d \neg(\psi_1 \wedge \cdots \wedge \psi_j) \tag{13}$$

and thereby, by applying the $(\Diamond \Box)$-interchange axiom [2], we get

$$\vdash_\Lambda \Diamond_d(\varphi_1 \wedge \cdots \wedge \varphi_i) \Rightarrow \neg\Box_d(\psi_1 \wedge \cdots \wedge \psi_j) \tag{14}$$

Since $\Box_b\varphi_1, \ldots, \Box_b\varphi_m \in \omega$, so is $\Box_b(\varphi_1 \wedge \cdots \wedge \varphi_n)$. Hence, by $\omega \mathfrak{R}^a \omega_1$ and by (10) we must have $\Diamond_a\Box_b(\varphi_1 \wedge \cdots \wedge \varphi_n) \in \omega$. But ω contains the instance

$$\Diamond_a\Box_b(\varphi_1 \wedge \cdots \wedge \varphi_n) \Rightarrow \Box_c\Diamond_d(\varphi_1 \wedge \cdots \wedge \varphi_n)$$

of $\mathbf{G}^{a,b,c,d}$ and therefore we must have $\Box_c\Diamond_d(\varphi_1 \wedge \cdots \wedge \varphi_n) \in \omega$. Since $\omega \mathfrak{R}^c \omega_2$, by (9), we have $\Diamond_d(\varphi_1 \wedge \cdots \wedge \varphi_n) \in \omega_2$ and, by (14), this means that

$$\neg\Box_d(\psi_1 \wedge \cdots \wedge \psi_m) \in \omega_2.$$

which contradicts the assumption that $\Box_d\psi_1, \ldots, \Box_d\psi_m \in \omega_2$, and then $\Box_d(\psi_1 \wedge \cdots \wedge \psi_m) \in \omega_2$. Thus Λ is consistent and completeness is thereby proved.

5   Discussion and Related Work

The main contribution of this paper is the proof related to the characterisation theorem as given in Theorem 6. This result provides answer to two questions which is commonly raised in the area of combining logics namely (1) Is there a way to specify interaction between the logics in the fibred logic? and (2) How do interactions between the logics translate into restrictions of the fibring function? It should be kept in mind that we can apply results related to *fusion* [7] and *independent combination* [4] to prove that the BDI logic

$$\mathbb{L}' \equiv (\otimes_{i=1}^n \mathbf{KD45}_{\text{BEL}_i}) \otimes (\otimes_{i=1}^n \mathbf{KD}_{\text{DES}_i}) \otimes (\otimes_{i=1}^n \mathbf{KD}_{\text{INT}_i}) \tag{15}$$

is sound, complete and decidable but these results do not transfer to the logic $\mathbb{L}$ as given in equation (1) when we add the required interaction axioms. This means that in the case of BDI we have transfer of properties for the three components *fused* together as in equation (15) but we do not have a result that we can apply in the case of interaction axioms being present in the combination. The point is that it is sometimes possible to recognise some existing combined systems as fibrings or dovetailings but difculties arise when the combination is not a simple fusion, but an interaction between the components is present. As pointed out in [8] results of properties transfer even if limited to very small classes of interaction axioms would be of extreme importance to the whole area of Multi-Agent System theories. As far as related work is concerned, the fibring technique outlined in this paper is closely related to that of [5]. There are a

---

[2] If φ is any wff which contains an unbroken sequence of $\Box$ and/or $\Diamond$ and ψ results from φ by replacing $\Box$ by $\Diamond$ and $\Diamond$ by $\Box$ throughout that sequence and also inserting or deleting a $\neg$ both immediately before and after that sequence, then $\vdash \varphi \Leftrightarrow \psi$ (and hence if $\vdash \varphi$ then $\vdash \psi$).

few other variants of fibring and related results in the Literature. There is a constrained version of fibring (any symbols common to both logic systems are shared) as defined in [15] wherein a category-theoretical approach is given importance in fine tuning the semantics of fibring. This is not the case in our work where no symbols appear in the intersection of the two signatures and the underlying semantic structure is that of possible worlds. There is also another constrained version of fibring using general semantics [19] in which results related to completeness preservation is shown. They do not consider property transfer in the case of interaction axioms. Fibring technique has also been applied to non-truth functional logics [1] as well as first-order modal logics [16].

References

1. Caleiro, C., Carnielli, W.A., Coniglio, M.E., Sernadas, A., Sernadas, C.: Fibring non-truth-functional logics: Completeness preservation. Journal of Logic, Language and Information 12(2), 183–211 (2003)
2. Catach, L.: Normal multimodal logics. In: Proceedings of the 7th National Conference on Artificial Intelligence (AAAI), pp. 491–495 (1988)
3. Chellas, B.F.: Modal Logic: An Introduction. Cambridge University Press (1980)
4. Finger, M., Gabbay, D.M.: Combining temporal logic systems. Notre Dame Journal of Formal Logic 37(2), 204–232 (1996)
5. Gabbay, D.M.: Fibring Logics. Oxford University Press, Oxford (1999)
6. Governatori, G., Padmanabhan, V., Sattar, A.: On Fibring Semantics for BDI Logics. In: Flesca, S., Greco, S., Leone, N., Ianni, G. (eds.) JELIA 2002. LNCS (LNAI), vol. 2424, pp. 198–210. Springer, Heidelberg (2002)
7. Kracht, M., Wolter, F.: Properties of independently axiomatizable bimodal logics. The Journal of Symbolic Logic 56(4), 1469–1485 (1991)
8. Lomuscio, A.: Information Sharing Among Ideal Agents. PhD thesis, School of Computer Science, University of Brimingham (1999)
9. Padmanabhan, V.: On Extending BDI Logics. PhD thesis, School of Information Technology, Griffith University, Brisbane, Australia (2003)
10. Padmanabhan, V., Governatori, G.: A Fibred Tableau Calculus for Modal Logics of Agents. In: Baldoni, M., Endriss, U. (eds.) DALT 2006. LNCS (LNAI), vol. 4327, pp. 105–122. Springer, Heidelberg (2006)
11. Padmanabhan, V., Governatori, G.: On Constructing Fibred Tableaux for BDI Logics. In: Yang, Q., Webb, G. (eds.) PRICAI 2006. LNCS (LNAI), vol. 4099, pp. 150–160. Springer, Heidelberg (2006)
12. Popkorn, S.: First Steps in Modal logic. Cambridge University Press (1994)
13. Rao, A.S., Georgeff, M.P.: Modelling rational agents within a BDI-architecture. In: Principles of KRR (KR 1991). Morgan Kaufmann (1991)
14. Rao, A.S., Georgeff, M.P.: Formal models and decision procedures for multi-agent systems. Technical note 61, Australian Artificial Intelligence Institute (1995)
15. Sernadas, A., Sernadas, C., Caleiro, C.: Fibring of logics as a categorial construction. J. Log. Comput. 9(2), 149–179 (1999)
16. Sernadas, A., Sernadas, C., Zanardo, A.: Fibring modal first-order logics: Completeness preservation. Logic Journal of the IGPL 10(4), 413–451 (2002)
17. Wolter, F.: Fusions of modal logics revisited. In: Advances in Modal Logic. CSLI Lecture notes 87, vol. 1 (1997)
18. Wooldridge, M.: Reasoning About Rational Agents. MIT (2000)
19. Zanardo, A., Sernadas, A., Sernadas, C.: Fibring: Completeness preservation. J. Symb. Log. 66(1), 414–439 (2001)

Reasoning about DNSSEC

Kollapalli Ramesh Babu, Vineet Padmanabhan, and Wilson Naik Bhukya

Department of Computers & Information Sciences,
University of Hyderabad, Hyderabad - 500046, India
krubabu@gmail.com,
{vineetcs,naikcs}@uohyd.ernet.in

Abstract. This Paper outlines a logic based formal approach to represent and reason about the DNSSEC (Domain Name System Security Extensions) protocol. DNSSEC provides security services to the existing DNS protocol mainly through public key cryptography. But, it is well known that even the use of the most perfect cryptographic tools does not always ensure the desired security goals. This situation arises because of *logical flaws* in the design of protocols. Our aim is to represent and reason about DNSSEC protocol using the Modal Logic system SVO so as to derive the desired goals of the protocol.

Keywords: Security Protocols, Modal Logic, Knowledge Representation & Reasoning.

1 Introduction

Nowadays, security protocols are widely used, to provide security services in different distributed systems. Deficiencies in the design of these protocols could have negative consequences over the system they are supposed to protect. There is a strong requirement of verification of the protocols before using it. Logic-based Specification and Verification is one of the widely used formal technique in the domain of security protocols. Many Modal logic Based systems like BAN[6], AT, GNY[9] and SVO [10] were proposed and used in successful specification and verification of security protocols. In this paper we formally analyze DNSSEC using the modal logic system SVO which was intended to unify its predecessors like BAN, GNY and AT. DNSSEC is a security extension to the existing Domain Name System which can achieve Data Integrity and Origin Authentication for security purposes.

2 DNSSEC

The Domain Name System (DNS) [2] is a hierarchically distributed database that provides information fundamental to Internet operations, such as translating human readable host names to Internet Protocol (IP) addresses and vice versa. This is commonly known as *name-address resolution*[2]. A Client entity known as a Resolver submits queries to, and receives responses from, the DNS server.

C. Sombattheera et al. (Eds.): MIWAI 2011, LNAI 7080, pp. 75–86, 2011.

The responses contain Resource Records (RRs)[4] which provides the desired name-address resolution information. Users accessing hosts on the Internet rely on the correct translation of host names to IP addresses which is served by the DNS servers. Because of the importance of the information served by the DNS server, there is a strong demand for authenticating the server and the information served by that server in a DNS system. Currently DNS system does not prevent attackers from modifying or injecting DNS messages. A typical attack, referred to as *DNS spoofing* [5], allows an attacker to manipulate DNS answers on their way to the users. If an attacker make changes in the DNS tables of a single server, those changes will propagate across the Internet. To stop these attacks on DNS system it is necessary to add security to the existing DNS System. To do this Domain Name System Security Extensions (DNSSEC) [3][4] were defined. Securing DNS means providing data origin authentication (i.e., data is received from a party from which it was sent) and integrity (i.e., data is same as it was sent and not modified in between) to the DNS system. Confidentiality is not required, since the information stored in the DNS database is supposedly public so that anyone in the Internet can see the DNS replies. All answers from DNSSEC servers are digitally signed. By checking the signature, a DNS Client is able to check whether the information was originated from a legitimate server and whether the data is identical to the data on the DNS server.

To achieve Security in Domain Name System, DNSSEC adds four records namely DNS Public Key (DNSKEY), Resource Record Signature (RRSIG), Delegation Signer (DS), and Next Secure (NSEC) [8]to the existing DNS System. These are explained as follows;

1. **DNSKEY:** DNSSEC uses public key cryptography to sign and authenticate DNS resource record sets (RRsets). The public keys are stored in DNSKEY resource records [8] and are used in the DNSSEC authentication process.
2. **RRSIG:** The digital signatures of DNS replies are stored in RRSIG record. RRSIG value [8] is created by encrypting the hash value of the DNS reply with private key of the zone.
3. **DS:** Contains the hash value[8] of a child zone's DNSKEY which is needed in authenticating Client zone DNSKEY.
4. **NSEC:** The NSEC RR [8] points to the next valid name in the zone file and is used to provide proof of non-existence of any name within a zone. The last NSEC in a zone will point back to the zone root or apex.

The DNS server in a zone creates public key and private key pair and publishes the public key in the zone[3]. The private key is kept in secrecy. Private key is used to create signature, and the public key is used to verify the signature. There will be a single private key that signs a zones data but there may be keys for each of several different digital signature algorithms. If a security aware resolver learns a zones public key, it can authenticate that zones signed data. Security-aware resolvers authenticate zone information by forming an authentication chain from a newly learned public key back to a previously known authentication public key, which in turn must have been learned and verified previously.

An alternating sequence of DNS public key (DNSKEY) RRsets and Delegation Signer (DS) RRsets forms a *chain of trust*[3]. A DNSKEY RR is used to verify the signature covering a DS RR and allows the DS RR to be authenticated. The DS RR contains a hash of another DNSKEY RR and this new DNSKEY RR is authenticated by matching the hash in the DS RR. This process is continued until the chain finally ends with a DNSKEY RR whose corresponding private key signs the desired DNS data. For instance, consider the URL `"www.dcis.uohyd.ernet.in."`. Here the root DNSKEY RRset can be used to authenticate the DS RRset for the `"in"` domain. The `"in"` domain DS RRset contains a hash that matches some `"ernet"` domain DNSKEY and the `"ernet"` domain DS RRset contains a hash that matches some "uohyd" domain DNSKEY. This DNSKEY's corresponding private key signs the "dcis" DNSKEY RRset. Private key counterparts of the "dcis" DNSKEY RRset signs data records such as `"www.dcis.uohyd.ernet.in."`

3 How DNSSEC Works: A Formal Interpretation

When Client sends request to DNS Server, DNSSEC adds additional data to the DNS protocol responses that provide extra information (RRSIG, DNSKEY) so as to allow the Client to authenticate the RRset data response[1] The Client can take the RRset response and use the algorithm referenced in the RRSIG record to generate the hash value of the data. The RRSIG value can be encrypted using the DNSKEY public key which will, in effect, decrypt the hash value in the RRSIG record. This operation allows the Client to check that the hash value of the RRset data matches the decrypted RRSIG hash value. The DNSKEY would normally be provided as part of the additional section of a DNSSEC response. If the Client has not validated the DNSKEY within some locally defined period, then the Client should also validate the DNSKEY value. This entails verifying the RRSIG record on the DNSKEY value, using the same procedure as for the RRset validation.

However domain zone key validation also entails the construction of a trust chain back to a trust anchor point. If this domain key is not already a trust anchor then the Client needs to query the parent zone for the DS record of the child zone, which returns a DNSKEY RR, RRSIG(DS) RR, and a DS RR. This DS RR needs to be validated using the DNSKEY of the parent zone. This parent zone public key, in turn, must be validated. This iterative process constructs a trust chain that, hopefully, leads back to a trust anchor. At that point the DNS response can be considered to be validated. Figure [1] explains how the authentication chain will be established using DS RRset and DNSKEY RRset. Consider that the host `"dcis"` in `"uohyd"` domain has made a DNS Request for `"D.com"` whose RRset is available in `"com"` domain. Then the name resolution process involves the following steps;

---

[1] RRset = It is a collection of RRs in a DNS ZONE that share a common name, class and type.

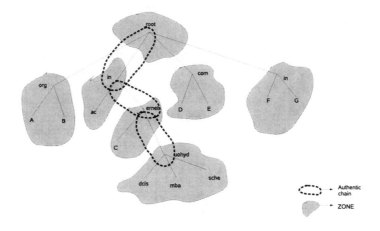

Fig. 1. A sample scenario

- M_{cs}: $dcis \longrightarrow uohyd$:$\langle DNSReq., D.com.\rangle$
- M_{cs}: $uohyd \longrightarrow ernet$:$\langle DNSReq., D.com.\rangle$
- M_{cs}: $ernet \longrightarrow in$:$\langle DNSReq., D.com.\rangle$
- M_{cs}: $in \longrightarrow root$:$\langle DNSReq., D.com.\rangle$
- M_{cs}: $root \longrightarrow com$:$\langle DNSReq., D.com.\rangle$
- M_{sc}: $com \longrightarrow root$:$\langle RRset_{D.com.}, RRSIG_{D.com.}, DNSKEY_{com}\rangle$
- M_{sc}: $root \longrightarrow in$:$\langle RRset_{D.com.}, RRSIG_{D.com.}, DNSKEY_{com}\rangle$
- M_{sc}: $in \longrightarrow ernet$:$\langle RRset_{D.com.}, RRSIG_{D.com.}, DNSKEY_{com}\rangle$
- M_{sc}: $ernet \longrightarrow uohyd$:$\langle RRset_{D.com.}, RRSIG_{D.com.}, DNSKEY_{com}\rangle$
- M_{sc}: $uohyd \longrightarrow dcis$:$\langle RRset_{D.com.}, RRSIG(RRset_{D.com.}), DNSKEY_{com}\rangle$

where M_{cs} stands for Message send from client to server, M_{sc} stands for Message
send from server to client and $\langle DNSReq., D.com.\rangle$ stands for DNS Request for
D.com domain. After receiving the DNS Response form "uohyd" server, "dcis"
host will try to construct **chain of trust** between the source of response and
trust of anchor as follows;

- M_{cs}: $dcis \longrightarrow uohyd$:$\langle DSReq., com.\rangle$
- M_{cs}: $uohyd \longrightarrow ernet$:$\langle DSReq., com.\rangle$
- M_{cs}: $ernet \longrightarrow in$:$\langle DSReq., com.\rangle$
- M_{cs}: $in \longrightarrow root$:$\langle DSReq., com.\rangle$
- M_{sc}: $root \longrightarrow in$:$\langle DS_{com}, RRSIG(DS_{com}), DNSKEY_{root}\rangle$
- M_{sc}: $in \longrightarrow ernet$:$\langle DS_{com}, RRSIG(DS_{com}), DNSKEY_{root}\rangle$
- M_{sc}: $ernet \longrightarrow uohyd$:$\langle DS_{com}, RRSIG(DS_{com}), DNSKEY_{root}\rangle$
- M_{sc}: $uohyd \longrightarrow dcis$:$\langle DS_{com}, RRSIG(DS_{com}), DNSKEY_{root}\rangle$

where $\langle DSReq., com.\rangle$ stands for Delegation Signer Request for com domain.

3.1   Origin Authentication and Data Integrity:

Authentication will be achieved by establishing Authentication chain between the zone's with the help of DS RRset and DNSKEY RRset's. For instance, in our example "dcis" already knows the authentication public key(DNSKEY) of root. To make newly learned DNSKEY as authentic it need to establish an authentication chain back to known DNSKEY i.e. root's DNSKEY. The steps given below shows how this chain of trust helps in verifying the Origin of the response;

1. Verifying Sender DNSKEY (i.e. $DNSKEY_{com}$)
   (a) $DNSKEY_{root}\{RRSIG(DS_{com})\} == hash(DS_{com})$
   (b) $DS_{com} == hash(DNSKEY_{com})$
   Initially the senders (i.e., .com's) DNSKEY has to be verified (1). In order to do this the hash value of the DS record of .com should match to the decrypted value of RRSIG of DS_{com} as shown in (a). Finally the hash value of the DNSKEY of .com is compared with DS_{com} record as given in (b). In the next step we have to verify the DNSKEY of parent zone of .com which is Root as given below.
2. Verifying Parent Zone DNSKEY(i.e. $DNSKEY_{root}$). The DNSKEY of root Zone is believed by every one. Therefore it is not required to be verified and from this we can get authentication chain to the root node.

Data Integrity will be achieved if the following condition is true

$$hash(RRset_{D.com}) == \{RRSIG_{D.com}\}DNSKEY_{com}$$

i.e., first the hash value is computed for the received RRset. Second RRSIG value is decrypted using DNSKEY and finally both the values are compared. If both values are equal then it implies that the received data is correct. If not we can arrive at the conclusion that it was modified in between.

4   Formal Analysis of DNSSEC Using SVO-logic

Formal methods are widely used for evaluating the design issues of security protocols. Modal logic systems like BAN, AT, GNY and SVO [6,9,1,11] logics are widely used in the analysing security protocols. These Modal logic systems analyze protocols by deriving beliefs that honest principals can get by executing the protocol correctly. We are using SVO logic as outlined in [10] for representing and reasoning about the DNSSEC protocol. The Inference rules and Axioms of SVO are as follows;

4.1   SVO Inference Rules

F1: Modus Ponens: From φ and $(\varphi \rightarrow \psi)$ *infer* ψ
F2: Necessitation: $\vdash \varphi$ *infer* $\vdash P$ *believes* φ

It should be noted that $\Gamma \vdash \varphi$ means that φ is derivable from the set of formulae Γ and the respective axioms which we are going to state below. $\vdash \varphi$ means that φ/P *believes* φ is a theorem, i.e., derivable from axioms alone.

4.2   SVO Axioms

A1: (Distributive Axiom) : P believes $\varphi \wedge P$ believes $(\varphi \rightarrow \psi) \rightarrow P$ believes ψ.
A1 states that a Principal believes all that logically follows from his beliefs.

A2: (Truth Axiom): P believes $\varphi \rightarrow \varphi$
The axiom states that the beliefs held by Principal is true.

A3: (Positive Introspection): P believes $\varphi \rightarrow P$ believes $(P$ believes $\varphi)$
A3 states that a Principal can tell what he believes.

A4: (Negative Introspection): $\neg(P$ believes $\varphi) \rightarrow P$ believes $(\neg P$ believes $\varphi)$
The axiom states that the Principal cannot tell what he does not believe.

4.3   Axioms for Reasoning about DNSSEC

A5:   **Received Axiom**
(a) P received $(X_1, \ldots, X_n) \rightarrow P$ received X_i
(b) $(P$ received $\{X_k\} \wedge P$ sees $\tilde{K}) \rightarrow P$ received X
The Principal P can receive concatenates of messages $X_1, \ldots, X_n$ and also decryptions with available keys so as to decrypt the encrypted message with available key K.
A6:   **Source Association**
(a) $(PK_\sigma(Q, K) \wedge$ received $X \wedge SV(X, K, Y)) \rightarrow Q$ said Y
The keys and signatures are used to identify the sender of the message. $(PK_\sigma(Q, K)$ represents the fact that K is the public signature verification key for principal Q. Similarly SV(X,K,Y) represents that, given a signed message X, by applying key K to it will verify the message Y which was signed with private key $\tilde{K}$.
A7:   **Seeing Axiom**
(a) P received $X \rightarrow P$ sees X
(b) $(P$ sees $X1 \wedge \ldots \wedge P$ sees $X_n) \rightarrow (P$ sees $F(X1, \ldots, X_n))$

The Principal P can see all the things that he receives. He can also see the messages that can be computed from the received messages.
A8:   **Freshness Axiom**
(a) $(fresh(X_i) \rightarrow fresh(X1, \ldots, X_n)$
(b) $(fresh(X1, \ldots, X_n) \rightarrow fresh(F(X1, \ldots, X_n))$
The Principal believes concatenated message is fresh, if one of it's message is fresh. The function of the message is also fresh.
A9:   **Saying Axiom**
(a) P said $(X_1, \ldots, X_n) \rightarrow P$ said $X_i \wedge P$ has $X_i,$ for $i = 1, \ldots, n.$
(b) P says $(X_1, \ldots, X_n) \rightarrow (P$ said $(X_1, \ldots, X_n) \wedge P$ says $X_i),$ for $i = 1, \ldots, n.$
A principal who has said a concatenated message has also said and has the concatenates of that message. A principal who has recently said X has said X.
A10: **Jurisdiction and Nonce verification Axiom**

(a) $(P \ controls \ \varphi \wedge P \ says \ \varphi) \rightarrow \varphi$
(b) $(fresh(X) \wedge P \ said \ X) \rightarrow P \ says \ X$
Part (a) of axiom 10 says that φ is under the absolute control of the Principal and part (b) distinguishes a message from having been said (sometime) to having been said during the current interval of time.

A11: **Possession Axiom**
(a) $P \ received \ X \rightarrow P \ has \ X$
(b) $P \ has(X1, ..., X_n) \rightarrow P \ has X_i$
(c) $(P \ has \ X_1 \wedge ... \wedge P \ has \ X_n) \rightarrow P \ has \ F(X_1, ..., X_n)$

Since the main aim of this paper is to give a syntactic analysis of DNSSEC we do not get into the semantic interpretation or truth conditions of the logical formulae. For an in depth analysis of the truth conditions involved in SVO logic in terms of cryptographic protocols one can refer [10].

4.4   Formal Analysis of DNSSEC

It is to be noted that in order to analyse a protocol in SVO logic it is common to have the following steps

1. Write assumptions about initial state
2. Annotate the protocol
3. Assert comprehensions of received messages
4. Assert interpretations of comprehended messages
5. Use the logic to derive beliefs held by protocol principals

In the first step we write initial conditions of the protocol, which includes the beliefs held by the principals, the possessions of keys or any other prior assumptions the principals might be holding. It should be kept in mind that in DNSSEC the Client establishes authentication chain back to the previously known DNSKEY. As noted earlier, since DNS is having a hierarchical structure wherein the trace goes back to the root key the initial assumption is that everyone believes root zones DNSKEY. i.e.

    A0 —*client believes $DNSKEY_{root}$* which can be rewritten as
    A1 —*client believes $PK(Root, DNSKEY_{root})$*

i.e., client believes the public key of root which is $DNSKEY_{root}$. Premises P1 to P5 as given below also falls into the category of initial assumptions. In the second step we write the messages that are exchanged between principals which includes the received messages, that is the messages are not lost in transit. Premises P6 and P7 as given below represents the annotation. In the third step we assert that the messages that are received by the principals are comprehended (eg. decryption of received message by using a key that is known already) as shown in premises P8 and P9. In the fourth step we write the inferred messages by principals with the received messages and the knowledge that principals initially have as outlined below;

$$client\ received\ (DNSKEY_{Sender}) \wedge\ client\ believes\ fresh(DS_{Sender})\ \wedge$$
$$(\{Hash(DNSKEY_{Sender})\} \equiv$$
$$DS_{Sender}) \rightarrow client\ believes\ fresh\ (DNSKEY_{Sender})$$

$$client\ received\ X \wedge\ client\ received\ SIG(X) \wedge$$
$$client\ believes fresh(DNSKEY_{Sender}) \wedge\ (\{SIG(X)\}_{DNSKEY_{Sender}} \equiv$$
$$Hash(X)) \rightarrow client\ believes\ X$$

In fifth step we use axioms and premises to derive the goals of the protocol.

4.5   Protocol Analysis

The following are the Set of premises derived from the operation of a protocol.

- P1: C believes fresh(PK(R,K))
- P2: R believes fresh(PK(R,K))
- P3: S believes fresh(PK(S,K))

  The above premises are derived based on the initial assumptions of the protocol. Client(C) believes public key K of Root(R), similarly Root(R) and Server(S) believes their own public keys.

- P4: C believes R controls (fresh(PK(R,K))
- P5: C believes S controls (fresh(PK(S,k))
  The above premises says that C believes R and S have control over freshness of the their public keys.

- P6: C received $\{S, C, RRSet, SV(SIG(RRSet), PK_\sigma(S, K), RRSet),$
  $PK(S, K)\}$
- P7: C received $\{R, C, DS_S, SV(SIG(DS_S), PK_\sigma(R, K), DS_S), PK(R, K)\}$
- P8: C believes C received $\{S, C, RRSet, SV(SIG(RRSet), PK_\sigma(S, K),$
  $RRSet), PK(S, K)\}$
- P9: C believes C received $\{R, C, DS_S, SV(SIG(DS_S), PK_\sigma(R, K), DS_S),$
  $PK(R, K)\}$

The above premises says that Client(C) believes that it received Resource Record Set(RRSet), signature verification of RRSet and public key K required to verify the signature of the message received from server(S). It also believes that it received Delegation Signer (DS_S) record, corresponding signature verification record $SIG(DS_S)$ and the public key K required to verify the signature of the message received from Root(R).

Objective 1: Verifying Origin Authentication: To say DNSSEC achieves Origin Authentication we need to prove the rule given below

$$client\ believes\ DNSKEY_{sender}i.e.\ "dcis"believes\ DNSKEY_{com}$$

i.e if Client believes in sender zones DNSKEY then he will believe the public key signature made by the sender using private key which can be verified using corresponding public key i.e. zone DNSKEY. To verify "com" zone's DNSKEY, "dcis" send a request to root i.e. com zone's parent for DS record set and "dcis" receives DS record set from root, which can be written as

$$dcis received \langle DS_{com}, RRSIG(DS_{com}), DNSKEY_{root} \rangle$$

from, A5.(a). we can derive

O1—$dcis\ received\ DS_{com}$
O2 —$dcis\ received\ RRSIG(DS_{com})$
O3 —$dcis\ received\ DNSKEY_{root}$
O4 —$dcis\ received\ DS_{com}, RRSIG(DS)$

When "dcis" receives this DS Record Set it compares it with

$$\{RRSIG(DS)\}_{DNSKEY_{root}}.$$

If the data has been received without any modifications in between then

O5 —$DS_{com} \equiv \{RRSIG(DS_{com})\}_{DNSKEY_{root}}$
And if the Above condition is satisfied then dcis believes DS_{com} is fresh
O6 —$dcis\ believes\ DS_{com}isfresh$
O7: —$dcis\ received\ DNSKEY_{com}$
From O7,A7(b)
O8: —$dcis\ sees\ hash(DNSKEY_{com})$
O9:—$DS_{com} \equiv hash(DNSKEY_{com})$
And if the above condition is satisfied then $dcis$ believes $DNSKEY_{com}$
From O9,O6,A1 we can get
O10 — **$dcis\ believes\ DNSKEY_{com}$**

Objective 2: Verifying Data Integrity: When "dcis" send a request to uohyd for D.com. name resolution, And receives DNS reply which contains the naming resolution "RRset", Digital signature "RRSIG" and "DNSKEY" of com zone. And it is proved that (In Origin Authentication Check)

$dcis\ believes\ DNSKEY_{com}$ which can be rewritten as
N1 —$dcis\ believes\ PK(com,DNSKEY_{com})$
N2 —$dcis\ received\ \langle RRset_{D.com.}, RRSIG_{D.com.}, DNSKEY_{com} \rangle$

From A5.(a)

N3 —$dcis\ received\ RRSET_{D.com}$

N4 —*dcis received $DNSKEY_{com}$*
N5 —*dcis received $RRSIG_{D.com}$*

If DNSKEY of received zone is fresh then

N6 —*Fresh($DNSKEY_{com}$)*

To verify Integrity **"dcis"** compares calculated RRSET's hash value with

$$\{RRSIG_{D.com}\}_{DNSKEY_{com}}$$

If the data is received with out any alterations then

N7 —*hash($RRSET_{D.com}$) $\equiv \{RRSIG_{D.com}\}_{DNSKEY_{com}}$*

From N2,N3, N6, N7 and from A1 we can get

N8 — dcis believes $RRSET_{D.com}$

5   Implementation Details

The implementation shows a trace of the path established between the client and the server while name-address resolution process takes place. It also shows how a chain of trust path is created between the server and the root during the process of origin authentication phase. The system takes the details about the DNS tree from a file which contains the information about each node in the network like parent and the children of the node. In this implementation we are assuming that the parent of each node will be its zone server. We considered each name server as a recursive name server i.e. if the desired naming resolution is not present at any server then server will forward that DNS request to its parent. The example given below shows the DNS tree we have used.

root$NULL$comorgin$net
in$root$ernet$ac
ac$in
ernetinuohyd$jnu
net$root$F$G
uohyd$ernet$mba$dcis$sche
dcis$uohyd
sche$uohyd
jnu$ernet
mba$uohyd
com$root$D$E
org$root$A$B
A$org
B$org
D$com
E$com

F$net
G$net

Each row contains the information about name of the node, parent name and its child names. By taking this information as input, the program will generate how the DNS resolution takes place from one node in the network to the other node in the network. In our example scenario we verified the correctness of DNSSEC protocol at "dcis.uohyd.ernet.in" for the DNS resolution D.com. The program will generate the trace of how the request is routed to the name server "com"

REQUEST IS SENT TO : uohyd
REPLY SENT FROM uohyd TO dcis TO CONTACT ernet
REQUEST IS SENT TO : ernet
REPLY SENT FROM ernet TO dcis TO CONTACT in
REQUEST IS SENT TO : in
REPLY SENT FROM in TO dcis TO CONTACT root
REQUEST IS SENT TO : root
REPLY SENT FROM root TO dcis TO CONTACT com
REQUEST IS SENT TO : com

And the program will generate the rule base which contains the set of rules being held by the client. For our example scenario this program will generate following rule basc for the node "dcis"

I1- dcis bel DNSKEY_root
A1- dcis bel DNSKEY $\longrightarrow$ DNSKEY(axiom-T)
A2- dcis bel DNSKEY $\land$ dcis receive$\{X\}$ DNSKEY $\longrightarrow$ dcis bel X (axiom-K)
D1- dcis sent Message:uohyd
D2- dcis receive Message:uohyd
D3- dcis sent Message:ernet
D4- dcis receive Message:ernet
D5- dcis sent Message:in
D6- dcis receive Message:in
D7- dcis sent Message:root
D8- dcis receive Message:root
D9- dcis sent Message:com
D10- dcis receive RRSET:com
D11- dcis sent Message:root
D12- dcis receive Message:root
D13- dcis bel DNSKEY_com
D14- dcis bel RRSET:com

From the above, it is seen that DNSSEC will help Clients to believe the received RRSET's and DNSKEY of the sender by verifying Origin Authentication and Integrity of sender's data.

6   Conclusion and Future Work

Logic based frameworks are widely used in specifying and verifying security protocols. DNSSEC is a security enabled DNS System, for which we are using SVO logic in formalizing it. By representing protocol messages in SVO we derived proof for Origin Authentication and Data Integrity from the axioms defined. To the best of our knowledge, this is the first work which addresses a formal framework for DNSSEC.

Since our formal model provides only a syntactic analysis (we did not provide any semantics in this paper) of DNSSEC the future work would be to give an appropriate semantics for the syntax outlined in this paper. Though it is well known that an interpreted system semantics as outlined in [7] would work well for protocols of the type of DNSSEC most of the current work addresses only a single hierarchy of message passing. As outlined earlier DNS has a distributed database kind of structure with a multi-level hierarchy. So we need to find an appropriate semantics suitable for describing such distributed protocol structure.

References

1. Abadi, M., Tuttle, M.: A semantics for a logic of authentication. In: Proceedings of the ACM Symposium of Principles of Distributed Computing, pp. 201–216. ACM Press (1991)
2. Albitz, P., Liu, C.: DNS and BIND, 4th edn. O'Reilly (April 2001)
3. Arends, R., Austein, R., Larson, M., Massey, D., Rose, S.: Dns security introduction and requirements. RFC 4033, Internet Engineering Task Force, 1 (March 2005)
4. Arends, R., Austein, R., Larson, M., Massey, D., Rose, S.: Resource records for the dns security extensions. RFC 4034, Internet Engineering Task Force, 1 (March 2005)
5. Ariyapperuma, S., Mitchell, C.J.: Security vulnerabilities in dns and dnssec. In: ARES, pp. 335–342 (2007)
6. Burrows, M., Abadi, M., Needham, R.M.: A logic of authentication. ACM Trans. Comput. Syst. 8(1), 18–36 (1990)
7. Fagin, R., Halpern, J., Moses, Y., Vardi, M.: Reasoning about knowledge. MIT Press (1995)
8. Huston, G.: Dnssec - the theory. The ISP Column, 1 (August 2006)
9. Mathuria, A.M., Safavi-naini, R., Nickolas, P.R.: On the automation of gny logic. In: Proceedings of the 18th Australian Computer Science Conference, pp. 370–379 (1995)
10. Syverson, P.F., Van Oorschot, P.C.: A unified cryptographic protocol logic. Technical report, NRL Publication 5540-227, Naval Research Lab (1996)
11. van Oorschot, P.: Extending cryptographic logics of belief to key agreement protocols. In: Proceedings of the 1st ACM Conference on Computer and Communications Security, CCS 1993, pp. 232–243. ACM (1993)

Formalizing and Reasoning with P3P Policies Using a Semantic Web Ontology

Boontawee Suntisrivaraporn[1,*] and Assadarat Khurat[2]

[1] School for Information and Computer Technology,
Sirindhorn International Institute of Technology,
Thammasat University, Thailand
sun@siit.tu.ac.th

[2] Institute for Security in Distributed Applications,
Hamburg University of Technology, Germany
khurat@tu-harburg.de

Abstract. Privacy has become a crucial issue in the online services realm. P3P policy, which is a privacy policy, enables websites to express their privacy practices so that users can be well-informed about the data collection and its usage. Besides, this privacy policy can be checked against its users' privacy preferences to help decide whether or not the service should be used. However, the interpretation of a P3P policy is unwieldy due to the lack of a precise semantics of its descriptions and constraints. For instance, it is admissible to have purpose and recipient values that have inconsistent meaning. There is a need for an explicit formal semantics for P3P policy to mitigate this problem. In this paper, we propose to use an OWL ontology to systematically and precisely describe the structures and constraints inherent in the P3P specification. Additional constraints are also defined and incorporated into the ontology in such a way that P3P policy verification can be automated with the help of an OWL reasoner.

1 Introduction

Privacy has become an important issue for the online world. To provide a service, online service providers (e.g. in the area of e-commerce and social networks) may collect and store users' sensitive data. It is thus essential to consider how they will treat the data. Governments of many countries and organizations are concerned with privacy as can be seen from enactment of privacy legislations—e.g. Privacy Acts in the USA, EU Directives in European Community and OECD Guidelines on the protection of personal data for international recommendations—to protect against misuses of users' data.

The *Platform for Privacy Preferences (P3P) Policy*, standardized by W3C [6,5], is a technology that stems from this privacy concern. It can be used by websites to express their practices about customers' data in the machine-readable format

---

* This work is partially supported by the National Research University Project of Thailand Office for Higher Education Commission and by Thailand Research Fund.

C. Sombattheera et al. (Eds.): MIWAI 2011, LNAI 7080, pp. 87–99, 2011.

XML. A P3P user agent embedded in e.g. a web browser can compare P3P policies of service providers with the user's privacy preferences specified beforehand. The comparison result enables the user to decide whether to use the services or not.

To be competitive in versatile online markets that change rapidly, more service providers have modified their services from standalone to composite services. Existing services are combined to form new ones resulting in less development cost and time than creating them from scratch. By the nature of composite services, more data need to be shared between service providers; therefore, checking the privacy policies across participating providers must be considered. However P3P policy may contain internal semantic inconsistencies far from being obvious. Therefore, to detect existing discrepancies and regain consistency, the formal semantics for P3P is compulsory and it needs to be explicitly formalized.

The Web Ontology Language (OWL) [3], a W3C recommendation, is a famous semantic web technology on which some policy languages such as Rei [18] and KAoS [17] are based. Due to its well-known capabilities in expressing logical formalism (Description Logic) and reasoning; and both the structures of P3P policy documents and dependencies therein can be described as an ontology, we decide to use OWL ontology to provide formal semantics for P3P. The benefits of employing OWL for P3P are twofold: *(i)* the logical underpinning of OWL guarantees preciseness of the definitions and constraints, i.e. ambiguity is reduced; and *(ii)* an OWL reasoning tool can be exploited to automatically check consistency of a particular P3P policy. Our proposed framework essentially makes use of an OWL ontology for P3P, designed specifically for the data–purpose centric interpretation. Several design decisions must be made during ontology development to realize our aims to be able to detect inconsistencies or other unethical practices in a P3P policy, and to explain which part is the culprit.

In this paper, we first describe the P3P Policy Language and its potential semantic inconsistencies in Sec.2. Inherent and ad-hoc constraints in P3P are identified in Sec.4 and then formulated in OWL in Sec.5. We discuss related works and give conclusions, respectively, in the last two sections.

2   P3P Policy

In P3P, not only how websites treat the collected data is expressed, but other aspects concerning privacy practices can be also described. The overall structure of a P3P policy is illustrated in Fig.1 *(left)*, in which the first line shows: *Entity*, the policy issuer; *Access*, the ability of individuals to access their data; and *Dispute-Group*, resolution procedures when disputes between privacy policies occur. How the websites may deal with the collected data is described in *Statement(s)*. A policy may contain one or more *Statement* elements, each consisting of *Data-Group*, *Purpose*, *Recipient* and *Retention*. The *Data-Group* element contains a list of data (*Data* element) which the services may collect and possibly data categories (*Categories* element). P3P specifies the categories for its defined standard set of the *Data* elements. The data standard set is structured in a hierarchy and grouped in four sets; *dynamic*, *user*, *thirdparty* and *business*.

Policy{Entity, Access, Disputes-Group,
  Statement(s){Purpose [Required],
          Recipient [Required],
          Retention,
          Data-Group{
              Data [Optional]{
                  Categories}}}}

Policy{Entity(#business.name): walmart.com,...,
  S1{Purpose:(current,contact [opt-in]),
      Recipient:(ours),
      Retention:(indefinitely),
      Data:(#user.login,#user.home-info)}
  S2{Purpose:(current,develop [opt-in],contact [opt-in]),
      Recipient:(ours),
      Retention:(stated-purpose),
      Data:(#user.name,#user.login,#user.home-info)}}

Fig. 1. The P3P policy structure (*left*) and an example from `walmart.com` (*right*)

Some *Data* elements can be placed in more than one group. The elements *Purpose*, *Recipient* and *Retention* describe, respectively, for which purpose the data may be used, to whom the data may be distributed, and for how long the data will be kept. The *Purpose* and *Recipient* elements can have multiple values while the *Retention* element can have only one value. P3P specification defines twelve values for *Purpose*, six values for *Recipient* and five values for *Retention*.

Besides, web sites/services can inform their users whether particular *Data*, *Purpose* and *Recipient* elements are either optional or mandatory through an optional attribute called *Optional* for the former and *Required* for the latter two as shown in square brackets in Fig.1 (*left*). The value of the *Optional* attribute is either *no* (default value) when the data is needed by the service or *yes* when the data is optional. The value of the *Required* attribute can be *always* (default value), *opt-out* or *opt-in*; *always* means this purpose/recipient value is always required; *opt-out* means the data may be used for this purpose/may be distributed to this recipient unless the users request not to; whereas *opt-in* means the data may be used for this purpose/ may be distributed to this recipient only when the users request so. An example P3P policy from Walmart (`http://www.walmart.com/w3c/global-p3ppolicy.xml`) is shown in Fig.1 (*right*). The first statement collects user's contact information and allows her to create an account. The second statement collects other personal information, viz. name, email, postal address for conducting surveys.

Potential Inconsistencies of a P3P Policy: Though P3P can be used to describe websites' privacy practices, several issues on its ambiguities were discussed in [15,10,12]. Some of them were clarified and addressed in the latest version of P3P specification [5]. We analyzed and categorized causes of P3P policy ambiguities into (*i*) syntax issue and (*ii*) pre-defined vocabularies.

P3P Policy Syntax: P3P allows multiple statements in a policy. This syntactic flexibility potentially causes semantic conflicts. For instance, a data item can be mentioned in different statements, assigning different *Retention* values to it. As *Retention* values are mutually exclusive, it is not sensible to allow such multiple values. In addition, P3P defines optional attributes expressing whether *Data*, *Purpose* and *Recipient* elements are required or optional. But, ambiguities arise when, e.g., *Data* element is required while *Purpose* and *Recipient* elements are optional. It is unclear whether or not the data is collected in the first place.

Table 1. Pertinent OWL 2.0 constructors

Name	Syntax	Semantics
top	**Thing**	$\Delta^{\mathcal{I}}$
bottom	**Nothing**	$\emptyset$
conjunction	C **and** D	$C^{\mathcal{I}} \cap D^{\mathcal{I}}$
disjunction	C **or** D	$C^{\mathcal{I}} \cup D^{\mathcal{I}}$
negation	(**not** C)	$\Delta^{\mathcal{I}} \backslash C^{\mathcal{I}}$
exists restriction	(r **some** C)	$\{x \in \Delta^{\mathcal{I}} \mid \exists y \in \Delta^{\mathcal{I}} : (x,y) \in r^{\mathcal{I}} \wedge y \in C^{\mathcal{I}}\}$
universal restriction	(r **only** C)	$\{x \in \Delta^{\mathcal{I}} \mid \forall y \in \Delta^{\mathcal{I}} : (x,y) \in r^{\mathcal{I}} \Rightarrow y \in C^{\mathcal{I}}\}$
min card restriction	(r **min** n C)	$\{x \in \Delta^{\mathcal{I}} \mid n \leq \sharp\{y : (x,y) \in r^{\mathcal{I}} \wedge y \in C^{\mathcal{I}}\}\}$
max card restriction	(r **max** n C)	$\{x \in \Delta^{\mathcal{I}} \mid n \geq \sharp\{y : (x,y) \in r^{\mathcal{I}} \wedge y \in C^{\mathcal{I}}\}\}$
concept inclusion	$C \sqsubseteq D$	$C^{\mathcal{I}} \subseteq D^{\mathcal{I}}$
role inclusion	$r \circ s \sqsubseteq t$	$r^{\mathcal{I}} \circ s^{\mathcal{I}} \subseteq t^{\mathcal{I}}$
concept assertion	$a : C$	$a^{\mathcal{I}} \in C^{\mathcal{I}}$
role assertion	$a \, r \, b$	$(a^{\mathcal{I}}, b^{\mathcal{I}}) \in r^{\mathcal{I}}$

Pre-defined Vocabularies: With the pre-defined values of *Purpose, Retention, Recipient* and *Data Category* elements, some combination of values between them are inconsistent. Consider, e.g., a statement containing *Purpose* value *develop* and *Retention* value *no-retention*. This introduces a conflict since *develop* is used "*...to enhance, evaluate, or otherwise review the site, service, product, or market ...*" [5] which requires to store data for longer than a brief period of time as stated by *no-retention*. The P3P specification only defines few constraints to check inconsistencies between *Purpose* and *Data Category*.

3 Semantic Web Ontology Language

To develop an ontology, one begins by defining *individuals, concepts* and *roles*. These entities represent particular individual objects in the domain, classes of individuals, and relationships among them, respectively. More complex *concept descriptions* can be built using OWL constructors[1] shown in the upper part of Tab.1. An OWL ontology comprises axioms (i.e. general knowledge about the domain of interest) and assertions (i.e. knowledge about particular individuals in the domain). Several kinds of axioms can be specified in OWL and can be generally categorized into *concept inclusions (CI)* and *role inclusions (RI)* as shown in the middle part of Tab.1. Note that a *concept definition (CD)* $A \equiv D$ is an abbreviation of two CIs $A \sqsubseteq D$ and $D \sqsubseteq A$. Knowledge about individuals can be specified in OWL through *concept assertions* and *role assertions* defined in the bottom part of Tab.1.

The set-theoretic semantics of OWL stems from that of Description Logics and is defined by means of *interpretations*. An interpretation $\mathcal{I}$ comprises a domain $\Delta^{\mathcal{I}}$ and a mapping $\cdot^{\mathcal{I}}$ that maps individuals to elements in, concepts to subsets of, and roles to binary relations on the domain. Axioms and assertions are mapped by $\cdot^{\mathcal{I}}$ to subset and instance relations, respectively. We summarize the

---

[1] See http://www.w3.org/TR/owl2-manchester-syntax/ for more constructors.

semantics of OWL constructors in the right column of Tab.1 and refer interested readers to [2] for more details. Consider, for example, a concept definition:

Professor $\equiv$ Lecturer and (teaches max 2 Course) and (isHeadOf some ResearchGroup)

Professor is defined to be those "lecturers that teach no more than 2 courses and are a head of some research group."

4   Data–Purpose Centric Semantics for P3P

As described in Sec.2, the interpretation of a P3P policy is cumbersome due to the lack of sufficient and clear descriptions and constraints. The work from Ting Yu et al. [15] proposed a formal semantics for P3P employing a data-centric view and the work from Agrawal et al. [19] proposed a strawman for privacy-aware database systems using purpose-centric base. We agree with the latter that the purpose of data usage is an important information for data practices, i.e. there must be a reason to collect the data. In addition, how long the data should be retained depends on the purpose of collection. Moreover, this way of interpretation also complies with the Purpose Specification Principle of OECD [13] and the EU Directive 95/46/EC Article 10(b) [1] that requires the data controller (website) to inform the data subject (user) at least about the identity of the controller and the purposes of collecting her data. We, therefore, propose to use both the data and purpose as the keys in our formal semantics for P3P. Based on Ting Yu et al.'s work, we have proposed a semantics for P3P in our previous work [11] employing a data–purpose centric relational table. However, this work was focused in determining privacy policy of composite services in which constraints for pre-defined vocabularies and the automated reasoning for checking semantic inconsistency was not considered. In what follows, we describe constraints for checking potential semantic conflicts:

Multiple statements: P3P policy allows specifying more than one statement in a policy. Thus, multiple values can be assigned to some elements that should have only one value. These values are the values of *Retention* element, and the values of *Optional* and *Required* attributes. Under the data–purpose based interpretation, we define that in a policy there must be only one value of these entities for each data–purpose pair, otherwise the policy is considered invalid.

For *Retention* element (referred as **Case1**), we define its constraint that in a policy, with the same data–purpose pair, its associated *Retention* element must have only one value. Similar constraints are defined for *Required* attribute of *Purpose* and *Recipient* elements for the same data–purpose pair but for *Optional* attribute the constraint is defined for each data alone, not data–purpose pair, since this attribute only belongs to the *Data* element.

Data hierarchy: P3P specification defines its base data schema in a hierarchy. It does not make sense if the upper level data (e.g. *#user.bdate*) has more restrictions than its lower level (e.g. *#user.bdate.ymd.year*). For instance, if the *Optional* attribute of *#user.bdate* is optional, the *Optional* attribute of *#user.bdate.ymd.year* can be optional or required. But if the *Optional* attribute of *#user.bdate* is required, the *Optional* attribute of *#user.bdate.ymd.year* must be required. Therefore, we define a constraint for this condition that a policy containing data where one is an ancestor of the other, if the *Optional* value of the ancestor is *no* then the *Optional* value of the other must be *no*; where we also define that the value *no* is more restrictive than *yes*. The *Required* values of *Purpose* and *Recipient* elements must conform to this condition. Their constraints are defined in the same way; where we define that *always* is more restrictive than *opt-out*, and *opt-out* is more restrictive than *opt-in*.

Optional attributes: Due to unclear meanings of some combinations of optional attributes (*Optional* and *Required*) in the P3P specification, we define a constraint (referred as **Case2**) that in a policy that contains data where all of its associated *Purpose* values have *Required* attributes *opt-in*, the *Optional* attribute of the data must be *yes*. This is because, for *opt-in*, the services may use the data only when the users specifically request to. Thus, before this request is made, the services should not collect the data.

Inconsistent Meaning between Purpose, Recipient, Retention and Data Category values: Except the pair between *Data Category* and *Retention*, we define eight constraints to check semantic consistency of each pair between *Purpose*, *Recipient*, *Retention* and *Data Category*. Four constraints are defined for the pair *Purpose* and *Data Category* according to the User Agent Guidelines [4] which has been appended to P3P1.1 specification. For the rest pairs i.e. between *Purpose* and *Recipient*; *Purpose* and *Retention*; *Retention* and *Recipient*; and *Recipient* and *Data Category*, one constraint is defined for each. Due to space limitation we give an example of two constraints between *Purpose* and *Data Category* (referred as **Case3**); and between *Purpose* and *Recipient* (referred as **Case4**) respectively as below:

A policy containing *Purpose* value *contact* must contain some *Data* element, associated with this *Purpose*, from one of *physical* and *online* categories.

In a policy, when the *Purpose* value is one of *admin*, *historical*, *develop* and *tailoring*, its associated *Recipient* value must be at least *ours*.

5   An Ontology for P3P

We propose to use an OWL ontology to systematically and precisely describe the structures and constraints inherent in the P3P specification. Once an ontology has been deployed, any P3P policy can be verified against this ontology with the help of an OWL reasoner. Our aim is to be able to verify whether a given policy is valid; and if not, what is wrong.

As described in Sec.2, a policy comprises at least one *Statement*, which in turn comprises several elements such as *Data*, *Purpose*, *Recipient*, and *Retention*. Note that other elements are admissible, but we restrict our attention to these four for clarity of discussion. An obvious modeling choice is to define a class for each of these elements and relate them with appropriate properties; see Fig.2 (*left*). To make sure that the purpose for one data is not grouped with another

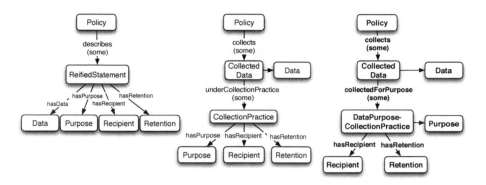

Fig. 2. *Paradigm♯1 (left)*: data, purpose, and other classes are at the same level. *Paradigm♯2 (center)*: data-centric modeling with purpose and other classes grouped at the same level. *Paradigm♯3 (right)*: data–purpose centric with the other elements grouped at the same level. The unlabeled arrow represents owl:subClassOf.

data, we propose here to flatten original P3P statements such that each resulting *reified statement* has exactly one *Data* and one *Purpose*. When adopting the data-centric interpretation of the P3P policy [15], the Paradigm♯2 could be used; see Fig.2 (*right*). In this paradigm, each data collected by a policy may be collected under different conditions. For instance, a birthdate (CollectedData) is collected indefinitely (*Retention*) for the historical purpose (*Purpose*), and also collected with no retention (*Retention*) only for individual analysis (*Purpose*). It should be clear that *Retention* and *Purpose* values, among other things, must be grouped correctly, i.e. not intertwined. Otherwise, a misinterpretation may arise, namely "a birthdate is collected with no retention for the historical purpose", which is clearly unintuitive. This issue can be systematically addressed by employing the "role grouping" technique introduced for the medical ontology SNOMED CT [14]. It means, in the context of P3P, that Purpose, Recipient and Retention must be grouped together under the class CollectionPractice, and each collected data may have relationships to more than one CollectionPractice. Despite being relatively straightforward, the two modeling paradigms do not support sufficient query answering and semantic constraint checking, e.g. to check if the retention value is unique for a data and purpose. To this end, we design a third modeling paradigm which reflects the data–purpose centric interpretation of the P3P policy. In this view, the purpose of the collected data is considered important for data practices. For instance, how long the birthdate should be retained depends also on its purpose of usage. In Fig.2 (*right*), Paradigm♯3 improves the second paradigm by promoting the purpose of data up one level in the ontological structure. The corresponding OWL definitions for Paradigm♯3 are given by α_1–α_3 in Fig.3.

With this paradigm it is possible to realize the constraints pointed out in the previous section. There are generally two approaches for checking constraint violation in any given P3P policy. The first, and probably the most intuitive, approach is to translate each constraint into a logical expression which then

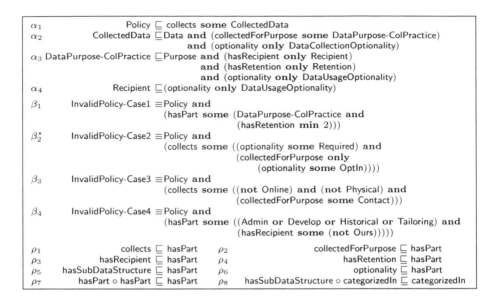

Fig. 3. A core extract of the OWL ontology for validity checking of P3P policies

forms (part of) a definition in the ontology. For instance, constraint **Case1** will impose functionality on the role hasRetention, i.e. (hasRetention **max** 1). Use of ontology reasoning on these logical constraints can help detect inconsistencies whenever a P3P policy under consideration is invalid for some reason. In other words, violation of any of the P3P constraints automatically triggers a logical inconsistency in the ontology. This appears quite a natural way to go at first, but it is insufficient for our original aim of being able to explain what is wrong in the P3P policy. This is due to the fact that, once an ontology is inconsistent, nothing can be reasoned about. An alternative approach is to allow arbitrary ontological structures depicted by a P3P policy of interest. Some parts of the ontology however may violate the constraints but will not raise logical inconsistencies. We then define special classes with specific definitions to represent these constraint violations. This approach not only can detect whether a given policy is valid, but also can provide reasons for its invalidity.

At the bottom of Fig.3 are role inclusions required for reasoning. The role hierarchy (see ρ_1–ρ_6) specifies that hasPart is a superrole of every other role, and ρ_7 specifies that it is transitive. For convenience and conciseness, hasPart is often used to reach a nested part in the policy structure. Assume, e.g., that we are interested in referring to policies that collects some data for some purpose with retention value *Indefinitely*, a straightforward description would be:

(collects **some** (collectedForPurpose **some** (hasRetention **some** Indefinitely)))

By using the superrole hasPart, the cumbersome description can be abbreviated as (hasPart **some** Indefinitely). The hierarchical structures of data in P3P are organized using an aggregation role hasSubDataStructure, and every leaf data item relates to their corresponding data category via categorizedIn. This design enhances the modeling in [7,9] by adding the left-identity role inclusion ρ_8. With this RI, any category of a sub-data structure is automatically propagated to its super-data structure. Note that listing of all data structures and relationships to data categories are out of scope of this paper and not included in Fig.3.

Checking Invalid P3P Policies: Following the alternative approach to checking P3P validity, various special OWL classes[2] are defined to capture the violation of constraints discussed in Sec.4. To this end, we describe four InvalidPolicy classes (see definitions β_1–β_4 in Fig.3) as follows:

InvalidPolicy-Case1 represents the class of invalid P3P policies that have multiple retention values for the same data–purpose collection practice. Multiple retention values are captured with the help of *at-least* number restrictions.

InvalidPolicy-Case2 represents the class of invalid P3P policies that have incompatible optionality values between data collection and data–purpose usage. Incompatibility occurs when a data collection is required (i.e. its optionality is *No*), but all its purposes' usage optionality is *opt-in*. Due to the *open-world assumption* adopted in OWL, $\beta_2^\star$ will not correctly capture undesired policies because (collectedForPurpose **only** ...) refers to *all* possible purposes, be it stated or inferred. One solution is to add a *closure assertion* that closes other possibly inferred purposes.

InvalidPolicy-Case3 represents the class of invalid P3P policies that collect some data that is neither *Online* nor *Physical* for *Contact* purpose.

InvalidPolicy-Case4 represents the class of invalid P3P policies that collect some data for a non-*Ours* recipient for any of the purposes *Admin*, *Develop*, *Historical* or *Tailoring*.

A given P3P policy (in XML syntax) can easily be translated into an ontological individual with associated assertions, and then these assertions will be verified against the ontology. With our design the ontology would remain consistent in most cases, while the P3P individual may be "inferred" to be an instance of one or more of the above InvalidPolicy classes.

The example policy from `walmart.com` can be translated to ontological assertions as depicted in Fig.4. We create a fresh individual (π in our example) for each P3P policy document and add a concept assertion $\pi : C$ to the ontology, where C describes all the data–purpose collection practices in the policy π as governed by Paradigm♯3. Since C tends to be large, it is broken down to pieces in Fig.4 to improve readability. This is possible because $\pi : (C$ **and** $D)$ is equivalent to the set of $\pi : C$ and $\pi : D$. The assertions specify that π is a Policy that collects data items Login, HomeInfo and Name. Login's collection is Required (default value), and it is collected for purposes Current, Contact and Develop. Furthermore, the remaining parts concern Retention, Recipient and Optionality aspects of each of the three data–purpose centric collection practices. Assertions for HomeInfo's and Name's collection are analogous and thus left out as exercise.

---

[2] Due to the space limitation, 4 out of 12 defined classes are presented here. Interested readers may find other classes at `http://ict.siit.tu.ac.th/~sun/p3p`.

```
π : Policy
π : collects some ( Login and
                    (optionality some Required)
                    (collectedForPurpose some (Current  and (hasRecipient some Ours)
                                                          and (hasRetention some Indefinitely)
                                                          and (hasRetention some StatedPurpose))
                    (collectedForPurpose some (Contact  and (hasRecipient some Ours)
                                                          and (hasRetention some Indefinitely)
                                                          and (hasRetention some StatedPurpose)
                                                          and (optionality some OptIn))
                    (collectedForPurpose some (Develop  and (hasRecipient some Ours)
                                                          and (hasRetention some StatedPurpose)
                                                          and (optionality some OptIn))))
π : collects some (HomeInfo and ···)
π : collects some (Name and ···)
```

Fig. 4. Ontological assertions describing the structures of the policy from Fig.1

Axioms in Fig.3 augmented with assertions in Fig.4 form a knowledge base about the P3P privacy policy issued by `walmart.com`. With the help of an OWL reasoning tool, this is processed and thereby additional knowledge can be inferred as to which InvalidPolicy classes the policy individual π belongs. Our experiments implementing in Protégé with the OWL reasoner Hermit 1.3.3 showed that π is an inferred instance of InvalidPolicy-Case1 and InvalidPolicy-Case3, i.e. π : InvalidPolicy-Case1 and π : InvalidPolicy-Case3. In other words, the P3P policy from Fig.1 (*right*) does not comply with at least two desired constraints. More precisely, **Case1** stems from the fact that the Login–Current collection practice has multiple retention values, viz. Indefinitely and StatedPurpose; whereas, **Case3** is due to the incompatibility between the purpose Contact and the data item Login, which is neither Online nor Physical.

Notes on Logical Constraints: Due to space limitations, several definitions/axioms must be excluded from Fig.3. We discuss here a few important ones that are indirectly required for reasoning.

- Each of the classes Data, Purpose, Retention and Recipient has subclasses representing their possible values in a specific policy. These subclasses are stated to be disjoint as they are intended to have different meaning. Also disjoint are optionality values for data collection, Optional and Required; and optionality values for data usage, Always, OptIn and OptOut.
- Domain and range restrictions are imposed on most roles. In particular, the role collects has domain Policy and range CollectedData, which help simplify the process of making assertions. Due to the domain restriction, the first assertion in Fig.4 could have been omitted. Due to the range restriction, the constraints for CollectedData come for free and are imposed on all data items collected in a policy.
- Paradigm♯3 depicts that CollectedData has some DataPurpose-ColPractice which is also specified by α_2. To realize the data–purpose centric viewpoint, it is mandatory that there is precisely one individual representing each

data–purpose pair. What this means in our ontology is that CollectedData can have at most one relationship to each Purpose subclass, i.e.

(collectedForPurpose **max** 1 Admin)
(collectedForPurpose **max** 1 Current)
(collectedForPurpose **max** 1 Historical)
(collectedForPurpose **max** 1 IndividualAnalysis)

- A role optionality is defined for CollectedData, DataPurpose-ColPractice and Recipient to represent this optional attribute according to the P3P specification. Whenever this attribute is missing from an original P3P document, the default value has to be asserted explicitly into the ontology, e.g. (optionality **some** Required) in Fig.4.
- The category of a data is defined by role categorizedIn, not directly by the subclass relation. To allow reasoning that data D is subclass of its category C, we add a CI: (categorizedIn **some** C) $\sqsubseteq$ C, for each data category C.

Several constraints must be withdrawn from the ontology since we have adopted the alternative approach to handling invalidity by allowing arbitrary structures for P3P policies. Consider constraint **Case1**, for example, which says that each data–purpose collection practice must have at most one retention value. This constraint can easily be modeled in the ontology by *(i)* replacing (hasRetention **only** Retention) in α_3 with (hasRetention **max** 1) or by *(ii)* specifying that role hasRetention is functional. If this logical constraint was incorporated into our ontology, then invalid structures corresponding to InvalidPolicy-Case1 would never be allowed in the first place and thus would be inconsistent. As argued earlier, it is more informative for ontology users if the ontology remains consistent and certain invalidity cases are represented by special classes. For this reason, we do not impose functionality on roles hasRetention, hasRecipient and optionality.

6   Related Work

A work on formalizing P3P in an ontology [8] was proposed as a W3C working group note. This and our work share the ideas of modeling most P3P entities as concepts (classes of individuals), of doing away with the notion of *Statement* by flattening them, of modeling data nested structures by an aggregation role instead of the subclass relation, and modeling data categories as superclasses. The modeling choice made in [8] could be said to correspond to Paradigm♯1 in which each policy statement is flattened to a few ReifiedStatement objects, each describing a collection practice of a data item. This class is referred to in [8] as CollectionPractice and related from Policy via a role describes. A subtle difference however remains in the choice between OWL quantifications. We reckon that a sensible policy should describe at least one collection practice of a data item, so **some** is chosen instead of **only**. In addition, we use roles subDataStructureOf and hasSubDataStructure in place of may-include-members-of, which is rather confusing. The fact that a super-data structure *may or may not* include a sub-data structure is straightforwardly modeled in our ontology using a number restriction, such as User ⊑ (hasSubDataStructure **max** 1 Login).

Damiani et al. [7] and Hogben [9] proposed a way to represent P3P-based data schema in the Semantic Web, focusing on data schema of P3P 1.0. In these works, data items are similarly modeled as classes, but they are interrelated via three roles, viz. is-a, part-of, and member-of which is unnecessarily complex and error-prone. A work by Li and Benbernou [16] proposed to model a policy and user preference as Description Logic classes, and matching between the two can be resorted to checking subsumption. Constraints within a policy structure were not considered in that work, and the definition for TBox subsumption introduced by the authors is rather obscured.

Since our fundamental view on privacy policy is data–purpose centric, it is important that the ontology also reflects this. This makes our proposed Paradigm♯3 and the ontology (extension of Fig.3) of fundamental difference compared to all the mentioned related works. Not only does this design make clear the semantics of the P3P, it also fully utilizes the facilities of OWL and its reasoning tools for knowledge retrieval and constraint checking.

7   Conclusion

We described three ontology modeling paradigms for P3P and implemented the most suitable one for the data–purpose centric view of user's data collection. Several constraints required to prevent certain semantic inconsistencies have been identified and formalized in an OWL ontology. We proposed two approaches to dealing with constraint violation detection when it comes to ontological reasoning: one is to translate it to a logical inconsistency; and the other is to retain logical consistency but capture constraint violation in OWL classes. The second approach was adopted, and OWL classes were defined with full definitions sufficient to detect semantic problems in P3P policy.

As future work, we plan to extend our paradigm to represent policies for composite services with potential cross-policy inconsistencies.

References

1. Directive 95/46/EC of the European Parliament and of the Council of 24 October 1995 on the protection of individuals with regard to the processing of personal data and on the free movement of such data. Official Journal of the European Communities (November 1995)
2. Baader, F., Calvanese, D., McGuinness, D., Nardi, D., Patel-Schneider, P. (eds.): The Description Logic Handbook: Theory, Implementation and Applications, 2nd edn. Cambridge University Press (2007)
3. Bechhofer, S., van Harmelen, F., Hendler, J., Horrocks, I., McGuinness, D.L., Patel-Schneider, P.F., Stein, L.A.: OWL Web Ontology Language reference. W3C Recommendation, February 10 (2004)
4. Cranor, L.: P3P 1.1 user agent guidelines. P3P User Agent Task Force Report 23 (May 2003)

5. Cranor, L., Dobbs, B., Egelman, S., Hogben, G., Hamphrey, J., Langheinrich, M., Marchiori, M., Presler-Marshall, M., Reagle, J., Schunter, M., Stampley, D.A., Wenning, R.: The Platform for Privacy Preference 1.1 (P3P1.1) Specification. W3C Working Group Note 13 (November 2006)
6. Cranor, L., Langheinrich, M., Marchiori, M., Presler-Marshall, M., Reagle, J.: The Platform for Privacy Preference 1.0 (P3P1.0) Specification. W3C Recommendation (April 2002)
7. Damiani, E., De Capitani di Vimercati, S., Fugazza, C., Samarati, P.: Semantics-aware privacy and access control: Motivation and preliminary results. In: 1st Italian Semantic Web Workshop, Ancona, Italy (December 2004)
8. Hogben, G.: P3P using the semantic web (web ontology, rdf policy and rdql rules). In: W3C Working Group Note 3 (September 2004)
9. Hogben, G.: Describing the P3P base data schema using OWL. In: WWW 2005, Workshop on Policy Management for the Web (2005)
10. Karjoth, G., Schunter, M., Herreweghen, E.V., Waidner, M.: Amending P3P for clearer privacy promises. In: 14th International Workshop on Database and Expert Systems Applications, IEEE Computer Society (September 2003)
11. Khurat, A., Gollmann, D., Abendroth, J.: A Formal P3P Semantics for Composite Services. In: Jonker, W., Petković, M. (eds.) SDM 2010. LNCS, vol. 6358, pp. 113–131. Springer, Heidelberg (2010)
12. Li, N., Yu, T., Antón, A.: A semantics-based approach to privacy languages. Technical Report TR2003-28, CERIAS (November 2003)
13. OECD Guidelines on the Protection of Privacy and Transborder Flows of Personal Data. Organisation for Economic Co-operation and Development (OECD) (September 1980)
14. Spackman, K.A., Dionne, R., Mays, E., Weis, J.: Role grouping as an extension to the Description Logic of Ontylog, motivated by concept modeling in SNOMED. In: Proceedings of the 2002 AMIA Annual Symposium, Hanley&Belfus (2002)
15. Yu, T., Li, N., Antón, A.: A formal semantics for P3P. In: ACM Workshop on Secure Web Services (October 2004)
16. Li, Y.H., Benbernou, S.: Representing and Reasoning About Privacy Abstractions. In: Ngu, A.H.H., Kitsuregawa, M., Neuhold, E.J., Chung, J.-Y., Sheng, Q.Z. (eds.) WISE 2005. LNCS, vol. 3806, pp. 390–403. Springer, Heidelberg (2005)
17. Uszok, A., Bradshaw, J., Jeffers, R., Suri, N., Hayes, P., Breedy, M., Bunch, L., Johnson, M., Kulkarni, S., Lott, J.: KAoS Policy and Domain Services: Toward a Description-Logic Approach to Policy Representation, Deconfliction, and Enforcement. In: IEEE Policy Workshop (June 2003)
18. Kagal, L.: Rei Ontology Specifications version 2.0, http://www.cs.umbc.edu/~lkagal1/rei/
19. Agrawal, R., Kiernan, J., Srikant, R., Xu, Y.: Hippocratic Databases. In: Proceedings of the 28th International Conference on Very Large Data Bases, VLDB 2002 (2002)

Structural Distance between $\mathcal{EL}^+$ Concepts*

Boontawee Suntisrivaraporn

School of Information and Computer Technology
Sirindhorn International Institute of Technology, Thammasat University, Thailand
sun@siit.tu.ac.th

Abstract. The inexpressive Description Logics in the $\mathcal{EL}$ family have been successful mainly due to their tractability of standard reasoning tasks like subsumption, adoption in modeling of biomedical ontologies, and standardization as an OWL 2 EL profile. This paper proposes two enhanced subsumption algorithms that not only test whether a particular subsumption holds but also give a numeric indicator showing the structural distance between the two concepts in the subsumption relationship. Structural distance is defined in terms of the effort required to obtain the subsumption in question. Both algorithms extend the standard subsumption algorithm for $\mathcal{EL}^+$ by an axiom labeling technique, originally proposed for finding justifications.

Keywords: Description logic, Subsumption, Structural distance.

1 Introduction

Description Logics (DLs) [3] are a family of logic-based knowledge representation formalisms, which can be used to develop ontologies in a formally well-founded way. This is true both for expressive DLs, which are the logical basis of the Web Ontology Language OWL 2, and for lightweight DLs of the $\mathcal{EL}$ family [1], which are used in the design of large-scale medical ontologies such as SNOMED CT [12] and form one of the W3C-recommended tractable OWL profiles, OWL 2 EL [9]. One of the main advantages of employing a logic-based ontology language is that reasoning services can be used to derive implicit knowledge from the one explicitly represented. DL systems can, for example, classify a given ontology, i.e., compute all the subsumption (i.e. subclass–superclass) relationships between the concepts defined in the ontology and arrange these relationships as a hierarchical graph. The advantage of using a lightweight DL of the $\mathcal{EL}$ family is that classification is tractable, i.e. a subsumption hierarchy of a given ontology can be computed in polynomial time.

Computation of a subsumption hierarchy is crucial to the ontology development life cycle because it graphically depicts *inferred* subsumption among those explicitly *stated* in the ontology. Apart from the fact that a particular subsumption in the hierarchy is stated or inferred, however, the ontology developer knows

---

* *This work is partially funded by Thailand Research Fund under grant MRG5380245 and the NRU project of Thailand Office for Higher Education Commission.*

C. Sombattheera et al. (Eds.): MIWAI 2011, LNAI 7080, pp. 100–111, 2011.

nothing concerning the effort required to compute it. Stated subsumptions are trivial to compute and do not require actual reasoning beyond transitive closure computation. On the other hand, inferred subsumptions may or may not be difficult to compute, and this fact is completely invisible to the ontology developer. For example, w.r.t. an example ontology $\mathcal{O}_{med}$ in Fig.1, both Pancarditis and Pericarditis are inferred subsumees of HeartDisease and will be positioned alongside each other beneath it in the hierarchy. Though observed from the subsumption hierarchy to be symmetric, the structures of their definitions differ which directly affect the effort required to compute them. At the minimum, it requires 4 steps to obtain the former subsumption, whereas the latter requires 6 steps. For larger ontologies with more complex nested structures, this difference will be greater. We believe that the *structural distance* between concepts in a subsumption, i.e. the minimum effort required internally by the reasoning algorithm, has merit for ontology design. When the subsumption hierarchy is equipped with this information, the ontology developer is better-informed about subsumption links as to how structurally distant they are from the subsumer. Statistics on the structural distance can help visualize locations of difficult subsumptions and may reveal structural discrepancies in the ontology.

In this paper, we present two algorithms for computing structural distance for a given subsumption. Both extend the polynomial-time subsumption algorithm for $\mathcal{EL}^+$ [1,2] with axiom labeling strategies, originally proposed for axiom pinpointing [11,4]. The first algorithm is shown to retain tractability of the original algorithm, but whenever the number of axioms is considered, exponential blowup arises. The rest of the paper is organized as follows. The next section introduces the DL $\mathcal{EL}^+$ together with its polynomial-time subsumption algorithm. Our extensions for computing structural distance are presented in Section 3. Related work is discussed in Section 4, and conclusion is given in the last section.

2   Preliminaries

In DLs, *concept descriptions* are inductively defined with the help of a set of *constructors*, starting with a set CN of *concept names* and a set RN of *role names*. $\mathcal{EL}^+$ concept descriptions are formed using the constructors shown in the upper part of Table 1. An $\mathcal{EL}^+$ *ontology* or *TBox* is a finite set of *general concept inclusion (GCI)* and *role inclusion (RI)* axioms, whose syntax is shown in the lower part of Table 1. Conventionally, r, s possibly with subscripts are used to range over RN, A, B to range over CN, and C, D to range over concept descriptions. It is worth noting that GCIs generalize primitive concept definitions $(A \sqsubseteq C)$ and full concept definitions $(A \equiv C)$, whereas RIs generalize transitivity $(r \circ r \sqsubseteq r)$ and reflexivity $(\epsilon \sqsubseteq r$, where ϵ stands for composition of zero roles).

The semantics of $\mathcal{EL}^+$ is defined in terms of *interpretations* $\mathcal{I} = (\Delta^\mathcal{I}, \cdot^\mathcal{I})$, where the domain $\Delta^\mathcal{I}$ is a non-empty set of individuals, and the interpretation function $\cdot^\mathcal{I}$ maps each concept name $A \in$ CN to a subset $A^\mathcal{I}$ of $\Delta^\mathcal{I}$ and each role name $r \in$ RN to a binary relation $r^\mathcal{I}$ on $\Delta^\mathcal{I}$. The extension of $\cdot^\mathcal{I}$ to arbitrary concept descriptions is inductively defined, as shown in the semantics column of

Table 1. Syntax and semantics of $\mathcal{EL}^+$

Name	Syntax	Semantics
top	$\top$	$\Delta^{\mathcal{I}}$
bottom	$\bot$	$\emptyset$
concept name	A	$A^{\mathcal{I}} \subseteq \Delta^{\mathcal{I}}$
conjunction	$C \sqcap D$	$C^{\mathcal{I}} \cap D^{\mathcal{I}}$
exists restriction	$\exists r.C$	$\{x \in \Delta^{\mathcal{I}} \mid \exists y \in \Delta^{\mathcal{I}} : (x,y) \in r^{\mathcal{I}} \wedge y \in C^{\mathcal{I}}\}$
GCI	$C \sqsubseteq D$	$C^{\mathcal{I}} \subseteq D^{\mathcal{I}}$
RI	$r_1 \circ \cdots \circ r_k \sqsubseteq s$	$r_1^{\mathcal{I}} \circ \cdots \circ r_k^{\mathcal{I}} \subseteq s^{\mathcal{I}}$

ω_1	Pericardium $\sqsubseteq$ BodyPart $\sqcap$ $\exists$part-of.Heart
ω_2	Pericarditis $\equiv$ Inflammation $\sqcap$ $\exists$has-loc.Pericardium
ω_3	Pancarditis $\equiv$ Inflammation $\sqcap$ $\exists$has-loc.Heart
ω_4	Inflammation $\sqsubseteq$ Disease
ω_5	HeartDisease $\equiv$ Disease $\sqcap$ $\exists$has-loc.Heart
ω_6	has-loc $\circ$ part-of $\sqsubseteq$ has-loc

Fig. 1. An example $\mathcal{EL}^+$ ontology $\mathcal{O}_{med}$

Table 1, where $\circ$ means composition of binary relations. An interpretation $\mathcal{I}$ is a *model* of an ontology $\mathcal{O}$ if, for each inclusion axiom in $\mathcal{O}$, the conditions given in the semantics column of Table 1 are satisfied. The main inference problem for $\mathcal{EL}^+$ is the subsumption problem:

Definition 1 (concept subsumption). *Given two $\mathcal{EL}^+$ concept descriptions C, D and an $\mathcal{EL}^+$ TBox $\mathcal{O}$, C is subsumed by D w.r.t. $\mathcal{O}$ (written $C \sqsubseteq_{\mathcal{O}} D$) if $C^{\mathcal{I}} \subseteq D^{\mathcal{I}}$ in every model $\mathcal{I}$ of $\mathcal{O}$.*

In the following, we will restrict the attention to subsumption between concept names. This is justified by the fact that subsumption between concept descriptions can be reduced to subsumption between concept names: we have $C \sqsubseteq_{\mathcal{O}} D$ iff $A \sqsubseteq_{\mathcal{O} \cup \{A \sqsubseteq C, D \sqsubseteq B\}} B$ where A, B are new concept names not occurring in C, D and $\mathcal{O}$. Fig.1 shows an example $\mathcal{EL}^+$ ontology from the medical domain. Relative to its axioms, it can be inferred that each of Pericarditis and Pancarditis is subsumed by HeartDisease.

Before the distance-labeled algorithm can be presented, we must briefly recall the original polynomial-time subsumption algorithm for $\mathcal{EL}^+$ [1,5,2]. As a preprocessing step, this algorithm transforms a given ontology into a *normal form* where all GCIs have one of the following forms: $A_1 \sqcap \ldots \sqcap A_k \sqsubseteq B$, $A \sqsubseteq \exists r.B$, $\exists r.A \sqsubseteq B$, and where all RIs are of the form $r \sqsubseteq s$ or $r \circ r' \sqsubseteq s$, where $r, r', s \in$ RN, $k \geq 1$, and $A, A_1, \ldots, A_k, B$ are elements of CN^+, i.e. $\mathsf{CN} \cup \{\top, \bot\}$. This normalization can be achieved in linear time using simple transformation rules, which

CR1	If $\{(X,A_1),\ldots,(X,A_k)\} \subseteq \mathcal{A},\ A_1 \sqcap \cdots \sqcap A_k \sqsubseteq B \in \mathcal{O}$,	then add (X,B) to $\mathcal{A}$.
CR2	If $(X,A) \in \mathcal{A},\ A \sqsubseteq \exists r.B \in \mathcal{O}$,	then add (X,r,B) to $\mathcal{A}$.
CR3	If $\{(X,r,Y),(Y,A)\} \subseteq \mathcal{A},\ \exists r.A \sqsubseteq B \in \mathcal{O}$,	then add (X,B) to $\mathcal{A}$.
CR4	If $\{(X,r,Y),(Y,\bot)\} \subseteq \mathcal{A}$,	then add $(X,\bot)$ to $\mathcal{A}$.
CR5	If $(X,r,Y) \in \mathcal{A},\ r \sqsubseteq s \in \mathcal{O}$,	then add (X,s,Y) to $\mathcal{A}$.
CR6	If $\{(X,r,Y),(Y,s,Z) \subseteq \mathcal{A},\ r \circ s \sqsubseteq t \in \mathcal{O}$,	then add (X,t,Z) to $\mathcal{A}$.

Fig. 2. Completion rules for the original $\mathcal{EL}^+$ subsumption algorithm

basically break down complex GCIs into simpler ones (see [1] for details). For instance, ω_3 from Fig.1 can be transformed to four GCIs:

$$\alpha_1 : \text{Pancarditis} \sqsubseteq \text{Inflammation}, \qquad \alpha_2 : \quad \exists\text{has-loc.Heart} \sqsubseteq X,$$
$$\alpha_3 : \text{Pancarditis} \sqsubseteq \exists\text{has-loc.Heart}, \qquad \alpha_4 : \text{Inflammation} \sqcap X \sqsubseteq \text{Pancarditis};$$

where X is a fresh concept name not used in $\mathcal{O}_{\text{med}}$. Given a ontology $\mathcal{O}$ in normal form over the concept names CN and role names RN, *the subsumption algorithm for $\mathcal{EL}^+$* employs completion rules to extend an initial set of assertions until no more assertions can be added. Assertions are of the forms (A,B) or (A,r,B) where $A,B \in \text{CN}^+$, and $r \in \text{RN}$. Intuitively, the assertion (A,B) expresses that $A \sqsubseteq_{\mathcal{O}} B$ holds and (A,r,B) expresses that $A \sqsubseteq_{\mathcal{O}} \exists r.B$ holds. The algorithm starts with a set of assertions $\mathcal{A}$ that contains:

- $(A,\top)$ and (A,A) for every concept name A
- (A,r,A) for r a role name such that $\mathcal{O} \models \epsilon \sqsubseteq r$, i.e. there exist RI axioms $\epsilon \sqsubseteq r_1$ and $r_i \sqsubseteq r_{i+1} \in \mathcal{O}$ with $1 \leq i < m$ with $r_m = r$.

It then exhaustively employs the rules shown in Fig.2 to extend $\mathcal{A}$. Note that such a rule is only applied if it really extends $\mathcal{A}$, i.e., if the assertion added by the rule is not yet contained in $\mathcal{A}$. The following theorem, originally shown in [1], summarizes the important properties of this algorithm.

Theorem 1. *Given an $\mathcal{EL}^+$ ontology $\mathcal{O}$ in normal form, the subsumption algorithm terminates in time polynomial in the size of $\mathcal{O}$. After termination, the resulting set of assertions $\mathcal{A}$ satisfies $A \sqsubseteq_{\mathcal{O}} B$ iff $(A,B) \in \mathcal{A}$, for all concept names A,B occurring in $\mathcal{O}$.*

3 Distance-Labeled Subsumption Algorithms

Standard reasoning algorithms can be extended with a *labeling strategy* to perform axiom pinpointing. This idea was originally conceived for tableau-based algorithms [4,11,10] and later established for polynomial-time subsumption algorithms, particularly for the $\mathcal{EL}^+$ subsumption algorithm [6]. In essence, for each inferred assertion, it stores a label (or a set of labels) which keeps track of the axioms in the ontology used by the algorithm to obtain that assertion. Any such algorithm applying this labeling technique for finding justifications is generally regarded as in the *glass-box* approach, which, in contrast to the black-box approach, sees and modifies the internal of the original algorithm.

In this paper, we propose a new extension to the original $\mathcal{EL}^+$ subsumption algorithm using a similar labeling technique. This extension is designed to compute a structural distance between two concepts. Instead of keeping track of the axioms in the ontology used to obtain an assertion of interest, we here keep track of the number of rule applications required to obtain the assertion. Note that there can be different paths of rule applications which may result in different numbers of rule applications. We define our first structural distance to be the minimum required effort in terms of numbers of rule applications as follows:

Definition 2. *Let $\mathcal{O}$ be an $\mathcal{EL}^+$ ontology in normal form, and A, B concept names such that $A \sqsubseteq_{\mathcal{O}} B$. Then, the structural distance w.r.t. rule applications between A and B, in symbols $\mathsf{dist1}(A, B)$, is the minimum number of rule applications required to obtain the assertion (A, B) in $\mathcal{A}$.*

In what follows, we describe a labeled extension that counts the number of rule applications for each inferred assertion. By nature of the $\mathcal{EL}^+$ algorithm, counting is carried out in a bottom-up fashion, i.e. more distant subsumptions will be computed after less distant ones. In the *distance-labeled* subsumption algorithm, each assertion π is labeled with some $n \in \mathbf{N}$, where $\mathbf{N}$ is the set of non-negative integers. Formally, we maintain *the set of labeled assertions*:

$$\mathcal{A}^{\mathsf{d}} \subseteq \left(\mathsf{CN}^+ \times \mathsf{CN}^+ \times \mathbf{N}\right) \cup \left(\mathsf{CN}^+ \times \mathsf{RN} \times \mathsf{CN}^+ \times \mathbf{N}\right).$$

Observe that, unlike labeled assertions in the pinpointing algorithm [6], an assertion π in the distance-labeled subsumption algorithm may occur in $\mathcal{A}^{\mathsf{d}}$ at most once with a presently minimum value n.

The labeled algorithm initializes $\mathcal{A}^{\mathsf{d}}$ with the smallest set consisting of:

- $(A, A)^0$ and $(A, \top)^0$, for all concept names $A \in \mathsf{CN}^+$;
- $(A, r, A)^m$, for r a role name such that $\mathcal{O} \models \epsilon \sqsubseteq r$, where m is the minimum number of RI axioms $\epsilon \sqsubseteq r_1$ and $r_i \sqsubseteq r_{i+1} \in \mathcal{O}$ with $1 \leq i < m$ with $r_m = r$.

After initialization, the set of assertions $\mathcal{A}^{\mathsf{d}}$ is extended by applying the *distance-labeled* completion rules shown in Fig.3 until no more rule applies. The update operator $\oplus$ is defined as follows:

$$\mathcal{A}^{\mathsf{d}} \oplus \pi^{\delta} \equiv \left(\mathcal{A}^{\mathsf{d}} - \{\pi^{\delta'}\}\right) \cup \{\pi^{\delta}\}$$

Throughout the course of execution, a smaller label δ may arise for a particular assertion π. Intuitively, the update operator $\oplus$ does not simply add a new labeled assertion but rather replaces an existing one, if any. Observe that a labeled completion rule may be applied several times to assert the same assertion base but with declining label values. We denote by $[\mathcal{A}^{\mathsf{d}}]$ the completed set of labeled assertions obtained after the labeled subsumption algorithm terminates and by $lab^*(\pi)$ the final label value of π. Recall that the original subsumption algorithm

DCR1 If $\{(X, A_1)^{\delta_1}, \ldots, (X, A_k)^{\delta_k}\} \subseteq \mathcal{A}^\mathsf{d}$, $\alpha : A_1 \sqcap \cdots \sqcap A_k \sqsubseteq B \in \mathcal{O}$
and there is *no* $(X, B)^\delta$ in $\mathcal{A}^\mathsf{d}$ such that $\delta \leq \delta_1 + \cdots + \delta_k + 1$
then $\mathcal{A}^\mathsf{d} := \mathcal{A}^\mathsf{d} \oplus (X, B)^{\delta_1 + \cdots + \delta_k + 1}$

DCR2 If $(X, A)^{\delta_1} \in \mathcal{A}^\mathsf{d}$, $\alpha : A \sqsubseteq \exists r.B \in \mathcal{O}$,
and there is *no* $(X, r, B)^\delta$ in $\mathcal{A}^\mathsf{d}$ such that $\delta \leq \delta_1 + 1$
then $\mathcal{A}^\mathsf{d} := \mathcal{A}^\mathsf{d} \oplus (X, r, B)^{\delta_1 + 1}$

DCR3 If $\{(X, r, Y)^{\delta_1}, (Y, A)^{\delta_2}\} \subseteq \mathcal{A}^\mathsf{d}$, $\alpha : \exists r.A \sqsubseteq B \in \mathcal{O}$,
and there is *no* $(X, B)^\delta$ in $\mathcal{A}^\mathsf{d}$ such that $\delta \leq \delta_1 + \delta_2 + 1$
then $\mathcal{A}^\mathsf{d} := \mathcal{A}^\mathsf{d} \oplus (X, B)^{\delta_1 + \delta_2 + 1}$

DCR4 If $\{(X, r, Y)^{\delta_1}, (Y, \bot)^{\delta_2}\} \subseteq \mathcal{A}^\mathsf{d}$,
and there is *no* $(X, \bot)^\delta$ in $\mathcal{A}^\mathsf{d}$ such that $\delta \leq \delta_1 + \delta_2 + 1$
then $\mathcal{A}^\mathsf{d} := \mathcal{A}^\mathsf{d} \oplus (X, \bot)^{\delta_1 + \delta_2 + 1}$

DCR5 If $(X, r, Y)^{\delta_1} \in \mathcal{A}^\mathsf{d}$, $\alpha : r \sqsubseteq s \in \mathcal{O}$,
and there is *no* $(X, s, Y)^\delta$ in $\mathcal{A}^\mathsf{d}$ such that $\delta \leq \delta_1 + 1$
then $\mathcal{A}^\mathsf{d} := \mathcal{A}^\mathsf{d} \oplus (X, s, Y)^{\delta_1 + 1}$

DCR6 If $\{(X, r, Y)^{\delta_1}, (Y, s, Z)^{\delta_2}\} \subseteq \mathcal{A}^\mathsf{d}$, $\alpha : r \circ s \sqsubseteq t \in \mathcal{O}$,
and there is *no* $(X, t, Z)^\delta$ in $\mathcal{A}^\mathsf{d}$ such that $\delta \leq \delta_1 + \delta_2 + 1$
then $\mathcal{A}^\mathsf{d} := \mathcal{A}^\mathsf{d} \oplus (X, t, Z)^{\delta_1 + \delta_2 + 1}$

Fig. 3. Distance-labeled completion rules

for $\mathcal{EL}^+$ is polynomial, whereas its extension for glass-box pinpointing may not terminate after a polynomial number of rule applications. In contrast to that extension, we show that the distance-labeled subsumption algorithm continues to enjoy the tractability of the original algorithm:

Lemma 1 (tractability). *Given an $\mathcal{EL}^+$ ontology $\mathcal{O}$ in normal form. The distance-labeled subsumption algorithm terminates in time polynomial in the size of $\mathcal{O}$.*

Proof. Each rule application updates $\mathcal{A}^\mathsf{d}$ with a new labeled assertion π^δ by the operator $\oplus$. Any existing assertion $\pi^{\delta'}$ in $\mathcal{A}^\mathsf{d}$ with $\delta' > \delta$ will be removed. This together with the preconditions of the distance-labeled completion rules, it is ensured that each labeled assertion is added to $\mathcal{A}^\mathsf{d}$ at most once. It remains to be shown that there are polynomially many such labeled assertions.

Let n be the size of $\mathcal{O}$. The number of assertion bases of the form (A, B) is bounded by n^2, and that of the form (A, r, B) is bounded by n^3. Since the number of assertion bases is polynomial, it suffices to show that label values are also bounded by a polynomial in n. We show this by induction in applications of the distance-labeled completion rules:

- *Base:* The label values set by the initialization are either 0 (for the form (A, B)) or bounded by the number of role inclusions (for the form (A, r, B)).
- *Induction:* Consider an exemplary rule **DCR1**. By induction hypothesis, all δ_i are polynomial, for $1 \leq i \leq k$. Since the number of conjuncts k is bounded

by the size of the ontology n, the new label added by this rule $\delta_1 + \cdots + \delta_k + 1$ is also a polynomial. Other cases can be argued in an analogous way.

$\square$

The algorithm terminates when no more rule applies, and non-applicability occurs only when no new assertion or no smaller label for an existing assertion base can be obtained. Also, the new label is calculated based on the effort in getting the used assertions and is augmented by one for the current rule application. It follows that:

Lemma 2. *Let $\mathcal{O}$ be an $\mathcal{EL}^+$ ontology and A, B concept names such that $A \sqsubseteq_{\mathcal{O}} B$. After the distance-labeled subsumption algorithm terminates on $\mathcal{O}$, we have that $lab^*(A, B) = \mathsf{dist1}(A, B)$.*

Example 1. Consider an ontology $\mathcal{O}$ comprising the following axioms in normal form. It is easy to see that $U \sqsubseteq_{\mathcal{O}} B$ and $U \sqsubseteq_{\mathcal{O}} D$.

$$\begin{array}{lll} \alpha_1 : A \sqsubseteq B & \alpha_4 : \quad U \sqsubseteq \exists r.A & \alpha_7 : V \sqsubseteq A \\ \alpha_2 : B \sqsubseteq C & \alpha_5 : \exists r.B \sqsubseteq V & \alpha_8 : V \sqsubseteq C \\ \alpha_3 : C \sqsubseteq D & \alpha_6 : \exists r.C \sqsubseteq W & \end{array}$$

Applying the distance-labeled algorithm to $\mathcal{O}$, $\mathcal{A}^d$ will be initialized with labeled assertions $(X, X)^0$ and $(X, \top)^0$ for all concept names X in $\mathcal{O}$. Then, distance-labeled completion rules are applied arbitrarily. Table 2 demonstrates one possible trace starting with an application of rule **DCR1** on assertion $(A, A)^0$ (from the initialization) and axiom $\alpha_1 \in \mathcal{O}$. This first rule application results in a new labeled assertion $\pi_1 : (A, B)^1$. Note that the superscript over this assertion suggests that it is a result of one rule application. This process continues and generates π_2, $\dots$, π_{10}, etc. With 5 rule applications, it can be proved that $U \sqsubseteq_{\mathcal{O}} B$, shown as π_6 in the table. Applying **DCR1** twice more, assertion π_8 will be added which means that $U \sqsubseteq_{\mathcal{O}} D$ with a distance of 7. However, this is not minimum because two subsequent applications of **DCR1** to α_8 and α_3 result in π_{10} with a smaller label 5. Note that, by adding π_{10}, the update operator $\oplus$ will effectively remove π_8, so at any point there can be at most one assertion with the same base.

Taking into Account the Axioms

Recall that the notion of "structural distance w.r.t. rule applications" in Definition 2 refers *merely* to the minimum number of rule applications required by the $\mathcal{EL}^+$ subsumption algorithm. In some situations, however, it may be more appropriate to take into account the (minimum) number of axioms required to obtain the assertion in question. Consider, for instance, $U \sqsubseteq_{\mathcal{O}} B$ and $U \sqsubseteq_{\mathcal{O}} D$ from Example 1. The structural distance w.r.t. rule applications of both subsumptions is the same, i.e. $\mathsf{dist1}(U, B) = \mathsf{dist1}(U, D) = 5$. However, observe that the axioms required for the former subsumption are α_1, α_4, α_5 and α_7, while those for the latter subsumption are α_1, α_3, α_4, α_5 and α_8. Although the number of rule applications and pattern of reasoning are analogous for both subsumptions, D can be perceived as *more distant* from U than B is in the sense that

Table 2. A trace of the distance-labeled subsumption algorithm for Example 1

Rule	Preconditions	New assertion
DCR1	$(A, A)^0, \alpha_1$	$\pi_1 : (A, B)^1$
DCR1	$(C, C)^0, \alpha_3$	$\pi_2 : (C, D)^1$
DCR2	$(U, U)^0, \alpha_4$	$\pi_3 : (U, r, A)^1$
DCR3	π_1, π_3, α_5	$\pi_4 : (U, V)^3$
DCR1	π_4, α_7	$\pi_5 : (U, A)^4$
DCR1	π_5, α_1	$\star \; \pi_6 : (U, B)^5$
DCR1	π_6, α_2	$\pi_7 : (U, C)^6$
DCR1	π_7, α_3	$\star \; \pi_8 : (U, D)^7$
DCR1	π_4, α_8	$\pi_9 : (U, C)^4$
DCR1	π_9, α_3	$\star \; \pi_{10} : (U, D)^5$

$$\vdots$$

it requires one more axiom. To this end, a refined notion of structural distance can be defined:

Definition 3. *Let $\mathcal{O}$ be an $\mathcal{EL}^+$ ontology in normal form, and A, B concept names such that $A \sqsubseteq_{\mathcal{O}} B$. Then, the structural distance w.r.t. rule applications and axioms between A and B, in symbols $\mathsf{dist2}(A, B)$, is the sum of the minimum number of rule applications and the minimum number of axioms required to obtain the assertion (A, B) in $\mathcal{A}$.*

Intuitively, the new structural distance $\mathsf{dist2}(A, B)$ between two concept names is a numerical representation that suggests the overall cost of computing their subsumption relationship, both in terms of the number of axioms and of the number of rule applications. Unfortunately, this structural distance value is *hard* to compute since it relies on the minimum number of supporting axioms, i.e. it requires to compute the cardinality of the smallest justification. The following hardness result will be used to show that computing $\mathsf{dist2}(A, B)$ is not tractable, unless of course P=NP.

Theorem 2 (originally shown in [6]). *Let $\mathcal{O}$ be an $\mathcal{EL}^+$ ontology, A, B concept names such that $A \sqsubseteq_{\mathcal{O}} B$, and n a natural number. It is NP-hard to determine whether there exists a subset $\mathcal{S} \subseteq \mathcal{O}$ such that $|\mathcal{S}| < n$ and $A \sqsubseteq_{\mathcal{S}} B$.*

The subsequent corollary shows hardness of the corresponding decision problem:

Corollary 1. *Let $\mathcal{O}$ be an $\mathcal{EL}^+$ ontology, A, B concept names such that $A \sqsubseteq_{\mathcal{O}} B$, and d a natural number. It is NP-hard to determine whether $\mathsf{dist2}(A, B) < d$.*

Proof. Assume to the contrary of what is to be shown: it is polynomial to determine if $\mathsf{dist2}(A, B) < d$ for some given A, B, d. Let δ be the minimum number of rule applications required for $A \sqsubseteq_{\mathcal{O}} B$ which by Lemma 1 can be computed in polynomial time. By Definition 2, $\mathsf{dist2}(A, B) - \delta$ holds the minimum number of axioms for $A \sqsubseteq_{\mathcal{O}} B$. But, this can be computed in polynomial time, contradicting the above theorem from [6]. ❑

SCR1	If $\{(X, A_1)_{\Sigma_1}^{\delta_1}, \ldots, (X, A_k)_{\Sigma_k}^{\delta_k}\} \subseteq \mathcal{A}^{\mathsf{ds}}$, $\alpha : A_1 \sqcap \cdots \sqcap A_k \sqsubseteq B \in \mathcal{O}$ and there is *no* $(X, B)_{\Sigma}^{\delta}$ in $\mathcal{A}^{\mathsf{ds}}$ such that $\Sigma \subset \Sigma_1 \cup \cdots \cup \Sigma_k \cup \{\alpha\}$ or such that $\Sigma = \Sigma_1 \cup \cdots \cup \Sigma_k \cup \{\alpha\}$ and $\delta \leq \delta_1 + \cdots + \delta_k + 1$ then $\mathcal{A}^{\mathsf{ds}} := \mathcal{A}^{\mathsf{ds}} \oplus (X, B)_{\Sigma_1 \cup \cdots \cup \Sigma_k \cup \{\alpha\}}^{\delta_1 + \cdots + \delta_k + 1}$
SCR2	If $(X, A)_{\Sigma_1}^{\delta_1} \in \mathcal{A}^{\mathsf{ds}}$, $\alpha : A \sqsubseteq \exists r.B \in \mathcal{O}$, and there is *no* $(X, r, B)_{\Sigma}^{\delta}$ in $\mathcal{A}^{\mathsf{ds}}$ such that $\Sigma \subset \Sigma_1 \cup \{\alpha\}$ or such that $\Sigma = \Sigma_1 \cup \{\alpha\}$ and $\delta \leq \delta_1 + 1$ then $\mathcal{A}^{\mathsf{ds}} := \mathcal{A}^{\mathsf{ds}} \oplus (X, r, B)_{\Sigma_1 \cup \{\alpha\}}^{\delta_1 + 1}$
SCR3	If $\{(X, r, Y)_{\Sigma_1}^{\delta_1}, (Y, A)_{\Sigma_2}^{\delta_2}\} \subseteq \mathcal{A}^{\mathsf{ds}}$, $\alpha : \exists r.A \sqsubseteq B \in \mathcal{O}$, and there is *no* $(X, B)_{\Sigma}^{\delta}$ in $\mathcal{A}^{\mathsf{ds}}$ such that $\Sigma \subset \Sigma_1 \cup \Sigma_2 \cup \{\alpha\}$ or such that $\Sigma = \Sigma_1 \cup \Sigma_2 \cup \{\alpha\}$ and $\delta \leq \delta_1 + \delta_2 + 1$ then $\mathcal{A}^{\mathsf{ds}} := \mathcal{A}^{\mathsf{ds}} \oplus (X, B)_{\Sigma_1 \cup \Sigma_2 \cup \{\alpha\}}^{\delta_1 + \delta_2 + 1}$
SCR4	If $\{(X, r, Y)_{\Sigma_1}^{\delta_1}, (Y, \perp)_{\Sigma_2}^{\delta_2}\} \subseteq \mathcal{A}^{\mathsf{ds}}$, and there is *no* $(X, \perp)^{\delta}$ in $\mathcal{A}^{\mathsf{ds}}$ such that $\Sigma \subset \Sigma_1 \cup \Sigma_2$ or such that $\Sigma = \Sigma_1 \cup \Sigma_2$ and $\delta \leq \delta_1 + \delta_2 + 1$ then $\mathcal{A}^{\mathsf{ds}} := \mathcal{A}^{\mathsf{ds}} \oplus (X, \perp)_{\Sigma_1 \cup \Sigma_2}^{\delta_1 + \delta_2 + 1}$
SCR5	If $(X, r, Y)_{\Sigma_1}^{\delta_1} \in \mathcal{A}^{\mathsf{ds}}$, $\alpha : r \sqsubseteq s \in \mathcal{O}$, and there is *no* $(X, s, Y)_{\Sigma}^{\delta}$ in $\mathcal{A}^{\mathsf{ds}}$ such that $\Sigma \subset \Sigma_1 \cup \{\alpha\}$ or such that $\Sigma = \Sigma_1 \cup \{\alpha\}$ and $\delta \leq \delta_1 + 1$ then $\mathcal{A}^{\mathsf{ds}} := \mathcal{A}^{\mathsf{ds}} \oplus (X, s, Y)_{\Sigma_1 \cup \{\alpha\}}^{\delta_1 + 1}$
SCR6	If $\{(X, r, Y)_{\Sigma_1}^{\delta_1}, (Y, s, Z)_{\Sigma_2}^{\delta_2}\} \subseteq \mathcal{A}^{\mathsf{ds}}$, $\alpha : r \circ s \sqsubseteq t \in \mathcal{O}$, and there is *no* $(X, t, Z)^{\delta}$ in $\mathcal{A}^{\mathsf{ds}}$ such that $\Sigma \subset \Sigma_1 \cup \Sigma_2 \cup \{\alpha\}$ or such that $\Sigma = \Sigma_1 \cup \Sigma_2 \cup \{\alpha\}$ and $\delta \leq \delta_1 + \delta_2 + 1$ then $\mathcal{A}^{\mathsf{ds}} := \mathcal{A}^{\mathsf{ds}} \oplus (X, t, Z)_{\Sigma_1 \cup \Sigma_2 \cup \{\alpha\}}^{\delta_1 + \delta_2 + 1}$

Fig. 4. Distance-labeled completion rules

Hardness stems from the fact that, for a given subsumption, there may potentially be exponentially many supporting sets of axioms. The algorithm for dist1 can be extended to "remember" sets of axioms used thus far to obtain the assertion in question. The set of labeled assertions $\mathcal{A}^{\mathsf{ds}}$ is subset of:

$$\left(\mathsf{CN}^+ \times \mathsf{CN}^+ \times \underbrace{\mathbf{N} \times 2^{\mathcal{O}}}_{\text{labels}} \right) \cup \left(\mathsf{CN}^+ \times \mathsf{RN} \times \mathsf{CN}^+ \times \underbrace{\mathbf{N} \times 2^{\mathcal{O}}}_{\text{labels}} \right).$$

Each assertion π_{Σ}^{δ} in $\mathcal{A}^{\mathsf{ds}}$ contains two labels δ and Σ which remember the number of rule applications and the axiom set required to obtain π.

The labeled algorithm initializes $\mathcal{A}^{\mathsf{ds}}$ with the smallest set consisting of:

- $(A, A)_{\emptyset}^{0}$ and $(A, \top)_{\emptyset}^{0}$, for all concept names $A \in \mathsf{CN}^+$;
- $(A, r, A)_{\Sigma}^{m}$, for r a role name such that $\mathcal{O} \models \epsilon \sqsubseteq r$, where Σ is a minimal set of RI axioms $\epsilon \sqsubseteq r_1$ and $r_i \sqsubseteq r_{i+1} \in \mathcal{O}$ with $1 \leq i < m$, $r_m = r$.

After initialization, the set of assertions $\mathcal{A}^{\mathsf{ds}}$ is extended by applying the *new distance-labeled* completion rules shown in Fig.4 until no more rule applies. Essentially, the new distance-labeled completion rules apply and add a new assertion π_Σ^δ when one of the following general conditions holds true:

- Σ is incompatible with any existing support set for the same assertion base.
- $\Sigma \subset \Sigma'$ for some $\pi_{\Sigma'}^{\delta'}$.
- $\Sigma = \Sigma'$ and $\delta < \delta'$ for some $\pi_{\Sigma'}^{\delta'}$.

In the latter two cases, any previous assertions $\pi_{\Sigma'}^{\delta'} \in \mathcal{A}^{\mathsf{ds}}$ that fall into these conditions will be replaced with the new one, whereas nothing is removed in the first case. The update operator $\oplus$ is defined as follows:

$$\mathcal{A}^{\mathsf{ds}} \oplus \pi_\Sigma^\delta \equiv \left(\mathcal{A}^{\mathsf{ds}} - \{\pi_{\Sigma'}^{\delta'} \mid \Sigma' \supset \Sigma\} - \{\pi_{\Sigma'}^{\delta'} \mid \Sigma' = \Sigma \text{ and } \delta' > \delta\}\right) \cup \{\pi_\Sigma^\delta\}$$

We denote by $[\mathcal{A}^{\mathsf{ds}}]$ the completed set of labeled assertions obtained after the labeled subsumption algorithm terminates and by $lab^{\mathsf{ds}}(A, B)$ the minimum sum of the final number of rule applications and cardinality of the support set, i.e.:

$$lab^{\mathsf{ds}}(A, B) = min\{\delta + card(\Sigma) \mid (A, B)_\Sigma^\delta \in [\mathcal{A}^{\mathsf{ds}}]\}$$

Lemma 3 (termination). *Given an $\mathcal{EL}^+$ ontology $\mathcal{O}$ in normal form. The modified distance-labeled subsumption algorithm terminates in time exponential in the size of $\mathcal{O}$.*

Proof. This label extension of the original $\mathcal{EL}^+$ subsumption algorithm is similar to the one for axiom pinpointing. The number of base assertions of the form (A, B) and (A, r, B) is polynomial in the size of $\mathcal{O}$, but each may be equipped with an exponential number of the Σ label (i.e. the number of subsets of $\mathcal{O}$).

The new update operator $\oplus$ makes sure that each labeled assertion is added to $\mathcal{A}^{\mathsf{ds}}$ only once. A labeled assertion may be removed, but then another labeled assertion with converging labels must be added. Since the number of labeled assertions is exponential and each rule application takes at most exponential steps, the algorithm terminates in time exponential in the size of $\mathcal{O}$.   ❏

As the algorithm exhaustively applies the rules whenever a smaller δ or Σ is identified, the labels in the completed set of assertions $[\mathcal{A}^{\mathsf{ds}}]$ contains, among other distance values and support sets, the minimum combination of both.

Lemma 4. *Let $\mathcal{O}$ be an $\mathcal{EL}^+$ ontology and A, B concept names such that $A \sqsubseteq_{\mathcal{O}} B$. After the modified distance-labeled subsumption algorithm terminates on $\mathcal{O}$, we have that $lab^{\mathsf{ds}}(A, B) = \mathsf{dist2}(A, B)$.*

Example 2. Consider again the subsumptions $U \sqsubseteq_{\mathcal{O}} B$ and $U \sqsubseteq_{\mathcal{O}} D$ from Example 1. An extract of a possible trace of rule applications is shown in Table 3. Like the previous example, after five rule applications, assertion π_6 is added to $\mathcal{A}^{\mathsf{ds}}$ with labels 5 and $\{\alpha_1, \alpha_4, \alpha_5, \alpha_7\}$. It is not difficult to see that π_6 is the only labeled assertion for base (U, B), and as such $lab^{\mathsf{ds}}(U, B) = \mathsf{dist2}(U, B) = 9$.

Table 3. An extract of a trace of the modified distance-labeled subsumption algorithm on the ontology of Example 1; discussed in Example 2

Rule	Preconditions	New assertion
SCR1	$(A, A)_\emptyset^0, \alpha_1$	$\pi_1 : (A, B)_{\{\alpha_1\}}^1$
SCR1	$(C, C)_\emptyset^0, \alpha_3$	$\pi_2 : (C, D)_{\{\alpha_3\}}^1$
SCR2	$(U, U)_\emptyset^0, \alpha_4$	$\pi_3 : (U, r, A)_{\{\alpha_4\}}^1$
SCR3	π_1, π_3, α_5	$\pi_4 : (U, V)_{\{\alpha_1, \alpha_4, \alpha_5\}}^3$
SCR1	π_4, α_7	$\pi_5 : (U, A)_{\{\alpha_1, \alpha_4, \alpha_5, \alpha_7\}}^4$
SCR1	π_5, α_1	$\star\ \pi_6 : (U, B)_{\{\alpha_1, \alpha_4, \alpha_5, \alpha_7\}}^5$
SCR1	π_6, α_2	$\pi_7 : (U, C)_{\{\alpha_1, \alpha_2, \alpha_4, \alpha_5, \alpha_7\}}^6$
SCR1	π_7, α_3	$\star\ \pi_8 : (U, D)_{\{\alpha_1, \alpha_2, \alpha_3, \alpha_4, \alpha_5, \alpha_7\}}^7$
SCR1	π_4, α_8	$\pi_9 : (U, C)_{\{\alpha_1, \alpha_4, \alpha_5, \alpha_8\}}^4$
SCR1	π_9, α_3	$\star\ \pi_{10} : (U, D)_{\{\alpha_1, \alpha_3, \alpha_4, \alpha_5, \alpha_8\}}^5$

$$\vdots$$

If two more rule applications are carried out following π_6, then π_8 can be obtained. However, another path of rule applications is possible that yield the same assertion base (U, D) with different labels. Since the support set for π_{10} is incomparable to that of π_8, the former is added into $\mathcal{A}^{ds}$. Unlike Example 1, this addition does not replace π_8 and thus both remain in $[\mathcal{A}^{ds}]$ after exhaustion of rule applications. By definition, the minimum sum is of interest, so $lab^{ds}(U, D) = dist2(U, D) = 10$. Note that although the two subsumptions $U \sqsubseteq_\mathcal{O} B$ and $U \sqsubseteq_\mathcal{O} D$ have the same structural distance w.r.t. the first definition, they differ w.r.t. the second definition. This is because the first definition of structural distance is oblivious to the number of axioms used for reasoning.

4   Related Work

In [7], the authors present the algorithm used in the LinKFactory, the ontology authoring environment designed specifically for LinKBase ontology. Relative to a particular concept, the algorithm ranks other concepts according to their semantic distances which can be judged inaccurate or approved by an expert. Though no detailed description of this algorithm is presented, the given example suggests that it uses the mere subsumption hierarchy, i.e. the semantic distance is defined to be the length of a path between two concepts in the hierarchy. A similar approach to computing distances between concepts is presented in [8], where the depth of concept in the hierarchy also plays a role.

5   Conclusion

In this paper, we present two notions of structural distance between $\mathcal{EL}^+$ concepts, one relative to the number of rule applications alone and the other relative to both the number of rule applications and number of axioms involved. The well-known labeling technique from axiom pinpointing is employed to extend the original $\mathcal{EL}^+$ subsumption algorithm for computing structural distances.

For future work, the first algorithm which is tractable shall be implemented and evaluated on real-world ontologies such as the Gene Ontology or SNOMED CT. We believe that the statistics on the structural distances between inferred subsumptions can reveal structural discrepancies that are invisible through a mere classification. Other interesting future work is to investigate the compatibility of our structural distance with the notion of semantic distance in [8]. Here, a stated subsumption and an inferred subsumption on the same level could be differentiated by assigning different distance values which could be suggested by the structural distances.

References

1. Baader, F., Brandt, S., Lutz, C.: Pushing the $\mathcal{EL}$ envelope. In: Proceedings of the 19th International Conference on Artificial Intelligence (IJCAI 2005). Morgan-Kaufmann Publishers, Edinburgh (2005)
2. Baader, F., Brandt, S., Lutz, C.: Pushing the $\mathcal{EL}$ envelope further. In: Clark, K., Patel-Schneider, P.F. (eds.) Proceedings of the OWLED 2008 DC Workshop on OWL: Experiences and Directions (2008)
3. Baader, F., Calvanese, D., McGuinness, D., Nardi, D., Patel-Schneider, P. (eds.): The Description Logic Handbook: Theory, Implementation and Applications, 2nd edn. Cambridge University Press (2007)
4. Baader, F., Hollunder, B.: Embedding defaults into terminological knowledge representation formalisms. Journal of Automated Reasoning 14, 149–180 (1995)
5. Baader, F., Lutz, C., Suntisrivaraporn, B.: Is tractable reasoning in extensions of the Description Logic $\mathcal{EL}$ useful in practice? Journal of Logic, Language and Information, Special Issue on Method for Modality, M4M (2007)
6. Baader, F., Peñaloza, R., Suntisrivaraporn, B.: Pinpointing in the Description Logic $\mathcal{EL}^+$. In: Hertzberg, J., Beetz, M., Englert, R. (eds.) KI 2007. LNCS (LNAI), vol. 4667, pp. 52–67. Springer, Heidelberg (2007)
7. Ceusters, W., Smith, B., Kumar, A., Dhaen, C.: SNOMED CT's problem list: Ontologists' and logicians' therapy suggestions. In: Jack, Y.-C., Fieschi, L.M., Coiera, E. (eds.) Proceedings of the Medinfo 2007 Congress. Studies in Health Technology and Informatics (SHTI-series), pp. 482–491. IOS Press (2004)
8. Ge, J., Qiu, Y.: Concept similarity matching based on semantic distance. In: Proceedings of the Forth International Conference on Semantics, Knowledge and Grid, pp. 380–383. IEEE Computer Society (2008)
9. Motik, B., Cuenca Grau, B., Horrocks, I., Wu, Z., Fokoue, A., Lutz, C.: OWL 2 web ontology language profiles (2009), http://www.w3.org/TR/owl2-profiles/
10. Parsia, B., Sirin, E., Kalyanpur, A.: Debugging OWL ontologies. In: Proceedings of the 14th International Conference on WWW 2005, pp. 633–640. ACM (2005)
11. Schlobach, S., Cornet, R.: Non-standard reasoning services for the debugging of Description Logic terminologies. In: Gottlob, G., Walsh, T. (eds.) Proceedings of IJCAI 2003, Acapulco, Mexico, pp. 355–362. Morgan-Kaufmann Publishers (2003)
12. Stearns, M.Q., Price, C., Spackman, K.A., Wang, A.Y.: SNOMED clinical terms: Overview of the development process and project status. In: Proceedings of the 2001 AMIA Annual Symposium, pp. 662–666. Hanley&Belfus (2001)

Fuzzy-Based Trusted Ant Routing (FTAR) Protocol in Mobile Ad Hoc Networks

Srinivas Sethi[1] and Siba K. Udgata[2]

[1] Department of CSE,
IGIT, Saranag, Orissa
srinivas_sethi@igitsarang.ac.in
[2] Department of Computer & Information Sciences,
University of Hyderabad, Hyderabad, 500046
udgatacs@uohyd.ernet.in

Abstract. This paper proposes a novel approach called Fuzzy-based Trusted Ant Routing (FTAR) using fuzzy logic and swarm intelligence to select optimal path by considering optimization of multiple objectives. It retains the advantages of swarm intelligence algorithm and ensures trusted routing protocol by implementing fuzzy logic. It uses trust-evaluation scheme using dropped packet and Time-Ratio parameters which calculate trust values for nodes in MANETs to distinguish between healthy and malicious nodes. FTAR considers not only shortest path but also the trusted level of neighbors or intermediate nodes.

Keywords: MANET, Routing Protocol, Fuzzy, Antnet.

1 Introduction

A mobile ad hoc network (MANET) is becoming popular day to day due to its easy deployability, low cost infrastructure special purpose applications etc.. It is a self-organized network of mobile devices connected by wireless links. Each device in a MANET is free to move independently in any direction, and will therefore change its links to other devices frequently. Since, nodes in MANET can move in an arbitrarily manner, the network topology may change rapidly and unpredictably.

Each node acts as a router and takes part in discovery and maintenance of routes to other nodes in the network. So router has different activities at the same time. To support robust and efficient operations in mobile wireless networks, routing functionality is included in mobile nodes along with tests for trusted nodes as well.

The proposed protocols can be grouped into three different categories: table-driven/ pro-active, on-demand/ reactive, and hybrid [1]. However, due to security vulnerabilities of the routing protocols, mobile ad-hoc network is unprotected to attacks by the malicious nodes. So, it has to address new kinds of security issues which require new evaluation schemes to protect the network from different attacks of malicious nodes. The different attacks are blackhole attack [2], grayhole attack [3], Selective Existence attack [4], etc.

C. Sombattheera et al. (Eds.): MIWAI 2011, LNAI 7080, pp. 112–123, 2011.

In blackhole attack, malicious nodes never send true control messages. To carry out a blackhole attack, when the malicious node receives a route request (RREQ) message, without checking its routing table, immediately sends a false route reply (RREP) message assigning a high sequence number to settle in the routing table of the victim node, before other nodes send a true one. So, requesting nodes assume that route discovery process is successfully completed and ignore other RREP messages and begin to send packets over malicious node. In this way malicious node attacks all RREQ messages and packets are dropped without forwarding anywhere. Blackhole attack affects the whole network if it is in central place of network.

In the grayhole attack of malicious node initially forward the packets and then fails to do so. Initially the node replays true RREP messages to nodes that initiate RREQ message and it takes over the sending packets. Afterwards, the node just drops the packets to launch a denial of service. This is known as routing misbehavior.

The node is not participating in the network operations but, use the network for its advantage to enhance performance and save its own resources such as power. These types of selfish node behaviors are known as selective existence attacks [3]. It does not send any HELLO messages and drop all packets. In this paper, we introduce a trust-evaluation scheme which calculates trust values for nodes in MANET to successfully distinguish between healthy and malicious nodes.

The rest of the paper is organized as; section 2 discusses related works. Section 3 describes the method for detection of trusted node using fuzzy logic. New proposed routing protocol is described in section 4. Simulation environment is discussed in section 5 followed by performance evaluation parameters in section 6. Section 7 discusses results of routing protocol followed by conclusions in section 8.

2   Related Works

The basic idea of the ant colony optimization (ACO) [5] meta-heuristic is taken from the food searching behavior of real ants. It often gives better results for hard combinatorial optimization problems. The study of ant's behavior exhibits the capability of finding the shortest path from the ant's nest to the food source. In AntNet[6][7], ants explore the network building paths from source to destination nodes using a stochastic policy dependent on the past and current network states and collect on-line information on the network status. The disadvantage of AntNet is that it is intrinsically slow.

AntHocNet [8], a meta-heuristic ant based routing protocol for routing in mobile ad hoc networks, which has been designed after the Ant Colony Optimization (ACO) framework and its general architecture shares strong similarities with the architectures of typical ACO implementations for network routing. It is a hybrid protocol consists of both reactive and proactive components.

ANT-E [9] is a novel meta-heuristic on-demand routing protocol using the Blocking Expanding Ring Search (Blocking-ERS) to control the overhead and local retransmission to improve the reliability in term of packet delivery ratio (PDR).

Ant-Colony-Based Routing Protocol (ARA) [10], has been described as on-demand routing protocols for MANET. In [11] the authors correlate different route selection parameters that affect the network performance is captured by fuzzy ant technology and the results show that fuzzy ant colony based routing protocol is very promising to take care of various uncertainties of MANET effectively. In [12], authors have presented a self-healing technique based on Fuzzy concepts for mobile Ad hoc networks. The basic idea is to modify the entries of the neighbor table and the time-stamp of the entry each based on the fuzzy system. The performance of Dynamic Source Routing (DSR) is improved by adding a congestion level of each mobile node, together with number of hops, as a mixed metric that will be considered during route selection decision in source node using fuzzy logic [13].

The authors investigate the development of protocols which are resilient to Byzantine Attacks in [14] and presented a Byzantine Secure Link State routing protocol for wired environments. In [15], the On-Demand Secure Byzantine Routing (ODSBR) routing protocol was proposed for MANETs. The ODSBR is secure against known outsider attacks due to presence of cryptographic mechanisms. In [3], [16] proposed several passive methods to monitor the behavior of neighboring nodes in order to determine whether they are acting in a faulty manner. In these works, if the neighbor is deemed to be misbehaving, the monitoring node suggests or carries out a path reroute around the faulty neighboring node.

3   A Fuzzy-Based Trusted Node

3.1   Fuzzy Logic

Fuzzy logic is used to approximate functions and can be used to model any continuous function or system. The advantages of fuzzy logic are easy to understand, flexible, tolerant of imprecise data and can model nonlinear functions of arbitrary complexity. The fuzzy logic has been used to solve several routing protocols and handover problems efficiently in wireless networks [18] [19].

3.2   Design of Fuzzy Interface System

Fuzzy inference is the process of formulating the mapping from a given input to an output using fuzzy logic and the mapping provides a basis from which decisions can be made, or patterns recognized. The process of fuzzy inference involves all of the pieces: membership functions, if-then rules etc.

In this paper, neighbor nodes are evaluated for their Trustfulness using a fuzzy logic approach and compare its performance with that of the Ant-U. The inputs to the fuzzy controller for routing are: (i) Time-ratio and (ii) Dropped packet. These two selection parameters make the node's ability to trust deliver network packets. Fig.-1 shows the generalized block diagram of fuzzy system for trusted node.

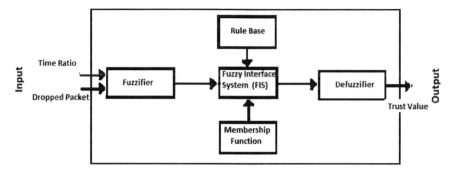

Fig. 1. Generalized Block Diagram of fuzzy system for trusted node

The basic functions of the different components of fuzzy interface system design in the scheme are described as follows.

3.2.1 Fuzzification

The fuzzifier performs the fuzzification process that converts two types of input data and one output which are needed in the inference system. The input to the fuzzifier 'time-ratio' is the ratio between route reply time and time-to-live whereas, dropped packets is numbers of packet dropped at the node. These two parameters are used to measure the trusted node where trusted value of node is output.

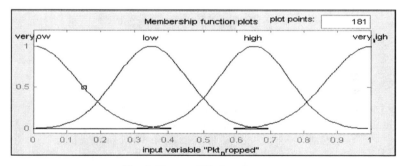

Fig. 2. Dropped Packets fuzzy set

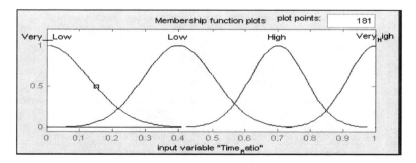

Fig. 3. Time-Ratio fuzzy set

Fuzzification of inputs: It obtains inputs and determines the degree to which they belong to each of the appropriate fuzzy sets via membership functions. It may be a table lookup or a function evaluation. Trusty node performs the node evaluation process in order to determine the trustworthiness of a neighbor node after establishing the route. The trust-value of a node evaluated through two inputs. They are dropped packet and Time-ratio, which get fuzzified in order to give a step-less indication as Fig-2 and Fig-3 respectively.

Fuzzification of outputs: After creating fuzzy sets from all inputs, output fuzzy sets are evaluated by rule evaluation where, the rule evaluation consists of "if-then"-statements that give evidence of how to proceed with a node with certain fuzzy-sets. The fuzzy sets as in Fig.-4, are used to appraise each constraint as being Very Low, Low, Medium, High or Very High, assigning each a value between {0,1}. These evaluations are passed to a fuzzy inference system that applies a set of fuzzy rules that determines the node is trusted or not.

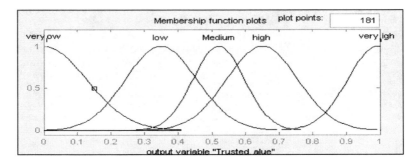

Fig. 4. Trust value of node

3.2.2   Inference System with Rule Base and Membership Function

Fuzzy Inference System is the system that simulates human decision-making based on the fuzzy control rules and the related input linguistic parameters. The low-high inference method is used to associate the outputs of the inferential rules [20][21]. The

```
1. If (Pkt_Dropped is very_high) or (Time_Ratio is Very__Low) then (Trusted__Node is very_low) (1)
2. If (Pkt_Dropped is very_high) and (Time_Ratio is Low) then (Trusted__Node is very_low) (1)
3. If (Pkt_Dropped is very_high) and (Time_Ratio is High) then (Trusted__Node is low) (1)
4. If (Pkt_Dropped is very_high) and (Time_Ratio is Very_High) then (Trusted__Node is Medium) (1)
5. If (Pkt_Dropped is high) and (Time_Ratio is Very__Low) then (Trusted__Node is very_low) (1)
6. If (Pkt_Dropped is high) and (Time_Ratio is Low) then (Trusted__Node is low) (1)
7. If (Pkt_Dropped is high) and (Time_Ratio is High) then (Trusted__Node is Medium) (1)
8. If (Pkt_Dropped is high) and (Time_Ratio is Very_High) then (Trusted__Node is Medium) (1)
9. If (Pkt_Dropped is low) and (Time_Ratio is Very__Low) then (Trusted__Node is very_low) (1)
10. If (Pkt_Dropped is low) and (Time_Ratio is Low) then (Trusted__Node is low) (1)
11. If (Pkt_Dropped is low) and (Time_Ratio is High) then (Trusted__Node is very_high) (1)
12. If (Pkt_Dropped is low) and (Time_Ratio is Very_High) then (Trusted__Node is very_high) (1)
13. If (Pkt_Dropped is very_low) and (Time_Ratio is Very__Low) then (Trusted__Node is very_low) (1)
14. If (Pkt_Dropped is very_low) and (Time_Ratio is Low) then (Trusted__Node is low) (1)
15. If (Pkt_Dropped is very_low) and (Time_Ratio is High) then (Trusted__Node is high) (1)
16. If (Pkt_Dropped is very_low) and (Time_Ratio is Very_High) then (Trusted__Node is very_high) (1)
```

Fig. 5. Fuzzy control rules for Trusted value of node

rule base is composed of a set of linguistic control rules and the accompanying control goals. Using the rule-based structure of fuzzy logic, a series of IF-THEN rules are defined for the output response given the input conditions. There are sixteen (4x4) possible logical-product output response conclusions, as shown in Fig.-5.

3.2.3 Defuzzification

The Defuzzification is the process of conversion of fuzzy output set into a single number and the method used for the defuzzification is smallest of minimum (SOM). The input for the defuzzification process is a fuzzy set. The aggregate of a fuzzy set includes a range of output values, and be defuzzified in order to resolve a single output value from the fuzzy set. Defuzzifier adopts the aggregated linguistic values from the inferred fuzzy control action and generates a non-fuzzy control output, which represents the trusted node adapted to node conditions. The defuzzification method is employed to compute the membership function for the aggregated output [20][21].

4   Description of Proposed Protocol

In this section, we discuss the adaptation of the fuzzy based trusted node for ant colony optimization meta-heuristic in MANET and describe the Fuzzy-based Trusted ant Routing (FTAR) protocol.

Data packets and control packets are two different types of packets used in the network. Forward ant (FANT) and a backward ant (BANT) are two classes of control packets used to update the routing tables and distribute information about the traffic load in the network. Apart from the control packets, the neighbor control packets are used to maintain a list of available nodes to which packets can be forwarded. The data packet represents the information which is exchanged among end-users. In ant-routing, data packets use the information stored at routing tables for moving from the source to the destination node. The HELLO messages are broadcasted periodically from each node to all its neighbors to check if the ant has arrived or not, as the destination address will change at every visited node. Birth time of an ant is the time when the ant has been generated and arrival time at the final destination is used to calculate the trip time.

FANT and BANT are used to discover the route in route discovery phase. A FANT is an agent which establishes the pheromone track to the source node and it gathers information about the state of network. Similarly, a BANT establishes the pheromone track to the destination node and use the collected information to adapt the routing tables on their path. The FANT is a small packet with a unique sequence number and the sequence number is used to distinguish duplicate packets. It creates a set of routing agents called FANT to search for the destination host. The source node would initiate a route discovery mechanism when a path to destination needs to be established and disseminate FANT to all its one-hop neighbors. While the destination is still not found, the neighbor would keep forwarding the FANTs to their own neighbors and so on. This process continues until a route to the destination is found using Blocking-ERS [22]; otherwise it sends a reply message to the source node. To prevent cycles, each node stores recently forwarded route request in a buffer.

The node interprets the source address of the FANT as destination address of BANT. The address of the previous node as the next hop and computes the pheromone value depending on the number of hops the FANT needs to reach the node. The node then relays the FANT to its neighbors. When the FANT reaches the destination node, the destination node extracts the information of the FANT and destroys it. Afterward, it creates a BANT and sends it to the source node. If any malicious node is available in the network, the above process may be deviated by black hole attack or gray hole attack or selective attack. To avoid this problem, we propose to check the fuzzy trust value of node in the network. The trusted neighbor nodes will be selected and the ant will be forwarded to it.iWhen the sender receives the BANT from the proper destination node, the path is established from source and destination and data packets can be sent.

Once the FANT and BANT have established the pheromone tracks for the source and destination nodes, subsequent data packets are used to maintain the path and strengthen the path during the communication. When a node relays a data packet towards the destination node, it increases the pheromone value of the entry, to strengthen the route to the destinations by the data packets as per following equation.

$$P_{new} = P_{id} + \Phi P_{id} \qquad (1)$$

Where, P_{new} is the new updated value, by P_{id} which is the previous pheromone value before reinforcement and Φ is a scaling factor.

All pheromone values in the routing table decreases over time. It shows the utilization rate of a route in the network. When the pheromone entry reaches a minimum threshold, it is considered a stale route and will be discarded from the routing table. The evaporation function is defined as:

$$P_{new} = P_{id} - \delta P_{id} \qquad (2)$$

Where, δ is the evaporation scaling factor. This helps the ant to find out the maximum probability of an ant to choose the path at time $t+1$.

FTAR recognizes a route failure through a missing acknowledgment within predefined time-to-live and a node gets a route error (RERR) message for a certain link, it deactivates this link by setting the pheromone value to 0. Then the node searches for an alternative link in its routing table and it sends the packet via this alternate path, if there exist one; otherwise the node informs its neighbors, to relay the packet. If the packet does not reach the destination, the source has to initiate a new route discovery phase. By using trusted value of the node in the network the proposed routing protocol FTAR is more secure or trust than Ant routing with unsafe or malicious nodes.

5   Simulation

We implemented these protocols in the discrete time network simulator (NS-2)[23], which offers high fidelity in wireless ad hoc network. NS-2 is used under Linux platform to evaluate the performance of proposed routing protocol. Simulations have been carried out using the parameters given table-1 for different mobility rate, area size and number of nodes. Random waypoint mobility model is used for modeling the mobility of nodes.

Table 1. Parameter values of FTAR and Ant-U for simulation

S. No	Parameters	Values
1	Area size	700x700 m.
2	Transmission range	250 m.
3	Number of Nodes	50, 100, 150, 200 Nos.
4	Simulation time	900 s.
5	Nodes Mobility	1,5,10,15,20 m/s.
6	Pause times	10 s.
7	Data rate	1 Kbps.
8	No. Of experiments	5 times.

6   Performance Evaluation Parameters

The standard performance metrics like packet delivery ratio (PDR), overhead and delay are used for evaluating the performance of routing protocols are chosen.

The packet delivery ratio in this simulation is defined as the percentage of the ratio between the number of packets sent by constant bit rate sources and the number of received packets by sink/ destination. This performance evaluation parameter measures the delivery reliability, effectiveness and efficiency of the routing protocol.

$$PDR = \frac{\sum P_d}{\sum P_s} * 100 \tag{3}$$

where, P_d =Number of packets sent at destinations,

and P_s = number of received packets at sources.

Average End-to-end Delay is used to measure as the time elapsed from the time when a data packet is originated from a source and it is successfully received by receiver. This includes all possible delays caused by buffering during route discovery latency, queuing at the interface queuing transmission delays at MAC, and propagation and transfer times of data packets. This is the average overall delay for a packet to traverse from a source node to a destination node. So,

$$Avg.End - to - end - Delay = \frac{\sum e}{P} \tag{4}$$

where, $e = T_d - T_s$,

T_d =Time when packet received at destination,

T_s =Time when packet created by source,

and P =Total Generated Packet.

Overhead is the total number of routing packets transmitted during simulation. It is important to compare the adoption to low-bandwidth environments and its efficiency in relation to node battery power (in that sending more routing packets consumes more power). Sending more routing packets also increases the probability of packet collision and can delay data packets in the queues.

7   Result and Discussion

In this paper, trusted value of the node is calculated by using fuzzy logic to make the protocol more secure. At the same time it also improves the PDR which denotes the efficiency, reliability and effectiveness of proposed routing protocol. It also reduces the total routing overhead by checking the malicious node in the network. It is able to control the overhead by detecting blackhole attack, grayhole attack and selective existence attack of malicious or unsafe node in the network.

Fig.-6 shows, the PDR of FTAR is more than other Ant-U with malicious or unsafe node in respect all mobility rate. Similarly from Fig.-7, it is observed that PDR of FTAR is more than Ant-U with any unsafe node in the network in respect to numbers of node. It shows improved reliability, effectiveness and efficiency of FTAR in comparison to Ant-U.

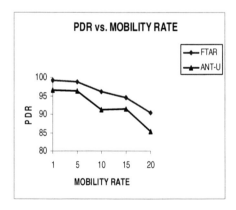

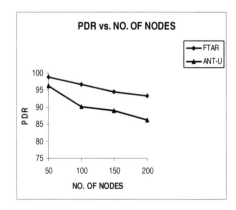

Fig. 6. PDR vs. Mobility Rate at 50 nodes   **Fig. 7.** PDR vs. No. of Nodes at 5 m/s

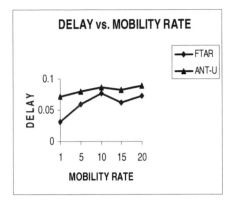

Fig. 8. Delay vs. Mobility Rate at 50 nodes

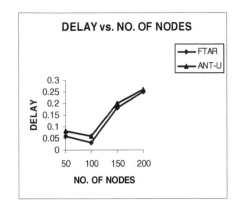

Fig. 9. Delay vs. No. of Nodes at 5 m/s

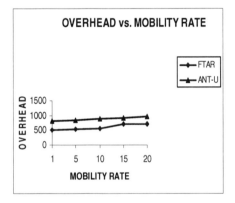

Fig. 10. Overhead vs. Mobility Rate at 50 nodes

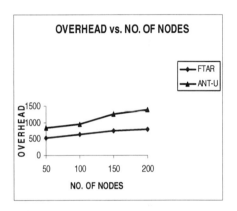

Fig. 11. Overhead vs. No. of Nodes at 5 m/s

In real time application, end-to-end delay is one of the important parameter to measure performance of routing protocol. Now, from Fig.8; it can be concluded that, end-to-end delay for FTAR is less than Ant-U for all mobility rates. Similarly end-to-end delay for FTAR is less than Ant-U for various node sizes as Fig. 9.

The overhead of FTAR is controlled by avoiding blackhole attack, gray hole attack and selective existence attack of malicious or unsafe node in the network. From Fig.-10, it is observed that the total overhead of proposed routing FTAR protocol is better than Ant-U for different mobility rates. Fig.11, show the total overhead of proposed routing FTAR protocol is better than Ant-U for various node sizes.

From the above results, it is observed that, the performance of FTAR is better than Ant-U for all possible combination of mobility rates and node sizes. This shows that the proposed routing protocol FTAR outperforms ANT-U.

8   Conclusions

In this paper, we proposed a Trust-node approach in the MANET based on Fuzzy concepts. The basic idea in this proposed work is to modify the entries of the dropped packets and the time-stamp of each entry based on the fuzzy system. This proposed approach shows an improvement over the Ant-U (with unsafe or malicious node). It avoids different attacks, which try to produce more routing overhead leading to blocking of the network and unnecessary increasing traffic. As trusted nodes are establishing the path from source to destination, it improves the PDR and decrease end-to-end delay and routing overhead. Since trust value of nodes is considered, the proposed routing protocol is highly reliable in real time environments.

References

1. Abolhasan, M., Wysocki, T., Dutkiewicz, E.: A Review of Routing Protocol for Mobile Ad hoc Networks. Elsevier Ad Hoc Nwtworks Journal 2(1), 1–22 (2004)
2. Deng, H., Li, W., Agrawal, D.: Routing Security in Wireless Ad Hoc Networks. IEEE Communication Magazine, 70–75 (October 2002)
3. Marti, S., Giuli, T.J., Lai, K., Baker, M.: Mitigating routing misbehavior in mobile ad hoc networks. In: Mobile Computing and Networking (MobiCom 2000), pp. 255–265 (2000)
4. Vigna, G., Gwalani, S., Srinivasan, K.: An Intrusion Detection Tool for AODV-Based Ad hoc Wireless Networks. In: Proc. of the 20th Annual Computer Security Applications Conference (ACSAC 2004) (2004)
5. Dorigo, M., Gambardella, L.M.: Ant colony system: a cooperative learning approach to the traveling salesman problem. IEEE Transactions on Evolutionary Computation 1(1), 53–66 (1997)
6. Di Caro, G.A., Dorigo, M.: Ant Colonies for Adaptive Routing in Packet-Switched Communications Networks. In: Eiben, A.E., Bäck, T., Schoenauer, M., Schwefel, H.-P. (eds.) PPSN 1998. LNCS, vol. 1498, pp. 673–682. Springer, Heidelberg (1998)
7. Dhillon, S.S., Van Mieghem, P.: Performance Analysis of the AntNet Algorithm. International Journal of Computer Networks, 2104–2125 (2007)
8. Di Caro, G.A., Ducatelle, F., Gambardella, L.M.: AntHocNet: An Ant-Based Hybrid Routing Algorithm for Mobile Ad Hoc Networks. In: Yao, X., Burke, E.K., Lozano, J.A., Smith, J., Merelo-Guervós, J.J., Bullinaria, J.A., Rowe, J.E., Tiňo, P., Kabán, A., Schwefel, H.-P. (eds.) PPSN 2004. LNCS, vol. 3242, pp. 461–470. Springer, Heidelberg (2004)
9. Sethi, S., Udgata, S.K.: The Efficient Ant Routing Protocol for MANET. International Journal on Computer Science and Engineering (IJCSE) 02(07), 2414–2420 (2010)
10. Güneş, M., Sorges, U., Bouazizi, I.: ARA - The Ant-Colony Based Routing Protocol for MANETs. In: International Conference on Parallel Processing Workshops, pp. 1530–2016 (2002)
11. Goswami, M.M., Dharaskar, R.V., Thakare, V.M.: Fuzzy Ant Colony Based Routing Protocol For Mobile Ad Hoc Network. In: International Conference on Computer Engineering and Technology, ICCET 2009, pp. 438–448 (2009)
12. Venkatesh, C., Yadaiah, N., Natarajan, A.M.: Dynamic Source Routing Protocol using Fuzzy Logic Concepts for Ad hoc Network. Accademic Open Internet Journal 15, 1–15 (2005)

13. Wagyana, A., Hendrawan, Rachmana, N.: Performance Improvement of Dynamic Source Routing on Manet using Fuzzy Logic. In: Proceedings of MoMM 2006, pp. 251 258 (2006)
14. Avramopoulos, I., Kobayashi, H., Wang, R., Krishnamurthy, A.: Highly Secure and Efficient Routing. In: INFOCOM 2004 (2004)
15. Awerbuch, B.R., Holmer, D., Nita-Rotaru, C., Rubens, H.: An on-demand secure routing protocol resilient to byzantine failures. In: ACM Workshop on Wireless Security, WiSe (2002)
16. Hu, Y.-C., Perrig, A., Johnson, D.B.: Ariadne: A secure on-demand routing protocol for ad hoc networks. In: Hu, Y.-C., Perrig, A. (eds.) Proceedings of the Eighth ACM International Conference on Mobile Computing and Networking, MobiCom 2002 (2002)
17. Belding-Royer, E.M., Parkins, C.E.: Evolution and future directions of the ad hoc on-demand distance vector routing protocol. Ad Hoc Network (Elsevier) 1(1), 125–150 (2003)
18. Wong, Y.F., Wong, W.C.: A fuzzy-decision-based routing protocol for mobile ad hoc networks. In: 10th IEEE International Conference on Network, pp. 317–322 (2002)
19. Raju, G.V.S., Hernandez, G., Zou, Q.: Quality of service routing in ad hoc networks. In: IEEE Wireless Communications and Networking Conference, vol. 1, pp. 263–265 (2000)
20. Pedrycz, W., Gomide, F.: An introduction to fuzzy sets: analysis and design (complex adaptive systems). MIT Press, Cambridge (1998)
21. Buckley, J.J., Eslami, E., Esfandiar, E.: An introduction to fuzzy logic and fuzzy sets (advances in soft computing). Physica Verlag (2002)
22. Park, I., Kim, J., London, I.P.: Blocking Expanding Ring Search Algorithm for Efficient energy Consumption in Mobile Ad Hoc Networks. In: Proceedings of the WONS, Les Menuires, France, pp. 185–190 (2006)
23. NS-2 Manual (2009),
    http://www.isi.edu/nsnam/ns/nsdocumentation.htm

Pattern Synthesis Using Fuzzy Partitions of the Feature Set for Nearest Neighbor Classifier Design

Pulabaigari Viswanath*, S. Chennakesalu, R. Rajkumar, and M. Raja Sekhar

Department of Computer Science and Engineering,
Rajeev Gandhi Memorial College of Engineering & Technology,
Nandyal - 518501, A.P., India
{viswanath.pulabaigari,schennakesavcse,m.rajasekhar.cse}@gmail.com,
rajsri1229@yahoo.co.in
https://sites.google.com/site/viswanathpulabaigari/

Abstract. Nearest neighbor classifiers require a larger training set in order to achieve a better classification accuracy. For a higher dimensional data, if the training set size is small, it suffers from the curse of dimensionality effect and performance gets degraded. Partition based pattern synthesis is an existing technique of generating a larger set of artificial training patterns based on a chosen partition of the feature set. If the blocks of the partition are statistically independent then the quality of synthetic patterns generated is high. But, such a partition, often does not exist for real world problems. So, approximate ways of generating a partition based on correlation coefficient values between pairs of features were used earlier in some studies. That is, an approximate hard partition, where each feature belongs to exactly one cluster (block) of the partition was used for doing the synthesis. The current paper proposes an improvement over this. Instead of having a hard approximate partition, a soft approximate partition based on fuzzy set theory could be beneficial. The present paper proposes such a fuzzy partitioning method of the feature set called fuzzy partition around medoids (fuzzy-PAM). Experimentally, using some standard data-sets, it is demonstrated that the fuzzy partition based synthetic patters are better as for as the classification accuracy is concerned.

Keywords: Pattern synthesis, fuzzy partition, nearest neighbor classifier, partition around medoids.

1 Introduction

Nearest neighbor classifier (NNC) and its variants like k-nearest neighbor classifier (k-NNC) are widely used and are well studied [6]. Theoretically, it is shown that the error rate of NNC is bounded by twice the Bayes error rate when the

---

* Corresponding author.

C. Sombattheera et al. (Eds.): MIWAI 2011, LNAI 7080, pp. 124–135, 2011.
© Springer-Verlag Berlin Heidelberg 2011

training set size is infinity [5]. Similarly, k-NNC, asymptotically is equivalent to the Bayes classifier [7].

Curse of dimensionality effect [3] is a problem because of which, when the dimensionality is large, with a limited training set, the classifier becomes a biased one, resulting in increased error rates. The curse of dimensionality refers to the exponential growth of hyper-volume as a function of dimensionality [4].

Obtaining a larger training set is difficult in some real world problems, like emotion recognition from speech signals, hand-drawn shape recognition, etc., where human beings have to generate the examples. As for nearest neighbor based classifiers, it requires to store the training set and search the training set. So, its classification time complexity and space complexity, both are $O(n)$, where n is the training set size.

Pattern synthesis [14,13,15,12,11] is a technique of generating *artificial (synthetic)* patterns from the given training patterns(original training patterns)[1]. Several studies shows that having a larger synthetic training set is beneficial. A bootstrapping method given by Hamamoto *et al.* [8] which generates new training examples by locally combining original training samples. NNC with bootstrapped training set is shown to perform better.

Partition based pattern synthesis [14], which is described in detail in the following sections, generates artificial patterns for a class based on a chosen partition of the feature set (which is specific for the chosen class). If the blocks of the partition are statistically independent for the given class, then the synthetic patterns generated are from the same distribution as the original patterns. This gives a quality measure for the synthetic patterns. But, very often, for real world problems, such a partition of the feature set does not exist. Partition based pattern synthesis finds an approximate hard partition by using correlation coefficient between pairs of features, and by employing *average linkage* [7] clustering method. The present paper, proposes an improvement over this, where (i) a fuzzy Partition Around Medoids (fuzzy-PAM) is employed to derive a fuzzy partition of the feature set, (ii) a fuzzy partition based synthesis method to generate synthetic patterns, and (iii) a greedy divide and conquer based nearest neighbors classifier, which, for a given test pattern, does classification in $O(n)$ time, where n is the number of given original patterns. This is done in a similar way, as done in [14]. Note that, the size of the synthetic training set is $O(n^p)$, where p is the number of blocks of the partition. Experimental studies are done with several standard data-sets, and it is shown that, fuzzy partition based pattern synthesis, often gives better classification accuracy than hard partition based pattern synthesis.

Partition based pattern synthesis [14] is renamed as *hard partition based pattern synthesis*, and the proposed method of this paper is called *fuzzy partition based pattern synthesis*.

The rest of the paper is organized as follows. Notation and definitions used are described in Section 2. Section 3 describes partition based pattern synthesis,

---

[1] The given training patterns, to distinguish from the synthetic training patters, are called *original* training patterns.

using both hard and soft (fuzzy) partitions. Section 4 describes partition finding methods where the proposed fuzzy-PAM method is described which finds a fuzzy clustering of the feature set. Section 5 presents nearest neighbor based classifiers which uses synthetic training sets. Section 6 describes about the experimental studies performed. Finally, Section 7 concludes the paper.

2 Notation and Definitions

Notation and definitions used are similar to that used in [14] and are described below.

Pattern: A pattern (data instance) is described as an assignment of values $X = (x_1, \ldots, x_d)$ to a set of features $F = (f_1, \ldots, f_d)$. $X[f_i]$ is the value of the feature f_i in the instance X. That is, if $X = (x_1, \ldots, x_d)$, then $X[f_i] = x_i$.

Sub-pattern: Let A be some subset of F and X be a feature-vector. Then, we use X_A to denote the projection of X onto the features in A. X_A is called a sub-pattern of X.

Set of sub-patterns: Let $\mathcal{Z}$ be a set of patterns. Then $\mathcal{Z}_B = \{Z_B \mid Z \in \mathcal{Z}\}$ is called the set of sub-patterns of $\mathcal{Z}$ with respect to the subset of features B.

Set of classes: $\Omega = \{\omega_1, \omega_2, \ldots, \omega_c\}$ is the set of classes.

Set of training patterns: $\mathcal{X}$ is the set of all training patterns.
$\mathcal{X}^l$ is the set of training patterns for class ω_l.
$\mathcal{X} = \mathcal{X}^1 \cup \mathcal{X}^2 \cup \ldots \cup \mathcal{X}^c$.

Hard Partition: $\pi = \{B_1, B_2, \ldots, B_p\}$ is a partition of F, i.e.,
$B_i \subseteq F$, $\forall i$,
$\bigcup_i B_i = F$, and $B_i \cap B_j = \emptyset$, if $i \neq j$, $\forall i$, $\forall j$.

Fuzzy Partition: Assuming there are p blocks, the ith block is described by a membership function $\mu_i : F \to [0, 1]$, such that $\sum_{i=1}^{p} \mu_i(f) = 1$, where f is a feature in F. So, the fuzzy partition is represented by $\mu = (\mu_1, \mu_2, \ldots, \mu_p)$. Further, $\mu_i(f_j)$ is denoted by μ_{ij}. So, each block μ_i of the partition is represented by $\mu_i = (\mu_{i1}, \mu_{i2}, \ldots, \mu_{id})$. A block of a fuzzy partition is called a fuzzy-block.

Fuzzy sub-pattern: Let $\mu_i = (\mu_{i1}, \mu_{i2}, \ldots, \mu_{id})$ be a fuzzy-block of a fuzzy partition. Then, for pattern X, X_{μ_i} is a fuzzy sub-pattern such that $X_{\mu_i}[f_j] = \mu_{ij} x_j$. That is, $X_{\mu_i} = (\mu_{i1} x_1, \mu_{i2} x_2, \ldots, \mu_{id} x_d)$ is a fuzzy sub-pattern. Note that, a fuzzy sub-pattern is a d dimensional pattern.

3 Partition Based Pattern Synthesis

3.1 Hard Partition Based Pattern Synthesis [14]

Let $X^1, \ldots, X^p$ be p training patterns (need not be distinct) in a class ω_l, where $\omega_i \in \Omega$ and $\pi = \{B_1, \ldots, B_p\}$ be a partition of F. Then $X = (X_{B_1}^1, X_{B_2}^2, \ldots, X_{B_p}^p)$ is a synthetic pattern belonging to the same class, i.e., ω_l, such that, $X[f_i] = X^j[f_i]$ if $f_i \in B_j$, for $1 \leq i \leq d$ and $1 \leq j \leq p$. Note that, a pattern Y can be equivalently represented as $(Y_{B_1}, Y_{B_2}, \ldots, Y_{B_p})$. That is, all projections of Y can be combined to get back that pattern.

Formally, for a given class of patterns $\mathcal{X}^l$ and for a given partition $\pi = \{B_1, \ldots, B_p\}$, $SS_\pi(\mathcal{X}^l) = \{(X_{B_1}^1, X_{B_2}^2, \ldots, X_{B_p}^p) \mid X^1, \ldots, X^p \in \mathcal{X}^l\}$ is the synthetic set of patterns for the class.

Example 1: Let $F = (f_1, f_2, f_3, f_4)$. Let the partition chosen for the class ω_l is $\{\{f_1, f_2\}, \{f_3, f_4\}\}$. Let $\mathcal{X}^l = \{(1, 2, 3, 4), (10, 11, 12, 13), (5, 6, 7, 8)\}$. Considering $X^1 = (1, 2, 3, 4)$ and $X^2 = (10, 11, 12, 13)$, the synthetic pattern that can be generated is: $(1, 2, 12, 13)$. We get, $SS_{\pi_l}(\mathcal{X}^l) = \{(1, 2, 3, 4), (1, 2, 12, 13), (1, 2, 7, 8), (10, 11, 3, 4), (10, 11, 12, 13), (10, 11, 7, 8), (5, 6, 3, 4), (5, 6, 12, 13), (5, 6, 7, 8)\}$, which is the entire synthetic set.

3.2 Fuzzy Partition Based Pattern Synthesis

Let $X^1, \ldots, X^p$ be p training patterns (need not be distinct) in a class ω_l, where $\omega_l \in \Omega$ and let the fuzzy partition, consisting of p blocks, be $\mu = (\mu_1, \mu_2, \ldots, \mu_p)$. See Section 2 for the notation used. Then, X is a synthetic pattern which belongs to the same class (*i.e.*, ω_l), such that,

$$X[f_i] = \mu_{1i}X^1[f_i] + \mu_{2i}X^2[f_i] + \cdots + \mu_{pi}X^p[f_i], \text{ for } i = 1 \text{ to } d.$$

So, $X = X_{\mu_1}^1 + X_{\mu_2}^2 + \cdots + X_{\mu_p}^p$. Formally, for a given class of patterns $\mathcal{X}^l$ and for a given fuzzy partition $\mu = (\mu_1, \mu_2, \ldots, \mu_p)$, $FSS_\mu(\mathcal{X}^l) = \{X = X_{\mu_1}^1 + X_{\mu_2}^2 + \cdots + X_{\mu_p}^p \mid X^1, \ldots, X^p \in \mathcal{X}^l\}$ is the synthetic set of patterns for the class.

Example 2: Considering the data given in Example 1, let the fuzzy partition chosen for the class be (μ_1, μ_2), where $\mu_1 = (1, 0.9, 0.2, 0)$ and $\mu_2 = (0, 0.1, 0.8, 1)$. Considering $X^1 = (1, 2, 3, 4)$ and $X^2 = (10, 11, 12, 13)$, the synthetic pattern generated is $X_{\mu_1}^1 + X_{\mu_2}^2 = (1, 1.8, 0.6, 0) + (0, 1.1, 9.6, 13) = (1, 2.9, 10.2, 13)$. The entire synthetic set is, $FSS_\mu(\mathcal{X}^l) = \{(1, 2, 3, 4), (1, 2.9, 10.2, 13), (1, 2.4, 6.2, 8), (10, 10.1, 4.8, 4), (10, 11, 12, 13), (10, 10.5, 8, 8), (5, 5.6, 3.8, 4), (5, 6.5, 11, 13), (5, 6, 7, 8)\}$.

Example 3: Figure 1 illustrates hard and fuzzy partition based synthesis for hand written digit data. Here, a digit is drawn on a 16×12 grid. If ink is present in a cell, the cell will have value 1 (black color), otherwise 0 (white color). Figure 1(a) shows two given images for digit '1'. Each pattern is represented as a 192 dimensional binary valued tuple. First row of the image forms the first 12 features $f_1, f_2, \ldots, f_{12}$, second row forms features $f_{13}, \ldots, f_{24}$, and so on, to form the 192 dimensional pattern. Hard partition based synthesis is done by taking a two block partition, such that first 96 features are in one block, the remaining are in the other block. Two synthetic patterns generated using hard partition based synthesis are shown in Figure 1(b). For doing fuzzy partition based synthesis, a fuzzy partition (μ_1, μ_2) is taken as $\mu_1 = (0.6, 0.6, \ldots, 0.6)$ and $\mu_2 = (0.4, 0.4, \ldots, 0.4)$. Fuzzy synthetic patterns, now can have non-binary values, and hence are shown as appropriate gray shades. See Figure 1(c).

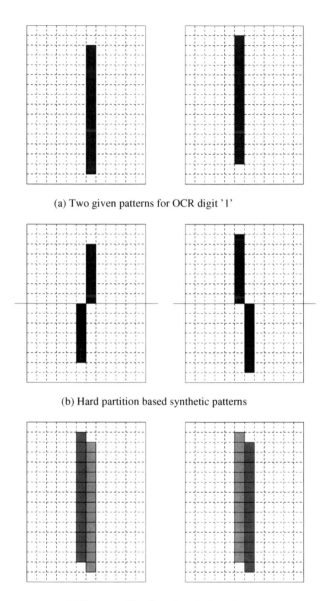

(a) Two given patterns for OCR digit '1'

(b) Hard partition based synthetic patterns

(c) Fuzzy partition based synthetic patterns

Fig. 1. Illustration of synthetic patterns with OCR data. In (a) and (b), each cell is either black or white. Whereas in (c) each cell could be any gray level (gray shade) between black and white.

4   Partition Finding Methods

Paper [14] shows that, for hard partition based synthesis, if the blocks of the partition are statistically independent then the synthetic set is simply a larger set, that can be seen as generated from the same distribution as the original training set. In real world problems, such a partition may not exist at all. So, the paper [14] gave an approximate way of finding a hard partition based on correlation coefficient between pairs of features. Correlation coefficient, $Cor(f_i, f_j)$, between two features f_i and f_j is,

$$Cor(f_i, f_j) = \frac{\text{Co-variance}(f_i, f_j)}{\text{Stddev}(f_i) \ \text{Stddev}(f_j)},$$

where $\text{Stddev}(f_i)$ is the standard deviation of feature f_i. Paper [14] uses average-linkage clustering method [7] to find a hard partition of the feature set F.

This paper proposes to use a fuzzy partitioning method called fuzzy partitioning around medoids (fuzzy-PAM) which is similar to *partitioning around medoids (PAM)* method [9] and *fuzzy k-means* clustering method [7] which are used to find a clustering of a data-set. fuzzy-PAM, in order to find a p block fuzzy partition (assuming $p \leq d$, where d is the number of features), finds p features from F, denoted as $f^{(1)}, f^{(2)}, \ldots, f^{(p)}$ such that

$$J(\{f^{(1)}, f^{(2)}, \ldots, f^{(p)}\}) = \sum_{i=1}^{p} \sum_{j=1}^{d} (\mu_{ij})^b |Cor(f^{(i)}, f_j)|$$

is maximized, where $1 \leq b < \infty$ is the fuzzifier, and

$$\mu_{ij} = \frac{|Cor(f^{(i)}, f_j)|^{1/(b-1)}}{\sum_{r=1}^{p} |Cor(f^{(r)}, f_j)|^{1/(b-1)}}.$$

Algorithm 1 gives the fuzzy-PAM method which finds a fuzzy partition of the feature set F and is similar to Partition Around Medoids (PAM) method, which is a k-medoid clustering method [9]. It starts with a randomly chosen p features to represent the p medoids. A medoid is swapped with a non-medoid, if the criterion J increases. The method ends, if no such swap exists, otherwise continues to do successive swaps.

5   Nearest Neighbor (NN) Classification Methods

This Section presents two NN-based methods to work with synthetic training sets generated using fuzzy partition based pattern synthesis, which are, (i) NNC(SP) and (ii) GDC-k-NNC. NNC(SP) explicitly generates all the synthetic patterns first and then implements k-NNC method using the synthetic data-sets as training sets. Even-though, this approach is simple, space and time requirements, both are $O(n^p)$, where p is the number of blocks in the fuzzy-partition and n is

---

Algorithm 1. Fuzzy-PAM($\{Cor(f_i, f_j)|1 \leq i, j \leq d\}$, p, m)

{Inputs are correlation coefficients between all pairs of features, number of blocks (p) and the parameter m.}

Let $j = 0$.

Let $S_j = \{f^{(i_1)}, f^{(i_2)}, \ldots, f^{(i_p)}\}$ be a randomly chosen p distinct features from F.

Find a feature $f^{(i_k)} \in S_j$ and a feature $f_l \in F - S_j$ such that $J((S_j - \{f^{(i_k)}\}) \cup \{f_l\}) > J(S_j)$.

while such a pair $(f^{(i_k)}, f_l)$ exists **do**

    $S_{j+1} = (S_j - \{f^{(i_k)}\}) \cup \{f_l\}$.

    $j = j + 1$.

    Find a feature $f^{(i_k)} \in S_j$ and a feature $f_l \in F - S_j$ such that $J((S_j - \{f^{(i_k)}\}) \cup \{f_l\}) > J(S_j)$.

end while

Let $S = S_{j-1} = \{f^{(1)}, f^{(2)}, \ldots, f^{(p)}\}$.

for $i = 1$ to p **do**

    for $j = 1$ to d **do**

        Find $\mu_{ij} = \dfrac{|Cor(f^{(i)}, f_j)|^{1/(b-1)}}{\sum_{r=1}^{P} |Cor(f^{(r)}, f_j)|^{1/(b-1)}}$.

    end for

end for

Output $\{\mu_{ij}|1 \leq i \leq p \text{ and } 1 \leq j \leq d\}$.

---

the number of original training patterns. Hence a greedy k-NNC method, which uses divide-and-conquer strategy, called GDC-k-NNC is proposed. This is similar to the greedy method that uses hard-partition based synthetic patterns which is given in [14]. Space and time complexity, both are $O(n)$ for GDC-k-NNC.

5.1 Greedy Divide-and-Conquer k-NNC (GDC-k-NNC)

From each class of synthetic patterns, this method, first finds k representatives called k *local-greedy-neighbors* of the given test pattern T in that class. Then it finds, k global greedy neighbors from the union of all local-greedy-neighbors.

1. Find k local-greedy-neighbors of the test pattern T in each class of synthetic patterns. Let $\mathcal{G}^l$ be the set of local-greedy-neighbors for class ω_l, for $1 \leq l \leq c$.
2. Find k global greedy-neighbors from union of all local greedy-neighbors, that is from $\mathcal{G}^1 \cup \ldots \cup \mathcal{G}^c$.
3. Classify T to the class based on majority vote among the k global greedy-neighbors.

First step in GDC-k-NNC is elaborated in Algorithm 2.

Space and time requirements of GDC-k-NNC. Assuming that k is a small constant when compared with n, the time required to find k nearest neighbors is $O(nk)$, which is $O(n)$. Since there are p blocks, for each block, for each class, k nearest neighbors needs to be found, so the time complexity is $O(np)$. Since, p is a small constant, it is $O(n)$ only. Similarly the space requirement is $O(n)$ only.

Algorithm 2. Step 1 of GDC-k-NNC( )

{ Let T be the given test pattern, $\mathcal{X}^l$ be the set of given original training patterns belonging to the class ω_l, for $1 \leq l \leq c$. }

for each class ω_l, *i.e.*, for $l = 1$ to c **do**

    for each fuzzy-block μ_i, *i.e.*, for $i = 1$ to p **do**

        Find k nearest neighbors of T_{μ_i} in $\mathcal{X}^l_{\mu_i} = \{X_{\mu_i} \mid X \in \mathcal{X}^l\}$. Let these k nearest neighbors be $\mathcal{V}_i = \{X^{i1}_{\mu_i}, X^{i2}_{\mu_i}, \ldots, X^{ik}_{\mu_i}\}$, and let $X^{ij}_{\mu_i}$ be the jth nearest neighbor.

    end for

    $\mathcal{G}^l = \{(X^{11}_{\mu_1} + X^{21}_{\mu_2} + \cdots + X^{p1}_{\mu_p}), (X^{12}_{\mu_1} + X^{22}_{\mu_2} + \cdots + X^{p2}_{\mu_p}), \ldots, (X^{1k}_{\mu_1} + X^{2k}_{\mu_2} + \cdots + X^{pk}_{\mu_p})\}$

    is taken to be the set of k greedy-neighbors in the class ω_l.

end for

Output $\mathcal{G}^l$, for $1 \leq l \leq c$.

---

6 Experiments

This section describes the experimental studies performed.

6.1 Data-Sets

Seven data-sets are used for experimental study. These are OCR, Hand-drawn Symbols, WINE, VOWEL, THYROID, GLASS and PENDIGITS data-sets. Except OCR and Hand-drawn Symbols data-sets, all are available at the UCI machine learning repository [10]. OCR data-set is also used in [2,1,14]. The properties of the data-sets are given in Table 1. Hand-drawn symbols data-set is generated by drawing 16 different symbols (see Figure 2). Zernike moments are used (after scale and translation normalization) to represent the symbols, since they possess rotation invariance. Note that Hand-drawn Symbol recognition should be invariant to scale, translation, rotation and mirror-reflection. Hence an appropriate representation needs to be chosen. In this paper, we used magnitude of the Zernike moments. For OCR, VOWEL, THYROID and PENDIGITS data-sets, the training and test sets are separately available. For the remaining data-sets 100 patterns are chosen randomly as the training patterns and the remaining as the test patterns. All the data-sets have only numeric valued features. The OCR data-set has binary discrete features, while the others have continuous valued features. Except OCR and Hand-drawn Symbols data-sets, all other data-sets are normalized to have zero mean and unit variance for each feature. Distance measure used is the Euclidean distance.

6.2 Classifiers for Comparison

The classifiers chosen for comparison purposes are as follows.

NNC: This is the conventional nearest neighbor (NN) classifier with original training patterns. Space and time requirements are $O(n)$ where n is the number of original training patterns.

Table 1. Properties of the data-sets used

Data-set	Number of features	Number of classes	Number of training examples	Number of test examples
OCR	192	10	6670	3333
Hand-drawn Symbols	8	16	1200	400
WINE	13	3	100	78
VOWEL	10	11	528	462
THYROID	21	3	3772	3428
GLASS	9	7	100	114
PENDIGITS	16	10	7494	3498

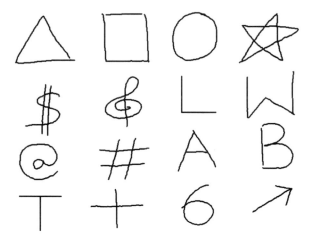

Fig. 2. Hand-drawn symbols used for experimental study

k-NNC: This is conventional k-NN classifier with original training patterns. Three-fold cross validation is done to choose the k value. Space and classification time requirements of the method are both $O(n)$ when k is assumed to be a constant when compared with n.

NNC with bootstrapped training set(NNC(BS)): We used the bootstrap method given in [8] to generate an artificial training set. The bootstrapping method is as follows. Let X be a training pattern and let $X_1, \ldots, X_r$ be its r nearest neighbors in its class. Then $X' = (\sum_{i=1}^{r} X_i)/r$ is the artificial pattern generated for X. Bootstrapping step requires $O(n^2)$ time, whereas space and classification time requirements are both $O(n)$.

GDC-k-NNC(Hard-partition): In this method a hard partition of the set of features is found by using average-linkage clustering method as given in [14]. This method is briefly explained in Section 5. The classifier used is Greedy Divide-and-Conquer k-NNC method given in [14]. Space and time

Table 2. A comparison between the classifiers (showing classification accuracy (%)). Values for parameters p and b are also shown for methods that uses synthetic patterns.

Data-set	NNC	k-NNC	NNC(BS)	GDC-k-NNC (hard-partition)	GDC-k-NNC (soft-partition)	NNC(SP) (soft-partition)
OCR	91.12	92.68	92.88	94.89 (p = 3)	95.01 (p=3,b=2)	94.92 (p=3,b=2)
Hand-drawn Symbols	79.20	87.80	88.15	89.60 (p = 2)	91.20 (p=2,b=2)	90.40 (p=2,b=2)
WINE	94.87	96.15	97.44	98.72 (p = 2)	98.72 (p=2,b=2)	98.72 (p=2,b=2)
VOWEL	56.28	60.17	57.36	60.17 (p = 1)	61.03 (p=2,b=2.1)	60.61 (p=2,b=2.1)
THYROID	93.14	94.40	94.57	97.23 (p = 2)	97.66 (p=3,b=2)	97.43 (p=3,b=2)
GLASS	71.93	71.93	71.93	72.06 (p = 1)	75.43 (p=2,b=2.1)	73.68 (p=2,b=2.1)
PENDIGITS	96.08	97.54	97.54	97.54 (p = 1)	97.77 (p=2,b=2)	97.65 (p=2,b=2)

requirements of this method are $O(n)$. The parameters are chosen as done for NNC(SP).

GDC-k-NNC(Fuzzy-partition): In this method a fuzzy partition of the set of features is found by using fuzzy-PAM clustering method as given in Algorithm 1. Space and time requirements of this method are $O(n)$. The parameters are chosen as done for NNC(SP), as given below.

NNC(SP): This method first generates the synthetic set using the fuzzy partition based pattern synthesis. Then k-NNC is done by using the synthetic set as the training set. This method has space and time requirements $O(n^p)$. The number of blocks (*i.e.*, the parameter p), the fuzzifier (*i.e.*, the parameter b), and the k value used are chosen by performing three-fold cross validations. Best b value obtained is around 2 for all data-sets.

6.3   Experimental Results

Table 2 shows the comparison between various classifiers on various data-sets. It is observed that GDC-k-NNC using fuzzy partitions outperforms all other listed classifiers, except in case of the WINE data-set, where it shows same classification accuracy as that of the GDC-k-NNC which uses hard partitions.

Figures 3 gives the comparison of classification accuracy with respect to the number of blocks (p) used in the synthesis for the OCR data-set.

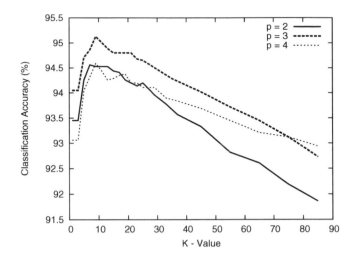

Fig. 3. Results of GDC-k-NNC (soft-partition): CA vs. k for various p values, for OCR data-set

7   Conclusions

Using a larger synthetic training set is better than using the given smaller training set. The paper [14] presented such a synthetic set generation method which
is based on hard partitions of the feature set. This method is called partition
based pattern synthesis. It is shown that, if the blocks of the partition are statistically independent then the synthetic set is from the same distribution as
the given data-set. Very often, such a partition does not exist for real world
data-sets. Hence an approximate hard partitioning method using correlation coefficient between features is proposed in [14]. The present paper, proposed to use
a fuzzy partition of the feature set and fuzzy partition around medoids (fuzzy-
PAM) method is given for this. Experimentally, fuzzy partition based synthetic
patterns are shown to be better (as for as classification accuracy) than hard
partition based synthetic patterns.

Acknowledgments. This work is sponsored by an AICTE Project under RPS
scheme. Ref: "F.No: 8023/BOR/RID/RPS-51/2009-10".

References

1. Ananthanarayana, V., Murty, M., Subramanian, D.: An incremental data mining
   algorithm for compact realization of prototypes. Pattern Recognition 34, 2249–2251
   (2001)
2. Babu, T.R., Murty, M.N.: Comparison of genetic algorithms based prototype selection schemes. Pattern Recognition 34, 523–525 (2001)

3. Bellman, R.: Adaptive Control Processes: A Guided Tour. Princeton University Press, New Jersey (1961)
4. Bishop, C.: Neural Networks for Pattern Recognition. Clarendon Press, Oxford (1995)
5. Cover, T., Hart, P.: Nearest neighbor pattern classification. IEEE Transactions on Information Theory 13(1), 21–27 (1967)
6. Dasarathy, B.V.: Nearest neighbor (NN) norms: NN pattern classification techniques. IEEE Computer Society Press, Los Alamitos (1991)
7. Duda, R.O., Hart, P.E., Stork, D.G.: Pattern Classification, 2nd edn. A Wiley-interscience Publication, John Wiley & Sons (2000)
8. Hamamoto, Y., Uchimura, S., Tomita, S.: A bootstrap technique for nearest neighbor classifier design. IEEE Transactions on Pattern Analysis and Machine Intelligence 19(1), 73–79 (1997)
9. Han, J., Kamber, M.: Data Mining: Concepts and Techniques. Academic Press (2001)
10. Murphy, P.M.: UCI Repository of Machine Learning Databases. Department of Information and Computer Science, University of California, Irvine, CA (2000), http://www.ics.uci.edu/mlearn/MLRepository.html
11. Viswanath, P., Murty, M., Bhatnagar, S.: Fusion of multiple approximate nearest neighbor classifiers for fast and efficient classification. Information Fusion 5(4), 239–250 (2004)
12. Viswanath, P., Murty, M., Bhatnagar, S.: A pattern synthesis technique with an efficient nearest neighbor classifier for binary pattern recognition. In: Proceedings of the 17 th International Conference on Pattern Recognition (ICPR 2004), Cambridge, UK, vol. 4, pp. 416–419 (2004)
13. Viswanath, P., Murty, M., Bhatnagar, S.: Overlap pattern synthesis with an efficient nearest neighbor classifier. Pattern Recognition 38, 1187–1195 (2005)
14. Viswanath, P., Murty, M., Bhatnagar, S.: Partition based pattern synthesis technique with efficient algorithms for nearest neighbor classification. Pattern Recognition Letters 27, 1714–1724 (2006)
15. Viswanath, P., Murty, M., Kambala, S.: An Efficient Parzen-Window Based Network Intrusion Detector Using a Pattern Synthesis Technique. In: Pal, S.K., Bandyopadhyay, S., Biswas, S. (eds.) PREMI 2005. LNCS, vol. 3776, pp. 799–804. Springer, Heidelberg (2005)

Data Clustering Using Modified Fuzzy-PSO (MFPSO)

Suresh Chandra Satapathy[1,*], Sovan Kumar Patnaik[2],
Ch. Dipti.Prava. Dash[3], and Soumya Sahoo[4]

[1] Anil Neerukonda Institute of Technology and Sciences, Vishakapatnam, India
sureshsatapathy@ieee.org
[2] Directorate of Horticulture. Odisha, Bhubaneswar
patnaiksovankumar@yahoo.co.in
[3] The Panchayat Samit, Satyabadi
ch.dipti@gmail.com
[4] C.V. Raman College of Engineering, Bhubaneswar
ritun_08@yahoo.co.in

Abstract. This paper presents an efficient hybrid method, namely fuzzy particle swarm optimization (MFPSO) to solve the fuzzy clustering problem, especially for large sizes. When the problem becomes large, the FCM algorithm may result in uneven distribution of data, making it difficult to find an optimal solution in reasonable amount of time. The PSO algorithm does find a good or near-optimal solution in reasonable time .In our work it is shown that its performance may be improved by seeding the initial swarm with the result of the c-means algorithm. Various clustering simulations are experimentally compared with the FCM algorithm in order to illustrate the efficiency and ability of the proposed algorithms.

Keywords: Particle Swarm Optimization, Cluster Centroid, Fuzzy C-means.

1   Introduction

Data clustering is the process of grouping together similar multi-dimensional data vectors into a number of clusters. Clustering algorithms have been applied to a wide range of problems, including exploratory data analysis, data mining [1], image segmentation [2] and mathematical programming [3,4]. Clustering techniques have been used successfully to address the scalability problem of machine learning and data mining algorithms. Clustering algorithms can be grouped into two main classes of algorithms, namely supervised and unsupervised. unsupervised clustering. Many unsupervised clustering algorithms have been developed one such algorithm is Kmeans which is simple, straightforward and is based on the firm foundation of analysis of variances. The main drawback of the K-means algorithm is that the result is sensitive to the selection of the initial cluster centroids and may converge to the local optima[5] . Fuzzy algorithms can assign data object partially to multiple clusters. The degree of membership in the fuzzy clusters depends on the closeness of

---

* Sr Member IEEE.

C. Sombattheera et al. (Eds.): MIWAI 2011, LNAI 7080, pp. 136–146, 2011.
© Springer-Verlag Berlin Heidelberg 2011

the data object to the cluster centers. The most popular fuzzy clustering algorithm is fuzzy c-means (FCM) which introduced by Bezdek [6] in 1974 and now it is widely used. Fuzzy c-means clustering is an effective algorithm, but the random selection in center points makes iterative process falling into the local optimal solution easily. For solving this problem, recently evolutionary algorithms such as genetic algorithm (GA), simulated annealing (SA), ant colony optimization (ACO), and particle swarm optimization (PSO) have been successfully applied. Particle Swarm Optimization (PSO) is a population based optimization tool, which could be implemented and applied easily to solve various function optimization problems, or the problems that can be transformed to function optimization problems [7].

In this work we have implemented a modified Fuzzy-PSO for effective data clustering. The proposed approach yield better clustering results when the data set size grows in terms of more number of records and clusters. The simulation results compare the basic Fuzzy C-means (FCM) with our suggested approach. The results clearly reveal the claim mentioned above.

The rest of the paper is organized in the following manner. In Section 2, we investigate the related works and section 3 introduces k-mean, section 4 tells about fuzzy c-means clustering, in Section 5 PSO algorithm for clustering is discussed; Section 6 presents our hybrid clustering method fuzzy-PSO techniques , and section 7 reports the experimental results. Finally section 8 concludes this work.

2   Related Works

There are some works from the literature that modify the particle swarm optimization algorithm to solve clustering problems. The PSO algorithm was used for solving clustering tasks. Runkler and Katz [10] introduced two new methods for minimizing the reformulated objective functions of the fuzzy c–means clustering model by particle swarm optimization: PSO–V and PSO–U. In PSO–V each particle represents a component of a cluster center, and in PSO–U each particle represents an unscaled and unnormalized membership value. In [11] In order to overcome the shortcomings of Fuzzy C-means, a PSO-based fuzzy clustering algorithm is discussed. The proposed algorithm uses the capacity of global search in PSO algorithm to overcome the shortcomings of FCM. Gan et al. [12] proposed the genetic fuzzy k-Modes algorithm for clustering categorical data sets. They treated the fuzzy k-Modes clustering as an optimization problem and used Genetic algorithm to solve the problem in order to obtain globally optimal solution. To speed up the convergence process of the algorithm, they used the one-step fuzzy k-Modes algorithm in the crossover process instead of the traditional crossover operator. In [13] authors used a Fuzzy C-Mean algorithm based on Picard iteration and PSO (PPSO-FCM), to overcome the shortcomings of FCM. Also in [14] authors hybridized PSO algorithm with FCM algorithm to find more appropriate cluster centers.

3   Fuzzy C-Mean Algorithms

Fuzzy c-means partitions set of n objects $o=\{o_1,o_2,...o_n\}$ in R^d dimensional space into c ($1< c < n$) fuzzy clusters with $Z = \{Z_1,Z_2,...Z_c\}$ cluster centers or centroids.

The fuzzy clustering of objects is described by a fuzzy matrix μ with n row and c columns in which n is the number of data objects and c is the number of clusters μ_{ij}, the element in the ith row and jth column in μ, indicates the degree of association or membership function of the ith object with the jth cluster. The characters of μ are as follows:

$$\mu_{ij} \in [0,1] \qquad i = 1,2,\ldots\ldots,n; \quad j = 1,2,\ldots.,c \tag{1}$$

$$\sum_{j=1}^{c} \mu_{ij} = 1 \qquad i = 1,2,\ldots\ldots,n \tag{2}$$

$$0 < \sum_{j=1}^{c} \mu_{ij} < n \qquad i = 1,2,\ldots\ldots,c \tag{3}$$

The objective function of FCM algorithm is to minimize the Eq. (4):

$$j_m = \sum_{j=1}^{c}\sum_{i=1}^{n} \mu_{ij}^m d_{ij} \tag{4}$$

$$d_{ij} = \|o_i - z_j\| \tag{5}$$

in which, m (m >1) is a scalar termed the weighting exponent and controls the fuzziness of the resulting clusters and d_{ij} is the Euclidian distance from object o_i to the cluster center z_j The z_j, centroid of the jth cluster, is obtained using Eq. (6).

$$z_j = \frac{\sum_{i=}^{n} \mu_{ij}^m o_i}{\sum_{i=1}^{n} \mu_{ij}^m} \tag{6}$$

Fuzzy c- mean Algorithm

1. Select , m (m >1); initialize the membership function values μ_{ij} , $i = 1,2,\ldots,n$; $j = 1,2,\ldots.,c$

2. Compute the cluster centers z_j , j= 1,2,.....,c according to Eq. (6).

3. Compute Euclidian distance d_{ij} i= 1,2,....,n; j= 1,2,.....,c

4. Update the membership function μ_{ij} , i= 1,2,....,n; j =1,2,.....,c according to Eq. (7).

$$\mu_{ij} = \frac{1}{\sum_{k=1}^{c} \left(\dfrac{d_{ij}}{d_{ik}}\right)^{\frac{2}{m-1}}} \tag{7}$$

5. If not converged, go to step 2.

4   Particle Swarm Optimization

The PSO method is an optimization method introduced by Eberhart and Kennedy in 1995 [7]. It is inspired by the social behavior of flock of birds and fish. The method uses a swarm of agents named particles which cooperate to find an optimal solution to a problem. Each particle corresponds to a feasible solution and represents a point in multidimensional space. New solutions are discovering by the movement of the particles from a location to another.

The algorithmic flow in PSO starts with a population of particles whose positions represent the potential solutions for the studied problem, and velocities are randomly initialized in the search space. In each iteration, the search for optimal position is performed by updating the particle velocities and positions. Also in each iteration, the fitness value of each particle's position is determined using a fitness function. The velocity of each particle is updated using two best positions, personal best position and global best position. A particle's velocity and position are updated as follows.

$$V(t+1) = \omega V(t) + c1 \ r1(pbest(t) - X(t)) + c2r2(gbest(t) - X(t)) \quad (8)$$

$$X(t+1) = X(t) + V(t+1) \quad (9)$$

Where X and V are position and velocity of particle respectively and w is inertia weight, c1 and c2 arc positive constants, called acceleration coefficients which control the influence of pbest and gbest on the search process, P is the number of particles in the swarm, r1 and r2 are random values in range [0, 1].

5   Modified Fuzzy-PSO (MFPSO)

Peng et al. [8] proposed a modified particle swarm optimization called fuzzy particle swarm optimization (MFPSO). In their proposed method the position and velocity of particles redefined to represent the fuzzy relation between variables. In this sub-section we describe this method for fuzzy clustering problem.

In MFPSO algorithm X, the position of particle, shows the fuzzy relation from set of data objects, $o = \{o_1, o_2.o_3..., o_n\}$, to set of cluster centers, $z = \{z_1, z_2,...z_c\}$ X Can be expressed as follows:

$$X = \begin{vmatrix} \mu_{11} & \cdots & \mu_{1c} \\ \vdots & \ddots & \vdots \\ \mu_{n1} & \cdots & \mu_{nc} \end{vmatrix} \quad (10)$$

In which μ_{ij} is the membership function of the ith object with the jth cluster with constraints stated in (1) and (2). Therefore we can see that the position matrix of each particle is the same as fuzzy matrixμ in FCM algorithm. Also the velocity of each particle is stated using a matrix with the size n rows and c columns the elements of which are in range [-.5, .5]. We get the equations (11) and (12) for updating the positions and velocities of the particles based on matrix operations.

$$V(t+1) = w \otimes V(t) \oplus (c1r1 \otimes (pbest \ominus X(t))) \oplus (c2r2 \otimes (gbest - X(t)))$$
(11)

$$X(t+1) = X(t) \oplus V(t+1)$$
(12)

After updating the position matrix, it may violate the constraints given in (1) and (2). So it is necessary to normalize the position matrix. First we make all the negative elements in matrix to become zero. If all elements in a row of the matrix are zero, they need to be re-evaluated using series of random numbers within the interval [0, 1] and then the matrix undergoes the following transformation without violating the constraints:

$$X_{normal} = \begin{vmatrix} \mu_{11} \Big/ \sum_{j=1}^{c} \mu_{1j} & \cdots & \mu_{1c} \Big/ \sum_{j=1}^{c} \mu_{1j} \\ \vdots & \ddots & \vdots \\ \mu_{n1} \Big/ \sum_{j=1}^{c} \mu_{nj} & \cdots & \mu_{nc} \Big/ \sum_{j=1}^{c} \mu_{nj} \end{vmatrix}$$
(13)

In MFPSO algorithm the same as other evolutionary algorithms, we need a function for evaluating the generalized solutions called fitness function. In this paper Eq. (14) is used for evaluating the solutions.

$$f(X) = \frac{K}{J_m}$$
(14)

therein K is a constant and Jm is the objective function of FCM algorithm (Eq. (4)). The smaller is Jm , the better is the clustering effect and the higher is the individual fitness $f(X)$. The MFPSO algorithm for fuzzy clustering problem can be stated as follows:

1. Initialize the parameters including population size P, c1, c2, w, and the maximum iterative count.
2. Create a swarm with P particles (X, pbest, gbest and V are $n \times c$ matrices).
3. Initialize X, V, pbest for each particle and gbest for the swarm.
4. Calculate the cluster centers for each particle using Eq. (6).
5. Calculate the fitness value of each particle using Eq. (14).
6. Calculate pbest for each particle.
7. Calculate gbest for the swarm.
8. Update the velocity matrix for each particle using Eq. (11).
9. Update the position matrix for each particle using Eq. (12).
10. If terminating condition is not met, go to step 4.

The termination condition in proposed method is the maximum number of iterations or no improvement in gbest in a number of iterations.

6   Cluster Validity

The main subject of cluster validation is "the evaluation of clustering results to find the partitioning that best fits the underlying data" .In other word cluster validity – measuring goodness of a clustering relative to others created by other clustering algorithms, or by the same algorithms using different parameter values. Hence, cluster validity approaches are approaches used to quantitatively evaluate the result of a clustering algorithm. These approaches have representative indices, called validity indices. The quality of a partition can be judged by an appropriate cluster validity index. Cluster validity indices correspond to the statistical-mathematical functions used to evaluate the results of a clustering algorithm on a quantitative basis. Generally, a cluster validity index serves two purposes. First, it can be used to determine the number of clusters, and secondly, it finds out the corresponding best partition. The traditional approach to determine the "optimum" number of clusters is to run the algorithm repetitively using different input values and select the partitioning of data resulting in the best validity measure. Two criteria that have been widely considered sufficient in measuring the quality of partitioning a data set into a number of clusters are

☐ **Compactness:** samples in one cluster should be similar to each other and different from samples in other clusters. An example of this would be the variance of a cluster.
☐ **Separation:** clusters should be well-separated from each other. An example of this criterion is the Euclidean distance between the cancroids of clusters.

There are a lot of approaches to find the best number of clusters well separated. For any partition of clusters, where ci represent the i-cluster of such partition. Here I have used Bezdek method for the purpose of cluster validation.
    A Fuzzy clustering validity function Bezdek[9] designed the partition coefficient F to measure the amount of overlap between clusters.

$$F = \frac{1}{n} \sum_{i=1}^{c} \sum_{j=1}^{n} (\mu_{ij})^2$$

In this form F is inversely proportion to the overall average overlap between pairs of fuzzy sub sets. In particular, there is no membership sharing between any pair of fuzzy clusters if F=1.Solving max_c {$max_{\Omega c}${F}} ($c = 2,3,\ldots\ldots,n-1$) is assumed to produce valid clustering of the dataset X.

7   Experimental Results

In the experiment five different data sets (iris, wine, Pima Indian Diebets, Blood Transfusion, and Glass) have been taken for observation. The resulting clusters have been validated by Bezdek index.   The MFPSO model has been designed in the in the dual core machine having 1.6 Gz speed with help of MatlabR2010a code. The details of datasets are mentioned below. The abstract of all databases has been shown in Table-1

Table 1. Description of datasets

Datasets	Instances	Features	No.of Class
Iris	150	4	3
Wine	178	13	3
Pima Indian	768	8	2
Blood Transfusion	748	5	2
Glass	214	10	6

In our experiment, we have used PSO. The details of parameters used in PSO is given in Table-2

Table 2. PSO Parameter

Parameter Name	Val
Swarm Size	20
Max iteration	100
Acceleration	1.49
Acceleration	1.49
Inertia of weight(w)	0.7

In 1st attempt, the objective function of each datasets has been optimized through FCM using the algorithm-1 and later same objective function optimized by MFPSO. The convergence value of objective function is called optimized value. In each case the compactness and the separability have been calculated at the optimized objective value. The table-3 and table-4 have shown the comparison of compactness & separability value of each dataset in FCM and MFCM respectively. The convergence of each dataset has been investigated and it is seen that for all dataset the MFCM converges faster than FCM.. The compactness and separabilty of two different models have been compared by equation (15) & (17).

$$cmp = \frac{1}{C} \sum_{1}^{C} \frac{v(C_i)}{v(X)} \tag{15}$$

$$v(X) = \sqrt{\frac{1}{N} \sum_{i=1}^{N} d^2(x_i, \bar{x})} \tag{16}$$

Where cmp =compactness, C is no of Cluster $v(C_i)$ is variance of cluster,v(X) is variance of datasets, $\bar{x}$ is the mean of X. The Separability (sep) have been determined by equation-17. Dc is the inter cluster distances.

$$sep = MAX\left\{D_C\right\} \tag{17}$$

$$\%\text{GAIN} = \frac{MFPSO-FCM}{MFPSO}*100 \tag{18}$$

Table 3. Comparison of Cluster

Data set	Compactness			
	Criterion	FCM	MFPS0	%Gain
Iris	Cluster1	17.03	18.5895	0.09
	Cluster2	18.58	21.4640	0.15
	Cluster3	24.80	28.5092	0.15
Wine	Cluster1	47.91	52.8768	0.10
	Cluster2	39.81	46.9354	0.18
	Cluster3	37.62	40.3589	0.07
Pima Indian Diabetes	Cluster1	305.7	351.358	0.15
	Cluster2	369.1	405.687	0.10
Blood Transfusion Service	Cluster1	294.5	315.698	0.07
	Cluster2	228.2	249.175	0.09
Glass	Cluster1	16.44	18.3546	0.12
	Cluster2	7.149	9.3654	0.31
	Cluster3	18.37	21.3569	0.16
	Cluster4	21.96	23.1456	0.05
	Cluster5	9.982	11.2457	0.13
	Cluster6	20.31	20.9875	0.03

Table 4. Cluster Separability

Data Set	FCM	MFPSO	%Gain
Iris	0.482	0.5421	0.12
Wine	0.312	0.5841	0.87
Pima Indian Diabetes	0.193	0.2896	0.50
Blood Transfusion Service	0.129	0.1589	0.23
Glass	0.431	0.4963	0.15

A Fuzzy clustering validity function Bezdek designed for the partition coefficient F to measure the amount of overlap between clusters. The Bezdek cluster validity has been mentioned at table 5.

Table 5. Cluster Validation By Bezdek's Index

Data Set	FCM	MFPSO
Iris	0.742	0.8934
Wine	0.5033	0.6632
Pima Indian Diabetes	0.5732	0.8475
Blood Transfusion Service	0.7791	0.9851
Glass	0.3799	0.4563

The details performances of both models are summarized at table -6. The MFPSO obtains superior result in all of data sets while escaping from local optima. Also the experimental results show that in the increased size of the data set (No of objects or clusters) the MFPSO surpasses FCM. All the values reported are estimated over 20 simulation runs.

Table 6. Performance Result For Clustering

Data Set	Objective Function		
	Criterion	FCM	MFPSO
Iris	Best	64.5446	48.6512
	Worst	62.2564	44.9878
	Average	63.4994	47.2647
Wine	Best	78.4571	79.3659
	Worst	77.8561	70.1234
	Average	78.2099	72.5824
Pima Indian Diabetes	Best	78.6986	75.3201
	Worst	77.5632	73.8561
	Average	78.2491	74.4630
Blood Transfusion Service	Best	78.6986	79.3659
	Worst	0.4563	44.9878
	Average	33.1590	29.3307
Glass	Best	8.3658	7.0131
	Worst	7.8625	6.1231
	Average	8.2058	6.4761

8   Conclusions

This paper presented a clustering approach based on modified Fuzzy PSO in comparison to basic Fuzzy C-means clustering. It is having a basic objective of minimizing the objective function and maximizing cluster compactness . We have shown the MFPSO based clustering on some well known data sets. Although FCM clustering is a very well established approach, however it has some demerits of initialization and falling in local minima. Modified Fuzzy PSO being a randomized based approach has the capability to alleviate the problems faced by FCM. In this paper we have shown that the MFPSO algorithm produces better results with reference to inter and intra cluster distances. This paper is also calculated the gain percentage to differentiate between the results. The performance of MFPSO and FCM were investigated and the results suggested that MFPSO performs better in comparison to FCM.

References

1. Evangelou, I.E., Hadjimitsis, D.G., Lazakidou, A.A., Clayton, C.: Data Mining and Knowledge Discovery in Complex Image Data using Artificial Neural Networks. In: Workshop on Complex Reasoning an Geographical Data, Cyprus (2001)
2. Lillesand, T., Keifer, R.: Remote Sensing and Image Interpretation. John Wiley & Sons (1994)
3. Andrews, H.C.: Introduction to Mathematical Techniques in Pattern Recognition. John Wiley & Sons, New York (1972)
4. Rao, M.R.: Cluster Analysis and Mathematical Programming. Journal of the American Statistical Association 22, 622–626 (1971)
5. Satapathy, S.C., Pradhan, G., Pattnaik, S., Murthy, J.V.R., Prasad Reddy, P.V.G.D.: Performance Comparisons of PSO based Clustering (2010)
6. Bezdek, J.: Fuzzy mathematics in pattern classification, Ph.D. thesis, Ithaca. Cornell University, NY (1974)
7. Kennedy, J., Eberhart, R.: Swarm Intelligence. Morgan Kaufmann (2001)
8. Pang, W., Wang, K., Zhou, C., Dong, L.: Fuzzy Discrete Particle Swarm Optimization for Solving Traveling Salesman Problem. In: Proceedings of the Fourth International Conference on Computer and Information Technology, pp. 796–800. IEEE CS Press (2004)
9. Bezdek, J.C.: Pattern Recognition with Fuzzy Objective Function Algorithms. Plenum Press, NY (1981)
10. Runkler, T.A., Katz, C.: Fuzzy Clustering by Particle Swarm Optimization. In: 2006 IEEE International Conference on Fuzzy Systems, Canada, pp. 601–608 (2006)
11. Li, L., Liu, X., Xu, M.: A Novel Fuzzy Clustering Based on Particle Swarm Optimization. In: First IEEE International Symposium on Information Technologies and Applications in Education, pp. 88–90 (2007)

12. Gan, G., Wu, J., Yang, Z.: A genetic fuzzy k-Modes algorithm for clustering categorical data. Expert Systems with Applications (2009)
13. Liu, H.C., Yih, J.M., Wu, D.B., Liu, S.W.: Fuzzy C-Mean Clustering Algorithms Based on Picard Iteration and Particle Swarm Optimization. In: 2008 International Workshop on Education Technology and Training & 2008 International Workshop on Geoscience and Remote Sensing, pp. 838–842 (2008)
14. Mehdizeded, E., Sadinezhad, S., Tavakkolimoghaddam, R.: Optimization of Fuzzy Criteria by a Hybrid PSO and Fuzzy C-Means Clustering Algorithm. Iranian Journal of Fuzzy Systems, 1–14 (2008)

Crisp and Soft Clustering of Mobile Calls

Pawan Lingras[1,2], Parag Bhalchandra[1], Santosh Khamitkar[1],
Satish Mekewad[1], and Ravindra Rathod[1]

[1] Swami Ramanand Teerth Marathwada University, Nanded, India
[2] Saint Mary's University, Halifax, Nova Scotia, Canada
pawan@cs.smu.ca

Abstract. Mobile communication devices are gaining even faster acceptance than the proliferation of web in 1990's. Mobile communication spans a wide variety of protocols ranging from phone calls, text messages/SMS, e-mail data, web data, to social networking. Characterization of users is an important issue in the design and maintenance of mobile services with unprecedented commercial implications. Analysis of the data from the mobile devices faces certain challenges that are not commonly observed in the conventional data analysis. The likelihood of bad or incomplete mobile communication data is higher than the conventional applications. The clusters and associations in phone call mining do not necessarily have crisp boundaries. Researchers have studied the possibility of using fuzzy sets in clustering of web resources. The issues from web mining are further compounded due to multi-modal communication in the mobile world. This paper compares crisp and fuzzy clustering of a mobile phone call dataset. This emerging area of application is called mobile phone call mining, which involves application of data mining techniques to discover usage patterns from the mobile phone call data. The analysis includes comparison of centroids, cluster quality of crisp and fuzzy clustering schemes and analysis of their semantics. Since fuzzy clustering is descriptive, equivalent rough clustering schemes are used for succinct comparison of cluster sizes.

1 Introduction

Customer profiling is one of the preliminary and primary aspects of a customer relationship management strategy. An unsupervised identification of customer profiles makes it possible for an organization to identify previously unknown characterizations of groups of customers. Clustering is one of the most frequently used unsupervised data mining technique. Clustering has been used in a wide variety of applications from engineering [24,12], web mining [10,13,14,16], to retail data mining [15]. Conventional crisp clustering techniques categorize objects precisely into one group. However, in real-world applications, an object may exhibit characteristics from different groups. This is especially true in the new and emerging field of mobile call mining [5]. Soft clustering techniques such as fuzzy [3,2] and rough clustering [14,21] make it possible for an object to belong to multiple clustering leading to fuzzy or rough and overlapping boundary regions.

C. Sombattheera et al. (Eds.): MIWAI 2011, LNAI 7080, pp. 147–158, 2011.
© Springer-Verlag Berlin Heidelberg 2011

Mobile phones usage has topped five billion mark, with more than a billion new mobile phone connections added in 2009 and first half of 2010. The total number of mobile phones as a percentage of world population now stands at 72%, with ratios above 100% in many European regions. Mobile devices are going to be a dominant competitor to the personal computer based communication. Mobile phone data offers a fertile ground for data mining research as well as business analysis. This paper uses a dataset created by Eagle, et al. [5] for granular clustering. The dataset includes a detailed logs of more than a 100 users' mobile phone activity over a nine month period. The logs are further supported with the help of descriptive surveys of all the users. Eagle, et al. [5] used the dataset for studying the social relationship between the users. The analysis described here can also be useful supplement to the work by Eagle, et al. [5] for further research in mobile phone call mining.

The paper focuses on clustering of phone calls and phone numbers for a single customer from the dataset. The objective is to identify the calling pattern of the customer using two complementary clustering paradigms, namely crisp and fuzzy clustering. Crisp clustering mandates that an object can belong to one and only one cluster. This restriction is relaxed in soft clustering techniques such as fuzzy and rough clustering, where an object can belong to more than one cluster.

The calling pattern can be useful in suggesting appropriate modifications to the customer's calling plan. Extending the analysis for all the users can be useful for the phone companies to better manage their resources as well as to maximize utilization and profits. All the phone calls made by a customer over the nine month period are clustered based on a number of attributes including, day, time, duration, call direction, data/voice, successful connection. We use two popular clustering techniques, namely, K-Means algorithm [8,18] for crisp clustering and fuzzy C-means algorithm [2,3] for fuzzy clustering. The study describes a process to identify the best representation of mobile customers, and design semantically meaningful crisp and fuzzy clustering schemes. The crisp clustering scheme is useful for a concise description of the clusters, while fuzzy clustering scheme is used for memberships of individual objects to different clusters, which is descriptive. Therefore, a procedure proposed by Joshi et al. [11] is used for creating a rough clustering scheme from the fuzzy clustering for concise comparison of cluster cardinalities, while still maintaining the overlapping nature of the fuzzy clustering scheme.

The paper is organized as follows. Section 2 provides a review of clustering algorithms. Preparation of dataset and experimental design is presented in section 3. Section 4 discusses the results and their application in the world of mobile phone call mining. A summary and conclusions based on the findings from this paper are described in section 5.

2   Review of Clustering

First, we describe the notations that will appear in this section. Let $X = \{x_1, \ldots, x_n\}$ be a finite set of objects. Assume that the objects are represented by m-dimensional vectors. A clustering scheme groups n objects into k clusters $C = \{c_1, \ldots, c_k\}$.

2.1   K-Means Clustering

K-means clustering is one of the most popular statistical clustering techniques [8,18]. The name K-means originates from the means of the k clusters that are created from n objects. Let us assume that the objects are represented by m-dimensional vectors. The objective is to assign these n objects to k clusters. Each of the clusters is also represented by an m-dimensional vector, which is the centroid or mean vector for that cluster. The process begins by randomly choosing k objects as the centroids of the k clusters. The objects are assigned to one of the k clusters based on the minimum value of the distance $d(\mathbf{v}, \mathbf{x})$ between the object vector $\mathbf{v} = (v_1, ..., v_j, ..., v_m)$ and the cluster vector $\mathbf{x} = (x_1, ..., x_j, ..., x_m)$. The distance $d(\mathbf{v}, \mathbf{x})$ is given by:

$$d(\mathbf{v}, \mathbf{x}) = \sqrt{\frac{\sum_{j=1}^{m}(v_j - x_j)^2}{m}} \tag{1}$$

After the assignment of all the objects to various clusters, the new centroid vectors of the clusters are calculated as:

$$x_j = \frac{\sum_{\mathbf{v} \in \mathbf{x}} v_j}{\text{Size of cluster } \mathbf{x}}, \text{where } 1 \leq j \leq m. \tag{2}$$

The process stops when the centroids of clusters stabilize, i.e. the centroid vectors from the previous iteration are identical to those generated in the current iteration.

2.2   Fuzzy c-Means Algorithm

The conventional clustering assigns various objects to precisely one cluster. Therefore, the conventional clustering is sometimes called crisp clustering. Soft clustering schemes such as fuzzy and rough clustering allow for an object to belong to more than one cluster. A fuzzy generalization of the clustering uses a fuzzy membership function to describe the degree of membership (ranging from 0 to 1) of an object to a given cluster. There is a stipulation that the sum of fuzzy memberships of an object to all the clusters must be equal to 1.

The algorithm was first proposed by Dunn [3]. Subsequently, a modification was proposed by Bezdek [2]. Fuzzy C-means algorithm is based on minimization of the following objective function:

$$\sum_{i=1}^{n} \sum_{j=1}^{k} u_{ij}^m \, d(\boldsymbol{x_i}, \boldsymbol{c_j}) \quad , \quad 1 < m < \infty \tag{3}$$

where n is the number of objects and each object is a d dimensional vector. A parameter m is any real number greater than 1, u_{ij} is the degree of membership of the ith object ($\boldsymbol{x_i}$) in the cluster j, and $d(\boldsymbol{x_i}, \boldsymbol{c_j})$ is the Euclidean distance between an object and a cluster center c_j.

The degree of membership given by a matrix $\boldsymbol{u}$ for objects on the edge of a cluster, may have a lesser degree than objects in the center of a cluster. However, the sum of these coefficients for any given object x_i is defined to be 1.

$$\sum_{j=1}^{k} u_{ij} = 1 \quad \forall i \tag{4}$$

The centroid of a fuzzy cluster is the weighted average of all objects, where the weights of each object is its degree of membership to a cluster:

$$c_j = \frac{\sum_{i=1}^{n} u_{ij}^{m} \ x_i}{\sum_{i=1}^{n} u_{ij}^{m}} \tag{5}$$

FCM is an iterative algorithm that terminates if

$$max \left(\left| u_{ij}^{t+1} - u_{ij}^{t} \right| \right) < \delta \tag{6}$$

where δ is a termination criterion between 0 and 1, and t is the iteration step.

2.3   Deriving Rough Clustering from Fuzzy Clustering

While fuzzy clustering is less restrictive than crisp clustering by permitting an object to belong to multiple clusters, it can be too descriptive - with potentially a list of possible memberships for every object. Rough clustering [12,13,14,15,16] is less restrictive than crisp clustering as it allows an object to belong to multiple clusters. However, the cluster representation is based on a lower and upper bounds of a cluster using rough set theoretic properties. The lower and upper bound representation of a cluster is more concise than the detailed and descriptive list of membership values. Rough K-means (RKM) [14,21] is one of the popular rough clustering algorithms. Since we are deriving the rough clustering scheme from a fuzzy clustering algorithm, we will forgo the description of RKM. Combination of these two approaches are also proposed [9,19] to fully utilize inherent strengths of each technique.

Joshi et al. [11] proposed an algorithm for deriving a rough clustering scheme that determine whether an object with a certain fuzzy membership values belongs to a lower bound of a cluster or belongs to upper bounds of multiple clusters. Joshi et al. suggested the use of $ratio_{ij} = \frac{max(\boldsymbol{u_i})}{u_{ij}}, \forall i = 1$ to n and $\forall j = 1$ to k , where $max(\boldsymbol{u_i})$ is the maximum of u_{ij} over j i.e. the maximum fuzzy coefficient value for an ith object. For an object if the fuzzy coefficients are (0.5, 0.4, 0.1) for 3 clusters then the corresponding ratios are (1(05/0.5), 1.25(0.5/0.4), 5(0.5/0.1)), respectively. If $ratio_{ij} \leq threshold$ then object x_i belongs to upper bound of cluster c_j, where $threshold \geq 1$. If an object x_i belongs to upper bound of one and only one cluster c_j, then it also belongs to the lower bound of c_j. We will use Joshi et al.'s approach for deriving a rough clustering scheme from a fuzzy clustering scheme.

3 Data and Experimental Design

This section describes data preparation applied to the original dataset provided by Eagle [4] followed by the design of the experiment.

3.1 Data Preparation and Experimental Design

In order to conduct a detailed study, the paper focuses on all the calls made by a single user. The dataset consisted of a total of 60,779 call to or from 62 distinct phone numbers. One of the phone numbers appeared in 36,369 calls, with 35,989 of these calls were packet data. Moreover, none of the other phone numbers were involved in Packet data transmission. This phone number was clearly an outlier and possibly a server. Hence, it was eliminated from the analysis. That left us with a total of 24.410 records made to 61 distinct phone numbers. Further analysis showed that a number of records were repeated. Choosing distinct values of start time, end time, and phone number resulted in a total of 2,014 distinct phone calls. Based on Eagle et al. [5], we chose the following six variables to represent a phone call:

1. Weekend/Weekday (1/0)
2. Daytime/night-time (1/0) (8 am - 7:59 pm was designated as daytime.)
3. Duration of the phone call (normalized using different weighting schemes)
4. Direction (outgoing/incoming = 1/0. Here missed call was considered an incoming message.)
5. Type of call (SMS/voice = 1/0)
6. Missed call (yes/no = 1/0. It was assumed that missed call was a special message. That is, the person did not want to talk to the caller. In some cases, missed call is used to deliver an agreed upon message without having to waste time or money through the connection.)

Except for the duration of the call, all the variables had binary values while clustering phone calls.

The dataset for phone numbers consisted of an additional variable corresponding to the number of phone calls made from that number. All the remaining variables were essentially the same, but represented the average over all the phone calls. It represented proportion of 1's. For example, a value of 0.4 for weekday/weekend meant that 40% of the calls to and from that phone number were on a weekend.

This resulted in a total of seven variables for representing a phone number:

1. Average number of Weekend/Weekday (1/0)
2. Average number of Daytime/night-time (1/0)
3. Average duration of phone calls
4. Average number of incoming/outgoing (1/0) calls. Here missed call was considered an incoming message.
5. Average number of SMS/voice (1/0)
6. Average number of missed calls (yes/no = 1/0).

4   Results and Discussions

We used an open-source software called R for all the experiments [23]. R is a free software environment for statistical computing and graphics.

Table 1. Distribution of variables representing phone calls

Variable	weekend=1 weekday=0	day=1 night=0	duration	out=1 in=0	missed=1	voice=1 sms=0
Minimum	0.00000	0.0000	0.0	0.0000	0.00000	0.0000
1st Quartile	0.00000	0.0000	0.0	0.0000	0.00000	1.0000
Median	0.00000	0.0000	18.0	1.0000	0.00000	1.0000
Mean	0.04518	0.3396	113.7	0.6112	0.05462	0.7731
3rd Quartile	0.00000	1.0000	54.0	1.0000	0.00000	1.0000
Maximum	1.00000	1.0000	6730.0	1.0000	1.00000	1.0000

As mentioned earlier, the mobile phone call data was used to extract datasets of phone calls and phone numbers. First dataset consisted of 2,014 phone calls, while the second dataset consisted of 61 phone numbers. While most of the variables were binary or in the range between $[0, 1]$, duration ranged from 0 to 6,000 seconds. Table 1 shows a detailed distribution of all the six variables in the phone calls dataset. We use minimum, maximum, mean, 1st, 2nd, 3rd quartile values to get a detailed picture of the distribution. At least 25% of the values are less than or equal to 1st quartile value. 2nd quartile value is also known as median. At least 50% of the values are less than or equal to the median. Similarly, at least 75% of the values were less than or equal to 3rd quartile value. Table 1 tells us that 95% of the calls were on weekdays, two-thirds were during the night, 75% were of less than one minute duration, 5% were missed calls, and 77% were voice calls. Similar conclusions can be drawn from Table 2 which shows distribution of variables for phone numbers.

Table 2. Distribution of variables representing phone numbers

Variable	No. of Calls	weekend=1 weekday=0	day=1 night=0	duration	out=1 in=0	missed=1	voice=1 sms=0
Minimum	1.00	0.00000	0.0000	0.00	0.0000	0.00000	0.0000
1st Quartile	3.00	0.00000	0.0000	5.50	0.5000	0.00000	1.0000
Median	6.00	0.00000	0.2581	37.06	0.6667	0.00000	1.0000
Mean	33.02	0.02278	0.3141	77.40	0.6625	0.07337	0.9275
3rd Quartile	31.00	0.00000	0.4603	84.00	1.0000	0.07140	1.0000
Maximum	309.00	0.33330	1.0000	626.49	1.0000	1.00000	1.0000

The value of duration for phone calls can be as high as 6730 (almost two hours), which is significantly higher than other binary variables. Similarly values of duration and number of calls from a phone number are significantly larger than other five variables. Such large values would normally dominate the clustering criteria. Therefore, three different weighting schemes were used in the experiments. The first weighting scheme used the raw values of duration. The second weighting scheme used maximum value of duration to normalize the duration to a number between $[0, 1]$. However, due to skewed distribution, this weighting scheme led to a large number of small values. For example, 75th percentile value was 0.008, i.e. 75% of the values were less than or equal to 0.008. Therefore, it was decided to normalize the duration using the average value of duration and number of calls.

Clustering of both phone calls and phone numbers was performed using K-means for different values of K. The values of K ranging from 2 to 100 were used for clustering phone calls. The range of K for clustering phone numbers was 2 to 10 as there are only 61 distinct phone numbers. We identified a reasonable range for the number of clusters using, the total within cluster scatter as a measure of cluster quality. The scatter provides a measure of spread of the clusters within a clustering scheme. It tends to drop with the increase in the number of clusters, as the clusters start becoming more homogeneous. The knee of the curve of the graph of sum of within group distances provides a good starting point for clustering.

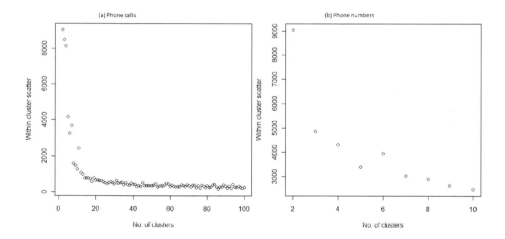

Fig. 1. Sum of within cluster scatter for phone calls and numbers

Figure 1(a) shows the graph of total within cluster scatter for the phone calls. The total rises sharply when the number of clusters become less than five. Figure 1(a) seems to suggest that the knee of curve appears between 5 to 15 clusters. Figure 1(b) shows the graph of total within cluster scatter for the phone numbers, which seems to suggest that the knee of curve appears between 5 to 9 clusters.

Table 3. Results of phone call clustering

Variable	weekend=1 weekday=0	day=1 night=0	duration	out=1 in=0	missed=1	voice=1 sms=0		
Crisp clustering, K = 2							Size	
C1	0.07	0.45	13.26	0.63	0.00	1.00	84	
C2	0.04	0.33	0.47	0.61	0.06	0.76	1930	
Soft clustering, K = 2							Lower	Upper
S1	0.05	0.47	12.07	0.66	0.00	1.00	90	98
S2	0.04	0.33	0.40	0.61	0.06	0.76	1916	1924
Crisp clustering, K = 4							Size	
C1	0.07	0.35	0.00	0.31	0.00	0.00	457	
C2	0.04	0.32	0.49	0.70	0.08	1.00	1438	
C3	0.06	0.50	8.71	0.70	0.00	1.00	104	
C4	0.07	0.33	27.34	0.47	0.00	1.00	15	
Soft clustering, K = 4							Lower	Upper
S1	0.05	0.35	0.26	0.22	0.09	0.49	694	912
S2	0.03	0.25	0.37	0.89	0.02	0.93	984	1203
S3	0.06	0.51	8.64	0.72	0.00	1.00	99	108
S4	0.07	0.33	24.15	0.42	0.00	1.00	16	18
Crisp clustering, K = 6							Size	
C1	0.03	1.00	0.34	0.79	0.04	0.89	489	
C2	0.05	0.00	0.39	0.97	0.00	1.00	662	
C3	0.05	0.16	0.09	0.13	0.13	0.41	682	
C4	0.06	0.49	4.66	0.67	0.00	1.00	111	
C5	0.04	0.47	10.93	0.67	0.00	1.00	55	
C6	0.07	0.33	27.34	0.47	0.00	1.00	15	
Soft clustering, K = 6							Lower	Upper
S1	0.02	0.91	0.34	0.86	0.03	0.93	470	523
S2	0.02	0.03	0.29	0.92	0.02	0.97	631	824
S3	0.04	0.18	0.10	0.09	0.06	0.25	537	725
S4	0.05	0.51	5.67	0.74	0.00	1.00	95	102
S5	0.04	0.50	10.86	0.76	0.00	1.00	49	51
S6	0.08	0.33	24.45	0.42	0.00	1.00	15	16

4.1 Analysis of Crisp and Fuzzy Clustering

Since we had identified fifteen as the highest possible number of clusters for
phone calls, we varied the value of number of clusters from 2 to 15 and performed
both crisp and fuzzy clustering. Table 3 shows the results for a select number of
clustering schemes, namely K = 2, 4, 6. These values of K are chosen because
there was a good correspondence between crisp and soft clustering. The labels
C1, C2, C3, etc. are used to denote crisp clusters, while labels S1, S2, S3, etc.
are their soft clustering equivalents. One can see the general similarity between
crisp and fuzzy centroids. The lower and upper bounds of the rough sets derived
from the fuzzy clustering are related to the corresponding crisp cluster sizes. In
most cases, size of a crisp cluster tends to fall between sizes of lower and upper
bounds.

The clustering schemes for different values of K also help us qualitatively analyze which value of K provides meaningful grouping. For example, clustering with K = 2 separates a small number of phone calls with minimal duration from those with large duration. However, when we increase K to 4, we see a better distribution among clusters. Clusters C3 and C4 are distinguished by the duration. Clusters C1 and C2 have similar durations, so the distinction is based on less dominant attribute, namely, outgoing/incoming and voice/sms. C1 exclusively consists of sms and has larger proportion (69%) of incoming calls, while C2 is exclusively voice based with larger proportion (70%) of outgoing calls. The corresponding fuzzy centroids for S1, S2, S3, and S4 display similar characteristics. We can make similar observations for K = 6, where clusters C4, C5, and C6 are now distinguished based on the duration. Clusters C1 consists of all daytime calls, while C2 has only night time calls. Cluster C3 distinguished itself from C1 and C2 by low percentage (13%) of outgoing calls. The centroids of S1-S6 provide a similar semantic explanation of the centroids. Further increase in values of K tends to make it difficult to provide semantic analysis. The soft clustering that agrees with the crisp clustering in terms of semantic analysis is especially useful, since we are able to identify a core group of objects that strongly demonstrate semantic traits of a cluster (lower bound) from those with significant traces (boundary region) of those traits.

Table 4. Results of phone number clustering

Variable	No. of Calls	weekend=1 weekday=0	day=1 night=0	duration	out=1 in=0	missed=1	voice=1 sms=0		
Crisp clustering, K = 3								Size	
C1	0.37	0.02	0.31	0.68	0.68	0.08	0.96	52	
C2	6.25	0.06	0.34	0.84	0.63	0.04	0.65	6	
C3	1.48	0.05	0.37	6.83	0.35	0.08	0.99	3	
Soft clustering, K = 3								Lower	Upper
S1	0.33	0.02	0.30	0.60	0.69	0.07	0.96	52	52
S2	5.89	0.06	0.33	0.61	0.60	0.05	0.61	6	6
S3	1.49	0.04	0.35	6.70	0.37	0.08	0.99	3	3
Crisp clustering, K = 4								Size	
C1	0.17	0.02	0.27	0.26	0.67	0.08	0.94	34	
C2	0.73	0.02	0.37	1.49	0.71	0.06	0.98	18	
C3	6.25	0.06	0.34	0.84	0.63	0.04	0.65	6	
C4	1.48	0.05	0.37	6.83	0.35	0.08	0.99	3	
Soft clustering, K = 4								Lower	Upper
S1	0.21	0.02	0.25	0.30	0.72	0.06	0.95	34	37
S2	0.61	0.01	0.38	1.47	0.70	0.07	0.97	15	18
S3	6.01	0.06	0.33	0.54	0.59	0.04	0.59	6	6
S4	1.47	0.04	0.34	7.50	0.32	0.08	1.00	3	3

Since we have a significantly smaller sample of sixty-one phone numbers as opposed to 2,014 phone calls, we could experiment with a smaller number of clustering schemes ranging from K = 2 to 7. Table 4 shows the results for K = 3 and 4, where the crisp and fuzzy centroids were reasonably similar, and it was possible to conduct meaningful semantic analysis. Higher values of K tended to create much smaller clusters. The resulting grouping from K-means and fuzzy C-means do not always match very well for these largely indistinguishable small clusters.

For K = 3, we see a large nondescript cluster C1 of 52 phone numbers. Here we define nondescript to be a cluster with very little meaningful values for any of the attributes. Two clusters C2 and C3 distinguish themselves based on the number of calls and durations. Cluster C2 comprises of phone numbers with highest number of phone calls and also consisting of 35% sms traffic. Cluster C3 has moderate number of phone calls with highest values for average duration. Both clusters C2 and C3 are very small. It is interesting to note that the membership in the corresponding soft clusters, S1, S2, and S3 is exactly the same. This means that there is no ambiguous membership for K = 3. Moreover, 85% of the phone numbers belong to a nondescript cluster labeled C1. Increasing K to 4, remedies the situation. While the last two clusters, C3 and C4 are still the same as C2 and C3 from K = 3, the previous large cluster is now split into two clusters, one with longer average duration phone calls (cluster C2) and cluster C1 remains nondescript as before, but with much smaller proportion (56%) of the total. Another important feature for K = 4 is the appearance of soft clusters S1 and S2, which correspond very well with cluster C1 and C2. There are three phone numbers in the boundary region of S1 and S2, which were forced into cluster C2 by the crisp clustering. This observation further underlines the importance of soft clustering for mobile phone call mining.

One could summarize the conclusions from Tables 3 and 4 as follows. In both cases, both crisp and fuzzy clustering are helpful in identifying the appropriate clustering schemes. The optimal clustering should be determined based on analysis of quality of clusters such as sum of within cluster scatter. The knee of curve can identify the range of optimal number of clusters. The number of clusters can be further narrow down by focusing on the cluster schemes where there is an agreement between crisp and fuzzy clustering. Since fuzzy clustering does not provide cluster sizes, its transformation to rough clustering provides lower and upper bounds of the soft clusters. These rough set representations of the clusters help further comparison between crisp and soft clustering. Based on these steps, we can identify six as the optimal number of clusters for phone calls and four as the optimal number for phone numbers. The use of rough clustering schemes derived from fuzzy clustering is helpful in identifying the core of each clusters as well as the objects that may straddle boundaries of multiple clusters.

5   Conclusions

This paper describes crisp and soft clustering of mobile phone calls and phone numbers based on a number of attributes ranging from duration, time of the day, day of the week, incoming or outgoing, voice or text, missed call or not, and number of calls made. K-means algorithm is used for crisp clustering and fuzzy C-means creates fuzzy clustering. Since fuzzy clustering creates fuzzy sets for an object but do not provide succinct representation of soft clusters. An algorithm by Joshi et al. [11] is used to create equivalent rough cluster representation with lower and upper bounds.

Experimentation with different numbers of clusters shows an interesting semantic view of how the clustering focus shifts from dominant attributes to less dominant attributes. When the number of clusters are increased, objects that were in a single cluster are invariably split into two or more clusters. Such a split leaves ambiguous memberships of certain objects that are captured very well by soft clustering.

Acknowledgment. The first author would like to thank the Natural Sciences and Engineering Research Council of Canada and the Faculty of Graduate Studies and Research, Saint Mary's University for funding. Data from Nathan Eagle [5] was instrumental in this study. Funding from the University Grants Commission (UGC) of India under the Scholar-in-Residence program made the collaboration among authors possible.

References

1. BBC News, Over 5 billion mobile phone connections worldwide (2010), http://www.bbc.co.uk/news/10569081
2. Bezdek, J.C.: Pattern Recognition with Fuzzy Objective Function Algorithms. Plenum Press, New York (1981)
3. Dunn, J.C.: Well separated clusters and optimal fuzzy partitions. Journal of Cybernetics 4, 95–104 (1974)
4. Eagle, N.: The Reality Mining Data Readme (2010), http://eprom.mit.edu/data/RealityMining_ReadMe.pdf
5. Eagle, N., Pentland, A., Lazer, D.: Inferring Social Network Structure using Mobile Phone Data. Proc. of the National Academy of Sciences 106(36), 15274–15278 (2009)
6. Farrugia, M., Quigley, A.: Cell phone Mini Challenge: Node-link animation award animating multivariate dynamic social networks. In: IEEE Symposium on Visual Analytics Science and Technology, VAST 2008, pp. 215–216 (2008)
7. Halkidi, M., Batistakis, Y., Vazirgianni, M.: Clustering Validity Checking Methods: Part II. ACM SIGMOD Record 31(3), 19–27 (2002)
8. Hartigan, J.A., Wong, M.A.: Algorithm AS136: A K-Means Clustering Algorithm. Applied Statistics 28, 100–108 (1979)
9. Hong, T.-P., Tseng, L.-H., Chien, B.-C.: Mining from incomplete quantitative data by fuzzy rough sets. Expert Systems with Applications 37(3), 2644–2653 (2010)
10. Joshi, A., Krishnapuram, R.: Robust Fuzzy Clustering Methods to Support Web Mining. In: Proceedings of the Workshop on Data Mining and Knowledge Discovery, SIGMOD, pp. 15/1-15/8 (1998)
11. Joshi, M., Lingras, P., Rao, C.R.: Correlating Fuzzy and Rough Clustering. Fundamenta Informaticae (to appear, 2011)
12. Lingras, P.: Unsupervised Rough Set Classification using GAs. Journal Of Intelligent Information Systems 16(3), 215–228 (2001)

13. Lingras, P.: Rough set clustering for Web mining. In: Proceedings of 2002 IEEE International Conference on Fuzzy Systems (2002)
14. Lingras, P., West, C.: Interval Set Clustering of Web Users with Rough K-means. Journal of Intelligent Information Systems 23(1), 5–16 (2004)
15. Lingras, P., Hogo, M., Snorek, M., Leonard, B.: Clustering Supermarket Customers Using Rough Set Based Kohonen Networks. In: Zhong, N., Raś, Z.W., Tsumoto, S., Suzuki, E. (eds.) ISMIS 2003. LNCS (LNAI), vol. 2871, pp. 169–173. Springer, Heidelberg (2003)
16. Lingras, P., Hogo, M., Snorek, M.: Interval Set Clustering of Web Users using Modified Kohonen Self-Organizing Maps based on the Properties of Rough Sets. Web Intelligence and Agent Systems: An International Journal 2(3), 217–230 (2004)
17. Lingras, P., Yan, R., West, C.: Fuzzy C-Means Clustering of Web Users for Educational Sites. In: Xiang, Y., Chaib-draa, B. (eds.) Canadian AI 2003. LNCS (LNAI), vol. 2671, pp. 557–562. Springer, Heidelberg (2003)
18. MacQueen, J.: Some Methods fir Classification and Analysis of Multivariate Observations. In: Proceedings of Fifth Berkeley Symposium on Mathematical Statistics and Probability, vol. 1, pp. 281–297 (1967)
19. Maji, P., Pal, S.K.: Rough Set Based Generalized Fuzzy C-Means Algorithm and Quantitative Indices. IEEE Transactions on Systems, Man, and Cybernetics, Part B 37(6), 1529–1540 (2007)
20. Nanavati, A.A., Gurumurthy, S., Das, G., Chakraborty, D., Dasgupta, K., Mukherjea, S., Joshi, A.: On the structural properties of massive telecom call graphs: findings and implications. In: Proc. of 15th ACM Conference on Information and Knowledge Management, pp. 435–444 (2006)
21. Peters, G.: Some Refinements of Rough k-Means. Pattern Recognition 39(8), 1481–1491 (2006)
22. Peters, J.F., Skowron, A., Suraj, Z., Rzasa, W., Borkowski, M.: Clustering: A rough set approach to constructing information granules. In: Proc. of 6th International Conference Soft Computing and Distributed Processing, SCDP 2002, pp. 57–61 (2002)
23. R, The R Project for Statistical Computing (2010), http://www.r-project.org
24. Sharma, S.C., Werner, A.: Improved method of grouping provincewide permanent traffic counters. Transportation Research Record 815, 13–18 (1981)
25. Ye, Q., Zhu, T., Hu, D., Wu, B., Du, N., Wang, B.: Cell phone mini challenge award: Social network accuracy - exploring temporal communication in mobile call graphs. In: IEEE Symposium on Visual Analytics Science and Technology, VAST 2008, pp. 207–208 (2008)

Association Rule Centric Clustering of Web Search Results

Hima Bindu Kommanti and Raghavendra Rao Chillarige

Department of Computer and Information Sciences, University of Hyderabad,
Hyderabad, Andhra Pradesh, India
himagopal@gmail.com, crrcs@uohyd.ernet.in

Abstract. Information abundance induced due to the ambiguous queries demands soft computing strategies. This problem can be addressed by Search Results Clustering. This paper presents a novel approach to the web search results clustering based on association rules using the Snowball technique. Association rule mining is employed on terms extracted from title and snippet of the search results. The detailed algorithm and experimental results on data sets of ambiguous queries are presented.

Keywords: Search results clustering, web mining, association rules, Snowball technique.

1   Introduction

Search engines are in wide use for information retrieval on the Web. Search engines display relevant results when the queries are descriptive enough. But most of the queries are short and ambiguous, usually containing less than three words ([19], [21],[22]) for example: "jaguar" , "apple". In such cases, the number of results returned by the search engine explodes and even runs into millions. It is a painful task to sift through the long list of results for the relevant one. And users hardly check beyond the first few pages of search results. Search result clustering is a solution to this problem.

Search Result Clustering (SRC) is defined as an automatic, on-line grouping of similar documents in search results list returned from a search engine [17]. SRC presents the results in thematic groups which helps the user to get an overview of the topics covered by search engine and to focus on a specific group of documents. This avoids the tedious task of verifying a long list of search results especially when the user's search intention is not expressed by the query terms. With SRC, user can quickly focus on the relevant cluster without exploring the long list of results. This is a viable solution for web search, as users hardly submit sufficiently descriptive queries and the user's search intention is not clear. Based on the clusters displayed as a result of the initial ambiguous query, it is possible to perform query reformation also. SRC can also be used to identify the keywords used for the search topic.

SRC is a post processing technique; the first few hundreds of search results are clustered. Each search result contains URL, title and a short text description called as

C. Sombattheera et al. (Eds.): MIWAI 2011, LNAI 7080, pp. 159–168, 2011.

snippet. Yahoo! Directory and Open Directory Project [18] organize web documents into various categories as a pre processing method. But these face limitatins due to the highly dynamic nature of the web. These are static and cover only a small portion of the web and they classify web pages based on coarse categories.

SRC is an ephemeral clustering and is very different from classical text clustering. SRC requires meaningful and human readable cluster labels. In addition, short text snippets are to be clustered and the number of clusters is highly dynamic and they can be overlapping. The short text snippets bring in another challenge – data sparsity.

Association rule mining, which is based on frequent item sets of market basket analysis [7] can be applied to the search results to identify frequently co-occurring terms. We introduce Association Rule Centric Clustering (ARCC), a novel search result clustering algorithm. ARCC follows the Snowball technique [20] to form the clusters. ARCC considers strong association rules and forms base clusters with the search results covered by them. These base clusters are grown by inclusion of search results satisfying the association rules holding in majority in the base clusters. This process is repeated till it is not possible to grow the clusters any longer.

This paper is organized as follows. The next section gives an overview of related work on web search result clustering techniques. The following section describes ARCC in detail. Subsequently, the experimental results are reported. We conclude by summarizing our contributions with directions for future work.

2   Related Work

Many attempts for SRC exist from classical text clustering to specialized clustering techniques for search results. Classical text clustering techniques fail to address SRC due to their inability to generate dynamic clusters with human readable labels [23]. The approaches for SRC extend from "data based" methods to "label based" methods. There are several clustering search engines like vivismo.com, grokker.com, carrot2.org, clusty.com, iBoogie.com.

Approaches to search result clustering can be classified as data–centric, description–aware and description–centric [4]. Scatter/Gather [5] is the earliest work on post retrieval clustering systems. It divides the search results into a small number of clusters along with short description. After the user selects some of these groups, clustering is performed again. Most frequently occurring keywords are selected as cluster digests. But this method and the data-centric methods in general fail to generate meaningful clusters. TRSC [14] is also a data centric method but tries to create understandable labels. TRSC enriches the missing features in the documents by using Tolerance Rough Set model.

The first description-aware clustering algorithm is "Suffix tree clustering" (STC) [23]. It creates clusters based on frequent phrases shared between documents. STC uses "suffix tree" to efficiently identify the sets of documents that share common phrases. STC has linear time complexity, is incremental and can form overlapping clusters. But when documents belonging to different topics have a common phrase, precision of STC is lower than the approaches based on similarity computation. HSTC [12] and SnakeT [6] are improvements over STC.

Description centric philosophy is followed by most of the commercial search results clustering systems. Lingo [17] is an example for description centric algorithm and it is used in the Carrot2 open source framework[1]. Lingo uses suffix arrays [10] for frequent phrase extraction and LSI to discover any existing latent structure of diverse topics in the search results. Lingo identifies the abstract topics present in the search results and the frequent phrases (becomes labels) which best match them. SHOC [25] is also based on suffix array and LSI and is designed to work in Chinese. Other methods in this category are SRC [24], Discover [9] and CREDO [3] system. In SRC, Salient phrases are extracted and ranked as candidate labels by using regression models learned from training data. *Discover* system works by selecting concepts based on noun phrases and salient keywords. CREDO system is based on concept lattices. Word Sense Induction(WSI) is used for automatic discovery of word senses in [14]. Given a query, word senses of it are acquired by using a text corpus. Clustering is performed on the basis of word senses. Search Results Clustering Based on Suffix Array and VSM is proposed in [1], they compared various clustering algorithms with varying sizes of results from 50 to 200.

3   Proposed Method

Frequent patterns are useful to identify the associations and correlations existing in the data. Frequent patterns help in data classification, clustering [7]. Frequent itemsets are used for document clustering in [8]. This motivated us to propose Association Rule Centric Clustering, ARCC.

The search results are obtained by using the APIs of the search engines like Google and Yahoo!. First few hundreds of the search results are used for clustering. The search results are preprocessed by stemming (Porter stemmer) and stop word removal. Each search result is treated as a transaction. The terms occurring in title and snippet of the search results are treated as items. The frequent itemsets are obtained by using Apriori algorithm [7]. The stronger association rules are generated from these frequent itemsets[7]. Then the rules are sorted in decreasing order of confidence values.

The clustering procedure is as follows. Let the list of search results be denoted as SR and the rule set as RS. Until RS is empty the following procedure is repeated. The best ranked rule BR is extracted from RS. The search results in which BR is satisfied are collected from SR to form a new cluster NC and they are removed from SR. The rules from RS which hold on NC above a minimum threshold percentage θ are extracted and form a set ER. The results from SR which obey the rules of ER are extracted and appended to NC. This process is repeated until there is no change in NC. If SR is not empty when RS has become empty, this set of results require further processing as they could not be clustered due to data sparsity. Some of them may not be satisfying the association rules even if they contain related words, but does not contain exactly the same words present in the rules. To group such related results with

---

[1] http://search.carrot2.org

their respective clusters, nearest neighbor classification is performed. For this frequency count of the search result terms in each cluster is used as the distance metric. To avoid favoring the larger clusters, the frequency count is expressed as a percentage of the number of terms of each cluster. Among the clusters with normalized frequency count above *theta2* for the search result, the cluster which contains the maximum value is the nearest, hence the result is assigned to it. If SR is not empty after repeating this procedure, SR is treated as the cluster with label "*other*". *Cosine similarity* is the other distance metric used.

From the association rules holding in the each cluster, the terms in each rule except the query term are used to form the label. As these terms are not human readable due to the pre processing task, using these terms as the root form, original terms/phrases are extracted from the original list of results. The results which do not fall in any cluster are placed in a cluster with the label "other", ARCC comes under data-centric category of the search results clustering techniques as the clusters are formed first and then the labels are generated.

The algorithm of this proposed method is presented next. The worst case time complexity of the core part of ARCC is $O(mn^2)$ with m search results and n association rules.

Algorithm. ARCC(Q, *min_sup*, *min_conf*, θ)
```
    1.//  Q is the  Search query
    2.//   min_sup is the minimum support
    3.//   min_conf  is the minimum confidence
    4.// θ is the threshold on number of documents
    5.//for which a rule is satisfied in the cluster
    6.// returns the clusters of search results C₁,C₂, ….Cᵢ
    7.//with the labels  L₁, L₂ , …Lᵢ
    8.{
    9.        results := Search_engine(Q);
   10.        D := PreProcess(results);
   11.        frequent_itemsets :=  Apriori (D, min_sup);
   12.        ARules := RuleGen(frequent_itemsets,min_conf);
   13.        R := Sort(ARules);  // sort in  decreasing
   14.                            // order of confidence
   15.        i  := 1;
   16.   while (|R|≠ 0 ) do
   17.        {
   18.         r  :=  R[0];
   19.         Cᵢ :=  { d | d   D, and r holds on d };
   20.         D :=  D - Cᵢ ;
   21.         Rᵢ  :=   {r};
   22.         R :=  R - { r };
   23.   repeat{
   24.         M :=  | Cᵢ |;    // size of the cluster Cᵢ
   25.         N :=  | Rᵢ |;  //  size of Rᵢ
```

```
26. // when the rule from R is satisfied in a
27.//number of documents above θ, add the rule to R′
28.         R ′:= { r | r ∈ R and
29.            |{ d | d ∈ C_i and r holds on d}| > θ };
30.         D′ := {d |d ∈ D, ∃ r   R′ and r holds on d};
31.         R_i :=  R_i ∪ R′;
32.         C_i :=  C_i ∪ D′;    // grow the cluster
33.         D :=  D - D′ ;
34.         R :=  R - R′;
35.         M′ := | C_i |;   N′ := | R_i |;
36.        }until (M′ =  M and  N′ = N); // stop
37.//growing the cluster when no more documents or
38.//rules can be added
39.        i  :=  i+1; // to form next cluster
40.     }
41. // perform NearestNeighbour classification of D
42.        D′ = NearestNeighbour({C_1, C_2, ….C_{i-1}},D);
43.     for j := 1 to i-1 do
44.        L_j :=  LabelGenerator( C_j);
45.        C_i := D′;  // documents which do not fall in
46. //any cluster
47.        L_i :=  "other";   // label "other" for C_i
48.        cluster = record
49.        {  set results;
50.           string label;
51.        }C;
52.     for j := 1 to i do
53.        {
54.            C[j].results := C_j;
55.            C[j].label := L_j;
56.        }
52. return cluster C;
53. }
```

4   Experiment and Results

To evaluate subtopic information retrieval, AMBIENT[2] (AMBIguous ENTries) test collection is used [4]. It consists of 44 ambiguous queries, each with a list of subtopics and a list of 100 search results. These results were obtained from Yahoo! in 2008. So far this dataset is the most recent to experiment the search result clustering. The queries are taken from a list of Wikipedia entries and the subtopics were manually assigned. [17] experimented with top 100 results from some search engines

---

[2] http://credo.fub.it/ambient

which are then manually grouped into various sub topics. But such an attempt is highly subjective, hence the experiments are conducted on AMBIENT data set and the results are presented here.

Table 1. ARCC evaluation on AMBIENT dataset

S. No	Query	Precision1	Recall1	F-measure1	Precision2	Recall2	F-measure2
1	Aida	60.00	50.00	54.55	37.63	58.33	45.75
2	B-52	100.00	24.00	38.71	100.00	24.00	38.71
3	Beagle	89.00	36.05	51.24	40.96	39.53	40.24
4	Bronx	83.00	48.68	61.16	69.14	73.68	71.34
5	Cain	49.00	65.79	55.56	30.11	73.68	42.75
6	Camel	67.74	30.00	41.58	50.91	40.00	44.80
7	Coral Sea	47.46	65.12	54.90	34.38	76.74	47.48
8	Cube	26.67	16.67	20.51	26.67	16.67	20.51
9	Eos	63.04	45.31	52.73	40.22	57.81	47.44
10	Excalibur	70.00	21.88	33.33	70.00	21.88	33.33
11	Fahrenheit	59.52	37.31	45.87	45.74	64.18	53.42
12	Globe	35.71	18.87	24.69	16.92	20.75	18.64
13	Hornet	55.56	34.09	42.25	31.48	38.64	34.69
14	Indigo	23.40	28.95	25.88	19.57	47.37	27.69
15	Iwo Jima	43.75	32.56	37.33	37.63	40.70	39.11
16	Jaguar	70.18	50.00	58.39	52.87	57.50	55.09
17	La Plata	67.24	58.21	62.40	51.58	73.13	60.49
18	Labyrinth	21.74	19.23	20.41	21.74	19.23	20.41
19	Landau	41.67	12.50	19.23	41.67	12.50	19.23
20	Life on Mars	89.04	77.38	82.80	80.21	91.67	85.56
21	Locust	30.95	27.08	28.89	28.89	54.17	37.68
22	Magic Mountain	69.70	56.10	62.16	36.71	70.73	48.33
23	Matador	26.09	32.43	28.92	17.86	40.54	24.79
24	Metamorphosis	88.57	56.36	68.89	46.67	63.64	53.85
25	Minotaur	66.67	27.45	38.89	66.67	27.45	38.89
26	Mira	26.09	31.58	28.57	18.89	44.74	26.56
27	Mirage	16.67	5.88	8.70	16.67	5.88	8.70
28	Monte Carlo	68.12	65.28	66.67	60.00	79.17	68.26
29	Oppenheim	16.13	12.20	13.89	16.67	34.15	22.40
30	Out of Control	21.05	22.22	21.62	21.05	22.22	21.62
31	Pelican	32.35	18.33	23.40	30.77	40.00	34.78
32	Purple Haze	32.65	59.26	42.11	20.22	66.67	31.03
33	Raam	73.08	32.76	45.24	73.08	32.76	45.24
34	Rhea	75.00	46.15	57.14	39.29	63.46	48.53
35	Scorpion	9.09	2.27	3.64	9.09	2.27	3.64
36	The Little Mermaid	51.22	43.75	47.19	35.16	66.67	46.04
37	Tortuga	10.42	17.24	12.99	13.64	41.38	20.51
38	Urania	78.57	25.00	37.93	78.57	25.00	37.93
39	Wink	46.15	39.13	42.35	25.93	45.65	33.07
40	Xanadu	66.67	61.22	63.83	40.48	69.39	51.13
41	Zebra	58.54	33.80	42.86	40.51	45.07	42.67
42	Zenith	28.57	33.33	30.77	22.47	66.67	33.61
43	Zodiac	6.25	15.00	8.82	14.61	65.00	23.85
44	Zombie	10.26	11.76	10.96	12.22	32.35	17.74

The results of ARCC on the queries are reported in Table 1, with Precision, Recall and F-measure values. Evaluating the clustering performance with comparison to the manually assigned subtopics has some justified differences. An example for such differences is when a larger human identified group gets split into smaller pure groups [15, 16]. Evaluation of cluster validity is not straight forward as 'm' manually assigned sub topics can be clustered into 'n' clusters by the algorithm. And also there may not be a direct mapping between the clusters obtained in these two approaches.

Hence we computed *tf-idf* values for the terms obtained after pre-processing. Using the *tf-idf* vectors, the centroids of the manually assigned clusters and the ARCC clusters are computed. Then the Cosine similarity measure is used to identify the mapping between the clusters obtained with the two approaches to enable cluster validity measures' computation. In Table 1, Precision1, Recall1 and F-measure1 are the results of ARCC with frequency count as the distance measure for the Nearest Neighbor classification of the results which do not satisfy the association rules. Precision2, Recall2 and F-measure2 are computed with Cosine similarity as the distance measure.

As assessing the quality of clustering is a hard problem, Rand index (RI) is a quality measure proposed in the literature [11]. RI can be computed when the gold standard $\mathcal{G}$ is given. Rand Index of a collection $\mathcal{C}$ is determined as

$$RI(C) = \frac{\Sigma_{(w,w') \in W \times W, w \neq w'} \, \delta(w,w')}{|\{(w,w') \in W \times W : w \neq w'\}|} \tag{1}$$

where W is the union set of all the words in $\mathcal{C}$ and $\delta(w,w') = 1$ if any two words w and w' are in the same cluster both in $\mathcal{C}$ and in the gold standard $\mathcal{G}$ or they are in two different clusters in both $\mathcal{C}$ and $\mathcal{G}$, otherwise $\delta(w,w') = 0$. In other words, the percentage of word pairs that are in the same configuration in both $\mathcal{C}$ and $\mathcal{G}$ are calculated. The average Rand index values of our method when compared against Lingo [17], Suffix Tree Clustering (STC) [23] and KeySRC [2] are reported in Table 2. The values reported in tables 1 and 2 are in percentages.

Table 2. Average Rand index

Clustering method	Rand index
Lingo	62.75
STC	61.48
KeySRC	66.49
ARCC with frequency count	56.57
ARCC with Cosine similarity	58.83

The inferiority of our approach when compared with other approaches can be attributed to the lack of natural language processing techniques. But our approach has less preprocessing overhead when compared with the other techniques. Even though frequent item set mining is a complex task, it does not have a serious impact on our algorithm. The reasons for this are, search results clustering deals with first few hundred search results and the association rule mining is performed only once.

Label generation is a quite simple in our approach when compared to the other approaches. We generate the labels based on the association rules related to the cluster. The following table shows the cluster labels for the queries "Beagle" and "Jaguar". It can be observed that the labels are human readable. Our results show that ARCC algorithm is able to produce clusters of search results which are potential for user acceptable labeling without human interference.

Table 3. Cluster labels

Query	AMBIENT sub topics	ARCC clusters
Beagle	Dog breed(55)	Hound (9)
	HMS beagle(2)	Dog breed (53)
	Mars (12)	Breed information (2)
	Search (18)	Mars (9)
	Other (23)	Search (9)
		Other (22)
Jaguar	Jaguar(Panthera onca)(22)	Cat (11)
	Jaguar(car) (47)	World(6)
	Atari Jaguar(5)	Car XK (29)
	Fender Jaguar (2)	Car new model (6)
	Jaguar, the codename for Mac OS X v10.2 (2)	Car price review (3)
	SEPECAT Jaguar, a military aircraft (2)	Motor (6)
	Other (20)	Dealer (3)
		Other (36)

5   Conclusion

In this paper a novel approach to Web search result clustering based on association rules is presented. Our idea is to find out the word associations automatically and build the clusters using Snowball technique. Our approach is able to generate clusters along with labels without human intervention. In future we intend to study various natural language processing approaches to improve the precision of our algorithm.

References

1. Bai, S., Zhu, W., Zhang, B.: Search Results Clustering Based on Suffix Array and VSM. In: 2010 IEEE/ACM International Conference on Green Computing and Communications & 2010 IEEE/ACM International Conference on Cyber, Physical and Social Computing (2010)
2. Bernardini, A., Carpineto, C., D'Amico, M.: Full subtopic retrieval with keyphrase –based search results clustering. In: Proceedings of WI 2009, pp. 206–213 (2009)
3. Carpineto, C., Romano, G.: Exploiting the potential of concept lattices for information retrieval with CREDO. J. Univ. Comput. Sci. 10(8), 985–1013 (2004)

4. Carpineto, C., Osiński, S., Romano, G., Weiss, D.: A survey of Web clustering engines. ACM Computing Surveys (CSUR) 41(3) (July 2009) ISSN:0360-0300
5. Cutting, D.R., Pedersen, J.O., Karger, D., Tukey, J.W.: Scatter/Gather: A cluster-based approach to browsing large document collections. In: Proceedings of the 15th Annual International ACM SIGIR Conference on Research and Development in Information Retrieval, pp. 318–329. ACM Press (1992)
6. Ferragina, P., Gullì, A.: The Anatomy of SnakeT: A Hierarchical Clustering Engine for Web-Page Snippets. In: Boulicaut, J.-F., Esposito, F., Giannotti, F., Pedreschi, D. (eds.) PKDD 2004. LNCS (LNAI), vol. 3202, pp. 506–508. Springer, Heidelberg (2004)
7. Han, J., Kamber, M.: Data mining Concepts and Techniques, 2nd edn. Morgan Kauffman Publishers (2006)
8. Kiran, G.V., Shankar, R., Vikram, P.: Frequent Itemset Based Hierarchical Document Clustering Using Wikipedia as External Knowledge. In: Setchi, R., Jordanov, I., Howlett, R.J., Jain, L.C. (eds.) KES 2010, Part II. LNCS (LNAI), vol. 6277, pp. 11–20. Springer, Heidelberg (2010)
9. Kummamuru, K., Lotlikar, R., Roy, S., Singal, K., Krishnapuram, R.: A hierarchical monothetic document clustering algorithm for summarization and browsing search results. In: Proceedings of the 13th International Conference on World Wide Web, pp. 658–665. ACM Press (2004)
10. Manber, U., Myers, G.: Suffix Arrays: A new method for on-line string searches. SIAM J. Comput. 22(5), 935–948 (1993)
11. Manning, C.D., Raghavan, P., Schutze, H.: Introduction to Information Retrieval. Cambridge University Press, New York (2008)
12. Maslowska, I.: Phrase-Based Hierarchical Clustering of Web Search Results. In: Sebastiani, F. (ed.) ECIR 2003. LNCS, vol. 2633, pp. 555–562. Springer, Heidelberg (2003)
13. Navigli, R., Crisafulli, G.: Inducing Word Senses to Improve Web Search Result Clustering. In: Proceedings of the 2010 Conference on Empirical Methods in Natural Language Processing, pp. 116–126. MIT, Massachusetts (2010)
14. Ngo, C., Nguyen, H.S.: A Tolerance Rough Set Approach to Clustering Web Search Results. In: Boulicaut, J.-F., Esposito, F., Giannotti, F., Pedreschi, D. (eds.) PKDD 2004. LNCS (LNAI), vol. 3202, pp. 515–517. Springer, Heidelberg (2004)
15. Osinski, S.: Improving Quality of Search Results Clustering with Approximate Matrix Factorisations. In: Lalmas, M., MacFarlane, A., Rüger, S.M., Tombros, A., Tsikrika, T., Yavlinsky, A. (eds.) ECIR 2006. LNCS, vol. 3936, pp. 167–178. Springer, Heidelberg (2006)
16. Osiński, S., Stefanowski, J., Weiss, D.: Lingo: Search Results Clustering Algorithm Based on Singular Value Decomposition. In: Proceedings of the International IIS: IIPWM 2004 Conference, Advances in Soft Computing, Intelligent Information Processing and Web Mining, Zakopane, Poland, pp. 359–368 (2004)
17. Osinski, S., Weiss, D.: A concept-driven algorithm for clustering search results. IEEE Intell. Syst. 20(3), 48–54 (2005)
18. Project, T.O.D.: http://dmoz.org/
19. Silverstein, C., Henzinger, M., Marais, H., Moricz, M.: Analysis of a very large altavista query log. Tech. Rep. 1998-014, Digital SRC (1998)
20. Snowball technique, http://en.wikipedia.org/wiki/Snowball_sampling
21. Spink, A., Wolfram, D., Jansen, B., Saracevic, T.: Searching the web: The public and their queries. Journal of the American Society for Information Science and Technology 52(3), 226–234 (2001)

22. http://www.forwardleap.com/number-of-words-per-search-query-increases/
23. Zamir, O., Etzioni, O.: Web document clustering: A feasibility demonstration. In: Proceedings of the 21st International ACM SIGIR Conference on Research and Development in Information Retrieval, pp. 46–54. ACM Press (1998)
24. Zeng, H.-J., He, Q.-C., Chen, Z., Ma, W.-Y., Ma, J.: Learning to cluster Web search results. In: Proceedings of the 27th ACM International Conference on Research and Development in Information Retrieval, pp. 210–217. ACM Press (2004)
25. Zhang, D., Dong, Y.: Semantic, Hierarchical, Online Clustering of Web Search Results. In: Yu, J.X., Lin, X., Lu, H., Zhang, Y. (eds.) APWeb 2004. LNCS, vol. 3007, pp. 69–78. Springer, Heidelberg (2004)

Handwritten Kannada Vowel Character Recognition Using Crack Codes and Fourier Descriptors

Ganapatsingh G. Rajput and Rajeswari Horakeri

Department of Computer Science, Gulbarga University, Gulbarga-585106,
Karnataka State, India
{ggrajput,rajeshwari_horakeri}@yahoo.co.in

Abstract. In this paper, we present an efficient method for recognition of basic characters (vowels) of handwritten Kannada text, which is thinning free and independent of size of handwritten characters. Crack codes and Fourier descriptors are used for computing features. The recognition accuracy has been studied by comparing the performances of well known K-NN and SVM classifiers. Five-fold cross validation technique is used for result computation. Experiments are performed on handwritten Kannada vowels consisting of 6500 images with 500 samples for each class. The mean performance of the system with these two shape based features together is 91.24% and 93.73% for K-NN and SVM classifiers, respectively, demonstrating the fact that SVM performs better over K-NN classifier. The system methodology can be extended for the recognition of remaining set of Kannada characters.

Keywords: Kannada, Fourier descriptors, crack codes, K-NN, SVM.

1   Introduction

Character recognition is a classic pattern recognition problem for which many researchers are working due to its lot of potential application areas including postal address reading, bank cheque sorting, and automated data entry. Different pattern classifiers like Neural networks, Hidden Markov model, Quadratic classifiers, and Fuzzy based classifiers are used for character recognition. A review on different pattern recognition methods is reported in [1]. Different feature extraction methods reported in the literature include Zernike moments, invariant moments, Hough transform, direction chain codes, wavelets, and Gabor filter banks. A survey on different feature extraction methods for character recognition is presented in [2, 3]. Substantial amount of work has been reported for recognition of characters in many non Indian scripts like English, Chinese, and Arabic [4, 5, 6]. Lot of contribution can be found for printed characters compared to handwritten characters. A brief review of work done related to handwritten characters written in different Indian scripts is given below.

1.1   Related Work

Different methodologies in OCR development as well as research work done on Indian scripts character recognition is presented in [7]. Printed and handwritten

C. Sombattheera et al. (Eds.): MIWAI 2011, LNAI 7080, pp. 169–180, 2011.

character recognition of Devanagari script using Gradient features is presented in [8]. Gradient features are extracted using Sobel and Robert operators and input to SVM classifier to study the accuracy of both printed and handwritten characters. Recognition of off-line Bangla handwritten compound characters using modified quadratic discriminant function (MQDF) is reported in [9]. Features used for recognition purpose are based on directional information obtained from the arc tangent of the gradient. A Roberts's filter is applied on the normalized image to obtain gradient image. Next, the arc tangent of the gradient is initially quantized into 32 directions and the strength of the gradient is accumulated with each of the quantized direction. Finally, the frequencies of these directions are down sampled using Gaussian filter to obtain 392 dimensional feature vectors. Recognition accuracy of 85.9% is reported. Recognition of handwritten Bangla basic characters is reported in [10]. The features are obtained by computing local chain code histograms of input image and the classification results are obtained after down sampling the histogram feature by applying Gaussian filter. Multilayer perceptrons (MLP) trained by back propagation (BP) algorithm are used as classifiers. Recognition accuracies on the training and the test sets obtained are respectively 94.65% and 92.14%. Recognition of handwritten Devanagari characters is presented in [11]. The directional chain code information of the contour points of the characters area used as features. Using quadratic classifier for recognition the recognition accuracy of 98.86% and 80.36% is reported for Devanagari numerals and characters, respectively. Fuzzy model based recognition of handwritten Hindi characters is presented in [12]. Features consists of normalized distances obtained using the box approach. The overall recognition rate reported is 90.65%.

Good quality of research has been carried out for recognition of handwritten Kannada numerals [13, 14]. To the best of our knowledge very few attempts have been made towards recognition of handwritten Kannada characters. In [15], a quadratic classifier based scheme for the recognition of off-line handwritten characters of three popular south Indian scripts: Kannada, Telugu, and Tamil is presented. The bounding box of a character is segmented into blocks, and the directional features are computed in each block. These blocks are then down-sampled by a Gaussian filter, and the features obtained from the down-sampled blocks are fed to a modified quadratic classifier for recognition. The mean accuracy of 90.34%, 90.90%, and 96.73% is reported for Kannada, Telugu, and Tamil characters, respectively. FLD based unconstrained handwritten Kannada characters recognition is presented in [16]. The mean recognition accuracy of 68% is reported using Euclidean distance measure. In [17], handwritten Kannada character recognition system based on spatial features is proposed. Directional spatial features viz stroke density, stroke length and the number of stokes are employed as features to characterize the handwritten Kannada vowels using k-NN classifier. The average recognition accuracy of 90.1% is reported for vowel characters. In [18], moment based features are used for recognition of Kagunita (the Kannada compound characters resulting from the consonant and vowel combination). These features are extracted using Gabor wavelets from the dynamically preprocessed original image. Multi Layer Perceptron with Back Propagation Neural Networks are employed for character classification.

Average recognition rate of 86% is reported for vowels and for consonants the average recognition reported is 65%. From the literature survey, it is evident that there is still lot of research scope for handwritten character recognition for Indian languages and in particular for Kannada language. In this paper, we propose a multi feature based approach for handwritten character recognition. Features are extracted combining two shape descriptors namely, crack codes and Fourier descriptors. These features accommodate the variability of samples of handwritten characters images in different domains (spatial domain and frequency domain, respectively). We present a novel method of extracting the features using crack codes and use Fourier descriptors to support the crack code features. The extracted features are fed to trained K-NN and SVM classifiers to study the recognition rate. As an initial attempt, we restrict our work to vowels rather than considering entire character set.

The rest of the paper is organized as follows. In Section 2, handwritten Kannada characters database creation is presented. Section 3 deals with the feature extraction and section 4 describe classification. The experimental results are presented in Section 5 and conclusion is given in section 6.

2   Database Creation

Kannada, the official language of the southern Indian state of Karnataka, is a Dravidian language. The Kannada alphabet was developed from the Kadamba and Chalukya scripts used between the 5th and 7th centuries AD. Under the influence of Christian missionary organizations, Kannada script was standardized at the beginning of the 19th century. The writing style is from left to right. Kannada is built up from a base character set of 49 characters: 15 vowels and 34 consonants. Further there are about as many stress marks as there are base characters. Stress marks (vothus) modify the base characters and are appendages. Fig. 1 present a listing of the characters (vowels and consonants) used in Kannada scripts.

(a) Kannada Vowels   (b) Kannada Consonants

Fig. 1. Kannada Character set

Since, the standard database of handwritten character images is not available in Kannada script; we created our own database for the proposed method. Dataset of handwritten Kannada characters (vowels and consonants) is created by collecting the handwritten documents from writers belonging to different professions. Sample image of Kannada handwritten vowels and consonants, in gray scale, is shown in Fig. 2.

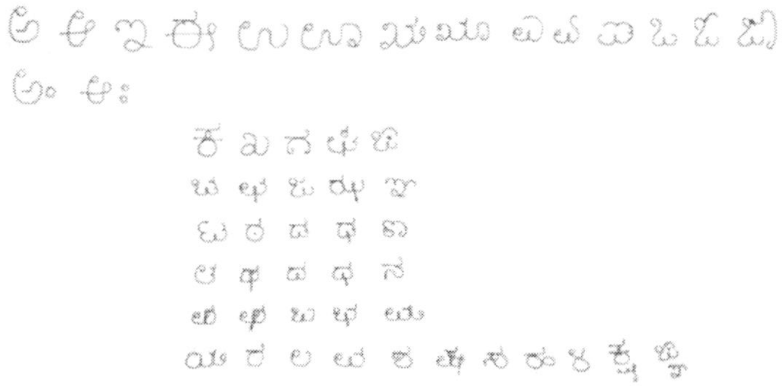

Fig. 2. Kannada handwritten vowels and consonants

The collected data sheets were scanned using a flat bed scanner at a resolution of 300 dpi and stored as grayscale images. The raw input of the digitizer typically contains noise due to erratic hand movements and inaccuracies in digitization of the actual input. The noise present in the image is removed by applying median filter three times. Image binarization is performed using Otsu's method [19]. The noise at isolated locations and spikes around the end of the characters are removed using morphological open and close operations. A minimum bounding box is then fitted to the character and the character is cropped. To bring uniformity among the handwritten characters, each image (located in bounding box) is size normalized to a size of 36x36 pixels. A total of 6500 binary digital images representing Kannada handwritten vowels are thus obtained. Each image represents a handwritten character (binary 1) that is unconstrained, isolated and clearly discriminated from the background (binary 0). Sample binary images of handwritten Kannada vowels are shown in Fig. 3.

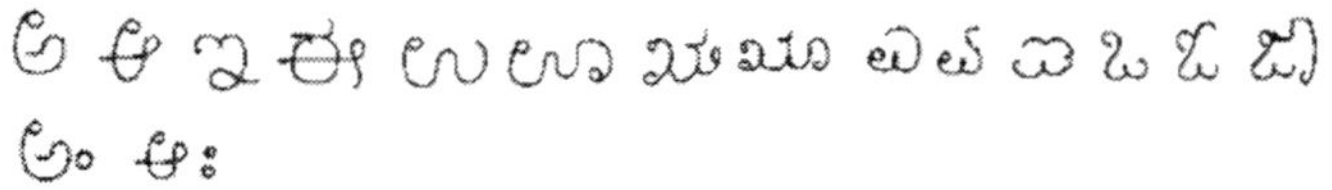

Fig. 3. Preprocessed handwritten character binary images (image inverted for display)

3   Feature Extraction

The traditional goal of the feature extractor is to characterize an object by making numerical measurements. Feature extraction is very problem dependent. Good features are those whose values are similar for objects belonging to the same category and distinct for objects in different categories. For extracting the features we have used boundary-based descriptors, namely, crack codes and Fourier descriptors. A brief description about crack codes and Fourier descriptors is given below.

3.1   Crack Codes

One of the ways to encode the contour or boundary by a connected sequence of straight line segments of specified length and direction is Chain code [19]. Another view is the crack code, the crack belongs to the boundary lies between a foreground and background pixel. Encoding this line (a sequence of horizontal and vertical pixel edges) yields the crack code of the digitized object boundary (identified as the bold line in Figure 4). Codes are represented with 4 possible directions as shown in Fig. 5. Crack codes are efficient in representing the region borders.

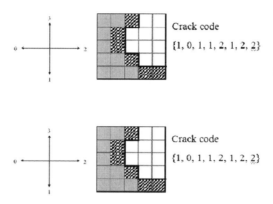

Fig. 4. a) Direction b) The "crack" is shown with the thick black line

Crack code for sample image of ಉ and ಋ is shown in Fig. 5. Arrow mark indicates the starting pixel which is the first on pixel scanned during column wise.

{1 2 1 2 2 3 2 2 1 ....}   {1 1 1 1 1 1 1 2 1 ...}

Fig. 5. Vowels ಉ and ಋ (image inverted for display)

In our proposed method, the normalized character image is scanned horizontally by keeping a window map of size 6x6 on the input image from top left to bottom right of the image (36 non overlapped blocks). For each block the crack code of image, representing the line between the object pixel and the background (the crack), is generated by traversing it in anticlockwise direction and stored in a vector V, the method of computing being defined in our earlier work [20]. The frequency of the codes 0, 1, 2, 3 is computed from vector V1. The normalized frequency, represented by vector V3, is then computed using the formula

$$V3= V2 \,/\, |V1| \quad where \quad |V1| = \sum V2 \tag{1}$$

Finally, concatenating the vectors V2 and V3 we get the required feature vector of size 8. We compute the feature vector of size 8 for all 36 blocks to obtain feature vector of size 288. The window size of 6x6 has been made choice by performing the experiments with different window sizes.

3.2   Fourier Descriptors

Fourier transformation is widely used for shape analysis [21, 22]. The Fourier transformed coefficients form the Fourier descriptors of the shape. These descriptors represent the shape in a frequency domain. The lower frequency descriptors contain information about the general features of the shape, and the higher frequency descriptors contain information about finer details of the shape. Although the number of coefficients generated from the transform is usually large, a subset of the coefficients is enough to capture the overall features of the shape. The high frequency information that describes the small details of the shape is not so helpful in character shape discrimination, and therefore, they can be ignored. As the result, the dimensions of the Fourier descriptors used for capturing shapes are significantly reduced. The method of computing the transform is explained below.

Suppose that the boundary of a particular shape has K pixels numbered from 0 to $K - 1$. The k-th pixel along the contour has position (x_k, y_k). Therefore, we can describe the contour as two parametric equations:

$$x(k) = x_k , \quad y\,(k) = y_k \tag{2}$$

The (x, y) coordinates of the point are presented in the complex plane by writing

$$s(k) = x(k) + i\, y(k) \tag{3}$$

The discrete Fourier Transform of this function is computed to end up with frequency spectra.

The discrete Fourier transform of s(k) is written as

$$a(u) = \frac{1}{K} \sum_{k=0}^{K-1} s(k)\; e^{-j2\pi uk/K} \quad , u = 0,1,2, \dots , K-1 \tag{4}$$

The complex coefficients a(u) are called the Fourier descriptors of the boundary. The inverse Fourier transform of these coefficients restores s(k).

In our proposed method, the contour is extracted from the normalized character image (Fig. 6) and is represented in complex plane. Fourier transform for this boundary is computed. The invariance is obtained by nullifying the 0-th Fourier descriptor (position invariance), dividing all Fourier descriptors by the magnitude of the 1-st Fourier descriptor (size invariance) and only considering the magnitude of the Fourier descriptors (orientation and starting point invariance). Only first 32 descriptors are computed, the size being determined empirically.

Fig. 6. Contour of sample Vowels (image inverted for display)

3.3   Feature Extraction Algorithm

Input: Pre processed size normalized character image
Output: 320 dimensional feature vector.
Method:
- Perform steps 1 and 2 on the input image.
- STEP 1
    1. Scan the image horizontally by keeping a window map of size 6x6 on the input image from top left most point to right most point (36 non overlapped blocks).
    2. Compute crack code for each block by traversing the image in anti clock wise direction and determine the crack code values[18].
    3. Normalize the crack code values for each block to obtain feature vector of size 288.
- STEP 2
    1. Extract the boundary of the character image.
    2. Represent the boundary in the complex plane where the column-coordinate is the real part and the row-coordinate the imaginary part.
    3. Compute Fourier transform and obtain the invariant 32 dimensional Fourier descriptors.
- STEP 3
    1. Combine features obtained in step 1 and step 2 to get feature vector of size 320.

4   Classification

The recognition accuracy of the proposed system is studied using K-NN classifier and SVM classifiers. The choice of these classifiers has been done based upon their extensive use in character recognition in literature. A brief description of these classifiers is given below.

4.1   K-NN Classifier

Classification typically involves partitioning samples into training and testing categories (unknown samples). The k- nearest neighbor (K-NN) technique classifies the unknown sample as belonging to the class most frequent among its k≥1 nearest neighbors, where the value of k is a design choice that one can make. Euclidean distance between the training pattern and unknown sample is computed to determine the k≥1 nearest neighbors.

4.2   SVM Classifier

Basically, Support Vector Machines (SVM)[23] is defined for two-class problem and it finds the optimal hyper-plane which maximizes the distance, the margin, between the nearest examples of both classes, named support vectors (SVs). Given a training database of M data { x_m | m=1, . . ., M},the linear SVM classifier is defined as:

$$F(x) = \sum \alpha_j \, x_j \, . \, x + b \qquad (5)$$

where {xj} are the set of support vectors and the parameters j and b have been determined by solving a quadratic problem.

The linear SVM can be extended to a non-linear classifier by replacing the inner product between the input vector x and the SVs xj, through a kernel function K defined as

$$K(x,y) = \phi(x) \, . \, \phi(y) \qquad (6)$$

This kernel function should satisfy the Mercer's Condition. The performance of SVM depends on the kernel used. A number of simple kernels include polynomial SVM, Radial Basis Function (RBF) SVM, and Two-layer neural network SVM. We have chosen RBF (Gaussian) kernel due to its better performance compared to other kernels. A SVM based classifier contracts all the information contained in the training set relevant for classification, into the support vectors. This procedure reduces the size of the training set by identifying its most important points. The SVM is applied to our multiclass character recognition problem by using one-versus-rest type method. More detailed treatment on principles and applications of SVM can be found elsewhere [24].

5   Experimental Results

Experiments are carried out on 6500 samples of the handwritten Kannada characters restricting to vowels only. The entire image set is partitioned into training set and test set. During training phase, the invariant Fourier descriptors and normalized crack codes for each character image is computed by performing feature extraction algorithm. The features are computed for all samples of the character images in the training set and stored in the respective classes. These features are then input to SVM. The result of the training step consists of the (Model) set of support vectors determined by the SVM based method. During the recognition phase, the Fourier Descriptors and normalized crack codes are computed for the test image in the same way, and the model determined during the training step is used to perform the SVM decision. The output is the image class. In the similar way we perform experiments using K-NN classifier.

The performance of the classifier is evaluated through k-fold cross-validation, with k=5, which involves the determination of classification accuracy for multiple partitions of the input samples used in training. For each validation step, 5200 images are used for training and 1300 images used for testing.

Table 1 presents recognition results using SVM multi-class classifier. Table 2 presents the confusion matrix for character images. The average recognition accuracy of 93.73% is achieved. Table 3 presents the recognition results using K-NN classifier with K=1. The average recognition rate of 91.24% is observed. The results for K=3, 5, and 7, respectively were 90.11%, 89.45% and 88.77%. Clearly, SVM performed better than K-NN. The misclassification of the vowels observed in the proposed method is attributed to following reasons. Since, the features extracted are global in nature, any changes in the local regions of the vowels, written by different persons, are not noticed in the features. Further, in certain cases a pair of handwritten vowels looks similar, giving similar features. This is evident from Table 2 for vowel pair ⟨ᴐ⟩ and ⟨ᴎ⟩, vowel pair ⟨ᴏ⟩ and ⟨ᴐ⟩, and vowel pair ⟨ᴋ⟩ and ⟨ᴏ⟩. Since the shape of the handwritten characters in these pairs is very similar, most of the pairs are misclassified. Further, the situation of misclassification continues for vowels written such as ⟨ᴏ⟩ (ᴎ or ᴃ ?). These problems pose some challenges to increase efficiency of the proposed method. In order to compare the results obtained by our method with the results reported in the literature [15-18], it is required to implement their methods and perform experiments on our database. However, the overall recognition rate is impressive compared to other works [15 – 18].

Table 1. Recognition results using SVM classifier

Kannada Vowels	Fivefold cross validation					Overall Recognition
	Fold-1	Fold-2	Fold-3	Fold-4	Fold-5	
ಅ	90	84	84	94	92	88.8
ಆ	95	91	89	90	90	91.0
ಇ	98	94	99	95	96	96.4
ಈ	97	97	97	96	96	96.6
ಉ	95	95	96	94	96	95.2
ಊ	99	94	93	97	97	96.0
ಋ	97	96	98	97	96	96.8
ಎ	84	87	90	94	94	89.8
ಏ	92	93	97	88	88	91.6
ಐ	82	94	94	96	96	92.4
ಒ	97	95	98	96	96	96.4
ಓ	92	94	88	97	97	93.6
ಔ	95	95	93	94	93	94
Overall recognition	93.30	93	93.53	94.46	94.38	93.73

Table 2. Confusion Matrix using SVM classifier

Vowels	ಅ	ಆ	ಇ	ಈ	ಉ	ಊ	ಋ	ಎ	ಏ	ಐ	ಒ	ಓ	ಔ
ಅ	**444**	32	1	1	1	0	2	0	3	8	5	2	1
ಆ	34	**455**	0	5	0	0	0	0	3	0	0	1	2
ಇ	1	4	**482**	2	0	1	1	0	0	3	3	3	0
ಈ	2	8	2	**483**	1	0	2	0	0	2	0	0	0
ಉ	1	0	0	0	**476**	13	2	3	1	1	1	1	1
ಊ	0	0	0	0	15	**480**	1	0	1	1	1	0	1
ಋ	0	3	1	2	3	0	**484**	0	0	4	0	0	3
ಎ	2	0	0	1	5	0	7	**449**	7	20	3	0	2
ಏ	1	1	1	0	0	2	0	25	**458**	11	1	0	0
ಐ	1	3	1	0	1	0	0	18	11	**462**	0	0	3
ಒ	1	0	1	4	3	0	0	0	0	3	**482**	4	2
ಓ	0	3	1	0	0	0	3	0	0	2	19	**468**	4
ಔ	2	0	1	6	0	0	1	0	4	7	0	9	**470**

Table 3. Recognition results using K-NN classifier with K=1

Kannada Vowels	Fivefold cross validation					Overall Recognition
	Fold-1	Fold-2	Fold-3	Fold-4	Fold-5	
ಅ	89	92	89	91	89.6	90.12
ಆ	88	89	84	79	84.6	84.92
ಇ	97	94	94	95	94.8	94.96
ಈ	94	97	95	89	93.8	93.76
ಉ	97	96	92	94	94.8	94.76
ಊ	96	97	93	93	94.4	94.68
ಋ	92	96	94	94	94	94
ಎ	91	95	96	96	93.8	94.36
ಏ	89	89	94	91	90.8	90.76
ಐ	79	77	79	79	79	78.6
ಒ	94	95	96	95	94.6	94.92
ಓ	97	89	93	95	93.4	93.48
ಔ	85	85	87	89	88.2	86.84
Overall recognition	91.38	91.61	91.23	90.76	91.21	91.24

6   Conclusions

In this paper we have presented an efficient method for recognition of Kannada handwritten basic characters (vowels) using crack codes and Fourier descriptors. The K-NN and SVM classifiers are used for classification and recognition. Five-fold cross validation technique is used to study the recognition accuracy of the proposed method. SVM classifier performed better than K-NN classifier. The average recognition of 93.73% is obtained for vowels using SVM demonstrating the fact that the combination of frequency and spatial information of the character image as features yields encouraging results. The novelty of the paper lies in the choice of the number of Fourier descriptors and the method of generating crack codes. Further, the proposed method is thinning free and independent of size of handwritten characters. However, the limitation is that present method has been experimented on vowels only. Our future plan is to extend the proposed method for the entire character set of Kannada script and study the performance of the system on a large dataset.

Acknowledgments. The authors thank the referees for their helpful comments.

References

1. Duda, R.O., Hart, P.E., Stork, D.G.: Pattern Classification, 2nd edn. Wiley, New York
2. Plamondon, R., Srihari, S.N.: On-Line and off-line handwritten recognition: A comprehensive survey. IEEE Trans. on PAMI 22, 62–84 (2000)
3. Jain, A.K., Taxt, T.: Feature extraction methods for character recognition-A Survey. Pattern Recognition 29(4), 641–662 (1996)
4. Liu, C.-L., Jaeger, S., Nakagawa, M.: Online recognition of Chinese characters: The-state-of-the-art. IEEE Trans. on PAMI 26, 198–213 (2004)
5. Yamada, K.: Optimal sampling intervals for Gabor features and printed Japanese character recognition. In: Proceedings of the Third International Conference on Document Analysis and Recognition, August 14-15, vol. 1, p. 150 (1995)
6. Cheung, A., Bennamoun, M., Bergmann, N.W.: An Arabic Optical Character Recognition system using Recognition based Segmentation. Pattern Recognition 34(2), 215–233 (2001)
7. Pal, U., Chaudhuri, B.B.: Indian script character recognition: a survey. Pattern Recognition 37(9), 1887–1899 (2004)
8. Holambe, A.N., Thool, R.C., Jagade, S.M.: Printed and Handwritten Character & Number Recognition of Devanagari Script using Gradient Features. International Journal of Computer Applications 2(9), 975–8887 (2010)
9. Pal, U., Wakabayashi, T., Kimura, F.: Handwritten Bangla Compound Character Recognition Using Gradient Feature. In: 10th International Conference on Information Technology (ICIT 2007), December 17-20, pp. 208–213 (2007)
10. Bhattacharya, U., Shridhar, M., Parui, S.K.: On Recognition of Handwritten Bangla Characters. In: Kalra, P.K., Peleg, S. (eds.) ICVGIP 2006. LNCS, vol. 4338, pp. 817–828. Springer, Heidelberg (2006)
11. Sharma, N., Pal, U., Kimura, F., Pal, S.: Recognition of Off-Line Handwritten Devnagari Characters Using Quadratic Classifier. In: Kalra, P.K., Peleg, S. (eds.) ICVGIP 2006. LNCS, vol. 4338, pp. 805–816. Springer, Heidelberg (2006)
12. Hanmandlu, M., Ramana Murthy, O.V., Madasu, V.K.: Fuzzy Model based recognition of handwritten Hindi characters. In: 9th Biennial Conference of the Australian Pattern Recognition Society on Digital Image Computing Techniques and Applications, December 3-5, pp. 454–461. IEEE (2007)
13. Rajashekararadhya, S.V., Ranjan, V.: Zone based Feature Extraction Algorithm for Handwritten Numeral Recognition of Kannada Script. In: Proc. of IEEE International Advance Computing Conference (IACC 2009), pp. 525–528 (2009)

14. Rajput, G.G., Horakeri, R., Mali, S.M.: Handwritten Numerals Recognition Using Shape Descriptors for Devanagari and Kannada Scripts. In: Li, Y. (ed.) Proc. of IEEE 2011 International Conference on Digital Convergence (ICDC 2011), pp. 1–7 (2011)
15. Pal, U., Sharma, N., Wakabayashi, T., Kimura, F.: Handwritten Character Recognition of Popular South Indian Scripts. In: Doermann, D., Jaeger, S. (eds.) SACH 2006. LNCS, vol. 4768, pp. 251–264. Springer, Heidelberg (2008)
16. Niranjan, S.K., Kumar, V., Hemantha Kumar, G., Aradhya, M.: FLD based Unconstrained Handwritten Kannada Character Recognition. International Journal of Database Theory and Application 2(3) (September 2009)
17. Dhandra, B.V., Hangarge, M., Mukarambi, G.: Spatial Features for Handwritten Kannada and English Character Recognition. IJCA, Special Issue on RTIPPR (3), 146–151 (2010)
18. Ragha, L.R., Sasikumar, M.: Feature Analysis for Handwritten Kannada Kagunita Recognition. International Journal of Computer Theory and Engineering, IACSIT 3(1), 1793–8201 (2011)
19. Gonzalez, R.C.G., Woods, R.E.: Digital Image Processing, 2nd edn. Pearson Education Asia (2002)
20. Rajput, G.G., Horakeri, R., Chandrakant, S.: Printed and Handwritten Kannada Numeral Recognition Using Crack Codes and Fourier Descriptors. IJCA, Special Issue on RTIPPR (1), 53–58 (2010)
21. Smach, F., Lemaître, C., Gauthier, J.-P., Miteran, J., Atri, M.: Generalized Fourier Descriptors with applications to Objects Recognition in SVM Context. J. Math. Imaging Vis. 30, 43–71 (2008)
22. Mahmoud, S.A., Mahmoud, A.S.: Arabic Character Recognition using Modified Fourier Spectrum vs. Fourier Descriptors. Cybernetics and Systems 40(3), 189–210 (2009)
23. Vapnik, V.N.: The Statistical Learning Theory. Springer, Berlin (1998)
24. Boser, B.E., Guyon, I.M., Vapnik, V.N.: A training algorithm for optimal margin classifiers. In: Proceedings of the Fifth Annual Workshop on Computational Learning Theory, pp. 144–152 (1992)

A Rule-Based Approach to Form Mathematical Symbols in Printed Mathematical Expressions

P. Pavan Kumar*, Arun Agarwal, and Chakravarthy Bhagvati

Dept. of Computer and Information Sciences,
University of Hyderabad, Hyderabad 500 046, India
pavan.ppkumar@gmail.com, {aruncs,chakcs}@uohyd.ernet.in

Abstract. Automated understanding of mathematical expressions (MEs) is currently a challenging task due to their complex two-dimensional (2D) structure. Recognition of MEs can be online or offline and in either case, the process involves symbol recognition and analysis of 2D structure. This process is more complex for offline or printed MEs as they do not have temporal information. In our present work, we focus on the recognition of printed MEs and assume connected components (ccs) of a given ME image are labelled. Our approach to ME recognition comprises three stages,namely symbol formation, structural analysis and generation of encoding form like LATEX. In this paper, we present symbol formation process, where multi-cc symbols (like =, ≡ etc.) are formed, identity of context-dependent symbols (like a horizontal line can be MINUS, OVERBAR, FRACTION etc.) are resolved using spatial relations. Multi-line MEs like matrices and enumerated functions are also handled in this stage. A rule-based approach is proposed for the purpose, where the heuristics based on spatial relations are represented in the form of rules (knowledge) and those rules are fired depending on input data (labelled ccs). As knowledge is isolated from data like an expert system in our approach, it allows for easy adaptability and extensibility of the process. Proposed approach also handles both single-line and multi-line MEs in an unified manner. Our approach has been tested on around 800 MEs collected from various mathematical documents and experimental results are reported on them.

Keywords: Mathematical expressions, connected components, symbol formation, rule-based approach.

1 Introduction

Mathematical expressions (MEs) form a significant and an essential part in the scientific and engineering disciplines. In view of applications like digitizing scientific documents, generating braille script for visually impaired etc, recognition of MEs is currently a challenging pattern recognition problem. Recognition of mathematical notation avoids the tedious task of typing LATEX expressions by

---

* Corresponding author.

C. Sombattheera et al. (Eds.): MIWAI 2011, LNAI 7080, pp. 181–192, 2011.
© Springer-Verlag Berlin Heidelberg 2011

allowing the users to write MEs on a data tablet. As MEs are two-dimensional (2D) in nature, their online or offline recognition involves two stages: Symbol recognition and Structural analysis. Labels are assigned to the symbols by the symbol recognition process and the relationships like subscript, superscript etc, among the symbols of ME are found in structural analysis stage. This entire process is much more complex for offline MEs than for online MEs due to lack of temporal information. A survey of existing works in this field is found in [5].

In our present work, we focus on the recognition of offline or printed MEs and assume connected components (ccs) of a given ME image are labelled. Our approach to ME recognition comprises three stages, namely symbol formation, structural analysis and generation of encoding form like LATEX. In this paper, we present symbol formation process and the remaining stages are outside the scope of the paper. Symbol formation process takes the labelled ccs of ME image as input and forms multi-cc symbols like =, ≡ etc, resolves the identity of context-dependent symbols like a horizontal line can be MINUS, OVERBAR, FRACTION etc. Multi-line MEs like matrices and enumerated functions are also handled at this stage.

In the literature, works on the complete offline systems are found in [11,6,13] and on the complete online systems in [8,14,9,20,3]. In the above works, symbol formation process has not been explained in a detailed manner. In [16], symbol formation is performed as part of recognition process by using a recognition threshold. In [20], multi-stroke symbols in handwritten MEs are formed by maintaining a list of strokes for various groupings. Zannibi et al, [21] form symbols after structural analysis by applying certain transformation rules on the generated tree. In [17] and [19], ccs are unified into symbols based on their sizes and the relative distances between their centroids. Yuko Eto et al, [7] constructs a network which represents possible relations and the associated costs among the symbols for a given ME and use the recognition results of the link structure to handle multi-cc symbols. Tapia et al, [15], handle multi-stroke symbols based on a minimum spanning tree construction and symbol dominance for online handwritten MEs.

All of the above approaches have not focused on the symbol formation process in detail and even the heuristics used to form symbols are loosely defined. They also lack an unified approach to handle all types of MEs: Single-line and Multi-line MEs (MLMEs) like matrices and enumerated functions. In our present work, we have proposed a rule-based approach for symbol formation, where the heuristics based on spatial relations are represented in the form of rules (knowledge) and those rules are fired depending on input ccs (data). Therefore, in the proposed approach, as knowledge is isolated from data like an expert system [4], it allows for easy adaptability and extensibility of the process. In addition, our proposed approach handles both single-line and multi-line MEs in an unified manner.

The paper is organized as follows: An overview of our approach to ME recognition is discussed in Section 2. In Section 3, proposed rule-based approach for symbol formation is presented. Section 4 presents the experimental results and the paper is concluded in Section 5.

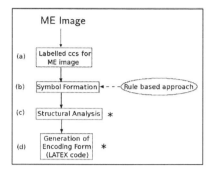

Fig. 1. Various stages of our approach to ME recognition

2 An Overview of Our Approach to ME Recognition

In this section, an overview of our approach to ME recognition is presented and its various stages are shown in Fig. 1. For a given input ME image, after its binarization, ccs are extracted and in the process, their minimum bounding rectangles (MBRs) are obtained, then labels are assigned for its connected components (ccs) in stage (a) of the figure. The process of ME recognition comprises three stages namely symbol formation (stage (b)), structural analysis (stage (c)) and generation of encoding form like LATEX code (stage (d)).

Symbol formation stage takes the labelled ccs given by stage (a) and forms multi-cc symbols and also resolves the identities of context dependent symbols using their spatial properties. For example, $\div$ is a multi-cc symbol and has three ccs (one horizontal line and two DOTs) and these three ccs are combined to form the single composite symbol $\div$. An unique label is given to the composite symbol and its MBR is computed in such a way that it exactly fits all its ccs. Similarly, a horizontal line is a context-dependent symbol as it can be MINUS, FRACTION, OVERBAR or UNDERBAR and the label of the horizontal line is changed to that of one of the above symbols based on the spatial properties of its neighbouring symbols. Mathematical functions like lim, min, max, arg etc, also formed in this stage as they can be considered as multi-cc symbols. For example, in $\max_{y} f(y)$, m, a and x are combined to form the composite symbol **max**. MLMEs like matrices and enumerated functions are also handled in this stage and their elements are extracted in the process by analyzing the spatial properties of ccs between their delimiters. A rule-based approach that has similar behaviour to that of an expert system is adopted in this stage and is discussed in the next section.

Structural analysis stage (stage (c)) takes the symbols formed in the previous stage, then finds the relationships like superscript, subscript etc among these symbols and an intermediate representation is generated for the given ME. In stage (d), encoding form like LATEX is generated from the intermediate representation given by stage (c). Discussion of these two stages (c) and (d) (shown as * in Fig. 1) is outside the scope of the paper.

3   Proposed Rule-Based Approach to Symbol Formation

As mentioned earlier, multi-cc mathematical symbols and the identity of context-dependent symbols are resolved by the symbol formation process. As mathematical functions are considered as multi-cc symbols, they are also formed in this stage. The starting and ending delimiters like $(, [, \{, \langle, |$ and $),], \}, \rangle, |$ respectively are also context-dependent symbols as they can be normal or MLME (matrices or enumerated functions) delimiters. Connected components between the delimiters are analyzed to find whether a MLME is present or not. If a MLME is present, its elements are also extracted in the process and the labels of the delimiters are changed to those of MLME delimiters. Therefore, our approach handles single-line as well as multi-line MEs in an unified manner.

As explained in the previous section, this stage takes as input the labelled ccs along with their MBRs for a given ME image. These ccs are sorted in the increasing order of x-co-ordinates. Here, it is assumed that x-axis is horizontal (from left to right) and y-axis is vertical (from bottom to top). If two or more ccs have same x-co-ordinate values, then they are sorted in the increasing order of y-co-ordinates. These ordered ccs are scanned from left to right to form symbols. In the process of scanning, if a sequence of ccs that corresponds to a multi-cc symbol is found, then based on spatial properties, its ccs are combined to form a single composite symbol and the individual ccs no longer exist after combination. Similarly, if a context-dependent symbol is found, based on spatial arrangement of its neighbouring symbols, its identity is resolved. After this stage, symbols ordered in a left to right manner are obtained. Let us consider a ME: $\tan\frac{x}{2} = \sqrt{\frac{1-\cos x}{1+\cos x}}$. Its left to right ordered ccs are as follows, in which horizontal line is denoted by h: t, a, n, -(h), 2, x, - (h), - (h), $\sqrt{}$, - (h), 1, 1, +, - (h), c, c, o, o, s, s, x, x. Symbols formed from these ccs are as follows: tan, - (FRACTION), 2, x, = (EQUAL TO), $\sqrt{}$, - (FRACTION), 1, 1, +, - (MINUS), cos, cos, x, x. Here, multi-cc symbol = is formed from two adjacent horizontal lines, three mathematical functions (tan and two cos functions) are formed and the remaining three single horizontal lines are resolved to FRACTION, FRACTION and MINUS respectively in that order. For further discussion, we define and use the following spatial relationships among the ccs.

Definition 1. Two ccs are horizontally (vertically) overlapped if their MBRs overlap after they are projected onto the horizontal (vertical) axis. For example, in $\frac{x}{y}$, each pair of ccs among x, y and $-$ are horizontally overlapped as their MBRs overlap after projected onto the horizontal axis. Similarly, in $a + b$, a, $+$ and b are vertically overlapped.

Definition 2. Two ccs are horizontally (vertically) adjacent if no other cc is present between them in the horizontal (vertical) direction. For example, in $\frac{x}{y}$, ccs x and $-$ (FRACTION) as well as $-$ and y are vertically adjacent, but x and y are not vertically adjacent as $-$ is present between them in vertical direction.

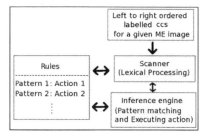

Fig. 2. Proposed symbol formation process

Similarly, in $a+b$, a and $+$ as well as $+$ and b are horizontally adjacent, but a and b are not horizontally adjacent as $+$ is present between them in the horizontal direction.

Let us consider the formation of the multi-cc symbol EQUIVALENT ($=$) as an example. In a ME, if a sequence of three adjacent horizontal line ccs occur, their spatial properties are examined to find whether this sequence forms EQUIVALENT symbol or not. For that, the three ccs are first sorted in the increasing order of y-co-ordinates. If each of the first two and the last two pairs of ccs are horizontally overlapped and vertically adjacent and if all the three ccs do not overlap horizontally with any other cc, then the three ccs form $\equiv$. Likewise, heuristics based on spatial relations have to be designed for other multi-cc and context-dependent symbols.

Heuristics designed to form symbols may fail in some cases and they need to be improved over time. If new symbols are added, heuristics have to be defined for them. If the heuristics are hard-coded in a procedural manner, it is difficult to handle the above two scenarios: Adaptability and Extensibility. Therefore, we have proposed a rule-based approach for symbol formation. In this approach, heuristics are designed in the form of rules and a knowledge base of rules for different symbols is created. These rules are fired depending on input data (here ccs). As knowledge is isolated from data, our symbol formation process behaves like an expert system [4] and is shown in Fig. 2. Proposed symbol formation process shown in Fig. 2 is discussed below:

1. Rules framed for different symbols are stored in the form of (Pattern, Action) pairs, which can be considered as a knowledge base. Pattern is a sequence of ccs that can form a multi-cc symbol or context-dependent symbol. Action part has a piece of code that checks for spatial properties among the ccs in the pattern. If those spatial properties are satisfied, some action is performed on them like forming multi-cc symbol, resolving context-dependent symbol etc. Otherwise, the rule is rejected.
2. Scanner scans the ordered list of labelled ccs of ME image and identifies a pattern which forms a multi-cc or a context-dependent symbol that is present in knowledge base. This is similar to compiler's style of lexical processing.
3. Inference engine takes the matched pattern and executes action associated with it. If a rule is rejected, last cc is eliminated from the pattern and the

resultant pattern is searched in the knowledge base. This process is continued until a matching pattern is found or no more ccs are remained. Now the scanning is resumed from the cc next to the matching pattern.

If a rule to form a symbol needs to be improved, its corresponding action part only has to be modified (easy adaptability). To add a new symbol, it is sufficient to design pattern and action parts for it (easy extensibility) and thus avoids major re-organization of the entire process. Using the above approach, we have framed a total of 74 rules for 61 multi-cc mathematical symbols and 13 context-dependent symbols. For our implementation, we have used C++, a high-level programming language in conjunction with **flex++** [2], a tool to generate lexical analyzer (scanner) in C++ under LINUX operating system. **flex++** takes the rule base, which is a set of (Pattern, Action) pairs, as input and generates a C++ lexical analyzer. The generated C++ scanner also performs the task of inference engine, in addition to scanning an ordered list of labelled input ccs.

Considering the same example as discussed above, for EQUIVALENT symbol, scanner finds the sequence of three adjacent horizontal line ccs (pattern). Inference engine searches for the pattern in the knowledge base and executes the corresponding action which examines the spatial properties (horizontal and vertical overlap as well as adjacency) among the three ccs. If the spatial properties are satisfied, it forms the required multi-cc symbol. Otherwise, it eliminates the last horizontal line cc from the pattern and searches for the pattern of two horizontal line ccs (this pattern may form =) in the knowledge base. If spatial properties are satisfied, = is formed. Otherwise, the single horizontal line cc (context-dependent symbol) is inspected if it is a MINUS, FRACTION etc, and accordingly its label is changed (action). The rules for some of the symbols are discussed below:

Multi-cc symbols

1. $\div$: If the two DOTS are horizontally overlapped and vertically adjacent to the horizontal line cc, then the three ccs (pattern) as discussed in Section 2, are combined to form $\div$ (action).
2. =: If the two horizontal line ccs (pattern) are horizontally overlapped and vertically adjacent and if the two ccs do not have horizontal overlap with any other cc, then the two ccs are combined to form = (action).
3. Similarly, symbols like $i, j, \doteq, \overset{\triangle}{=}, \cong, \approx, \subseteq, \supseteq, \simeq, \leq, \geq, \ll, \gg, \Theta, \odot, \%$ etc, are formed based on the horizontal and vertical overlap as well as adjacency properties.
4. Mathematical functions:
   Let us consider **lim** : If a cc l (pattern) is encountered, then the ccs, bottom part of i, DOT and m are inspected to the right of it. If they are present and each pair of ccs (except the pair, bottom part of i and DOT) are checked whether they are vertically overlapped and horizontally adjacent in that order. The pair, bottom part of i and DOT is checked for horizontal overlap and vertical adjacency. If they are, all the ccs are combined and the label corresponding to **lim** is assigned to the composite symbol. Similarly, other functions like inf, min, max etc, are handled.

Context-dependent symbols

1. **Horizontal line:** If a horizontal line cc (pattern) is encountered, it is checked whether atleast one cc which is not a mathematical operator (non-operator cc), is present in the above as well as in the below of it. If present and that non-operator cc is horizontally overlapped and vertically adjacent to the current horizontal line cc, then the label of this horizontal line is changed to FRACTION.

   Otherwise, if a non-operator cc is present only below the current horizontal line cc and its x-centroid (x-co-ordinate of mid-point of its MBR) lies within the left and right boundaries of the horizontal line, then the label of the horizontal line is changed to OVERBAR.

   Otherwise, if a non-operator cc is present only above the current horizontal line cc and its x-centroid lies within the left and right boundaries of the horizontal line, then the label of the horizontal line is changed to UNDERBAR.

2. **DOT** : If atleast one non-operator cc is present below and is horizontally overlapped and vertically adjacent to DOT (pattern), then label of the current cc DOT is changed to that of accent DOT symbol ($\dot{\ }$). If it is accent DOT, then inspect for an other DOT that is vertically overlapped and horizontally adjacent to the right of it. If one is present, then check whether this second DOT has the same non-operator cc present below and is horizontally overlapped and vertically adjacent to it. If so, both the DOT symbols are combined and the label for the composite symbol is assigned to that of accent double DOT symbol($\ddot{\ }$).

3. **Starting and Ending delimiters:** If a starting delimiter (pattern) is encountered, its corresponding ending delimiter is found and ccs between them are analyzed to find whether those delimiters are for MLME or not. As enumerated functions do not have ending delimiters, a dummy one is assumed. If a MLME is detected, the labels of the delimiters are changed to those for MLMEs and in the process of ccs' analysis, the elements of MLME are also extracted. Detailed process of MLME detection and its element extraction is discussed below. At present, both matrices and enumerated functions are handled.

MLME detection and its element extraction. In a MLME, each element can be again a ME. Chuan et al [12] propose a method for element segmentation of online matrices based on spacing algorithm that leverages symbol identities, sizes and their relative location. Kanahori et al, [18], [10] detect offline matrices based on a threshold (1.5 times the average height of the characters) on the height of starting delimiter. They perform element segmentation by inflating symbols and combining with the neighbouring symbols if they overlap with the inflated symbols and different inflation factors are chosen for different symbols.

Our approach handles both matrices and enumerated functions in an uniform manner except that a dummy ending delimiter is assumed for enumerated functions. To discuss our approach, some terminology is defined below:

Definition 3. A mathematical operator is called a *Horizontal (H) operator* (Eg: $+$, $-$, $*$, $<$, $\leq$, $\geq$, $=$ etc.) if it does not have symbols above and below of it.

Otherwise, it is a *Non-Horizontal* (*NH*) *operator*. Eg: Sum like operators like $\sum, \int, \prod, \sqrt{\ }$ and accent symbols like OVERBAR, UNDERBAR, VECTOR etc.

Definition 4. *NH* operators are termed as *Two-Sided* (*2S*) (Eg: $\sum, \int, \prod, \sqrt{\ }$ etc.) if they can have symbols in both the above and below of them and they are termed as *One-Sided* (*1S*) (Eg: Accent symbols) if they have symbols in only one of the above or below of them.

The process for MLME detection and its element extraction is discussed below:

1. If a starting delimiter is encountered, inspect to its right for the corresponding ending delimiter such that their heights are almost same in the sense, the ratio of smaller to larger heights is almost 1 (greater than 0.8 is taken in our experimentation).
2. If the ending delimiter is not found and the starting delimiter is {, it can be an enumerated function and so all the ccs after the starting delimiter are captured. Otherwise, if the ending delimiter is not found and the starting delimiter is not {, do nothing and exit.
3. If the ending delimiter is found, capture all the ccs between the starting and ending delimiters.
4. Find average height of all the captured ccs which gives an estimate of font size and let it be f.
5. Extract rows of MLME using the captured ccs as described below:
   (a) As ccs in any row are vertically overlapped, each such set of ccs forms a row. The sets of vertically overlapped ccs are found using a graph-based approach. Assume an undirected graph with each cc as a node and an edge is drawn between two nodes (ccs) if the ccs are vertically overlapped. The connected components of the graph are found. The connected component of a graph (ccg) is a sub-graph in which there is a path between any two nodes in it. That means, each ccg contains all the ccs that are vertically overlapped either directly or indirectly and hence forms a row. The number of ccgs gives the number of rows. In degraded documents, adjacent rows may be overlapped and so the condition for the vertical overlap of two ccs is tightened. Instead of just vertical overlap, a vertical overlap of atleast $x\%$ (x can be 50) of the minimum of the heights of the two ccs can be considered.
   (b) If there is only one row, go to element extraction procedure (step 6). Otherwise, go to next step.
   (c) Order the rows in a top to bottom manner. Now there is a need to merge rows as the horizontal, vertical and diagonal dots as well as the super and sub-scripts of *NH* operators may go to different rows.
   (d) Inspect all the rows and merge the rows which form horizontal, vertical and diagonal dots. For that, check if there is a sequence of rows which contains only the dots. If so, merge the successive rows until they overlap after their row heights are doubled. Row height is taken as maximum of the heights of all the ccs in that row.

(e) Scan the resultant rows and for each row do the following: If a $1S - NH$ operator is found and if it does not have any horizontally overlapped ccs in the current row, merge the next row with the current row if the next row overlaps with the current row after the current row height is doubled.

(f) Scan the resultant rows and for each row do the following:
  - If a cc (X) that is a $2S - NH$ operator or a horizontal straight line (note that we do not know whether this is a FRACTION, accent symbol or MINUS at this stage) is found, perform the next two steps.
  - Expand MBR of X vertically on both the sides, by a factor of the maximum of its height and width.
  - If the expanded X overlaps with atleast one non-operator cc in the previous (next) row, then shift all the ccs that are enclosed in the expanded MBR from the previous (next) row to the current row.

(g) In the above process, some rows may become empty as the ccs in them are moved to the neighbouring rows and so eliminate them.

(h) For each resultant row, order the ccs in the left to right manner.

6. Perform element extraction for each row as follows:

(a) Form sets of horizontally overlapped ccs of the current row using graph-based approach in a similar manner as discussed earlier. Initially, each set of ccs is an element. Now there is a need to merge elements as the operands of H as well as NH operators may be in different elements.

(b) For each element – Examine its ccs and if a cc (X) which is a $2S - NH$ operator is found, shift the first cc Y (operand) from the next element along with the horizontally overlapped ccs of Y to the current element.

(c) For each resultant element – Examine its ccs and if a cc (X) which is a H operator is found, expand X horizontally on both the sides by a factor of its width and if the expanded X overlaps with the previous and the next elements, merge the current element with the previous and next elements.

(d) Merge the resultant elements that are closer to one another based on font size (f) – If the gap between last cc of a element and the first cc of its next element is less than $0.5 * f$, merge the two elements.

7. If the above process gives only one row and one element, it is not MLME.

8. Otherwise, change the labels of the starting and ending delimiters to those of the corresponding MLME delimiters. As each element is again a ME, send each of them to symbol formation process so that symbols are formed for all the elements recursively. This recursion handles nested MLMEs.

An illustration of the above process is shown in Fig. 3. A matrix image is shown in Fig. 3(a). In Fig. 3(b), initial rows obtained based on vertical overlap are shown (step 5(a) in the above process). It is observed that nine rows are obtained. As second, fifth and eighth rows have horizontal line ccs, ccs from their previous and next rows are shifted to these rows and as a result only three rows are obtained as shown in Fig. 3(c) (step 5(f)). In Fig. 3(d), initial elements obtained based

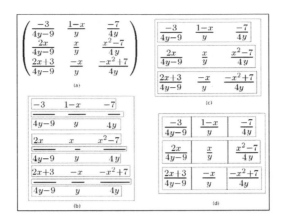

Fig. 3. Illustration of MLME row and element extraction algorithm:(a)A matrix image (b) Initial row extraction (based on vertical overlap)(c) Final row extraction (d) Initial (based on horizontal overlap) as well as Final element extraction for each row

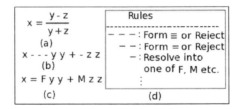

Fig. 4. (a)A ME image (b) Left to right ordered ccs (c) Symbols formed from the ccs; Here, F denotes FRACTION and M denotes MINUS (d) Required rules

on horizontal overlap for each row are shown (step 6(a)). In this example, as the adjacent elements are not closer to one another (based on font size) (step 6(d)), the final elements are same as the initial ones.

4   Results and Discussion

Our approach is tested on about 800 MEs [1] taken from various mathematical documents collected from the internet. Those MEs cover various branches of mathematics like Algebra, Trigonometry, Geometry, Calculus etc. In Fig. 4(a), a ME image is shown and its left to right ordered ccs are shown in (b). Left to right ordered symbols that are formed from its ccs are shown in (c) and the required rules are shown in (d). As discussed in Section 3, scanner first picks a pattern of three horizontal line ccs and as the rule is rejected, = is formed and the remaining two horizontal lines are resolved to FRACTION and MINUS respectively. A MLME image and its result after applying symbol formation process are shown in Fig. 5. It can be seen in Fig. 5, = is formed, horizontal line is resolved to FRACTION, elements are extracted in each determinant (shown in boxes in Fig. 5) and the labels of corresponding delimiters are accordingly

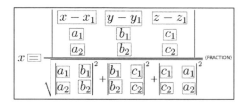

Fig. 5. Symbol formation process on a ME image with determinants

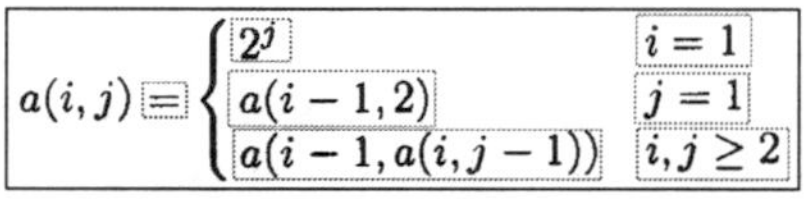

$$a(i,j) = \begin{cases} 2^j & i = 1 \\ a(i-1,2) & j = 1 \\ a(i-1, a(i, j-1)) & i, j \geq 2 \end{cases}$$

Fig. 6. Symbol formation process on an enumerated function image

changed. Each element is again subjected to symbol formation process and the horizontal line ccs in those elements are resolved to MINUS (not shown in the figure). An enumerated function and its result of symbol formation process are shown in Fig. 6. In that figure, = and elements extracted are shown in boxes. Of course, mulit-cc symbols i and j formed in $a(i,j)$ as well as in each element of the function are not shown in the figure.

From our experimentation on 826 MEs, it is observed that for some MEs, non-MLMEs are taken as MLMEs and vice-versa and for a few other MEs, elements are not correctly extracted. Out of 826 MEs, there are 757 non-MLMEs and 69 MLMEs. Of 69 MLMEs, there are 60 matrix expressions and 9 enumerated functions in which elements of all the 60 matrix expressions and 8 enumerated functions are correctly extracted. Among 757 non-MLMEs, 500 MEs have delimiters, in which only 20 MEs are taken as MLMEs and the remaining non-MLMEs without delimiters have well formed symbols. In our approach, further improvement in MLME detection and its element extraction can be accomplished by just modifying action parts associated with starting delimiters (easy adaptability).

5   Conclusion

In this paper, we focus on the symbol formation process in printed MEs in which multi-cc symbols and the context-dependent symbols are resolved using spatial relations. A rule-based approach is proposed for the purpose which handles both single-line and multi-line MEs in an unified manner. Our approach has been tested on around 800 MEs collected from various mathematical documents and experimental results are reported on them.

References

1. http://dcis.uohyd.ernet.in/~pavanp/mathocr/PrintedMEs.zip
2. flex++(1):fast lexical analyzer generator-Linux man page,
   http://linux.die.net/man/1/flex++

3. Awal, A.-M., Mouchere, H., Viard-Gaudin, C.: Towards handwritten mathematical expression recognition. In: ICDAR 2009, pp. 1046–1050. IEEE Computer Society, Washington, DC (2009)
4. Buchanan, B.G., Shortliffe, E.H.: Rule Based Expert Systems: The Mycin Experiments of the Stanford Heuristic Programming Project. Addison-Wesley (1984)
5. Chan, K.-F., Yeung, D.-Y.: Mathematical expression recognition: a survey. IJDAR 3, 3–15 (2000)
6. Chaudhuri, B.B., Garain, U.: An approach for recognition and interpretation of mathematical expressions in printed document. Pattern Analysis and Applications 3, 120–131 (2000)
7. Eto, Y., Suzuki, M.: Mathematical formula recognition using virtual link network. In: ICDAR 2001, pp. 762–767. IEEE Computer Society, Washington, DC (2001)
8. Fukuda, R., Sou, I., Tamari, F., Ming, X., Suzuki, M.: A technique of mathematical expression structure analysis for the handwriting input system. In: ICDAR 1999, p. 131. IEEE Computer Society, Washington, DC (1999)
9. Garain, U., Chaudhuri, B.B.: Recognition of online handwritten mathematical expressions. IEEE Transactions on Systems, Man, and Cybernetics, Part B: Cybernetics 34(6), 2366–2376 (2004)
10. Kanahori, T., Suzuki, M.: Detection of matrices and segmentation of matrix elements in scanned images of scientific documents. In: ICDAR 2003, vol. 1, p. 433. IEEE Computer Society, Washington, DC (2003)
11. Lee, H.J., Wang, J.S.: Design of a mathematical expression recognition system. In: ICDAR 1995, vol. 2, pp. 1084–1087 (1995)
12. Li, C., Zeleznik, R.C., Miller, T., LaViola, J.J.: Online recognition of handwritten mathematical expressions with support for matrices. In: ICPR 2008, pp. 1–4 (2008)
13. Suzuki, M., Tamari, F., Fukuda, R., Uchida, S., Kanahori, T.: Infty- an integrated OCR system for mathematical documents. In: Proceedings of ACM Symposium on Document Engineering 2003, pp. 95–104. ACM Press (2003)
14. Tapia, E., Rojas, R.: Recognition of on-line handwritten mathematical formulas in the E-Chalk System. In: ICDAR 2003, vol. 2, p. 980 (2003)
15. Tapia, E., Rojas, R.: Recognition of On-Line Handwritten Mathematical Expressions Using a Minimum Spanning Tree Construction and Symbol Dominance. In: Lladós, J., Kwon, Y.-B. (eds.) GREC 2003. LNCS, vol. 3088, pp. 329–340. Springer, Heidelberg (2004)
16. Tian, X.-D., Li, H.-Y., Li, X.-F., Zhang, L.-P.: Research on symbol recognition for mathematical expressions. In: International Conference on Innovative Computing, Information and Control, vol. 3, pp. 357–360. IEEE Computer Society, Los Alamitos (2006)
17. Tian, X., Fan, H.: Structural analysis based on baseline in printed mathematical expressions. In: International Conference on Parallel and Distributed Computing Applications and Technologies, PDCAT 2005, pp. 787–790. IEEE Computer Society, Los Alamitos (2005)
18. Toshihiro, K., Masakazu, S.: A Recognition Method of Matrices by Using Variable Block Pattern Elements Generating Rectangular Area. In: Blostein, D., Kwon, Y.-B. (eds.) GREC 2001. LNCS, vol. 2390, pp. 320–329. Springer, Heidelberg (2002)
19. Twaaliyondo, H.M., Okamoto, M.: Structure analysis and recognition of mathematical expressions. In: ICDAR 1995, vol. 1, p. 430. IEEE Computer Society, Washington, DC (1995)
20. Vuong, B.-Q., Hui, S.-C., He, Y.: Progressive structural analysis for dynamic recognition of on-line handwritten mathematical expressions. Pattern Recognition Letters 29, 647–655 (2008)
21. Zanibbi, R., Blostein, D., Cordy, J.R.: Recognizing mathematical expressions using tree transformation. IEEE Transactions on PAMI 24, 1455–1467 (2002)

PCA Plus LDA on Wavelet Co-occurrence Histogram Features: Application to CBIR

Shivashankar S[1,*], Parvati Vasudev K.[2], Pujari Jagadesh D.[2],
and Sachin Kumar S. Veerashetty[3]

[1] Department of Computer Science, Karnatak Science College,
Dharwad, Karnataka, India
[2] Department of Information Science, SDM College of Engineering and Technology,
Dharwad, Karnataka, India
[3] Department of Computer Science, VTU,
Belgaum, Karnataka, India
s_shivashankar@rediffmail.com, jaggudp@yahoo.com,
{vkparvati,sveerashetty}@gmail.com

Abstract. In this paper, we propose a novel wavelet based PCA-LDA approach for content Based Image Retrieval. The color and texture features are extracted based on the co-occurrence histograms of wavelet decomposed images. The features extracted by this method form a feature vector of high dimensionality of 1152 for the color image. A combination of Principal Component Analysis (PCA) and Linear Discriminate Analysis (LDA) was applied on feature vector for dimension reduction and to enhance the class separability. By applying PCA to the feature vectors, low dimensionality feature sets were obtained and processed using LDA. The vectors obtained from the LDA are representative of each image. It is evident from the experimental results that the proposed method exhibits superior performance in the reduced feature set (i.e., retrieval efficiency 87% for proposed method, 66% for PCA and 35% for original set based on wavelet feature).

Keywords: Texture, Wavelet, PCA, LDA, CBIR, Dimensionality Reduction.

1   Introduction

With the development of the Internet, and the availability of image capturing devices such as digital cameras, image scanners, the size of digital image collection is increasing rapidly. Efficient image searching, browsing and retrieval tools are required by users from various domains, including remote sensing, fashion, crime prevention, publishing, medicine, architecture, etc. For this purpose, many general purpose image retrieval systems have been developed [1]. The goal of content based image retrieval (CBIR) is to retrieve desired images from large image databases, based on visual contents, such as color, texture and shape. The main tasks in CBIR are extracting features of every image based on its pixel values. These extracted

---

* Corresponding author.

C. Sombattheera et al. (Eds.): MIWAI 2011, LNAI 7080, pp. 193–200, 2011.

features form the image representation for measuring similarity with other images in the database. Region Based Image retrieval (RBIR) is a special type of CBIR. A region is seen as a part of an image with homogeneous low-level features. Depending on the query specification type, the RBIR systems are categorized as Whole Image as Query (WIQ) and Image Region as Query (IRQ). In WIQ type RBIR, users provide the example image and the system uses information from the whole image for query [2]. The similarity measure of two images is computed using feature information of regions of the whole image. The SIMPLIcity system [3] uses this type of approach, named as Integrated Region Matching (IRM), for image similarity.

In the CBIR system, images are usually represented by high dimensional visual perceptive feature vectors. However, the difficulty to index high-dimensional vectors and the gap between low-level visual features and high-level semantic concepts makes it ineffective to achieve good performance. In the last decade, Fisher linear discriminant analysis has been demonstrated to be a successful discriminant analysis algorithm in face recognition [5], [6], [7], [8]. It performs dimensionality reduction by trying to find a mapping from originally high-dimensional space to a low-dimensional space in which the most discriminant features are preserved. As LDA has been broadly applied and well studied in recent years, a series of LDA algorithms have been developed, the most famous method of which is Fisherface [7], [8]. It uses a PCA plus LDA as a two-phase framework. Its recognition effectiveness has been widely proved [4], [7], [8], [9], [10].

The major problem with RBIR based system is poor performance of segmentation algorithms. Semantic segmentation has been a challenge and not very effectively addressed till date [3]. Hence in this research, color and texture features are extracted based on the co-occurrence histograms of wavelet decomposed images, which capture the information about relationship between each high frequency subband and that in low frequency subband of the transformed image at the corresponding level [16]. The features extracted by this method form a feature vector of dimensionality 1152 for the color image. Despite having excellent discriminative power the feature set suffers from high dimensionality. A combination of Principal Component Analysis (PCA) and Linear Discriminate Analysis (LDA) was applied on feature vector for dimension reduction and to enhance the class separability. By applying PCA to the feature vectors, low dimensionality feature sets were obtained and processed using LDA. The vectors obtained from the LDA are representative of each image. The experimental results are encouraging. This paper is organized as follows: In Section 2, the proposed method is discussed in detail. The experimental results are explained in Section 3. Finally, section 4 concludes the discussion.

2   Proposed Method

The Fig. 1. represents the architecture of the proposed system, which consists of two Modules. Each is described below.

2.1   Image Representation Module

2.1.1 Wavelet Feature

We extract wavelet based co-occurrence histogram features [16] on each of the channels of the image in RGB space. The image is represented by a t dimensional vector x_i (where t=1152). These texture features capture the significant information about color and texture for characterizing an image. The vectors obtained in this manner from all N images will be denoted by $X = \{x_1, x_2 \dots, x_n\}$. Further these features are used for dimensionality reduction.

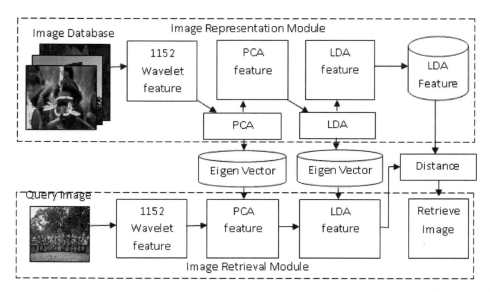

Fig. 1. Architecture of the proposed system

2.1.2 The PCA Space

Given a set of data, PCA finds the linear lower-dimensional representation of the data such that the variance of the reconstructed data is preserved [14], [15]. So, the main idea behind using PCA in our approach is to reduce the dimensionality of the wavelet co-occurrence histogram features.

Given a t dimensional vector representation of each image, the Principal Component Analysis (PCA) is used to find a subspace whose basis vectors correspond to the maximum-variance directions in the original space. Let W represent the linear transformation that maps the original t-dimensional space onto a f-dimensional feature subspace where normally f≪t. The new feature vectors $y_i \in \Re^f$ are defined by $y_i = W^T x_i, i = 1, \dots, N$. The columns of W are the eigenvectors e_i obtained by solving the eigenstructure decomposition $\lambda_i e_i = Q e_i$, where $Q = XX^T$ is the covariance matrix and λ_i the eigenvalue associated with the eigenvector e_i. Before obtaining the eigenvectors of Q, the eigen vectors are normalized such that $\|x_i\|=1$ to make the system invariant to the intensity of the illumination source. The eigenvectors are stored in the database and is called as PCA eigenvectors. A PCA feature vector is obtained with reduced dimension of 40 features for each image (empirical results showed better performance for 40 features).

2.1.3   The LDA Space

Linear Discriminant Analysis (LDA) searches for those vectors in the underlying space that best discriminate among classes (rather than those that best describe the data). More formally, given a number of independent features relative to which the data is described, LDA creates a linear combination of these which yields the largest mean differences between the desired classes. Mathematically speaking, for all the samples of all classes, we define two measures:

1) One is called within-class scatter matrix, as given by

$$S_w = \sum_{j=1}^{C} \sum_{i=1}^{N_j} (y_i^j - \mu_j)(y_i^j - \mu_j)^T \qquad (1)$$

where y_i^j is the ith sample of class j, μ_j is the mean of class j, C is the number of classes, and N_j the number of samples in class j.

2) The other is called between-class scatter matrix

$$S_b = \sum_{j=1}^{C} (\mu_j - \mu)(\mu_j - \mu)^T \qquad (2)$$

where μ represents the mean of all classes.

The goal is to maximize the between-class measure while minimizing the within-class measure. One way to do this is to maximize the ratio $\frac{det\ |S_b|}{det|S_w|}$. The advantage of using this ratio is that it has been proven [12] that if S_w is a nonsingular matrix then this ratio is maximized when the column vectors of the projection matrix, W, are the eigenvectors of $S_w^{-1}S_b$. It should be noted (and it is very easy to prove) that:

1) There are at most C-1 nonzero generalized eigenvectors and, so, an upper bound on f is C - 1,

2) We require at least f + C samples to guarantee that S_w does not become singular (which is almost impossible in any realistic application). To solve this, [13] and [11] proposed the use of an intermediate space. In both cases, this intermediate space is chosen to be the PCA space.

Thus, the original t-dimensional space is projected onto an intermediate f-dimensional space using PCA and then onto a final g-dimensional space using LDA. These LDA features for each image are stored in the database which is further used for retrieval.

2.2   Image Retrieval Module

In this module, 1152 wavelet based co-occurrence histogram features are extracted from the query image. These features are projected on PCA eigen vector to obtain PCA feature of dimensionality 40. Further these features are projected on LDA eigen vector which produce LDA features. These LDA features are compared with those stored in the database by using Euclidean distance measure. The following show the formula of Euclidian distance

$$D(M) = \sqrt{\sum_{j=1}^{N} \left(f_j[X] - f_j[M] \right)^2} \quad (3)$$

where, N is the number of features, $f_j[X]$ represents j^{th} feature of the query image X, while $f_j[M]$ represents the jth feature of the Mth image in the database. The result of image retrieval is a list of image valued by images distance with the query image.

3   Experimental Results

The proposed system is implemented on WANG database [17] which is a subset of Corel images consisting of 1000 images of natural scenes divided into 10 labeled categories of 100 images each. These images were arranged in 10 semantic groups: tribesmen, elephants, horses, flowers, foods, greek architecture, buses, Dinosaurs, mountains, and beaches.

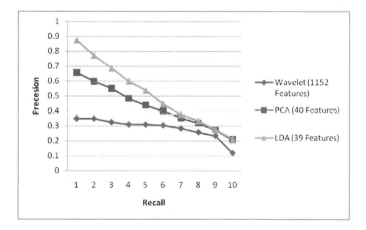

Fig. 2. Average Precesion~Recall Graph of 10 images one image choosen from each category

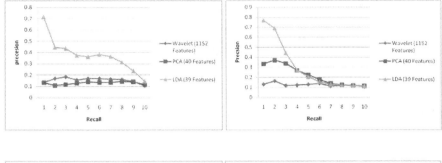

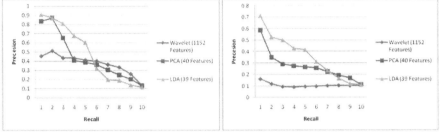

Fig. 3. Precesion~recall graph Top-Left : tribesmen (43), Top-Right: Monuments(204), Bottom-Left : Elephant (510), Bottom-Right : Food(955)

The experimental results of the proposed method is compared with wavelet (1152 features) and PCA (40 features). The Fig. 2. shows a precesion~recall graph with the averaging done over 10 query images one image randomly choosen from each category. It is evident that the result of the proposed method outperforms the other two methods in the reduced feature set (i.e., retrieval efficiency 87% for proposed method, 66% for PCA and 35% for original set based on wavelet feature). The precesion~recall graph for few queries are shown in Fig. 3. The Fig. 4. shows the sample query images and top 10 retrievals for each query obtained by the proposed method. The first image is the query image, followed by the corresponding retrieved images. We are able to retrieve all the top 10 images for buses, Dinosaurs, flowers, horses and mountains Categories. For greek architecture, elephants and food categories top 9 images are of the same category, top 8 images are from tribesman category, whereas a poor of only 6 images are retrieved for beaches category.

4   Conclusion

A novel wavelet based PCA-LDA approach for content Based Image Retrieval has been presented in this paper. The texture features are extracted based on the co-occurrence histograms of wavelet decomposed images. A combination of Principal Component Analysis (PCA) and Linear Discriminate Analysis (LDA) was applied on feature vector for dimension reduction and to enhance the class separability. The vectors obtained from the LDA are representative of each image. It was found to be robust against changes in illumination. The experimental results demonstrate the efficacy of the proposed method for image retrieval. The results are encouraging.

Fig. 4. Sample query image followed by top ten retrievals in ten examples

References

1. Liua, Y., Zhanga, D., Lua, G., Mab, W.-Y.: A survey of content-based image retrieval with high-level semantics. Pattern Recognition 40, 262–282 (2007)
2. Hiremath, P.S., Shivashankar, S., Pujari, J.: Wavelet Based Features for Color Texture Classification With Application To CBIR. International Journal of Computer Science and Network Security 6(9A), 124–133 (2006)
3. Wang, J.Z., Li, J., Wiederhold, G.: SIMPLIcity: Semantics-Sensitive Integrated Matching for picture Libraries. IEEE Trans. Pattern Analysis and Machine Intelligence 23(9), 947–963 (2001)

4. Ye, F., Shi, Z., Shi, Z.: A Comparative Study Of PCA, LDA And Kernel LDA For Image Classification. In: International Symposium on Ubiquitous Virtual Reality, pp. 51–54 (2009)
5. Cheng, Y., Zhuang, Y., Yang, J.: Optimal Fisher discriminant analysis using the rank decomposition. Pattern Recognition 25(1), 101–111 (1992)
6. Yu, H., Yang, J.: A Direct LDA Algorithm for High-Dimensional Data with Application to Face Recognition. Pattern Recognition 34(10), 2067–2070 (2001)
7. Swets, D.L., Weng, J.: Discriminant analysis and eigenspace partition tree for face and object recognition from views. In: Proceedings of the 2nd International Conference on Automatic Face and Gesture Recognition (FG 1996), October 14-16, p. 192. IEEE Computer Society, Washington, DC (1996)
8. Belhumeur, N., Hespanha, J., Kriegman, D.: Eigenfaces vs.Fisherfaces: Recognition Using Class Specific Linear Projection. In: Buxton, B.F., Cipolla, R. (eds.) ECCV 1996. LNCS, vol. 1065, pp. 45–58. Springer, Heidelberg (1996)
9. Zhao, W., Chellappa, R., Phillips, J.: Subspace Linear Discriminant Analysis for Face Recognition. Technical Report CS-TR4009, Univ.of Maryland (1999)
10. Lu, J., Plataniotis, K.N., Venetsanopoulos, A.N.: Face Recognition Using Kernel Direct Discriminant Analysis Algorithms. IEEE Transactions on Neural Networks 14(1), 117–126 (2003)
11. Belhumeour, P.N., Hespanha, J.P., Kriegman, D.J.: Eigenfaces vs. Fisherfaces: Recognition Using Class Specific Linear Projection. IEEE Trans. Pattern Analysis and Machine Intelligence 19(7), 711–720 (1997)
12. Fisher, R.A.: The Statistical Utilization of Multiple Measurements. Annals of Eugenics 8, 376–386 (1938)
13. Swets, D.L., Weng, J.J.: Using Discriminant Eigenfeatures for Image Retrieval. IEEE Trans. Pattern Analysis and Machine Intelligence 18(8), 831–836 (1996)
14. Sengur, A.: An expert system based on principal component analysis, artificial immune system and fuzzy k-NN for diagnosis of valvular heart diseases. Comp. Biol. Med (2007), doi:10.1016/j.compbiomed.2007.11.004
15. Duda, R.O., Hart, P.E., Stork, D.G.: Pattern Classification. Wiley, New York (2001)
16. Hiremath, P.S., Shivashankar, S.: Wavelet based co-occurrence histogram features for texture classification with an application to script identification in a document image. Pattern Recognition Letters 29, 1182–1189 (2008)
17. http://wang.ist.psu.edu/

Printed Text Characterization for Identifying Print Technology Using Expectation Maximization Algorithm

Maramreddy Umadevi, Arun Agarwal, and Chillarige Raghavendra Rao

Department of Computers and Information Science, University of Hyderabad,
Hyderabad, Andhra Pradesh, India
sriuma28@yahoo.co.in, {aruncs,crrcs}@uohyd.ernet.in

Abstract. Forensic analysis of printed documents is a multi objective activity with intrinsic data as inputs which demands efficient techniques. Recent trends suggest the need for good preprocessors and post analysing tools which characterize printed text for identification of print technology. Each printing technology differs in their process of placing marking material on the target. The paper focuses on frequently used word like 'the' as test sample for characterizing printed text. The novelty of the proposed algorithm is that the selected printed text is modelled as mixture of three Gaussian models namely text, noise and background. The associated patterns and features of the models are derived using Expectation Maximization(EM) algorithm and few indices are proposed based on these parameters. One of the indices called Print Index(PI) for text is used for basic print technology discrimination.

Keywords: Index Terms- EM algorithm, Gaussian Mixture Model and Print Index.

1 Introduction

Documents are any material containing marks, symbols, or signs that convey meaning or message to someone[1]. Printed material like documents of agreements related to authority or ownership of properties, identity cards have text content which is often forged by antisocial elements for performing criminal activities. Forgery is done by altering any of the contents of the document or reproducing the whole document with evolving digital imaging techniques. One can easily add text to the margin of the document or with in the document. People print their names by removing genuine name in identity cards or change the names in the mark sheets for achieving certain targets. Therefore determining genuineness of a document is critical and needs to be established. These documents are also referred to as questioned documents, which are submitted for forensic examination. Document Examination starts from general to specific. Document examiner needs to answer questions about the consistency of the document, i.e., whether the content in the document is printed using one

C. Sombattheera et al. (Eds.): MIWAI 2011, LNAI 7080, pp. 201–212, 2011.
© Springer-Verlag Berlin Heidelberg 2011

source printer or more than one printer. There is need for an extensive knowledge of emerging print technologies to identify the class characteristics of the document. Printed text characterization assists forensic examiner in identifying printing process or techniques by identifying spatial pattern of text produced by that printing mechanism.

We now discuss characterization of printed text for identification of print technology. Assume that each word in the printed text contains three main components namely printed text, noise which is scattered around the edges of printed text due to the spatial distribution of the marking material and the back ground. Each component is modelled as Gaussian distribution and the printed text is represented by mixture of these three Gaussian distributions. These models are built using EM algorithm which returns parameters with mean, mixed proportion and variance for each of the three components. The Print Index(PI) proposed based on these parameters is taken as feature to characterize printed text. The contribution in this paper can be presented in two ways: one building the classifier and second identification of print technology as inkjet or laserjet.

The rest of the paper is organized as follows: Section 2 discusses related work in the field of forensic analysis of printed documents for identification of print technology, Section 3 describes EM algorithm, Section 4 presents algorithm for characterization of printed text and calculation of print index. It also presents experimental results, evaluates performance and robustness of the proposed method, Section 5 concludes and suggests future work.

2   Related Work

Recent research publications demonstrate various approaches suggested for discriminating printing techniques. Research activities at Purdue University are on characterization of Electro photographic printers[2], the gray level co-occurrence feature[3] of the most frequently occurring letter 'e' and Gaussian Mixture Model(GMM) [4] are used for printer identification.

In GMM, Principal component analysis is used as dimension reduction technique by 1-D projections of the extracted text character. These researches are exclusively for the identification of Electro photographic printers.

Machine Identification code project by Electronic Frontier Foundation identifies presence of pattern of yellow dots [5] in colour laser printouts which represent printer serial number. This is not applicable to all Electro-photographic printers as some printers do not show the presence of these yellow dots.

Identification of printing process using HSV color space by Haritha[6][7], is based on hue histogram for identification of printing process and photocopy. Hue contrast, periodicity and ink over spray are the features selected for classifying ink jet, laser jet and photocopies. This is color image processing technique using HSV color space.

Gray level features proposed by Lambert[8] for discriminating ink jet from laser jet print is dependent on high resolution scanned images, 3200 dot per inch. Recent research is concentrated on evaluation of gray level features like perimeter based edge roughness of the text[9] for print technique classification, based on low resolution image for high through put document management system. In Beusekom [10] proposed a method to detect misalignment of text lines that are additionally inserted in a document. If the forged text line alignment is same as original text line, it is difficult to find out the forged document.

Forensic examination of printed document needs high resolution scanned images of the text as input for pixel level comparison. When the large number of documents are to be examined, then there is need to manage huge data for identification of print pattern. Dimension reduction of input data helps in preprocessing of the forensic analysis of printed text documents. Hence, From literature review it can be seen that there is need for techniques for characterization of printed text based on feature set selection to reduce data dimension. The selected features assists the forensic examiner in identifying the basic print technology like ink jet or laser jet, which printed the text.

3   Expectation Maximization Technique

3.1   Introduction

Statistical partitioning of image into meaningful regions is goal of many image analysis algorithms[11]. The segmentation process will group the components existing in the image which are strongly related to the image objects. EM space partitioning algorithm is convergent and optimize partitioning decisions based on the initial set of Gaussian Mixture Models[12]. A proper initializing condition is important, otherwise the algorithm will be forced to converge to numerous local minima.

Each iteration of the EM algorithm follows two steps: E-step and M-step. E-step is an Expectation step, once observed data and current model parameters are given, expectation step involves estimation of missing data. Gaussian mixture density parameter is one of the widely used applications of EM algorithm in pattern recognition. Assume probabilistic model of mixed distribution:

$$p(x|\Theta) = \sum_{i=1}^{C} \alpha_i p_i(x|\theta_i) \qquad (1)$$

where the parameters $\Theta = \{\alpha_1, \alpha_2, ...\alpha_C, \theta_1, \theta_2, ..., \theta_C\}$ such that

$$\sum_{i=1}^{C} \alpha_i = 1 \qquad (2)$$

Here, C component densities are mixed together with C mixing coefficients α_i. Here i=1, 2, ...,C. where C is number of mixing components. The function p_i is the density function of Gaussian distribution and parametrized θ_i and is defined as follows:

$$p_i(x|\theta_i) = \frac{1}{\sigma_i\sqrt{(2\pi)}} exp\left[-\frac{|x-M_i|^2}{2\sigma_i^2}\right] \tag{3}$$

where x is the value of the observed variable, $\theta_i = \{M_i, \sigma_i^2, \alpha_i\}$, M_i, σ_i^2, and α_i are the mean, the variance and the corresponding mixing parameter for i^{th} gaussian distribution of that observed data.

The Expectation step is represented by log likelihood function as follows

$$Q(\Theta, \Theta(t)) = E[\log p(X, Y \mid \Theta) \mid X, \Theta(t)] \tag{4}$$

where $\Theta(t)$ are the current parameters and Θ are the new parameters that optimize the increase of Q. The M step is applied to maximize the result obtained from the E-step.

$$\Theta(t+1) = argmaxQ(\Theta \mid \Theta(t)) \text{ and } Q(\Theta(t+1), \Theta(t)) \geq Q(\Theta, \Theta(t)) \tag{5}$$

Expectation maximization steps are applied repeatedly until specified number of iterations or the log likelihood function is smaller than the specified values.

$$\alpha_i(t+1) = \frac{\sum_{j=1}^{N} p(i \mid x_j, \theta(t))}{N} \tag{6}$$

$$M_i(t+1) = \frac{\sum_{j=1}^{N} x_j p(i \mid x_j, \theta(t))}{\sum_{j=1}^{N} p(i \mid x_j, \theta(t))} \tag{7}$$

$$\sigma_i^2(t+1) = \frac{\sum_{j=1}^{N} p(i| x_j, \theta(t))|x_j - M_j(t+1)|^2}{\sum_{j=1}^{N} p(i| x_j, \theta(t))} \tag{8}$$

where

$$p(i| x_j, \phi) = \frac{\alpha_i p_i(x_j| \theta_i)}{\sum_{k=1}^{C} \alpha_k p_k(x_j|\theta_k)} \tag{9}$$

The following section discusses the application of EM for segmentation of text sample into meaningful regions.

3.2 Application of EM for Text Sample

Assume that the test document has the word 'the' printed in Times New Roman font with font size of 12pt. Each test document is printed on white paper where text is in foreground, white paper as background and some pixels distributed all over the document as noise. Scanned image of printed word 'the' is taken as text sample which is shown in Figure 1. This scanned image 'the' is taken as input to EM algorithm for segmenting it into a strongly related component. Each word is assumed as a mixture of foreground text, back ground white colour and intermediate intensities which are known as noise. Thus, each printed text

(a) Scanned sample word 'the'   (b) Segmented text after applying EM

Fig. 1. Segmenting text using EM algorithm

is assumed as mixture of these three Gaussian distributions. Associated patterns of these three Gaussian distributions of text is built using the EM algorithm. Gray scale image of printed text is submitted to EM algorithm considering three classes, which are fore ground text, noise and background. Each pixel in the image is assigned a posterior probability of belonging to one of the three classes. Based on posterior probability of each pixel, it is classified as belong to one of the three classes and is shown in Figure 1.

4   Algorithm for Characterization of Printed Text

In this section, we developed a novel Print Index(PI) based on the printed text. Algorithm 1 describes procedure for characterization of printed text. The following systematic procedure has been developed to obtain the print index for a given printer.

1. Print a word say 'the' on white paper at 600 dpi.
2. Scan the printed text at 2400dpi.
3. Extract the word 'the' from scanned image and fix it to minimum bounded rectangle(MBR)
4. Normalize the MBR to fixed size using nearest neighbour interpolation[13]. Each text sample 'the' is resized to [300,400] and text sample 'The' is resized to [300,600].
5. Resized sample is given as input to EM Algorithm. Determine EM parameters $\{M_i, \sigma_i^2, \alpha_i\}$ for i=1,2,3 where C=3, i.e., number of classes=3.

EM algorithm segment each sample into 3 clusters namely text, noise, background (white). For each cluster we compute parameters mean intensity, mixing proportion and variance. The data generated for bench mark data set is given to EM algorithm, which returns parameters to formulate Print Index. The following sub section is devoted to methodology for classification of printer technology based on Print Index and its performance.

Algorithm 1. PRINTCHAR(Textsample)

//Algorithm for Characterization of printed text//
Input:
       Textsample: resized image of printed text
Output:
       PI: Print Index
Method:
1: Give Textsample as input to EM algorithm {EM parameters for text are $\{M_{text}, \alpha_{text}, \sigma_{text}^2\}$, for noise are $\{M_{noise}, \alpha_{noise}, \sigma_{noise}^2\}$ and for background component are $\{M_{background}, \alpha_{background}, \sigma_{background}^2\}$ respectively}
   {Cumulative Mean, μ is defined as follows}
2: $\mu \leftarrow \mu_{text} + \mu_{noise} + \mu_{background}$
   $\{\mu_{text} \leftarrow M_{text} * \alpha_{text}\}$
   $\{\mu_{noise} \leftarrow M_{noise} * \alpha_{noise}\}$
   $\{\mu_{background} \leftarrow M_{background} * \alpha_{background}\}$
3: Print Index of text is defined as $PI \leftarrow 100 * \frac{(I_{noise} - I_{text})}{(I_{text})}$
   {Index of text, $I_{text} \leftarrow 100 * \frac{\mu_{text}}{\mu}$}
   {Index of noise, $I_{noise} \leftarrow 100 * \frac{\mu_{noise}}{\mu}$}
   {Index of background, $I_{background} \leftarrow 100 * \frac{\mu_{background}}{\mu}$}
4: Return PI

4.1 Classification of Printed Text

Classification of printed text is the process which selects various text samples produced using various print technology and compute print index of these samples. For classification, group these Print Indexes to identify the print technology of given test sample. Hence, selection of text sample is significant in building the methodology for characterization of printed text. This section discusses about preparation of text samples.

Selection of text samples. Three types of text documents are prepared for selection of text samples. Each text document has Times New Roman font with font size of 12pt. These documents are printed on white paper at 600 dpi and scanned at 2400 dpi using HP Scanjet scanner.

First type of text document contains most frequently occurring word 'the' and it is taken as Type 1 text sample. Second type of document contains word 'The' and it is taken as Type 2 text sample. Some general text document is taken as third type of text document, in which all three letter word are taken as Type 3 text sample. Each word in the document is selected by application of minimum bounded rectangle [14]. For sample of any small case three letter word like 'the' are resized to a fixed size of 300 by 400, where as the sample of type like 'The' is resized to 300 by 600 for characterization of text. Rapid changes in availability of printers created constraints in selection of text sample. Therefore, text sample on available printers was considered. The text samples are selected from the printers listed in Table 1 and Table 2. First and third type of text documents was printed on printers listed in Table 1. Second type of text documents are printed on printers listed in Table 2. which shows printer id, no of samples collected and printer name.

Table 1. Printers used for printing 'the' and general three letter word

P. id	No. of words 'the' Collected	No of general 3 letter words	printer	Print technology
1	100	34	Hppsc1608	Inkjet
2	100	34	Officejet6110	Inkjet
3	100	34	Hplaser4550N	Colorlaserjet
4	100	34	Hplaser1200	Laserjet
5	100	34	SamsungML2010	Laserjet

Table 2. Printers used for printing Text sample 'The'

P. id	No. of words Collected	printer	Print technology
1	200	Hppsc1608	Inkjet
2	200	Officejet6110	Inkjet
3	100	Hplaser4550N	Colorlaserjet
4	100	Hplaser1200	Laserjet
5	100	SamsungML2010	Laserjet
6	100	Xeroxwcpe220	Black and white laser
7	100	Hplaser 9040	Black and white laser
8	82	CannonIR3530	Black and white laser
9	100	Cannon LBP2900	Black and white laser

Segmentation of text samples using EM. Selection of text samples and preprocessing of samples is followed by segmentation using Expectation Maximization algorithm. Text 'the' referred to as Type 1 samples are printed on printers listed in Table 1 and shown in Figure 2. Application of Expectation Maximization technique for segmenting each text into three components is shown in Figure 3.

Fig. 2. Type 1 samples printed on printers listed in Table 1

Fig. 3. Segmented words of Figure 2

Characterization of Printed Text. Each sample is characterized using Print Index measure which uses modelled Gaussian parameters of each sample. Application of EM to each printed image of text sample, it returns modelled Gaussian distribution parameters for fore ground text, background and noise. Cumulative mean for each sample and Index of text, back ground and noise of each sample is calculated as shown in Algorithm 1. Cumulative mean and Index of text and noise is used to formulate Print Index measure.

Total of 500 samples of 'the' are collected from 5 different printers listed in Table 1. Sample versus Index of each component in that sample is shown in Figure 4. From Figure 4 it is clearly noticed that index of text is more for inkjet samples compared to laserjet samples whereas index of noise is more in laserjet samples compared to inkjet samples.

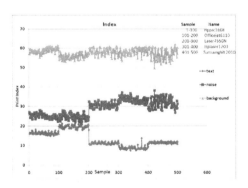

Fig. 4. Printer sample Vs index of text, noise and back ground for Type 1 samples

Print Index of each sample is shown in Figure 5. From Figure 5 it is observed that the PI of ink jet printers is less compared to the print index of laser jet. It is clearly visible that upper bound of print index of most inkjet printers are near value 70 while it is lower bound for the print index of laserjet sample. From the Figure 5, it is also observed that the randomness in Print Index of laserjet samples is more compared to inkjet samples. This indicates that index

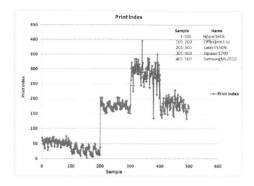

Fig. 5. Sample Vs Print index of printers listed in Table 1

of noise is more and random in laser jet compared to the noise in ink jet. Type 1 samples, 'the' are used to build the classifier and Type 2, Type 3 samples are used for demonstrating the performance of classifier or methodology. It can be observed from the print index that the whole Print Indexes can be divided into 2 categories of data and labelled as 1 and 2. As two classes of data is available for classification, one is for inkjet and the other is for laserjet print, first label of data represents inkjet Print Indices and the second label represents for laserjet Print Indices.

Experiment results. The Print Indices calculated are given as input to EM algorithm for classification of print technology. As text samples are collected from various ink and laserjet prints, the calculated print index can be grouped to form different labels based on their common class characteristics.

For Type 2 text sample 'The', classification accuracy is as follows. Out of 9 printer data, the characterized print index are labelled 1 to 2 and classified as inkjet or laser jet. Total 1082 'The' are collected from 9 printers listed in Table 2 and Print Index is calculated for each resized sample of size [300,600]. Print Indices of 'The' are shown in Figure 6. Ten fold test [15] is adopted for demonstrating performance of classification. Ten percent of the total samples are set aside as test data and remaining is taken as training data. Training data along with number of classes is given as input to the EM algorithm which returns the mixed proportion and mean of each class. Based on these parameters, the test data is classified. The test data contain 108 samples and are selected randomly out of 1082 collected samples and the experiment is repeated for each iteration. Number of classes is 2(inkjet and laser jet). For 10 iterations, the total test data contains 1080 sample. This classification is shown in Table 3.

Out of 1080 samples, 7 samples of laserjet are misclassified as inkjet print. Performance analysis of proposed method is explained in terms of 'Kappa'[16], a statistical measure for calculating correct chance of agreement. 'Kappa' value of 98% chance of agreement is achieved and it indicates near perfect performance.

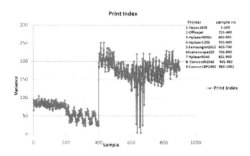

Fig. 6. Print Indices of Type 2 sample 'The'

Table 3. Classifying print Technology

	Classified as		
	Ink jet	Laser Jet	Error
Ink jet	400	0	0 in 400
Laser Jet	7	673	7 in 680
Total	407	673	1080

4.2   Robustness of Printed Text Characterization

Printed text characterization is demonstrated on the general text document (Type 3 sample)containing some general text which is shown Figure 7. Thirty four Three letter words are contained in the document and these words are selected as text samples from this document for validating the Print Index methodology.

Identification of all types of printing, especially when it is of traditional printing style, can be accomplished by consideration of the design (font) of type, the spacing between letters, words, lines, and sections of the copy; the malalignment of letters; defective or damaged typefaces or uneven type impressions; and actual printing errors. If the material is produced by letterpress, each letter represents a separate type unit and may contain some identifying factor. If the material is set by offset, the various letter impressions come from a common source, but, of course, there is always the slight variation possible in the imprinting of one impression compared to another. By studying the combination of these various factors, it is possible to say whether two identical texts were produced by the same type or plate.

It is always possible to reproduce the same subject matter by a second printing. If there is a lapse of time between the two, it may mean that the original was reset if letterpress was used, or the original copy was prepared again if offset methods were employed. A second production of this nature may produce slight variants that will distinguish between the two printings.

Fig. 7. Three letter words contained in general text documents

Type 3 document was printed on five printers listed in Table 1. The samples numbered 1 to 68 are inkjet print samples and the samples from 69 to 170 are laserjet samples. Print Index of Type 3 samples are plotted in Figure 8 which clearly forms two groups: one is from 1-68 representing inkjet print and the other is from 69 to 170 representing laserjet print. Hence, the proposed method clearly distinguishes inkjet print from laserjet for general three letter text.

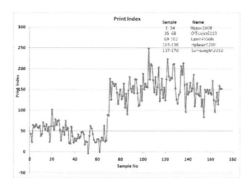

Fig. 8. Print index of Type 3 samples

5   Conclusion and Future Work

PI calculated from reduced feature space of printed text works successfully in classification of laser print technology from inkjet print technology. This work can be further extended to discriminate between photocopy and offset technology and identification of printer type.

Acknowledgements. The author(1) would like to thank Mohinder Singh, Government Examiner of Questioned Documents, Hyderabad, India for their valuable suggestions.

References

1. Hilton, O.: Scientific Examination of Questioned Documents. CRC Press (1993)
2. Khanna, N., Mikkilineni, A.K., Martone, A.F., Ali, G.N., Chiu, G.T., Allebach, J.P., Delp, E.J.: A Survey of Forensic Characterization Methods for Physical Devices. Digital Investigation3s, s17–s28 (2006)
3. Mikkilineni, A.K., Chiang, P.J., Ali, G.N., Chiu, G.T., Allebach, J.P., Delp, E.J.: Printer Identification based on Graylevel Co-occurrence Features for Security and Forensic Applications. In: Proceedings of the SPIE International Conference on Security, vol. 5681, pp. 430–440 (2005)
4. Ali, G.N., Chiang, P.J., Mikkilineni, A.K., Chiu, G.T., Delp, E.J., Allebach, J.P.: Application of Principal Components Analysis and Gaussian Mixture Models to Printer Identification. In: Proceedings of the IS & Ts NIP20: International Conference on Digital Printing Technologies, vol. 20, pp. 301–305 (2004)
5. http://www.eff.org/issues/printers
6. Haritha, D., Chakravarthy, B.: Identification of Printing Process using HSV Colour Space. In: Narayanan, P.J., Nayar, S.K., Shum, H.-Y. (eds.) ACCV 2006. LNCS, vol. 3852, pp. 692–701. Springer, Heidelberg (2006)
7. Chakravarthy, B., Haritha, D.: Classification of Liquid and Viscous Inks using HSV Color Space. In: Proceedings of Eight International Conference on Document Analysis and Recognition, pp. 660–664 (2005)

8. Lampert, C.H., Mei, L., Breuel, T.M.: Printing Technique Classification for Document Counterfeit Detection. In: IEEE International Conference on Computational Intelligence and Security, pp. 639–644 (2006)
9. Schulze, C., Schreyer, M., Stahl, A., Breuel, T.M.: Evaluation of Graylevel-Features for Printing Technique Classification in High-Throughput Document Management Systems. In: Srihari, S.N., Franke, K. (eds.) IWCF 2008. LNCS, vol. 5158, pp. 35–46. Springer, Heidelberg (2008)
10. Beusekom, J.V., Shafait, F., Breuel, T.M.: Document Inspection Using Text-Line Alignment. In: Document Analysis Systems, pp. 263–270 (2010)
11. Ilea, D.E., Whelan, P.F.: Color Image segmentation using A Self-Initialization EM algorithm. In: Proceedings of Sixth IASTED International Conference, pp. 417–424 (2006)
12. Zhang, Z., Chen, C., Sun, J., Chan, K.L.: EM Algorithms for Gaussian Mixtures with Split and Merge Operation. Pattern Recognition, 1973–1983 (2003)
13. http://www.cs.umd.edu/~djacobs/CMSC427/Interpolation.pdf
14. http://en.wikipedia.org/wiki/Minimumboundingrectangle
15. Ye, N.: The Hand book of Data Mining. Lawrence Erlbaum Associates Inc., New Jersy (2003)
16. http://en.wikipedia.org/wiki/Cohen's--kappa

A Shape Representation Scheme for Hand-Drawn Symbol Recognition

Pulabaigari Viswanath*, T. Gokaramaiah, and Gouripeddi V. Prabhakar Rao

Departments of CSE and IT,
Rajeev Gandhi Memorial College of Engineering & Technology,
Nandyal - 518501, A.P., India
{viswanath.pulabaigari,tgokari,gvprabha}@gmail.com
https://sites.google.com/site/viswanathpulabaigari/

Abstract. Pen based inputs are natural for human beings. A hand-drawn shape (symbol) can be used for various purposes, like, a command gesture, an input for authentication purpose, etc. Shape of a symbol is invariant to scale, translation, mirror-reflection and rotation of the symbol. Moments, like Zernike moments are often used to represent a symbol. Descriptors based on Zernike moments are rotation invariant, but since they are neither translation nor scale invariant, a normalization step as pre-processing is required. Apart from this, higher order Zernike moments are error prone. The present paper, proposes to use probability distributions of some local moments of lower order, as a representation scheme. Theoretically it is shown to possess all invariance properties. Experimentally, using the k-nearest neighbor classifier (with Kullback-Leibler distance), it is shown to perform better than Zernike moments based representation scheme.

Keywords: handwritten symbol recognition, moments, moment invariants, probability distribution, nearest neighbor classification.

1 Introduction

Similar to speech input, pen based input is natural for human beings to work with machines. For small devices like mobile phones and PDAs, providing input using the small key-pad (comprising mostly of 12 to 20 keys) that comes as part of the device is very cumbersome. Nowadays, most of these devices are equipped with a touch-screen that can be used for pen inputs. Various hand-drawn shapes can be used as command gestures (like drawing '$' symbol on the touch-screen opens accounting software), for authentication purposes, etc [7][12][1]. A shape [1], or more specifically, a hand-drawn shape, is composed by writing various strokes which are lines and or curves on a writing pad. A shape is invariant to translation, scale, rotation, mirror-reflection and for small distortions. A good representation

---

* Corresponding author.
[1] *Shape* and *symbol* are used interchangeably throughout the paper. Similarly, *hand-drawn* and *hand-written* are used interchangeably.

C. Sombattheera et al. (Eds.): MIWAI 2011, LNAI 7080, pp. 213–224, 2011.

of a shape should possess all these invariance properties, so that, similar shapes will get similar representations.

Hand-written character recognition is a related problem [14]. It is often done by modeling a character as a composition of various strokes. So, stroke recognition is done first, later the relationship between strokes is identified. A segmental two layered HMM based model is used in [1] where strokes (one of several base shapes) are recognized first, later relationship between them.

Recognition of objects in an image is yet another related problem. An image is seen as a two dimensional function $f(x, y)$. Normally, first the image is segmented to extract the boundary of the object. Then the object is brought into a standard orientation and size. Then feature extraction is done. Various boundary based (also called contour based) shape representation schemes uses *shape signature, signature histogram, shape invariants, curvature, shape context, shape matrix, spectral features, etc.* A detailed review of existing methods are given by Zhang *et. al.* [19]. A recent centroid-contour signature based scheme which possess all invariance properties is given by Gokaramaiah *et. al.* [8]. Another approach is to use global descriptors of the image as features. Among various global descriptors, moments are well suited and some moments possess invariance properties as well [11][15][4][5][6]. Zernike moments are a class of orthogonal moments. They possess good reconstruction capability. From Zernike moments, it is possible to derive descriptors which are rotation invariant. Zernike moments for image analysis were first used by Teague [16] which were later studied by several researchers [6]. Heloise Hse *et. al.* [10] used them for hand-written symbol recognition. More recently, Jiangsheng Gui *et. al.* [9] used them for fruit shape classification.

Some limitations of Zernike moments are, (i) they are neither translation nor scale invariant, so pre-processing is required to bring the symbol to a standard size and location, and (ii) since they are defined over a unit circle, they suffer from discretization errors, called geometric errors [13]. Higher order Zernike moments are more vulnerable to these errors.

The present paper proposes to use distribution of some properties (like local variance which can be seen as a local moment) of points that comprise the symbol. It is theoretically shown that the proposed representation possess all invariance properties. Experimentally, the proposed representation is compared with Zernike moments. K-nearest neighbor classifier is used to compare the representation schemes. Since the proposed representation uses distributions, Kullback-Leibler distance is used. Whereas, for Zernike moments representation, Euclidean distance is used. The proposed scheme can be seen as a variation and a generalization of centroid-distance histogram and k^{th} order difference histogram given in [8], which were suitable only for convex and closed shapes.

The rest of the paper is organized as follows. Section 2 gives some definitions and notation used throughout the paper. Section 3 briefs about moments and Zernike moments. Section 4 presents the proposed shape representation schemes. Section 5 gives details about the experimental studies performed. Finally, Section 6 concludes the paper.

2   Notation and Definitions

1. **Point**: $P = (x, y)^T$ is a point in a two dimensional Euclidean space where x and y are its co-ordinates. A point is specified as a column vector having two components.

2. **Shape**: Shape is a discrete and finite set of points $\{P_1, P_2, \ldots, P_n\}$ where $P_i = (x_i, y_i)^T$, for $i = 1$ to n. Note that a shape (especially a hand-drawn shape) is normally formed with various curves and lines which are theoretically continuous. But, practically, every curve or line is a finite set of discrete points, since any sensing device will have a finite sensitivity and a finite acquisition rate.

3. **Shape-transformation**: Shape-transformation is a transformation (function) which maps one shape to other shape and which is one of the following defined transformations, *viz.*, translation, scaling, rotation and mirror-reflection. See Figure 1. Note, each of these transformations, is a one-to-one mapping. That is, for each shape-transformation there is an inverse shape-transformation. A composition of two or more shape-transformations is a shape-transformation. It is easy to verify that composition of shape-transformations is both commutative and associative.

4. **Translation**: For given constants a and b, translation of shape S is $tr(S) = \{(x + a, y + b)^T \mid (x, y)^T \in S\}$.

5. **Scale (Scaling)**: For a given positive constant c, scaling of shape S is $sl(S) = \{(cx, cy)^T \mid (x, y)^T \in S\}$.

6. **Rotation**: For a given constant θ, let R be a matrix called *the rotation matrix*, and

$$R = \begin{bmatrix} \cos\theta & \sin\theta \\ -\sin\theta & \cos\theta \end{bmatrix}.$$

Given θ, rotation of shape S is $rt(S) = \{RP \mid P \in S\}$

7. **Flip (mirror-reflection)**: For a shape S, its mirror-reflection is $fp(S) = \{(-x, y)^T \mid (x, y)^T \in S\}$. Here, mirror reflection is defined only using the Y-axis (vertical axis). But, in general any straight line can act as a flipping axis. A series of translation and rotations along with the defined flip achieves general flip transformation.

3   Moments and Zernike Moments

This section briefs about an existing shape representation method which is based on Zernike moments. For a two dimensional image function $f(x, y)$, defined over a domain $D \subset \mathbb{R} \times \mathbb{R}$, which is piece-wise continuous having a finite nonzero integral, its general moment M_{pq}, where p and q are non-negative integers, is

$$M_{pq} = \iint_D P_{pq}(x, y) f(x, y) dx dy. \tag{1}$$

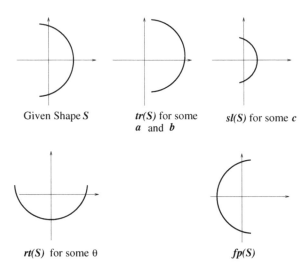

Fig. 1. An example of various transformations. Note, even-though shape is given as a continuous curve, practically it is a discrete and finite set of points.

Here, $p_{pq}(x, y)$ is a polynomial basis function and $r = p + q$ is called order of the moment. Geometric moments are obtained when $p_{pq}(x, y) = x^p y^q$, a monomial. That is, geometric moment

$$m_{pq} = \iint_D x^p y^q f(x, y) dx dy. \tag{2}$$

There are other types of moments like orthogonal moments which are obtained by considering an orthogonal polynomial basis, like Legendre and Zernike polynomials. There is no information redundancy in these moments and have good reconstruction capabilities. However, Legendre moments do not possess invariance to linear transformations, hence are not suitable for shape representation. From Zernike moments, it is possible to derive descriptors having all invariance properties. Zernike moments for image analysis were first used by Teague [16] which were later studied by several researchers [6]. Heloise Hse *et. al.* [10] used them for hand-written symbol recognition. More recently, Jiangsheng Gui *et. al.* [9] used them for fruit shape classification.

Zernike moment of order p with repetition q is

$$A_{pq} = \iint_D f(x, y) V_{pq}(x, y) dx dy, \tag{3}$$

where $x^2 + y^2 \leq 1$, and V_{pq} is the respective Zernike polynomial. Zernike polynomials are complex and orthogonal polynomials defined as

$$V_{pq}(x, y) = V_{pq}(\rho, \theta) = R_{pq}(\rho) e^{jq\theta}, \tag{4}$$

$$R_{pq}(\rho) = \sum_{s=0}^{\frac{p-|q|}{2}} (-1)^s \frac{(p-s)!}{s!(\frac{p+|q|}{2} - s)!(\frac{p-|q|}{2} - s)!} \rho^{p-2s}, \tag{5}$$

where p is a non-negative integer, q is an integer such that $p-|q|$ is even, $|q| \le p$, $\rho = \sqrt{x^2 + y^2}$, and $\theta = \tan^{-1}(y/x)$.

Discrete version of the Zernike moment [10] of order p with repetition q is

$$A_{pq} = \frac{p+1}{\pi} \sum_x \sum_y f(x,y)V_{pq}(x,y), \quad x^2 + y^2 \le 1. \tag{6}$$

If the image plane is a $N \times N$ grid, then a mapping is needed in order to get the image inside a unit circle, as given below. For more details refer [2].

$$\rho = \sqrt{(c_1x + c_2)^2 + (c_1y + c_2)^2}, \tag{7}$$

$$\theta = \tan^{-1} \frac{c_1y + c_2}{c_1x + c_2}, \tag{8}$$

where $c_1 = \frac{\sqrt{2}}{N-1}$, and $c_2 = -\frac{1}{\sqrt{2}}$.

Magnitude of a Zernike moment, *i.e.*, $|A_{pq}|$ is rotation and mirror reflection invariant. Zernike moments are neither scale nor translation invariant. So, a preprocessing step involving normalization against scale and translation are done first. Further, in case of hand-written symbol recognition, it depends on number points in the symbol. So, normalization using interpolation is done. In [10], for a given threshold value T, a point is inserted in between two points that are more than T distance apart. Further, since $A_{p,-q} = A_{pq}$, and since $|A_{00}|$, $|A_{11}|$ are same for all of the normalized symbols, extracted features are of order two or more. In [9], further, only first few principal components are used as features. For more details of using Zernike moments refer to [10,9].

Zernike moments, since are defined over a unit circle, they suffer from discretization errors, called geometric errors [13]. Higher order Zernike moments are more vulnerable to these errors. The present paper proposes to use distribution of local geometric moments of lower order to represent a hand-written symbol.

4 The Proposed Shape Representation Scheme

The proposed scheme is a variation and a generalization of contour based object representation techniques called centroid-distance histogram and k^{th} order difference histogram given by Gokaramaiah *et. al.* [8]. These were based on centroid-contour distance (CCD) curve given by Wang *et. al.* [18]. CCD curve, which is also called centroid distance signature, is a one dimensional function $s : [0, 2\pi] \to \mathbb{R}^+$, where $\mathbb{R}^+$ is the set of non-negative real numbers. Here, first centroid of the contour is obtained. Distance from centroid to contour is seen as the function of angle (with a predefined axis). But this representation is suitable only for closed and convex contours. For non-convex shapes, s need not be a function of angle. See Figure 2. Further, hand-drawn symbols mostly can be open shapes like those shown in Figure 1, where centroid contour distance becomes infinity for some angles.

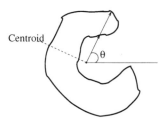

Fig. 2. Centroid distance signature for non-convex shapes need not be a function of angle. For some angles, there can be more than one centroid contour distance.

In this paper, distribution of centroid to contour distances and distribution of local variance are proposed as shape representation schemes. These can be seen as local moment distributions. For a shape $S = \{P_1, \ldots, P_n\}$, its centroid is $\bar{P} = \frac{1}{n} \sum_{i=1}^{n} P_i$.

Centroid-point-length, which is similar to centroid contour distance in [8] and [18], of a point $P_i = (x_i, y_i)^T$ in S is the Euclidean distance between P_i and the centroid $\bar{P}$. It is denoted by $l(P_i, S)$, where

$$l(P_i, S) = \|P_i - \bar{P}\| = \sqrt{(x_i - \bar{x})^2 + (y_i - \bar{y})^2}. \tag{9}$$

We define

$$l_{\max}(S) = \text{Maximum}\{l(P_i, S) | P_i \in S\}, \tag{10}$$

normalized-centroid-point-length of $l(P_i, S)$ is

$$\bar{l}(P_i, S) = \frac{l(P_i, S)}{l_{\max}(S)}. \tag{11}$$

For a point $P_i \in S$, let $N(P_i, r, S) = \{P_j \in S \mid \|P_i - P_j\| \le r\}$, called *the neighborhood* of P_i in S of radius r, be the points in S which are within distance r from P_i. Here, r is called *the neighborhood-radius*. Let

$$L(P_i, r, S) = \{\bar{l}(P_j, S) \mid P_j \in N(P_i, r, S)\} \tag{12}$$

be the set of normalized-centroid-point-lengths of points in $N(P_i, r, S)$. For a finite set of numbers R, let $Avg(R)$ denote its average, and $Var(R)$ denote its variance. For a given shape S and neighborhood-radius r, we define two random variables A and V as follows. $A : S \to \mathbb{R}^+$, where $A(P_i) = Avg(L(P_i, r, S))$, and $V : S \to \mathbb{R}^+$, where $V(P_i) = Var(L(P_i, r, S))$. Similarly, we define distributions F_A, F_V and probabilities P_A, P_B as follows.

$$F_A(t) = P_A(A \le t) = \frac{|\{A(P_i) \le t | P_i \in S\}|}{|\{A(P_i) | P_i \in S\}|} \tag{13}$$

and

$$F_V(t) = P_V(V \le t) = \frac{|\{V(P_i) \le t | P_i \in S\}|}{|\{V(P_i) | P_i \in S\}|}. \tag{14}$$

Note that, P_A and P_V satisfies all axioms of the probability theory [17]. Further, for an interval (t_1, t_2),

$$P_A(t_1 < A \le t_2) = F_A(t_2) - F_A(t_1) \tag{15}$$

and

$$P_V(t_1 < A \le t_2) = F_V(t_2) - F_V(t_1). \tag{16}$$

For appropriate quantization of A and V, we get histograms (of average normalized-centroid-point-lengths and its variance over a neighborhood of radius r) that are similar to histogram representations used in [8]. These histograms are called *average histogram* and *variance histogram*, respectively.

Let $\nu \in [0, 1]$ be a constant. For a given shape S, the neighborhood-radius r is chosen as

$$r = \nu \, l_{\max}(S). \tag{17}$$

For a given shape S, for a given ν, average and variance histograms are used to represent the shape. Figure 3 gives distribution function F_A for the hand-drawn symbol '+' and '@', when $\nu = 0.3$, whereas Figure 4 shows probability functions P_A for same symbols.

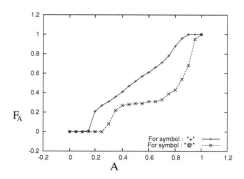

Fig. 3. Distribution function F_A for hand-drawn symbol '+' and '@', when $\nu = 0.3$

Next, we formally establish that F_A and F_V have all invariance properties for a given shape.

Theorem 1. *For a given shape S, let S' be its transformation obtained by applying any one of shape-transformations, viz., translation, scale, rotation, or mirror-reflection to S. For a given $\nu \in [0, 1]$, the distribution function F_A for shapes S and S' are same. Also, the distribution function F_V for shapes S and S' are same.*

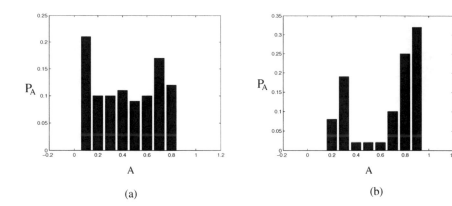

Fig. 4. Probability function P_A (average histogram), (a) for symbol '+' and (b) for symbol '@', when $\nu = 0.3$

Proof: We prove the theorem for shape-transformations scale and rotation. It is similar to this for the other two transformation, hence are not given.

For a point $P \in S$, let P' be its corresponding point in S'.

For scaling, $P' = cP = (cx, cy)^T$, if $P = (x, y)^T$, where c is a positive constant. It is easy to see that the centroid $\bar{P}'$ of S' is related to the centroid $\bar{P}$ of S, which is

$$\bar{P}' = c\bar{P}. \tag{18}$$

Similarly

$$l(P', S') = c\,l(P, S), \tag{19}$$

and

$$l_{\max}(S') = c\,l_{\max}(S). \tag{20}$$

So,

$$\bar{l}(P', S') = \frac{l(P', S')}{l_{\max}(S')} = \frac{c\,l(P, S)}{c\,l_{\max}(S)} = \bar{l}(P, S). \tag{21}$$

Let neighborhood-radius for S' be r', while that for S be r. We get, for given ν,

$$r' = \nu\,l_{\max}(S') = \nu\,c\,l_{\max}(S) = c\,r. \tag{22}$$

Let P_i and P_j be two points in S. Let their corresponding points in S' be P'_i and P'_j, respectively. Then, if $P_j \in N(P_i, r, S)$, then $\|P_i - P_j\| \leq r$. Since $\|P'_i - P'_j\| = c\|P_i - P_j\|$, we get $\|P'_i - P'_j\| \leq c\,r$. That is, $\|P'_i - P'_j\| \leq r'$. So, we get, $P'_j \in N(P'_i, r', S')$.

Next, we show that $L(P_i, r, S) = L(P'_i, r', S')$.

$$
\begin{aligned}
L(P_i, r, S) &= \{\bar{l}(P_j, S) \mid P_j \in N(P_i, r, S)\} \\
&= \{\bar{l}(P'_j, S') \mid P'_j \in N(P'_i, r', S')\} \\
&= L(P'_i, r', S').
\end{aligned}
$$

Hence, for any point $P_i \in S$,

$$Avg(L(P_i, r, S)) = Avg(L(P'_i, r', S')),$$

and,

$$Var(L(P_i, r, S)) = Var(L(P'_i, r', S')).$$

So, for a given positive constant ν, F_A for S and S' are same, and, F_V for S and S' are same. This proves invariance with respect to scaling.

For rotation, $P' = RP$, where R is the rotation matrix, for some angle θ. For details about this notation, see Section 2. Note that, R is an orthogonal matrix. That is, $\|P_i - P_j\| = \|P'_i - P'_j\|$. Since $\bar{P}' = R\bar{P}$, we get, $l_{\max}(S) = l_{\max}(S')$. Hence, the neighborhood-radius for S', i.e., r' is

$$r' = \nu\, l_{\max}(S') = \nu\, l_{\max}(S) = r. \tag{23}$$

So, it directly follows that, $P_j \in N(P_i, r, S) \Rightarrow P'_j \in N(P'_i, r', S')$. Hence, $L(P_i, r, S) = L(P'_i, r', S')$. So, the distribution functions F_A and F_V for a shape S are same before and after rotation   □

5 Experimental Study

Sixteen hand-drawn symbols, as shown in Figure 5 are used. Ten different persons are asked to draw each symbol for ten times. So, a total of 1600 hand-drawn symbols database is created. Each symbol's coordinates are collected by drawing it on a 512×512 writing pad. 400 randomly chosen symbols (out of 1600 symbols) are separated by doing sampling without replacement, and is used as the test set. Remaining 1200 symbols constitutes the training set. The problem addressed in this paper is *writer independent* hand-drawn symbol recognition.

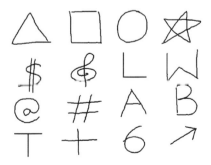

Fig. 5. Hand-drawn symbols used for experimental study

The classifier used is the k-nearest neighbor classifier(k-NNC) [3]. Two representation schemes, *viz.*, Zernike moments based one and the proposed probability distributions are compared. Parameters, like order of the Zernike moments, k in k-NNC and ν used in the proposed representation scheme are chosen based on three-fold cross validations. The order of the Zernike moments is chosen from $\{3, 4, \ldots, 12\}$. k used in k-NNC is chosen from $\{1, 2, \ldots, 19\}$, whereas ν is chosen from $\{0.1, 0.2, \ldots, 1.0\}$.

With Zernike moments, distance measure used is the Euclidean distance. Whereas, with the proposed probability distributions, the distance used is the Kullback-Leibler distance (KL-distance) [3], since this is more appropriate to compare divergence between probability distributions. To find P_A and P_V based on the proposed scheme, A is quantized in to intervals $[0, 0.1], (0.1, 0.2], \ldots, (0.9, 1]$, and V is quantized in to intervals $[0, 0.05], (0.05, 0.10], (0.10, 0.15] \ldots, (0.95, 1]$.

Let the probability function P_A for a shape S is denoted as $P_{A,S}$, and P_V is denoted by $P_{V,S}$. Let A is divided in to intervals $a_1, a_2, \ldots, a_p$. KL-distance from P_{A,S_i} to P_{A,S_j} is

$$D_{KL}(P_{A,S_i}, P_{A,S_j}) = \sum_{i=1}^{p} P_{A,S_i}(a_i) \log \frac{P_{A,S_i}(a_i)}{P_{A,S_j}(a_i)}. \tag{24}$$

Similarly assuming that V is divided in to intervals $v_1, v_2, \ldots, v_q$, KL-distance from P_{V,S_i} to P_{V,S_j} is

$$D_{KL}(P_{V,S_i}, P_{V,S_j}) = \sum_{i=1}^{q} P_{V,S_i}(v_i) \log \frac{P_{V,S_i}(v_i)}{P_{V,S_j}(v_i)}. \tag{25}$$

Since, KL-distances given in Equations 24 and 25 are not symmetric, following symmetric KL-distances, respectively, are used.

$$D_{KLS}(P_{A,S_i}, P_{A,S_j}) = D_{KL}(P_{A,S_i}, P_{A,S_j}) + D_{KL}(P_{A,S_j}, P_{A,S_i}). \tag{26}$$

$$D_{KLS}(P_{V,S_i}, P_{V,S_j}) = D_{KL}(P_{V,S_i}, P_{V,S_j}) + D_{KL}(P_{V,S_j}, P_{V,S_i}). \tag{27}$$

Distance between two shapes S_i and S_j, according to the proposed representations is

$$D(S_i, S_j) = D_{KLS}(P_{A,S_i}, P_{A,S_j}) + D_{KLS}(P_{V,S_i}, P_{V,S_j}). \tag{28}$$

Zernike moments are neither scale nor translation invariant. Hence, pre-processing is done to bring a shape to a standard location (center of the 512×512 grid) and size (to fill the 512×512 grid without changing the aspect ratio). Further, it depends on number points. So points are added or deleted to a shape such that two adjacent points (in a stroke) should be at a distance of less than or equal to $\sqrt{2}$.

Figures 6(a) shows validation results of Zernike moments based representation for $k = 3, 7$ and 11. It shows classification accuracy (CA) Vs. order of the Zernike moments. It is found that, based on the validation, Zernike moments of order 8 with $k = 7$ gives best performance. Similarly, Figure 6(b) shows some of the validation results for the proposed representation scheme. Here, k Vs. CA is shown for $\nu = 0.1, 0.3$ and 0.7. From validation results, it is found that, for the proposed representation scheme, $\nu = 0.3$ and $k = 9$ gives the best results. With these chosen parameters, results on the test set are given in Table 1.

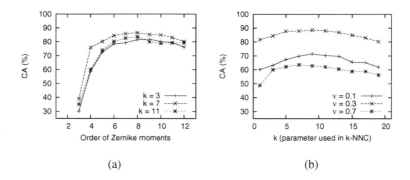

(a)   (b)

Fig. 6. (a)Validation results for Zernike moments representation, showing order of Zernike moments Vs. CA, for varied k in k-NNC. (b) Validation results for the proposed representation, showing k (used in k-NNC) Vs. CA, for varied ν values.

Table 1. Results on the test set

Representation	k	CA(%)
Zernike Moments(Order = 8)	7	87.8
Proposed Method ($\nu = 0.3$)	9	89.2

6   Conclusion

The paper proposed a shape representation scheme based on local moment distributions, like local variance of some properties of points that comprise the symbol. The proposed representation scheme possess all invariance properties needed, and is theoretically verified. Further, based on the experimental studies performed, it is shown to be better than Zernike moments based representation.

Acknowledgments. This work is sponsored by an AICTE Project under RPS scheme. Ref: "F.No: 8023/BOR/RID/RPS-51/2009-10".

References

1. Artieres, T., Marukatat, S., Gallinari, P.: Online handwritten shape recognition using segmental hidden Markov models. IEEE Transactions on Pattern Analysis and Machine Intelligence 29(2), 205–217 (2007)
2. Chong, C.W., Raveendran, P., Mukundan, P.: A comparitive analysis of algorithms for fast computation of Zernike moments. Pattern Recognition 36, 731–742 (2003)
3. Duda, R.O., Hart, P.E., Stork, D.G.: Pattern Classification, 2nd edn. A Wiley-interscience Publication, John Wiley & Sons (2000)
4. Flusser, J.: On the independence of rotation moment invariants. Pattern Recognition 33(9), 1405–1410 (2000)

5. Flusser, J.: Moment invariants in image analysis. Proceedings of World Academy of Science, Engineering and Technology 11, 196–201 (2006)
6. Flusser, J., Suk, T., Zitova, B.: Moments and Moment Invariants in Pattern Recognition. John Wiley & Sons, UK (2009)
7. Frankish, C., Hull, R., Morgan, P.: Recognition accuracy and user acceptance of pen. In: Proceedings of SIGCHI Conference on Human Factors in Computing Systems, pp. 503–510 (1995)
8. Gokaramaiah, T., Viswanath, P., Reddy, B.: A novel shape based hierarchical retrieval system for 2D images. In: 2010 IEEE International Conference on Advances in Recent Technologies in Communication and Computing (ARTCom), pp. 10–14 (October 2010)
9. Gui, J., Zhou, W.: Fruit shape classification using zernike moments. In: Proceedings of International Conference on Image Processing and Pattern Recognition in Industrial Engineering, vol. 7820 (August 2010)
10. Hse, H., Newton, A.R.: Sketched symbol recognition using Zernike moments. In: Proceedings of ICPR 2004, vol. 1, pp. 367–370. IEEE Computer Society, Los Alamitos (2004)
11. Hu, M.K.: Visual pattern recognition by moment invariants. IRE Transactions on Information Theory 8(2), 179–187 (1967)
12. Kenzie, I.M., Zhang, S.: The immediate usability of graffiti. In: Proc. Graphics Interface, pp. 129–137 (1997)
13. Lio, S.X., Pawlak, M.: On the accuracy of zernike moments for image analysis. IEEE Transactions on Pattern Analysis and Machine Intelligence 20(12), 1358–1364 (1996)
14. Pal, U., Chaudhuri, B.B.: Indian script character recognition: a survey. Pattern Recognition 37(9), 1887–1899 (2004)
15. Reiss, T.: The revised fundamental theorem of moment invariants. IEEE Transactions on Pattern Analysis and Machine Intelligence 13(8), 830–834 (1991)
16. Teague, M.R.: Image analysis via the general theory of moments. Journal of Optical Society of America 70(8), 920–930 (1980)
17. Rohatgi, V.K., Ehsanes Saleh, A.K.: An Introduction to Probability and Statistics. A Wiley-Interscience Publication, John Wiley & Sons, Inc. (2002)
18. Wang, Z., Chi, Z., Feng, D.: Shape based leaf image retrieval. IEE Proc.-Vis. Image Signal Process. 150 (February 2003)
19. Zhang, D., Lu, G.: Review of shape representation and description techniques. Pattern Recognition 37, 1–19 (2004)

On Modeling the Affective Effect on Learning

Arunkumar Balakrishnan

Department of Computer Technology and Applications,
Coimbatore Institute of Technology, Coimbatore, India
arunkumar.cta.cit@gmail.com

Abstract. This paper presents an approach to modeling the affective state of a student. The model represents the learning process used by the student including the affective state. The student modeling is built upon an ontology of machine learning strategies. This paper describes how the ontology is extended to include affective knowledge. The recommended learning strategies for a situation are ordered based on the affective state of the learner.

Keywords: Student modeling, affective modeling, integrated machine learning.

1   Introduction

Affective computing is defined as "computing that relates to, arises from or deliberately influences emotion" [15]. Affect is linked to thinking and performing functions in the context of rational behavior, memory, decision making and creativity [15]. The affective state of the learner influences the learning. With the crux of intelligent tutoring systems being learner directed teaching, knowledge of the affective state can orient the teaching process to provide a 'motivational' and 'psychological' presence [15].

The activities towards realizing the goal of utilizing the affective state effectively are: [15] [4] a) affective state detection b) modeling the affective state and c) using the knowledge about the affective state to effect required changes in behavior. This paper focuses on, 'modeling the affective state'. The modeling is done in the context of learning during teaching. The affective model is built by extending the architecture of an existing system that uses an ontology of learning strategies to model the learning behavior of a student[1]. First the architecture of the integrated machine learning system is described. Next the application of that system to learning student models in the domain of multi-digit subtraction including the additional modules, to handle the domain of subtraction and to model students are explained. Section 4 describes the enhancements to the system in order to model affective states. Section 5 describes the application to model the affective state of the student in the context of multi-digit subtraction.

2   Architecture of the Multi Strategy Machine Learning System

This section explains the architecture of the system, which allows it to select the learning strategy for a particular situation. Research on multi strategy task-adaptive

C. Sombattheera et al. (Eds.): MIWAI 2011, LNAI 7080, pp. 225–235, 2011.

learning has attempted to develop a methodology, which for any learning task can recognize what learning strategy, or combination thereof, is likely to be the most effective (the 'learning strategy selection problem').

The objective of the multi strategy machine learning system described here is to solve this problem. [1] describes the usage of an ontology of machine learning strategies to handle the learning strategy problem. To maintain the learning status during a problem solving process a 'plausible justification tree' [18] is used. The multi strategy machine learning system was coded in XLISP.

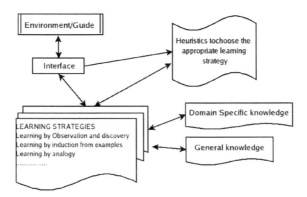

Fig. 1. The architecture of the Multi-strategy machine learning system [1]

The ontology of machine learning strategies

The data structure used to represent the 'relations and attributes' of the learning strategies is a 'property-list'.

The twenty six relations and attributes of learning strategies are [1]:

What-is-it, General-principles, Basics-of, General-paradigm, Research-paradigm, Features, Stages-in, Tasks-of, Subcomponents, Types-of, Interesting-subset-of-category, Important-examples-of, Superior-case-of, Requirements, Applicability-conditions, Constraints-problems, Solutions-to-a-problem, Representation, Evaluation-criteria-of-result, Method-alg-heuristics, Operators, Fundamental-operator, Relationship, Generates, Cause, Equal-name-wise.

The process of learning strategy selection

The current situation is represented in a plausible justification tree.

Procedure 1: The current situation in the environment is matched with the applicability-conditions of each of the learning strategies in the ontology. The search does not stop with the first learning strategy that has its applicability-conditions matching the current state; it searches the complete ontology for all learning strategies that may be found applicable.

Procedure 2: a) The 'applicability-conditions', 'implementation-requirements' and 'certainty-of-results' of the selected learning strategies are retrieved. b) The ordered list of 'preferred-application-features' and the degree of match of 'applicability-conditions' are used to sort the learning strategies in decreasing order of preference. c) The learning strategy on top of this list is now suggested for application. The sorting will not necessarily result in only one learning strategy on top. At such stages the selection is random if the situation is a new one (The steps b and c are modified in Section 4). d) The suggested learning strategy is applied and the change in the situation is represented in the plausible justification tree. e) The 'chosen / correct' learning strategy is also stored in a list along with a description of the particular situation. The list also records the learning strategies that were nearly correct for the situation.

Procedure 3: The 'preferred-application-features' list stores the used learning strategies with a weight marker for each. This weight is incremented each time the learning strategy is used successfully.

3   Application of the Ontology of Learning Strategies to the Generation of Student Models

The modules added to the Ontology were:

a) A procedural representation of the subtraction sub procedures. The seven primary procedures that are involved in subtraction are represented [14]: i) Add-ten (number, row, column) - Replace number with number + ten ii) Decrement (number, row, column) iii) Find-difference (number1, number2, column) iv) Find-top (column) - Take number from the top row of a column as the result. v) Shift-column (column) - Shift both (focus and process) to the column on the left of the current focus. vi) Shift-left (column) - Shift focus to the column on the left of the current focus. vii) Shift-right (column) - Shift focus to the column to the right of the current focus.
b) An ordered list to store the examples presented with a tag specifying each example's sequence number.
c) A knowledge base (XLISP property lists) storing the subject knowledge of student.
d) A mapping from the 'applicability-conditions' of a machine learning strategy to the domain terminology of subtraction. The 'applicability-conditions' are mapped to situations present in the teaching of subtraction like 'example provided', 'counter example provided' and 'new topic presented'.
e) A mapping from the machine learning strategies to specific learning routines applicable in the subtraction domain. (The template of each machine learning strategy is used to create domain specific learning routines.)

Figure 2 provides the architecture of the system including the above additions.

The process

The generation of student models is done off-line. The system is provided with the example sequence that is to be given to the students. After each example is presented the Multi strategy Machine Learning system is invoked. A Plausible Justification tree is constructed of the subtraction procedure that can be generated with each example, after application of the learning strategy.

The system tries to use all the learning strategies that get selected in order to model wrong application of the learning strategies. The mapping procedure has two environment state values of: 1) Example(s) presented and 2) the student's knowledge in mathematics. These map to the applicability conditions of 'learning by induction from training instances' and 'learning by analogy', respectively. The learning by analogy is restricted to analogical inferences in the mathematical knowledge learned up to that point by the student [8].

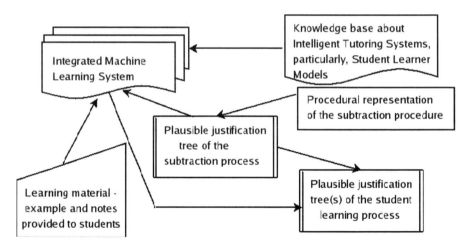

Fig. 2. Architecture of the system including the student model generation components

Modeling the errors of the student

Plausible justification trees (PJT) are generated for application of the highest recommended machine learning strategy and also for the other recommended learning strategies. The PJT for the application of the 'other recommended' learning strategies are maintained along the problem solving process. One of these alternative PJT provides a result equal to the erroneous result given by the student.

This 'erroneous' PJT is used to show where the student has mis-applied a learning strategy. The student is also shown what should have been the correct learning strategy at that place of problem solving. This should correct the learning behavior of the student, hopefully not only in the subject being taught but overall in the student's learning personality.

Results

In addition to demonstrating the learning strategies that map to the 47 buggy rules recorded by Brown and Burton [6], learning by induction and learning by analogy are also found to be applicable. VanLehn [19] and [20] notes three sources of impasses: a) mistaken or excessive generalization b) over-specificity and c) deletion. Here, we saw that the previously acquired knowledge for the student (about Addition) influences the learning of subtraction. The student while being taught borrowing is told to add ten to the number being borrowed-to. The associative link to addition can suppress the rest of the borrowing procedure. An instance of the procedural errors of students given by Brown and VanLehn [5] demonstrates a result of such a learning error: Result of 732 minus 484 was given as 258. In this, 2 of the first number was made 12 by adding 10. But the adjacent column number of 3 was not decremented thus resulting in the wrong value of 5.

For the above case, two PJTs are generated; one using the influence of addition (which models the error) and the other without (which is the expected behavior). These are shown in Figure 3.

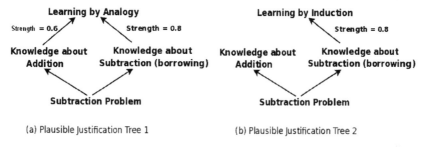

(a) Plausible Justification Tree 1   (b) Plausible Justification Tree 2

Fig. 3. The two plausible justification trees

The above demonstrates the ability of the system to provide a model of the learning errors of the student in the subject of subtraction. The influence of the examples and the prior knowledge of the student (these are the cognitive relvance features) are shown to affect the learning process. More results are provided of this nature are provided in [1].

The reader is referred to [1] for more details of the architecture of the integrated machine learning system , the ontology of learning and the application to generate student models with the subject domain of subtraction.

4   Enhancements to Handle Affective States

The knowledge about each learning strategy present in the system, as described above refers to the attributes of each learning strategy with respect to the external environmental attributes. For example - availability of an example favors inductive learning from examples. Mapping affective states to the learning strategies introduces a new dimension – internal attributes. One option is to maintain the relationship between affective states and learning strategies in a separate ontology. The preferred option taken here is to include the relationships between affective state and learning in the same ontology. This allows us to maintain all factors that affect the learning behavior in a single framework allowing for possible interplay between these knowledge entities. The change done to the existing system is in the processing of the ontology. The attributes referring to the applicability of a learning strategy are used as before, when the learning strategy is chosen for the problem situation. This is the favored or recommended learning strategy. It is in the tracking of a bug (mistake) that the affective state's effect is used. Previously the other 'less' recommended learning strategies were tried in the preferred order to see which sequence reproduced the bug. Now, the affective state of the learner is used to order these alternative learning strategies. The effect of the affective state is thus brought to bear upon the learning behavior.

In order to map the effect of affect on learning, two relationships are added to the set of knowledge relations. First representation about 'affect' is introduced by an 'affect-types-of' relation. This lists out the different types of affect_states [4]   - good_mood, sad_mood, angry_mood, confusion, flow, fear and the 22 emotion categories in the OCC model (which are based on valenced reactions to situations constructed either as being goal relevant events, as acts of an accountable agent or as attractive or unattractive objects) [3]. Next a relation that connects the influence of the mood on a learning strategy is added. This is 'affect-influence-of' relationship. This relationship shows the effect of each type of affect on a particular learning strategy. The possible values are –

positive_influence,   negative_influence,   no_effect,   transitionary_effect, long_term_effect, distraction.

The relationships added to the ontology were based on the affective states described in [4] and [17] which summarized the interaction between affect and learning related activities. This paper extends their work by relating the favored learning strategy to each affective state. 1) More 'interest and attention' in the state of the learner is linked to more 'effort' on the current task. This situation indicates a higher chance for learning by experimentation to be used. This link is therefore added to the ontology as an attribute of the 'affect-influence-of' property of 'learning by experimentation'. Using the same reasoning the situation is also linked negatively to learning by being told, learning by deduction and learning by explanation based induction. 2) Positive moods are linked to higher rating for tasks. This indicates that the task will be stored with a higher value. This is indicative of a higher utility being conferred on the task. Accordingly a positive mood is linked as adding to the utility of a task; this utility is used in learning by reinforcement [12]. 3) Positive moods are linked to problem solving strategies being initiated. Therefore the situation is added to increase the likelihood of 'learning by induction' including 'learning by experimentation'. Positive moods are also linked negatively to learning strategies that are deductive. 4) Positive moods enhance memorization. This is represented within the ontology of learning strategies by increasing the link for multiple associations to be formed. The learning by induction strategy that is invoked at this stage is encouraged to create more 'sets of relations'. 5) Positive moods influence inclusive forms of thinking- directly impacting the quality of responses and indirectly impacting the quantity. These aspects are linked within the ontology as a) influencing the scope of the learning by induction process, b) encouraging learning by analogy and c) multiple versions of hypotheses being maintained for consideration. 6) Sad moods encourage creativity. This point is used to establish a link between 'sad moods' and learning by discovery and learning by abduction. 7) Happy individuals tend to do top down processing. Pre-existing knowledge structures are used and details of the current situation are not focused on. These facts increase the likelihood of using learning by analogy when the student is in a happy mood. Accordingly happy moods are linked to the learning by analogy strategy as a contributing factor. 8) A sad mood encourages the learner to base decisions on a rational analysis of the game. This is represented as a link between sad moods and learning by deduction, learning by being told and less with learning by induction.

The above knowledge pieces were added based on the relationships between moods and cognitive activities suggested by [4]. In addition moods such as 'aloofness', as opposed to 'mingling with other human beings' are also linked to leaning strategies. (Learning by being told and asking questions is encouraged by an attitude of seeking help from others.) [17] identifies the basic set of emotion- learning attributes as 'interest', 'engagement', 'confusion', 'frustration', 'boredom', hopefulness', 'satisfaction' and 'disappointment'. 'Interest' and 'engagement' is linked to enabling the learning activity and is directly proportional to the 'degree of deployment' of the chosen learning strategy. The higher these affective states, the more correctly and completely these learning strategies will be used. 'Confusion' and 'frustration' will add to a heightened focus on the learning activity but will be for a shorter period if the affective states continue! (The application monitors the situation when these affective states are encountered and will change the effect when the time increases beyond a threshold level.) Moods are also noted to change. An initial mood that encourages discovery (and the corresponding learning strategies) may after a period of failures result in a mood of irritability and despair which would then call for invoking 'learning by being told'.

Working of the enhanced system

Given the learning situation, the system identifies the possible learning strategies that are applicable and orders them based on their cognitive relevance. Now the process that led to the observed error is discovered by considering which learning strategy would have been used if the affective state of the learner was different from a 'normal' state. Primarily, the effect of all the possible affective states is realized on the set of suggested learning strategies for a particular situation. This could lead to a different choice of learning strategy from the recommended one. The plausible justification tree for this 'different' choice of learning strategy is generated and the process continues to see which of the choices, generates the error committed by the learner. The identification of the 'wrong' choice is now 'reverse inferred' to the affective state of the learner.

We now consider the effect of affect on the same example used to demonstrate the selection of learning strategies in Section 3. It was shown that learning by induction and learning by analogy are both suggested, based on the previously learnt lesson, resulting in a correct or an incorrect solution. The result / problem solution can differ, based on the affective state of the learner also. The affective states are:

a) Happy b) Sad c) Angry d) Interested e) Frustrated f) Bored g) Distracted h) Focused i) Confused.

In a 'happy', 'focused', 'interested' state the student is open to learning the presented matter completely. The differences between the applicability conditions between learning by induction and learning by analogy are appreciated by the learner and the correct approach is used; resulting in the proper learning. In a 'happy' 'distracted' 'interested' state, the learner can miss out important differentiator – this leads to a partial learning of the situation and the applicable method. This behavior is implemented in the learning strategy with a random skip of a step in the process. In states where 'angry' mood comes into play, the effect is one where the subject is learnt with no scope for irregularities - the 'lesson' has to be perfect, failing which the whole subject may be lost on the learner. This situation is implemented by a choice of a rigid learning method and immediate dropping of the learning process in the event of any discrepancy between the instance and the expected transition states. In 'sad' states, the learner at the first instance of a block in the learning will resort to an imaginative inference; which could result in a creative method being discovered or a surprisingly erroneous one. These are realized by a probabilistic choice step within the learning strategy (an 'impasse' [11] case!). The representation for 'confused' state differs from the above, by the random choice focusing towards less relevant activities (justified by a lack of knowledge which is the reason for the confusion). The effect of a 'frustrated' state is realized through combining the effects of angry and confused states. 'Bored' state results in lesser attention to the subject, resulting in incompletely learnt procedures.

A sample is provided of the results that the system generated for each of the moods of a learner, while being taught the multi-digit subtraction problem:

Sad – learning to subtract even when not required and learning to borrow without decrementing.

Angry – questioning the need for decrementing while borrowing and learning to not decrement while borrowing.

Bored – learning to enter default values (digits of the first number).

Distracted – learning to enter approximate results for the subtraction.

Confused – learning to borrow without decrementing or, learning to not accept a negative result and therefore changing the sign of the result to a positive one.

The plausible justification trees for the above states are presented in Figure 4.

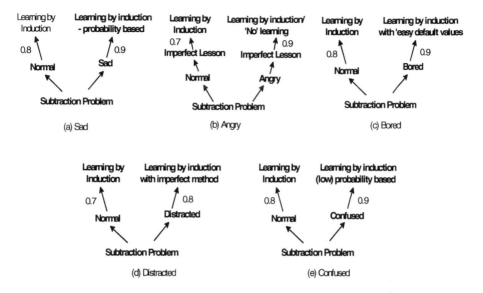

Fig. 4. Plausible justification trees for the affective states

5   Related Work

Conati worked on the probabilistic assessment of affect in educational games [7]. A system that uses dynamic posture information to classify interest levels in learning environments has been done by Mota and Picard [13]. The OCC theory [3] provides a means to relate emotions to underlying goals and perception of relevant events. This provides a reason for the presence of emotions. Jacques and Vicari [10] used the 'Belief Desire and Intention' approach for inferring a student's emotions, modeling these emotions and deciding on a suitable affective action. AutoTutor [9] utilized the techniques of emote-aloud to uncover affective states of confusion frustration and delight (eureka). The log files of the interactions between the user and the system were mined to identify characteristics of the dialogues and the learner's knowledge states that were correlated with these affect states. [22] presents an affective behavior model for intelligent tutoring systems. The paper presents tutorial actions that are based on a Bayesian model of the affective and pedagogic state of the student. Three affective states of 'absorbed', 'neuter' and 'fatigue' are modeled based on the facial expression in [21]. [23] utilizes a Dynamic Decision Network to select a tutorial action based on the combination of two utility measures, one on learning and the other on affect. [16] built personality profiles of students and augmented them with goal orientation and empathetic tendency information. These were found to provide significant affective information.

The focus in this paper is on modeling the effect of affect on learning rather than identifying the 'affective state' of the learner.

6   Results

From the learning strategies perspective the enhancement is in the manner of application of each learning strategy. From being only cognitive oriented and limiting the scope to the learning strategy selection problem, affective influences are analyzed and affective effects converted into actions and mis-actions. Differences are noticed in the way a chosen strategy is executed, in a particular situation. The strategy is executed completely and meticulously at times when there is more interest and focus while at times of boredom the chosen strategy is executed with less care. These differences in execution 'intensity' result in mis-learning(s) of subject concepts and are displayed in the types of errors seen while solving problems. This results in a new cause for observed errors / bugs. Among other observations, the results extend the concepts of 'impasse' learning [11]. The state of impasse can be reacted to in different manners based on the affective state leading to different results.

The ontology of learning strategies now combines both cognitive and affective influences on learning. It is hoped that this integration will prove beneficial to the study as previous approaches have kept the two influences separate, even though their interplay has been realized to be a major factor in the learning exhibited by animals and children [15].

From the perspective of teaching, the learner is allowed to view his 'learning processes' and the effect of his affective state on the learning process. This should enable the learner to reflect on his learning behavior and his emotions, as both the representation of the learning process and the emotions are externalized.

The next work is to influence the teaching strategy based on the recognized affective state. [2] refers to twenty instructional strategies designed to reduce negative feelings and to enhance positive feelings. These strategies have to be interwoven within the state model. In parallel experiments are to be carried out on the modeling accuracy. This is planned to be done utilizing feedback from human school and college teachers on the same test domain as that used by the system.

References

[1] Balakrishnan, A.: Development of an ontology of learning strategies and its application to generate open learner models. In: IEEE Proceedings of the 8th International Conference on Machine Learning and Applications 2009, USA (2009)

[2] Astleitner, H.: Designing emotionally sound interaction: The FEASP approach. Instructional Science 28(3), 169–198 (2000)

[3] Bartneck, C.: Integrating the OCC model of emotions in Embodied characters. In: Workshop on Virtual Conversational Characters: Applications, Methods and Research Challenges (2002)

[4] Blanchard, E.G., Volfson, B., Hong, Y.-H., Lajoie, S.P.: Affective Artificial Intelligence in education: From detection to adaptation. In: Int. Conference on AI in Education (2009)

[5] Brown, J.S., VanLehn, K.: Repair theory: A generative theory of bugs in procedural skills. Cognitive Science 4, 379–426 (1980)

[6] Burton, R.: Diagnosing bugs in a simple procedural skill. In: Sleeman, D.H., Brown, J.S. (eds.) Intelligent Tutoring Systems. Academic Press (1982)

[7] Conati, C.: Probabilistic assessment of user's emotions in educational games. Journal of Applied Artificial Intelligence 16(7-8), 555–575 (2002); Managing cognition and affect in HCI

[8] Forbus, K., Gentner, D.: Learning physical domains: Toward a theoretical framework. In: Anderson, J.R., et al. (eds.) Machine Learning 2 -An Artificial Intelligence Approach, ch. 12. Morgan Kaufmann (1986)

[9] Graesser, A.C., McDaniel, B., Chipman, P., Witherspoon, A., D'Mello, S.: Detection of emotions during learning with AutoTutor. In: The Proceedings of the Cognitive Science Society. Erlbaum, Mahwah (2006)

[10] Jaques, P.A., Viccari, R.M.: A BDI Approach to Infer Student's Emotions in Intelligent Learning Environments. In: Lemaître, C., Reyes, C.A., González, J.A. (eds.) IBERAMIA 2004. LNCS (LNAI), vol. 3315, pp. 901–911. Springer, Heidelberg (2004)

[11] John, S.B., Van Lehn, K.: Repair theory: A generative theory of bugs in procedural skills. Cognitive Science 4(4), 379–426 (1980)

[12] Kaelbling, L.P., Littman, M.L., Moore, A.W.: Reinforcement Learning: A survey. Journal of Artificial Intelligence Research 4, 237–285 (1996)

[13] Mota, S., Picard, R.W.: Automated posture analysis for detecting learner's interest level. In: Proceedings of Computer Vision and Pattern Recognition, Workshop on HCI, pp. 724–736 (2003)

[14] Pat, L., James, W., Stellan, O.: Rules and principles in cognitive diagnosis. In: Frederiksen, N., et al. (eds.) Diagnostic Monitoring of Skill and Knowledge Acquisition. Lawrence Erlbaum Associates Publishers (1990)

[15] Picard, R.W., Papert, S., Bender, W., Blumberg, B., Breazeal, C., Cavallo, D., Machover, T., Resnick, M., Roy, D., Strohecker, C.: Affective learning – a manifesto. BT Technology Journal 22(4) (2004)

[16] Robison, J., McQuiggan, S., Lester, J.: Developing Empirically Based Student Personality Profiles for Affective Feedback Models. In: Aleven, V., Kay, J., Mostow, J. (eds.) ITS 2010. LNCS, vol. 6094, pp. 285–295. Springer, Heidelberg (2010)

[17] Shen, L., Wang, M., Shen, R.: Affective e-learning: Using "emotional" data to improve learning in pervasive learning environment. Journal of Educational Technology and Society 12(2) (2009)

[18] Tecuci, G., Kodratoff, Y.: Apprenticeship Learning in Imperfect Domain Theories. In: Kodratoff, Y., Michalski, R.S. (eds.) Machine Learning: An Artificial Intelligence Approach, vol. 3. Morgan Kaufmann (1990)

[19] Van Lehn, K.: Learning one subprocedure per lesson. Artificial Intelligence 31, 1–40 (1987)

[20] Van Lehn, K.: Towards a theory of impasse-driven learning. In: Mandl, H., Lesgold, A. (eds.) Learning Issues for Intelligent Tutoring Systems. Springer, Heidelberg (1988)

[21] Yanwen, W., Tingting, W., Xiaonian, C.: Affective modeling and recognition of learning emotion: Application to E-learning. Journal of Software 4(8) (2009)

[22] Yasmin, H., Juliata, N., Enrique, S., Gustava, A.-F.: Incorporating an affective model to an intelligent tutor for mobile robotics. In: 36th ASEE/IEEE Frontiers in Education Conference. IEEE (2006)

[23] Hernández, Y., Sucar, L.E., Conati, C.: An Affective Behavior Model for Intelligent Tutors. In: Woolf, B.P., Aïmeur, E., Nkambou, R., Lajoie, S. (eds.) ITS 2008. LNCS, vol. 5091, pp. 819–821. Springer, Heidelberg (2008)

Machine Learning Based Performance Prediction
for Multi-core Simulation

Jitendra Kumar Rai[1,2], Atul Negi[2], and Rajeev Wankar[2]

[1] ANURAG, Hyderabad, India
jk.anurag@yahoo.com
[2] Department of Computer & Information Sciences,
University of Hyderabad, Hyderabad, India
atulcs@uohyd.ernet.in
wankarcs@uohyd.ernet.in

Abstract. Programs co-running on cores share resources on multi-core processor systems. It is now well known that interference between the programs arising from the sharing may result in severe performance degradations. It is the objective of recent research in system scheduling to be aware of shared resource requirements of the running programs (threads). To this end AKULA is a toolset recently developed that provides a platform for experiments and developing thread scheduling algorithms on multi-core processors. In AKULA a bootstrapping module works on the basis of previously collected performance data of programs to simulate program execution on multi-cores. In this paper we describe a different approach where that augments such a bootstrapping module with a model built using machine learning techniques. The proposed model will extend the bootstrapping module's ability to predict degradation in performance due to sharing where previous performance data is not available for pairing /co-scheduling of applications. Also the proposed approach allows greater scalability for variable number of processor cores sharing the resources.

Keywords: Multi-core simulation, Performance prediction, Machine learning techniques, AKULA toolset, CPU Scheduling, Co-runner interference.

1 Introduction

Multi-core processors have multiple execution cores on a single processor chip. These cores share various resources such as caches, memory bus and memory controller. Programs co-running on the cores, which share the resources, interfere with each other. Such interference causes degradation in the performance of the programs. Improving the thread scheduling have been suggested [1], [2] as one of the solution to alleviate such performance bottlenecks.

Recently Zhuravlev et al. developed AKULA [3] toolset to aid the developers in narrowing down and rapidly exploring the design space of scheduling algorithms for multi-core processors. AKULA provides user friendly APIs to prototype thread placement algorithms at user level and also provides facility to rapidly test the algorithms using multi-core simulation provided by the bootstrap module.

C. Sombattheera et al. (Eds.): MIWAI 2011, LNAI 7080, pp. 236–247, 2011.

In this paper we propose machine learning based performance prediction method to improve the multi-core simulation provided by bootstrapping module of AKULA toolset [3]. The rest of the paper is organized as follows. In Section 2 we describe about the AKULA toolset. Section 3 describes our proposal for using machine learning trained model to improve multi-core simulation provided by bootstrap module of AKULA. In section 4 we describe the experimental methodology to build model by training machine learning algorithms. Section 5 and section 6 mention prediction accuracy and transferability results of the trained model. Section 7 mentions related works. Last section mentions conclusions and future work.

2   Overview of the AKULA Toolset

The AKULA toolset [3] helps the algorithm developers in quickly converting an idea for the scheduling algorithm into a working scheduling algorithm, which can then be rapidly evaluated. AKULA consists of three modules: *profiler*, *bootstrap* and *wrapper* modules. The profiler module is provided for collecting the performance data for workload consisting of a pair of programs. The performance data is collected for solo-run and concurrent-run (paired-run) of the programs on a real multi-core system. The concurrent-run involves co-running the pair of programs on processor cores, which share the resources such as last level caches and bus.

Bootstrap module simulates the multi-core system for rapid evaluation of proposed scheduling algorithms with the workloads for which the performance data have already been collected by the *profiler*.

If the rapid evaluation of a scheduling algorithm by bootstrap module shows fulfillment of the objective e.g. improvement in performance then the scheduling algorithm can be further tested on real multi-core based systems using *wrapper* module. Otherwise the algorithm developer can further improvise the proposed algorithm or work on a different idea.

The key components of the bootstrap data are the solo-run and concurrent-run (paired-run) performance data. Solo-run data include execution time of the application measured on the real system, when the application runs alone without interference from the applications co-running on other core sharing the resources. The concurrent-run data is kept in the form of degradation matrix, which contains for a set of target applications, performance degradation values when each application is co-scheduled with every other application on the core sharing the resources. For example in case of four programs A, B, C and D which run on the system where two cores share the resources, the performance data collected could be shown as Table 1 and Table 2.

Table 1. Solo-run performance data

Program name	Solo-run Time (sec.)
A	100
B	150
C	175
D	200

Table 2. Performance degradation matrix for concurrent-run

Program name	Alone	With A	With B	With C	With D
A	1.00	0.75	0.50	0.98	0.99
B	1.00	0.60	0.30	0.95	0.97
C	1.00	0.99	0.98	1.00	1.00
D	1.00	1.00	1.00	1.00	1.00

The bootstrap module performs the simulated run of the threads in given schedule by using the collected performance data. For every scheduling time interval (called *tick*) it calculates the progress of the threads using bootstrap data and the formula shown in equation 1:

$$Pg(A) = \frac{tick}{Solo(A)} * dg(A, Neighb(A)) \tag{1}$$

Where *Pg(A)* refers to the fraction of total work that a thread completes in a given scheduling interval. *Tick* refers to the length of the scheduling time interval. *Solo(A)* is the solo-run completion time of the thread and *dg(A,Neighb(A))* is the degradation that a thread *A* experience due to sharing of the resources by co-running thread *Neighb(A)* on other core. Both *Solo(A)* and *dg(A,Neighb(A))* are obtained from previously collected bootstrap data.

When a thread executes solo, the progress made by it is equal to length of the scheduling clock interval (i.e. *tick*) divided by the time to execute the entire thread. When the other co-running threads compete for the resources shared by the cores, the progress made by the thread needs to be scaled by the performance degradation observed by it in concurrent-run (paired-run) as shown in equation 1.

Since time needed to calculate the progress of a thread over a *tick* using above methodology is usually much shorter than the *tick* itself, this methodology allows very fast evaluations of the scheduling algorithms by simulated run of the threads.

3   Improving Multi-core Simulation in AKULA

We propose to use machine learning techniques to generate the model for bootstrap module of AKULA toolset [3]. The model trained using proposed methodology would replace the bootstrap data i.e. the performance degradation matrix. The advantages gained by using machine learning trained model for multi-core simulation in AKULA will be as follows:

1. The current bootstrap method in AKULA performs the multi-core simulation using data from performance degradation matrix, which works for pair of applications for which such data have already been collected. It does not provide the facility of predicting the performance degradation for pairs of applications for which such data have not been collected.

The offline-trained model proposed in this paper has the ability to predict performance degradation for unknown pairs of applications, which is reflected in terms of prediction accuracy metrics of the trained model, mentioned in section 5.

2. The AKULA bootstrap works using the data from performance degradation matrix for pairs of applications, which works for the case where the pair of applications is co-scheduled on two processor cores, which share the resources. The method becomes unwieldy when the number of processor cores sharing the resources is more than two. The architectural trends for multi-core processors indicate towards growth in number of cores sharing the resources. For example on Intel Core i5 and Intel Core i7 processors [4], four cores share the last level cache. On AMD Phenom 8450 processor [5] three cores present on the chip share the last level cache, while on AMD Phenom 9650 processor [5], four cores share the last level cache. On Sun Ultrasparc T1 (Niagara1) eight cores each with four threads i.e. total 32 threads share the last level caches [11], while on Ultrasparc T2 (Niagara2) processor there are eight cores each with eight threads i.e. total 64 threads sharing the last level caches [12].

The methodology proposed in this paper uses fractional solo-run programs attributes (described in section 4.3), which enables the offline trained model to predict the performance degradation even in the case when the number of cores sharing the resources is more than two.

3. The methodology proposed in AKULA collects bootstrap data for one minute run of the application. The real life applications have quite larger runtimes, and also the applications have different phase behaviors during their entire run [10]. The application requirements of the shared resources change with the phases. The proposed model having the prediction capability would be more amenable to take phase behaviors of the applications into account.

Our previous work [6] describes the methodology using machine learning techniques for building performance prediction model for multi-cores. The model developed in the work predicts the concurrent-run (paired-run) performance of a program using solo-run attributes of the program and its co-running program as inputs. For two applications A and B co-running on two cores which share the resources the model predicts the concurrent-run performance of A as shown below:

$$f((a_{1A}, a_{2A}, ...a_{nA}), (a_{1B}, a_{2B}, ...a_{nB})) \rightarrow concurrent\_run\_CPI_A \qquad (2)$$

Where $concurrent\_run\_CPI_A$ is concurrent-run performance of program A in terms of cycles per instructions (CPI) and $(a_{1A}, a_{2A}, ..., a_{nA})$ and $(a_{1B}, a_{2B}, ..., a_{nB})$ are set of solo-run program attributes of A and B respectively. The limitation of the above model is that it needs to be retrained for the case where the number of cores sharing the resources are more than two, e.g. the number of cores sharing last level caches are four on Intel Xeon E5630 [4], three on AMD Phenom 8450 [5] and four on AMD Phenom 9650 [5].

The model proposed in this paper takes fractional solo-run program attributes as inputs (mentioned in section 4.2), which enables the offline trained model to predict the concurrent-run performance of applications for the cases when the number of cores sharing the resources is more than two. The proposed model gives concurrent-run performance in terms of cycles per instruction (*concurrent_run_CPI$_A$*) by taking proposed new solo-run attributes as inputs. Thus the calculation of the progress a thread makes in a *tick* (mentioned in section 2, equation 1) can be done like this:

$$Pg(A) = \frac{tick}{Solo(A)} * \frac{solo\_run\_CPI_A}{concurrent\_run\_CPI_A} \tag{3}$$

Where the *solo_run_CPI$_A$* is solo-run performance of application A, which is collected in solo-run experiment (described in section 4). The *concurrent_run_CPI$_A$* is concurrent-run performance of application A, predicted by the offline-trained model. The ratio of the two as mentioned in (equation 3), basically is the degradation in performance of application A, when sharing the resources with another application co-running on other core of the processor. In next section we describe about the experimental methodology and new solo-run program attributes to train the model for performance prediction.

4   Model Building

Data collected from the hardware performance counters of the processors were used to train the machine learning algorithms. Hardware performance counters are special registers, provided by modern processors to measure counts of various performance events like L2 cache misses, instructions completed, cycles consumed etc. Processor manuals [4] provide information for configuring hardware performance counters to measure various performance events of interest.

4.1   Experimental Setup

The first experimental platform was based on Intel quad-core Xeon X5482 processor, which generated the train-set. The test set was generated from AMD Phenom 9650 processor based platform. We used perfmon2 interface [7] with linux kernel 2.6.30 on both platforms to collect the hardware performance counters data. We used SPEC cpu2006 [8] benchmark applications with reference inputs as workload, which include total 55 programs.

The two platforms used for generating the train and test data-sets have differences in terms of organization of caches and their sharing among the cores. The Intel Xeon X5482 processor has four cores on it. The processor cache organization of Intel Xeon X5482 processor is described in Table 3. Each core on the processor has level-1 (L1) instruction and level-1 (L1) data cache, each of size 32 KB. There is level-2 (L2) cache of size 12 MB, which is unified in nature i.e. it contains both data as well as instructions. It is organized in two blocks, each of size 6MB. On Intel Xeon X5482 processor, two processor cores share each block of the last level (L2) cache and Front Side bus (FSB) [4].

Table 3. Organization of caches on Intel Xeon X5482 processor, which was used to generate train-set

Item	Specifications
L1 Instruction Cache	32KB 8-way set-associative per core
L1 Data Cache	32KB 8-way set-associative per core
L2 Unified Cache	Total 12MB, Each 6MB 24-way set-associative L2 cache block is shared by two cores

The AMD Phenom 9650 processor also has four cores on it. The processor cache organization of AMD Phenom 9650 processor is described in Table 4. Each core on the processor has level-1 (L1) instruction and level-1 (L1) data cache, each of size 64 KB. Each core has its own private level-2 (L2) cache of size 512KB. The level-2 (L2) cache is unified in nature i.e. it contains both data as well as instructions. There is unified level-3 (L3) cache of size 2MB, which is shared by all the four processor cores.

Table 4. Organization of caches on AMD Phenom 9650 processor, which was used to generate test-set

Item	Specifications
L1 Instruction Cache	64KB 2-way set-associative per core
L1 Data Cache	64KB 2-way set-associative per core
L2 Unified Cache	512KB 16-way set-associative per core
L3 Unified Cache	2MB 32-way set-associative, shared by four cores

The two platforms used for generating the train-set and test-set differ in terms of the organization of processor memory hierarchy resources on them. The organization of processor caches differs mainly on following aspects: number of levels of caches, size of the caches, associativity of caches and number of cores sharing the last level caches as described in Table 3 and Table 4. Moreover the caches present at different levels (i.e. L1, L2 etc.) are inclusive on Intel Xeon X5482 processor [4], while on AMD Phenom 9650 they are exclusive [13].

4.2   Experiments

Train-set and test-set data were collected by conducting solo-run and concurrent-run experiments on experimental platforms as described in our previous work [6]. In solo-run experiment each SPEC cpu2006 [8] application was run on a core and the performance counter data for complete run were collected. The solo-run performance counter data were used to generate the solo-run program attributes.

In concurrent-run experiment on Intel Xeon X5482 processor based platform, two SPEC cpu2006 [8] applications were run simultaneously, as there are two cores on the processor sharing the last level (L2) caches. One application was run on a core along with other on the core sharing the resources with the first. The performance counter data for complete run of the first application were collected. As the applications have different run-times, the other application was re-run if it finished before the completion of the first application. Data collected during concurrent-run experiment were used to generate the class variable concurrent-run performance.

In concurrent-run experiment on AMD Phenom 9650 processor based platform, four SPEC cpu2006 [8] applications were run simultaneously, because on AMD Phenom 9650 processor four cores share the last level (L3) cache. One application was run on a core along with other three on the cores sharing the resources with the first. The performance counter data for complete run of the first application were collected. As the applications have different run-times, each of the other three applications was re-run if it finished before the completion of the first application. Data collected during concurrent-run experiment were used to generate the class variable concurrent-run performance.

4.3   Solo-run Program Attributes and Class Variable

The performance events which can be collected on the two experimental platforms differ [4] [13], as the performance monitoring unit of a processor is specific to its micro-architecture. We collected the performance events which are specific to utilization of the memory hierarchy resources shared among the cores. The performance events data collected during the experiments are mentioned below:

INSTRUCTIONS_RETIRED
Number of instructions completed. The performance event used for collecting this data is named INSTRUCTIONS_RETIRED on Intel Xeon X5482 processor. On AMD Phenom 9650 processor the performance event used for collecting this data is named RETIRED_INSTRUCTIONS.

UNHALTED_CORE_CYCLES
Number of core cycles completed. The performance event used for collecting this data is named UNHALTED_CORE_CYCLES on Intel Xeon X5482 processor. On AMD Phenom 9650 processor the performance event used for collecting this data is named CPU_CLK_UNHALTED.

LAST_LEVEL_CACHE_REFERENCES
Number of references to last level cache. The performance event used for collecting this data is named LAST_LEVEL_CACHE_REFERENCES on Intel Xeon X5482 processor. On AMD Phenom 9650 processor, we can not count core specific events for last level (L3) cache [13] [14] [15]. Though the processor manual specifies cores select masks [13] for getting the core specific events from last level (L3) cache, the prescribed masks do not work in practice [14] and there is an official erratum from

AMD [15] regarding this issue. Due to this we used event data for level-2 (L2) cache for generating the solo-run program attributes. Hence on AMD Phenom 9650 processor the performance event used for collecting this data is named REQUESTS_TO_L2__ALL, which basically collects the number of references to level (L2) cache.

LAST_LEVEL_CACHE_MISS
Number of misses and prefetch occurring at last level cache. The performance event used for collecting this data is named L2_LINES_IN__SELF__ANY on Intel Xeon X5482 processor. Due to non functioning of the core specific event mask for last level (L3) cache on AMD Phenom 9650 processor, we used event data for level-2 (L2) cache for generating the solo-run program attributes. On AMD Phenom 9650 processor the performance event used for collecting this data is named L2_CACHE_MISS__ALL, which basically collects the number of misses and prefetches to to level (L2) cache.

   The event data collected from the solo-run of the programs were used to calculate the solo-run program attributes. The list of the solo-run program attributes calculated from the afore-mentioned performance event data is given below:

LAST_LEVEL_CACHE_REFERENCES_PKI
Number of references to last level cache per kilo instructions.

LAST_LEVEL_CACHE_MISS_PKI
Number of misses and prefetches occurring at last level cache per kilo instructions.

LAST_LEVEL_CACHE_MISS_PK_LAST_LEVEL_CACHE_REFERENCES
Number of misses and prefetches occurring at last level cache per kilo references. This gives a rough estimate of cache re-referencing property of the program at last level cache.

Fr_LAST_LEVEL_CACHE_REFERENCES_PKI
Fraction of number of references to last level cache per kilo instructions of the program as compared to its co-running programs.

Fr_ LAST_LEVEL_CACHE_MISS_PKI
Fraction of number of misses and prefetches to last level cache per kilo instructions of the program as compared to its co-running programs.

Fr_CPI
Fraction of cycles per instruction of the program as compared to its co-running programs. It encapsulates the effect of overall resource utilization behavior of the program as compared to its co-running programs.

solo_run_CPI
Cycles per instruction of the program for its solo run. It encapsulates the effect of overall resource utilization behavior of the program.

The class variable (i.e. the dependent variable to be predicted later) is concurrent-run cycles per instruction (*concurrent_run_CPI*) for each program for its complete run, calculated from data collected from concurrent-run experiment. The model *f* (generated by training machine learning algorithms) to predict the concurrent-run performance of program A can be expressed in the form of equation shown below:

$$f(a_{1A}, a_{2A}, a_{3A}, a_{4A}, a_{5A}, a_{6A}, a_{7A}) \rightarrow concurrent\_run\_CPI_A \quad (4)$$

Where a_{1A}, a_{2A},....., a_{7A} are seven solo-run attributes for program A as mentioned above. Due to use of new program attributes especially the fractional attribute, the model shown by equation 4 always needs seven attributes for a program to predict its concurrent-run performance. It is an improvement over our previously proposed model [6] shown in equation 2, which takes solo-run attributes of two applications to predict the concurrent-run performance (where the two applications will be co-running on two core sharing the resources). The model shown in equation 2 needs to be rebuilt to consider the case when the number of cores sharing the resources is more than two.

5   Results on Prediction Accuracy of Model

We used supervised learning, in which the machine learning algorithms are trained with supplied data-set (also called train-set) to build the models. On training the machine learning algorithms   generate regression models, which later on can be used for predicting the variable of interest in a real world scenario. The machine learning algorithms used in the study are: Linear Regression (LR), Artificial Neural Networks (ANN), Model Trees (M5'), K-nearest neighbors classifier (IBK), KStar (K*) and Support Vector Machines (SVM). We used weka-3.6.2 machine learning workbench [9]. Default settings of the parameters (as provided in weka-3.6.2) to the above-mentioned machine learning algorithms were used. The total number of instances used in the study is 3025, which were generated from Intel Xeon X5482 processor based platform.

Table 5. Prediction accuracy metrics in 10 times10-fold cross validation for performance prediction on Intel Xeon X5482 processor

Algor-ithms	Correlation coefficient (C)	Mean absolute error (MAE)	Root mean squared error (RMSE)	Relative absolute error (RRSE %)	Root relative squared error (RAE %)
LR	0.97	0.18	0.31	24.99	21.06
ANN	0.99	0.14	0.20	16.41	15.82
IBK	0.98	0.11	0.22	17.63	12.80
K*	0.99	0.08	0.20	15.72	9.73
M5'	0.99	0.09	0.17	13.95	10.66
SVM	0.97	0.15	0.33	26.82	17.52

We used 10-fold cross validation [9] to evaluate the prediction accuracy of the trained model. The values of prediction accuracy metrics for 10 times 10-fold cross validation [9] observed in the study are mentioned in Table 5. The prediction accuracy metrics indicate that the best performing algorithms are KStar (K*) and Model Trees (M5'), mainly based on the values of correlation coefficient and mean absolute error.

6   Transferability of Trained Regression Models

We used test-set data from other experimental platform based on AMD Phenom 9650 processor, to assess the transferability of the trained regression models. The number of instances of test-set data generated from AMD Phenom 9650 processor is 123. These numbers of test instances are generated based on the availability of the platform for performing experiments. The assessment for transferability of trained regression models across two processors having different cache organizations was performed for the three best performing algorithms in 10-fold cross validation i.e. KStar (K*), Model Trees (M5') and K-nearest neighbors classifier (IBK). The prediction accuracy metrics of the trained regression models on the test data-set are shown in Table 6. The prediction accuracy metrics for the test data indicate that the regression models trained by data from Intel Xeon X5482 processor are reasonable for performing performance predictions on other processor i.e. AMD Phenom 9650 processor and the Model Trees (M5') algorithm seem to perform best.

Table 6. Prediction accuracy metrics for test data from AMD Phenom 9650 processor for performing performance prediction

Algorithms	Correlation coefficient (C)	Mean absolute error (MAE)	Root mean squared error (RMSE)
IBK	0.95	0.34	0.53
K*	0.87	0.30	0.86
M5'	0.99	0.16	0.26

7   Related Work

Among previous works Chandra, D. et al. [16] proposed analytical models for predicting miss rates for processes sharing the same cache. These models are fairly involved and require the reuse distance or stack distance profiles for each thread to predict the inter thread cache contention. Recently Zhuravlev et al. [17] proposed performance estimate of co-scheduled programs using stack distance profile. Obtaining stack distance profile is a costly operation. They obtained it using Pin binary instrumentation [18] [19], which is very time consuming. Xu, C. et al. [20] proposed shared cache aware performance model for multi-core processors. The model estimates the performance degradation due to shared cache contention between co-running processes on multi-cores. Their model uses reuse distance diagram of the program. Their method to obtain the reuse distance diagram involves multiple runs of the given program with a synthetic benchmark called stressmark.

The proposed use of machine learning technique does not require time-consuming program run under binary instrumentation [17] [18] [19] for collecting the information about program behaviors in the form of stack distance profiles for generating the performance prediction model. It can also reduce the time required for performance prediction as a trained model could be used for performance prediction afterwards, thus amortizing the efforts required for training the algorithm to build the model.

8   Conclusion and Future Work

We proposed the use of model trained by machine learning to improve the multi-core simulation provided by bootstrap module of AKULA [3] toolset. The offline-trained model will enable the bootstrap module to predict the performance degradation for new workload schedules, while the current implementation works for known workload pairings by using the previously stored performance data. The model will also be useful for performance prediction when the number of cores sharing the resources (e.g. last level caches) is more than two. We believe that by virtue of storing the knowledge the offline-trained model may be able to consider the applications phase behaviors [10]. Exploring the applicability of the proposed model to phase behaviors and integrating with AKULA toolset [3] are part of our future work.

References

1. Zhuravlev, S., Blagodurov, S., Fedorova, A.: Addressing Shared Resource Contention in Multicore Processors via Scheduling. In: Fifteenth International Conference on Architectural Support for Programming Languages and Operating Systems (ASPLOS 2010), Pittsburgh, Pennsylvania, USA, pp. 129–142 (March 2010)
2. Rai, J.K., Negi, A., Wankar, R., Nayak, K.D.: A Machine Learning based Meta-Scheduler for Multi-core Processors. International Journal of Adaptive, Resilient and Autonomic Systems (IJARAS) 1(4), 46–59 (2010)
3. Zhuravlev, S., Blagodurov, S., Fedorova, A.: AKULA: A Toolset for Experimenting and Developing Thread Placement Algorithms on Multicore Systems. In: Proceedings of the 19th International Conference on Parallel Architectures and Compilation Techniques (PACT 2010), Vienna, Austria, pp. 249–260 (2010)
4. Intel® 64 and IA-32 Architectures Software Developer's Manuals,
   http://www.intel.com/products/processor/manuals
5. AMD-phenom-processor-model-numbers-feature-comparison,
   http://www.amd.com/us/products/desktop/processors/
   phenom/Pages/AMD-phenom-processor-model-numbers-
   feature-comparison.aspx

6. Rai, J.K., Negi, A., Wankar, R., Nayak, K.D.: Performance Prediction on Multi-core Processors. In: The IEEE 2010 International Conference on Computational Intelligence, Communication Systems and Networks (CICN 2010), Bhopal, India, November 26-28, pp. 633–637 (2010)
7. Eranian, S.: Perfmon2: The Hardware-based Performance Monitoring Interface for Linux. In: 2006 Linux Symposium, vol. 1, pp. 269–288 (2006)
8. Standard performance evaluation corporation. SPEC CPU2006,
   http://www.spec.org/cpu2006/
9. Witten, I.H., Frank, E.: Data Mining: Practical machine learning tools and techniques, 2nd edn. Morgan Kaufmann, San Francisco (2005)
10. Sherwood, T., Perelman, E., Hamerly, G., Sair, S., Calder, B.: Discovering and Exploiting Program Phases. IEEE Micro 23(6), 84–93 (2003)
11. Poonacha, K., Kathirgamar, A., Kunle, O.: Niagara, a 32-way Multithreaded Sparc Processor. IEEE Micro, 21–29 (March-April 2005)
12. Niagara2: A Highly Threaded Server-on-a-Chip,
    http://www.opensparc.net/pubs/preszo/06/04-Sun-Golla.pdf
13. BIOS and Kernel Developer's Guide (BKDG) For AMD Family 10h Processors,
    http://developer.amd.com/documentation/guides/
    pages/default.aspx
14. Eranian, S.: (on mailing list) Re: [perfmon2] CORE_0_SELECT Umask for L3 events on AMD F10h (2011),
    http://permalink.gmane.org/gmane.comp.linux.perfmon2.devel/
    3014
15. Revision Guide for AMD Family 10h Processors 41322 Rev. 3.82 (2011),
    http://support.amd.com/us/Processor_TechDocs/41322.pdf
16. Chandra, D., Guo, F., Kim, S., Solihin, Y.: Predicting Inter-Thread Cache Contenton on a Chip Multi-Processor Architecture. In: Proceedings of the 11th International Symposium on High Performance Computer Architecture, HPCA 2005, San Francisco, CA, USA, pp. 340–351 (2005)
17. Zhuravlev, S., Blagodurov, S., Fedorova, A.: Addressing Shared Resource Contention in Multicore Processors via Scheduling. In: Proceedings of the 15th International Conference on Architectural Support for Programming Languages and Operating Systems, ASPLOS 2010, Pittsburgh, Pennsylvania, USA, pp. 129–142 (2010)
18. Luk, C.K., Cohn, R., Muth, R., Patil, H., Klauser, A., Lowney, G., Wallace, S., Reddi, V.J., Hazelwood, K.: Pin: Building Customized Program Analysis Tools with Dynamic Instrumentation. In: Proceedings of the 2005 ACM SIGPLAN Conference on Programming Language Design and Implementation, PLDI 2005, pp. 190–200 (2005)
19. Hoste, K., Eeckhout, L.: Microarchitecture-Independent Workload Characterization. IEEE Micro 27(3), 63–72 (2007)
20. Xu, C., Chen, X., Dick, R.P., Mao, Z.M.: Cache Contention and Application Performance Prediction for Multi-Core Systems. In: Proceedings of the 2010 IEEE International Symposium on Performance Analysis of Systems and Softwares IEEE ISPASS 2010, White Plains NY, USA, pp. 76–86 (2010)

Forecasting Using Rules Extracted from Privacy Preservation Neural Network

Nekuri Naveen[1,2], Vadlamani Ravi[1,*], and Chillarige Raghavendra Rao[2]

[1] Institute for Development and Research in banking Technology, Castle Hills Road #1,
Masab Tank, Hyderabad – 500 057 (AP) India
[2] Department of Computer & Information Sciences, University of Hyderabad,
Hyderabad – 500 046 (AP) India
naveen.nekuri@gmail.com, rav_padma@yahoo.com,
crrcs@uohyd.ernet.in

Abstract. Privacy preserving data mining is of paramount importance in many areas. In this paper, we employ Particle Swarm Optimization (PSO) trained Auto Associative Neural Network (PSOAANN) for preservation privacy in input feature values. The privacy preserved input features are fed to the Dynamic Evolving Neuro Fuzzy Inference System (DENFIS) and Classification and Regression Tree (CART) separately for rule extraction purpose. We also propose a new feature selection method using PSOAANN. Thus, in this study, PSOAANN accomplishes privacy preservation as well as feature selection. The performance of the hybrid is tested using 10 fold cross validation on 5 regression datasets viz. *Auto MPG, Body Fat, Boston Housing, Forest Fires* and *Pollution*. The study demonstrates the effectiveness of the proposed approach in generating accurate regression rules with and without feature selection. The t-test at 1% level of significance is performed to see whether the difference in results obtained in the case of with and without feature selection is statistically significant or not. In the case of PSOAANN + CART, it is observed that the result is statistical insignificant between with and without feature selection in four datasets. In the case of PSOAANN + DENFIS, it is observed that statistical significance between with and without feature selection for three datasets. Hence, from the t-test it is concluded that the proposed feature selection method yielded better or comparable results.

Keywords: Privacy Preservation, Privacy Preserved Auto Associative Neural Network, Dynamic Evolving Fuzzy Inference System, CART, Feature Selection, Rule Extraction, Regression.

1 Introduction

In areas like banking, business, finance and medical sectors are very much concerned about the privacy of the data for the last few decades. The privacy of the data throws new challenges for decision making based on data mining. The advantage of privacy

---

* Corresponding author.

C. Sombattheera et al. (Eds.): MIWAI 2011, LNAI 7080, pp. 248–260, 2011.
© Springer-Verlag Berlin Heidelberg 2011

preserving data mining (PPDM) is that it ensures privacy before actually mining the data. The concept of PPDM was introduced by Agrawal and Srikant [1] and Lindell and Pinkas [2]. Some PPDM algorithms were developed in the security and data mining [3]. PPDM is being used in real world applications like healthcare [4], medicine [5], counter-terrorism [6], homeland security [7], bio-terrorism surveillance [8], business collaboration [9], etc. In medical appliance Boyens et al [10] proposed a new aggregation methodology without disclosing the data and also its usage. Later, many PPDM techniques were proposed. Classifying the existing PPDM algorithms taxonomy was proposed by Bertino [11]. Granmo and Oleshchuk [12] briefly presented some PPDM approaches. PPDM algorithms were classified into 3 major classes by Vaidya et al [13] based on the type of changes upon the original data. (i) Value Distortion methods (or) Perturbative methods: transforming the original data by using some mathematical functions. (ii) Value transformation methods (or) Non-perturbative methods: a partial suppression of the original data is taking place. Crises [14] summarized some of the non-perturbative techniques like data swapping and k-anonymity. (iii) Cryptographic methods, which are used in distributed data mining [15]. Ramu and Ravi [16] proposed a novel PPDM method by hybridizing random projection and random rotation and applied it to solve some benchmark problems and bankruptcy prediction in banks. Bansal et al [17] reported privacy preserving algorithm for neural network. Recently, Paramjeet et al [18] proposed a new architecture for privacy preservation using auto-associative neural network. Very recently, Naveen et al [19] used the same architecture used by Paramjeet et al [18] for extracting rules from it to solve classification problems. The work of Naveen et al [21] is different from that of Paramjeet et al [18] as follows: (i) They used Logistic Regression (LR) and DT as classifiers, whereas Naveen et al [19] employed Ripper rule induction system in addition to DT and dropped LR (ii) Naveen et al [19] presented the '*if-then*' rules in this paper, whereas they did not. (iii) Naveen et al [19] presented the coverage of each rule here, whereas they did not. (iv) Naveen et al [19] performed the t-test to compare the performance of the classifiers on the original and the transformed data and to compare the performance of DT and Ripper on the transformed data. (v) The experimental setup is different in both studies. In the current study also, we used the same architecture for privacy preservation. But, for solving regression problems using 'if-then' rules, we used DENFIS and CART in the present study. Both are versatile in that they can solve classification as well as regression problems. The current study is different from that of Paramjeet et al [18] and Naveen et al [19] as follows: (i) Here, we solved regression problems, but those studies solved classification problems only. (ii) Also, a feature selection method is proposed in PSOAANN whereas they did not.

The rest of the paper is organized as follows. Section 2 presents an overview of the Particle Swarm Optimization (PSO) and DENFIS. Section 3 describes the proposed methodology. Section 4 describes the feature selection. Section 5 presents results and discussion. Finally section 6 concludes the paper.

2   Overview of PSO, DENFIS and CART

2.1   PSO

In 1995, Kennedy and Eberhart [20] proposed the PSO algorithm which is a population based optimization technique. PSO mimics the behavior of bird flocking, fish schooling or the social behavior of group of people. Each individual particle is considered to be a point in the N dimensional space. The procedure of PSO mainly consists of initialization and velocity updation. In initialization phase, randomly generate a population of solutions called particles with each particle assigned with random velocity V_{id}^{Old}. The neighborhood best p_{id} is the best path traveled by each of the particle. The global best p_{gd} is the best path from the entire population. In velocity updation, each particle's velocity is vigorously adjusted with respect to its position x_{id}^{old} using neighborhood best or global best particle. The velocity V_{id}^{New} and position x_{id}^{New} of each particle are updated by following the equations:

$$V_{id}^{New} = w * V_{id}^{Old} + c_1 * rand * \left(p_{id} - x_{id}^{old}\right) + c_2 * rand * \left(p_{gd} - x_{id}^{old}\right) \qquad (1)$$

$$x_{id}^{New} = x_{id}^{Old} + V_{id}^{New} \qquad (2)$$

Where c_1 and c_2 are two predefined positive constants (usually c_1=2, c_2 =2), w is the inertia weight value, which is continuously decreased as the iterations pass, rand is a random number generated from uniform distribution U(0,1).

2.2   DENFIS

The dynamic evolving neural-fuzzy inference system (DENFIS) for online learning is proposed by Kasabov and Song [21]. While it has both on-line and off-line versions, it uses Takagi-Sugeno type fuzzy inference engine to generate fuzzy rules. DENFIS evolves through incremental, hybrid of supervised/unsupervised learning and adopt new input data. Fuzzy rules are generated and updating during the process by using the local element. When data is presented to the DENFIS, new fuzzy rules are created and the rules are updated. Cluster the input data to find the cluster centers by using off-line evolving clustering method called Evolving Clustering Method (ECM) which is fast and one pass algorithm for the input data. A new fuzzy rule is created if a new cluster centre is found by the ECM. The antecedent part of the new fuzzy rule is generated using position of the cluster centre. For each data pair, some existing fuzzy rules are updated, if their rule nodes distances to the data point are not greater than 2 × Dthr, Dthr is the user defined threshold value of the a cluster. The fuzzy rule antecedent part is updated when the clusters are changed with ECM. The consequent part of the rules is created and updated using the least square estimators.

2.3   Classification and Regression Tree (CART) [22]

CART is an algorithm to generate tree for solving both classification and regression problems. It implements binary recursive portioning procedure. First, root node or parent node is selected based on a splitting criterion and then the data is partitioned into two child nodes. This binary splitting process is repeated with the two child nodes treating them as the parent node until further splitting is not possible. CART use GINI index for splitting the attribute with all the possible and best splits of the data used for analysis. A tree is being generated after all the best splits taken for all the attributes which may overfit the information contained in the training dataset. Now, tree pruning takes place which will reduce the tree branches. In other words, the tree is simpler without compromising the accuracy after pruning takes place.

3   Proposed Methodology

A. Particle Swarm Optimization Trained Auto-associative Neural Network

The PSOAANN consists of three layers: input layer, hidden layer and output layer. The input and output layers consists of equal number of nodes which represent the same input features. The number of hidden nodes is a user defined parameter. This architecture resembles multi layer perceptron without bias node.   Sigmoid activation function is used in the hidden and output layers. After the training process is completed, the output nodes contain the transformed values of the original input features. Earlier, Hrushka and Natter [23] used the architecture for market segmentation, where the hidden nodes are treated as clusters. They used sigmoid activation function in hidden and output layers and the backpropagation algorithm for training the network. Some drawbacks are there in backpropagation algorithm like trapping in local minima and slow convergence. To overcome these drawbacks PSO is employed for weight updation, instead of the backpropagation. The main advantage of proposing a three layered AANN for privacy preservation over the traditional five layered AANN [24, 25] is the decrease in computations. For more details of the training algorithm of PSOAANN the reader is referred to Paramjeet et al [18].

B. Proposed Hybrid Methodology

The proposed hybrid consists of two phases.

Phase 1: PSOAANN is employed to transform data M to M^1. Then, the actual output labels are appended to the M^1 and the resulting data matrix is fed to the second phase. Privacy is measured in terms of the optimal NRMSE value obtained by PSOAANN. It is evident that the NRMSE value is directly proportional to the amount of privacy preserved for a dataset i.e., the more the NRMSE value, the more the privacy is preserved. The transformed data matrix is shared with the data miner for the purpose of regression.

Phase 2: Regression task is performed on the M^1 by using the rules generated by DENFIS / CART. The block diagram of the proposed hybrid is depicted in Figure 1.

C. Experimental Setup

In Phase 2, the privacy preserved dataset is split into 80% and 20%. 10-fold cross validation (10-fcv) is performed on the 80% part and 20% of the dataset is named as a validation set and stored for evaluating the efficacy of the rules. The rules generated using DENFIS / CART are tested against the validation set.

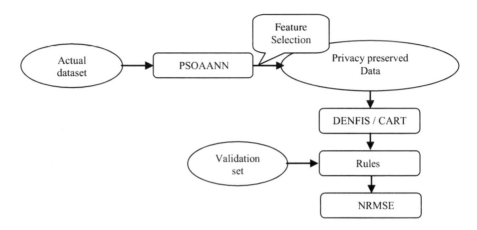

Fig. 1. Flow diagram of the proposed hybrid approach

4   Proposed Feature Selection Method

Feature selection is a procedure to select the important features from a given dataset. Guyon and Elisseeff [26] indicated that there are many benefits of feature selection: (i) facilitating data visualization and data understanding, (ii) reducing the measurement and storage requirements, (iii) reducing training and utilization times, and (iv) defying the curse of dimensionality to improve prediction performance.

We proposed a new method of feature selection between input and hidden layers only. Our objective is to select the most important features such that they are half in number of the total features for a given dataset. Since the input and output layer represent the same input features, we consider the input and hidden layers in this architecture for feature selection. The proposed feature selection method cannot be compared with the existing methods because it is implemented between the input and the hidden layer of the PSOAANN.

The proposed method of feature selection is as follows:

1. For each hidden node j, sum the absolute weights as $S_j = \sum_{i=1,j=1}^{nin,nhn}|w_{ij}|$, where w_{ij} represents the weight between the ith input and j^{th} hidden node. nin and nhn denote number of input and hidden nodes respectively.
2. Each of the weight connection from all the input nodes to each of the hidden layer is converted into the contribution of each input nodes with respect to each of the hidden node as follows.

$$r_{ij} = \frac{|w_{ij}|}{S_j} * 100$$

This percentage serves the measure of importance of each of the input features at each of the hidden node in the hidden layer.

3. Each of the input features is ranked based on the percentage of its importance at each of the hidden nodes. Based on this ranking, at each of the hidden node, a few (While this number varies between 2 to 5, exact number depends on the dataset.) top ranked features are considered. Because each hidden node yields different ranks to the same features, we compute the frequency of occurrence (FREQ) of the selected input features across all the hidden nodes and rank them again with respect to the FREQ value. Then, we considered 50% of the total features in number. Then the selected features are fed to the DENFIS / CART for the rule generation purpose. It should be noted that by changing the number of hidden nodes of the PSOAANN, the optimal feature subset would turn out to be different.

5   Results and Discussion

To demonstrate the effectiveness of the proposed hybrid, five benchmark regression datasets namely *Auto MPG*, *Body Fat*, *Boston Housing*, *Forest Fires* and *Pollution* are solved. *Auto MPG dataset* concerns city-cycle fuel consumption in miles per gallon. This dataset contains 398 instances with 8 features. This dataset is available in UCI machine learning repository [27]. *Body Fat dataset* is obtained from StatLib repository http://lib.stat.cmu.edu . It estimates the percentage of *Body Fat* determined by underwater weighing and various body circumference measurements for 252 men with 14 features [28]. *Boston Housing dataset* is obtained from UCI machine learning repository [27]. It concerns housing values in suburbs of Boston and contains 506 instances with 14 features. *Forest Fires dataset* is obtained from UCI machine learning repository [27]. It contains 517 instances with 13 features [29]. *Pollution dataset* is obtained from StatLib repository http://lib.stat.cmu.edu . This dataset contains 60 instances with 16 features [30].

We coded PSOAANN in ANSI C and implemented it on a Pentium 4 machine 2 GB RAM and 2.3GHz clock speed in Windows environment. We ran PSOAANN for 1000 iterations for all the problems before extracting rules from it. We found that 1000 iterations yielded considerably less NRMSE value at convergence thereby suggesting that reasonable amount of privacy is preserved in all datasets. We employed DENFIS for extracting rules from PSOAANN. DENFIS is available in NeuCom tool, whose student version is freely available at http://www.aut.ac.nz . Also, we employed CART for extracting rules from PSOAANN. CART is freely available at www.saflord-systems.com .

Average NRMSE values, obtained over 10-folds for the hybrid PSOAANN + DENFIS, with and without feature selection, are tabulated in Table 1. From Table 1, it is observed that the reduced feature set yielded better NRMSE values compared to that of the full feature set in three datasets namely *Auto MPG*, *Boston Housing*, and

Forest Fires. Percentage relative difference between NRMSE values yielded by full feature set and reduced feature set is also computed and presented in Table 1. Since the obtained average NRMSE values for with and without feature selection are numerically close to each other, we performed t-test whether they are statistically significant or not. The t-test is performed on the hybrid of PSOAANN + DENFIS on full features and reduced features at 1% level of significance, presented in Table 1. The t-test indicates that on *Auto MPG, Boston Housing, Forest Fires* and *Pollution dataset* with full features and reduced features are statistically significant. However in the case of *Body Fat dataset* the NRMSE values are insignificant.

Table 1. Average NRMSE values over 10-folds

Dataset	Validation set (PSOAANN +DENFIS)			
	Full features	Reduced features	% Relative Difference	t-test values (1% level)
Auto MPG	0.11505	**0.09384**	18.43546	4.799471
Body Fat	**0.04759**	0.04789	0.630385	0.28197
Boston Housing	0.41484	**0.17154**	58.64912	5.205724
Forest Fires	0.02393	**0.01735**	27.49687	5.624731
Pollution	**0.02306**	0.11185	385.039	30.16919

Average NRMSE values, obtained over 10-folds for the hybrid PSOAANN + CART, with and without feature selection are tabulated in Table 2. From Table 2, it is observed that the full feature set yielded better NRMSE values compared to reduced feature set in all the datasets except in Forest fires *dataset*. Percentage relative difference between NRMSE values yielded by full feature set and reduced feature set is also computed and presented in Table 2. Since the obtained average NRMSE values for with and without feature selection are numerically close to each other, we performed t-test whether they are statistically significant or not. The t-test is performed on the hybrid of PSOAANN + CART on full features and reduced features at 1% level of significance, tabulated in Table 2. In the case of *Auto MPG, Boston Housing, Forest Fires* and *Pollution* both the full feature set and reduced feature set hybrid are statistically insignificant.

Table 2. Average NRMSE values over 10-folds

Dataset	Validation set (PSOAANN+CART)			
	Full features	Reduced features	% Relative Difference	t-test values (1% level)
Auto MPG	**0.10750**	0.10944	1.804534	0.537005
Body Fat	**0.10187**	0.11815	15.98233	3.717352
Boston Housing	**0.18098**	0.18379	1.553729	0.384312
Forest Fires	0.01956	**0.01409**	27.95869	0.980145
Pollution	**0.11549**	0.12541	8.590848	0.774523

Average rule base size over 10-folds is computed and presented in Table 3, for full feature set and reduced feature set for all the datasets. In the case of PSOAANN + DENFIS hybrid, the rule base size of reduced features is higher than that of rule base size of full feature set in all the datasets except forest fires *dataset*. The length of the rule has reduced with reduced feature set and achieved better NRMSE value in the case of *Auto MPG, Boston Housing* and *Forest Fires dataset*. In the case of PSOAANN + CART hybrid the rule base size of *Boston Housing, Forest Fires* and *Pollution dataset* has reduced with reduced features set compared to full features set.

Table 3. Average rule base size of full features and reduced feature

Dataset	PSOAANN + DENFIS		PSOAANN + CART	
	Full Features	Reduced Features	Full Features	Reduced Features
Auto MPG	3.2	5.5	21	23
Body Fat	3	6.1	19.8	19.9
Boston Housing	2.4	3	8.1	4.3
Forest Fires	3.9	3.1	4.2	3.1
Pollution	3.8	3.9	4	3.8

The rules obtained in the best fold (in terms of NRMSE values) of the hybrid PSOAANN + DENFIS and PSOAANN + CART with feature selection are presented in Appendix A and Appendix B respectively. From the experimental study, it is inferred that the proposed feature selection method using auto associative networks is an efficient method. Also, we observed that the proposed rule generation hybrid is viable in solving regression problems.

6   Conclusions

In this paper, we presented a hybrid method to extract rules using DENFIS and CART from PSOAANN to solve regression problems. We tested the efficiency of the proposed hybrid on five benchmark regression datasets viz. *Auto MPG, Body Fat, Boston Housing, Forest Fires* and *Pollution*. We proposed a new method of feature selection using PSOAANN. In the current study, PSOAANN accomplish in preserving the privacy of the input features and as well as feature selection. The rule base size obtained with and without feature selection overall the datasets is also compared. Since the obtained NRMSE values over with and without feature selection are close to each other, we perform t-test at 1% level of significance to find whether they are statistically significant or not. In the case of PSOAANN + CART, it is observed that the results are statistically insignificant between with and without feature selection overall datasets except *Body Fat*. In the case of PSOAANN + DENFIS, it is observed that the results are statistically significant between with and without feature selection for four datasets. From the results, we also conclude that the proposed hybrid is viable in solving the regression problems with and without the proposed feature selection method.

References

1. Agrawal, R., Srikant, R.: Preserving Privacy in Data Mining. In: ACM SIGMOD International Conference on Management of Data (May 2000)
2. Lindell, Y., Pinkas, B.: Privacy Preserving in Data Mining. In: Proceeding of the 20th Annual Cryptology Conference in Advances on Cryptology, pp. 36–54 (2000)
3. Xiao-Dan, W.U., Dian-Min, Y.U.E., Feng-Li, L.I.U., Yun-Feng, W., Chao-Hsien, C.H.: Privacy Preserving Data Mining Algorithms by Data Distortion. Management Science and Engineering, 223–228 (2006)
4. Behlen, F.M., Johnson, S.B.: Multicenter Patient Records Research: Security Policies and Tools. J. Am. Med. Inform. Assoc. 6(6), 435–443 (1999)
5. Berman, J.J.: Confidentiality Issues for Medical Data Miners. Artificial Intelligent Med. 26(1-2), 25–36 (2002)
6. Thuraisingham, B.: Web Data Mining and its Applications in Business Intelligence and Counter-terrorism. CRC Press (2003)
7. Fienberg, S.E.: Homeland insecurity: Data mining, terrorism detection, and confidentiality. In: Australian Bureau of Statistics, 55th Session of the International Statistical Institute (ISI), Sydney (2005)
8. Sweeney, L.: Privacy-Preserving Bio-terrorism Surveillance. In: AAAI Spring Symposium, AI Technologies for Homeland Security (2005)
9. Oliveira, S.R.M., Zaiane, O.R.: A privacy-preserving clustering approach toward secure and effective data analysis for business collaboration. Journal of Computer and Security 26, 81–83 (2007)
10. Boyens, C., Krishnan, R., Padman, R.: On privacy-preserving access to distributed heterogeneous healthcare information. In: Proceedings of the 37th International Conference on Annual Hawaii System Sciences (2004)
11. Bertino, E.: A Framework for Evaluating Privacy Preserving Data Mining Algorithms. Data Mining and Knowledge Discovery 11, 121–154 (2005)
12. Granmo, O.C., Oleshchuk, V.A.: Privacy Preserving Data Mining in Telecommunication Services. International Journal of Computing 3(4), 85–90 (2005)
13. Vaidya, J., Clifton, C., Zhu, M.: Privacy Preserving Data Mining. In: Advances in Information Security, vol. 19. Springer, Heidelberg (2006) ISBN: 978-0-387-25886-7
14. Crises, G.: Non-Perturbative Methods for Microdata Privacy in Statistical Databases (2004), http://citeseer.ist.psu.edu/crises04nonperturbative.html
15. Pinkas, B.: Cryptographic techniques for privacy-preserving data mining. SIGKDD Explorations 4 (2002)
16. Ramu, K., Ravi, V.: Privacy preservation in data mining using hybrid perturbation methods: an application to bankruptcy prediction in banks. International Journal Data Analysis Techniques and Strategies 1(4), 313–331 (2009)
17. Bansal, A., Chen, T., Zhong, S.: Privacy Preserving Back-Propagation neural network learning over arbitrarily partitioned data. Journal of Neuro Computing and Applications, 1433–3058 (2010)
18. Paramjeet, Ravi, V., Naveen, N., Raghavendra Rao, C.: Privacy Preserving Data Mining using Particle Swarm Optimization trained Auto-Associative Neural Network: an Application to Bankruptcy Prediction in Banks (Accepted International Journal of Data Mining Modeling and Management)
19. Naveen, N., Ravi, V., Raghavendra Rao, C.: Rule Extraction from Privacy Preserving Neural Network: Application to Banking. In: International Conference on Control, Robotics and Cybernetics (ICCRC 2011), India, March 21-24, pp. 408–412 (2011)

20. Kennedy, J., Eberhart, R.C.: Particle Swarm Optimization. In: Proceeding of IEEE International Conference on Neural Networks, Piscataway, NJ, USA, pp. 1942–1948 (1995)
21. Kasabov, N., Song, Q.: DENFIS: Dynamic, evolving neural-fuzzy inference systems and its application for time-series prediction. IEEE Transactions on Fuzzy Systems 10, 144–154 (2002)
22. Breiman, L., Friedman, J.H., Olshen, R.A., Stone, C.J.: Classification and Regression Trees. Wadsworth International Group, Belmont, California (1984)
23. Hruschka, H., Natter, M.: Comparing performance of feedforward neural nets and K-means for cluster-based market segmentation. European Journal of Operational Research 114, 346–353 (1999)
24. Kramer, M.A.: Nonlinear principal component analysis using auto associative neural networks. AIChE Journal 37(2), 233–243 (1991)
25. Ravi, V., Pramodh, C.: Non-linear principal component analysis-based hybrid classifiers: an application to bankruptcy prediction in banks. International Journal of Information and Decision Sciences 2(1), 50–67 (2010)
26. Guyon, B., Elisseeff, A.: An introduction to variable and feature selection. Journal of Machine Learning Research 3, 1157–1182 (2003)
27. Asuncion, A., Newman, D.J.: UCI Machine Learning Repository. University of California, School of Information and Computer Science, Irvine, CA (2007)
28. Penrose, K.W., Nelson, A.G., Fisher, A.G.: FACSM, Human Performance Research Center, Brigham Young University. Provo, Utah 84602 as listed in Medicine and Science in Sports and Exercise 17(2), 189 (1985)
29. Cortez, P., Morais, A.: A Data Mining Approach to Predict Forest Fires using Meteorological Data. In: Neves, J., Santos, M.F., Machado, J. (eds.) New Trends in Artificial Intelligence, Proceedings of the 13th EPIA 2007 - Portuguese Conference on Artificial Intelligence, Guimarães, Portugal, pp. 512–523 (2007)
30. McDonald, G.C., Schwing, R.C.: Instabilities of regression estimates relating air Pollution to mortality. Technometrics 15, 463–482 (1973)

Appendix A

PSOAANN + DENFIS

Auto MPG

1. If X1 is GMF(0.50 0.49) & X2 is GMF(0.58 0.25) & X3 is GMF(0.20 0.26) & X4 is   GMF(0.60 0.26) then Y = 1.35- 0.83* X1- 0.33* X2+ 1.45*X3- 0.01*X4

2. If X1 is GMF(0.10 0.90) & X2 is GMF(0.66 0.19) & X3 is GMF(-3.29 0.41) & X4 is GMF(0.12 0.21) then Y = 1.40-1.31*X1-0.58*X2+2.26*X3+0.11*X4

3. If X1 is GMF(0.10 0.73) & X2 is GMF(0.42 0.48) & X3 is GMF(0.41 0.94) & X4 is GMF(0.16 0.66) then Y = 1.40 -1.42*X1+0.65*X2+2.65*X3-2.09*X4

4. If X1 is GMF(0.33 0.42) & X2 is GMF(0.08 0.73) & X3 is GMF(0.51 0.59) & X4 is GMF(0.17 0.54) then Y = 1.90-1.74*X1+ 0.20*X2+2.49*X3- 1.98*X4

5. If X1 is GMF(0.43 0.85) & X2 is GMF(0.14 0.72) & X3 is GMF(1.53 0.65) & X4 is GMF(0.38 0.34) then Y = 0.79-0.47*X1+0.60*X2+1.71*X3-0.79*X4

6. If X1 is GMF(0.14 0.06) & X2 is GMF(0.46 0.81) & X3 is GMF(0.46 0.53) & X4 is GMF(0.15 0.93) then Y = 2.07-2.00*X1-0.11*X2+2.43*X3-1.76*X4

Body Fat

1. If X1 is GMF(0.45 0.61) & X2 is GMF(0.25 0.31) & X3 is GMF(0.45 0.61) & X4 is GMF(0.44 0.61) & X5 is GMF(0.44 0.61) &X6 is GMF(0.39 0.38) & X7 is GMF(0.43 0.64) then Y = 7.21+35.46*X1-3.62*X2-157.05*X3+165.24*X4-56.95*X5-6.80*X6+ 9.62* X7

2. If X1 is GMF(0.42 0.25) & X2 is GMF(0.43 0.47) & X3 is GMF(0.41 0.23) & X4 is GMF(0.41 0.23) & X5 is GMF(0.42 0.26) & X6 is GMF(0.45 0.55) & X7 is GMF(0.43 0.34) then Y = 5.25-41.94*X1-1.32*X2-17.82*X3+81.91*X4-47.99*X5-5.32*X6+23.19*X7

3. If X1 is GMF(0.44 0.44) & X2 is GMF(0.36 0.03) & X3 is GMF(0.43 0.46) & X4 is GMF(0.43 0.46) & X5 is GMF(0.44 0.40) & X6 is GMF(0.24 0.75) & X7 is GMF(0.43 0.39) then Y = 5.83-19.30*X1-3.37*X2+8.06*X3+29.27*X4-40.33*X5-5.55*X6+19.79*X7

4. If X1 is GMF(0.52 0.07) & X2 is GMF(0.51 0.32) & X3 is GMF(0.52 0.05) & X4 is GMF(0.52 0.05) & X5 is GMF(0.52 0.06) & X6 is GMF(0.49 0.77) & X7 is GMF(0.52 0.12) then Y = 5.39-39.11*X1- 0.35*X2-46.36*X3+115.67*X4-55.58*X5-5.74*X6+22.36*X7

5. If X1 is GMF(0.47 0.39) & X2 is GMF(0.18 0.90) & X3 is GMF(0.44 0.31) & X4 is GMF(0.45 0.32) & X5 is GMF(0.48 0.44) & X6 is GMF(0.53 0.08) & X7 is GMF(0.50 0.65) then Y = - 0.53-249.51*X1+2.05*X2+420.11*X3-223.39*X4-8.78*X5-0.22*X6+62.81*X7

6. If X1 is GMF(0.54 0.94) & X2 is GMF(0.51 0.47) & X3 is GMF(0.55 0.94) & X4 is GMF(0.55 0.94) & X5 is GMF(0.55 0.94) & X6 is GMF(0.55 0.06) & X7 is GMF(0.53 0.95) then Y = - 0.20-353.18*X1+7.35*X2+397.33*X3-81.98*X4-57.90*X5-2.77*X6+94.30*X7

Boston Housing

1. IfX1 is GMF(-0.26 0.34) & X2 is GMF(-0.09 0.62) & X3 is GMF(0.09 0.38) & X4 is GMF(0.24 0.81) & X5 is GMF(0.11 0.45) then Y = 1.20-4.92*X1+0.74*X2+3.24*X3-0.41*X4+1.41*X5

2. If X1 is GMF(0.35 0.06) & X2 is GMF(0.13 0.30) & X3 is GMF(0.41 0.06) & X4 is GMF(0.19 0.33) & X5 is GMF(0.34 0.07) then Y = 1.62-3.46*X1+1.42*X2+1.09*X3-1.63*X4+2.15*X5

3. If X1 is GMF(0.23 0.83) & X2 is GMF(0.19 0.81) & X3 is GMF(0.24 0.85) & X4 is GMF(0.50 0.74) & X5 is GMF(0.20 0.83) then Y = - 3.77-22.04*X1-16.83*X2+39.64*X3+ 19.26 * X4-13.43*X5

Forest fires

1. If X1 is GMF(0.49 0.04) & X2 is GMF(0.46 0.75) & X3 is GMF(0.45 0.89) & X4 is GMF(0.49 0.30) & X5 is GMF(0.48 0.12) & X6 is GMF(0.45 0.14) then Y = 2.27-0.03*X1+ 2.41*X2-3.33*X3-0.15*X4+0.41*X5-0.54*X6

2. If X1 is GMF(0.49 0.69) & X2 is GMF(0.39 0.85) & X3 is GMF(0.36 0.94) & X4 is GMF(0.50 0.51) & X5 is GMF(0.49 0.45) & X6 is GMF(0.46 0.41) then Y = 2.50-0.04*X1+ 2.78*X2-3.91*X3-0.04*X4+0.57*X5-0.81*X6

3. If X1 is GMF(0.53 0.80) & X2 is GMF(0.50 0.07) & X3 is GMF(0.51 0.20) & X4 is GMF(0.51 0.46) & X5 is GMF(0.52 0.95) & X6 is GMF(0.50 0.90) then Y = 1.05+0.00*X1-0.09*X2+0.07*X3+0.06*X4+0.01*X5-0.05*X6

Pollution

1. If X1 is GMF(0.44 0.59) & X2 is GMF(0.47 0.65) & X3 is GMF(0.45 0.68) & X4 is GMF(0.27 0.58) & X5 is GMF(0.19 0.52) & X6 is GMF(0.27 0.58) & X7 is GMF(0.46 0.60) then Y = 3.71+2.05*X1-8.27*X2-2.18*X3-3.40*X4-4.01*X5 +5.05*X6 +7.56*X7

2. IfX1 is GMF(0.45 0.04) 7 X2 is GMF(0.31 0.13) & X3 is GMF(0.37 0.04) & X4 is GMF(0.46 0.80) & X5 is GMF(0.61 0.17) & X6 is GMF(0.59 0.26) & X7 is GMF(0.38 0.16) then Y = 14.68+36.47*X1+76.41*X2-17.94*X3-2.71*X4+21.04*X5-35.19 *X6-102.83*X7

3. If X1 is GMF(0.43 0.24) & X2 is GMF(0.49 0.58) & X3 is GMF(0.44 0.67) & X4 is GMF(0.24 0.06) & X5 is GMF(0.49 0.06) & X6 is GMF(0.32 0.05) & X7 is GMF(0.51 0.52) then Y = - 1.17+3.08*X1+70.19*X2+1.63*X3+14.35*X4+34.44*X5-45.35*X6-77.50*X7

PSOAANN + CART: In the following rules for all the datasets $y^{\wedge}$ stands for mean predicted values of the output variable

Auto MPG

1. If (MODEL_YEAR <= 0.363079 && ORIGIN <= 0.284024) then $y^{\wedge}$ = 0.146703
2. If (MODEL_YEAR <= 0.363079 && ORIGIN > 0.284024) then $y^{\wedge}$ = 0.3524
3. If (MODEL_YEAR > 0.363079 && MODEL_YEAR <= 0.387028 && ORIGIN <= 0.282366) then $y^{\wedge}$ = 0.276508
4. If (MODEL_YEAR > 0.363079 && MODEL_YEAR <= 0.387028 && ORIGIN > 0.282366) then $y^{\wedge}$ = 0.424724
5. If (MODEL_YEAR > 0.387028 && MODEL_YEAR <= 0.409424 && ORIGIN <= 0.262815) then $y^{\wedge}$ = 0.7713
6. If (MODEL_YEAR > 0.387028 && MODEL_YEAR <= 0.409424 && ORIGIN > 0.262815 && ACCELERATION <= 0.3677 && WEIGHT <= 0.580048) then $y^{\wedge}$ = 0.240025
7. If (MODEL_YEAR > 0.387028 && MODEL_YEAR <= 0.409424 && ORIGIN > 0.262815 && ACCELERATION <= 0.3677 && WEIGHT > 0.580048) then $y^{\wedge}$ = 0.39839
8. If (MODEL_YEAR > 0.387028 && MODEL_YEAR <= 0.409424 && ACCELERATION > 0.3677 && ORIGIN > 0.262815 && ORIGIN <= 0.28284) then $y^{\wedge}$ = 0.441009
9. If (MODEL_YEAR > 0.387028 && MODEL_YEAR <= 0.409424 && ACCELERATION > 0.3677 && ORIGIN > 0.28284 && ORIGIN <= 0.296171 && WEIGHT <= 0.573617) then $y^{\wedge}$ = 0.475286
10. If (MODEL_YEAR > 0.387028 && MODEL_YEAR <= 0.409424 && ACCELERATION > 0.3677 && ORIGIN > 0.28284 && ORIGIN <= 0.296171 && WEIGHT > 0.573617) then $y^{\wedge}$ = 0.6531
11. If (MODEL_YEAR > 0.387028 && MODEL_YEAR <= 0.409424 && ACCELERATION > 0.3677 && ORIGIN > 0.296171 && ORIGIN <= 0.304303) then $y^{\wedge}$ = 0.287683
12. If (MODEL_YEAR > 0.387028 && MODEL_YEAR <= 0.409424 && ACCELERATION > 0.3677 && ORIGIN > 0.304303) then $y^{\wedge}$ = 0.45063
13. If (MODEL_YEAR > 0.409424 && WEIGHT <= 0.567021) then $y^{\wedge}$ = 0.605614
14. If (MODEL_YEAR > 0.409424 && WEIGHT > 0.567021 && WEIGHT <= 0.567886) then $y^{\wedge}$ = 0.395367
15. If (MODEL_YEAR > 0.409424 && WEIGHT > 0.567886 && ACCELERATION <=0.385558) then $y^{\wedge}$ = 0.643297
16. If (MODEL_YEAR > 0.409424 && WEIGHT > 0.567886 && ACCELERATION > 0.385558) then $y^{\wedge}$ = 0.781033

Body Fat

1. If (HIP <= 0.369299 && HEIGHT <= 0.616522 && ABDOMEN <= 0.335662) then $y^{\wedge}$ =0.270877
2. If (HIP <= 0.369299 && ABDOMEN > 0.335662 && HEIGHT <= 0.603009) then $y^{\wedge}$ = 0.541377
3. If (HIP <= 0.369299 && ABDOMEN > 0.335662 && HEIGHT > 0.603009 && HEIGHT <= 0.615732) then $y^{\wedge}$ = 0.430292
4. If (HIP <= 0.369299 && ABDOMEN > 0.335662 && HEIGHT > 0.615732 && HEIGHT <= 0.616522) then $y^{\wedge}$ = 0.661053
5. If (HIP <= 0.369299 && HEIGHT > 0.616522 && ABDOMEN <= 0.327975) then $y^{\wedge}$ = 0.13979

6. If $(HIP <= 0.369299$ && $ABDOMEN > 0.327975$ && $HEIGHT > 0.616522$ && $HEIGHT <= 0.640913$ && $FOREARM <= 0.567538)$ then $y^{\wedge} = 0.395684$

7. If $(HIP <= 0.369299$ && $ABDOMEN > 0.327975$ && $HEIGHT > 0.616522$ && $HEIGHT <= .640913$ && $FOREARM > 0.567538$ && $THIGH <= 0.389392)$ then $y^{\wedge} = 0.532632$

8. If $(HIP <= 0.369299$ && $ABDOMEN > 0.327975$ && $HEIGHT > 0.616522$ && $HEIGHT <= 0.640913$ && $FOREARM > 0.567538$ && $THIGH > 0.389392)$ then $y^{\wedge} = 0.280982$

9. If $(HIP <= 0.369299$ && $ABDOMEN > 0.327975$ && $HEIGHT > 0.640913$ && $FOREARM <= 0.49268)$ then $y^{\wedge} = 0.56$

10. If $(HIP <= 0.369299$ && $ABDOMEN > 0.327975$ && $FOREARM > 0.49268$ && $FOREARM <= 0.552787$ && $HEIGHT > 0.640913$ && $HEIGHT <= 0.670625)$ then $y^{\wedge} = 0.353918$

11. If $(HIP <= 0.369299$ && $ABDOMEN > 0.327975$ && $FOREARM > 0.49268$ && $FOREARM <= 0.552787$ && $HEIGHT > 0.670625)$ then $y^{\wedge} = 0.203684$

12. If $(HIP <= 0.369299$ && $ABDOMEN > 0.327975$ && $HEIGHT > 0.640913$ && $FOREARM > 0.552787)$ then $y^{\wedge} = 0.226566$

13. If $(HIP > 0.369299$ && $HEIGHT <= 0.595437)$ then $y^{\wedge} = 0.753383$

14. If $(HIP > 0.369299$ && $WEIGHT <= 0.416667$ && $HEIGHT > 0.595437$ && $HEIGHT <= 0.632087$ && $FOREARM <= 0.540211)$ then $y^{\wedge} = 0.638196$

15. If $(HIP > 0.369299$ && $WEIGHT <= 0.416667$ && $HEIGHT > 0.595437$ && $HEIGHT <= 0.632087$ && $FOREARM > 0.540211)$ then $y^{\wedge} = 0.511292$

16. If $(HIP > 0.369299$ && $WEIGHT <= 0.416667$ && $HEIGHT > 0.632087)$ then $y^{\wedge} = 0.428722$

17. If $(HIP > 0.369299$ && $HEIGHT > 0.595437$ && $WEIGHT > 0.416667)$ then $y^{\wedge} = 0.71579$

Boston Housing

1. If $(CRIM <= 0.29449)$ then $y^{\wedge} = 0.55045$
2. If $(CRIM > 0.29449$ && $CRIM <= 0.31266)$ then $y^{\wedge} = 0.426722$
3. If $(CRIM > 0.31266$ && $CRIM <= 0.364969)$ then $y^{\wedge} = 0.324014$
4. If $(CRIM > 0.364969)$ then $y^{\wedge} = 0.183918$

Forest Fires

1. If $(DC <= 0.339062)$ then $y^{\wedge} = 0.00974743$
2. If $(DC > 0.339062$ && $DC <= 0.339085)$ then $y^{\wedge} = 0.684146$
3. If $(DC > 0.339085)$ then $y^{\wedge} = 0.00859632$

Pollution

1. If $(SO <= 0.289196)$ then $y^{\wedge} = 0.619402$
2. If $(SO > 0.289196)$ then $y^{\wedge} = 0.391931$

Typhon - A Mobile Agents Framework for Real World Emulation in Prolog

Jatin Matani and Shivashankar B. Nair

Department of Computer Science & Engineering,
Indian Institute of Technology, Guwahati, India
{j.matani,sbnair}@iitg.ernet.in

Abstract. In this paper, we present a mobile agent framework nicknamed *Typhon*, based on LPA Prolog's *Chimera* agent system, which allows users to go in for rapid emulation of algorithms and test beds rather than their mere simulation. This framework provides for agent migration, cloning, payload carrying abilities, state saving and security and also facilitates a reduced deployment time. The framework allows users to exploit the intelligence programming abilities of Prolog and integrate them with the inherent parallelism exhibited by mobile agents. To portray the versatility of the system we describe implementations of a typical resource discovery application for a robot tethered to a node in a network.

Keywords: Intelligent Agents, Mobile Agents, Prolog.

1 Introduction

Mobile agents form software entities capable of exhibiting autonomous behaviour. They are capable of migrating from one networked node to another and also preserving their states. Intelligence can be embedded within and also acquired by them during their visits to the nodes. Intelligent mobile agents can gather precious information in a distributed manner while also exchanging them amongst themselves. Mobile agents are particularly useful in fragile networks due to their autonomous and asynchronous execution. Their ability to react dynamically to environmental changes makes them highly robust and fault tolerant [1].

The use and applications of such agents has always been a hot area of research. Their use has been grossly limited mainly because of the non-availability of an easy-to-use framework which can provide for their deployment, programming and testing. A significant number of mobile agent frameworks have been developed in the past which include - Aglets [2], AgentSpace [3] and JADE [4] - all of which are based on a Java platform. Java has been the most effective platform mainly because it is an interpreted language and the Java Virtual Machine satisfies some aspects of security. However, these platforms offer weak mobility. For example, most Java based frameworks offer mobility via serialization and de-serialization of agents. In other words, the agent code is converted to byte streams and sent to the next remote host

C. Sombattheera et al. (Eds.): MIWAI 2011, LNAI 7080, pp. 261–273, 2011.

where it is once again reassembled. Their execution at the new location starts afresh and not from the last state.

There are yet other frameworks that make use of Prolog to realize such platforms. Prolog is well suited for developing intelligent solutions due to its inherent features which include unification, resolution and depth first search. Its declarative nature and efficient handling of tree structures makes it highly efficient and productive. Prolog also offers dynamic code, which allows traits such as learning and intelligence to be easily incorporated.

Jini [5] and Movilog [6] reportedly use a combined Java and Prolog based framework for creating agent based systems. The use of two different languages generally deters a developer from using such platforms as it makes the knowledge of these concerned languages mandatory. A pure Prolog based mobile agent framework possibly could serve the purpose better. ALBA [7] and IMAGO [8] cater to a Prolog-only environment for mobile agent based system development. ALBA is more of a library rather than a platform, and uses SICStus Prolog for commissioning agents. IMAGO [7] on the other hand is a hierarchy based mobile agent system. Agents in IMAGO are categorized into three types - *Stationary imagos* which are powerful but lack mobility, *Worker imagos* which are mobile but limited in ability and *Messenger imagos* which are used for communications between different *imagos*. IMAGO however comes as a separate package and cannot be used in tandem with other interpreters.

This paper describes *Typhon*, a mobile agent framework which uses LPA Prolog (*http://www.lpa.co.uk*). *Typhon* (a mythical monster) assisted by the *Chimera* (the offspring of *Typhon*) Agent System provided with LPA Prolog facilitates an environment to create and program mobile agents with logic embedded within. This version of Prolog was chosen as the base since it comes with numerous toolkits such as those for developing graphical user interfaces, ProData for database support, Data Mining, Flint for fuzzy logic, etc. Developing a mobile agent framework on LPA Prolog would mean that these agents will be in a position to easily make use of these toolkits to provide the extra features required for the mobile agents to exhibit intelligence. LPA Prolog also provides an Intelligence server toolkit which allows for programs written in Prolog to communicate with those written in other languages such as C and Java. The framework allows a user to exploit the intelligence programming abilities inherent in Prolog and at the same time program and rapidly emulate complex parallel algorithms.

2   *Typhon*: The Mobile Agent Framework

Typhon requires LPA Prolog and its *Chimera* Agent system to be running on all the nodes that form the network. *Typhon* can then be installed from within the environment on each node. A description of the framework along with its features has been presented in the subsequent sections.

2.1   Overview

The *Chimera* agent system, which provides the base for *Typhon*, allows for the creation of multiple static agent applications across any TCP/IP network. It combines the intelligence modelling of logic programming with an event driven paradigm. Events are raised and responded to, locally and across the network. A *Chimera* agent is composed of two entities: a *Socket* and a *Handler*. The former is a Microsoft Windows' socket and serves to connect an agent to its environment which could in turn comprise other such agents. The latter comprises Prolog code which defines the behaviour of the agent when an event occurs. Agents in *Chimera* are straightforward to implement and handle since only the concerned events need to be coded. There are no agent loops or special modes as also no explicit waiting for input. Thus a *Chimera* agent can run within the LPA Prolog environment even when the latter is being used interactively for others purposes. Such agents can thus run as servers on several nodes in a network to form a system that can facilitate their mobile meta level counterparts to migrate to and co-exist within a node. The *Typhon* framework depicted in Figure 1, is composed of – A *Typhlet* platform which rides on the *Chimera* agent system running on each node of the network and the *Typhlets* that constitute the mobile agents. *Typhon* uses functions defined by *Chimera* to provide inter-platform connectivity and *Typhlet* migration. It also offers special mobile agent based features that aid the programmer to realize the mobile *Typhlets*. The following sections describe some of the major features of the framework.

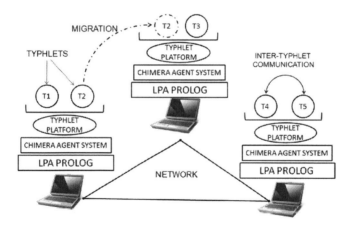

Fig. 1. *Typhon* - The Mobile Agent Framework running on top of the LPA *Chimera* Agent System on a network of nodes

3   *Typhlets* and *Typhclones*: Creation, Migration and Payloads

Typhlets can clone to create *Typhclones* which are also capable of creation, migration and payload carrying. The manner in which *Typhlets* and *Typhclones* are created, loaded and invoked to migrate are discussed in the subsequent sections.

3.1   Agent Creation

The mobile agents or the *Typhlets* can be created using a simple Prolog predicate –
typhlet_create(TYPHLID, Handler, Port)
(output) TYPHLID   :   *<atom>*
(input) Handler   :   *<atom>*
(input/output) Port   :   *<integer>*

To maintain the uniqueness, *Typhon* christens every newly created *Typhlet* with a unique 8-character identifier viz. the *TYPHLID* and outputs the same for use by the programmer. Further references to this *Typhlet* by the programmer can be done using this *TYPHLID*. The second parameter is the *Handler* which is the predicate that handles the events perceived by a *Typhlet* from its environment. The third parameter is the *Port* number which may be assigned by either the user or the system. A simple handler could be as portrayed –

handler(typhlid , Link, incoming_message(X)):-
            write('IncomingMessage:'),write(X), typhlet_post(typhlid,Link,message_ack(X)).

The above handler will receive an incoming message and post the same message back to the sender. The framework always asserts a generic handler in the form of a dynamic database which is eventually replicated with bound *Typhlet* identifiers generated at run-time. This allows for multiple *Typhlets* to have separate handler clauses, all of which are generated at run-time.

3.2   Agent Migration

Typhon provides two migration scenarios viz. *move* and *clone*. *Typhlets* can be moved to other platforms running on other nodes in the network by using the predicate –

move_typhlet(TYPHLID,Link).

A link indicates an already established connection between the platforms and is achieved using the predicate –

connect(IP,Port,Link)

which creates a TCP/IP connection between the two connected nodes. Once the link is created, the *Typhlet* whose identifier is TYPHLID can migrate across network through this link. The other movement mechanism allows for the *Typhlet* to send a copy of itself to the other node while retaining the original in the current node. The clone referred to as a *Typhclone*, is conferred a new global identifier, its own specific handler and code and then transported to the other node. The *Typhclone*-specific handler and code are *logically* the same as that of its parent *Typhlet* but are cast in a manner so as to differentiate them from those of its parent. This is done because as the agents migrate across the network their inherent logic code may evolve. After such an evolution, if a *Typhlet* and its clone once again populate the same node, such specificity will allow for differentiating between their respective codes, which otherwise would have the same predicate names resulting in a conflict in the embedded logic. The relevant predicate that handles cloning is *clone_typhlet(TYPHLID, Link)*.

3.3   Payloads

In agent based environments, each agent would be assigned code or logic that allows it to perform a set of tasks. A programmer can write such code or *payload* for a *Typhlet* which could be carried by it across nodes and executed therein, if required. Payloads in *Typhon* comprise Prolog code which the programmer can attach to a *Typhlet*. Since Prolog facilitates dynamic code, payloads may get bulkier as a *Typhlet* migrates across a network. *Typhon* thus provides for Addition (*add_payload/2*), Removal (*remove_payload/2*), Copying (*copy_payload/2*) and even Shedding (*shed_payload/2*) of code. *Typhlets* can also provide copies of their payloads to their peers and even to *Typhclones*. These features allow programmers to embed on-the-fly learning mechanisms onto the *Typhlets* or their clones.

3.4   Network Management

An intelligent system can be created only if many of its parameters are available for study and tuning. *Typhon*, thus provides the programmer with useful information that can be procured and used on-the-fly to change the behaviour of the system under development. It provides for statistics such as individual *Typhlet* hop-times and network traffic information in the form of a history within a platform. Since mobile agents can work autonomously, they are well suited for networks with low connectivity. Keeping such statistics helps manage the migration of *Typhlets* by giving a fair idea of the local conditions that prevail around a particular node. For instance, the hop-time, maintained by each platform individually, provides part of such information. The hop-time is defined as the time taken in the recent past for a *Typhlet* to migrate to another node. These times prove to be a valuable heuristic in time critical and dynamic scenarios where *Typhlets* need to migrate along the shortest path. The *hoptime/4* predicate gives information about 4 parameters viz. the number of *Typhlets* or *Typhclones* that arrived at the current node, their average arrival time, the number of such agents that departed this node and the average departure time. Similarly using the *neighbour* predicate, a mobile agent can find the number and relevant information of neighbouring nodes in its locality.

3.5   Security

Security in *Typhon* is currently based on a token authentication mechanism. Each platform can be considered to have a lock, key to which is specific and pre-defined by the programmer. Only *Typhlets* holding the key specific to the platform are authorized to enter it while others are denied entry. The keys are initially conferred to the the *Typhlets* or *Typhclones* either at the time of writing the program or their creation or on-the-fly by a user or some such mechanism. Keys can also be attached and removed on-the-fly using the *add_token/2* and *remove_token/2* predicates. A *Typhlet* can also hold multiple keys to enable migration across multiple platforms. Token based security restricts unauthorized access. Apart from this, the scheme helps form virtual networks wherein agents from one virtual network cannot migrate to nodes of another unless granted the concerned tokens. This greatly aids privacy when multiple agent based systems or applications share the same network.

3.6   Restore Points

At any point of time, a node may host numerous *Typhlets* or *Typhclones* along with their associated code. The *save_state/1* and *restore_state/1* predicates allow a user to save the state of the platform at a node. Saving a state would cause all pertinent *Typhlet* information, their most recent behaviours, associated data and payload code including existing code available at the platform to be saved into a file. Restoring would mean this saved information could be used to once again bring back a platform back to the same state. Saving and restoring can be ideal when a prototype of a system is being tested or when a system wishes to backtrack to a point or state it encountered in the past. From a meta level perspective, this feature can help us create global restore points. Such restore points might be particularly useful while devising multi-mobile agent based learning mechanisms such as Genetic or other Bio-inspired algorithms. A state inspector tool is currently under development which will allow a user to analyze different states and then resume from a specific state.

4   Implementation

In order to portray the versatility of the framework, *Typhlets* were used to implement a resource discovery process in a network. Resource discovery in peer to peer networks can make use of the inherent parallelism and the distributed nature of multiple mobile agents instead of a centralised approach. One of the implementations carried out to authenticate this mobile agent framework, is based on a simulated resource discovery algorithm reported by Gaber and Bakhouya [9].

Agents dispatched by a node which requires the resource, clone and percolate through the network to culminate in a faster search process. Excessive cloning can cause flooding. Thus each agent or clone is conferred a dynamic *Time to Live* (TTL) which reduces with every hop. When the agent's TTL becomes zero it contacts the requestor to find whether or not the request is satisfied by other agents. If so it *dies*; else it extends its life time and continues its quest into the network. Alternative approaches involve using pheromones [10] or modelling such a system based on an artificial immune system [11].

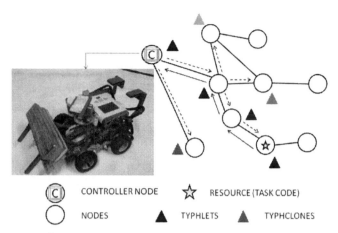

Fig. 2. The Lego NXT® Robot and the network showing the movement and cloning of *Typhlets* for the resource discovery

In our implementation of the Gaber and Bakhouya resource discovery algorithm [9], we have used a robot that acts as a requestor as shown in Figure 2. A robot tethered to a node (a computer), referred to as a controller, in a network, senses its environment using on-board sensors. Initially the robot is devoid of any behaviours (control programs) that are needed to react to its sensors. Since it has no idea as to how to react to a particular state of the environment as reported by its sensors, it instructs the node to spawn a *Typhlet* which in turn commences its journey within the network, to find the relevant task (or code) to be executed for this particular state of the robot. This *Typhlet* clones as it migrates to produce several *Typhclones* to achieve a parallel search within the nodes of the network. Eventually one of them finds the code for the task to be performed hosted at a node. The *Typhlet* that is successful in reaching this node uploads the relevant code for the task as its payload and returns to the requestor node. The code is then downloaded onto the robot and executed by it to effect the appropriate actuation. This in turn causes a change in the environment of the robot and hence the values reported by its sensors. Once again if the robot does not know what it needs to perform so as to counter the change in the values reported by its sensors, the requesting and spawning process is repeated. We have used a Lego NXT® robot running LeJOS connected to a node via Bluetooth. The *Typhlets* connect to the robot via a Java server. As seen in Figure 2, when the robot has a wooden block on its gripper, it does not know what it needs to do next. It thus sends a *Typhlet* which in turn clones and brings back the code for the task to be performed. The major portion of the *Typhlet* code to implement the algorithm has been listed in the Appendix A.

A pheromone based approach has been reported by Nair and Godfrey in [12,13]. As seen in Figure 3, the requestors generate and diffuse pheromones in their neighbourhood. Several *Typhlets* move around the network and migrate between different nodes in a conscientious manner such that they avoid recently visited nodes. This is achieved by carrying a list of visited nodes. When a *Typhlet* carrying the

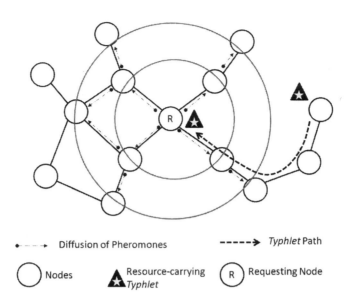

Diffusion of Pheromones   - - - - → *Typhlet* Path

Nodes   Resource-carrying *Typhlet*   (R) Requesting Node

Fig. 3. Typhlets sensing the pheromone trail and moving towards the requestor node

requested service senses a pheromone trail, it tracks and travels towards the pheromone diffusing node at the epicentre of the pheromoned network and services it.

In order to implement the mechanism cited by Nair and Godfrey [12], we developed a pheromone diffusion interface which was loaded at each *Typhlet platform*. Pheromone based signals were emulated such that they possess information like their concentration and volatility (life-time). These pheromones carry information about the request, the requestor node identifier and parameters like its concentration and life-time. When a node requests for a service, it diffuses pheromones onto its immediate (one-hop) neighbours with a life-time and the maximum concentration. When a pheromone reaches a node, the latter diffuses it further into its neighbourhood but with a decreased concentration and life-time. When the appropriate *Typhlet* (the one capable of fulfilling the request) senses the pheromone trail, it moves along the pheromone concentration gradient and services the request as shown in Figure 3. The portion of the *Typhlet* code to implement the migration routine cited in [12] has been listed in Appendix B.

It can be inferred from the conciseness of the code that writing equivalent simulators to realize such algorithms is a far more complex task. Moreover these applications can be developed, tested and studied in real networks unlike in its equivalent simulation where many assumptions need to be made. These implementations clearly highlight the versatility of *Typhlets* and their use in conjunction with hardware. The integration of the *Typhon* framework on LPA Prolog enables the development and use of custom interfaces such as those used for generating and diffusing pheromones and also others that facilitate the connections to specific hardware (such as the LEGO NXT® robot) with ease. These experiments validate *Typhon's* rapid prototyping ability even in real-world applications where a hardware component is prominent.

5   Conclusions

The mobile agent framework based on LPA Prolog nicknamed *Typhon* described herein, couples the inherent rapid prototyping ability of a Prolog engine and the parallelism exhibited by mobile agents to allow emulation of complex algorithms. *Typhon* thus facilitates efficient real-world implementations and testing of a range of algorithms that otherwise can only be studied in a limited and simulated way. The framework also provides novel features for network management, evolution of code, saving and restoring states apart from standard ones like cloning, pay load carrying abilities and also security. Such features are comparatively hard to realize in existing frameworks like Jade and AgentSpace. A typical application of the use of *Typhon* for resource discovery over a real network with hardware in-the-loop has also been discussed, which throws more light on its versatility and ease of development. The conciseness of the code listed in the appendix when compared with the equivalent code written to realize the same in simulation, is negligible. Further, simulations are always in a closed-world normally with many assumptions to aid them. In *Typhon*, the mobile agents are real and thus facilitate an open-world testing while also minimizing the coding effort.

Typhon can be used in a range of scenarios and with the use of LPA Prolog's add-on toolkits the implementation and testing of real systems that exhibit intelligence and distributed parallelism can be greatly eased. We are currently investigating the use of *Typhon* to realize complex bio-inspired systems, such as ACO, PSO, etc. that can learn in a distributed and parallel manner over a real network.

Acknowledgments. The authors acknowledge the help rendered by Shashi Shekhar Jha, Research Scholar, Department of Computer Science & Engineering, Indian Institute of Technology Guwahati, India, in realizing the link between *Typhon* and the Lego NXT® robot.

References

1. Lange, D., Oshima, M.: Reactions on Java Aglets: Seven Issues for the next Generation of Mobile Agent Systems. In: Second International ACTS Workshop on Advanced Services in Fixed and Mobile Telecommunications Networks, Singapore (1999)
2. Lange, D., Oshima, M.: Programming and Deploying Java Mobile Agents Aglets, 1st edn. Addison-Wesley Longman Publishing Co., Inc., Boston (1999)
3. Rodrigues da Silva, A., Mira da Silva, M., Delgado, J.: An Overview of AgentSpace: A Next-Generation Mobile Agent System. In: Rothermel, K., Hohl, F. (eds.) MA 1998. LNCS, vol. 1477, pp. 148–159. Springer, Heidelberg (1998)

4. Bellifemine, F., Bergenti, F., Caire, G., Poggi, A.: Jade - A Java Agent Development Framework. In: Multi-Agent Programming, Multiagent Systems, Artificial Societies, And Simulated Organizations, vol. 15, pp. 125–147. Springer, US (2005)

5. Tarau, P.: Jinni: Intelligent Mobile Agent Programming at the Intersection of Java and Prolog. In: Proceedings of the Fourth International Conference on Practical Application of Intelligent Agents and Multi-Agents, London, pp. 109–123 (1999)

6. Zuzino, A., Campo, M., Mateos, C.: Movilog: A platform for Prolog Based Strong mobile agents on the WWW. In: Inteligencia Artificial, Revista Iberoamericana de I.A., Valencia, pp. 83–92 (2003)

7. Devèze, B., Chopinaud, C., Taillibert, P.: ALBA: A Generic Library for Programming Mobile Agents with Prolog. In: Bordini, R.H., Dastani, M.M., Dix, J., El Fallah Seghrouchni, A. (eds.) PROMAS 2006. LNCS (LNAI), vol. 4411, pp. 129–148. Springer, Heidelberg (2007)

8. Li, X.: IMAGO: A Prolog-based System for Intelligent Mobile Agents. In: Pierre, S., Glitho, R.H. (eds.) MATA 2001. LNCS, vol. 2164, pp. 21–30. Springer, Heidelberg (2001)

9. Gaber, J., Bakhouya, M.: Mobile Agent-Based Approach for Resource Discovery in Peer-to-Peer Networks. In: Joseph, S., Despotovic, Z., Moro, G., Bergamaschi, S. (eds.) AP2PC 2006. LNCS (LNAI), vol. 4461, pp. 63–73. Springer, Heidelberg (2008)

10. Amin, K., Mikler, A.: Dynamic agent population in agent-based distance vector routing. In: Second International Workshop on Intelligent Systems Design and Applications, Atlanta, pp. 543–549 (2002)

11. Bakhouya, M., Gaber, J.: Adaptive Approach for the Regulation of a Mobile Agent Population in a Distributed Network. In: Proceedings of the Fifth International Symposium on Parallel and Distributed Computing (ISPDC 2006), Romania, pp. 360–366 (2006)

12. Nair, S.B., Godfrey, W.: A Pheromone based Mobile Agent Migration Strategy for Servicing Networked Robots. In: Proceedings of the 5th International ICST Conference on Bio-Inspired Models of Network, Information, and Computing Systems (BIONETICS), Boston (2010); To appear in Springer

13. Nair, S.B., Godfrey, W.: Mobile Agent Cloning for Servicing Networked Robots. In: Proceedings of the 13th International Conference on Principles and Practice of Multi-Agent Systems (PRIMA 2010), Kolkata (2010); To appear in Springer

Appendix A

Typhlet Code to Emulate the Resource Discovery Algorithm by Gaber and Bakhouya [9].

```
% Creates the Typhlet and attaches necessary payloads. Robot calls create/0. %
create:-      .
typhlet_create(TYPHLID,event_handler,Port),
add_payload(TYPHLID,[(visited,5),(start_algorithm,1),
(ttl,2),(ntable,4),(requester_node,4),
(populate_ntable,1),(send_typhclones,1),
(can_do_task,2),(check_resource,1)]).
```

% On creation of an agent, the *Typhlet* needs to complete the task. However if the task code is unknown, the *can_do_task* fails; start the search algorithm at the local node using the payload : *start_algorithm*/1. %

```
event_handler(typhlid,Link,(create,P)):-
can_do_task(typhlid,1)->task_code(typhlid)
;start_algorithm(typhlid).
```

% On expiry of time-to-live (TTL), the *Typhlet* asks the requester whether resource has been discovered or not. This handler is invoked when the requester replies with negatively. The TTL is thus extended to 2. %

```
event_handler(typhlid,Link,not_discovered(X)):-
retract(ttl(typhlid,0)),assert(ttl(typhlid,2)),
send_typhclones(typhlid).
```

% Initiates the algorithm by checking for the presence of resource. Presence of resource decides addition of resource or cloning. %

```
start_algorithm(typhlid):-
retractall(ntable(typhlid,_,_,_)),
check_resource(typhlid).
```

% Payload function to check the presence of the resource. If the resource is present, add it as payload and return to the robot else populate neighbour table to send clones. %

```
check_resource(typhlid):-
resource(1)->add_payload(typhlid,[(task_code,1)]),
retract(can_do_task(typhlid,0)),
assert(can_do_task(typhlid,1)),
requester_node(N,IP,Port),connect(IP,Port,Link),
move_typhlet(typhlid,Link);populate_ntable(typhlid).
```

% Populates the information of the neighbouring nodes. If a node has already been visited, it is not added to table viz. *ntable*. This table contains the list of 'possible resource nodes.' %

```
populate_ntable(typhlid):-
forall(neighbours(Name,Ip,Port),
(not visited(typhlid,_,Name,_,_),
assert(ntable(typhlid,Name,Ip,Port)))).
```

% Checks the time-to-live (TTL) value for the *Typhlet*. If 0, the *Typhlet* contacts the requester to find whether the request has been fulfilled or not. %

```
checkttl(typhlid):-
ttl(typhlid,0),requester_node(typhlid,Name,IP,Port),
typhlet_create(typhlid,Link,IP,Port),
typhlet_post(typhlid,L,discovered(typhlid)).
```

% Send *Typhclones* to neighbours not yet visited. In the process, time-to-live (TTL) is reduced by 1. All nodes, where *Typhclones* are sent, are added to the visited list. %

```
send_typhclones(typhlid):-
node_info(CurrNode,_,_),forall(ntable(typhlid,Name,IP,Por
t),  assert(visited(typhlid,CurrNode,Name,IP,Port))),
not ttl(typhlid,0),retract(ttl(typhlid,X)),Y is X -1,
assert(ttl(typhlid,Y)),forall(ntable(typhlid,N2,IP2,P2),
(connect(IP2,Port2,L),clone_typhlet(typhlid,L))),
typhlet_kill(typhlid).
```

/*In this program, a considerable part of the implementation is shown. The above code is that of the agent code which intiates the resource discovery in the peer to peer network. When a mobile agent or a *Typhlet* is created, the *create* event occurs which in turn attempts to complete the task. If the task code is not available locally, the search algorithm is invoked which spawns a *Typhlet* to discover the resource (task code). When the *Typhlet* (or *Typhclone*) discovers the node where the resource exists, it uploads the task onto itself and returns to the requester agent. The *create* event is triggered again. However this time, the predicate *can_do_task(1)* succeeds, and hence the relevant task is performed.*/

Appendix B

Typhlet Code to Emulate the Pheromone-Conscientious Migration Strategy [12] for Mobile Agents Servicing Networked Robots

% On migration to a node, the hop count of the *Typhlet* is incremented. The presence of pheromone is checked via *check_pheromone*/1. Presence of pheromones leads to migration along the pheromone concentration gradient towards the epicentre i.e. the requestor node; else it reverts to the conscientious migration strategy. %

```
typhlet_handler(typhlid,Link,migration(ID,P)):-
pheromone(T_ID,C,L,NextNode)->
move_to_epicenter(typhlid,NextNode);cons_move(typhlid).
```

% The following payload predicates guides the *Typhlet* towards the source of pheromones. It prints out a message and performs the servicing when it reaches the epicenter. %

```
move_to_epicenter(typhlid,NextNode):-
node_info(Name,_,_),
neighbors(NextNode,IP,Port),not Name = NextNode->
connect(IP,Port,Link),move_typhlet(typhlid,Link)
;write('I have reached the epicenter'), do_task(typhlid).
```

% *cons_move*/1 takes the decision of migration to the next node based on a conscientious strategy. A neighbour is chosen as the destination which has been least recently visited. This neighbour is added into the visited_nodes list%

```
cons_move(guid):-
(neighbors(N,IP,P), not visited_nodes(guid,N))->
(connect(IP,P,LINK),assert(visited_nodes(guid,N))),
```

```
move_typhlet(guid,LINK));
(visited_nodes(guid,V),neighbors(V,VIP,VP),
connect(VIP,VP,VLINK),retract(visited_nodes(guid,V)),
assert(visited_nodes(guid,V)),
move_typhlet(guid,VLINK)).
```

/* This code belongs to the *Typhlet* travelling in the network. It follows a conscientious strategy for migration via *cons_move*/1 in absence of pheromones. When a *Typhlet* senses a pheromone trail, it moves towards the source using *move_toward_epicenter*/2. When it reaches the epicenter, it prints out a message and performs the service it is capable of. */

Optimal Service Composition via Agent-Based Quality of Service

Chattrakul Sombattheera

Faculty of Informatics
Mahasarakham University
Mahasarakham
Thailand 44150
chattrakul.s@msu.ac.th

Abstract. Optimal service allocation has gained a lot of attention from researchers recently. We address this problem by proposing an agent-based composite web-services framework to allocate to the tourist an optimal service composition, one which maximally satisfies the tourist. By saying optimal service composition, we take into account a number of factors including i) the number of visited places must be maximal, ii) the number of redundant places must be minimal, iii) the total price is within the budget, and iv) the time constraint must be obeyed. We propose an approach to allow service requesters for choosing the optimal service. Our architecture deploys agents in order to provide flexibility and efficiency to the system.

Keywords: Optimal service composition, optimal coalition structure, multiagent systems.

1 Introduction

Among many real world domains where composite web services can be applied, tourism industry is also a very common area in which researchers in composite web services are interested. A common scenario in tourism industry is for a web service to compose a trip based on the requirement given by the traveler. Such a requirement is usually composed of the budget, the time frame, the preferences on accommodation and food, etc., the traveler has. The task of the web service is to compose a set of service providers, e.g. hotels, airliners, etc., as per request. In this research we consider a domain where the traveler is interested in visiting as many places as possible, given a number of constraints the person has.

It is quite common in tourism industry that a tourist, who is under budget and time constraints, would prefer to visit places as many as possible in one trip. However, it is also quite common that multiple service providers offer redundant services to tourists, i.e. their traveling packages include the same places. It is obviously unnecessary and, to some extent, boring for the tourist to visit any place more than once. This issue is not so easy to manage in real world because traveling agencies, as service providers, are competitors and are unlikely to cooperate. In order to convince service providers to cooperate, the payoffs to all the service providers must be acceptable and fair to those who

C. Sombattheera et al. (Eds.): MIWAI 2011, LNAI 7080, pp. 274–285, 2011.

are interested in cooperation. Hence it is a challenge, from research perspective, to find a solution to satisfy the tourist. This problem is clearly a complex task of class NP-hard. The question here is that how could we allocate available resources in web services to service requesters appropriately, taking into account performance and economic point of view.

We address this problem by proposing an agent-based composite web-services framework to allocate to the tourist an optimal service composition, one which maximally satisfies the tourist. By saying optimal service composition, we take into account a number of commonly found factors including i) the number of places be visited must be maximal, ii) the number of redundant places must be minimal, iii) the total price is within the budget, and iv) the time constraint must be obeyed. Of course, these factors are not the only ones. The proposed framework can take into account more factors but the model of the problem needs appropriate modification. The framework also addresses weaknesses in current composite web-services technology that deploys a top-down approach, where service providers are to be chosen by a service broker. We propose an approach to allocate the optimal service composition, where agents are deployed to represent service providers. The optimal service will be chosen by the service requester from a number provides flexibility and efficiency to the system. In the framework, intermediate parties, such as request brokers, are less important and the system is more independent.

The remaining contents of this report is structured as following. Section 2 surveys related work in optimal composite web services as well as the coverage on the underpinning concept of a multiagent system concept used to solve the allocation problem. Section 3 describe the proposed architecture where each RCA proposes to the tourist its solution. Section 4 presents an example of how to use an algorithm to allocate service providers to satisfy the tourist optimally. Section 5 discusses the experiments and presents the results. Section 6 conclude the research conducted.

2   Related Work

While web services area has gain more and more attention from researchers, the need for more complex scenarios, where multiple layers of service providers are to cooperatively combine to solve the problem for requesters, has lead to another area of research in web services. This area is known as composite web services. The early work of composite web services focus merely on accomplishing the request of the requester.

However, this leaves a major flaw in composing such web services that the performance is not taken into account. This leads to a new area of research, known as optimal composite web services. Optimal composite web services is the area of web services that aims to construct the best services possible from available services providers based on certain criteria. In the following we will explore previous work in the area.

Huang, Lan and Yang [1], propose a QoS-based scheme to compose optimal services. Their work claims to "help service requesters select services by considering two different contexts: single QoS-based service discovery and QoS-based optimization of service composition." They take into account a number of attributes including i) response time, which is the time required for the service providers to get back to the requesters, ii) reliability, which is the ability to provide requested functionality, iii) availability, which is the degree or frequency that the service is accessible and operational, and iv) price, which is the cost of service request. They propose multiple criteria for making decision and select optimal service. They claim that the scheme is efficient and works well for complicated scenarios. This work's experiments look for number of tasks that can fit a request while we look for retrieving an optimal solution quickly. Furthermore, the number of tasks (98) involved in this work is far lower than what we do ($B_{15} = 1382958545$) packages.

Cheng and Koehler [2] study how to achieve optimal pricing policies for web-enabled application services. In their work, service providers are service firms that provide a contractual service offering to deploy, host, manage, and lease what is typically packaged application software from a centrally managed facility. The application these service providers "range from standard productivity tools to expensive applications such as Enterprise Resource Planning systems like SAP or PeopleSoft." They model the economic dynamics between these service providers and their potential customers. They consider a two-part pricing scheme to model the ASP problem. They do not consider balking but the service providers reimburses customers for time spent waiting for services. In addition, they require a minimal average performance guarantee. They define the "Short-Run Problem as the period during which the ASP cannot alter the service guarantee or the capacity". They also look at longer period in which the service providers "can increase server capacity and then provide better service and performance guarantees". They propose that "the optimal pricing policy need not be in the form of a fixed fee, metered price, two-part tariff, or two-part tariff plus reimbursement". They show that there exists a unique rational expectation equilibrium. This work differs from ours that we look into different domain and focus on achieving the optimal solution (package) quickly.

Lina, Liub, Xiab and Zhangb [3] consider the problem of "finding the optimal capacity allocation in a clustered Web system environment so as to minimize the cost while providing the end-to-end performance guarantees". They are interested in "constraints on both the average and the tail distribution of the end-to-end response times". They deploy a non-linear program to solve the problem, i.e. "to minimize a convex separable function of the capacity assignment vector". They claim that under a certain condition, their solution yield a nice geometric interpretation. They claim that their algorithm can yield asymptotically optimal solution for stringent service requirement. Although this work consider the problem a nonlinear function like we do, the problem domain is different. Furthermore, they are interested in end-to-end delay while we are interested in fitting maximal number of places to visit in timely fashion.

Tang and Cheng [4] study "the optimal pricing and location strategy of a Web service intermediary (WSI), which offers a time-sensitive composite Web service". They model the problem as a "linear city model" and then extend their research on the more general model. Their analyses show that the optimal strategy can be derived by delay cost, integration cost, and prices of the constituent Web services. Their results show that "the WSI can be optimally located between the Web service providers". The also found that a penetration price can be charged when the delay cost is low. Furthermore, they also propose that multiple optimal locations for the WSI can be obtained when the proximity of Web service providers are dispersed. This work differs from our work that we consider different domain and we look forward to achieve optimal solution in timely fashion.

As we have briefly discussed previous works in optimal composite web services, it is clearly shown that we need a new model for solving the problem of allocating optimal packages (service providers) to tourists as per requests. We therefore propose to deploy an idea of solving a multiagent system problem, known as *optimal coalition structure* problem, to solve our problem in tourism domain.

3   An Agent-Based Framework

Typical web-services composition architectures deploy request brokers to locate appropriate service providers and create the complete services. Request brokers play important roles in this kind of architecture that they impose their roles as the central command unit of the systems. However, this is also a threat to the availability, performance and security to the system. Furthermore, service providers may not be able to maximize the benefit out the resources because they cannot do much on negotiation in such architectures.

3.1   Architecture

In contrast to typical composite web-services architectures, we propose an architecture where the importance of centralized request brokers is minimized. We deploy agent technologies to help increase the performance of the system. Furthermore, service providers can leverage maximal benefits out of their resources.

Here we consider a tourism domain where a tourist wants to visit as many traveling places as possible in one trip. It will upset the tourist badly if any of the places is missed. The degree of satisfaction increases by the number of places be visited. Visiting a place only once is preferred. However, visiting a place more than once is doable, if it is inevitable, but will decrease the tourist's satisfaction to some extent because it is boring in general cases. We define the components of the aforementioned tourism scenario in terms of service oriented computing (SOC). A tourist is then considered as a service requester, from now on. In the following, we will define the stake holders in SOC in terms of an agent-based system.

A service requester will be represented by an agent which can be accessed from a computer connected to the Internet. We shall refer to such an agent as a requester agent (RA). An RA can be created by any requester. For a requester, its RA needs to know what is the goal of the requester. The goal of a requester, of course, varies depending on the type and activity of the requester. A goal, for example, may be to a traveling package satisfying the user's specification. Such a specification may include request for minimal number of star of each hotel, traveling time from the airport, traveling time from shopping centers, specific foods, and within a given budget. Based on composite services being proposed by several request collector agents, an RA will decide to choose the best service based on QoS. RAs will deploy its intelligent ability to gather goal and proactively ask for related information from the requester.

In order to deal with requests from RAs, we propose a request collector agent (RCA). On one hand, RCAs act as a blackboard to where RAs can post their requests, including information about preferences on the service. On the other hand, RCAs also maintain a list of available service providers and their relevant information, including type of services, area of services, prices, etc. The role of RCAs is not to be the decisive manager as a request broker in typical composite web services. Instead, they forward the details of up coming requests to service providers, whom RCAs believe they are capable of serving the request. RCAs then forward information about services proposed by service providers to the respective RAs. Once the decisions were made by the RAs, the winning services will be forwarded to respective service providers. Note that the final decisions for choosing the best services belong to RAs, not RCAs. This makes our architecture different from typical composite web services. There can be multiple RCAs in a system (which we assume can be a large one). RCAs can act proactively for communicating with RAs and service providers.

The last stakeholder is the service provider. We use service provider agent (SPA) to take care of utilizing the service provider's resources. Each SPA knows at least one RCA and will keep an eye on the availability of requests for services of which they are capabled, as well as other available SPAs. Each SPA uses its intelligence to prepare appropriate strategies to make an offer, i.e., cost and QoS, for its service. It consistently updates the new offer with its respective RCA. Given the available information of requests and SPAs at RCAs it knows of, each SPA can compute the optimal service for each RCA when the due time for proposing service has arrived. Each SPA has to be obliged to just one service whose QoS is the highest. The SPA with the least identification (in lexicographic order) will be acting on behalf of all SPAs for the service. This includes communicating with respective RCA and the member SPAs. A service provider can deploy an SPA and join the system by sending out a request to participate (RTP) to existing RCAs. An RTP is a message that specifies what is the service provider's capability, which is merely a set of places in its traveling packages.

We model the scenario as a service-oriented computing system and deploy the multiagent systems concept to enhance the performance. We firstly define optimal composite services, a multiagent system architecture, and a set of protocol in the system.

3.2   Optimal Composite Service as Quality of Service

Let $\mathfrak{P}$ be a set of traveling places, each of which, $P_i \in \mathfrak{P}$ is a place of interest and is available to tourists. The tourist is under a budget and time constraints.

We denote by $R = \langle BUDGET, TIME \rangle$ the request to visit traveling places with constraints $BUDGET \in \mathbb{Z}^+$ and $TIME \in \mathbb{Z}^+$. There is a set of traveling packages, $\mathfrak{S}$, proposed by travel agencies. Each package, $S \subseteq \mathfrak{S}$, is a plan to take the tourist to a number of places. We define the cost function $C : S \leftarrow \mathbb{Z}^+$, which associates to each S a monetary cost. We also define the time function $T : S \leftarrow \mathbb{Z}^+$, which associate to each plan an amount of time required to finish it.

In the context of tourism industry, the satisfaction of tourists is very important and can be regarded as quality of service. The quality of service to satisfy the tourists depends on

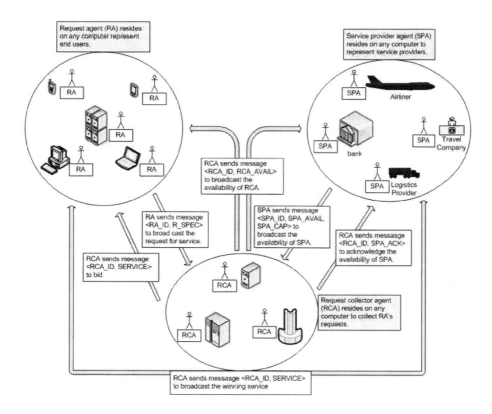

Fig. 1. Architecture We deploy agents to represent stakeholders. Request agents (RA) represent end users. Request collector agents (RCA) collect requests, allocate tasks, broadcast the allocation. Service provider agents represent service providers.

- The number of visited places must be maximized,
- The number of redundant places must be minimized,

We define a service structure $SS = \{S_i | S_i \in \mathfrak{S}$ and $\bigcup S_i = \mathfrak{P}\}$ is a set of services which cover all places.

The tourist will define the utility function for the services in order to measure QoS. In general, the number of visited places increase the satisfaction of the tourist. However, visiting the same place again will decrease his satisfaction. The tourist, for example, may define the utility function as follow:

- The utility increases by the number places visited,
- The utility decreases by half of the number of place visited more than once.

Therefore, the QoS function is defined below:

$$QoS(SS) = \sum |S_i| - \frac{|S_i \cap S_j|}{2} \tag{1}$$

where $S_i, S_j \in SS$, and $i \neq j$.

We are interested in finding for a given request an optimal composite service SS^* such that

$$SS^* = arg_{max}QoS(SS^*). \tag{2}$$

3.3 Communication Protocol

Since there are three stake holders involved in the architecture, there must be a way for each of them to know the existence of other agents before they can really compose services. As a standard means in multiagent systems, we introduce a protocol for the agents, who communicate to each other by sending messages. Here we are interested in high level communication, which can be extended by any real implementation via XML (and that is not the focus of this research).

We take into account what travel agencies do in real world tourism industry, where service providers are usually formed loosely-coupled associations. Travel agencies in an association usually cooperate to their associative members to some extent. Then a tourist is free to negotiate with any of them and chose the best option. We follow this real world setting by allowing SPAs to register themselves as a member of an association. This association will have just one registrater, which is represented by an RCA. The role of an RCA is to run the composite algorithm to find the optimal service composition of its members and proposes it to the requesting SPA, who will choose the optimal global composition.

- a message to broadcast the availability of a RCA. Any agent that wants to act as an RCA will broad cast the message which notifies other agents, including existing RCA, in the system that it wants to play the role of RCA. The message is of the form $\langle RCA\_ID, RCA\_AVAIL \rangle$, where RCA_ID is a high level identification of the agent and RCA_AVAIL is merely a plain text specifying this agent wants to be an RCA. Receiving RCAs and SPAs will update their databases accordingly.
- a message to broadcast the availability of SPA. Any agent that that wants to perform the SPA role for an RCA who belong to the same association has to make its availability and capability recognized by other agents. It will send the respective RCA the message $\langle SPA\_ID, SPA\_AVAIL, SPA\_CAP \rangle$, where SPA_ID is the identification of the agent, SPA_AVAIL is the a plain text specifying the agent wants to act as an SPA agent, and SPA_CAP is the plain text explaining the agent's capability.
- a message to acknowledge the availability of SPAs. Receiving RCAs will update their databases accordingly and send the acknowledgment message $\langle RCA\_ID, SPA\_ACK \rangle$ to the SPA in order to acknowledge the availability. Up on receiving the acknowledgment message, the new SPA updates its database for existing RCAs accordingly.
- a message between RA and RCA to broadcast the request for service. A demanding requester agent will send a message $\langle RA\_ID, R\_SPEC \rangle$, where RA_ID is the identification of the RA and R_SPEC is the request specification, which is merely the $\langle TIME, BUDGET \rangle$. Receiving RCAs will update their databases for

available requests accordingly. Each RCA will execute its composition algorithm which will derive its optimal composite service.

- a message between RCA and RA to launch a bid for service. Having obtained its optimal composite service, each RCA will send the message $\langle RCA\_ID, SERVICE \rangle$ directly to the respective RA who will determine the winning bid.
- a message to broadcast the wining bid. SPA will send message $\langle RCA\_ID, SERVICE \rangle$ to all bidding RCAs in order to announce the winner. The winner is then bound to contract and provide service to SPA.

4 Quality of Service

In this section, we will discuss about the model for computing quality of service proposed to use with the aforementioned framework.

There are two main steps in solving the problem:

- data preparation stage. In this stage, each RCA will sort services by lexicographic order in each cardinality,
- search for optimal composite service stage. In this stage, each RCA will apply the new algorithm to search for the optimal service composition.

After that, the respective RA will identify the most appropriate service composition for RA. RA will decide which one of the composite services being proposed will be the most appropriate one.

4.1 Data Preparation

In this research, we consider a set of places S as a coalition. The value of the coalition is merely the number of places. However, since the service composition is under budget constraint, we can generate coalitions in each cardinality in lexicographic order and sort them by costs. Note that coalitions in our context are a subset of places travel agencies offer in their packages. Hence it could easily be the case that they are equal. We consider them different coalitions, while traditional coalition formation considers them the same coalition and will have just one of them for each similarity.

We will use $C(S)$ to sort Ss in each cardinality. Table 1 shows an example in our setting. There are 3 places, $\mathcal{P} = \{P_1, P_2, P_3\}$, where tourists might be interested visiting. These places are offered to tourists via seven packages, $\mathcal{S} = \{S_1, S_2, \ldots, S_7\}$, each of which, $S_i \subseteq \mathcal{P}$, is a subset of all places. Attached to each S, is the cost function, $C(S)$, which takes as an input S and spits out a number as the (monetary) cost of operation for S. All the Ss can now be sorted (by any robust algorithm, such as merge sort algorithm) in ascending order.

4.2 Data Example

As shown in Table 1, all sorted Ss in each cardinality are placed in their respective columns from top to bottom. Apparently, we do not have any package of size 3. Furthermore, the number of Ss in each cardinality is not related to binomial coefficient

($^{n}C_{|S|}$). It is arbitrarily depending on the number of packages available in the system. Since each of these packages can be proposed individually by service providers in the system, acquiring, sorting, and storing these data will be done on the fly. In each sorted column of Ss, the respective $\bar{r}$ of each S is also shown in parenthesis.

Table 1. Example of data Coalitions (services in each cardinality are sorted by their costs, given by the cost function

$\mathcal{P}$	S	$\mathcal{C}$	$|S| = 1$	$|S| = 2$	$|S| = 3$
P_1	$S_1 = \{P_1, P_2\}$	$C(S_1) = 10$	$S_4\ (\bar{r} = 6)$	$S_1\ (\bar{r} = 5)$	
P_2	$S_2 = \{P_2, P_3\}$	$C(S_2) = 12$	$S_7\ (\bar{r} = 8)$	$S_2\ (\bar{r} = 6)$	
P_3	$S_3 = \{P_1\}$	$C(S_3) = 9$	$S_3\ (\bar{r} = 9)$	$S_6\ (\bar{r} = 7)$	
	$S_4 = \{P_2\}$	$C(S_4) = 6$		$S_5\ (\bar{r} = 9)$	
	$S_5 = \{P_1, P_3\}$	$C(S_5) = 18$			
	$S_6 = \{P_1, P_2\}$	$C(S_6) = 14$			
	$S_7 = \{P_3\}$	$C(S_7) = 8$			

4.3 Satisfaction-Cost Ratio as Quality of Service

The most important step in our algorithm is to identify the best candidate out of available packages in order to compose the SS. As in the algorithm on which this work is based, we need an indicative information which would direct the search towards optimality quickly. There are some issues involved in this. First, the number of unvisited places being offered in a package indicates the degree of satisfaction of the tourist and the satisfaction is decreased by visiting the same places more than once. Further more, we also have to take into account the cost of each package that governs the service composition. Let $|S\ CS|$ be the set of unvisited places in S. Let $CS \cap S$ be the set of visited places. Here we propose to use the *satisfaction-cost ratio*,

$$\bar{r} = \frac{|SCS| - |CS \cap S|}{C(S)}, \tag{3}$$

to identify the best candidate.

4.4 Computing Optimal Service Composition

There are multiple algorithms for solving the optimal coalition structure problem. Any of them can be applied to solve the problem of optimal service composition. The algorithm presented in [5] is quite suitable for solving this optimal service composition problem because it can be applied seamlessly. While it searches for the next best candidate coalition based on the "contribution value" in the original problem, it can be applied to search for next best service provider based on QoS. Furthermore, the algorithm can reach optimality quickly, which is a huge benefit for real world practice where anytime solution is highly preferred.

5 Experiments

With the modified algorithm of [5], we conduct experiments on $n \in [8 \ldots 10]$ places (due to the large search space in the exhaustive search for optimal results). The number of packages in each cardinality i in each of a variation of n is derived from $^{n}C_i$. The numbers of packages in each case of n are shown in Table 2. The numbers of $^{n}C_i$ across all cardinality form the bell shape of normal distribution with an extremely high mean. Furthermore, the distribution of the costs of the packages in each cardinality is of normal distribution as well. We conducted our experiment for the extreme cases, i.e. the tourists prefer no redundancy on the places to be visited. Therefore, the algorithm will use the utility function that gives $-\infty$ to any package that contains redundant places with those already placed in SS. In other words, the experiment is similar to that of [5].

Table 2. Number of Packages In each case of $8 \leq n \leq 10$, the table list the number of packages for each $1 \leq i \leq n$

	i=1	i=2	i=3	i=4	i=5	i=6	i=7	i=8		i=9	i=10	i=11	i=12	i=13	i=14	i=15
n=12	12	66	220	495	792	924	792	495	n=12	220	66	12	1			
n=13	13	78	286	715	1287	1716	1716	1287	n=13	715	286	78	13	1		
n=14	14	91	364	1001	2002	3003	3432	3003	n=14	2002	1001	364	91	14	1	
n=15	15	105	455	1365	3003	5005	6435	6435	n=15	5005	3003	1365	455	105	15	1

In each setting (a variant of n), we run our algorithm with the generated data against the exhaustive search, which guarantees optimal results. We run the experiments a number of times for each n and compare the results achieved from our algorithm against that of the optimal cases. The experiments are conducted on an AMD Turion 64 X2 2GHz machine with 896MB of RAM.

6 Results

The raw figures obtained from our experiments are presented in Table 3. The equivalent results are also depicted in Figure 2, where the x axis is the number of agents, ranging from 12 to 15 agents, and the y axis is the log(10) of execution time in milliseconds. Note that we can carry out the experiment with exhaustive search for merely 14 places, which take a lot of time to finish. We project the figure for the execution time of 15 places based on the previous cases. Although we can carry out the search with our algorithm for up to 26 places, we do not do so because the difference of the results of our algorithm and the exhaustive case will be too much. Note that whereas the execution time of the exhaustive search bursts exponentially, our algorithm yields pretty consistent execution time throughout all the cases, i.e. lower than 10 seconds (10^4 ms).

We have shown here how we can optimally allocate available service providers to perform tasks for requesters in global scale. Note that a number of available agents may not be allocated with any task. This means a number of these agents may not benefit from there existing resources. This is due to the fact that the allocation is focused on the benefit of the requesters. It is left open to further research to explore for the balance of being allocated with tasks and accruing benefit to service providers.

Table 3. Raw figure results

num-agent	exhaustive	converge	terminate
12	22610	4970	5424
13	212578	4968	5768
14	2189678	5507	5880
15	21896780	5037	6795

The table shows the raw execution times achieved from the exhaustive search and our algorithm in milliseconds.

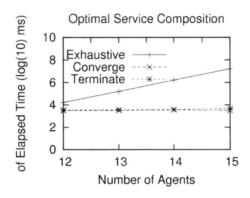

Fig. 2. Experiment Results The results of our experiments are shown here. The times required for exhaustive search grow exponentially while the convergence and termination times of our algorithm are quite consistent, i.e. around 4K and 5K ms respectively.

7   Conclusion

We address the optimal service composition problem by proposing an agent-based composite web-services framework to allocate to the tourist an optimal service composition, one which maximally satisfies the tourist. We take into account a number of factors including i) the number of places be visited must be maximal, ii) the number of redundant places must be minimal, iii) the total price is within the budget, and iv) the time constraint must be obeyed. We propose an approach to allocate the optimal service composition. We deploy a best first search algorithm that is used to solve the optimal coalition structure to solve this problem. Where other work in optimal service composition considers various aspects which are different from us. We seeks to find optimal packages for the tourist in timely fashion. The utility proposed can be substituted with other utility functions which can be more complex and appropriate to different domains. The results show that our approach can yield optimal results in less than 10 seconds for 15 places bundled in 1,382,958,545 packages, which would take around 21896 seconds for the exhaustive search.

References

1. Huang, A., Lan, C.W., Yang, S.: An optimal qos-based web service selection scheme. Information Science 179(19), 3309–3322 (2009)
2. Cheng, H., Koehler, G.: Optimal pricing policies of web-enabled application services. Decision Support Systems 35(3), 259–272 (2003)
3. Lina, W., Liub, Z., Xiab, C.H., Zhangb, L.: Optimal capacity allocation for web systems with end-to-end delay guarantees. Performance Evaluation 62(1), 400–416 (2005)
4. Tang, Q., Cheng, H.: Optimal location and pricing of web services intermediary. Decision Support Systems 40(1), 129–141 (2005)
5. Sombattheera, C., Ghose, A.: A best-first anytime algorithm for computing optimal coalition structures. In: Proceedings of the 7th International Joint Conference on Autonomous Agents and Multiagent Systems (AAMAS 2008), pp. 1425–1428. ACM Press (2008)

Enhanced Data Replication Broker

Rafah M. Almuttairi, Rajeev Wankar, Atul Negi,
and Chillarige Raghavendra Rao

University of Hyderabad, DCIS, Hyderabad, 500046, AP, India
rafahmohammed@gmail.com,
{wankarcs,atulcs,crrcs}@uohyd.ernet.in

Abstract. Data Replication Broker is one of the most important components in data grid architecture as it reduces latencies related to file access and file transfers (replica). Thus it enhances performance since it avoids single site congestion by the numerous requesters. To facilitate access and transfer of the data sets, replicas of data are distributed across multiple sites. The effectiveness of a replica selection strategy in data replication broker depends on its ability to serve the requirement posed by the users' jobs or grid application. Most jobs are required to be executed at a specific execution time. To achieve the QoS perceived by the users, response time metrics should take into account a replica selection strategy. Total execution time needs to factor latencies due to network transfer rates and latencies due to search and location. Network resources affect the speed of moving the required data and searching methods can reduce scope for replica selection. In this paper we propose an approach that extends the data replication broker with policies that factor in user quality of service by reducing time costs when transferring data. The extended broker uses a replica selection strategy called Efficient Set Technique (EST) that adapts its criteria dynamically so as to best approximate application providers' and clients' requirements. A realistic model of the data grid was created to simulate and explore the performance of the proposed model. The policy displayed an effective means of improving the performance of the network traffic and is indicated by the improvement of speed and cost of transfers by brokers.

Keywords: Data Grid, Replica Selection technique, Association Rules, Broker.

1 Introduction

Grid Computing emerges from the need to integrate collection of distributed computing resources to offer performance unattainable by any single machine [1]. Data Grid technology is developed to share data across many organizations in different geographical locations. The idea of replication is to move and cache data close to users to improve data access performance and to reduce the latency of data transfers. It is a solution for many grid-based applications such as climatic data analysis and physics grid network [2]. The scientists require downloading perhaps up to 1 TB of data at a time for locally responsive navigation and manipulation. When

C. Sombattheera et al. (Eds.): MIWAI 2011, LNAI 7080, pp. 286–297, 2011.
© Springer-Verlag Berlin Heidelberg 2011

different sites hold the required data (replicas), the selection process has a direct role on the efficiency of the service provided to the user [4]. Our experimental data has been taken from sites in world seen from *CH.CERN.N20* [7].

The rest of the paper is organized as follows: *Section 2* summarizes the statement of problem. *Section 3* explains the general aspect of the data grid architecture including the proposed approach. Our Intelligent optimizer with its two phases is explained in *Section 4, 5 and 6*. Simulation input is shown in *Section 7* and the results and their interpretation are presented in *Section 8*.

2   Problem Statements

In the context of data grid computing one of main key decision making tool in a data replication scheme is the *resource broker* that determines how and when to acquire grid services and resources for higher level components. Our proposed approach focuses on enhancing a resource broker to achieve the following:

1- Transfers of large amount of data (Terabyte or above) at a high speed.
2- Different sources may send the requested file(s) simultaneously.
3- Multiple data streams are used with each TCP connection between computing element and replica site to utilize the bandwidth.
4- Data consumers are allowed to get portions of data from different locations.
5- Dynamic and automatic replica data management.

3   Architecture of the Modified Data Replication Broker

In this section an extended version of a general Data Grid architecture is explained with functionality of its main components. The data replication broker (resource broker) resides in the middleware of data grid architecture and works as a resource manager. Figure 1 describes the services that are most commonly used in the proposed data selection scheme and shows where the data replication broker is situated. The data replication broker does the file transfer functionality in three cases:

1- Broker receives a request from data grid user/application.
2- Scheduler has signed for a replication needed somewhere in the grid sites.
3- Huge data has been generated and should be distributed in different grid sites. In all situations, the resource broker is given the identity of the file to be transferred from the "best" replica provider(s) [8][17][18][19].

3.1   Replica Management System (RMS)

As we see in the Figure 1, the main component of the Data Grid is the *Replica Management System (RMS)* [5] it acts as a logical single entry point to the system and interacts with the other components of the system. Some terms are used in Figure 1 that should be clearly defined, such as:

3.2   Replica Location Service (RLS)

RLS is the data grid service that keeps track of where replicas exist on physical storage systems. It is responsible for maintaining a catalog of files registered by the users or services when files are created. Later, users or services query *RLS* servers to find physical locations of replicas. It has:

- A *Logical file Name (LN)* is a unique identifier for the contents of a file (replica).
- A *Physical file Name (PN)* is the location of a replica on a storage system [8].

3.3   Replica Optimization Service (ROS)

ROS is used in the Optimization component to optimize replica selection process by minimizing different types of costs such as, *Price* and *Time* and so on. In our model, *ROS* is used to minimize the cost of the time. Minimizing the total transfer time of requested files is the main objective of our model which can be achieved by pointing the user/application requests to appropriate replica with respect to the network latency [19]. ROS gathers the information from the network monitoring service.

3.4   Network Monitoring Service (NMS)

Network Monitoring Service such as, *Iperf Service* [10], is used for monitoring network conditions of connected grid nodes. The *Bandwidth (BW)*, the *Distance* (Hops), the *Round Trip Time (RTT)* are examples of network conditions whose exact values can be measured using network services. In our model we propose a new network monitoring service called *One Way Ping* Service, *OWPS* to be used in *NMS* component. *OWPS* uses *One-Way Active Measurement Protocol (OWAMP)*[11]. *OWPS* is a command line client application and a policy daemon that is used to determine the one way latencies between hosts. In roundtrip-based measurements which can be measured by NWS/*Iperf* service, it is hard to isolate the direction in which congestion is experienced. One-way measurements would solve this problem and make the direction of congestion immediately apparent. This would prompt a better allocation of replicas by decreasing areas of congestion where ever possible.

3.5   Data Transport Service (DTS)

Standard tool for data transfer between the Gird sites or downloading from Grid sites is *GridFTP*. *GridFTP* is a high- performance, secure, reliable and multi streams, included in most of the storage management systems. It uses *TCP* as the transport layer protocol.

4   Intelligent Optimizer

This research shows a new optimization technique that considers link throughput (network latencies) when selecting the best replica. The new approach has two phases which are:

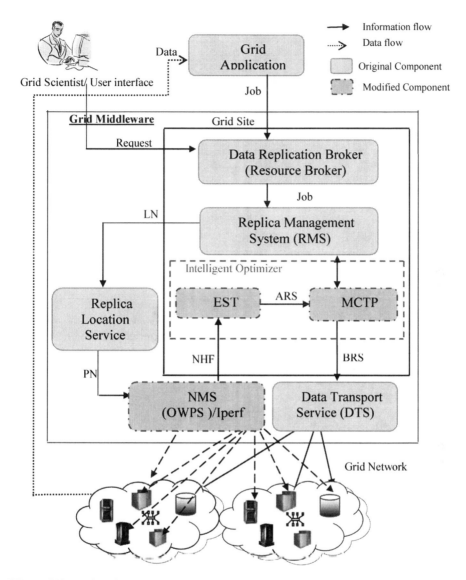

Where, *LN*: Logical file Name, *PN*: Physical file Name, *NHF*: Network History File, *EST*: Efficient Set of replicas Technique, *MCTP*: Minimum Cost and Time Policy, *ARS*: Associated Replica Sites and *BRS*: Best set of Replica Sites.

Fig. 1. Architecture of the enhanced Data Replication Broker

1- Coarse-grain selection criteria: It is for sifting replica sites which have low latency (uncongested links).
2- Fine-grain selection criteria: It is for extracting the associated replica sites have lowest prices.

The associated sites can work together to share transferring large file to be processed by dividing the file among them and each replica site sends only a part.

5   Coarse-Grain Phase Using Efficient Replica Set Technique (EST)

The first phase of the model is called Coarse-grain selection phase. In this phase *EST* [12] selection strategy is used to extract the replica sites having good latency. Association rule concept of data mining approach is used with the following metrics:

1.   *Single Trip Time (STT)*
Using *OWPS* we get *Single Trip Time (STT)*, *STT* is time taken by the small packet to travel from *Replica Sites (RS)* to the *Computing Site (CS)*.

2.   *Standardization Data*
Using a mapping function we can convert *STT/RTT* values to logical values and save the result in *Logical History File (LHF)*.

3.   *Association Rules Discovery*
One of popular association rules algorithms of data mining approach is an Apriori algorithm [12]. Here, it is used for discovering associated replica sites to work concurrently and minimize total time of transferring the requested file(s).

4.   *EST algorithm*
It is to extract the best set of replica sites to work concurrently and get the minimum transfer time of getting the requested files as shown in Figure 1.

6   Fine-Grain Phase Using Minimum Cost and Time Policy (MCTP)

MCTP represents the Fine-grain process. It is extracting the best replicas sets, *BRS* from associated replicas sites *ARS* is explained. The sites in *BRS* are used to send parts of requested large file or multiple related files to minimize the total transfer time. The following functions are used to represent the Fine-grain phase.

6.1   Delay Function

To determine the amount of data that can be transmitted in the network the *Bandwidth Delay Product (BDP)* should be calculated. *BDP* plays an especially important role in high-speed / high-latency networks, such as most broad band internet connections. It is one of the most important factors of tweaking *TCP* in order to tune systems to the type of network used. The *BDP* simply states that:

$$BDP = BW \times RTT \tag{1}$$

Initialize: $k=1$, $J=\{J_1,J_2,...,J_x\}$, where x is max. number of jobs in a *Queue (Q)*

Step I While ($Q \neq \{\}$) OR ($k \leq x$) Do

Step II Receive $J_k=\{f_1,f_2,...,f_c\}$ where c is the number of requested files in J_k

Step III Get S_i, *where* $i=\{1, 2, ...,M\}$ *and M represents number of replicas.*

Step IV Get *Network History File (NHF)*.

  - Rows = STTs / RTTs
  - Columns = S_i

Step V Convert *NHF* to *Logical History File (LHF)* that contains logical values *(LV)* applying the following mapping function for each column.

a) Calculate the Mean:

$$MSTT_{i,j} = \frac{(\sum\limits_{k=i}^{(l-1)+i} STT_{k,j})}{l}, \text{ where } l = 10$$

b) Calculate the Standard deviation:

$$STDEVi_{,j} = \sqrt{\frac{\sum\limits_{k=i}^{(l-1)+i} (STT_j - MSTT_{i,j})^{\wedge}2}{l}}$$

c) Find $\quad Q_{i,j} = \dfrac{STDEV_{i,j}}{MSTT_{i,j}} \times 100$

d) Find $\quad AVi = \dfrac{\sum\limits_{j=1}^{M} Q_{i,j}}{M}$

e) *Compare* IF $(AVi < Q_{i,j})$ then $LV = 0$ *Otherwise* $LV = 1$

Step VI Call *AT (LHF, c, s ,ARS)*

  Input- LHF: *Logical values of Network History File*

  c: Minimum confidence value.

  s: Minimum support value.

  Output- ARS: List of Associated Replica Sites, A_j , $j=\{1,2,...,n\}$, n represents number of associated sites and $n \leq M$..

Step VII Call *Fine-grain (A_j)*.

Step VIII $k=k+1$

Step IX Get next job J_k from the Q.

Fig. 2. The steps of the proposed selection algorithm

TCP Window is a buffer that determines how much data can be transferred before the server stops and waits for acknowledgements of received packets. Throughput is in essence bound by the *BDP*. Equation 1 is also used to determine the optimal size of receiver window size, *RWIN* to utilize the bandwidth [14] and *RTT* is the average round trip time of links. In case the *RWIN* is less than *BDP* that means the bandwidth is not fully used with single *TCP* stream, so multi data streams should be used [13].

6.2   Network Efficacy

The efficacy of the network can be calculated by:

$$f(s) = (k \times s / b) / (k \times s / b) + RTT \tag{2}$$

Where, k is number of bits in the sending frame. s is sending window size, b is the bit rate of the link and *RTT* is the average round trip time of links.

6.3   Multiple Data Stream Function

Multiple data streams can further utilize the bandwidth by the grid environment see Figure 3. *GridFTP* has an ability to send data using multiple streams. The number of streams, Ns, can be automatically calculated using the following formula [14]:

$$Ns = Bandwidth \times RTT / windowsize \tag{3}$$

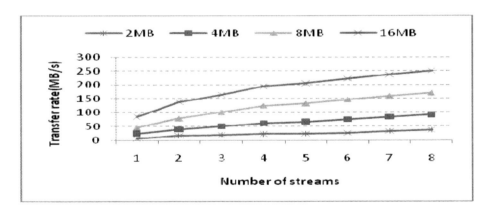

Fig. 3. Effects of varying window size and number of streams on the data transfer rate using GridFTP

7   Simulation Inputs

A *Large Hadron Collider (LHC)*, operated by the European Laboratory for Nuclear Research *(CERN)* [9], generates around thirty terabytes of data which needs huge storage and large number of processors to analyses it. This data will be accessed by researchers anywhere in the world, for downloading, reconstruction and analysis, so researchers can sit at their laptops, write small programs or macros, submit the programs through the agent, find the necessary data on servers and then run their jobs through supercomputer centers. The massive data sets are now being collected and distributed to researchers around the world through high-speed connections to the *LHC Computing Grid (LCG)*, a network of computer clusters at scientific institutions. The network employs the connectivity of private fiber-optic cable links, as well as existing portions of the public Internet.

Time and cost are the most important factors in the most of the selection processes in grids.ïIn this paper we present a dynamic replica selection strategy to enhance a replica broker. The new strategy aims to adapt at run-time its criteria to flexible *QoS* binding contracts, specified by the service provider and/or the client. The adaptability feature addressed by our replica selection strategy is inferred from the observation that the basic metrics, which influence the *QoS* that the user perceives when accessing a replica, depend directly on the application being replicated and on the clients' preferences. The enhanced replica broker takes into account these two factors in two phases:

1. *Coarse-grain:* It utilizes a data mining approach called the association rules to select the set of replicas from a number of sites that hold replicas.
2. *Fine-grain:* It works as a scoring function. It utilizes a grid core services such as replica location service and network monitoring services with transport service to select best replicas with respect to the cost and transfer time from uncongested set of replica sites.

To get logs files of the data grid networks and use them as an input files to our simulation, the site of *CERN* and 105 sites connected to it are used as a test bed form. All other site characteristics such as: number of jobs to be run, delays between each job submission, maximum queue size in each computing element, size and number of requested files and speed of I/O storage operations, assumed same for all replicas to see the effect of network resources only.

8   Performance Evaluation and Results

The implementation and performance evaluation of the proposed model are described in this section.

A)   Experimental Data

To test the performance of our model on real data grid environment, Internet end-to-end performance monitoring   reporting, *PingER* [7] is used to monitor the links between *CERN* and other sites [9]. The reports of *Feb.2011* are saved as text files. The implementation procedure for our model is done by writing a *C++* program with the following functions:

1. **Extracting RTT function:** This function extracts the *RTTs* from *PingER* report and save it in a text file called *Network History File (NHF)*.
2. **Converting function:** A mathematical standardization method is used to convert the real values of *RTTs* to logical values and save it in a text file called, *Logical History File LHF*.

3. *EST function:* The *LHF* with minimum *confidence (c)* and *support (s)* are used as input parameters to generate Associated Replica Sites, *ARS by* executing the *EST*.

B) Network Conditions effects

After examining *PingER* reports we noted that some sites at the same time having stability in the network links. In other words, at certain time of the day, some sites have *Round Trip Times* with almost constant values (good latency) as shown in *Figures 3*. It shows the status of the link between *CERN site* and *"81.91.232.2"*, *"waib.gouv.bj"*. As it is noted the stability of the link varies from time to time, so the link between the two sites was stable in the beginning of *2Feb2011*, then it became unstable in the mid of the day and after that again became stable and also the *"195.24.192.36"*, *"www.camnet.cm"* site,, has also a stabile link whereas the *"80.249.75.2"*, *"univ-sba.dz"* site has unstable link in the same time.

When user/application request is received at the beginning of the day by our proposed broker, both of stable links sites will be selected and appear in *ARS* after applying the *Coarse-grain* phase whereas site *"univ-sba.dz"*, will not be selected because it is unstable at the same time.

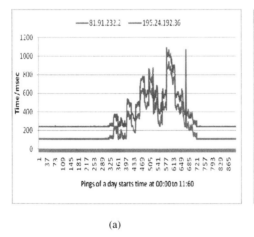
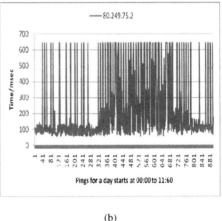

(a)   (b)

Fig. 4. RTT between number of data grid sites and "cern.ch" site

Another network condition effect is observed between distributed sites, the transfer rate of requested data files varies with the *TCP* window size of the sender and the number of streams used to transfer data as shown in *Figure 4* above.

The simulator consists of a hundred and five sites spread around the world that deal with *cern.ch, 192.91.244.6* via internet.

We simulate our work as the following steps:

1- The input log files are

a- Latency log file: In this file all round trips time between *cern.ch 192.91.244.6* and distributed sites for the date of date (2Feb2011) are saved.

b- Replica location log file: In this file we saved the IP addresses of sites with the name of their files which can be used for others. The cost per *MB* of the file, the *Bandwidth BW*, window size and *Maximum Transmission Unit MTU* [14].

2- Output file has set of association rules

To get the output file, let us see this scenario:

A data grid job *(J₁)* contains five file of 10GB size *(f₁f₂f₃f₄ and f₅) is* submitted to the *Replica broker*. The required files are distributed on the 105 replica sites (a site holding a copy of the file is called a replica). To execute J_1 on the computing element *"cern.ch"* that is referred by S_0, the required files should be available at S_0. After checking replica location log file, the files are found in the thirty distributed sites only, as shown in Figure 5. In order to minimize total executing time of J_1, the files should be concurrently taken from different sites. Selecting number of sites from these thirty sites represents first phase of our work, *Coarse-grain*.

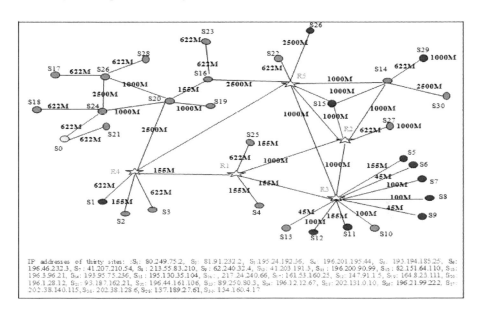

Fig. 5. The EU Data Grid Test bed of 30 sites connected to CERN and the approximate network Bandwidth

a-   Simulation result of the Phase one: Coarse-grain

When J_1 arrives at *2:00 Am*, the selected set of replica sites having a good latency are:*{S_2, S_3, S_4, S_5, S_{10}, S_{13}, S_{14}, S_{16}, S_{17}, S_{18}, S_{19}, S_{20}, S_{21}, S_{22}, S_{23}, S_{24}, S_{25}, S_{27}, S_{28}, S_{30}}*, this set is called *Associated set of Replica Sites (ARS)*.

b-   Simulation result of the Phase one: Fine-grain

Fine-grain is purifying the selection to get the *Best set of Replica Sites (BRS)*, sites with a good price and throughput. Using same scenario to get *BRS* from *ARS* we apply *MCTP* with the following steps:

1- Apply a scoring function, Equation 4 on *ARS* to determine *BRS*, Which is referred to as S_{ij}, sites with highest scores [8]. For simplicity, assumed an equal weight for both w_D and w_p that is 0.5.

$$S_{ij} = -w_D (D_{ij} / Ns) - w_p (P_j \times f) \qquad (4)$$

C)   Comparison with other methods

Replica broker is varying with different selection strategies that are used to get the best site having the requested file. In this section we explain the difference between our replica broker and others:

a-   EST with traditional model: In traditional data grid broker who uses traditional selection method, the best replica is the one which has the least number of *Hops* (routers), or the highest Bandwidth or the minimum *Round Trip Time (RTT)* to reach the computing site [15]. Figure 5 shows the comparison between EST and traditional model using highest Bandwidth as a criterion to select the best replica. As we can observe our technique has a better performance most of the times because it selects the sites which have the stable links. In traditional model the site which has the highest bandwidth does not always mean to be the best because sometimes this highest bandwidth link can be congested.

b- EST with Random model: In this model the replica is selected randomly to serve user's request [16]. The drawback of this model is it does not take care of   network conditions like BW and congested links. It selects random provider from the list of providers to get the requested file as shown in Figure 6.

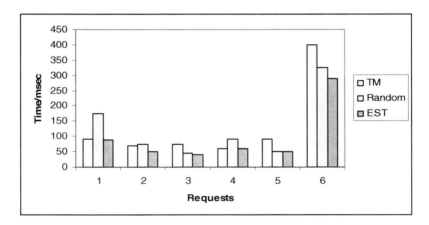

Fig. 6. Comparison of EST with TM and Random

Acknowledgments. Authors wish to express their sincere thanks to Prof. Arun Agarwal, from GridLabs Department of Computer and Information Sciences, University of Hyderabad, India for providing all the infrastructural and computational support required to carry out this work. His academic suggestions to improve the quality of the work are also highly appreciated and acknowledged.

References

1. Buyya, R., Venugopal, S.: The Gridbus toolkit for service oriented grid and utility computing: an overview and status report. In: 1st IEEE International Workshop Grid Economics and Business Models, GECON 2004, pp. 19–66, 23 (April 2004)
2. Abbas, A.: Grid Computing: A Practical Guide to Technology and Applications (2006)
3. Venugopal, S., Buyya, R., Ramamohanarao, K.: A taxonomy of Data Grids for distributed data sharing, managment, and proce. ACM Comput. Surv. 38(1), Article 3 (June 2006)
4. Vazhkudai, S., Tuecke, S., Foster, I.: Replica selection in the globus data grid. In: First IEEE /ACM Int. Conf. on Cluster Computing and the Grid, CCGrid 2001 (2001)
5. Rahman, R.M., Barker, K., Alhajj, R.: Replica selection strategies in data grid. Journal of Parallel and Dis. Computing 68(12), 1561–1574 (2008)
6. Almuttairi, R.M., Wankar, R., Negi, A., Rao, C.R., Almahna, M.S.: New replica selection technique for binding replica sites. In: 2010 1st International Conference on Data Grids, Energy, Power and Control (EPC-IQ), pp. 187–194 (December 2010)
7. https://confluence.slac.stanford.edu/display/IEPM/PingER
8. Lin, H., Abawajy, J., Buyya, R.: Economy-Based Data Replication Broker. In: Proceedings of the 2nd IEEE Int'l Con. on E-Science and Grid Computing (E-Science 2006), Amsterdam, Netherlands. IEEE CS Press, Los Alamitos (2006)
9. Earl, A.D., Menken, H.L.: Supporting the challenge of LHC produced data with ScotGrid, The University of Edinburgh CERN-THESIS-2006-014 (April 2006)
10. Tirumala, A., Ferguson, J.: Iperf 1.2 - The TCP/UDP Bandwidth Measurement Tool (2002)
11. http://www.internet2.edu/performance/owamp
12. Almuttari, R.M., Wankar, R., Negi, A., Rao, C.R.: Intelligent Replica Selection Strategy for Data Grid. In: Proceeding of the 10th Int. Conf. on Parallel and Distributed Proceeding Techniques and Applications, LasVegas, USA, vol. 3, pp. 95–100 (July 2010)
13. Matsunaga, H., Isobe, T., Mashimo, T., Sakamoto, H., Ueda, I.: Data transfer over the wide area network with large round trip time. In: IOP Science, 17th Int. Conf. in High Energy and Nuclear Physics (2010)
14. Wang, J., Huang, L.: Intelligent File Transfer Protocol for Grid Environment. In: Current Trends in High Performance Computing and Its Applications, Part II, pp. 469–476 (2005), doi:10.1007/3-540-27912-1_63
15. Kavitha, R., Foster, I.: Design and evaluation of replication strategies for a high performance data grid. In: Proceedings of Computing and High Energy and Nuclear Physics (2001)
16. Ceryen, T., Kevin, M.: Performance characterization of decentralized algorithms for replica selection in distributed object systems. In: Proceedings of 5th International Workshop on Software and Performance, Palma, de Mallorca, Spain, July 11 -14, pp. 257–262 (2005)
17. Almuttari, R.M., Wankar, R., Negi, A., Rao, C.R.: Smart Replica Selection for Data Grids Using Rough Set Approximations (RSDG). In: CICN, pp. 466–471 (November 2010)
18. Almuttari, R.M., Wankar, R., Negi, A., Rao, C.R.: Rough set clustering approach to replica selection in data grids (RSCDG). In: ISDA 2010, pp. 1195–1200 (November 2010)
19. Almuttari, R.M., Wankar, R., Negi, A., Rao, C.R.: Replica Selection in Data Grids Using Preconditioning of Decision Attributes by K-means Clustering (K-RSDG). In: Information Technology for Real World Problems (VCON), pp. 18–23 (December 2010)

A Modified Harmony Search Threshold Accepting Hybrid Optimization Algorithm

Yeturu Maheshkumar[1,2] and Vadlamani Ravi[1,*]

[1] Institute for Development and Research in Banking Technology, Castle Hills Road #1,
Masab Tank, Hyderabad – 500 057 (AP) India
[2] Department of Computer & Information Sciences, University of Hyderabad,
Hyderabad – 500 046 (AP) India
ymaheshkumar527@gmail.com, rav_padma@yahoo.com

Abstract. Hybrid metaheuristics are the recent trend that caught the attention of several researchers which are more efficient than the metaheuristics in finding the global optimal solution in terms of speed and accuracy. This paper presents a novel optimization metaheuristic by hybridizing Modified Harmony Search (MHS) and Threshold Accepting (TA) algorithm. This methodology has the advantage that one metaheuristic is used to explore the entire search space to find the area near optima and then other metaheuristic is used to exploit the near optimal area to find the global optimal solution. In this approach Modified Harmony Search was employed to explore the search space whereas Threshold Accepting algorithm was used to exploit the search space to find the global optimum solution. Effectiveness of the proposed hybrid is tested on 22 benchmark problems. It is compared with the recently proposed MHS+MGDA hybrid. The results obtained demonstrate that the proposed methodology outperforms the MHS and MHS+MGDA in terms of accuracy and functional evaluations and can be an expeditious alternative to MHS and MHS+MGDA.

Keywords: Harmony Search, Threshold Accepting, Hybrid Metaheuristic, Unconstrained Optimization, Metaheuristic.

1   Introduction

Optimization is a process of attempting to find the best possible solution out of all possible solutions. When we search for an optimal solution in the given search space we will come across two types of optimal solutions: *local optimum* and *global optimum*. A *local optimal solution* is a point in a search space where all the neighboring solutions are better than the current solution and the *global optimum solution* is a point in the search space where all other points in the search space are worse than or equal to the current solution. Many search methodologies including exhaustive search, heuristics and Metaheuristics were proposed to find the optimal solutions.

---

* Corresponding author.

C. Sombattheera et al. (Eds.): MIWAI 2011, LNAI 7080, pp. 298–308, 2011.
© Springer-Verlag Berlin Heidelberg 2011

Heuristics are generally referred to as trial-and-error methods. A heuristic is a method which seeks good solutions at a reasonable computation cost without being able to guarantee optimality, and possibly not feasibility and it is difficult to state how close to optimality the solution is [3]. *Metaheuristics* refers to set of concepts that can be used to define heuristic methods such that they can be applied to a wide set of different problems [4]. They can be seen as a general algorithmic framework which can be applied to solve different optimization problems with relatively few modifications to make. Metaheuristic can also be considered as a master strategy that guides and modifies other heuristics to produce solutions beyond those that are normally generated in a quest for local optimality. The heuristics guided by such a meta-strategy may be high level procedures or may embody nothing more than a description of available moves for transforming one solution into another, together with an associated evaluation rule. At present Metaheuristics is one of the important research areas in searching methodologies. In literature the term Metaheuristics refer to broad collection of relatively sophisticated heuristic methods like Particle Swarm Optimization (PSO), Harmony Search (HS) [5], Tabu Search (TS), Genetic Algorithm (GA), etc. This rapid focus on the area of metaheuristics led to development of new strategy named hybridization where more than one metaheuristics is employed such that the obtained hybrid will possess the advantage of both metaheuristics. Most commonly used hybrid strategy employs one or more metaheuristics to explore the search space and go near the optimal region where the probability of finding the global optimal solution is more than other regions and then other metaheuristic was used to exploit the near optimal region to find the global optimal solution. This strategy consists of employing both global search method and local search methods. There were many strategies adopted by researchers in developing hybrid metaheuristics.

The rest of the paper is organized as follows. Section 2 describes the literature survey of several metaheuristics. Section 3 describes the proposed strategy and how it is implemented. Section 4 presents the results and discusses the performance of the proposed hybrid by comparing with MHS and MHS+MGDA. Section 5 concludes the paper.

2   Literature Survey

The trend of hybridization of the existing Metaheuristics has started around 15 years ago. The hybrid optimization algorithms benefit from the advantages of the component metaheuristic algorithms. To start with, Ravi et al. [6] hybridized Non-Equilibrium Simulated Annealing (NESA) with a simplex like heuristic to develop a new algorithm called Improved Non-Equilibrium Simulated Annealing (INESA). This is one of the earliest hybrid algorithm proposed in the literature. In this paper, they improved Non-Equilibrium Simulated Annealing (NESA) by taking the solutions at regular intervals of the progress of NESA and then combining them with the best solutions obtained before the termination of NESA part of algorithm. At this stage they applied a simplex-like heuristic to obtain the global optimum. After that a hybrid metaheuristic in which 3 heuristics namely scatter search, GA and TS were employed in tandem was proposed [7]. In [7] the authors introduced the notion of memory to explore the solution space more extensively and also uses scatter search by combining the concepts of trajectory and clustering methods. The later stages of the algorithm combined the characteristics of TS and GA to test the status of new solutions and to direct the search towards global optimum. Later a hybrid Metaheuristic by hybridizing GA and NMSS was proposed [8]. In [8] the authors used GA to detect promising regions where we can find the optimal solution and uses NMSS for Intensification i.e., to locally search for global optimum in the promising region. A hybrid method [9] that hybridizes TA and DE was proposed in which TA is first applied to certain number of solutions of search space and the resultant set was passed to DE to move towards global optimal solution. After that a hybrid metaheuristic that hybridize DE by employing reflection property of the simplex method for fast convergence to global optima was developed [10]. Later, a hybrid metaheuristic using DE and Tabu Lists was developed for solving global optimization problems [11]. After that a hybrid metaheuristic, DETA was proposed [12]. In this model Differential Evolution (DE) is hybridized with Threshold Accepting (TA) that takes the advantage of efficient exploration of DE and exploitation of TA. They reported spectacular reduction in function evaluations when tested on test problems.

Many hybrid methodologies using harmony search have been proposed in the literature. To start with, a novel hybrid metaheuristic using harmony search and PSO was developed [13]. In this approach they induced harmony search inside the PSO such that before updating the position and velocity the solutions are passed as initial vector to harmony search such that a new solution generated every time is compared with worst solution and updated. Later a hybrid metaheuristic using harmony search and Sequential Quadratic Programming was developed [14]. In this approach after employing Harmony search, Sequential quadratic programming is employed on each solution to perform local search. The solution which provides better objective function value than other solutions is considered as the final accepted solution. Then two modified HS methods to deal with the uni-modal and multi-modal optimization problems have been proposed [15]. The first modified HS method is based on the fusion of the HS and Differential Evolution (DE) namely, HS-DE. The DE is employed here to optimize the members of the HS memory. The second modified HS method utilizes a novel HS memory management approach, and it targets at handling the multi-modal problems. Recently a heuristic particle swarm ant colony optimization (HPSACO) is presented for optimum design of trusses [16]. This algorithm is based on the particle swarm optimizer with passive congregation (PSOPC), ant colony optimization and harmony search scheme. HPSACO applies PSOPC for global optimization and the ant colony approach is used to update positions of particles to attain the feasible solution space. HPSACO handles the problem-specific constraints using a fly-back mechanism, and harmony search scheme deals with variable constraints. Later a new hybrid metaheuristics that includes the harmony search and MGDA [17] metaphors was proposed [1]. In this hybrid they first proposed a slight modification to harmony search and termed as modified harmony search (MHS). Then they employed MHS to explore the search space thoroughly and the best solution obtained is passed as initial solution to MGDA. The final solution obtained from MGDA is the global optimal solution.

3   MHSTA Hybrid

3.1   Overview of Harmony Search

Harmony search, proposed by Geem et al. [5] is one of the most recent meta-heuristic algorithms that found applications in science and engineering realms. The novelty in this algorithm lies in the fact that it is analogous to the improvisation technique of musicians. The algorithm in brief applies the idea of building an experience and then producing the best result that can be obtained from this experience. The analogy is such that a musical instrument represents a decision variable, its pitch range represents the value range, and solution vector is represented by the harmony and with thorough iterations (analogous to practice). The fitness value of the objective function is to be improved during iterations which is represented by the aesthetics. Given the random nature of the technique, it is highly likely that it will escape the local optima. An added benefit is that it performs very little operation on each prospective solution thereby substantially reducing program execution time. But, one of the major issues with Harmony Search is that for prolonged periods of time (in terms of iterations), during the execution of the program, its solution remains unchanged, especially during the final stages. As a result of which several unproductive iterations are performed with no genuine improvement to the solution. The modifications proposed by Choudhuri et al. [1] on Harmony Search are:

-- The value of *hmcr* is kept dynamically increasing from 0 to 1 during the execution of the program.
-- The HS algorithm is terminated when the difference between the best and the worst solution in the harmony memory is found to be less than some predefined constant.

The algorithm for Modified Harmony Search is explained in a step-by-step way as follows:

Here, we have two parameters: Harmony Memory Considering Rate (*hmcr*), which determines the percentage amount of the variable to be considered from memory and Pitch Adjusting Ratio (*par*),*which*   is the probability with which the value is considered.

1. Generate a set of *hms* number of solutions randomly and initialize harmony memory with this set.
2. Create a new solution vector with components of the solutions selected from harmony memory with a probability of *hmcr* such that the components when selected from the harmony memory are chosen randomly from different solutions within the harmony memory. Note that as the number of iterations increase the value of *hmcr* is increased linearly.
3. Perform the pitch adjustment operation by altering the variables' value by *delta* with a probability *par* ('*delta*' value is used in case of discrete optimization problems).

4. If the objective function value of this vector is found to be better than the worst solution in the memory then replace the worst solution with this vector.
5. Repeat this procedure (Steps 2 through 4) till the difference between the best and worst solutions within the harmony memory becomes less than some predefined *diff1* (a small value), or maximum number of iterations (predefined) is reached, whichever happens earlier. This step terminates MHS and the best solution in the memory is the optimal solution by MHS. Note that the value of *diff1* is set to larger value than usual in order to facilitate early termination of MHS and begin with the next phase.

3.2   Threshold Accepting Algorithm

Threshold Accepting algorithm was proposed by Dueck and Sheur [2]. It is a point based search technique. It is a variation of Simulated Annealing (SA) algorithm while in SA, a new solution is accepted on a probabilistic basis, but in TA the new solution is accepted based on a deterministic criterion. In TA any new solution that is not much worse than the previous solution is accepted.

The pseudo code of TA is as follows:

Initialize the solution randomly and set global iteration counter itr=0, old=99999, thresh=2

   f_i ← *fitness value of initial solution*
   while itr<gitr   // gitr is the number of global iterations
   DO
      itr ← *itr+1*
      ii ← *0*   *// ii - inner iteration value*
      while ii < limit or del1 > thresh
      DO
         ii ← *ii+ 1*
         Generate a candidate solution vector using the following equation
            candidate solution = old solution+(max-min)*(2*u-1)pindex
         f_j ← *fitness value for the candidate solution*
         del1 ← $f_i - f_j$
      END
   If del1 < thresh , set $f_i = f_j$
   If thresh < thrtol , set del2 = (new − old) / old
   Report current solution as the optimal one if abs (del2) < acc and exit if itr < gitr
   Else
      old ← *new*
      thresh = thresh * (1-eps)
   END

TA is applied on a single solution. The algorithm runs for '*gitr*' number of global iterations and for every inner iteration, a candidate solution is generated. The fitness value is calculated for each candidate solution and the solutions that are not much worse than the previous one are selected for exploring. The algorithm terminates when the difference between objective function values of previous and present is very small as determined by the parameter acc which is set to 10^{-6} to obtain highly accurate solution. The parameter *thresh* is used to determine the acceptance of candidate solution and is generally set to 2 at the beginning and is gradually decreased in a geometric progression based on an epsilon value that is generally set to 0.01. *limit* is the number of inner iterations. *max, min* are the boundaries of the decision variables and *pindex* is generally an odd integer between 3 and 33 and is used to generate a value that is added to the old solution to generate a neighborhood solution.

3.3   MHSTA Algorithm

MHSTA is a new hybrid metaheuristic that employs both MHS and TA. The proposed method is a 2 phase process. The first phase of hybrid metaheuristic starts with employing MHS to explore the search space thoroughly such that finally a near optimal region is obtained where there is high probability to find the global optimal solution. In this phase MHS is not employed to its full extent by terminating the algorithm by choosing a small value for *diff1* (in our proposed hybrid the value of *diff1* is set to 0.0001). The best solution out of all the solutions i.e., the solution which provides better fitness value than other solutions is considered for the second phase. In second phase, TA is employed by considering the best solution from the phase1 as its initial solution. Here TA tries to exploit the near optimal region to find the global optimal solution. The algorithm of MHSTA is as follows:

Start
*   Consider the objective function to optimize and the search space of the objective function and initialize the harmony memory.*
*   Phase 1*
*   Employ MHS to find the near optimal region (the algorithm for MHS is explained previously)*
*   The best solution obtained is considered for phase 2*
*   Phase 2*
*   Employ TA on the best solution obtained from phase1*
*   The final solution obtained is considered as the global optimal solution.*
End

The schematic view of the proposed approach was depicted in Figure 1. The 'problem' in the figure represents any optimization problem and 'N' represents the number of solutions to consider which is user defined. After employing MHS with N solutions the solution which gives the best optimal value is considered for the next phase which is represented as 'B' in the figure. Threshold Algorithm is invoked with 'B' as its initial solution. The optimal solution provided by the TA is the final solution obtained from the proposed hybrid model.

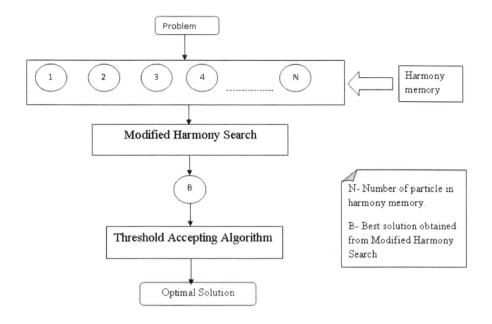

Fig. 1. Schematic view of MHSTA hybrid metaheuristic

4   Results and Discussions

The effectiveness of the proposed hybrid is analyzed by testing the proposed hybrid on 22 benchmark unconstrained optimization problems taken from [18]. The global optimal values obtained for each benchmark problem and the corresponding functional evaluations required are presented in Table 1. The results presented in Table 1 are the average results of 30 simulations with different seed values. In the Table 1 Function column contains the names of the benchmark problems and OPTIMAL VALUES represents average functional value obtained using the corresponding method (MHS, MHS+MGDA and MHSTA). The numbers 1-22 represents the serial number of the benchmark functions as per Table 1. FEval column contains the functional evaluations taken to provide the optimal value. The results clearly demonstrate that the proposed hybrid outperformed MHS and MHS+MGDA methods in terms of functional evaluations and optimal value. Out of 22 benchmark problems, in the case of 19 problems, the proposed hybrid produced better optimal value with less functional evaluations and in case of 3 problems the proposed hybrid yielded better optimal value than that of MHS and MHS+MGDA but after consuming little more functional evaluations. The proposed hybrid yielded better results on higher dimensional problems (sphere – 50 and 100 dimensions) with respect to functional evaluations and objective function values as well. Fig. 2 depicts the graphical comparison of functional evaluations consumed by MHS, MHS+MGDA, MHSTA hybrid Metaheuristics. The dark line represents MHS, the rounded dot line represents MHS+MGDA and the vertical dotted line represents MHSTA. Fig. 2 clearly demonstrates the supremacy of MHSTA over other Metaheuristics by consuming very less functional evaluations. The results clearly demonstrate the supremacy of MHSTA over other hybrid methods.

Table 1. Average optimal solutions and functional evaluations

		MHS		MHS+MGDA		MHSTA	
SNo	FUNCTION	OPTIMAL VALUES	FEval	OPTIMAL VALUES	FEval	OPTIMAL VALUES	FEval
1	Aluffi Penttini [19]	-0.352032	4497	-0.352226	3015	-0.352343	1408
2	Becker [20]	0.000013	6582	0.000261	2201	0.000027	1456
3	Bohachevsky1 [21]	0.009631	6619	0.0116	4162	0.000001	1883
4	Bohachevsky2 [21]	0.011379	7165	0.006072	4032	0.000001	1883
5	Camelback3 [22]	0.000263	4261	0.000317	4081	0.000050	1574
6	Camelback6 [22,23]	-1.031211	4478	-1.03113	4243	-1.031431	1336
7	Dekker's [24]	-24756.5839	3444	-24772.369	2276	-24771.979	1513
8	Easom [23]	-0.966595	5543	-0.96656	4038	-0.998774	1653
9	Goldstein [22]	3.01732	3888	3.060314	1033	3.002347	1432
10	Hartman3 [22]	-3.862748	5840	-3.86278	3661	-3.862746	1771
11	Miele [25]	0	7717	0.000018	2853	0.000025	1770
12	Mod.Rosenbrock [20]	0.020783	7353	0.0267	4570	0.005817	2104
13	Periodic [20]	0.900265	7015	0.90078	4480	0.906822	1869
14	Powell [25]	0.142005	10039	0.0134726	6687	0.022234	4952
15	Salomon 10 d [26]	0.042011	1480	0.05187	1042	0	1324
16	Schaffer2 [23]	0.710002	4234	0.0172575	3678	0.355321	1602
17	Schaffer1 [23]	0.014096	4442	0.012822	3107	0.012209	2217
18	Schwefel (10 d) [27]	-2094.040	8755	-2094.914	8726	-4187.6411	10039
19	Sphere (5d) [28]	0.005837	8577	0.001032	4771	0.000133	4037
20	Zakharov [29]	0.01826	9468	0.0015	5888	0.000215	5478
21	Sphere (50d) [28]	0.56729	13678	2.71172882	14267	0.052370	11075
22	Sphere (100d) [28]	0.58902	14478	3.11667	15167	0.37238	11075

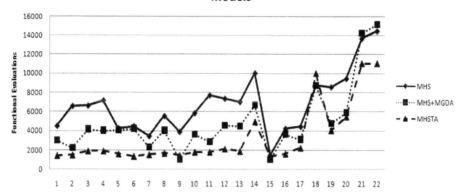

Fig. 2. Functional evaluations consumed by MHS, MHS+MGDA, MHSTA

5   Conclusions

MHSTA hybrid metaheuristic includes the advantages of efficient exploration of MHS combined with efficient exploitation of TA. The process of employing TA with best the solution produced by MHS helps to provide more accurate objective function value. The results demonstrate that the proposed hybrid metaheuristic is more expeditious than that of the exiting hybrid methodologies MHS, MHS+MGDA. The proposed hybrid produced better optimal value with almost 50% reduction in the consumption of functional evaluations which depicts its supremacy in terms of accuracy and speed.

References

1. Choudhuri, R., Ravi, V., Mahesh Kumar, Y.: A Hybrid Harmony Search and Modified Great Deluge Algorithm for Unconstrained Optimization. Int. Jo. of Comp. Intelligence Research 6(4), 755–761 (2010)
2. Dueck, G., Scheur, T.: Threshold Accepting: A General Purpose Optimization Algorithm appearing Superior to Simulated Annealing. Jo. of Comp. Physics 90, 161–175 (1990)
3. Edmund, K.B., Graham, K.: Search Methodologies: Introductory Tutorials in Optimization and Decission Support Techniques. Springer, Heidelberg (2005)
4. Glover, F.: Future Paths for Integer Programming and Links to Artificial Intelligence. Computers and Op. Research 13(5), 533–549 (1986)
5. Geem, Z., Kim, J., Loganathan, G.: A new heuristic optimization algorithm: harmony search. Simulation 76, 60–68 (2001)
6. Ravi, V., Murthy, B.S.N., Reddy, P.J.: Non-equilibrium simulated annealing-algorithm applied to reliability optimization of complex systems. IEEE Trans. on Reliability 46, 233–239 (1997)

7. Trafalis, T.B., Kasap, S.: A novel metaheuristics approach for continuous global optimization. Jo. of Global Optimization 23, 171–190 (2002)
8. Chelouah, R., Siarry, P.: Genetic and Nelder-Mead algorithms hybridized for a more accurate global optimization of continuous multi-minima functions. European Jo. of Op. Research 148, 335–348 (2003)
9. Schimdt, H., Thierauf, G.: A Combined Heuristic Optimization Technique. Advance in Engineering Software 36(1), 11–19 (2005)
10. Bhat, T.R., Venkataramani, D., Ravi, V., Murty, C.V.S.: Improved differential evolution method for efficient parameter estimation in biofilter modeling. Biochemical Eng. Jo. 28, 167–176 (2006)
11. Srinivas, M., Rangaiah, G.: Differential Evolution with Tabu list for Global Optimization and its Application to Phase Equilibrium and Parameter Estimation. Problems Ind. Engg. Chem. Res. 46, 3410–3421 (2007)
12. Chauhan, N., Ravi, V.: Differential Evolution and Threshold Accepting Hybrid Algorithm for Unconstrained Optimization. Int. Jo. of Bio-Inspired Computation 2, 169–182 (2010)
13. Li, H., Li, L.: A novel hybrid particle swarm optimization algorithm combined with harmony search for higher dimensional optimization problems. In: Int. Conference on Intelligent Pervasive Computing, Jeju Island, Korea (2007)
14. Fesanghary, M., Mahdavi, M., Joldan, M.M., Alizadeh, Y.: Hybridizing harmony search algorithm with sequential programming for engineering optimization problems. Comp. Methods Appl. Mech. Eng. 197, 3080–3091 (2008)
15. Gao, X.Z., Wang, X., Ovaska, J.: Uni-Modal and Multi Modal optimization using modified harmony search methods. IJICIC 5(10(A)), 2985–2996 (2009)
16. Kaveh, A., Talatahari, S.: PSO, ant colony strategy and harmony search scheme hybridized for optimization of truss structures. Computers and Structures 87, 267–283 (2009)
17. Ravi, V.: Optimization of Complex System Reliability by a Modified Great Deluge Algorithm. Asia-Pacific Jo. of Op. Research 21(4), 487–497 (2004)
18. Ali, M.M., Charoenchai, K., Zelda, B.Z.: A Numerical Evaluation of Several Stochastic Algorithms on Selected Continuous Global Optimization Test Problems. Jo. of Global Optimization 31, 635–672 (2005)
19. Aluffi-Pentini, F., Parisi, V., Zirilli, F.: Global optimization and stochastic differential equations. Jo. of Op. Theory and Applications 47, 1–16 (1985)
20. ˙Price, W.L.: Global Optimization by Controlled Random Search. Computer Jo. 20, 367–370 (1977)
21. Bohachevsky, M.E., Johnson, M.E., Stein, M.L.: Generalized simulated annealing for function optimization. Techno Metrics 28, 209–217 (1986)
22. Dixon, L., Szego, G.: Towards Global Optimization 2. North Holland, New York (1978)
23. Michalewicz, Z.: Genetic Algorithms + Data Structures = Evolution Programs. Springer, Heidelberg (1996)
24. Dekkers, A., Aarts, E.: Global optimization and simulated annealing. Mathematical Programming 50, 367–393 (1991)
25. Wolfe, M.A.: Numerical Methods for Unconstrained Optimization. Van Nostrand Reinhold Company, New York (1978)
26. Salomon, R.: Reevaluating Genetic Algorithms Performance under Co-ordinate Rotation of Benchmark Functions. Bio. Systems 39(3), 263–278 (1995)
27. Muhlenbein, H., Schomisch, S., Born, J.: The parallel genetic algorithm as function optimizer. In: Belew, R., Booker, L. (eds.) Proceedings of the Fourth Int. Conference on Genetic Algorithms, pp. 271–278. Morgan Kaufmann (1991)

28. Sphere problem; global and local optima,
    `http://www.optima.amp.i.kyoto.ac.jp/member/student/hedar/Hed`
    `ar_files/TestGO_files/Page113.html` (cited on November 20, 2010)
29. Zakharov Problem Global and local optima,
    `http://www.optima.amp.i.kyotoc.jp/member/student/hedar/`
    `Hedar_files/TestGO_files/Page3088.htm` (cited on November 20, 2010)

Differential Evolution Algorithm for Motion Estimation

Samrat L. Sabat*, K. Shravan Kumar, and P. Rangababu

School of Physics University of Hyderabad, Hyderabad -500046, India
slssp@uohyd.ernet.in, {shravana2,p.rangababu}@gmail.com

Abstract. Motion Estimation (ME) is computationally expensive step in video encoding. Exhaustive search technique for ME yields maximum accuracy at the cost of highest execution time. To overcome the computational burden, many fast search algorithms are reported that limit the number of locations to be searched. ME is formulated as an optimization problem and the Sum of Absolute Difference (SAD) is considered as an objective function to be minimized. SAD error surface is a multimodal in nature. Fast searching algorithms converge to a minimal point rapidly but they may be trapped in local minima of SAD surface. This paper presents an application of Differential Evolution algorithm for motion estimation. The performance of the DE algorithm is compared with Full search, three step search, Diamond search and Particle swarm optimization for eight QCIF video sequences. Four performance indicators namely Peak Signal to Noise Ratio (PSNR), Structural Similarity (SSIM), number of search points and run time are considered for performance comparison of algorithms. Simulation result shows that both PSO and DE algorithms are performing close to Full search and reduces computational overload significantly in all the sequences.

Keywords: Block matching, Motion estimation, Differential evolution, Particle swarm optimization.

1 Introduction

Motion estimation (ME) plays an important role in video coding. It is one of the most computational intense blocks in video coding. The exhaustive search algorithm is the optimal algorithm used for motion estimation. Since it performs exhaustive search, it takes more time to give optimal solution. To overcome the computational burden many fast search algorithms are reported that limit the number of locations to be searched. Developing fast algorithms for ME to reduce computational complexity in video coding has been an active area of research. Block matching algorithms (BMA) like full search, 2D-logarithm search (LOGS) [8], new three step search [10], four step search [11], diamond search [18], directional gradient descent search [12], adaptive motion estimation [1], are being popularly used in motion estimation for most of the video codecs. In a typical BMA, the current frame of a video sequence is divided into non-overlapping

---

* Corresponding author.

C. Sombattheera et al. (Eds.): MIWAI 2011, LNAI 7080, pp. 309–316, 2011.

square blocks of pixels called Macro Blocks (MB). For each reference block in the current frame, BMA searches for the best matched block within a search window of the previous frame. The full search (FS) block-matching algorithm is the simplest block matching algorithm (BMA) that performs exhaust search and gives optimal solution. Although this is the simple algorithm, it takes more time to give optimal solution because for each MB, it searches $(2p + 1)^2$ pixel locations, where p is the allowed maximum displacement i.e., the search window size. Fast search algorithms reduce computation time by reducing the number of search points. These search algorithm assumes that the SAD error surface is uni-modal in the search range [2]. In most of the real world video signals the SAD error surface is multimodal in nature. The objective of motion estimation is to find the set of parameters that best captures the motion and thereby minimizing an objective function.

Motion estimation is modeled as nonlinear optimization problem. This minimization can be done by using deterministic approach or stochastic approach. The disadvantage with deterministic approach is that if the search space is wide, then the algorithm may trap to local minima leading to sub optimal solutions. This is the main drawback of using deterministic approaches like full search, diamond search, three step search etc. Stochastic optimization techniques are proven to be more robust to local minima and converge rapidly to global solutions. Genetic algorithm (GA) has been proposed for motion estimation [16]. The genetic motion search algorithm (GMS) is proposed [6] to overcome the problem of trapping in local minima by first choosing a random search point and then using an algorithm similar to the genetic processes of mutation and evolution to find the global minimum of the matching distortion. Particle Swarm Optimization (PSO) is computationally simple compared to GA like algorithms as it does not require evolutionary operators, and has been applied to motion estimation problem [15].

Since Differential evolution is proven to work better compared to many stochastic techniques, and authors have applied to solve many real world optimization problems [13,3], this paper proposes an application of Differential evolution technique for motion estimation.

The rest of this paper is organized as follows. Section 2 reviews existing research on Motion Estimation. Section 3 provides the concept and implementation steps of Differential Evolution algorithm. Section 4 shows the experimental results and Section 5 concludes this paper.

2   Differential Evolution Method

Differential Evolution technique, proposed by Storn and Price [14], is a simple yet powerful algorithm for solving continuous parameter optimization problem. It has successfully been applied to diverse domains of science and engineering, such as signal processing, machine intelligence, pattern recognition among many others. It has been reported that DE performs better than GA and PSO [5] for optimizing several numerical benchmark functions [17]. Like other evolutionary algorithms, DE also involves (i) variation process, which enables exploring different regions of the search space and (ii) selection process, which ensures the exploitation of previous knowledge about the fitness landscape [17]. A complete survey of DE algorithm can be found in [3]. The implementation of DE algorithm requires following steps [13].

1. Parameter initialization: Initialize population size (NP), boundary constraints of optimization variables, mutation factor (F), crossover rate (CR), and the stopping criterion (t_{max}).
2. Initial population generation: Initialize the generations counter $(t = 0)$ and also initialize population of individuals (solution vectors) $\mathbf{x}_i(t)$ with random values generated according to a uniform probability distribution in the n-dimensional problem space. i denotes the population number.
3. Fitness evaluation: Evaluate the fitness value of each individual.
4. Mutation: For each vector $\mathbf{x}_i^t$, a mutant vector or a donor vector $\mathbf{v}_i^t$ is generated using one of the mutation equation. For generating the mutant vector different strategies are used [4]. Each strategy corresponds to a variant of DE. In this work, we have used DE/rand/2/bin (Strategy 2) that uses $\mathbf{v}_i^t = (\mathbf{x})_{r1}^i(t) + F_1 \cdot (\mathbf{x}_{r2}^i(t) - \mathbf{x}_{r3}^i(t) + F_2 \cdot (\mathbf{x}_{r4}^i(t) - \mathbf{x}_{r5}^i(t))$. Where, r_1^i, r_2^i, r_3^i are mutually exclusive integers $\in 1, 2, 3, ...NP$ chosen randomly. F_1 and F_2 $\in [0,2]$ is a real and constant factor called scaling factor. $\mathbf{x}_{best}(t)$ is the best individual vector in the population.
5. Crossover: In order to increase the potential diversity of the population and to have constant population size, a crossover operation is performed using binomial scheme. A random number is generated and cross over is performed on each of the D variables whenever the random number is less than the crossover probability (CR) value. A trail vector is generated after crossover operation as

$$\mathbf{u}_i^t = [u_{i,1}^t, u_{i,2}^t, ..., u_{i,D}^t] \tag{1}$$

In case of binomial crossover

$$u_{i,j}^t = \begin{cases} v_{i,j}^t & \text{if } rand(j) \leq CR \text{ or } j = randn(i) \\ x_{i,j}^t & \text{otherwise} \end{cases} \tag{2}$$

where, $i = [1, 2, ...NP]$ and $j = [1, 2, ..D]$, CR is $\in [0,1]$.
6. Selection: In this step the target vector $\mathbf{x}_i^t$ is compared with the trial vector $\mathbf{v}_i^t$ and the one with the lowest function value is admitted to the next generation.
7. Termination criteria: Update the generation number using $t = t + 1$. Proceed to Step 3 if $t < t_{max}$ or all the design specification not satisfied.
8. Output the best solution $\mathbf{x}_{best}$ and its fitness value.

3   Problem Formulation

In this work, Sum of Absolute Difference (SAD) is considered to be the objective function to be minimized. Mathematically it can be defined as

$$SAD_{i,j}^k = \sum_{m=1}^{N} \sum_{n=1}^{N} |b_{m,n}^{k,i,j} - b_{m+x_1,n+x_2}^{k-1,i,j}| \tag{3}$$

where b represents the macro-block of size N for $i = 1, 2, 3 ... N_{bh}$ and $j = 1, 2, 3 ... N_{bv}$, where N_{bh}, N_{bv} are number of macro-blocks in horizontal and vertical directions of the frame. Search algorithm is initiated to find the motion vector for each macro-block of the current frame k.

Each population member of the search algorithm is encoded as the co-ordinates of integer pixel locations (x_1, x_2) of the search window in the previous frame $k-1$, and the population member with global optimum SAD value is considered as the motion vector (MV). We used a motion field filtering technique [9] that eliminates spurious motion vectors from the spatial areas in the video frames where no actual motion exists. The basic idea in this algorithm is to compare the MAD between the corresponding blocks with the average SAD, and based on that we decide if motion is present or not. In this work, as a first step in finding MV, we decide whether motion exists in each block simply by comparing its SAD with the previously calculated Threshold (THR). If $SAD < THR$ both motion vector is set to zero. Otherwise, the algorithm continues search for motion vector in the search window. We define threshold for the k_{th} frame as:

$$THR = \gamma \frac{1}{N_{bh} N_{bv}} \sum_{i=1}^{N_{bh}} \sum_{j=1}^{N_{bv}} SAD_{i,j}^k \qquad (4)$$

where γ is a scalar. Different performance measurement metrices such as Average PSNR $(AVGPSNR)$ Average Structural Similarity index $(AVGSSIM)$, number of search points and run time are considered for performance evaluation of algorithm. Mathematically PSNR can be defined as

$$PSNR = 10 \times \log_{10}(\frac{MAX_I^2}{MSE}) \qquad (5)$$

where mean square error (MSE) is

$$MSE = \frac{1}{N_h N_v} \sum_{m=1}^{N_h} \sum_{n=1}^{N_v} (I^k(m, n) - I^{k_{orig}}(m, n))^2 \qquad (6)$$

In equation (6), I^k is the motion compensated k^{th} frame and $I^{k_{orig}}$ is the kth original frame. Additionally we also have used another performance indicator, namely Structural similarity (SSIM) [7] that considers structural information of image, to measure the quality of motion estimation algorithm.

4   Experimental Results and Analysis

Motion estimation problem and all the search algorithms were written in MATLAB scripting language, which are executed on a Intel Core2Duo processor with 3Ghz speed and 2GB RAM. The DE algorithm is applied to find motion vectors

of various QCIF resolution video sequences. The luminescence content of the
sequences are extracted and each frame is divided into macro blocks of fixed
size 16×16 pixels. The search range of all the algorithms are fixed as $p = \pm 7$
pixels which forms a 15×15 pixel search window. The scaling factor γ mentioned
in equation (4) is set to 0.45, which works for most of the sequences [9]. The
experiments are conducted by using the luminance component of eight video
sequences as tabulated in Table 1. In Table 1 presents the perfromance comparison of different algorithms such as exhaustive search (ES), PSO , DE, TSS
and DS. Average PSNR ($AVGPSNR$), Average SSIM ($AVGSSIM$), average
number of search points per MB (AVG SADS) and total runtimes are calculated
for 100 frames of the video sequences. The experimental results for comparison
are summarized in Table 1.

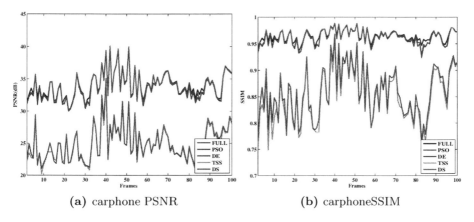

(a) carphone PSNR   (b) carphoneSSIM

Fig. 1. PSNR and SSIM of carphone sequence

From the table it is evident that both DE and PSO algorithm perfroms equally
well on the tested video sequences. It also can be observed that in case of complex
video sequences such as *foreman* and *carphone* video sequences DE algorithm
gives better PSNR and SSIM value compared to rest of the algorithms. Figure 1
and 2 presents the PSNR and SSIM of *foreman* and *carphone* video sequence.
In simulation, all the eight video sequences are of QCIF (176×144) resolution.
For both theese sequences, PSO and DE gives almost same PSNR and SSIM
as full search algorithm. Both PSO and DE improves average PSNR considerably. However the average number of search point for both PSO and DE are
considerable smaller than full search but more than fast search algorithm. From
Table 1, it is also clear that the run time for DE algorithm is more than fast
search algorithm. This concludes that fast search algorithm gives the suboptimal
solution in less time compared to PSO and DE. These algorithms take more run
time but gives optimal solution close to full search algorithm.

Table 1. Performance comparison of DE algorithm with FS,TSS, PSO and DS

Sequence	Algorithm	AVG PSNR	AVG SSIM	AVG SADS	TOT TIME
Akiyo	ES	43.670960	0.985452	225.000000	176.694751
	PSO	43.619033	0.985388	35.016937	28.492899
	DE	43.634904	0.985386	35.016937	28.038624
	TSS	42.665282	0.982531	25.000000	13.119886
	DS	42.665282	0.982531	11.434547	6.791996
Carphone	ES	33.665879	0.955197	225.000000	174.490402
	PSO	33.415856	0.951944	51.584634	40.662043
	DE	33.462047	0.952467	51.559637	41.049785
	TSS	24.569817	0.842305	25.000000	13.414832
	DS	24.731072	0.850120	12.953984	7.842295
Foreman	ES	32.397299	0.943979	225.000000	172.168027
	PSO	31.795191	0.931867	55.402408	43.486243
	DE	31.998536	0.935268	55.659627	44.613081
	TSS	23.381623	0.831569	25.000000	12.725047
	DS	24.195267	0.851165	13.173758	8.012334
Mobile	ES	25.837003	0.913603	225.000000	173.427359
	PSO	25.824509	0.913428	71.561677	57.068729
	DE	25.829658	0.913480	71.554331	61.431947
	TSS	25.353802	0.906752	25.000000	12.797778
	DS	25.362348	0.906856	11.454341	7.020376
Mother-Daughter	ES	40.235099	0.969844	225.000000	172.903151
	PSO	40.155449	0.969378	56.389960	43.885556
	DE	40.163574	0.969334	56.382920	46.038491
	TSS	31.416097	0.919111	25.000000	12.791876
	DS	32.220950	0.928021	11.836445	7.403744
News	ES	36.693778	0.972798	225.000000	172.994825
	PSO	36.665917	0.972596	36.746454	29.077052
	DE	36.646018	0.972619	36.727681	29.272656
	TSS	34.493078	0.957682	25.000000	12.728181
	DS	34.561214	0.958370	11.529946	6.800016
Salesman	ES	39.492695	0.974351	225.000000	171.398818
	PSO	39.451365	0.974137	69.138251	54.232535
	DE	39.447306	0.974143	69.139884	55.469899
	TSS	37.474067	0.961476	25.000000	12.918997
	DS	37.486132	0.961442	11.483624	7.270469
Silent	ES	35.172902	0.957340	225.000000	174.434319
	PSO	35.071236	0.956810	36.062851	29.940964
	DE	35.062172	0.956856	36.062443	29.035304
	TSS	31.032795	0.923496	25.000000	12.871285
	DS	31.133456	0.925052	11.887869	7.047756

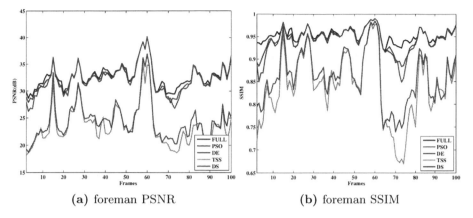

(a) foreman PSNR   (b) foreman SSIM

Fig. 2. PSNR and SSIM of foreman sequence

5   Conclusions

In this paper, differential evolution technique is applied for block motion estimation in video encoders. In terms PSNR and SSIM the differential evolution algorithm outperforms other fast block matching algorithm. In complex sequences
like *foreman* and *carphone*, DE and PSO both outperforms three step search
and diamond search algorithm. However three step search and diamond search
uses less number of search point compared to PSO and DE algorithm. This work
also gives a conclusion that fast search algorithm gives the suboptimal solution
in less time compared to PSO and DE. Both the PSO and DE algorithms gives
optimal solutions close to full search algorithm at the cost of more run time.

Acknowledgment. The authors are thankful to Department of Science & Technology, Govt of India for providing financial support to carryout this work.

References

1. Ahmad, I., Zheng, W., Luo, J., Liou, M.: A fast adaptive motion estimation algorithm. IEEE Transactions on Circuits and Systems for Video Technology 16(3),
   420–438 (2006)
2. Chan, Y.-L., Siu, W.-C.: An efficient search strategy for block motion estimation
   using image features. IEEE Transactions on Image Processing 10(8), 1223–1238
   (2001)
3. Das, S., Suganthan, P.N.: Differential evolution: A survey of the state-of-the-art.
   IEEE Transactions on Evolutionary Computation 15(1), 4–31 (2011)
4. Das, S., Abraham, A., Konar, A.: Automatic Clustering Using an Improved Differential Evolution Algorithm. IEEE Transactions on Systems Man and Cybernetics,
   Part A 38(1), 218–237 (2008)

5. Eberhart, R., Kenedy, J.: Particle swarm optimization. In: Proceedings of IEEE Int. Conference on Neural Networks, Piscataway, NJ, pp. 1114–1121 (November 1995)
6. Hung-Kei Chow, K., Liou, M.L.: Genetic motion search algorithm for video compression. IEEE Transactions on Circuits and Systems for Video Technology 3(6), 440–445 (1993)
7. Hung-Kei Chow, K., Liou, M.L.: A universal image quality index. IEEE Signal Processing Letters 9(3), 81–84 (2002)
8. Jain, J., Jain, A.: Displacement measurement and its application in interframe image coding. IEEE Transactions on Communications 29(12), 1799–1808 (1981)
9. Jovanov, L., Pizurica, A., Schulte, S., Schelkens, P., Munteanu, A., Kerre, E., Philips, W.: Combined wavelet-domain and motion-compensated video denoising based on video codec motion estimation methods. IEEE Transactions on Circuits and Systems for Video Technology 19(3), 417–421 (2009)
10. Li, R., Zeng, B., Liou, M.: A new three-step search algorithm for block motion estimation. IEEE Transactions on Circuits and Systems for Video Technology 4(4), 438–442 (1994)
11. Po, L.M., Ma, W.C.: A novel four-step search algorithm for fast block motion estimation. IEEE Transactions on Circuits and Systems for Video Technology 6(3), 313–317 (1996)
12. Po, L.M., Ng, K.H., Cheung, K.W., Wong, K.M., Uddin, Y., Ting, C.W.: Novel directional gradient descent searches for fast block motion estimation. IEEE Transactions on Circuits and Systems for Video Technology 19(8), 1189–1195 (2009)
13. Sabat, S.L., Udgata, S.K.: Differential evolution algorithm for mesfet small signal model parameter extraction. In: 2010 International Symposium on Electronic System Design (ISED), pp. 203–207 (December 2010)
14. Storn, R., Price, K.: Differential evolution: A simple and efficient adaptive scheme for global optimization over continuous spaces. J. Global Optimization 11, 341–359 (1997)
15. Yuan, X., Shen, X.: Block matching algorithm based on particle swarm optimization for motion estimation. In: Second International Conference on Embedded Software and Systems, pp. 191–195 (2008)
16. Yuelei, X., Duyan, B., Baixin, M.: A genetic search algorithm for motion estimation. In: 5th International Conference on Signal Processing Proceedings, WCCC-ICSP 2000, vol. 2, pp. 1058–1061 (2000)
17. Zaharie, D.: Influence of crossover on the behavior of differential evolution algorithms. Applied Soft Computing 9(3), 1126–1138 (2009)
18. Zhu, S., Ma, K.K.: A new diamond search algorithm for fast block-matching motion estimation. IEEE Transactions on Image Processing 9(2), 287–290 (2000)

Swarm Intelligence Based Localization in Wireless Sensor Networks

Dama Lavanya and Siba K. Udgata

Department of Computer and Information Sciences,
University of Hyderabad,
Hyderabad-500046, India
lavanya576@gmail.com,
udgatacs@uohyd.ernet.in

Abstract. In wireless sensor networks, sensor node localization is an important problem because sensor nodes are randomly scattered in the region of interest and they get connected into network on their own. Finding location without the aid of Global Positioning System (GPS) in each node of a sensor network is important in cases where GPS is either not accessible, or not practical to use due to power, cost, or line of sight conditions. The objective of this paper is to find the locations of nodes by using Particle Swarm Optimization and Artificial Bee Colony algorithm and compare the performance of these two algorithms. The term swarm is used in a general manner to refer to a collection of interacting agents or individuals. We also propose multi stage localization and compared multi stage localization performance with single stage localization.

Keywords: Wireless Sensor Networks, Localization, Beacon, Particle Swarm Optimization, Artificial Bee Colony Algorithm, Multi stage localization.

1 Introduction

Recent advances in integrated circuit design, embedded systems and novel sensing materials have enabled the development of low cost, low power, multi functional sensor nodes. These nodes with wireless interfaces and on-board processing capacity bring the idea of wireless sensor network into reality. It changes the way information is collected, specially in situations where information is hard to capture and observe.

Wireless Sensor Networks (WSNs) distinguish themselves from other traditional wireless or wired networks through sensor and actuator based interaction with the environment. A sensor network consists of number of sensor nodes scattered in the region of interest to acquire some physical data. The sensor node should have the ability of sensing, processing and communicating.

Localization is a very important issue in sensor networks. Finding the location of sensor nodes in a sensor network is known as Localization problem. In some

C. Sombattheera et al. (Eds.): MIWAI 2011, LNAI 7080, pp. 317–328, 2011.

areas like deep forests, humans are not able to go and fix the sensor nodes. In those areas, sensor nodes are deployed through random deployment and thus the sensors take random positions. In a sensor network, there will be a large number of sensor nodes densely deployed at positions which may not be predetermined. In most sensor network applications, the information gathered by these micro-sensors will be meaningless unless the location from where the information is obtained is known. This makes localization capabilities highly desirable in sensor networks. We can attach a GPS to a sensor node while deploying and find the location of the sensor node after deployment by using the GPS. However, attaching a GPS receiver to each node is not always the preferred solution for several reasons like cost, inaccessibility, nodes may be deployed indoors, or GPS reception might be obstructed by climatic conditions. We can attach GPS to some sensor nodes. After the sensor nodes are deployed the nodes which are attached with the GPS are aware of their locations. These nodes are called anchor nodes or beacon nodes or landmarks. By using the locations of the anchor nodes, unknown nodes estimate their location by using the Localization algorithms.

In recent years, a number of algorithms were proposed for the localization of sensor nodes, especially in applications involving monitoring, tracking and geographic routing. All these WSN localization algorithms share a common feature that they estimate the locations of sensor nodes with initially unknown positions using the a-priori knowledge of the absolute positions of a section of nodes (beacons or anchors). Thus WSN localization is a two phase process. In the first phase known as the ranging phase, the algorithms determine the distance between the node and the neighbouring beacons. In the second phase the position estimation of the nodes is carried out using the ranging information. The range can be determined using received signal strength (RSS), Angle of arrival (AOA) or any of the time based techniques like Time of arrival (TOA), Time difference of arrival (TDOA) or Round trip time (RTT). Whatever be the ranging method, there will be a measurement error in practical localization systems that result in noisy range estimations. Thus the accuracy in the position estimation phase is highly sensitive to the imprecise range measurements. The position estimation of the sensor nodes can be done either by using a geometric approach that gives exact solutions to a set of simultaneous nonlinear equations [1-2] or by using an optimization approach that minimizes the error in locating the coordinates of the nodes [3-5].

This paper uses swarm intelligence algorithms like Particle Swarm Optimization(PSO) algorithm and Artificial Bee Colony(ABC) algorithm for the localization problem and compares the performance of both. We also present a multistage localization method and compare the performance of single stage localization and multi stage localization.

The rest of the paper is organized as follows: section 2 briefs related work; section 3 presents the localization problem definition and proposed approach based on PSO and ABC algorithm; section 4 describes the experimental results; section 5 concludes the paper.

2   Related Work

Generally, it is assumed that there are number of anchor nodes in the sensor network. The locations of anchor nodes are known and they are used to fix the local coordinate system. However due to constraints on cost and complexity, most sensor nodes have unknown locations, which are to be estimated with respect to a set of anchor nodes with known location information.

Many researchers have approached the localization problem from different perspectives. Here we discuss some localization methods.

2.1   Distance Measurement

Distance measurements may be obtained by measuring signal propagation time or received signal strength (RSS) information.

Different ways of obtaining signal propagation time include time of arrival (ToA), round trip time of flight (RToF) or time difference of arrival (TDoA) of a signal [6]. Some of these propagation time based measurements require very accurate synchronization between the transmitter and the receiver. Furthermore, due to the high propagation speed of wireless signals, a small error in propagation time measurements may cause a large error in the distance measurements.

Since most of the mobile units in the market already have RSS indicator built in them, RSS method looks attractive for range measurements. But the accuracy of this method can be very much influenced by multi-path, fading, non-line of sight (NLoS) conditions and other sources of interference.

2.2   Coordinate Estimation

In the literature, different approaches are considered for coordinate estimation of the sensor nodes. The main aim of these methods is to estimate the coordinates of the sensor nodes with minimum error.

Niculescu et al. [7] proposed a distributed, hop by hop localization method. It uses a similar principle as that of GPS. Unlike in GPS, not all sensor nodes will have direct communication with anchors in a sensor network. They can only communicate with their one hop neighbors which are within their transmission range. Long-distance transmission is achieved by hop-by-hop propagation. Each non-anchor node maintains an anchor information table and exchanges updates only with its neighbors. Once all the anchors have received the distance of the other anchors measured in number of hops, they estimate the average distance for one hop. This information is broadcasted by the anchors as a correction factor to the entire network in hop-by-hop fashion. On receiving the correction factor, a non-anchor node may estimate distances to anchor nodes and perform trilateration to get its estimated coordinate. It is a simplest and distributed algorithm. In this algorithm error propagation is there and it depends on the location of the anchor nodes.

Savvides et al. [8] extended the single hop technique of GPS to multi-hop operation as in [7] thus waiving the line of sight requirement with anchors.

Non-anchor nodes collaborate and share information with one another over multiple hops to collectively estimate their locations. To prevent error accumulation in the network, they used least squares estimation with a Kalman filter to estimate locations of all non-anchor nodes simultaneously. To avoid converging at local minima, they used a geometrical relationship to obtain an initial estimate that is close to the final estimate. This algorithm is based on the assumptions that the distance measurements between the nodes and their neighbors are accurate.

In [9], a network containing powerful nodes with established location information is considered. In this work, anchors beacon their position to neighbors that keep an account of all received beacons. Using this proximity information, a simple centroid model is applied to estimate the listening nodes location.

In [10], Mayuresh et al. provide a Three Master method for localization. In this method, one of the beacon nodes transmits the localization packet. This packet contains transmitted power, its ID and its location. This packet is received by other beacon nodes and neighboring unlocalized nodes in the network. The other two beacon nodes do not transmit at same time as the first anchor node. They back-off by random time interval and transmit the localization packet. Some nodes in the neighborhood of beacons will receive the packet from all the three beacons. These nodes now can calculate their distances from beacons by measuring the received signal strength. Then these nodes will calculate their location using circular triangulation. These nodes can work as beacon nodes for the next iteration. Now the newly localized nodes will back-off by a random time and the one whose back-off period expires first will start the next iteration by transmitting a localization packet. To localize every node, it should have at least three anchor nodes within their transmission region and initially this algorithm needs three beacon nodes.

Doherty et al. [11] approached the problem using convex optimization based on semi-definite programming. The connectivity of the network was represented as a set of convex localizing constraints for the optimization problem. Pratik et al. [4] extended this technique by taking the non convex inequality constraints and relaxed the problem to a semi-definite program. Tzu-Chen Liang improved Pratik's method further by using a gradient-based local search method [12]. All these semi-definite programming methods require rigorous centralized computation.

3   Proposed Approach

Here we use swarm intelligence algorithms like Artificial Bee Colony algorithm and Particle Swarm Optimization algorithm for solving the localization problem in sensor network. The term swarm is used in a general manner to refer to any restrained collection of interacting agents or individuals. Also we propose multi stage localization and compared the multistage localization performance with that of single stage localization.

3.1 Problem Statement

The objective of WSN localization in a network of total m sensor nodes is to estimate the coordinates of n nodes using the a-priori information about the location of $m - n$ anchor nodes. Thus for a 2D localization problem, a total of $2n$ unknown coordinates, $\theta = [\theta_x, \theta_y]$, where $\theta_x = [x_1, x_2, x_3, ..., x_n]$ and $\theta_y = [y_1, y_2, y_3, ..., y_n]$ are to be estimated using the anchor node coordinates $[x_{n+1}, ..., x_m]$ and $[y_{n+1}, ..., y_m]$.

The position estimation of the coordinates of the nodes can be formulated as an optimization problem, involving the minimization of an objective function representing the error in locating the nodes. The sum of squared range errors between the nodes and neighboring anchor nodes can be considered as the objective function for this problem. The errors originate from the inaccuracies in the underlying range measurement techniques.

Let (x, y) be the coordinates of the node to be determined and d_i be the distance between the node and the ith anchor node.

$$d_i = \sqrt{(x - x_i)^2 + (y - y_i)^2} \tag{1}$$

Let $\widehat{d_i}$ be the value of d_i obtained from the noisy range measurements. The objective function for the localization problem can be framed as

$$f(x, y) = \frac{1}{M} \sum_{i=1}^{M} (d_i - \widehat{d_i}) \tag{2}$$

where,

$M \geq 3$ is the number of anchor nodes within the transmission range of the target node

(x, y) are the coordinates of the node to be estimated.

(x_i, y_i) are the coordinates of the ith anchor node.

3.2 Particle Swarm Optimization (PSO) Algorithm

Particle Swarm Optimization is an evolutionary computation technique developed by Kennedy et al. [13] in 1995. It belongs to the class of stochastic global optimization algorithms, which simulates the social behavior of bird flocking. The PSO algorithm is easy to implement and also computationally efficient.

The PSO technique employs a set of feasible solutions called particle's that are populated in the search space with random initial locations. The values of the objective function corresponding to the particle locations are evaluated. Then the particles are moved in the search space obeying rules inspired by bird flocking behavior [14-15]. Each particle is moved towards randomly weighted average of the best position that the particle has come across so far (*pbest*) and the best position encountered by the entire particle population (*gbest*).

Let $x_i = (x_{i1}, x_{i2}, ..., x_{iN})$ be the N dimensional vector representing the position of the ith particle in the swarm, $gbest = [g_1, g_2, ..., g_N]$ be the position vector of the best particle in the swarm (i.e., the particle with the smallest objective function value), $Pbest_i = [p_{i1}, p_{i2}, ..., p_{iN}]$ be the vector of the ith particles best and $v_i = [v_{i1}, v_{i2}, ..., v_{iN}]$ be the velocity of the ith particle. The particles evolve according to the equations

$$v_{id} = \omega v_{id} + c_1 r_1 (p_{id} - x_{id}) + c_2 r_2 (g_d - x_{id}) \qquad (3)$$

$$x_{id} = x_{id} + v_{id} \qquad (4)$$

where $d = 1, 2, ..., N; i = 1, 2, ..., K$; and K is the size of the swarm population. ω is the inertial weight, c_1 and c_2 are termed as cognitive and social scaling parameters respectively. r_1 and r_2 represent uniform random numbers in the interval [0,1]. The inertia factor determines the confidence of a particle in its own movement unaffected by pbest, and gbest. c_1 determines how much a particle is influenced by the memory of its best solution whereas c_2 is an indication of the impact of rest of the swarm on the particle.

The parameters ω, c_1 and c_2, have a critical role in the convergence characteristics of PSO. The coefficient ω should be neither too small, which results in an early convergence, nor too large, which on the contrary slows down the convergence process. A value of $\omega = 0.7$ and $c_1 = c_2 = 1.494$ were recommended for faster convergence by [16-17] after experimental tests.

3.3   PSO Based WSN Localization

We are using the concept of the Particle Swarm Optimization to the sensor node localization in wireless sensor networks as given in Algorithm 1.

For each unknown node, all these steps are executed. Each particle represents a solution i.e. each particle is a location of an unknown node.

Algorithm 1. Particle Swarm Optimization based WSN Localization

---

1: Selection of initial configuration
   The centroid of the anchor nodes within the transmission range of the node is a good initial estimate of the solution. The value of gbest is initialized with the position of the centroid.

$$(x_c, y_c) = \left(\frac{1}{M} \sum_{i=1}^{M} x_i, \frac{1}{M} \sum_{i=1}^{M} y_i \right)$$

2: The group of K particles is initialized with the random positions using polar coordinates, with the centroid as the origin. The $pbest_i$ is initialized with this value of particle positions. Also the initial velocity of all particles is set to zero.
3: For each particle, evaluate the objective function using Eqn. (2). If i^{th} particle's current objective function value is better than that of $pbest_i$, update $pbest_i$ with the current location of the particle.
4: Update gbest with the particle with best objective function value in the particle population.
5: For each particle, update the velocity and position according to the Eqns. (3) and (4) respectively.
6: Repeat 3-5 till either the threshold values of objective function or the maximum number of iterations are achieved.

3.4 Artificial Bee Colony (ABC) Algorithm

Artificial bee colony (ABC) algorithm is an optimization algorithm based on a particular intelligent behavior of honeybee swarms. Karaboga et al. [18] has proposed a bee swarm algorithm called artificial bee colony (ABC) algorithm.

In ABC algorithm [18], the colony of artificial bees consists of three groups of bees: employed bees, onlookers and scouts. First half of the colony consists of the employed artificial bees and the second half includes the onlookers. For every food source, there is only one employed bee. The employed bee whose food source has been abandoned becomes a scout.

In ABC algorithm, the position of a food source represents a possible solution to the optimization problem and the nectar amount of a food source corresponds to the quality (fitness) of the associated solution. The number of the employed bees or the onlooker bees are equal to the number of solutions in the population. At the first step, the ABC generates a randomly distributed initial population of SN solutions (food source positions), where SN denotes the size of population. Each solution x_i ($i = 1, 2, \ldots, SN$) is a D-dimensional vector. Here, D is the number of optimization parameters. After initialization, the population of the positions (solutions) is subjected to repeated cycles, $C = 1, 2, \ldots, MCN$, of the search processes of the employed bees, the onlooker bees and scout bees. An employed bee produces a modification on the position (solution) in its memory depending on the local information (visual information) and tests the nectar amount (fitness value) of the new source (new solution). Provided that the nectar amount of the new one is higher than that of the previous one, the bee memorizes the new position and forgets the old one. Otherwise it keeps the position of the previous one in its memory. After all employed bees complete the search process; they share the nectar information of the food sources and their position information with the onlooker bees on the dance area. An onlooker bee evaluates the nectar information taken from all employed bees and chooses a food source with a probability related to its nectar amount. As in the case of the employed bee, it produces a modification on the position in its memory and checks the nectar amount of the candidate source. An artificial onlooker bee chooses a food source depending on the probability value associated with that food source p_i calculated by the following expression

$$p_i = \frac{fit_i}{\sum_{n=1}^{sn} fit_n} \tag{5}$$

where fit_i is the fitness value of the solution i which is proportional to the nectar amount of the food source in the position i and SN is the number of food sources which is equal to the number of employed bees (BN).

In order to produce a candidate food position from the old one in memory, the ABC uses the following expression

$$v_{ij} = x_{ij} + \phi_{ij}(x_{ij} - x_{kj}) \tag{6}$$

Where $k = 1, 2, \ldots, SN$ and $j = 1, 2, \ldots, D$ are randomly chosen indexes. Although k is determined randomly, it has to be different from i. ϕ_{ij} is a random number between [-1, 1].

The food source of which the nectar is abandoned by the bees is replaced with a new food source by the scouts. In ABC, this is simulated by producing a position randomly and replacing it with the abandoned one. In ABC, if a position cannot be improved further through a predetermined number of cycles, then that food source is assumed to be abandoned. The value of predetermined number of cycles is an important control parameter of the ABC algorithm, which is called *limit* for abandonment. Assume that the abandoned source is x_i and $j = 1, 2, \ldots, D$, then the scout discovers a new food source to be replaced with x_i. This operation can be defined as follows

$$x_i^j = x_{min}^j + rand(0, 1)(x_{max}^j - x_{min}^j) \qquad (7)$$

A greedy selection mechanism is employed as the selection operation between the old and the candidate one.

3.5 ABC Based WSN Localization

Our implementation of the ABC method for WSN localization is described in Algorithm 2. For each node, all these steps are executed. Each food source represents a solution i.e. each food source is a location of the unknown node.

Algorithm 2. ABC based WSN Localization

1: Initialize the population of food sources associated with the employed bee x_{ij}, $i = 1, 2, \ldots, SN$, $j = 1, 2, \ldots, D$
2: Evaluate the population using Eqn. (2)
3: Produce candidate food source v_{ij} for the employed bees by using Eqn. (6) and evaluate them using Eqn. (2)
4: Apply the greedy selection process
5: Calculate the probability values p_{ij} for the solutions x_{ij} by Eqn. (5)
6: Produce the candidate food sources v_{ij} for the onlookers from the solutions x_{ij} selected depending on p_{ij} and evaluate them using Eqn. (2)
7: Apply the greedy selection process
8: Determine the abandoned food source for the scout, if exists, and replace it with a new randomly produced solution x_{ij} by Eqn. (7)
9: Memorize the best solution achieved so far
10: Repeat 3-9 until number of cycles is equal to MCN

3.6 Multi Stage Localization

Till now we discussed single stage localization i.e. all unknown nodes are localized in a single phase. In a single stage localization, unknown nodes which are having more number of neighbor anchor nodes will get good position estimates than the unknown nodes which are having less number of neighbor anchor nodes. If some unknown nodes does not have at least one neighboring beacon node, is unable to find its location. So in single stage localization the mean square error is more. To reduce the mean square error and improve the quality of solution, we propose a multi stage localization algorithm.

In multi stage localization, localization is done in multiple stages. We put a limit on the unknown nodes to be localized. We define anchor limit i.e. the number of neighboring anchor nodes of an unknown node. The nodes which are having the required number of neighboring anchor nodes are allowed to localize in the first stages. The nodes which are localized in the first stage become the anchor nodes for the second stage. In this way we will repeat the localization process until all the unknown nodes are localized.

The multi stage localization algorithm is given in Algorithm 3.

Algorithm 3. Multi Stage Localization

1: Initialize required neighboring beacon limit.
2: Find the unknown nodes which satisfy the required neighboring beacon limit.
3: Allow these unknown nodes to carry out localization process.
4: Run one of the localization algorithms i.e. ABC, PSO, etc to find the locations of the unknown nodes that satisfy the required neighboring beacon limit.
5: Add the localized nodes in this stage to the anchor node list and remove those from the unknown nodes list.
6: Repeat step 3-5 until all unknown nodes are localized.

---

4   Experimental Results

In this work, we implemented Particle Swarm Optimization algorithm and Artificial Bee Colony algorithm for the localization in wireless sensor networks.

We compared these two algorithms for different percentage of anchor nodes and transmission ranges. We observe that the localization error is not decreasing significantly with increase in percentage of anchor nodes but the error decreases significantly with increase in transmission range.

We also carried out the multi stage localization algorithm. Compared to the single stage localization, multi stage localization is giving better results at the cost of high computational overhead.

Table 1 shows the localization error observed for 1000 nodes with varying transmission range and beacon/ anchor node density. The anchor node density is chosen in a very small range of 2.5 to 10% of total nodes for Particle Swarm Optimization algorithm, Artificial Bee Colony algorithm and multi stage localization. In all the experimental cases, it is found that PSO algorithm is performing better than ABC both in case of single stage and multi-stage.

Table 1. Localization error for the different algorithms of various transmission ranges and % of beacon nodes

Algorithm name	Total number of nodes	% of Beacon nodes	Transmission Range	Grid Size	Localization Error
PSO	1000	2.5	20	100 * 100	28.1495
PSO	1000	5	20	100 * 100	27.273
PSO	1000	7.5	20	100 * 100	26.156
PSO	1000	10	20	100 * 100	25.2738
Multi Stage PSO	1000	2.5	20	100 * 100	27.6674
Multi Stage PSO	1000	5	20	100 * 100	27.0734
Multi Stage PSO	1000	7.5	20	100 * 100	26.0359
Multi Stage PSO	1000	10	20	100 * 100	25.0356
ABC	1000	2.5	20	100 * 100	45.128
ABC	1000	5	20	100 * 100	43.3864
ABC	1000	7.5	20	100 * 100	40.9254
ABC	1000	10	20	100 * 100	40.0794
Multi Stage ABC	1000	2.5	20	100 * 100	40.0384
Multi Stage ABC	1000	5	20	100 * 100	38.0384
Multi Stage ABC	1000	7.5	20	100 * 100	36.3748
Multi Stage ABC	1000	10	20	100 * 100	34.1936
PSO	1000	2.5	35	100 * 100	27.3207
PSO	1000	5	35	100 * 100	26.089
PSO	1000	7.5	35	100 * 100	25.1697
PSO	1000	10	35	100 * 100	24.763
Multi Stage PSO	1000	2.5	35	100 * 100	27.1672
Multi Stage PSO	1000	5	35	100 * 100	25.9365
Multi Stage PSO	1000	7.5	35	100 * 100	25.005
Multi Stage PSO	1000	10	35	100 * 100	24.5732
ABC	1000	2.5	35	100 * 100	43.9904
ABC	1000	5	35	100 * 100	41.7596
ABC	1000	7.5	35	100 * 100	40.2794
ABC	1000	10	35	100 * 100	38.4621
Multi Stage ABC	1000	2.5	35	100 * 100	39.2738
Multi Stage ABC	1000	5	35	100 * 100	35.2389
Multi Stage ABC	1000	7.5	35	100 * 100	33.2738
Multi Stage ABC	1000	10	35	100 * 100	30.283
PSO	1000	2.5	50	100 * 100	26.537
PSO	1000	5	50	100 * 100	25.5347
PSO	1000	7.5	50	100 * 100	24.8105
PSO	1000	10	50	100 * 100	24.4852
Multi Stage PSO	1000	2.5	50	100 * 100	25.8936
Multi Stage PSO	1000	5	50	100 * 100	25.3829
Multi Stage PSO	1000	7.5	50	100 * 100	24.673
Multi Stage PSO	1000	10	50	100 * 100	24.1093
ABC	1000	2.5	50	100 * 100	41.534
ABC	1000	5	50	100 * 100	40.1783
ABC	1000	7.5	50	100 * 100	38.2894
ABC	1000	10	50	100 * 100	36.9728
Multi Stage ABC	1000	2.5	50	100 * 100	35.9282
Multi Stage ABC	1000	5	50	100 * 100	33.229
Multi Stage ABC	1000	7.5	50	100 * 100	32.0374
Multi Stage ABC	1000	10	50	100 * 100	30.0283

5   Conclusions

This paper mainly concentrated on developing swarm intelligence based localization algorithm that gives the best location estimates for unknown nodes with less number of anchor nodes. We used two popular swarm intelligence algorithms namely Particle Swarm optimization and Artificial Bee Colony algorithm for localization in wireless sensor networks. We compared the performance of Particle

Swarm Optimization and Artificial Bee Colony algorithm. Among these two algorithms, Particle Swarm Optimization is showing better performance in terms of localization error compared to Artificial Bee Colony algorithm.

We also proposed multi stage localization and compared the performance of single stage localization with that of multi stage localization to observe that multi stage localization gives better results than single stage localization.

References

1. Yu, K., Oppermannr, I.: Performance of UWB position estimation based on TOA measurements. In: Proc. Joint UWBST and IWUWBS, Kyoto, Japan, pp. 400–404 (2004)
2. Chan, Y.T., Ho, K.C.: A Simple and Efficient Estimator for Hyperbolic Location. IEEE Transactions on Signal Processing 42(8), 1905–1915 (1994)
3. Doherty, L., Pister, K., El Ghaoui, L.: Convex Position estimation in wireless sensor networks. In: IEEE INFOCOM, vol. 3, pp. 1655–1663 (2001)
4. Biswas, P., Ye, Y.: Semidefinite programming for ad hoc wireless sensor network localization. In: Third International Symposium on Information Processing in Sensor Networks, pp. 46–54 (2004)
5. Kannan, A.A., Mao, G., Vucetic, B.: Simulated annealing based wireless sensor network localization. Journal of Computers (2), 15–22 (2006)
6. Vossick, M., Wiebking, L., Gulden, P., Wieghardt, J., Hoffmann, C., Heide, P.: Wireless local positioning. IEEE Microwave Magazine 4(4), 77–86 (2003)
7. Niculescu, D., Nath, B.: Ad hoc positioning system (aps). In: IEEE GLOBECOM 2001, vol. 5, pp. 2926–2931 (2001)
8. Savvides, A., Park, H., Srivastava, M.B.: The bits and flops of the n-hop multilateration primitive for node localization problems. In: International Workshop on Sensor Networks Application, pp. 112–121 (2002)
9. Bulusu, N., Heidemann, J., Estrin, D.: GPS-less Low Cost Outdoor Localization for Very Small Devices. IEEE Personal Communications Magazine 7(5), 28–34 (2000)
10. Patil, M.M., Shaha, U., Desai, U.B., Merchant, S.N.: Localization in Wireless Sensor Networks using Three Masters. In: ICPWC 2005, pp. 384–388 (2005)
11. Doherty, L., Pister, K., Ghaoui, L.E.: Convex position estimation in wireless sensor networks. In: IEEE INFOCOM 2001, vol. 3, pp. 1655–1663 (2001)
12. Liang, T.C., Wang, T.C., Ye, Y.: A gradient search method to round the semi definite programming relaxation solution for ad hoc wireless sensor network localization. Stanford University, formal report 5 (2004),
http://www.stanford.edu/yyye/formalreport5.pdf
13. Kennedy, J., Eberhart, R.C.: Particle Swarm Optimization. In: Proceedings of IEEE International Conference on Neural Networks, Piscataway, NJ, pp. 1942–1948 (1995)
14. Noel, M.M., Joshi, P.P., Jannett, T.C.: Improved Maximum Likelihood Estimation of Target Position in Wireless Sensor Networks using Particle Swarm Optimization. In: Third International Conference on Information Technology: New Generations, ITNG 2006, pp. 274–279 (2006)
15. Chen, Y., Dubey, V.K.: Ultra wideband source localization using a particle-swarm-optimized Capon estimator. In: IEEE International Conference on Communications, vol. 4, pp. 2825–2829 (2005)

16. Eberhart, R.C., Shi, Y.: Particle swarm optimization: developments, applications and resources. In: Proceedings of the IEEE Congress on Evolutionary Computation (CEC 2001), pp. 81–86 (2001)
17. Eberhart, R.C., Shi, Y.: Tracking and optimizing dynamic systems with particle swarms. In: Proceedings of the IEEE Congress on Evolutionary Computation (CEC 2001), pp. 94–97 (2001)
18. Karaboga, D., Basturk, B.: Artificial Bee Colony (ABC) Optimization Algorithm for Solving Constrained Optimization Problems. In: Melin, P., Castillo, O., Aguilar, L.T., Kacprzyk, J., Pedrycz, W. (eds.) IFSA 2007. LNCS (LNAI), vol. 4529, pp. 789–798. Springer, Heidelberg (2007)

Local and Global Intrinsic Dimensionality Estimation for Better Chemical Space Representation

Mohammed Hussein Shukur, T. Sobha Rani, S. Durga Bhavani,
G. Narahari Sastry, and Surampudi Bapi Raju

m.kurd@hotmail.com,
{tsrcs,sdbcs,bapics}@uohyd.ernet.in,
gnsastry@gmail.com

Abstract. In this paper, local and global intrinsic dimensionality estimation methods are reviewed. The aim of this paper is to illustrate the capacity of these methods in generating a lower dimensional chemical space with minimum information error. We experimented with five estimation techniques, comprising both local and global estimation methods. Extensive experiments reveal that it is possible to represent chemical compound datasets in three dimensional space. Further, we verified this result by selecting representative molecules and projecting them to 3D space using principal component analysis. Our results demonstrate that the resultant 3D projection preserves spatial relationships among the molecules. The methodology has potential implications for chemoinformatics issues such as diversity, coverage, lead compound selection, etc.

Keywords: Chemoinformatics Chemical Spaces, Bioinformatics, Intrinsic Dimensionality Estimation, Dimensionality Reduction.

1 Introduction

Chemical space is often characterized to be a high dimensional space due to huge number of molecule descriptors [10][11] where each molecular descriptor is considered as a dimension. The high dimensional space suffers from being too complex for conducting meaningful and inter-operable analyses. Critical chemoinformatics applications such as designing targeted lead compounds, generation of diverse library, and drug discovery require manageable space to accomplish the tasks with less effort, time and high accuracy.

Transforming chemical data in high-dimensional space to a space of fewer dimensions has always been problematic with respect to preserving intrinsic local and global features of the original space [1] [4]. Main challenge is to reduce the descriptor space significantly but at the same time retain the features of chemical space such as diversity, coverage, etc.

Ideally, the reduced representation has a dimensionality that corresponds to the intrinsic dimensionality of the data. The intrinsic dimensionality of data has the minimum number of parameters required to account for the observed properties of the

C. Sombattheera et al. (Eds.): MIWAI 2011, LNAI 7080, pp. 329–338, 2011.
© Springer-Verlag Berlin Heidelberg 2011

data [5]. These parameters should preserve both the local and global features of the high dimensionality space in lower dimensional representative space. In this paper we consider three-dimensional space to be an appropriate lower dimensional representative space. The reason for considering three-dimensional space is because it is convenient for visualization as compared to more high dimensions and further it is possible to represent more depth than two-dimensional space. Thus the choice of 3D as an appropriate space stems from pragmatic reasons. In recent years, a large number of new techniques for estimation of local and global intrinsic dimensionality have been proposed.

The outline of the remainder of this paper is as follows. Section 2 describes simplification of chemical space; Section 3 reviews intrinsic dimensionality estimation techniques; Section 4 describes datasets; Section 5 details experiments performed; Section 6 discusses representation of molecules in lower dimensional subspace, and finally in Section 7 conclusions are included.

2   Simplification of Chemical Space

The topic of reduction of chemical space to manageable size has not been investigated much in the literature. We give a brief glance of one approach that had been influential, that of BCUT approach [2, 9]. This approach attempts at designing low dimensional reference space and simplify the high dimensional space to two-dimensional or three-dimensional spaces with a loss of some information but enables visualization. The visualization of low dimensional space allows a more intuitive analysis and design. This most common technique BCUT, is devised by Pearlman and Smith [9] as an extended version of the original proposal (Burden-CAS-University of Texas) [2]. The method finds the two lowest eigenvalues of a matrix composed of uncorrelated molecular descriptors. As a result, the original molecular descriptors could be projected usually to a six-dimensional space. The downside of this approach is that the new reduced dimensions are not directly related to the original dimensions because of the eigenmatrix transformation. In the following we take a different approach. We first find out if 3D subspace could be a viable intrinsic dimension of the chemical descriptor space using intrinsic dimensionality estimation techniques. Then we use a standard dimensionality reduction technique such as principal component analysis to demonstrate that the spatial arrangement of chemical compounds is indeed preserved after projection to a lower dimensional subspace.

3   Techniques for Intrinsic Dimensionality Estimation

The intrinsic dimensionality is the number of appropriate local or global features needed for representing dataset in lower dimensional space. We discuss five techniques for intrinsic dimensionality estimation used in this paper.   For convenience, the dataset is denoted by X, intrinsic dimensionality by d, and its estimation by $\hat{d}$. There are two classes of intrinsic dimensionality estimation methods, one based on local properties analysis and the other by analysis of global properties. The description of the methods presented here is adapted from Maaten, 2007 [8].

3.1   Estimation of Local Properties

Local intrinsic dimensionality estimators are usually based on analysis of hypersphere that covers the data points and it is assumed to grow proportional to $r \times d$ where r is the radius and d is the intrinsic dimensionality. In the following we will describe three methods, namely, Correlation dimension, Nearest neighbor and Maximum likelihood estimation methods [8].

3.1.1 Correlation Dimension Estimator

The correlation dimension estimator uses relative amount of data points to initial state that lie within hypershper with radius r and is given by equation (1).

$$C(r) = \frac{2}{n(n-1)} \sum_{i=1}^{n} \sum_{j=i+1}^{n} c \quad \text{where } c = \begin{cases} 1, \text{if} \|x_i - x_j\| \leq r \\ 0, \text{if} \|x_i - x_j\| > r \end{cases} \tag{1}$$

As $C(r)$, the correlation dimension function is proportional to $r \times d$, by using the limit over r, we get the intrinsic dimensionality d as shown in equation (2).

$$d = \lim_{r \to 0} \frac{\log c(r)}{\log r} \tag{2}$$

While the limit in equation (2) cannot be solved, its value can be estimated by computing $C(r)$ for different values of r (usually two values are taken). Equation (3) shows the estimate of the intrinsic dimensionality as given by the following ratio:

$$\hat{d} = \frac{\log(C(r_2) - C(r_1))}{\log(r_2 - r_1)} \tag{3}$$

3.1.2 Nearest Neighbor Estimator

Nearest neighbor estimator is similar to correlation dimension estimator but it is based on analyzing the number of the neighboring data pints that are covered by a hypersphere of radius r. The minimum radius r of the hypersphere that is necessary to cover k nearest neighbors is computed instead of counting the number of the data points as in the correlation dimension estimation. Nearest neighbour estimator computes $C(k)$ as shown in equation (4).

$$C(k) = \frac{1}{n} \sum_{i} T_k(x_i) \tag{4}$$

where, $T_k(x_i)$ is the radius of the smallest hypersphere with centre x_i, which covers k neighboring data points. The final estimation of the intrinsic dimension is similar to what has been done in the case of correlation estimation using a ratio from two points as shown in equation (5).

$$\hat{d} = \frac{\log(C(K_2) - (C(K_1))}{\log(K_2 - K_1)} \tag{5}$$

3.1.3 Maximum Likelihood Estimator

Maximum likelihood estimator is similar to both the above techniques conceptually but the estimation procedure is different. In this method, the estimate is based on the number of data points covered by a hypersphere with a growing radius by modeling the number of data points inside the hypersphere as a *poisson* process [6]. The rate of the process $\lambda(t)$ at intrinsic dimensionality d is expressed by the following equation (6).

$$\lambda(t) = \frac{f(x)\pi^{d/2}dt^{d-1}}{\Gamma(\frac{d}{2+1})} \tag{6}$$

In equation (6), $f(x)$ represents density of sampling while $\Gamma(\bullet)$ is gamma function. With Poisson process, the maximum likelihood estimation of the intrinsic dimensionality d around data point x_i is given by k nearest neighbors as given in equation (7).

$$\hat{d}(x_i) = \left(\frac{1}{k-1} \sum_{j=1}^{k-1} \log\frac{T_k(x_i)}{T_j(x_i)}\right)^{-1} \tag{7}$$

In equation (7), $T_k(x_i)$ is the radius of the smallest hypersphere with centre x_i that covers k neighboring data points..

3.2   Estimation of Global Properties

As discussed in section 2.1, local methods derive their intrinsic dimensionality estimate from averaging over local data points. In contrast, global methods use the whole data for estimating the intrinsic dimensionality. In the following two such methods, namely, eigenvalue-based estimator and geodesic minimum spanning tree estimator are described [8].

3.2.1   Eigenvalue-Based Estimator
The eigenvalue-based intrinsic dimensionality estimator is based on principal component analysis (PCA) for original dataset and normalized datasets. As is well known, eigenvalues provide the amount of variance in the data. Using normalized data, the eigenvalues can be plotted to provide an estimate of the intrinsic dimensionality of the data by counting the number of the normalized eigenvalues that are higher than a small threshold value ε.

3.2.2   Geodesic Minimum Spanning Tree Estimator
The geodesic minimum spanning tree (GMST) estimator is based on minimum spanning tree length function, which is related to the intrinsic dimensionality d. In this procedure, a length function $L(X)$ is computed by summing the Euclidean distances corresponding to all edges in geodesic minimum spanning tree as shown in equation (8). A minimal graph over dataset X of geodesic minimum spanning tree is obtained where every data point x_i is connected to k nearest neighbors.

$$L(X) = \min_{T \in T} \sum_{e \in T} g_e \tag{8}$$

Where, T is the set of all sub-trees of graph G, e is an edge in tree T, and g_e is the Euclidean distance corresponding to the edge e. Subset A of various size m are constructed over the dataset X, *where* $A \subset X$, and the lengths $L(A)$ of the GMSTs of the subsets A are computed as shown in equation (8).

4   Data Set

The chemical datasets are collected from ZINC website [13]. 498,711 molecules are obtained after ensuring that there are no duplicates and also by deploying the Lipinski's Rules [7]. Molecular descriptors [10][11] are generated for each molecule by using CDK library. Data pre-processing on the molecular descriptors is accomplished by eliminating descriptors with more than 80% zero values. From pervious knowledge, it is known that highly correlated descriptors when used together, lead to dramatic distortion of the reference space because of over-representation and overlapping nature of the data. We eliminated correlated descriptors and selected only representatives from the set of correlated descriptors by using reverse nearest neighbor (RNN) clustering procedure [12]. We ended up with three different datasets, organized based on molecular descriptor categories, namely, 2D descriptors (59 numbers), 3D descriptors (48 numbers), and E-state descriptors (42 numbers). Each of the datasets had a size amounting to 498,711 molecules.

5   Experiments

Intrinsic dimensionality is an important concept in high dimensional datasets. If this can be estimated, dimensionality reduction can be accomplished without loss of information. It is also important in choosing a set of the descriptors that can reduce dimensions to lower dimensions by preserving local and global space features. At this stage we made several experiments by testing various datasets. Three datasets have been used in all the five experiments reported in here. Each dataset corresponds to one of the molecular descriptor category, 2D, 3D or E-State as mentioned in section 3. We conducted experiments starting with the original datasets and gradually removing some descriptors according to the nature of the values. The aim of these experiments has been to find appropriate descriptor set and datasets that give a mean estimation of the intrinsic dimension close to the value three over all the five techniques considered here.

5.1   Experiment 1: Estimating Using the Original Data

In this experiment, three different types of molecule descriptor datasets are used, each dataset containing 498,711 molecules with either 2D molecule descriptors (50 in number), or with 3D molecule descriptors (46 of them), or E-state molecule descriptors dataset with 24 descriptors. Each of these datasets is given as input to the five intrinsic dimensionality estimation methods. The results are shown in Table 1. As seen in the table, the mean dimensionality estimated for 2D dataset is 4.6, 3D dataset is 5.8 and E-state Dataset has 5.6. Clearly, the mean value for the intrinsic dimensionality estimated for the three datasets is well above the desired value of three. Obviously, if dimensionality reduction is forcibly applied on these datasets and data were to be reduced to three dimensions, it is expected that the lower space will suffer from missing local and the global features. Hence we experimented with removing certain redundant features from the feature set describing the molecules. Four such experiments have been conducted and they are described in sequence below.

Table 1. Result of Experiment 1: Estimation from the Original Data

	Dataset		
	2D	3D	Estate
Estimation Techniques / Dimension	50	46	24
Maximum likelihood	8.5	9.7	8.8
Correlation dimension	2.55	2.7	4.9
Nearest Neighbor	0.156	0.11	0.12
Eigenvalue-based	5	2	5
Geodesic minimum spanning tree	7	14.4	9.5
Mean No. of Dimensions	4.6	5.8	5.6

5.2 Experiment 2: Estimation from the Original Data without Negative Valued Descriptors

In this experiment, the same three different types of Molecule descriptor datasets are used as in the first experiment, except that now descriptors with negative values are removed. As seen in Table 2, mean dimensionality accomplished for 2D dataset is 5.0, 3D dataset is 9.3 and E-state Dataset has 4.6. Results from 2D and 3D datasets show that the intrinsic dimensionality estimate has gone up in this experiment. Thus, eliminating features with negative values does not seem to be sufficient. Hence we experimented next with eliminating features that have high variability.

Table 2. Result of Experiment 2: Estimation Original Data without negative Valued Descriptors

	Dataset		
	2D	3D	Estate
Estimation Techniques / Dimension	50	25	33
Maximum likelihood	8.5	9.7	7.2
Correlation dimension	2.5	2.7	4.2
Nearest Neighbor	0.13	0.11	0.14
Eigenvalue-based	5	2	4
Geodesic minimum spanning tree	9.8	31.4	7.5
Mean No. of Dimensions	5.0	9.3	4.6

5.3 Experiment 3: Original Data without Descriptors Has MAX Standard Deviation Estimation

In this experiment, the same three types of molecule descriptor datasets are used as in the first experiment, however now the descriptors with maximum standard deviation are removed. The idea behind this procedure is that descriptors with large variation in values do not facilitate representation of molecules in a lower dimensional subspace. As seen in Table 3, mean dimensionality estimated for 2D dataset is 4.8, 3D dataset is 5.0 and E-state Dataset has 6.03. These datasets yield estimates higher than the desired value of three.

Table 3. Result of Experiment 3: Estimation using Original Data without descriptors possessing maximum standard deviation

	Dataset		
	2D	3D	Estate
Estimation Techniques / Dimension	50	25	33
Maximum likelihood	7.3	9.7	8.7
Correlation dimension	2.0	2.7	4.6
Nearest Neighbor	0.16	0.11	0.12
Eigenvalue-based	3	2	6
Geodesic minimum spanning tree	11	10.6	10.7
Mean No. of Dimensions	4.8	5	6.03

5.4   Experiment 4: Estimation after Scale Normalization of Original Data

In this experiment, mainly two datasets are used, namely, 2D-A containing 50 uncorrelated 2D molecular descriptors, while 2D-B contains 122 uncorrelated and correlated 2D molecular descriptors. To ensure that all the descriptors have comparable range of values, scale normalization (to a range of [0,1]) is done on both the datasets. Experiments are conducted both on the un-normalized as well as normalized datasets. As seen in Table 5, mean dimensionality estimated for normalized datasets is higher than for original datasets. Although the difference in estimated dimensionality for 2D-A and 2D-B is less, overall the dimensionality is still far from the desirable value of three. In the following experiment, we tried to combine two of the above approaches that yielded in a successful result.

Table 4. Result of Experiment 4: Estimation Original Data and normalized dataset

	Dataset			
	2D-A	Normalized 2D-A	2D-B	Normalized 2D-B
Estimation Techniques / Dimension	59	59	122	122
Maximum likelihood	8.5	11.4	7.6	11.1
Correlation dimension	2.55	3.5	2.8	3
Nearest Neighbor	0.156	0.09	0.149	0.9
Eigenvalue-based	5	11	6	7
Geodesic minimum spanning tree	7	9.3	8.9	8
Mean No. of Dimensions	4.6	7.09	5.1	5.8

5.5   Experiment 5: Estimation Using Original Data without Negative-Valued Descriptors or Having Maximum Standard Deviation

In this experiment, three different types of molecule descriptor datasets are used as in the first experiment. However, in this case, descriptors that have negative values or having maximum standard deviation are both removed, combining the approaches of experiments 2 and 3. As seen in Table 4, mean dimensionality estimated for 2D dataset is 3.37, 3D dataset is 3.9 and E-state Dataset has 3.9. These datasets show nearest estimation to the desired value compared to all the previous experiments. Dimensionality reduction techniques are expected now to produce lower dimensional representation with minimum error with these datasets.

Table 5. Result of Experiment 5: Estimation Original Data without negative or maximum standard deviation valued Descriptors

	Dataset		
	2D	3D	Estate
Estimation Techniques / Dimension	41	40	24
Maximum likelihood	7.4	7.8	6.9
Correlation dimension	2.1	2.7	4.1
Nearest Neighbor	0.16	0.11	0.15
Eigenvalue-based	3	2	3
Geodesic minimum spanning tree	4	7	5.2
Mean No. of Dimensions	3.37	3.9	3.9

6   Representation of Molecules in Lower Dimensional Subspace

The experiments in the previous sections establish that it is possible to represent chemical compounds that have high dimensional descriptor vectors in a lower dimensional subspace. In particular, the surprising result is that by appropriate elimination of descriptors, it is possible to represent the molecules in a three-dimensional subspace. The next question then is to actually project the molecules into a 3D space and see if the resulting projection can preserve local and global features of relationship among the molecules.

Principal Component Analysis (PCA) is one of the most well-known linear dimensionality reduction techniques [3][8]. PCA has been used here to construct a 3D representation of molecules. First of all, several samples are generated, each sample containing 100 active-seed molecules. These molecules are selected by structure based clustering algorithm to verify if the reduced space has maintained the same local and global features for these molecules as in the high dimensional space. As can be seen from Figures 1 A and B, the two views of the 3D space generated shows that local and global features of the high dimensional space are preserved. The molecules that are "red" in colour are all together, similarly those in "blue" and "cyan" also cluster together in the 3D projection. This clearly points out that the spatial relations of the molecular representatives chosen in the high dimensional space are also preserved in the lower dimensional subspace of three dimensions. Although this kind of projection of few representative molecules does not serve as complete validation of the approach, this gives a tremendous hope that such low dimensional representations could be constructed for chemical compounds.

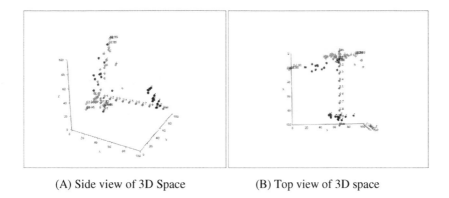

(A) Side view of 3D Space   (B) Top view of 3D space

Fig. 1.

7   Conclusion

This paper explores ways of estimating intrinsic dimensionality of high-dimensional descriptor representation of chemical compounds. High redundancy in the features leads to a potential representation of the compounds in lower dimensional subspace. We experimented with three local dimensionality estimation methods and two global estimation schemes. Local methods take into consideration local properties whereas global methods compute intrinsic dimensionality based on all the data items.

We conducted five experiments using several pre-processing steps applied on the datasets. About 400,000 compounds that are available publicly are used in the experiments. Our results point out that each of the 2D (about 50 descriptors), 3D (about 46 descriptors) or E-state (about 24 descriptors) features can potentially be reduced to three dimensions. Thus although the original descriptor space is very high, a huge reduction is possible. In order to verify this process, we have done extensive evaluation experiments by using active-seeded samples with principal component analysis. Our results verify that intrinsic dimensionality estimation helps to generate lower dimensional subspace representation that preserves various spatial relations enjoyed by the molecules in the higher dimensional representation. However, more robust validation techniques are required to demonstrate the complete usefulness of the proposed approach.

These results have potential implication for various critical chemoinformatic issues such as diversity, coverage, representative subset selection for lead compound identification, etc. Use of a lower dimensional representative space can speed up the virtual screening throughput of large chemical libraries. Virtual screening is a crucial step in drug discovery applications. The current proposal is suitable for integration into any cell-based approaches that are employed in design of targeted leads or diverse chemical subset selection applications in chemoinformatics.

References

[1] Brown, N.: Chemoinformatics – An Introduction for computer Scientists. ACM Computing Surveys 41(2), 8:1–8:36 (2009)

[2] Burden, F.R.: Molecular identification number for substructure searches. J. Chem. Inf. Comput. Sci. 29(3), 225–227 (1989)

[3] Burgess, C.J.C.: Dimension Reduction: A Guided Tour. Foundations and Trends in Machine Learning 2(4), 275–365 (2010)

[4] Consonni, V., Todeschini, R.: Challenges and Advances in Computational Chemistry and Physics (8), 29–102 (2010)

[5] Fukunaga, K.: Introduction to Statistical Pattern Recognition. Academic Press Professional, Inc., San Diego (1990)

[6] Levina, E., Bickel, P.J.: Maximum likelihood estimation of intrinsic dimension. In: Advances in Neural Information Processing Systems, vol. 17. The MIT Press, Cambridge (2004)

[7] Lipinski, C., Hopkins, A.: Chemical space and biology. Nature 432, 855–861 (2004)

[8] Maaten, L.: An Introduction to Dimensionality Reduction Using Matlab, Technical Report MICCIKAT 07-07 (2007)

[9] Pearlman, R.S., Smith, K.M.: Novel Software Tools for chemical Diversity. Perspectives in Drug Discovery and Design, 339–353 (1998)

[10] Todeschini, R., Consonni, V.: Handbook of Molecular Descriptors, vol. (1), pp. 20–100. Wiley-VCH, Weinheim (2002)

[11] Todeschini, R., Consonni, V.: Molecular Descriptors for Chemoinformatics, 2nd Revised and Enlarged edn., vol. (1)(2), pp. 39–77. Wiley-VCH (2009)

[12] Vadapalli, S., Valluri, S.R., Karlapalem, K.: A Simple Yet Effective Data Clustering Algorithm. In: Proceedings of the Sixth International Conference on Data Mining (ICDM 2006) (2006)

[13] ZINC Database, http://zinc.docking.org/

A Resilient Voting Scheme for Improving Secondary Structure Prediction

Chittaranjan Hota[1], Filippo Ledda[2], and Giuliano Armano[2]

[1] Dept. of Computer Science, BITS Pilani Hyderabad Campus, Hyderabad, India
[2] Dept. of Electronics & Computer Engineering, University of Cagliari, Italy
hota@bits-hyderabad.ac.in, {filippo,armano}@diee.unica.it

Abstract. This paper presents a novel approach called Resilient Voting Scheme (RVS), which combines different predictors (experts) with the goal of improving the overall accuracy. As combining multiple experts involves uncertainty and imprecise information, the proposed approach cancels out the impact of bad performers while computing a single collective prediction. RVS uses a genetic algorithm to assign a reliability to each expert, by using the Q3 measure as fitness function. A resilient voting is then used to improve the accuracy of the final prediction. RVS has been tested with well known datasets and has been compared with other state-of-the-art combination techniques (i.e., averaging and stacking). Experimental results demonstrate the validity of the approach.

Keywords: Artificial Neural Networks, Voting, Resilient Protocols, Protein Secondary Structure Prediction.

1 Introduction

The primary structure of a protein refers to its sequence of amino acids. Generally, the sequence contains hundreds of amino acids and different portions of this sequence fold into different shapes which are called secondary structure. There are three main classes of secondary structures, namely alpha-helices (H), which are spiral in shape, beta-sheets (E), which group together to form sheet-like conformations, whilst the rest are labelled as turns or coils (C). Fig. 1 shows an example of primary sequence and its corresponding secondary structure. The three dimensional (3-D) structure of a protein is related to its sequence of amino acids. Hence, it is possible to predict the structure of a protein from its sequence with high accuracy. The objective of Secondary Structure Prediction (SSP) is to extract maximum information from the primary sequence in the absence of a known 3-D structure or homologous sequence of known structures [19].

Let the primary sequence of a protein of length n be represented as a string (of the given length) in:

$$\{A, R, N, D, C, Q, E, G, H, I, L, K, M, F, P, S, T, W, Y, V\}$$

C. Sombattheera et al. (Eds.): MIWAI 2011, LNAI 7080, pp. 339–350, 2011.

where each letter denotes an amino acid residue (one-letter encoding). Let the secondary structure of the sequence having length n be represented as a string (of the given length) in:

$$\{H, E, C\}$$

Hence, for any target protein of length n, SSP tries to find a mapping as:

$$[A, R, N, D, C, Q, E, G, H, I, L, K, M, F, P, S, T, W, Y, V]^n \rightarrow [H, E, C]^n$$

While it is relatively inexpensive to sequence proteins, i.e., to find out the amino acid sequence they are made of, it is expensive to discover the way amino acids fold in 3-D space by using techniques like X-ray crystallography and Nuclear magnetic resonance [25]. Hence, over the past various years, several computational and statistical techniques have been developed to predict the tertiary structure from a sequence more accurately and effortlessly [17].

Predicting the secondary structure of a protein is often a preliminary step in the task of tertiary structure prediction. A wide variety of techniques like statistics [4], Artificial Neural Networks (ANNs) [8, 22, 23], Support Vector Machines [26], and Hidden Markov Models [3] have been adopted by researchers to improve the accuracy of SSP over time.

Primary Sequence:
KKVKVSHRSHSTEPGLVLTLGQGDVGQLGLGENVMERKKPALVSIPEDVVQAEAGGMHTV
CLSKSGQVYSFGCNDEGALGRDTSVEGSEMVPGKVELQEKVVQVSAGDSHTAALTDDGRV
FLWGSFRDNNGVIGLLEPMKKSMVPVQVQLDVPVVKVASGNDHLVMLTADGDLYTLGCG
EQGQLGRVPELFANRGGRQGLERLLVPKCVMLKSRGSRGHVRFQDAFCGAYFTFAISHEGH
VYGFGLSNYHQLGTPGTESCFIPQNLTSFKNSTKSWVGFSGGQHHTVCMDSEGKAYSLGRA
EYGRLGLGEGAEEKSIPTLISRLPAVSSVACGASVGYAVTKDGRVFAWGMGTNYQLGTGQ

Secondary Structure:
CCCCCCCCCCCCCCCEEEEEEEEECCCCCCCCCCCCCEEEEEEEEECCCCCEEEEEECCCCEEEEEE
CCCCEEEEECCCCCCCCCCCCCCCHHHCCEECCCCCCEEEEEECCCEEEEEECCCCEEEEEC
EEECCEEEECCEECECEEEEEEECCCCCEEEEEECCCEEEEEECCCCEEEEECCCCCCCCCCH
HHCCCCCHHHHHHHHHHCCEECCCECCCCCCECCEEEEEECCEEEEECCCCEEEEECCCC
CCCCCCCCCCEEEEEECHHHCCCCCCEEEEEECCCEEEEEECCCCEEEEECCHHHCCCCCCC
CCCEEEEEECCCCCCEEEEEECCCEEEEEECCCCEEEEECCCCCCCCCCCCCCEEEEEECCCC

Fig. 1. An example of mapping between a primary sequence and its secondary structure

We know that predictors based on multiple alignments allow to reach an accuracy of close to 80% (e.g., [21]), which makes them "good" predictors, whereas predictors that do not exploit multiple alignment never reach 70% of accuracy (e.g., [18]), which makes them "bad" predictors. To better assess the validity of the proposed combination method (RVS), we decided to perform experiments using some good predictors, together with bad predictors.

The rest of the paper is organized as follows. Section 2 discusses the related work done in combining classifier outputs, followed by the earlier developed [10] GAME generic architecture (Section 3), which has been used to implement the proposed RVS. Section 4 reports relevant techniques for combining classifiers, while Section 5 describes RVS. Section 6 summarizes experimental results and we conclude the paper in Section 7.

2   Related Work

Javid et al. [24] proposed a novel Secondary Structure Voting Scheme (SVSS) using Radial Basis Function ANNs to combine different votes suggested by different prediction techniques. Richard et al. [15] combined predictions of several separately trained neural networks whose errors are largely independent of each other. They used competitive learning to cluster the input patterns into subclasses of each category which is then recognized by a neural network having a hidden unit. Later they used backpropagation to refine this learning. These steps were repeated to create several networks that in combination generalize well. Jame et al. [5] proposed a consensus algorithm that combines predictions made by different techniques. For example, if four different predictors have predicted a single amino acid residue as H, H, E, and H, respectively, then the consensus prediction would be H. This consensus approach produced 1% improvement in average accuracy over the best single method. Ronnie et al. [7] proposed an approach to combine the output of multiple predictors based on their class-specific reliability rather than using an overall reliability measure. For example, how much correctly the classifier has predicted either alpha-helices, or beta-sheets, or coils instead of considering an average accuracy for all three classes.

The reliability of a predictor is modeled as prediction accuracy of that predictor using Evidential theory which is then mapped to a weight assigned to the predictor. Ahmed et al. [1] proposed a new combination technique based on Dempster-Shafer (DS) theory of evidence, which is based on adjusting the evidence of different predictors by minimizing the Mean Square Error (MSE) of training data, which resulted in improved overall performance and reduced error rate. Liu et al. [14] proposed a voting scheme to improve the prediction accuracy of a three state predictor (H,E,C). In place of combining the output from multiple predictors, the output of a single predictor is refined by assigning scores to each output state based on the probability of the classification technique, then ranking these scores by normalizing them, and finally computing a weight as an average of rank and score. Armano et al. [2] used multiple hybrid experts to perform prediction, each expert being composed by two parts: one that decides whether the expert is able to deal with the current input and the other involved in the actual prediction. Hsin-Nan et al. [12] combined the predictions of PROSP and PSIPRED using their confidence levels. Ken-Li et al. [13] proposed a combinatorial fusion technique to facilitate feature selection and combination for improving the accuracy.

3   GAME Generic Architecture

This section describes GAME [9, 10], the generic architecture used for implementing the proposed RVS. The choice of GAME depends on the fact that it supports rapid prototyping and testing of classifiers or predictors for real world problems, in particular SSP problems, from a multiple expert perspective. GAME is completely written in Java 6.0 with integrated development environment as NetBeans, and can be run in the most common operating systems, including all recent Windows and Linux versions. A module in GAME is a Java class in a specific package which implements a specific interface. The GUI used to generate configurations is implemented using the standard Java Swing lightweight library. Standard modules that are available to the developers in the GAME framework are shown in Fig. 2. Experiments are runnable modules which define a computation flow. A setting manager is responsible for setting data types, logging, caching dataset resource files. A module manager is responsible for system module handling. Fig. 3 shows the main interface, which can be used to configure and start experiments in the same session, alongwith multiple experts that can be configured for combination.

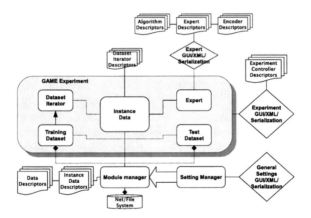

Fig. 2. Modules of GAME (a multiple sheet box represents alternate modules)

4   Combining Experts

In an SSP problem, a combination of experts is a set of experts whose individual decisions are combined to classify new instances more accurately [2, 13, 24, 25]. One reason for this could be that the training data may not provide sufficient information for selecting the expert that most likely will issue the correct prediction, so that combining the output of experts appears to be the best trade-off. Another reason could be that the adopted learning algorithm may not be able to solve the difficult problem posed in SSP with a monolithic predictor.

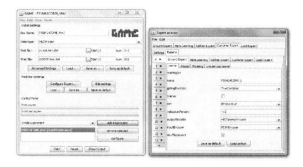

Fig. 3. GAME: Main configuration window with several experts

Several methods have been proposed to construct ensembles of classifiers or predictors. Bryll et al. [20] propose an approach that establishes an appropriate attribute subset size and then randomly selects subsets of features, creating projections of the training set on which the ensemble classifiers are built. The induced classifiers are then used for voting. Chen et al. [11] generated adaptively different ensembles of classifiers in the training phase by fitting the validation data globally with different degrees. The test data are then classified by each of the generated ensembles. The final decision is made by taking into consideration both the ability of each ensemble to fit the validation data locally and reducing the risk of overfitting. However, there is a need to combine the output of all the classifiers to observe a better output or accuracy.

In this paper, a new approach called RVS is proposed to combine smartly the involved predictors by proportionately assigning to each of them a reliability value R (i.e., the degree of confidence in its output). The best set of reliability values have been obtained using a genetic algorithm, which tried all possible assignments of R to each expert, with $R \in \{1, 3, 5, 7, 9, 11\}$ (ranging from 1 to 11 with a step size of 2 has demonstrated to be largely adequate to differentiate between experts' reliabilities). In Fig. 4, the SELECTION step takes 20% of the best individuals. The REPRODUCTION step is carried out by a combination of crossover and mutation functions. A random individual is taken from the selected set, and 80% of the time, the crossover with another randomly selected individual is added to the new population. The remaining 20% of the times mutation is applied randomly to individuals, and the mutated one is added to the new generation.

5   The Proposed Resilient Voting Scheme

We computed the weights (votes) W_i for every expert i using Equation 1, as shown below:

$$W_i = \begin{cases} R_i & \text{if } T_i = true \\ 0 & \text{otherwise} \end{cases} \tag{1}$$

where T_i is a binary rank, computed as follows:

```
1. Choose the initial population of individuals
2. valuate the fitness of each individual in that population
3. REPEAT on this generation UNTIL a termination criterion is satisfied:
     a. Select the best-fit individuals for reproduction
     b. Breed new individuals through crossover and mutation operations
     c. Evaluate the individual fitness of new individuals
     d. Replace least-fit population with new individuals
4. RETURN the best individual(s)
```

Fig. 4. Genetic algorithm that assigns reliability values as an evolutionary optimization process

$$\text{Output of an expert:} \begin{pmatrix} d_H \\ d_E \\ d_C \end{pmatrix} \rightarrow \begin{pmatrix} d_1 \\ d_2 \\ d_3 \end{pmatrix} \text{(sorted in descending order)} \quad (2)$$

so that:

$$T_i = \begin{cases} 1 & \text{if } (d_1 - d_2) \geq 0.4 \\ 0 & \text{otherwise} \end{cases} \quad (3)$$

Then we combine the predictions of all classifiers using the majority function shown in Equation 4:

$$l^* = \operatorname*{argmax}_{l \in \{H,E,C\}} \sum_{j=1}^{N} W_j \cdot V_j(l) \quad (4)$$

where i) l^* is the preferred class of the combiner, i.e., either H or E or C; ii) N is the number of experts; and iii) $V_j(l)$ is the prediction of expert e_j for the label $l \in \{H, E, C\}$.

The architecture of RVS is shown in Fig. 5. The working of our resilient scheme is explained with the help of the following example. A portion of primary sequence alongwith its secondary structure (stride) is shown in Fig. 6. Let expert1, expert2 and expert3 have weights W values as 3.6, 2.04 and 1.34 respectively. The bold-underlined characters are wrong predictions by RVS. The first column shows that expert3 is unable to produce an output satisfying Equation 1. Let other two, i.e., expert1 and expert2 output (0.1,0.2,0.9) and (0.3,0.2,0.8) respectively. Now the value of the preferred class $l^* = argmax[(3.60 * .1 + 2.04 * .3 + 0), (3.60*.2+2.04*.2+0), (3.60*.9+2.04*.8+0)] = argmax(.972, 1.128, 5.16) \rightarrow$ C. The fourth amino acid in the sequence, i.e., L whose 3-state structure H is predicted correctly although the most reliable agent has predicted wrongly. Here, $l^* = argmax[(3.60 * .2 + 2.04 * .8 + 1.34 * .9), (3.60 * .7 + 2.04 * .2 + 1.34 * .1), (3.60 * .1 + 2.04 * .3 + 1.34 * .2)] = argmax(3.558, 3.062, 1.24) \rightarrow H$, when the output of expert1 is (.2,.7,.1), expert2 is (.8,.2,.3) and expert3 is (.9,.1,.2). This shows the resilience of the proposed approach where we get correct prediction inspite of the most accurate agent making a wrong prediction. The worst case scenario is that when all or the majority of agents are unable to predict correctly (8th and 16th amino acids in Fig.6). In this case, RVS will also predict wrongly –which is unavoidable.

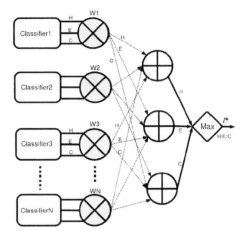

Fig. 5. Architecture of the Resilient Voting Scheme

Seq:	A	A	D	L	V	E	T	M	K	S	G	E	H	D	F	G	A
Stride:	C	H	H	H	H	H	H	H	H	H	C	C	C	C	E	E	E
Expert1:	C	H	H	E	H	H	H	C	H	H	C	C	-	C	E	H	E
Expert2:	C	H	H	H	H	H	H	C	H	H	C	C	-	H	E	H	H
Expert3:	-	H	H	H	H	H	H	-	H	H	E	C	C	C	E	E	C
RVS:	C	H	H	H	H	H	H	C	H	H	C	C	C	C	E	H	E

Fig. 6. An Example of Resilient Voting Scheme

6   Results and Discussions

6.1   Test Setup

We trained twelve experts with varying training-set size, window-size, and encoding scheme (Table 1) for every dataset. Each expert was designed as a multilayer feed-forward neural network having an input layer, one hidden layer, and output layer. We used backpropagation learning with a sigmoidal activation function. The first 200 proteins from the nrDSSP dataset [12] were used to train all the experts. The same dataset were also used for the calculation of Q_3 needed in the fitness function of the evolutionary algorithm.

Table 1 reports the assignments of R to all the predictors, together with their most relevant parameters, as assigned by the genetic algorithm. In particular, the size of the training-set (T), the window size (S), and the encoding scheme (L) have been reported. To evaluate the performance of RVS we have used standard datasets, RS126 [22], which contains 126 proteins, CB513 [5], with 513 non-redundant proteins, and EVA common set 6 (EVAc6) [6], with 212 protein chains. Let us remark that in particular the EVAc6 is a very difficult dataset whose proteins have no or very loose relationships with the proteins used for training.

Table 1. Final reliability values (R) for each expert

Expert	T	S	L	R
E1	100	15	PSSM	7
E2	100	5	PSSM	1
E3	100	15	SLB	1
E4	100	5	SLB	1
E5	100	15	SIMPLE	1
E6	100	5	SIMPLE	1
E7	200	15	PSSM	11
E8	200	5	PSSM	11
E9	200	15	SLB	5
E10	200	5	SLB	1
E11	200	15	SIMPLE	11
E12	200	5	SIMPLE	1

6.2   Performance Measures

Each test has been evaluated with the following standard metrics:

- Q_3 *index*. It is in fact a measure of accuracy, largely used for its simplicity. It is defined as:

$$Q_3 = \frac{\sum_{i \in \{h,e,c\}} tp_i}{\sum_{i \in \{h,e,c\}} N_i} = \frac{\sum_{i \in \{h,e,c\}} tp_i}{N} \tag{5}$$

  where N_i is the number of residues observed for structure category i (which sum to the total number of residues, say N) and tp_i, i.e., true positives, the corresponding correctly predicted residues.
- *Segment OVerlapping (SOV)*. Defined in [27], it accounts for the predictive ability of a system by taking into account the overlapping between predicted and actual structural segments.
- *Matthews Correlation Coefficients (MCCs)*. Defined in [16], the MCC measure relies on the concept of confusion matrix. Evaluated on a specific secondary structure, MCC is a good estimation of the prediction quality for that structure. For secondary structures, each MCC is defined as follows:

$$C_i = \frac{tp_i tn_i - fp_i fn_i}{\sqrt{(tp_i + fp_i)(tp_i + fn_i)(tn_i + fp_i)(tn_i + fn_i)}} \tag{6}$$

  where $i \in \{h, e, c\}$; tp_i represents the number of true positives for the class i, tn_i the true negatives, fp_i the false positives, and fn_i the false negatives.

6.3   Discussion

Table 2 shows that RVS improves Q_3 over averaging and ANN stacking for EVAc6 by 0.64% and 0.27%, respectively. Table 3 shows that RVS improves Q_3

over averaging and ANN stacking for CB513 by 0.68% and 0.01%, respectively. In Table 2 and Table 3, Qh, and Qe in RVS is lower than that in ANN stacking. However, considered alone, these metrics are not important, the overall Q3 matters –which is better in RVS over ANN stacking.

Inclusion of weights in RVS based on reliability and accuracy has shown improvements in SOV (in EVAc6) over averaging by 0.86% and over ANN stacking by 0.4%. Also, in CB513, RVS's improvement in SOV over averaging is 0.71%

Table 2. Qh, Qe, Qc, and Q3 measure for EVAc6

Experts	Qh	Qe	Qc	Q3
E1	60.87	70.86	75.14	67.91
E2	54.74	64.84	77.87	65.59
E3	68.61	60.61	76.09	70.18
E4	62.69	55.94	72.25	65.12
E5	46.59	53.82	68.26	58.87
E6	32.60	45.98	79.12	56.01
E7	70.91	67.37	72.15	69.97
E8	72.75	52.52	74.31	69.96
E9	68.03	58.42	81.10	71.09
E10	62.94	57.07	78.05	67.63
E11	53.06	47.16	73.48	62.45
E12	68.17	29.92	63.48	61.23
Averaging	66.97	60.95	81.17	71.90
ANN_Stacking	74.40	71.58	72.11	72.27
RVS	70.73	60.56	80.31	72.54

Table 3. Qh,Qe,Qc, and Q3 measure for CB513

Experts	Qh	Qe	Qc	Q3
E1	73.10	70.03	78.15	73.76
E2	69.59	63.22	80.54	72.31
E3	80.45	60.79	79.15	74.58
E4	73.20	53.32	79.09	70.64
E5	51.24	55.19	70.36	61.68
E6	37.20	44.52	81.38	60.07
E7	81.13	67.40	76.66	74.99
E8	82.54	50.81	78.36	72.78
E9	80.30	58.65	83.63	76.16
E10	74.92	54.14	82.07	72.73
E11	58.89	48.14	75.68	64.78
E12	72.32	28.57	66.07	60.07
Averaging	79.01	60.23	85.02	76.74
ANN_Stacking	83.24	63.19	82.04	77.41
RVS	81.70	60.17	84.60	77.42

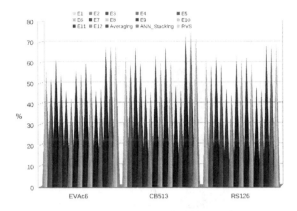

Fig. 7. Bar graph of SOV measure for EVAc6, CB513, and RS126

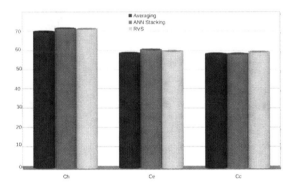

Fig. 8. MCC measure for Averaging, ANN Stacking, and RVS for CB513

and over ANN stacking 0.61%. In RS126, RVS's improvement in SOV over averaging is 0.81% and over ANN stacking is 1.44%. These results are plotted in Fig.7. Matthew's Correlation Coefficients (MCC) are plotted in Fig. 8 for CB513 dataset.

7   Conclusion

In this paper, a novel approach for combining predictors, called Resilient Voting Scheme, is proposed using weighted consensus. The approach is aimed at improving the accuracy in predicting protein secondary structures. The weights and ranks are efficiently calculated, based on the resiliency of the predictors. Well known benchmarks (i.e., CB513, RS126, EVAc6) have been used to measure the efficiency of the proposed approach. The Q3 measure (72.54%) shows its usefulness over standard averaging (71.90%) and ANN stacking (72.27%) on the EVAc6 dataset. Similar observations were also made on the CB513 dataset, reporting a Q3 measure of 77.42% for the proposed approach against 76.74% and 77.41% for averaging and ANN stacking respectively.

Acknowledgments. This work has been supported by the Italian Ministry of Education - Investment funds for basic research, under the project ITAL-BIONET - Italian Network of Bioinformatics.

References

1. Al-Ani, A., Duriche, M.: A new technique for combining multiple classifiers using dempster-shafer theory of evidence. Artificial Intelligence Research 17, 333–361 (2002)
2. Armano, G., Mancosu, G., Milanesi, L., Orro, A., Saba, M., Vargiu, E.: A hybrid genetic-neural system for predicting protein secondary structure. BMC Bioinformatics 6, S3 (2005)
3. Bystroff, C., Thousson, V., Baker, D.: Hmm-str: A hidden markov model for local sequence structure correlations in proteins. J. Mol. Biol. 301, 173–190 (2000)
4. Chou, P.Y., Fasman, G.D.: Conformational parameters for amino acids in helical, sheet, and random coil regions calculated from proteins. Biochemistry 13, 211–222 (1974)
5. Cuff, J.A., Barton, G.J.: Evaluation and improvement of multiple sequence methods for protein secondary structure prediction. Proteins: Structure, Function, and Genetics 34, 508–519 (1999)
6. Eyrich, A.V., Marti-Renom, M.A., Przybylski, D., Madhusudhan, M.S., Fiser, A., Pazos, F., Valencia, A., Sali, A., Rost, B.: Eva: continuous automatic evaluation of protein structure prediction servers. Bioinformatics 17(12), 1242–1243 (2001)
7. Johansson, R., Bostrom, H., Karlsson, A.: A study on class-specifically discounted belief for ensemble classifiers. In: Proceedings of IEEE International Conference on Multisensor Fusion and Integration for Intelligent Systems (MFI), pp. 614–619 (2008)
8. Jones, D.T.: Protein secondary structure prediction based on position specific scoring matrices. J. Mol. Biol. 292, 195–202 (1999)
9. Ledda, F.: Protein secondary structure prediction: Novel methods and software architectures. In: PhD Thesis, DIEE, University of Cagliari, Italy (2011)
10. Ledda, F., Milanesi, L., Vargiu, E.: Game: A generic architecture based on multiple experts for predicting protein structures. Communications of SIWN 3, 107–112 (2008)
11. Lei, C., Karel, M.S.: A generalized adaptive ensemble generation and aggregation approach for multiple classifier systems. Pattern Recognition 42, 629–644 (2009)
12. Lin, H.-N., Chang, J.-M., Wu, K.-P., Sung, T.-Y., Hsu, W.-L.: A knowledge based hybrid method for protein secondary structure prediction based on local prediction confidence. Bioinformatics 21, 3227–3233 (2005)
13. Lin, K.-L., Lin, C.Y., Huang, C.D., Chang, H.M., Yang, C.Y., Lin, C.T., Tang, C.Y., Hsu, D.F.: Feature seclection and combination criteria for improving accuracy in protein structure prediction. IEEE Transactions on Nanobioscience 6, 186–196 (2007)

14. Liu, Y.C., Lin, C.-Y., Yu, K.-M., Tang, C.-Y.: Rap: Refine a prediction of protein secondary structure. In: Proceedings of 23rd Workshop on Combinatorial Mathematics and Computation Theory, pp. 34–38 (2006)
15. Maclin, R., Shavlik, J.W.: Combining the predictions of multiple classifiers: Using competitive learning to initialize neural networks. In: Proceedings of 14th International Joint Conference on Artificial intelligence (IJCAI 1995), pp. 524–531 (1995)
16. Matthews, B.W.: Comparison of the predicted and observed secondary structure of t4 phage lysozyme. Biochim. Biophys. Acta 405, 442–451 (1975)
17. Mount, D.: Bioinformatics: Sequence and Genome Analysis, 2nd edn. CSHL Press, NY (2004)
18. Qian, N., Sejnowski, T.J.: Predicting the secondary structure of globular proteins using neural network models. Journal of Mol. Biology 202, 865–884 (1988)
19. Quali, M., King, R.D.: Cascaded multiple classifiers for secondary structure prediction. Protein Science 9, 1162–1176 (2000)
20. Robert, B., G-Osuna, R., Quek, F.: Attribute bagging: Improving accuracy of classifier ensembles by using random feature subset. Pattern Recognition 36, 1291–1302 (2003)
21. Rost, B.: Review: Protein secondary structure prediction continues to rise. J. Struct. Biol. 134, 204–218 (2001)
22. Rost, B., Sander, C.: Prediction of protein secondary structure at better than 70% accuracy. J. Mol. Biol. 232, 584–599 (1993)
23. Rus, S.K., Krogh, A.: Improving prediction of protein secondary structure using structured neural networks and multiple sequence alignments. J. Comp. Biol. 3, 163–183 (1996)
24. Taheri, J., Zomaya, A.Y.: A voting scheme to improve the secondary structure prediction. In: Proceedings of ACS/IEEE International Conference on Computer Systems and Applications (AICCSA), pp. 1–7 (2010)
25. Vogiatzis, D., Frosyniotis, D., Papadopoulos, G.A.: The protein structure prediction module of the prot-grid information system. In: Proceedings of ICEIS, pp. 372–378 (2003)
26. Ward, J.J., Mcguffin, L.J., Buxton, B.F., Jones, D.T.: Secondary structure prediction with support vector machines. Bioinformatics 19, 1650–1655 (2003)
27. Zemla, A., Vencolvas, C., Fidelis, K., Rost, B.: A modified definition of SOV, a segment-based measure for protein secondary structure prediction assesment. Proteins 34, 220–223 (1999)

Extensions to IQuickReduct

Sai Prasad P.S.V.S. and Raghavendra Rao Chillarige

Department of Computer and Information Sciences,
University of Hyderabad, Hyderabad
{saics,crrcs}@uohyd.ernet.in

Abstract. IQuickReduct algorithm is an improvement over a poplar reduct computing algorithm known as QuickReduct algorithm. IQuickReduct algorithm uses variable precision rough set (VPRS) calculations as a heuristic for determining the attribute importance for selection into reduct set to resolve ambiguous situations in Quick Reduct algorithm. An apt heuristic for selecting an attribute helps in producing shorter non redundant reducts. This paper explores the selection of input attribute in ambiguous situations by adopting several heuristic approaches instead of VPRS heuristic. Extensive experimentation has been carried out on the standard datasets and the results are analyzed.

Keywords: Rough Sets, Feature Selection, Reduct, Quick Reduct, IQuickReduct.

1   Introduction

Last three decades have seen an increased interest in the area of Rough Sets[10]. One of the important contributions of the Rough Sets for the Data mining and Soft Computing community is the concept of Reduct. Given a decision system consisting of several objects defined by conditional and decision attributes, reduct is a subset of the Conditional Attributes preserving the classification ability of the original system. Unlike Principle component analysis(PCA) for dimensionality reduction[19] reduct preserves the original semantics of the conditional attributes and gives dimensionality reduction with no loss of classification precision.

There are several approaches proposed for reduct calculations based on Discernibility matrix, Positive Region, Entropy and granularity based [2]. Quick Reduct Algorithm (QRA) is a reduct algorithm which is positive region based and has been used in several applications [1]. IQuickReduct algorithm (IQRA) [14] is proposed by the authors for overcoming some of the deficiencies of the QRA and has the advantages of finding the required subset of conditional attributes in less time and space complexity and also as an attempt to obtain shorter length reducts. "Searching for the shortest length reduct" has been the goal of several researchers [18,20]. But finding the shortest length reduct is found to be NP Hard[8]. IQRA is an attempt to use heuristic methods to get shortest length reduct or near to shortest length reduct.

In IQRA, VPRS heuristic is used to select an attribute when the kappa gain is zero in QRA instances. In soft computing domain there are various heuristics in practice

C. Sombattheera et al. (Eds.): MIWAI 2011, LNAI 7080, pp. 351–362, 2011.
© Springer-Verlag Berlin Heidelberg 2011

for selecting an attribute under uncertainty such as Information Gain(IG) [3], Gini Index[11]. In this paper relevance of such heuristics in IQRA is explored.

Section 2 gives the basics of QRA and IQRA. The proposed heuristic approaches in IQRA are given in section 3. In Section 4 illustration of algorithms is given using small examples. Section 5 contains the results of experimentation and analysis of the results.

2   QuickReduct and IQuickReduct

Let DT =<U,C∪{d}> be a decision system, where U is the set of objects, C is the set of conditional attributes and **d** is the decision attribute. QRA is a greedy algorithm for the calculation of a reduct. The algorithm starts with an empty set of conditional attributes R and in each iteration an attribute is added into R which increases the kappa, which is a measure of dependency of decision attribute on conditional attributes, in a maximum way. The algorithm terminates by retuning the R as a reduct set when the kappa of the R is equal to the kappa of C. IQRA is proposed to increase the efficiency of the QRA in following ways.

1. If an object is included in the positive region in current iteration it continues to be in the positive region in the future iterations. The current positive region will not add any more knowledge to the decision making in future iterations. Removal of the positive region obtained in current iteration helps in reducing the space and time complexity that is required for the QRA. In IQRA after the inclusion of an attribute into reduct set R the obtained positive region of objects are removed from the decision table and the modified table is used for future iterations.

2. In the iteration in which an inclusion of any available attribute does not increase the kappa then QRA needs to take an arbitrary decision and by default the first available attribute is included in the subset. This phenomenon is referred from now on as having zero kappa gain and such situation is referred as a trivial ambiguous situation. In such ambiguous situations IQRA uses the variable precision rough sets [4] as heuristic and includes that attribute which is giving a positive kappa with least reduction in the precision parameter β. Picking the attribute into R with the help of knowledge from the heuristic instead of a default choice is found to be helpful in avoidance of super reduct (a non trivial super set of reduct) and finding a shorter length reduct.

In this way IQRA is an improvement to the QRA and is found to give shorter length reducts (if not minimal length reducts) in less time and space requirements.

For completeness sake the algorithm IQRA given in [14] is presented here.

Algorithm IQuickReduct

Input: Decision table DT = (U, C∪D) where U is the set of objects and C is the set of conditional attributes and D is the set of decision attributes.

Output: Set of attributes R preserving the property $\gamma_R^1(D) = \gamma_C^1(D)$.

1. Calculate $\gamma_C^1(D)$.
2. $R = \Phi$. /* Initially R the reduct set is an empty set*/
3. Count=0. /* Count variable at any instance contain the number of objects in Positive region*/
4. While $\gamma_R^1(D) \neq \gamma_C^1(D)$, /*The loop continues till the kappa of R is not equal to kappa of C*/
5. do
6.   AvailableSet= $C - R$ /* AvailableSet contains attributes which are not included into R*/
7. $\beta = 1$, $\varepsilon = 0.1$. /* β is the precision parameter used in kappa calculation using VPRS. β is reduced by epsilon amount in step 9 in case there is no positive kappa gain and the steps 7i onwards are repeated*/
    i.   T=R
    ii. foreach $q \in AvailableSet$,
    iii. do
    iv. if $\varpi_{R\cup\{q\}}^{\beta}(D) > \varpi_T^{\beta}(D)$,
    v.   T= $R \cup \{q\}$
    vi. endfor
8.   if $T = R$, /* No kappagain*/
9. $\beta = \beta - \varepsilon$
10.   if $\beta \geq 0.5$,
11.   goto 7i
12.   else
13.   R=R $\cup$ {First attribute in AvailableSet}/*In case VPRS heuristic is not useful a default choice is made*/
14.   else /*for if in step 8*/
15.   R=T
16.   Set POSPARTIAL to $POS_R^1(D)$ for DT   /*For removal of redundant objects calculate Positive region with tolerance of 1*/
17. Reduce DT by removing the objects belonging to POSPARTIAL.
18. Count=Count+$|POSPARTIAL|$
19. $\gamma_R^1(D) = Count \div |U|$
20. endwhile
21. Return R

(Note: In the above algorithm $\varpi_R^{\beta}(D)$ is used to denote kappa value when calculated for reduced decision table using β precision and $\gamma_R^1(D)$ is used for denoting kappa value for original decision table.)

The two aspects mentioned earlier can be seen in the algorithm. The first aspect refers to removal of the POS region which is done in steps 15 to 19. The second aspect is using of heuristic when there is no kappa gain. This is done in steps 9 to 14. If there is a positive kappa gain in all iterations then IQRA result is same as QRA with a gain in computational time.

3   IQuickReduct Extensions

IQRA suffers when the kappa gain is zero for successive iterations. It is observed that sometimes choice of attribute at low precision will be detrimental to the objectives. To reduce the costlier computational part of IQRA i.e. steps 9-14, is considered to plug apt heuristics like Information Gain, Maximum Domain Cardinality and ensemble of Heuristics.

3.1   IQuickReduct Using Information Gain (IQRA_IG)

Using Information Gain for selecting attribute importance is explored in [15,17]. It is also given in [2] using IG alone for selecting attribute importance instead of kappa can result in many redundant attributes and results in super reduct. But when there is no kappa gain relying upon IG is a viable alternative and have less number of calculations than Variable precision calculations. So in this heuristic IG is calculated for all the available attributes and the attribute which has the maximum IG is selected into the Reduct set.

3.2   IQuickReduct Using Maximum Domain Cardinality (IQRA_MD)

The attribute that has the highest number of distinct values or domain cardinality is selected into the Reduct Set. This is a simple and less expensive heuristic. If the domain cardinality is high then there is more number of equivalence classes for the attribute. Hence there is a higher chance of having shorter length partitions. Having shorter length partitions gives higher chance of inclusion into the positive region in the later iterations. This heuristic is redundant if the attributes are not distinguishable with respect to domain cardinality like in binary datasets.

3.3   IQuickReduct Using Combination of Heuristics (IQRA_Comb)

A possibility for selection of attribute may not just rely upon one heuristic value but an attribute can be selected if it is good with respect to all the heuristic values. In this algorithm attributes are given rank values Rank_VP, Rank_IG, Rank_MD based on the three heuristics proposed earlier. All the three ranks are combined and the attribute which has the best combined rank is selected for inclusion into the reduct set.

3.4   Extensions in Non Trivial Ambiguity Situations

In our experiments it is observed that when QRA is choosing an attribute into reduct for a very small kappa gain (like in the order of <0.1 or <0.05) is resulting in reduct set of large size. In these cases IQRA and the above variations follow the path of QRA as there is a positive kappa gain. But if the gain is minimal a viable alternative is to pick the attribute based on heuristic and not based on kappa gain. With this motivation two extensions are proposed. This kind of ambiguity is named as *non trivial ambiguity* to differentiate from the zero kappa gain ambiguity which is named as the *trivial ambiguity*. The two improvements in this direction are

1) **IQRA_IMP1:** This is a variation of IQRA_Comb using the heuristic calculations when the kappa gain is <0.1. That is algorithm does not pick the attribute based on the kappa gain when the kappa gain is <0.1. Instead uses the heuristic calculation used in IQRA_Comb for selection of attribute.

2) **IQRA_IMP2:** This is a variation of IQRA_IG using the heuristic calculations when the kappa gain is <0.1.

4   Illustration of the Algorithms

4.1   Trivial Ambiguity Situation

The decision table DT1 given in Table 1 is illustrating *trivial ambiguity situation*. The conditional attributes are {A, B, C, D, E} and the decision attribute is 'F'. The reduct set obtained by QRA is <C,A,D,B>. The kappa of R after each iteration of QRA is <0.3846, 0.3846, 0.6154, 1.0>. In first iteration attribute 'C' has given maximum kappa of 0.3846 and is included into R without ambiguity. But in the second iteration of QRA none of the available attributes {A,B,D,E} are giving any increase or gain in kappa. This is the *trivial ambiguity situation* in which QRA adopts a default choice and includes the first available attribute 'A' into R. The third and fourth iterations are unambiguous and QRA terminates after inclusion of 'B' in the fourth iteration as the kappa of R has become equal to kappa of C which in this case is 1 indicating that the DT1 is a consistent decision table.

The reduct set obtained in IQRA algorithm for DT1 is <C, D, B>. The kappa of R after each iteration of IQRA is <0.3846, 0.3846, 1>. As before the first iteration is as same as QRA as there is no ambiguity and attribute 'C' is included in R. But in the second iteration instead of going for the default choice VPRS heuristic calculations are used. In this case when beta is 0.8 attribute 'D' acquired positive variable precision kappa and hence is included into R. The importance of this inclusion is that after third iteration itself we could obtain the required reduct set of attributes. This example also illustrates the utility of IQRA that of avoiding super reduct. The result of QRA is a super reduct and the result of IQRA is a reduct. For this dataset DT1 all other extensions of IQRA also were able to pick attribute '4' in second iteration and resulted in the same result as IQRA. For example IQRA_IG has chosen '4' in the second iteration because '4' has given the maximum Information Gain of 0.1589 compared to all the available attributes. The only exception is IQRA_MD as the example dataset has the same domain cardinality for all the conditional attributes and hence the result obtained in IQRA_MD is same as that of QRA.

Table 1. Decision table DT1 for illustrating trivial ambiguous situations

ObjId	A	B	C	D	E	F
1	1	1	1	1	0	0
2	0	1	1	1	1	0
3	0	1	1	0	0	1
4	0	0	1	1	1	1
5	1	1	1	1	1	0
6	0	1	2	0	0	1
7	0	0	0	1	0	1
8	1	1	0	1	0	1
9	0	1	1	1	1	0
10	1	1	0	0	1	1
11	0	0	1	0	0	0
12	1	0	2	1	0	1
13	1	1	1	0	0	1

4.2   Non Trivial Ambiguity Situation

The decision table DT2 given in table 2 is used for illustrating *non trivial ambiguity* situation. DT2 contains 35 objects, 6 conditional attributes and 1 decision attribute. For DT2 the reduct set R obtained in QRA is <F, D, A, B, E>. The kappa of R after each iteration is <0.0286, 0.4, 0.8286, 0.9429, 1.0>. It can be observed that there is a positive kappa gain in all iterations. Hence the results of QRA, IQRA, IQRA_IG, IQRA_MD, IQRA_Comb are same as there is no trivial ambiguous situation. But the obtained R is actually a super reduct. In first iteration it can be seen that attribute 'F' has given maximum kappa of 0.0286 which is very small and is less than 0.1. Such situation as per our terminology falls into non trivial ambiguous situation. For DT2 the result R obtained in IQRA_IMP1 using IG heuristic in *non trivial ambiguity* situations is <A, D, C, E> and the kappa of R after each iteration is <0, 0.4, 0.8286, 1.0>. The attribute 'A' is included in first iteration as 'A' gave a maximum IG value of 0.3963. The iterations 2,3,4 are all having positive kappa gain (>0.1) thus there is no need of adopting any heuristic. The result obtained using IQRA_IMP1 is a reduct and not a super reduct as it is the case with QRA. The result obtained in IQRA_IMP2 is <C,B,E,D> a shorter set compared to QRA but is still a super reduct only. Hence application of heuristic may not avoid all occurrences of super reduct but can at least reduce the size of the set obtained.

Table 2. Decision table DT2 for illustrating non trivial ambiguous situations

ObjId	A	B	C	D	E	F	G
1	2	0	3	0	2	0	4
2	4	3	0	3	2	1	4
3	0	0	4	3	0	4	4
4	1	1	4	3	0	0	1
5	0	3	0	0	4	4	1
6	1	3	1	1	4	3	3
7	4	3	0	4	2	1	2
8	3	0	3	0	3	0	2
9	3	4	0	4	1	1	4
10	1	3	2	2	2	0	4
11	0	2	4	1	3	0	1
12	4	1	1	3	1	3	4
13	2	0	4	4	1	4	2
14	0	3	3	2	0	0	2
15	2	3	2	1	1	4	0
16	3	1	2	1	4	4	2
17	3	0	0	2	2	0	3

18	0	2	1	1	2	4	0
19	1	2	3	1	1	0	4
20	4	0	1	2	3	3	1
21	2	2	0	0	2	3	3
22	3	4	4	4	4	0	1
23	1	4	0	2	2	1	1
24	1	0	0	4	4	3	0
25	4	4	4	3	4	0	1
26	0	3	1	1	3	4	3
27	1	3	3	2	1	4	1
28	1	3	2	4	4	3	4
29	2	3	4	3	0	0	1
30	4	3	4	3	1	1	4
31	1	1	4	3	4	0	3
32	0	4	1	4	3	3	3
33	1	0	4	1	2	4	4
34	3	4	3	3	2	2	4
35	1	3	3	0	1	4	1

5   Experiments and Results

Matlab environment [7] is opted for demonstrating the proposed hybrid IQRA extensions. The experiments are conducted on several datasets available from UCI Machine Learning Repository [16] and Richard Jensen's website [12]. We tried to completely enumerate all reducts of each dataset in the experiment using Rough Set Exploration tool (RSES) [13] for analyzing the ability of the proposed algorithms in reaching the shortest length reduct. RSES is having limitations in working only for datasets having less number (<20) of conditional attributes. In such cases we have used SAVGeneticInducer in Rosetta tool [9] and generated the reducts. Even though the results of the genetic algorithm are not exhaustive in enumerating all reducts they are a good approximation for the total possible reducts of a dataset.

5.1   Results for Extensions of IQuickReduct Algorithm for Trivial Ambiguity

For many datasets there is positive kappa gain in all iterations of QRA and hence all the extensions including IQRA are generating the same reduct as found by QRA. In all such datasets there is a significant time gain in IQRA and its extensions. Here the results are given only for those datasets which involve ambiguity in QRA implementation.

In table 3 the details of the datasets having ambiguity in QRA are given. The results of the experiments on these datasets are reported in Table 4 giving length of the reduct set obtained, the nature of the reduct set (SR for super reduct, R for reduct) and the computational time in seconds (shown in italics).

5.2   Analysis of the Results

In **Mofn** dataset all the extension methods except IQRA_MD could obtain the single reduct available for this dataset. As **Mofn, Exactly2, Exactly** are binary datasets the result in IQRA_MD is ineffective and is same as QRA.

IQRA_IG is proved to be better than IQRA in getting a shorter reduct and also in finding the reduct in shorter time period.

Exactly2 dataset results need further analysis. It appears that QRA has got better result than the IQRA, IQRA_IG. The kappa accumulated after each iteration of QRA is shown in Table 5. It can be seen that for the first four iterations there is no kappa gain. QRA has by default included [1 2 3 4] into the reduct set. The only reduct available to this dataset happens to be [1 2 3 4 5 6 7 8 9 10]. Because [1 2 3 4] is a subset of the expected reduct QRA is able to perform better. When we experimented by altering the order of the conditional attributes QRA gave a super reduct of 13 length. But the result of IQRA heuristic methods is near to length 10. Hence heuristic based methods can give almost invariant results even when order of conditional attributes is changed but it is not the case with QRA. If the default choice is good with respect to the expected outcome QRA performs well otherwise its performance can be unpredictable.

Table 3. Datasets used in *Trivial ambiguity* Experiments

Dataset	Rows	Attributes	Decision Classes	Reducts Count	(SRL,LRL)#
Mofn	1000	14	2	1	(6,6)
Exactly2	1000	14	2	1	(10,10)
Dna	318	58	8	50*	(5,7)
Exactly	1000	14	2	1	(6,6)
SyntheisDT$	999	27	3	237	(7,9)

*(#: SRL: Shortest Reduct Length LRL: Longest Reduct Length $: Dataset generated randomly *Reducts found using SAV Genetic Inducer in Rosetta)*

Datasets **Dna, SynthesisDT1** illustrate the use of simple heuristic IQRA_MD. Because of the varying sizes of the domains of conditional attributes in these datasets a simple heuristic calculation is able to give the better performance in these datasets. This heuristic is the most cost effective heuristic.

The best super reduct obtained for **Exactly** dataset is by IQRA_Comb. The reduct for **Exactly** dataset is [1 3 5 7 9 11] and that of obtained by IQRA_Comb is [1 2 3 7 5 9 11]. Still this result is misleading in the sense that for all the methods a positive kappa is obtained only after including the fifth attribute. Even the variable precision could give positive kappa at the low precision parameter value of 0.7 for first three iterations. The positive kappa seen at that low precision also is very small. Even the best information gain values for first four iterations of IQRA_Comb is [0.008 0.0014

0.0011 0.0013] which are negligible values. As the dataset is of binary MD heuristic also is ineffective. Because of such complicated nature of the dataset even though a combination heuristic could give near best solution all the methods are proved ineffective when the order of the conditional attributes is changed. Further exploration is required in seeing how to tackle such datasets for obtaining a shorter length reduct.

Table 4. Results Summary for trivial ambiguous datasets

Dataset	QRA	IQRA	IQRA_IG	IQRA_MD	IQRA_Comb
Mofn	7 SR	6 R	6 R	7 SR	6 R
	9.59	5.44	5.07	6.44	5.66
Exactly2	10 R	13 SR	11 SR	10 R	10 R
	27.37	19.67	17.16	15.74	17.46
Dna	7 R	6 R	5 R	5 R	5 R
	126.66	43.66	40.61	40.16	43.12
Exactly	8 SR	10 SR	9 SR	8 SR	7 SR
	13.72	22.3	15.47	11.46	10.58
SynthesisDT	7 R	7 R	6 R	6 R	6 R
	225.07	71.8	58.91	59.2	68.74

Table 5. Details of Kappa Obtained in Exactly2 Dataset in QRA

Attribute Included	1	2	3	4	10	9	6	8	7	5
Kappa	0	0	0	0	0.04	0.139	0.28	0.482	0.71	1

The results obtained for ***Exactly*** dataset depicts one exceptional situation. Here as for the first five iterations there is no positive kappa gain many iterations of kappa calculations on all available attributes is involved. Till sixth iteration there is no removal of positive region. Hence all the calculations till sixth iteration are on the original decision table in IQRA. Hence the time required for completion of IQRA happens to be more than QRA. We need to remember that this is an exceptional situation and occurred only once in many experiments that were conducted using these algorithms.

5.3   Results for Extensions of IQuickReduct Algorithm for Non Trivial Ambiguity

Here the results are given for those datasets in which there is positive kappa gain in each iteration of QRA. In this case all the extensions IQRA, IQRA_IG, IQRA_MD, IQRA_Comb will give the same result as QRA but in less time duration. Hence the results include only the result from QRA, IQRA_IMP1, IQRA_IMP2. The table 6 gives the nature of the datasets used.

Table 6. Details of the Datasets used in *non trivial ambiguity* experiments

Dataset	Rows	Attributes	Decision Classes	Reducts Count	(SRL,LRL)@
Chess	3196	37	2	4*	(29,29)
Heart	294	14	2	20	(6,8)
Letters	26	34	26	47*	(8,10)
Water[#]	521	39	3	234*	(6,7)
Water[$2]	521	39	3	11*	(23,23)
Water[$3]	521	39	3	43*	(14,18)
Isolet[$2]	34	618	17	87*	(8,10)
Isolet[#]	34	618	17	64*	(4,6)

(*Reducts found using SAV Genetic Inducer Algorithm in Rosetta
Discretization Applied: #: ChiMerge[5], $2: EqualWidth[6] with 2 bins, $3:
Equal Width with 3 bins
* @: SRL: Shortest Reduct Length LRL: Longest Reduct Length)*

The results obtained through QRA, IQRA_IMP1, IQRA_IMP2 are given in table 7 giving length of the reduct set obtained, the nature of the reduct set (SR for super reduct, R for reduct) and the computational time in seconds (shown in italics).

The results indicate the use of going for heuristic when kappa gain in iteration is not significant. One can see significant time reduction in IQRA_IMP1 and IQRA_ IMP2 algorithms and also achieving much shorter reducts. In some datasets even though super reducts are obtained they are near to shortest length reducts for the concerned dataset.

In the water dataset with ChiMerge Discretization realizing a reduct of size '5' is smaller than the reducts obtained through the popular SAVGeneticReducer of Rosetta tool prompts further exploration on these hybrid methods of Reduct Computation. It is to be noted that there is no bound on number of reducts to be generated in the SAVGeneticReducer module in Rosetta.

Table 7. Results Summary for Non Trivial Ambiguous Datasets

Dataset	QRA	IQRA_IMP1	IQRA_IMP2
Chess	31 SR	29 R	29 R
	2673.6	*74.9*	*64.6*
Heart	7 R	6 R	8 SR
	9.59	*2.18*	*2.14*
Letters	11 SR	10 SR	9 SR
	15.85	*6.49*	*3.83*
Water[#]	6 R	6 R	5 R
	83.68	*14.08*	*11.92*
Water[$2]	29 SR	24 SR	25 SR
	146.03	*26.46*	*16.52*
Water[$3]	17 SR	17 SR	15 R
	173.11	*15.91*	*13.63*
Isolet[$2]	12 SR	8 SR	9 SR
	336.11	*53.59*	*44.45*
Isolet[#]	3 R	3 R	2 R
	104.09	*74.19*	*58.94*

6   Conclusion

The experiments that were done by us using only the heuristics such as Information Gain or Maximum Domain Cardinality without using kappa information found to generate super reducts with lot of superfluous attributes. Hence we adopted the hybrid methods in which kappa information and heuristic information used to select the attribute into the reduct set. The extensions given to IQRA are found to be useful in generating shorter length reducts in less computational time. If researchers who are looking to get the shortest length reduct can adopt IQRA and classify the dataset into trivial ambiguous or nontrivial ambiguous nature. If the dataset is trivial ambiguous it is recommended to use IQRA_IG and IQRA_IMP2 is recommended for nontrivial ambiguous datasets. One need to generate informative metadata for designing apt agent for adopting appropriate IQRA extended hybrid methods.

References

1. Chouchoulas, A., Shen, Q.: Rough Set Aided Keyword Reduction for Text Categorization. Applied Artificial Intelligence 15, 843–873 (2001)
2. Ding, S., Ding, H.: Research and Development of Attribute Reduction Algorithm Based on Rough Set. In: 2010 Chinese Control and Decision Conference, pp. 648–653 (2010)
3. Guyon, I., Elisseeff, A.: An Introduction to Variable and Feature Selection. Journal of Machine Learning Research 3, 1157–1182 (2003)

4. Katzberg, J.D., Ziarko, W.: Variable precision rough sets with asymmetric bounds. In: Ziarko, W. (ed.) Rough Sets, Fuzzy Sets and Knowledge Discovery, pp. 167–177. Springer, Heidelberg (1994)
5. Kerber, R.: ChiMerge: Discretization of Numeric Attributes. In: Tenth National Conference on Artificial Intelligence, AAAI 1992, California, pp. 123–128 (1992)
6. Kotsiantis, S., Kanellopoulos, D.: Discretization Techniques, A Recent Survey. GESTS International Transactions on Computer Science and Engineering 32, 47–58 (2006)
7. Matlab Software, http://www.mathworks.com/
8. Nguyen, H.S., Skowron, A.: Boolean Reasoning for Feature Extraction Problems. In: Raś, Z.W., Skowron, A. (eds.) ISMIS 1997. LNCS (LNAI), vol. 1325, pp. 117–126. Springer, Heidelberg (1997)
9. Øhrn, A., Komorowski, J.: ROSETTA: A Rough Set Toolkit for Analysis of Data. In: Proc. Third International Joint Conference on Information Sciences, Fifth International Workshop on Rough Sets and Soft Computing (RSSC 1997), Durham, NC, USA, vol. 3, pp. 403–407 (1997)
10. Pawlak, Z.: Rough Sets. International Journal of Computer and Information Science 11, 341–356 (1982)
11. Ranabir Singh, S., Hema Murthy, A., Timothy Gonsalves, A.: Feature Selection for Text Classification based on Gini Coefficient of Inequality. In: Fourth International Workshop on Feature Selection in Data Mining, JMLR 2010, Hyderabad, pp. 76–85 (2010)
12. Richard Jensen collection of datasets, http://users.aber.ac.uk/rkj/datasets/index.php
13. Rough Set Exploration System, http://alfa.mimuw.edu.pl/~rses/
14. Sai Prasad, P.S.V.S., Raghavendra Rao, C.: IQuickReduct: An Improvement to QuickReduct Algorithm. In: Sakai, H., Chakraborty, M.K., Hassanien, A.E., Ślęzak, D., Zhu, W. (eds.) RSFDGrC 2009. LNCS, vol. 5908, pp. 152–159. Springer, Heidelberg (2009)
15. Slezak, D.: Approximate Entropy Reducts. Fundamenta Informaticae 53, 365–390 (2002)
16. UCI Machine Learning Repository, http://archive.ics.uci.edu/ml/datasets.html
17. Xinying, C., Yuefan, L.: A Heuristic Reduction Algorithm Based on Entropy of Attribute. Journal of Convergence Information Technology 6, 209–216 (2011)
18. Yue, B., Yao, W., Abraham, A., Liu, H.: A New Rough Set Reduct Algorithm Based on Particle Swarm Optimization. In: Mira, J., Álvarez, J.R. (eds.) IWINAC 2007, Part I. LNCS, vol. 4527, pp. 397–406. Springer, Heidelberg (2007)
19. Zeng, A., Pan, D., Zheng, Q.-L., Peng, H.: Knowledge acquisition based on rough set theoryand principal component analysis. IEEE Intelligent Systems 21(2), 78–85 (2006)
20. Zhang, J., Wang, J., Li, D., He, H., Sun, J.: A New Heuristic Reduct Algorithm base on Rough Sets Theory. In: Dong, G., Tang, C., Wang, W. (eds.) WAIM 2003. LNCS, vol. 2762, pp. 247–253. Springer, Heidelberg (2003)

Distributed Methodology of CanTree Construction

Swarupa Rani K. and Raghavendra Rao Chillarige

Department of Computer and Information Sciences,
University of Hyderabad,
Hyderabad
{swarupacs,crrcs}@uohyd.ernet.in

Abstract. Single pass construction process of the CanTree for deriving association rules has been attracting researchers for data mining and incremental data mining to accommodate growth of transactional logs. This paper proposes five step mechanism for building a CanTree in HPC. The Pima Indian Diabetes Data Set considered for demonstrating a proposed mechanism and its performance.

Keywords: Knowledge discovery and data mining, Tree Structure, Frequent Sets, Incremental Mining, CanTree, HPC.

1   Introduction

Data Mining has attracted a great deal of attention in the information domain, due to its wide availability of huge amounts of data and the imminent need for converting such data into useful information and knowledge. The knowledge gained can be used for applications such as market analysis, fraud detection, customer retention and scientific discovery [1, 3, 8, 9, 10, 18, 21].

Data mining refers to extracting or mining knowledge from large amounts of data. One of the fundamental and important tasks of data mining is the mining of frequent patterns. The main utility of Frequent Pattern is to derive association rules which in turn useful for building knowledge. Various types of Association Rules starts from Boolean Association rules to complex kind of generalized Association Rules [3].

Association rules represent an important class of knowledge that can be discovered from data repositories [3,4,5,6]. The filing up additional data may or may not consistent with association rules derived by that time posses challenging problems. Thomas, S. et.al [6] proposed a novel theme of incremental mining and demonstrated to address this type of problems. Since then incremental mining attracted several researchers in various domains of knowledge discovery. The objective of incremental mining is to avoid re-execution, excessive computation and I/O by developing apt representation systems for the meta data and the associated procedures for updating frequent patterns without referring once again the raw data.

C. Sombattheera et al. (Eds.): MIWAI 2011, LNAI 7080, pp. 363–372, 2011.

The work on association rule mining began with the development of the AIS algorithm (Agrawal, Imielinski, Swami algorithm) [8] for discovering association rules. [11,12,13] suggests several improvements. The FP-Tree algorithm [13] builds a special tree structure in main memory to avoid multiple passes over database.

In general association rule mining algorithm can be divided into two phases

1. Finding all frequent itemsets , each of these itemsets will occur at least as frequently as a pre-determined minimum support count.
2. Generating strong association rules from frequent itemsets.

The existing incremental mining association rule discovery [2,7,14,15,16,13] can be classified into two categories with and without candidate set.

CanTree[21] proposed modified algorithms of FP Tree without considering any candidate itemsets.. To overcome the limitations the present study proposes a five step mechanism (similar to [17]) i.e., sharding, constructing, merging, FP Tree generation, Association Rule discovery.   By adapting apt divide-and-conquer philosophy in sharding step. A heuristic is developed and demonstrated in Section 3 and 4 respectively.

2   An Overview of CanTree(CANonical-Order TREE)

The main concept of CanTree [19] is mainly designed for incremental mining. In this tree, items are arranged according to some canonical order, which can be determined by the user prior to the mining process.   The construction of the CanTree only requires one database scan. This is different from the construction of an FP-tree where two database scans are required. Specifically, items can be consistently arranged in lexicographic order or alphabetical order or items can be arranged according to some specific order depending on the item properties.

The following are the some properties of CanTree:

Property 1: Items are arranged according to a canonical order, which is a fixed global ordering.

Property 2: The ordering of items is unaffected by the changes in frequency caused by incremental updating

Property 3: The frequency of a node in the CanTree is at least as high as the sum of frequencies of all its children.

Once the CanTree is constructed, we can mine frequent patterns from the tree in a divide-and-conquer fashion [13].

2.1   Illustrations of CanTree

Table 1. Sample Transactions

TID	Transactions
t_1	{a,d,b,g,e,c}
t_2	{d,f,b,a,e}
t_3	{a}
t_4	{d,a,b}
t_5	{a,c,b}
t_6	{c,b,a,e}
t_7	{a,b,c}
t_8	{a,b,c}

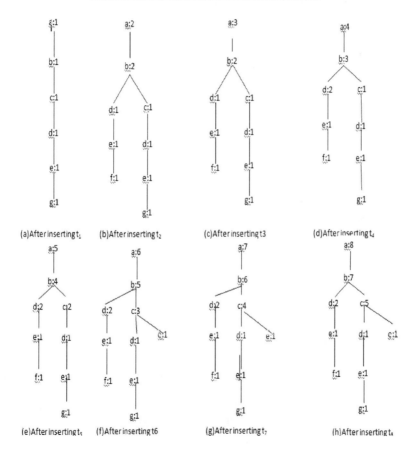

Fig. 1. The CanTree after each transaction is added

2.2   Complexity and Limitations

CanTree significantly reduce computation and time because they easily find mergeable paths and require only upward path traversals. The computation required to construct the CanTree is O(mn) where m is the maximum length of the transaction and n is the number of transactions. As a result, CanTree provide users with efficient incremental mining.

Although CanTree offers a simple single-pass construction process, it usually yields poor compaction in tree size compared to the FP-Tree. However tree-restructuring [20] process can be carried in order to reduce tree size, as it falls into postprocessing category and hence it demands several overheads.

3   An Improved CanTree Construction Methodology

In this paper we propose to parallelize the CanTree Construction on distributed environment. This method partitions the computations in such a way that each compute node executes independently. Such partitions eliminates computational dependencies between compute nodes and thereby communication among them.

This paper focused mainly on algorithms such as sharding and merging so that it will help in reducing memory use and computational cost on each node. The above factors leads to design the construction of CanTree in parallel and distributed environment.

This model adapts divide and conquer methodology. The given database is split into different parts and distributed over to different processors (Sharding Algorithm). This process of splitting database is called sharding [17]. Then in each processor, the transactions are ordered by the user prior to the mining process. The predefined canonical order has mainly two advantages.

1)   CanTree requires only one scan

2)   Canonical order makes the tree merging process simpler.

The distribution of data to different processors is done using threads. The tree construction is carried out using the OpenMP (Multi-processing tool). The synchronization between processors is achieved internally by these OpenMp.

Once the CanTrees are constructed at different processors they are united at the main computer (Merging Algorithm). Then the mining process is carried out by calling out FP-Growth process [13]. The association rules are generated from the frequent patterns. This divide and conquer approach can also be implemented in Map Reduce Environment of HPC(High Performance Computing)[17].

3.1   Illustrations of Improved CanTree Construction Methodology

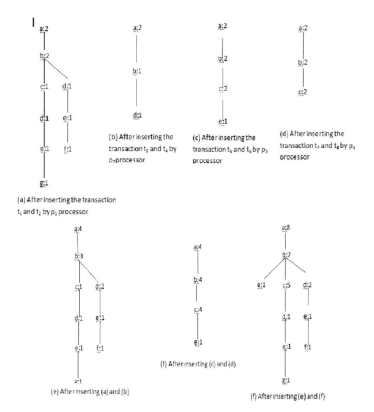

Fig. 2. Distributed methodology of CanTree Construction. The transaction are taken from table 1. and given an input value of p is 4(i.e., four processors).

3.2   Five Steps Mechanism for Improved CanTree Construction Methodology

Step 1: Sharding: Divide the Database into successive parts and storing the parts into different computers. Such division and distribution of data is called sharding, and each part is called shard.

Step 2: Tree Structure Generation: CanTree is generated for each shard. The CanTree is generated in multithreaded/multiprocessor environment. The resultant tree structure is sent to main computer.

Step 3: Merging: The tree structures are merged and FP-Growth method is applied on the merged tree to uncover frequent patterns.

Step 4: Pattern Generation: Mining is done on the CanTree to generate the frequent patterns [13].

Step 5: Association Rule Mining: This module is applied to extract the rules present.

The following are the subsections of steps 1,2,3 and steps 4 and 5 are carried from [13].

3.2.1   Algorithm of Distributed Methodology of CanTree Construction

3.2.1.1   Sharding Mechanism

Input:Transaction Database(D), Number of Processors (p)
Output:CanTrees CT_1, CT_2,..................,CT_p
Method:
1. Count the number of transactions in (D) as db
2. num:=floor(dp/p)
3. Divide (D) into p buckets each bucket having num transactions except may for the last bucket namely DB_1, DB_2,................,DB_p
4. Call in parallel for i=1 to p
             CTi:=CanTree($DB_{i)}$
    end
5. Return{ CT_1, CT_2,..................,CT_p }

3.2.1.2   Tree Structure Generation Mechansim

Input:Transaction Database(DB)
Output:CanTree(CT)
Method:
1. Define and clear the root r of CanTree r ;
2. For each transaction T_i in DB do
3. Make T_i ordering according to canonical order;
4. Call r = Construct Tree(T_i , r)
end
Method:
ConstructTree(T_i, r)
Input:Single Transaction(T_i), Root of the tree r
Output:Root of the tree r
1. Let the items in TRANS be [p/Y], where p is the first element and Y is the remaining sequence
2. Call Insert_Tree(p/Y,r)
3. return r
Method:
Insert_Tree(p/Y,T)
If T has a child such that
{
     n.itemname=p.itemname
     Then increment n's count by 1;
}

else
Create a new node N and let it count be 1 its parent link be linked to T
If Y is non-empty, call Insert_Tree(Y,N) recursively.

3.2.1.3 Merging Mechanism

Input:X,Y are the roots of CanTree1, CanTree2
Output:X
Method:
Merge(X,Y)
for each child node c of Y
do
If X has a child node x such that
x.item_name=c.item_name
then
increment x count value by the count value of c
call Merge(x,c) recursively
else
attach the sub_tree rooted at c in Y to X
MergeP(CT_1, CT_2,..................,CT_p,P)
If P > 2
T_1:=MergeP((CT_1, CT_2,..................,CT_p,P)
T2:=MergeP($CT_{p/2+1}$ ....CT_p,
return Merge(T_1,T_2)
else
Merge(CT_1,CT_2).

4   Experimental Results

Tests are performed using different size dataset and implemented the algorithm.
Experiments are performed using Intel processors on Java platform.   Different
libraries like JOMP and Xstream libraries are used. Performance is evaluated using
Pima Indian Diabetes Data Set.

4.1   Data Set Information

Data Set Used: Pima Indian Diabetes Data Set
Data Set Characteristics: Multivariate
Number of Transactions: 9000-35000
Area: Life
Attribute Characteristics: Integer, Real
Number of Attributes: 8
Date Donated: 1990-05-09
Associated Tasks: Classification
Missing Values: Yes

Several constraints were placed on the selection of these instances from a larger database. In particular, all patients here are females at least 21 year old of Pima Indian heritage

Attribute Information

1.   Number of times pregnant
2.   Plasma glucose concentration a 2hours in an oral glucose tolerance test
3.   Diastolic blood pressure(mm Hg)
4.   Triceps skin fold thickness(mm)
5.   2-Hour serum insulin(mu U/ml)
6.   Body mass index(weight in kg/(height in m) 2)
7.   Diabetes pedigree function
8.   Age(years)
9.   Class variable(0 or 1)

Table 2. The following table depicts computational time for conventional method [19] and the present five step methodology

S.No.	Number of Transactions	Conventional Model (Time in seconds)	Proposed Model (Time in Seconds)	Difference (Time in Seconds)
1	9750	0.88	0.78	0.10
2	17325	1.20	0.97	0.23
3	25850	1.61	1.08	0.53
4	34650	1.97	1.11	0.86

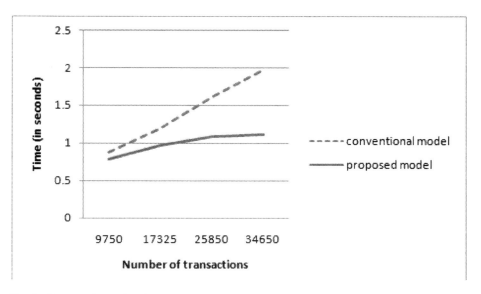

Fig. 3. Computational time involved in conventional and proposed model for different sizes of transactions

5   Conclusion and Future Work

The proposed model, which shards a large-scale mining task into independent, parallel tasks. Our study shows that the computational time in the conventional as well as five step mechanism almost linear with a significant slope. The graph indicates the transactions increasing and the five step mechanism outperforms in computation time. The proposed model achieves the performance gain during tree construction and can be effectively used in temporal and distributed environment. This can be included further tree restructuring to produce a highly compact frequency descending tree structure. CanTree occupies much of the space since it does not share any prefixes. So there is a scope to reduce its size in order to meet the memory requirements.

References

1. Zhang, S., Wu, X., Zhang, C.: Multi-Database Mining. IEEE Computational Intelligence Bulletin 2(1), 5–13 (2003)
2. Cheung, D.W., Han, J., Ng, V.T., Wong, C.Y.: Maintenance of Discovered Association Rules in Large Databases: An Incremental Updating Technique. In: Proc. the International Conference on Data Engineering, pp. 106–114 (1996)
3. Han, J., Kamber, M.: Data Mining: Concepts and Techniques. Morgan Kaufmann Publishers (2001)
4. Thomas, S., et al.: An Efficient Algorithm for the Incremental Updation of Association Rules in Large Databases. In: Knowledge Discovery and Data Mining (1997)
5. Thomas, S.: Architectures and optimizations for integrating Data Mining algorithms with Database Systems. In: CSE. University of Florida, Gainesville (1998)
6. Thomas, S., Chakravarthy, S.: Incremental Mining of Constrained Associations. In: Proc. of the 7th Intl. Conf. of High Performance Computing, HiPC (2000)
7. Cheung, D.W., Lee, S.D., Kao, B.: A general Incremental Technique for Mining Discovered Association Rules. In: Proc. International Conference on Database System for Advanced Applications, pp. 185–194 (1997)
8. Agrawal, R., Imielinski, T., Swami, A.: Mining Association Rules between sets of items in large databases. In: ACM SIGMOD International Conference on the Management of Data, Washington, D.C (1993)
9. Agrawal, R., Srikant, R.: Fast Algorithms for mining association rules. In: 20th Int'l Conference on Very Large Databases, VLDB (1994)
10. Savasere, A., Omiecinsky, E., Navathe, S.: An efficient algorithm for mining association rules in large databases. In: 21st Int'l Cong. on Very Large Databases (VLDB), Zurich, Switzerland (1995)
11. Chen, Y.: An Efficient Parallel Algorithm for Mining Association Rules in Large Databases. Georgia Institute of Technology, Atlanta (1998)
12. Shenoy, P., et al.: Turbo-charging Vertical Mining of Large Databases. In: ACM SIGMOD Int'l Conference on Management of Data, Dallas (2000)
13. Han, J., Pei, J., Yin, Y.: Mining Frequent Patterns without Candidate Generation. In: ACM SIGMOD Int'l Conference on Management of Data, Dallas (2000)
14. Tsai, P.S.M., Lee, C.C., Chen, A.L.P.: An Efficient Approach for Incremental Association Rule Mining, Technical Report (1998)

15. Masseglia, F., Poncelet, P., Teisseire, M.: Incremental mining of sequential patterns in large databases. Data Knowl. Eng. 46(1), 97–121 (2003)
16. Lee, C.-H., Lin, C.-R., Chen, M.-S.: Sliding-window filtering: An Efficient Algorithm for Incremental Mining. In: Proceedings of the Tenth CanTree International Conference on Information and Knowledge Management, Atlanta, Georgia, USA, pp. 263–270 (2001)
17. Li, H., Wang, Y., Zhang, D., Zhang, M., Chang, E.: Pfp: parallel fp-growth for query recommendation. In: Proceedings of the 2008 ACM Conference on Recommender Systems, pp. 107–114 (2008)
18. Sarawagi, S., Thomas, S., Agrawal, R.: Integrating Association Rule Mining with Relational Database System: Alternatives and Implications. In: ACM SIGMOD Int'l Conference on Management of Data, Seattle, Washington (1998)
19. Leung, C.K., Khan, Q.I., Li, Z., Hoque, T.: CanTree: A Canonical-Order Tree for Incremental Frequent-Pattern Mining. Knowledge and Information Systems 11(3), 287–311 (2007)
20. Tanbeer, S.K., Ahmed, C.F., Jeong, B.-S., Lee, Y.-K.: CP-Tree: A Tree Structure for Single-Pass Frequent Pattern Mining. In: Washio, T., Suzuki, E., Ting, K.M., Inokuchi, A. (eds.) PAKDD 2008. LNCS (LNAI), vol. 5012, pp. 1022–1027. Springer, Heidelberg (2008)
21. Mishra, P., Chakravarthy, S.: Evaluation of K-way Join and its variants for Association Rule Mining. Information and Technology Lab at The University of Texas at Arlington, TX (2002)

Investigative Behavior Profiling with One Class SVM for Computer Forensics

Wilson Naik Bhukya[1] and Sateesh Kumar Banothu[2]

[1] Department of Computer and Information Sciences,
University of Hyderabad, Hyderabad - 500046, India
naikcs@uohyd.ernet.in
[2] Department of Information Technology,
JNTUH College of Engineering, Jagityal, Karimnagar, India
sateeshbkumar@gmail.com

Abstract. Behavior profiling of a user or a system is of great importance and is a non-trivial task of system forensic experts. User profiling information is very much useful for forensic investigators by monitoring and collecting significant changes in user's behavior based on his/her computer usage patterns. Traditional investigation mechanisms are based on command line system events collected using log files. In a GUI based investigative profiling system, most of the user activities are performed using either mouse movements and clicks or a combination of mouse movements and keystrokes. The command line data cannot capture the complete GUI event behavior of the users hence it is insufficient to perform any forensic analysis in GUI based systems . Presently, there is no frame work available to capture the GUI based user behavior for forensic investigation. We have proposed a novel approach to capture the GUI based user behavior using a logging tool . Our experimentation results shows that, the GUI based investigative profiling forensic can give more accurate and leads to identify the culprits. We have shown how one class SVM is less overhead in terms of training and testing instances for computer forensic compared to two class SVM.

Keywords: GUI based Profiling, Mouse events, forensic investigation, User behavior, SVM.

1 Introduction

Computer Forensic is an emerging branch of forensic science pertaining to legal evidence found in digital medium used for Cyber crime. Cyber crime generally refers to criminal activity where a computer or network is the source, tool, target, or place of a crime. Computer crime can broadly be defined as criminal activity involving an information technology infrastructure, including illegal access (unauthorized access), illegal interception (by technical means of non-public transmissions of computer data to, from or within a computer system), data interference (unauthorized damaging, deletion, deterioration, alteration or

C. Sombattheera et al. (Eds.): MIWAI 2011, LNAI 7080, pp. 373–383, 2011.

suppression of computer data), systems interference (interfering with the functioning of a computer system by inputting, transmitting, damaging, deleting,
deteriorating, altering or suppressing computer data), misuse of devices, forgery
(ID theft), and electronic fraud [24]. The goal of computer forensic investiga-
tor is to perform the investigation using proper tools and procedures that are
validated in the court of law. There are many tools [29][30] available in the literature to assist the forensic investigators to reduce the time and complexity, all
these tools mainly try to find out the file modifications on the disc and network
and hardware usage statistics. However, these tools do not capture or analyze
any GUI usage profiling for Cyber crime. Investigative profiling is an essential
activity in computer forensic that can significantly narrow the search of Cyber
criminal and reason about his/her behavior. This is similar to criminal profiling
which focuses on personality features of an offender in order to identify the type
of the person [32]. Profiling can also help in detecting email or text authorship
[31]. A criminal can take over the account of legitimate user to utilize the priv-
ileges and rights to carry out the malicious agenda [6]. When a person from an
Intranet perpetrates most of his actions may be technically legal for the system
and hence it is more difficult to detect such perpetrations. Also, person inside
the Intranet has enough knowledge about the system as well as the behavior
of the victims so that he can escape detection for a longer period of time. The
only information, which can be used in forensic is to find these kind of crimi-
nals contained in the actions he/she performs. This set of actions is known as
behavioral profile forensic. Profile forensic techniques are based on the premise
that when a a person perpetrates the system, he will sufficiently deviate from
the users normal behavior and thus be caught [2].

To be able to make a distinction between normal and perpetrator behavior, the
computer forensic software plays vital role by monitoring, collecting and utilize
data form user sessions to build user profiles based on different Data Mining
techniques. Data Mining has been successfully used in a variety of domains with
large data sets. It has proven useful for a number of purposes, for example,
describing the contents of data with patterns to summarize the characteristics
of the data set even in the presence of noise and incomplete data [25]. Patterns
can also be viewed as descriptions of the behavior of the data and can be the basis
of the development of profiles (a set of statements about the behavior of what
is being investigated), an important resource for analysis in Computer Forensic
investigations.The user profiles can be build using command line sequences or
GUI events captured for the particular user or by using both. This data is initially
used to train the detection systems about what is normal, and later for detecting
malicious activity.

There have been attempts to capture the user profiles using process table
details and GUI event details for Windows Operating Systems [4][2][8]. However, no work has been done so far for capturing GUI user profile for forensic
investigation. In this paper, we have developed a GUI event logger which is
placed in the Intranet server to collect and analyze data of several users and

used it for forensic investigation. Our main aim was to collect and observe perpetrators abnormal deviation from users normal profile, therefore only binary classifier has been used to check the normal and abnormal user activities . We have used One-class SVM to build self profile with users legitimate sessions and detect perpetrator when significant deviation occurs. Though One-Class SVM has been proven [3][11] best for binary classification, for comparison purpose we have also experimented with Two-class SVM, which is similar to the other classification techniques.

This paper is organized as follows: In section 2, we have discussed background and related work. In section 3, we have described event logging and feature extraction . Section 4 describes our experimental setup for training and testing. Results are presented in section 5. Finally, section 6 outlines conclusions and future work.

2   Background and Related Work

2.1   User Profiling Based on Command Line Data Using Data Mining

Constructing personal profiles has been used in the context of customer personalization. Here, marketing content and services are tailored to an individual on the basis of knowledge about their preferences and behavior. Applications include content based and collaborative filtering-based recommendation systems,customer profiling [1][9], fraud detection [26] and web browsing activities [27][28][34][36]. Another relevant activity within Data Mining is the extraction of sequential patterns [35] which analyzes temporally ordered data in order to model repetitive behavior. [32] has build and analyzed only command line data and frequency of the the events.

2.2   Behavior Profile Based on GUI Data

Pausra and Brodley [8] focused on use of mouse while browsing the web pages in a browser, considering only mouse movements. This approach can be disadvantageous if a user uses an application other than the browser. The GUI based user behavior includes number of mouse clicks, mouse movements, mouse speed, keys pressed etc. This GUI behavior can be used for fraud detection. For this purpose, Garg and Kwait [2] developed an active system logger using Microsoft .NET framework and C# language on Windows XP System.

2.3   Behavior Profile Based on GUI Usage Analysis

The work of Imsand and John [5] is based on the notion of how the current user interacts with the graphical user interface. This method does not use mouse movements or keystroke dynamics, rather profiles how the user manipulates the windows, icons, menus, and pointers that comprise a graphical user interface.

This method has a number of disadvantages. Most of the user profiling seems to be manual then an automated process. This methodology is application specific rather than capturing overall system events and is not generalized for all users. The method of training the system is biased and it is much like a manual survey of the different users, which is very difficult in real world scenario. The use of time factor is not stated clearly in their work. [33] proposed a methodology of GUI user analysis for masquerade attacks which does not highlight anything related to computer forensic investigation and reporting. All the above related work does not show any methodology nor any mechanism for computer forensic.

3   Proposed Method

We have proposed a novel approach to monitor, capture, analyze and report the GUI based user behavior for forensic investigation. This behavior includes amount of mouse clicks, key board shortcuts, different attributes of clicks like, which button was pressed, co-ordinates of mouse, different mouse movements, wheel rotations (horizontal or vertical), and keys pressed during a user session. As there are no publicly available GUI data sets to test the methodology for the forensic investigation, we have developed a logging tool to collect the GUI event details of KDE (K Desktop Environment). We have collected data from 8 different users in the lab using this tool. A hashing technique(SHA-2) is used in order to maintain the integrity of captured data on the server, which is essential as a part of forensic procedure to re verify the integrity in the court of law. Our experimentation results shows that the GUI based behavior can be efficiently used for forensic investigation to achieve high rate of accuracy with less overhead of training and testing using One Class SVM. The above methodology will be useful not only to investigate the computers but also can be customized to investigate many other electronic gadgets which contain GUI applications (Apple iphone and other electronic gadgets).

3.1   KDE Application Structure and Event Capturing

KDE or the K Desktop Environment, is a network transparent contemporary desktop environment for UNIX workstations. KDE seeks to fulfill the need for an easy to use desktop for UNIX workstations, similar to desktop environments found on Macintosh and Microsoft Windows operating systems. Figure 1 shows the architecture of a typical KDE application. *KApplication* is a class that provides low-level KDE application services, and *KTMainWindow* serves as a programmer-friendly base class for our main application window, *KMyMainWindow*. The classes *KMenuBar*, *KToolBar*, and *KStatusBar* are created, positioned, and resized by *KTMainWindow*, but we can customize them from within *KMyMainWindow* [21].

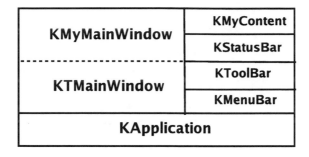

Fig. 1. KDE Application Structure

Widgets are graphical user-interface elements. Simple widgets can be controls or indicators such as a push button or a text label. In KDE, widgets are implemented using C++ classes. Usually there is a One-to-one widget-to-class correspondence. For example, a pushbutton is implemented by *QPushButton*. All widgets are ultimately derived from the *QWidget* base class. All these widgets ultimately interact with the user through the class *KApplication*. *KApplication* dispatches event messages that signal, for example, keypresses or mouse clicks to all the widgets used by an application. *KApplication* receives messages from *X*, the underlying windowing system, and distributes them to the widgets in your application.

System Events. Window system events tell the widget when it needs to repaint, reposition, or resize itself, when mouse clicks or keystrokes have been directed toward that widget, when the widget receives or loses the focus, and so on. *QWidget* handles the events by calling a virtual method for each event. Each method get passed, as an argument, a class containing information about the event. To handle the event, the corresponding method must be reimplemented in the subclass of *QWidget*. Figure 2 shows the event capturing procedure.

3.2   Experimental Setup

Data Collection. We have collected user behavior data for multiple users and extracted unique parameters to be able to construct the feature vectors which are similar to investigation clues to crack the case. For this purpose, we have developed an *active event logger* for KDE (K Desktop Environment) in Linux. KDE is one of most powerful desktop environments for Linux.

All the GUI event details are logged to log file on a NFS server. Event details include name of the event, time of event occurrence, and different attributes of the event. The following are the some of the event details from the log file required for investigative profiling:

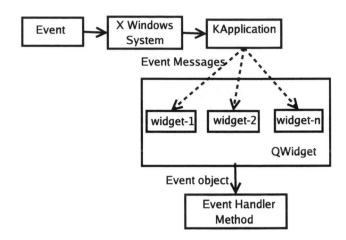

Fig. 2. Event capturing

User Session Started ....
Event Occurred at:Fri Apr 6 23:34:49 2007
Event :: Mouse Cursor entered the Window
Event Occurred at:Fri Apr 6 23:34:53 2007
Event :: Mouse clicked
Window Coordinates:27 39
Global Coordinates:132 163
Button Pressed : Left
Key Board Shortcut : Alt+c.

Feature Extraction. After collecting the user data, we have extracted useful and unique parameters of the user behavior to be able to construct unique feature vectors for training and testing with SVM [2]. We have extracted the following unique features from that of [2].

Mouse Clicks (lc, rc, dc): the average number of left, right, and double mouse clicks per user session as well as activity for each 10 minute window during the session.
Mouse Enter and Exit (en,ex): the average number of mouse entrance and exits in to the window per user session.
Wheel Rotations (wh, wv): the average number of horizontal and vertical wheel rotations per user session.
Key Pressed (kp): the average number of keys pressed per user session.
Keyboard shortcuts used (ks): the average number of keyboard shortcuts per user session.
Taking above features we have constructed the feature vectors for all the users.

Calculation of Features. Moreover, we have constructed 18 features for every user after extracting parameters as described in previous section. They are :

Mouse Clicks: *(lc,rc,dc)* = 3
Mouse Enter and Exit : *(en,ex)* = 2
Wheel Rotations : *(wh,wv)* = 2
Key Pressed : *(kp)* = 1
Keyboard shortcuts used: *(ks)*=1

The total of these raw features is 9. Additionally, we calculated the mean *'m'* and standard deviation *'sd'* for all the raw features above. This gives a total of 18 unique features represented as:

(lc,rc,dc,en,ex,wh,wv,kp,ks) * *(m,sd)*

we have applied sliding window technique on these features to generate the tuples. These tuples are given as input to the SVM [2], as SVMs have been known to be highly effective in text classification [16],[17].

We not only calculated all the features of the particular users but also we have the option of forensic report generated according to the law requirements, to show the authenticity and time of the collected features.

4   Applying One-Class Profile Identification

We have used a Two-class SVM for which both the positive and negative training is required. To improve the investigation time with large data which is created out of several GUI events, we have also applied *One-class profile identification.* One-class SVM requires only the user's legitimate sessions training to build up the user's profile and not the illegitimate sessions [3][11]. Therefore, when only user's legitimate sessions are available, one class training is the only viable approach.

4.1   One-Class SVM

Our main aim is to detect abnormal profiles and for that we have checked that new sessions does or doesn't belongs to the real user (a "Positive" or "Negative"). We have used one target user's some sessions as "positive data" to train a One-class SVM without any negative training data. We have used remaining sessions of that user for testing purpose. For each target user (User A, User B, User C, User D, ...), a set of the sessions from the target user are trained as positive with out any negative training. Then the remaining sessions from the target user are used for testing with each other user's sessions as negative.

We have used the data set from 8 user's for this One-class SVM approach. User A (10 sessions), User B (8 Sessions), User C (9 sessions), User D (8 sessions), User E (6 sessions), User F (7 sessions), User G (6 sessions), User H (8 sessions).

5   Results and Discussion

The collected data from 8 different users across the subnet was fed to the parsing engine, as described to obtain 18 features. These features were used to create tuples for providing input to the SVMs. The methodology to train and test the system was as follows:

- Data sets were obtained for four distinct users A(10 sessions), B(8 sessions), C(9 sessions), and D(8 sessions).
- The obtained data was split for training and testing as follows:

Table 1. Training and Testing sessions

User	Training sessions	Testing sessions
A	5	5
B	4	4
C	5	4
D	4	4

- Used the sliding window technique to generate feature vectors
- Used training and testing sets for SVM as described in previous section and calculated detection rates and error rates
- We have used SVM lite software, which implements Vapiniks Support vector machine[17].

5.1   One-Class SVM Results

We have used the data set from 8 user's for this One-class SVM approach. User A (10 sessions), User B (8 Sessions), User C (9 sessions), User D (8 sessions), User E (6 sessions), User F (7 sessions), User G (6 sessions), User H (8 sessions).

For each target user, we have trained the SVM using only the legitimate training sessions. Note that when only the user's own legitimate sessions are available, One-class training is the only viable approach [3][11].

For example, consider the training and testing strategy for User D. The User D is trained as positive. 4 positive sessions from User D are used for training and the remaining 4 positive sessions are tested with each other user's sessions as negative.

The average investigative detection rate is 94.88% for User D using One-class SVM approach.

5.2   Comparing with Two-Class SVM Approach

The same data set (8 users) is tested with the Two-class SVM. In this approach, we have trained both the positive and negative samples and the results are compared with the One-class SVM approach.

The average user profile forensic identification rate of our experiments is only 53.08%, compared to 94.88% of one-class approach. We observed that, we can obtain higher accuracy of forensic investigation with less time using One-class SVM approach compared to Two-class approach. Moreover, One-class approach requires less training data because there is no need of training the negative

Table 2. result of One-class SVM for User-D

User	Hits(%)	ERR
User E	97.24%	2.75%
User F	95.00%	5.00%
User G	94.87%	5.12%
User H	92.42%	7.8%
Average	94.88%	5.16%

sessions (illegitimate sessions). Which in turn reduces the overall investigation time. We have also compared our results with the previous work done in Microsoft Windows environment [4]. For 3 users and 8 features, their detection rate is 73.85% and false positive rate is 26.15% where as we achieved 94.88% using one class SVM.

6   Conclusions

We have designed and developed a new framework for monitoring, capturing and analyzing and reporting GUI based user behavior for system forensic investigation. We have collected data from a Linux system placed in an Intranet server using a logger developed for KDE(KDesktop Environment). We have constructed trivial features from these parameters and used support vector machine algorithms to first train and then classify the users using both One-class as well as Two-class SVMs to find the accurate perpetrators with less time of forensic investigation. Our results demonstrate that One-class SVM is far better than Two-class SVM for this problem of perpetrator identification not only in terms of finding accurate perpetrator but but also in terms of training and testing times. We have found that user behavior features based on mouse and keyboard activities on a GUI based system can be effectively used to uniquely identify users and thus provide very good forensic analysis.

As part of our future work, we plan to generalize the event capturing for all the GUI applications of different electronic gadgets . We also want to experiment for many users with huge data set. We have also observed that different events across the system can be collected and analyzed in the layered form. The layered architecture can give more accurate results for computer forensic investigation.

References

1. Adomavicius, G., Tuzhilin, A.: Expertdriven validation of rule-based user models in personalization applications. Data Mining and Knowledge Discovery 5(1/2), 33–58 (2001)
2. Garg, A., Rahalkar, R., Upadhyaya, S., Kwait, K.: Profiling Users in GUI Based Systems for Masquerade Detection. In: Proceedings of 7th Annual IEEE Information Assurance Workshop (IAW 2006), June 21-23. United States Military Academy, West Point (2006)

3. Heller, K.A., Svore, K.M., Keromytis, A.D., Stolfo, S.J.: One Class Vector Machines for Detecting Anomalous Windows Registry Accesses. In: Proceedings of 2003 International Conference on Data Mining (ICDM 2003), November 19 (2003)
4. Li, L., Manikopoulos, C.N.: Windows NT One-class Masquerade Detection. In: Proceedings of 2004 IEEE Information Assurance Workshop (IAW 2004). United States Military Academy, West Point (2004)
5. Imsand, E.S., Hamilton Jr, J.A.: GUI Usage Analysis for Masquerade Detection. In: Proceedings of 2007 IEEE, Information Assurance Workshop (IAW 2007), June 21-23. United States Military Academy, West Point (2007)
6. Coull, S.E., Branch, J.W., Szymanski, B.K., Breimer, E.A.: Sequence Alignment for Masquerade Detection (2006)
7. Coull, S., Branch, J., Szymanski, B., Breimer, E.: Intrusion detection: A bioinformatics approach. In: 19th Annual Computer Security Applications Conferences, Las Vegas, Nevada, December 8-12 (2003)
8. Pusara, M., Brodley, C.: User Re-authentication via mouse movements. In: Proceedings of the 2004 ACM Workshop on Visualization and Data Mining for Computer Security, Washington D.C., USA, October 29 (2004)
9. Hirsh, M., Basu, C., Davidson, B.: Learning to personalize. Communications of the ACM 43(8), 102–106 (2000)
10. Schonlau, M., DuMouchel, W., Ju, W.-H., Karr, A.F., Theus, M., Vardi, Y.: Computer Intrusion: Detecting Masquerades. Statistical Science 16, 58–74 (2001)
11. Wang, K., Stolfo, S.J.: One Class Training for Masquerade Detection. In: ICDM Workshop on Data Mining for Computer Security, DMSEC 2003 (2003)
12. Monrose, F., Rubin, A.: Authentication via Keystroke Dynamics. In: ACM Conference on Computer and Communications Security, pp. 48–56 (1997)
13. Pusara, M., Brodley, C.E.: User re-authentication via mouse movements. In: VizSEC/DMSEC 2004: Proceedings of the 2004 ACM Workshop on Visualization and Data Mining for Computer Security, Washington DC, USA, pp. 1–8 (2004)
14. Wespi, A., Dacier, M., Debar, H.: Intrusion Detection Using Variable-Length Audit Trail Patterns. In: Debar, H., Mé, L., Wu, S.F. (eds.) RAID 2000. LNCS, vol. 1907, pp. 110–129. Springer, Heidelberg (2000)
15. Feng, H., Kolesnikov, O., Fogla, P., Lee, W., Gong, W.: Anomaly Detection using Call Stack Information. In: Proceedings of IEEE Symposium on Security and Privacy, Oakland, California (May 2003)
16. Joachims, T.: Text Categorization with Support Vector Machines: Learning with Many Relevant Features. In: Nédellec, C., Rouveirol, C. (eds.) ECML 1998. LNCS, vol. 1398, pp. 137–142. Springer, Heidelberg (1998)
17. Joachims, T.: SVM light:Support Vector Machine (2004), http://www.cs.cornell.edu/People/tj/svmlight/index.html
18. Ghosh, A., Schwartzbard, A., Schatz, M.: Learning Program Behavior Profiles for Intrusion Detection. In: First USENIX Workshop on Intrusion Detection and Network Monitoring, pp. 51–62 (1999)
19. Levitt, K., Ko, C., Fink, G.: Automated Detection of Vulnerabilities in Privileged Programs by Execution Monitoring. In: Computer Security Application Conference (1994)
20. Schonlau, M.: Masquerading User Data (1998), http://www.schonlau.net/intrusion.html
21. http://developer.kde.org/documentation/books/kde-2.0-development

22. Dash, S.K., Reddy, K.S., Pujari, A.K.: Episode Based Masquerade Detection. In: Jajodia, S., Mazumdar, C. (eds.) ICISS 2005. LNCS, vol. 3803, pp. 251–262. Springer, Heidelberg (2005)
23. Kim, H.-S., Cha, S.-D.: Empherical evaluation of SVM-based masquerade detection using UNIX commands. Computers and Security 24, 160–168 (2005)
24. http://en.wikipedia.org/wiki/Cybercrime
25. Ester, M., Kriegel, H.-P., Sander, J., Xu, X.: A density-based algorithm for discovering clusters in large spatial databases with noise. In: Proceedings of the Second Int. Conference on Knowledge Discovery and Data Mining (1996)
26. Fawcett, T., Provost, F.: Adaptive fraud detection. Data Mining and Knowledge Discovery 1(3), 291–316 (1997)
27. Chan, P.K.: A Non-Invasive Learning Approach to Building Web User Profiles. In: Masand, B., Spiliopoulou, M. (eds.) WebKDD 1999. LNCS (LNAI), vol. 1836, pp. 39–55. Springer, Heidelberg (2000)
28. Mannila, H., Toivonen, H., Verkamo, A.: Discovery of Frequent Episodes in Event Sequences. Data Mining and Knowledge Discovery 1(3), 259–289 (1997)
29. http://www.opensourceforensics.org/tools/index.html
30. http://www.guidancesoftware.com
31. Van Halteren, H.: Radboud University Nijmegen, The Netherlands Author verification by linguistic profiling: An exploration of the parameter space. ACM Transactions on Speech and Language Processing (TSLP) Archive 4(1) (January 2007); table of contents Article No. 1 Year of Publication: 2007 ISSN:1550-4875
32. Abraham, T.: Event sequence mining to develop profiles for computer forensic investigation purposes. In: Proceedings of the 2006 Australasian Workshops on Grid Computing and e-research. ACM International Conference Proceeding Series, vol. 167(54) (2006)
33. Bhukya, W.N., Kommuru, S.K., Negi, A.: Masquerade Detection Based Upon GUI User Profiling in Linux Systems. In: Cervesato, I. (ed.) ASIAN 2007. LNCS, vol. 4846, pp. 228–239. Springer, Heidelberg (2007)
34. Tan, P.-N., Kumar, V.: Mining Indirect Associations in Web Data. In: Kohavi, R., Masand, B., Spiliopoulou, M., Srivastava, J. (eds.) WebKDD 2001. LNCS (LNAI), vol. 2356, pp. 145–166. Springer, Heidelberg (2002)
35. Srikant, R., Agrawal, R.: Mining generalized association rules. In: Proceedings of 21st VLDB Conference (1995)
36. Mobasher, B., Dai, H., Luo, T., Sun, Y., Wiltshire, J.: Discovery of aggregate usage profiles for web personalization. In: Proceedings of the Workshop on Web Mining for E-Commerce, WEBKDD 2000 (2000)

Compromise Matching in P2P e-Marketplaces: Concept, Algorithm and Use Case

Manish Joshi[1], Virendrakumar C. Bhavsar[2], and Harold Boley[3]

[1] Department of Computer Science,
North Maharashtra University, Jalgaon, India
joshmanish@gmail.com
[2] Faculty of Computer Science,
University of New Brunswick, Fredericton, Canada
bhavsar@unb.com
[3] Institute for Information Technology,
National Research Council Canada
harold.boley@nrc.gc.ca

Abstract. A basic component of automated matchmaking is the automatic generation of a ranked list of profiles matching with the profiles of a given participant. Identifying and ranking of matching profiles among thousands of candidate profiles is a challenging task. In order to determine the degree of matching between two profiles, corresponding pairs of constraints are compared and aggregated to the overall similarity between the two profiles.

This paper describes the structure and algorithm of a proposed matchmaking system with a focus on the central notion of compromise match. A compromise match is called for when either one or both constraints within a pair are soft and moreover their values do not match exactly. Two important aspects of compromise matching are discussed, namely *compromise count factor, compromise count reduction factor*; furthermore their effect on ranking is described. A use case with a sample set of home rental profiles from an existing e-marketplace is employed for demonstration.

Keywords: Matchmaking in e-marketplaces, soft constraints, compromise match.

1 Introduction

The use of automated matchmaking in e-marketplaces is increasing rapidly. Several matchmaking systems have been proposed with the objective to assist buyers and sellers in e-marketplaces [1–7]. In a peer-to-peer e-marketplace participants (sellers / buyers) can submit their profiles and browse through counterpart profiles. A profile is a collection of participants' expectations regarding products/services that are offered/sought.For any profile 'P' an automated matchmaking system would find the best available counterpart profiles that match the needs mentioned in the profile 'P'.

C. Sombattheera et al. (Eds.): MIWAI 2011, LNAI 7080, pp. 384–394, 2011.
© Springer-Verlag Berlin Heidelberg 2011

A participant may have numerous and multifaceted expectations, which are also called as *constraints*. To model such complex expectations and furthermore to appropriately represent profiles, is a key issue for the success of an automated matchmaking system.

The relative flexibility of participants regarding the fulfillment of a constraint gives an additional dimension to the problem. Hard and Soft constraints determine whether a participant can proceed with a match even if the condition value described by his/her constraint is not satisfied by the value of the corresponding constraint of the counterpart profile.

Soft constraints bring in flexibility and let participants negotiate on constraint facet value. Most of the profile matches in e-marketplaces lie in between a complete mismatch and an exact match (exact matching of all constraints of two profiles). The presence of soft constraints is mainly responsible for such matches. Hence, soft constraint matching needs explicit attention.

A review and comparison of many matchmaking systems is given in [9]. However, only two matchmaking systems [8] [12] explicitly defined Hard and Soft constraints. While computing the matchmaking results, these systems analyze the effect of mismatching software constraints.

In the system proposed by Veit et al. [8], declaration of a constraint type (hard or soft) for each constraint in a profile is mandatory. The type of a constraint plays an important role in the determination of an overall distance of a candidate profile from a centroid profile. Whereas, in Ragone et al. [12] matchmaking system constraints are split into strict requirements (hard constraints) and preferences (soft constraints). Participants have to assign utility values to soft constraints, which are used while computing the matchmaking score. These systems, however, cannot categorize the profiles depending upon the characteristics of soft constraints pertaining to the profiles.

In this paper, we discuss the role of soft constraints in *compromise matching* and describe how our matchmaking system effectively manages the issues related with soft constraints. With the help of an use case we demonstrate how user can influence ranking of matchmaking profiles according to his/her preferences.

The remaining paper is organized as follows. Section 2 elaborates our matchmaking system that is used to experiment with soft constraints. The concept of a compromise match and proposed solutions are discussed in section 3. Section 4 demonstrates the rank management by changing compromise match related parameters followed by conclusions in section 5.

2   Matchmaking System

Since ICEC-2010 proceedings are not readily available, we are giving some of the definitions about profile representation as a handy reference from [10] for various terminologies used while explaining compromise matching.

Following two subsections describe the profile representation and a modified matchmaking algorithm respectively.

Room to rent on Church Street, 10 to 15 min walk to Campus. Looking for a working professional or mature student (preferably male) to rent a one bedroom in a two bedroom apartment. Includes, heats / lights, phone, cable, high speed Internet, for $450.00 to $480.00. Laundry facilities on location. Parking available. If you are interested, please call me at XXX-XXXX or XXX-XXXX.

< area, {Church Street}, No, 1 >
< bedrooms,{1}, No, 1 >
< partner,{student, professional}, No, 1 >
< partnerGender,{male}, Yes, 1.1 >
< rent,{450 $\cdots$ 480}, No, 1 >
< type,{Shared Apartment}, No, 1 >

Fig. 1. Representation of a Seller Profile

2.1   Profile Representation

A participant profile $P = \{C_1, C_2, C_3, ..., C_m\}$ is a set of constraints. Each constraint is a quadruple $C_i = \langle a, d, f, p \rangle$, where a is an attribute, d is a set of values used to describe an attribute, flexibility that determines whether a constraint is a soft or a hard constraint which is indicated by f, and p is the priority of a constraint. All elements of a constraint are described below.

Attribute (a)- An attribute represents the facet. For example, if a participant has a constraint 'Looking for 3 bedrooms', then the attribute of this constraint is 'bedrooms'. This field always has an alphabetical value.

Description (d)- Description represents a set of values that can be assigned to an attribute of a constraint. In the example of 'Looking for 3 bedrooms', the attribute 'bedrooms' of the constraint has the description value '3'. Let D be the domain of d. $d \subset D$. D contains all possible member values that a description set can have. D contains alphabetical strings that describe an attribute, or numerical values that can be assigned to an attribute, or a combination of both, or a range value having a format like $num_1 \cdots num_2$ such that $num_1, num_2 \in R$.

Consider a user who asks for a '2 or 3 bedroom apartment'. In this case, the attribute 'bedrooms' have a description value that can be represented as a set of 'multiple values' or a 'range'. Hence <bedrooms, {2, 3}, f, p> and <bedrooms, {2 $\cdots$ 3}, f, p> are both valid representations and have identical meanings. Figure 1 shows the 'rent' constraint that has a range description.

Flexibility (f)- Flexibility indicates whether the constraint is a hard or a soft constraint. $f \subset F$, where $F = \{No, Yes\}$. A 'No' value of f (i.e. no flexibility) indicates a rigidness of the constraint, whereas a value 'Yes' represents a soft constraint. A soft constraint is matched with any value of the corresponding constraint of the counterpart profile as a compromise match. A constraint specification provided by a buyer as 'house rent must be 500' indicates a hard constraint and is represented as <rent, {500}, No, p>. A constraint description

'Smoking is not allowed, but can smoke in balcony', represents a soft constraint. It can be represented as <allowSmoke, {No}, Yes, p>.

Priority (*p*) - The priority describes the relative priority of soft constraints among other soft constraints, in a profile. The value of p can be any real value grater than 0. $p \in R$. All soft constraints are initialized with the priority values of 1. The priority values for all soft constraints are set automatically to match the preferences indicated by participants.

For example, if a buyer specifies that the facet 'pets' with value 'allowed' is more important to him than all remaining facets, then priority value for this constraint is set to a value grater than 1. The constraint is represented as <pets, {allowed}, Yes, 1.1>, and all remaining constraints will have *p* values as 1. Note that, the value of flexibility in this example, is 'Yes', indicating a soft constraint. These priority values ultimately used to rank the service represented by the facet. The 'partnerGender' attribute shown in Figure 1 has a priority for *male* and hence its priority value is set accordingly grater than 1.

Figure 1 illustrate how a profile can be represented in our model. The description of the participant profile is followed by a quadruple representation.

2.2   Algorithm

The similarity value between any two profiles is defined as a function of attribute, description, flexibility and priority values of all constraints from both profiles. For any two profiles P_x and P_y, where P_x has m constraints and P_y has n constraints, a similarity value Sim is obtained as described in an algorithm (Fig. 2).

```
Sim  = 1
for i = 1 to m
    for j = 1 to n
        if (S (Ci, Cj) > 0) then
            Sim * = S(Ci, Cj)
        if (S(Ci, Cj) < 0) then
            Sim - = OmissionPenalty
```

Fig. 2. Algorithm to compute similarity value

The function $S(C_i, C_j)$ calculates an **intermediate similarity value** using steps listed in the algorithm in Fig. 3. Note that the number of constraints in two profiles may not be the same. For a constraint C_i, its attributes, description, flexibility and priority values are represented using $C_{i.a}$, $C_{i.d}$, $C_{i.f}$, and $C_{i.p}$, respectively.

The algorithm (Fig. 3) considers a pair of constraints of two profiles. All constraints in a profile are lexicographically sorted on attribute values. Hence, if an attribute value of an ith constraint of the P_x profile is less than an attribute value of a jth constraint of the P_y profile, then next constraint of the profile P_x

```
if (C_{i.a} = C_{j.a}) then
    if (C_{i.d} = C_{j.d}) then
        S = C_{i.p} × C_{j.p}
    else
        if (C_{i.f} = No) AND (C_{j.f} = No) then
            S = C_{i.p} × C_{j.p} × relDiff(C_{i.d}, C_{j.d})
        elseif (C_{i.f} = Yes) AND (C_{j.f} = Yes)
            S = C_{i.p} × C_{j.p} × β
        else
            S = C_{i.p} × C_{j.p} × α
    C_i = C_{i++}
    C_j = C_{j++}
if (C_{i.a} < C_{j.a}) then
    C_i = C_{i++}
    return − 1
if (C_{i.a} > C_{j.a}) then
    C_j = C_{j++}
    return 0
return S
```

Fig. 3. Algorithm to compute intermediate similarity value

is obtained by setting $C_i = C_{i++}$. For such a missing constraint of the profile P_x, the similarity value is reduced by a certain fraction called as 'omissionPenalty'.

If the attributes of both the constraints are the same then an intermediate similarity value is calculated by checking the description values. For an exact match between the two constraints $(C_{i.d} = C_{j.d})$, the intermediate similarity value is obtained by multiplying priority values $(C_{i.p} \times C_{j.p})$. The multiplication of priority values of both the constraints ensures that a soft constraint with higher priority would secure higher intermediate similarity value.

If the description values are not same then an intermediate similarity value is calculated by considering the flexibility of the constraints. When hard constraints in two profiles do not match, instead of reducing the similarity value to zero, we compute a relative difference between the two corresponding description values of these attributes. For computing the relative difference, a routine *relDiff* is used. Note that for numeric and alphabetical values of d, separate routines are required to obtain relative differences. Since we are considering hard constraints, our algorithm for *relDiff* routine adjusts the difference by a factor so that the resulting intermediate similarity value is substantially small.

The parameters α and β are *compromise count reduction factors* used in a case of compromise match and its usage is elaborated in the next section.

A list of our use case profiles of landlords (LP-1 to LP-6) and Tenants (TP-1 to TP-6) is tabulated in Appendix A. Following example shows how similarity value is obtained when profile TP-1 is matched with profile LP-2.

Intermediate similarity values are computed when each constraint of TP-1 is compared with corresponding constraint of LP-2. One constraint of TP-1 with attribute 'available' does not have corresponding attribute match in LP-2 profile. The description values of both the profiles for constraints with attributes 'bedrooms' (2 each), 'rent' (600···900 and 625) and 'type' (apartment each) have an exact match. Whereas for 'allowSmoke' attribute, the description values mismatch (yes and no respectively). But both the 'allowSmoke' constraints are soft constraints and hence the similarity value is multiplied by an appropriate compromise count reduction factor β.

3 Compromise Match

The concept of soft constraints induces the notion of a compromise match. We define the concept of compromise matching and illustrate its implementation in this section.

As defined earlier, soft constraint indicates participant's approval to counterpart's facet value irrespective of match with his/her own facet value. Such soft constraints, in particular, lead to compromise matching between any two profiles in a matchmaking system. A pair of constraints from two profiles said to have a compromise match if, either one or both of the constraints in a comparison are soft constraints and the values of the facets of both the corresponding constraints do not match. In such a case, either one or both participants may compromise with the mismatching value mentioned in the counterpart constraint. Hence we refer to it as a 'compromise match'.

The 'allowSmoke' attribute of the first constraint of the TP-1 profile when compared with the 'allowSmoke' constraint of the profile LP-3, it results in an exact match for these constraints. The matching value 'yes' for these two constraints yield an exact match. However, when the same constraint from the TP-1 profile is compared with an appropriate constraint of the LP-2 profile, a compromise match emerges. Both the above mentioned conditions are satisfied. A compromise match would also result when the same constraint of TP-1 is compared with a corresponding constraint of profile LP-1.

A compromise match is not an exact match hence a similarity value between corresponding profiles should be reduced. In our matchmaking system, when there is a compromise match between two constraints, an intermediate similarity value (refer algorithm in Fig 3) is reduced by a certain factor. Consider an example of a soft constraint by a landlord, "rent is $700 and can be negotiated" (LP-4) and a tenant's (buyer's) soft constraint as "I am ready to pay $500 as rent but can pay more for additional services" (TP-3). These two constraints have a compromise match. As both the participants are ready to compromise with their preferred rent amounts, it is likely that these two participants can reach an agreement. Despite of a difference of $200 these two participants' willingness to negotiate on rent facet is a prominent factor that increases the likelihood of an agreement between these two participants.

In case of a comparison between the same LP-4 rent constraint with TP-2 rent profile constraint ($600 rent amount and a hard constraint), it is important to note that, only one participant (the landlord) is willing to negotiate. Although the difference in preferred amount is of $100, the likelihood of an agreement between these two profiles (LP-4 and TP-3) is relatively less than the participants in earlier example (LP-4 and TP-2).

Hence, we conclude that a similarity value in case of a compromise match is influenced by the count (*compromise count factor*) of participants (one or both) willing to compromise.

We propose two compromise count reduction factors, α and β to reduce an intermediate similarity value, in case of a compromise match. The compromise count reduction factor α is associated with compromise count factor value 1 while the β is associated with compromise count factor value 2. The values of α and β are parameters of our system and are set to less than 1. The algorithm given in the previous subsection to compute the intermediate similarity value S shows how these parameters are used in the calculation. The next section demonstrates effect of different values of α and β on ranking of the matching profiles.

Table 1. Results of Matchmaking

Profiles		Similarity Value	Category
LP-4	TP-4	0.995	Potential
	TP-1	0.990	Potential
	TP-5	0.985	Potential
	TP-3	0.9702	Compromise (both)
	TP-2	0.9504	Compromise (one)
	TP-6	0.0	Mismatch
TP-1	LP-3	1.0	Exact
	LP-4	0.990	Potential
	LP-2	0.975	Compromise (both)
	LP-5	0.0	Mismatch
	LP-6	0.0	Mismatch
	LP-1	0.0	Mismatch

If a compromise count is one, then there are relatively fewer chances of an agreement as only one participant is ready to compromise. The compromise count reduction factor α represents this case, while the factor β is used when compromise count is two. We set the values of parameters α and β such that a higher similarity value shall be resulted in a compromise match where both participants are ready to compromise and relatively a lower similarity value shall be resulted if only one participant is ready to compromise.

We have implemented the compromise matching in Java and incorporated it in our previous matchmaking system [11] for computing similarity between a set of given profiles. We have applied the system to find the similarity values for all possible combinations for the profiles LP-4 and TP-1 and the result is presented in Table 1. The table also specifies the category of the match between any two profiles P_x and P_y. The categories are defined as follows:

1. **Exact:** All constraints of profile P_x are present in profile P_y and have exact matches.
2. **Potential:** Some of the constraints from profile P_x are not present in profile P_y. However, all the remaining constraints of profiles P_x and P_y have exact matching constraints.
3. **Compromise:** At least one compromise match exists between the constraints of profile of P_x and profile P_y. Based on the compromise count factor we propose two subcategories as
   (a) **Compromise(both):** A compromise match with compromise count factor two.
   (b) **Compromise(one):** A compromise match with compromise count factor one.

4   Compromise Match Trade Off

Let profile P_A, P_B and P_C are three profiles. P_A has two soft constraints, P_B has one hard constraint and P_C has two soft constraints.

Let $Match1$ be a similarity value between P_A and P_B (single compromise match). Let $Match2$ be a similarity value between P_A and P_C (two compromise matches).

Table 2. Compromise Match and Ranking

Case 1: $Match3 > Match4$	
$\alpha = 0.93$, $\beta = 0.95$	
Similarity between P_A and P_B (One compromise match with compromise count factor as 1)	Similarity between P_A and P_C (Two compromise matches with compromise count factor as 2)
$Match3 : 1 \times \alpha = 0.93$	$Match4 : 1 \times \beta \times \beta = 0.9025$
Rank 1: P_A with P_B **Rank** 2: P_A with P_C	
Case 2: $Match4 > Match3$	
$\alpha = 0.88$, $\beta = 0.95$	
Similarity between P_A and P_B (One compromise match with compromise count factor as 1)	Similarity between P_A and P_C (Two compromise matches with compromise count factor as 2)
$Match3 : 1 \times \alpha = 0.88$	$Match4 : 1 \times \beta \times \beta = 0.9025$
Rank 1: P_A with P_C (In Case 1, this match was at rank 2) **Rank** 2: P_A with P_B (In Case 1, this match was at rank 1)	

It is obvious that user would wish ranking of these matches that comply $Match1 > Match2$.

But when compromise count factor is considered the ranking is not that obvious.

Let $Match3$ be a similarity value between P_A and P_B (single compromise match) with compromise count factor 1 (only one participant is ready to compromise, owner of P_A in this case). Let $Match4$ be a similarity value between P_A and P_C (two compromise matches) with compromise count factor 2 (both participants are ready to compromise).

In this case, one can not easily determine whether $Match3$ should be grater than $Match4$ or $Match4$ should be grater than $Match3$. Participants' choice should be decisive in this trade off.

By setting the values of compromise count reduction factors α and β as shown in table 2, we can manipulate ranks in such matchings.

This example illustrates how different values of compromise count reduction factors can be used for ranking matchmaking results according to user preferences.

5   Conclusion

The flexibility supported to participants by the soft constraints leads to compromise matching. We have explicitly defined compromise matching and identified important aspects associated with it. We have developed a matchmaking system in Java for computing similarity among a set of given profiles. We illustrated compromise matching using this matchmaking system. We have applied the system to determine the similarity among seller and buyer profiles that are obtained from an existing e-marketplace. The role of soft constraints in such compromise matches has been elaborated. We proposed and demonstrated the effect of compromise count reduction factors in ranking of matches.

References

1. Bhavsar, V.C., Boley, H., Lu, Y.: A Weighted-Tree Similarity Algorithm for Multi-Agent Systems in e-Business Environments. Computational Intelligence 20, 584–602 (2004)
2. Kuokka, D., Harada, L.: Integrating Information via Matchmaking. Journal of Intelligent Information Systems 6, 261–279 (1996)
3. Liesbeth, K., Rosmalen, P., Sloep, P., Kon, M., Koper, R.: Matchmaking in Learning Networks: Bringing Learners Together for Knowledge Sharing Systems. The Netherlands Interactive Learning Environments 15(2), 117–126 (2007)
4. Mohaghegh, S., Razzazi, M.R.: An Ontology Driven Matchmaking Process. World Automation Congress 16, 248–253 (2004)
5. Noia, T.D., Sciascio, E.D., Donini, F.M., Mongiello, M.: A System for Principled Matchmaking in an Electronic Marketplace. International Journal of Electronic Commerce 8, 9–37 (2004)

6. Subrahmanian, V.S., Bonatti, P., Dix, J., Eiter, T., Kraus, S., Ozcan, F., Ross, R.: Heterogenous Agent Systems. MIT Press (2000)
7. Sycara, K., Widoff, S., Klusch, M., Lu, J.: Larks: Dynamic Matchmaking among Heterogeneous Software Agents in Cyberspace. Autonomous Agents and Multi-Agent Systems 5, 173–203 (2002)
8. Veit, D., Mller, J.P., Weinhardt, C.: Multidimensional Matchmaking for Electronic Markets. International Journal of Applied Artificial Intelligence 16, 853–869 (2002)
9. Joshi, M.R., Bhavsar, V.C., Boley, H.: Knowledge Representation in Matchmaking Applications. In: Akerkar, R., Sajja, P. (eds.) Advanced Knowledge Based Systems: Models Applications and Research, pp. 29–49 (2010)
10. Joshi, M.R., Bhavsar, V.C., Boley, H.: Matchmaking in P2P e-Marketplaces: Soft Constraints and Compromise Matching In: 12th International Conference on e-Commerce (ICEC 2010), pp. 148–154 (2010)
11. Joshi, M.R., Bhavsar, V.C., Boley, H.: A Knowledge Representation Model for Matchmaking System in e-Marketplaces, In: 11th International Conference on e-Commerce (ICEC 2009) pp. 362–365. ACM (2009)
12. Ragone, A., Straccia, U.V.C., Noia, T.D., Sciascio, E.D., Donini, F.M.: Vague Knowledge Bases for Matchmaking in P2P E-Marketplaces. In: 4th European Conference on The Semantic Web (ECSW 2007), pp. 414–428. Springer, Heidelberg (2007)

Appendix A: Sample Profiles

A sample list of landlord profiles and tenant profiles obtained from an on-line free local classifieds service available at 'http://fredericton.kijiji.ca'.

LP-1
\<allowSmoke, {no}, No, 1\> \<available,{Sept-1},No,1\>
\<pets, {no}, No, 1\> \<rent, {395}, No,1\>
\<type,{bachelor},No, 1\>

LP-2
\<allowSmoke, {no}, Yes, 1\> \<bedrooms,{2},No,1\>
\<parking, {1}, No, 1\> \<rent, {625}, No,1\>
\<type,{apartment},No, 1\>

LP-3
\<allowSmoke, {yes}, No, 1\> \<available,{Sept-1},No,1\>
\<bedrooms,{2},No,1\> \<laundry, {yes}, No, 1\>
\<parking, {2}, No, 1\> \<rent, {900}, No,1\>
\<type,{apartment},No, 1\>

LP-4
\<bedrooms,{2},No,1\>\<lease,{year},No,1\>
\<laundry, {yes}, No, 1\> \<rent, {700}, Yes,1\>
\<type,{apartment},No, 1\>

LP-5
\<available,{Sept-01},No,1\> \<bedrooms,{3},No,1\>
\<rent, {600···900}, No, 1\> \<security,{700},No,1\>
\<type,{apartment},No, 1\>

LP-6
\<rent, {300}, No,1\> \<type,{room},No, 1\>

TP-1
\<allowSmoke, {yes}, Yes, 1\> \<bedrooms,{2}, No, 1\>
\<available,{Sept-1}, No, 1\> \<type,{apartment}, No,1\>
\<rent, {600···900}, No, 1\>

TP-2
\<bedrooms, {2}, No, 1\> \<kids,{yes}, No, 1\>
\<pets,{yes}, No, 1\> \<rent, {600}, No, 1\>
\<type,{apartment}, Yes,1\>

TP-3
\<laundry,{yes}, Yes, 1\> \<pets,{yes}, No, 1\>
\<rent, {500}, Yes, 1\> \<type,{apartment}, Yes,1\>

TP-4
\<area,{downtown}, No, 1\> \<available,{Sept-1},No,1\>
\<bedrooms,{2},No,1\> \<kids,{no}, No, 1\>
\<laundry, {yes}, No, 1\> \<pets, {yes}, No, 1\>
\<rent, {800}, Yes, 1\> \<type,{apartment}, No,1\>

TP-5
\<available,{Sept-1},No,1\> \<rent, {800}, No, 1\>
\<type,{apartment}, No,1\>

TP-6
\<available,{Sept-1},No,1\> \<parking, {1}, Yes, 1\>
\<rent, {500}, No, 1\> \<type,{bachelor}, No,1\>

Online Assignments of Containers to Trains Using Constraint Programming

Abder Aggoun, Ahmed Rhiat, and Jean-Pierre Grassien

KLS OPTIM, ICAM Lille, Port Autonome de Deunkerque, France
abder.aggoun@klsoptim.com

Abstract. In this article we are particularly interested in optimizing the assignment of containers of different sizes to wagons on a train while respecting the business constraints. We present a model of the problem based on Constraint Programming (CP) techniques.

Keywords: Optimization, Constraint Programming, online assignment, containers, wagons, Full Web.

1   Introduction

In this article we are particularly interested in optimizing the assignment of containers of different sizes to wagons on a train while respecting the business constraints. We present a model of the problem based on Constraint Programming (CP) techniques. The application is powered by a solver which is embedded in a full web application enriched with capabilities allowing online interactive operations.

2   SOCHART Project

The SOCHART project (competitiveness cluster I-Trans) addresses a niche market in logistics and especially multimodal platforms and therefore carriers, dockers, port platforms and all shippers who wish to improve and / or better control the logistical process of loading, unloading, packing, stripping and optimized management of areas and ways of handling. The project's goal is to provide tools for decision support, to cover all foreseeable and unforeseeable constraints (random) flow (between the terminal and multimodal platform). They offer means to :

- optimize the management area of the site,
- optimize the assignment of containers to wagons,
- improve the preparation of loading trains, ships, trucks and containers in various forms,
- anticipate the loading plans of trains based on interaction and forecasting planning of movements and equipment handling,
- optimize the loading plans of containers / trucks / barges,
- provide Web service tools to enhance collaboration between shippers and carriers. These tools feature a calendar of qualified international reservations and monitoring carrier schedules driven by an optimization engine to smooth the load of resources.

C. Sombattheera et al. (Eds.): MIWAI 2011, LNAI 7080, pp. 395–405, 2011.

3   Problem Definition

We distinguish three types of planning:

- **Strategic Planning:** this is for example the construction of new segments or the acquisition of rolling stocks.
- **Tactical planning:** this is for example the computation of hourly time-tabling of train staff or the planning of the train assignments according to demands.
- **Operational planning:** this it is for example the scheduling of trains, the assignment of containers to trains or the planning of the loading operations and the equipment handling.

This article deals with the operational planning of trains. Furthermore, assigning a destination of a train is treated beforehand and the results are inputs for component optimization developed in this article. The number of wagons and their specifications are also known. The planning of loading and handling equipment is not addressed in this article.

4   Objectives

The main objectives are:

- Development of an interactive Full Web application incorporating recent AJAX developments to minimize the flow between the workstation and server.
- Development of an optimization engine to compute an initial solution and to assist the operator when completing partial solutions.
- Development of a fast algorithm to assist the operator in choosing the right container for a wagon.

5   State of the Art

The problem is known in literature as "bin packing". The objective is to minimize the number of wagons (bins) while placing the maximum number of containers (items). Solving techniques based on mathematical models using integer linear programming in (Bursting) or metaheuristics [6, 7, 8, 9, 10] are the most well-known for this class of problems. The constraints taken into account are the maximum weight constraints attached to wagons, the maximum number of containers per wagon, the number of wagons attached to a train and its total weight. Within these limited number of constraints the problem can be solved to optimal degrees.

The application handles new additional business constraints, among them:

1. The handling of dangerous goods.
2. The incompatibilities between families of containers, e.g. two containers containing dangerous goods cannot be assigned to the same wagon.
3. The original constraints of wagon-makers which are configuration constraints.

These business constraints and especially the handling of constraints associated with configurations of the selected wagons make the problem difficult to solve. In addition, one must handle preference constraints to increase the quality of solutions.

Currently planning is carried out manually and requires several hours. The approach chosen in this article to model and solve the problem is Constraint Programming techniques.

6   Logistical Entities

6.1   Train

Every trip in a rail train with the logistical attributes: destination, speed, train length, estimated weight, route and departure and arrival times.

A first treatment determines the constraints to respect from these parameters: admissible gauges over rail lines (depending on the route to follow), the maximum length (hence the number of wagons), the maximum weight not to exceed.

6.2   Container

A container is characterized by a set of logistical attributes:

- Identification
- The empty weight
- The gauge constraint
- The size
- Indications of the content: code of the dangerous goods.

The main logistical attributes selected for optimization are the total weight of the container and the contents therein, the "content" attributes must take into account the constraints related to dangerous goods.

6.3   Wagon

A car (wagon) is defined by the logistical attributes:

- A number
- A type
- The empty weight
- The gauge
- The number of axles.

Constraints:

- The capacity of the wagon: the number of TEUs (Twenty foot Equivalent Unit).
- The length.
- The maximum permissible weight.

There are several types of wagons. Each car type has its own loading constraints. The plan of charging a car obeys models which are called loading configurations. To each wagon type one or more configurations is/are associated.

6.4   Configuration

A configuration corresponds to a type of pre-specified load plan by the manufacturer; they are patterns. It is structured into slots. A slot position describes the position of containers or unit loads on the vehicle. It is characterized by the following attributes:

- *The starting plot:* the first plot on which we place the transport unit.
- *The arrival plot:* the last slot used by the transport unit.

In the first rectangle, fig. 1, representing the car crosses "+" indicates the positions of the plots. The model presented in this figure comprises four configurations. Only the first two are detailed below.

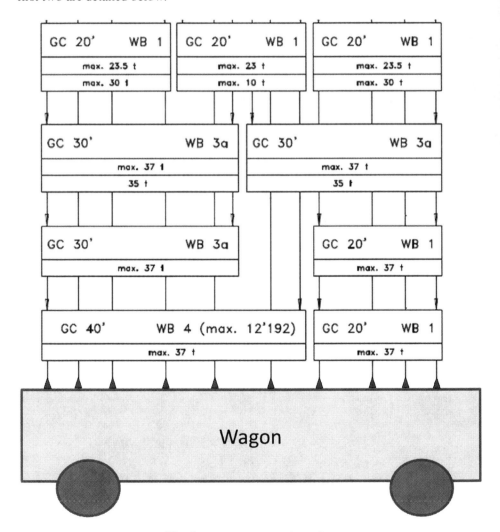

Fig. 1. Examples of configuration

Configuration 1: structured in three slots with weight constraints to receive three containers of 20 '.

- **Case 1:** it is possible to put three containers whose maximum weight are respectively 23.5 T, 23 T and 23.5 T.
- **Case 2:** it is possible to put three containers whose maximum weight are respectively 30T, 10 T and 30T.

Configuration 2: structured in two slots to accommodate two containers of 30 '. The weight of each container must be less than or equal to 37 T.

7   Modelling

Operations Research and Mathematical Optimization are increasingly used in the field of rail transport because they are employed to model and solve many problems encountered in this sector.   The potential gains are substantial (reduction of transportation costs, contribution to the environment by reducing CO_2, delay reduction ...).

In this section we will define the notation used to facilitate the understanding of the article.   Then we do a brief recall on Constraint Programming and optimization technology used. Finally, we focus on modelling and solving problems related to the assignment of containers to wagons with the respect of business constraints.

7.1   Notations

The notations are introduced to facilitate the understanding of modelling constraints.

Data:

- N: the maximum number of wagons
- M: the number of containers to plan
- W: the maximum permitted weight of the train
- NM: the maximum number of containers allowed
- w_i: $_i$ :: $1..M$, the weight of the container i.
- WM_i: Maximum Weight of wagon i.

Decision variables:

- $x_i: x_i\ 0..1$
  - ✓ $x_i = 1$: The container is assigned to a train wagon,
  - ✓ $x_i = 0$: the container is docked (remains on the platform).
- $S_i: S_i\ 0..N$
- $S_i = k$ means the container $_i$ is assigned to wagon k.
- FC_k : K configuration of a wagon.
- NS: number of different sizes of containers (20 ', 30', 40 ', ...).
- NF: number of configurations of a wagon, it differs from one wagon to another.

7.2 Constraint Programming

Constraint Programming (CP) [1, 2, 3, 4, 5] has become a reality in the industrial world. Its success represents an important development of Artificial Intelligence and a successful vulgarization of the techniques of operations research in decision-making solutions in various domains. Indeed, CP has effectively addressed a large class of combinatorial problems. The Constraint Programming system used is Choco [http://choco.emn.fr].

Choco is a Constraint Programming system designed to tackle real world "constrained search" problems with a short-term development time and good efficiency. The Choco system provides a number of constraint solvers over different computation domains. These domains have been chosen because of their interest for applications, but also since efficient specialized constraint solving methods exist for these domains. In this paper we focus on finite domains in Choco.

Constraint Programming is based on the idea that many interesting and difficult problems can be expressed declaratively in terms of variables and constraints. The variables range over a (finite) set of values and typically denote alternative decisions to be taken. The constraints are expressed as relations over subsets of variables and restrict feasible value combinations for these variables. A solution is an assignment of values (search) to variables, which satisfies all constraints. It is the ability of CP systems to effectively take into account heterogeneous constraints which, in the 90s, raised a commercial interest in this paradigm.

The cumulative constraint [1, 3] expresses resource constraints between sets of domain variables. It can be used for many types of problems, e.g. scheduling with resource constraints (machines, manpower etc), packing and placement problems (one-dimensional bin packing, 2D and 3D problems), or assignment problems (timetabling). The constraint uses rather complex propagation techniques to analyze and develop necessary conditions for consistency. A typical use of cumulative constraint is found in resource scheduling. We have to schedule a number of tasks (figure 2) of different durations where the tasks require certain amounts of resources (e.g. manpower), during their operation. The overall amount of manpower available during the scheduling period is fixed and the total requirements at each time point by all tasks should not exceed the available *limit*.

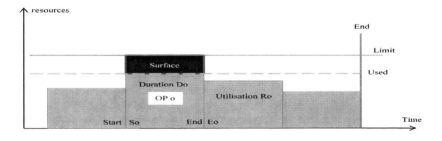

Fig. 2. Cumulative Constraint

Syntax: *cumulative({So, Do, Ro } o in O, H, Limit)*

  — *Starts*: a list of start dates S_i of operations O over a horizon H
  — *Durations:* a list of their durations D_i
  — *Resources:* list of quantities of resources they use R_i,
  — *Limit:* the maximum resources available,
  — *End:* the end date for all tasks.

The constraint holds if the following condition is satisfied.

$$\sum_{1 \le o \le n : S_o \le t \le S_o + D_o} R_o \le Limit , t = 1..H ; \max(S_o + D_o) \le H$$

7.3   Container Constraints Type

To each container is associated a decision domain-variable.

  — $S_i :: 0.. N$, $N' \ge N$ is the estimated maximum number of cars.
  — $S_i > N$ means the container is docked.

This model is used to construct the relaxation in conjunction with the following constraints:

  ✓ $S_i > N \rightarrow x_i = 0$
  ✓ $x_i = 0 \rightarrow S_i > N$

The first step of optimization is the adjustment of the domain of variables S_i.   For example, a container type trailer i can only go on certain wagons. Consequently, all wagons j which are incompatible are removed from its domain.

  — $j = 1 .. N$, incompatible $(i, j) \rightarrow S_i \neq j$.

7.4   Incompatibility Constraints

These constraints are necessary to model the referencing of containers of dangerous goods. Consider two containers i and j referenced as containing dangerous goods, a typical constraint is the placement of these two containers on different wagons. In CP [1], the constraint is modeled by constraint "different":

  — $S_i \neq S_{j, I} i \neq j$

7.5   Constraints of Maximum Weight per Car

The cumulative constraint is well-suited for modelling Bin Packing problems where:

  — H: the number of wagons.
  — *Limit:* the maximum total weight per wagon.
  — Each wagon is seen as a bin.
  — A container is modelled as an operation where:
      ✓ S_o models the bin (unknown)
      ✓ $D_o = 1$
      ✓   and W_o models the weight of the container (given).

The domain of S_o is *{1 : N'}..*

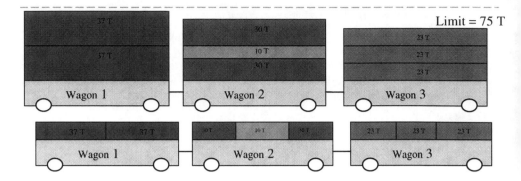

Fig. 3. Cumulative constraint

In Figure 3 all bins $_i$ (cars) have the same length $(D_o = 1)$.

7.6   Constraint Maximum Weight of the Train

The constraint is true if the following condition is satisfied; it is modelled with arithmetic constraints over finite domains.

$$\sum_{i=1}^{i=M} x_i * w_i \leq W$$

7.7   Constraints of Maximum Cardinality of the Train

The operator can specify the maximum number of candidate containers to load on the train. This constraint, if present, acts as a redundant constraint. The constraint is true if the condition is satisfied.

$$\sum_{i=1}^{i=M} x_i \leq NM$$

7.8   Wagon Cardinality Constraints

As shown in Figure 1, one or more configurations is/are associated for each container. The objective is to allocate container wagons while respecting the rules of the manufacturer. The cardinality type of wagon is to respect the number of wagons up to 20 ', 30', 40 '...

Let:

- k: index configurations of a wagon w.
- CF_k : $0..1$, a Boolean variable is assigned to a wagon for each corresponding configuration, the configuration is selected or not.
- M_k: the maximum number of containers of types i on the configuration CF_k.
- N_k : $0..M_k$, the number of assigned containers of type i.

The configuration is chosen if the cardinality constraints by type of containers are checked.

$$CF_k = and\ (\ N_{20} \leq M_{20}\ \&\ N_{30} \leq M_{30}\ \&\ N_{40} <= M_{40}\ )$$

If $\forall \kappa C_k = 0$, the wagon is empty.

If the wagon is not completely full, multiple configurations are candidates. During the enumeration phase, the engine optimization emphasizes the quality of the solution by choosing the most appropriate settings according to preferences.

7.9   Constraints Configuration

Redundant constraints are derived from configurations of the wagons. For each wagon, it is possible to calculate the maximum cardinality per type (size) of container (e.g. maximum of 30 containers that can be assigned to a wagon).

The cumulative constraint is well-suited to model such constraints. A wagon is seen as a bin. The height is the maximum of containers per type. The example of modelling is to model the maximum given weight per wagon.

7.10   Objective Function

The objective function consists in assigning all selected containers to wagons. The objective is to minimize the number of unassigned containers to wagons on the train. Some preference constraints like priorities, same destination and same clients are handled by the search strategies. A CP program is structured in three parts: declaration of decision variables, statement of constraints and enumeration.

The search combines constructive solution procedures and some CP strategies. It takes advantage of the constraint programming propagation (domain of variables is reduced after each step of assignment) and the strategies used to select each step, the best object (container, configuration), the best decision variable and the best value.

In practice the aim is to privilege preferences in order to compute quality solutions easing the work of operators and respecting their rules and constraints. In some cases the problem turns into a simplified one where the aim is to find a feasible solution respecting business constraints because the number of containers to load is computed by a separate module. If the computed solution shows empty cells in the wagon then operators might take decisions to add additional containers using online assignment capabilities.

7.11   Online Assignments

The problem solving is carried out in two steps. In the first step the application loads a new instance of data (train departure, wagons of the train, containers). After checking the validity of constraints and data, the application launches the first solver which is constraint programming based. The aim is to compute a first good solution respecting the business constraints.

By experience, the solution found is close to optimality. The average computation time is less than one minute on a standard desktop computer. This solution is called the base solution.

In a second step the operator starts some interactive actions. The application is Full Web featuring advanced interactive capabilities (WEB 2). Changes are required to take into account urgent constraints (e.g. assignment of an additional container to a given wagon), moving a container from one wagon to another, moving a container from one position in a wagon to another one. All these changes are performed online by the operator. They are implemented as imposed constraints. For the online assignment the constraint programming solver states the problem, sets the imposed constraints and starts the enumeration phase. The average computation time is a few seconds. For this step a second solver based on Tabou search is under development. If the imposed constraints are limited to a small set of moves this solver will be automatically launched.

8   Conclusion

This work uses Constraint Programming to solve the problem of allocation of container wagons, while respecting the constraints-business. The presence of inconsistent constraints reinforces the choice of Constraint Programming. One of the major contributions of the proposed modelling is the ability to exploit the incremental aspect of Constraint Programming to set strategies as well as the choice of containers/wagons to calculate quality solutions.

Experiments are underway using representative samples provided by our industrial partners to validate our work and extend this application to other areas.

The average time expected by the users is 15 minutes to compute a good first solution. The actual computation time is a few minutes for common data (35 wagons, 80 containers). This objective is reached. The online assignment of containers to wagons makes the improvement of existing solutions possible by handling some preference constraints which are not handled by the solver, offering flexibility and decision making capabilities.

References

[1] Aggoun, A., Vazacopoulos, A.: Solving Sports scheduling and timetabling problems with constraint programming. In: Btenko, S., Gil-Lafuente, J., Pardalos, P.M. (eds.) Economics, Management and Optimization in Sports. Springer, Heidelberg (2003)

[2] Aggoun, A., Beldiceanu, N., Bourreau, E., Simonis, H.: The contribution of global constraints for modeling and solving industrial applications. FRANCORO II Second Journées Francophones Operational Research, Sousse, Tunisia (1998)

[3] Aggoun, A., Beldiceanu, N.: Extending CHIP in Order to Solve Complex Scheduling Problems. Journal of Mathematical and Computer Modeling 17(7), 57–73 (1993)

[4] Beldiceanu, N.: Global Constraints as Graph Properties on a Structured Network of Elementary Constraints of the Same Type. In: Dechter, R. (ed.) CP 2000. LNCS, vol. 1894, pp. 52–66. Springer, Heidelberg (2000)

[5] Bockmayr, A., Pisaruk, N., Aggoun, A.: Network Flow Problems in Constraint Programming. In: Walsh, T. (ed.) CP 2001. LNCS, vol. 2239, pp. 196–210. Springer, Heidelberg (2001)

[6] Chen, L., Bostel, N., Dejax, P., Xi, L.: A simulation model of equipment to handle containers in the port of Shanghai. In: Francophone Conference of Modeling and Simulation - MOSIM 2006, Rabat - Morocco (2006)

[7] Corry, P., Kozan, E.: Optimsed loading patterns for intermodal trains. Spetrum GOLD 30(4), 721–750 (2008)

[8] Dash optimzation, Applications of optimization with XpressMP (2000)

[9] Gunther, H.O., Hwan Kim, K.: Container Terminals and Automated Transport Systems. Springer, Heidelberg (2005)

[10] Vacca, I., Bierlaire, M., Salani, M.: Optimization at Container Terminals: Status, Trends and Perspectives. STRC: Tth Siwss Transport Research Conference, Monte Verita, September 12-14 (2007)

A Binary-Real-Coded Differential Evolution for Unit Commitment Problem: A Preliminary Study

Saptarshi Dutta[1] and Dilip Datta[2]

[1] Department of Mechanical Engineering,
Royal School of Engineering and Technology, Royal Group of Institutions,
Guwahati - 781 035, India
saptarshidutta@gmail.com
[2] Department of Mechanical Engineering, National Institute of Technology,
Silchar - 788 010, India
datta_dilip@rediffmail.com

Abstract. Due to its economical importance, the unit commitment problem has become a matter of concern in power systems, and consequently an important area of research. It is a nonlinear mixed-integer optimization problem, in which a given number of power generating units are to be scheduled in such a way that the forecasted demand is met at minimum production cost over a time horizon. In this paper a binary-real-coded differential evolution along with some repairing mechanisms is investigated as the solution technique of the problem. In the computational experiment carried out with a hypothetical 10-unit power system over 24-hour time horizon, available in the literature, the proposed technique is found outperforming all the existing methods.

Keywords: Unit commitment problem, differential evolution, repairing mechanisms.

1 Introduction

The unit commitment problem (UCP) involves the optimum scheduling of power generating units as well as the determination of the optimum amounts of power to be generated by committed units, so as to meet the forecasted demand at minimum production cost over a daily to weekly time horizon. The problem is also subject to various generator- and system-based constraints. Since the size of the discrete search space increases exponentially with the increasing number of units to be scheduled, the UCP is known as one of the most difficult problems to be solved in power systems.

Although the exact solution of the UCP can be obtained by complete enumeration, but the approach is not applicable to realistic power systems due to its excessive computational time requirement [30]. This has motivated to investigate alternative algorithms, which can be applied to realistic power systems in order to obtain approximate solutions of the UCP in reasonable computational time. Such alternative algorithms studied for the UCP include both

C. Sombattheera et al. (Eds.): MIWAI 2011, LNAI 7080, pp. 406–417, 2011.
© Springer-Verlag Berlin Heidelberg 2011

deterministic methods and metaheuristic techniques, as well as metaheuristics hybridized with deterministic methods. The investigated deterministic methods include the priority list method [22], dynamic programming [25], branch-and-bound methods [6], mixed-integer linear programming [26], and Lagrangian relaxation (LR) method [17]. Because of the inadequacy of these methods in handling large-size instances and/or non-convex search space of the UCP, various metaheuristics are investigated, such as artificial neural networks [10], genetic algorithm (GA) [1, 2, 7, 13, 20], evolutionary programming [12], memetic algorithm (MA) [29], Tabu search [16], simulated annealing [33], particle swarm optimization (PSO) [15, 27, 32], and differential evolution [4, 11, 14, 19, 18, 28, 31]. Apart from these, some hybrid methods combining metaheuristics and deterministic methods are also investigated in order to reduce the search space in large-scale UCP. Such hybrid methods include LR and GA [5], LR and MA [29], and LR and PSO [3].

In the present work, a binary-real-coded differential evolution (DE) is investigated for the UCP, in which the binary part of the DE deals with the scheduling of units and the real part determines the amounts of power generated by committed units. Since the UCP is a hard mixed-integer problem, some mechanisms are also incorporated in the DE for forcibly repairing an infeasible solution. A hypothetical 10-unit power system available in the literature is used to evaluate the effectiveness of the approach over 24-hour time horizon. A comparison is made between the proposed method and other methods including both analytical and metaheuristic algorithms. Computational results show the potential of the proposed approach.

The rest of the article is organized as follows: the formulation of the UCP is presented in Section 2, followed by the binary-real-coded DE in Section 3 and the repairing mechanisms for the UCP in Section 4. The computational results and discussion are presented in Section 5. Finally, the article is concluded in Section 6 with the present findings and future planning of the current work.

2   Formulation of the UCP

As stated in Section 1, the UCP is a mixed-integer scheduling problem over a time horizon, in which the total production cost is to be minimized by satisfying a series of generator- and system-based equality and inequality constraints. It is formulated as two linked optimization processes, namely the unit-scheduling problem and the load dispatch problem. The entire UCP involves $\{0,1\}$ integer variables to represent on/off status of the units and real variables to represent the amounts of power to be generated by committed units. Accordingly, the formulation of the UCP is presented in the following two subsections.

2.1   Objective Function

The objective function in the UCP is to minimize the total production cost over the entire time horizon, which is the sum of operating fuel costs of the committed units and the start-up costs of the uncommitted units. It can be expressed as:

$$\text{Minimize}\quad F \equiv \sum_{t=1}^{T} \sum_{i=1}^{N} [\phi_i(p_{it}) \cdot u_{it} + \psi_{it} \cdot (1 - u_{i,t-1}) \cdot u_{it}] \tag{1}$$

where N is the number of units and T is the time horizon. p_{it} is the real variable of the UCP, which represents the amount of power generated by unit i at time t. u_{it} is the {0,1} binary variable of the UCP, representing the on/off status of unit i at time t; whose value is 1 if the unit is 'on' at that time, otherwise it is 0. The value of $u_{i,t=0}$ is to be obtained from the known initial status of unit i, which shows for how long the unit was on/off prior to the start of the time horizon.

The function $\phi_i(p_{it})$ in (1) is the operating fuel cost of unit i at time t, which is frequently expressed as:

$$\phi_i(p_{it}) = a_i + b_i p_{it} + c_i p_{it}^2 \tag{2}$$

where a_i, b_i and c_i are known cost coefficients of unit i.

Finally, the term ψ_{it} in (1) represents the start-up cost of unit i at time t, which was off prior to time t. This term is usually simplified as below:

$$\psi_{it} = \begin{cases} d_i, & \text{if } \Gamma_i^{\text{down}} \leq \tau_{it}^{\text{off}} \leq \Gamma_i^{\text{down}} + f_i \\ e_i, & \text{if } \tau_{it}^{\text{off}} > \Gamma_i^{\text{down}} + f_i \end{cases} \tag{3}$$

where d_i, e_i, f_i and Γ_i^{down} are, respectively, the known hot start cost, cold start cost, cold start time and minimum down time of unit i. τ_{it}^{off} is the continuously off time of unit i up to time t. It is to be mentioned that at the time of determining $\tau_{i,t=1}^{\text{off}}$ also, the known initial status of unit i is to be considered.

2.2   Constraints

The UCP basically involves four types of constraints: power balance, spinning reserve requirement, minimum up time of a unit, and minimum down time of a unit. Apart from these, a unit is to generate power within a given range. Accordingly, the formulations of the constraints are given below:

1. *Power balance constraints*: The total power generated by all the committed units at a time instant must meet the power demand at that time instant, i.e.,

$$\sum_{i=1}^{N} u_{it} p_{it} = D_t; \quad t = 1, 2, \ldots, T \tag{4}$$

   where D_t is the known (forecasted) power demand at time t.

2. *Spinning reserve constraints*: The sum of the maximum power generating capacities of all the committed units at a time instant should be at least equal to the sum of the known power demand and minimum spinning reserve requirement at that time instant, i.e.,

$$\sum_{i=1}^{N} u_{it} P_i^{\text{max}} \geq D_t + R_t; \quad t = 1, 2, \ldots, T \tag{5}$$

where P_i^{max} is the known maximum power that can be generated by unit i at any time instant, and R_t is the known minimum spinning reserve requirement at time t.

3. *Minimum up time constraints*: A unit must be continuously 'on' for a certain number of time instants before it can be switched off, i.e.,

$$s_{it}^{\mathrm{on}} \geq \Gamma_i^{\mathrm{up}}, \text{ if } t < T; \quad i = 1, 2, \ldots, N \qquad (6)$$

where Γ_i^{up} is the known minimum up time of unit i; and s_{it}^{on} is the continuous on-span of that unit up to time t, after which it is switched off at time $(t+1)$. It is to be mentioned that if unit i is 'on' at $t = 1$, the known initial status of the unit is also to be considered at the time of determining its first on-span.

4. *Minimum down time constraints*: A unit must be continuously off for a certain number of time instants before it can be switched on, i.e.,

$$s_{it}^{\mathrm{off}} \geq \Gamma_i^{\mathrm{down}}, \text{ if } t < T; \quad i = 1, 2, \ldots, N \qquad (7)$$

where s_{it}^{off} is the continuous off-span of unit i up to time t, after which it is switched on at time $(t+1)$. It is to be mentioned that if unit i is off at $t = 1$, the known initial status of the unit is also to be considered at the time of determining its first off-span.

5. *Ranges of generated power*: A committed unit must generate power within a given range, i.e.,

$$P_i^{\mathrm{min}} \leq p_{it} \leq P_i^{\mathrm{max}}; \quad i = 1, 2, \ldots, N \text{ and } t = 1, 2, \ldots, T \qquad (8)$$

where $(P_i^{\mathrm{min}}, P_i^{\mathrm{max}})$ is the range of power to be generated by unit i at any time instant.

3   The Binary-Real-Coded DE

The UCP is a mixed-integer scheduling problem over a time horizon, which involves $\{0,1\}$ binary variables to represent on/off status of the units and real variables to represent the amounts of power to be generated by committed units. That is, the UCP is a combination of two linked optimization processes, namely unit scheduling problem (USP) and load dispatch problem (LDP). Since the traditional DE [23, 24] is a real-coded algorithm, it is not directly applicable to the USP. Hence, different binary-coded versions of DE are applied to the USP [4,11,14,19,18,28,31]. However, for the LDP, usually some other schemes are employed along with a binary-coded DE used for the USP, such as the lambda-iteration method [14, 19, 31], linear programming method [18], and quadratic numerical method [11]. Only a limited number of works are found in the specialized literature, in which a real-coded DE is applied to the LDP along with a binary-coded DE used for the USP [4, 28]. This has motivated the present work to investigate the real-integer-discrete-coded DE, proposed by Datta and Figueira [8], for both the USP and LDP. This version of DE has the capability to handle any type of variables (real, integer and/or discrete) without any conversion. It is treated here as the binary-real-coded DE to work with the $\{0,1\}$ binary variables and real variables of the UCP. The basic steps of this binary-real-coded DE are addressed in the following subsections.

3.1   Vector Representation and Population Initialization

A vector (solution) of the binary-real-coded DE for the UCP is a two-dimensional array of variables. The first array represents the unit-schedule in terms of {0,1} binary variables, while the second array is to give real-valued amounts of power generated by committed units. Each of a {0,1} binary variable and a real variable is represented by a single dimension of a vector. Therefore, the number of dimensions required to represent all the {0,1} binary variables of the UCP is (number of units)×(time horizon). The same number of dimensions is required to represent all the real variables also. Once the total dimensions of a vector is determined, the population (a set of vectors) is initialized randomly before starting the DE operations. A real dimension is initialized by a random real value in the given range of the real variable which is represented by that dimension, while all the binary dimensions are initialized randomly by 0 or 1 with equal probability.

3.2   Mutation Operator

As in a traditional DE, in the mutation operation of the binary-real-coded DE also four distinct vectors are considered at a time, out of which one is called the target vector, one is the base vector, and the other two are random vectors. Then, a mutant $\bar{x}_j$ against a real variable x_j of a target vector is generated as follows:

$$\bar{x}_j^{(i,k)} = x_j^{(\alpha,k)} + F\left(x_j^{(\beta,k)} - x_j^{(\gamma,k)}\right); \ i = 1,\ldots,Q; \ j = 1,2,\ldots,D \qquad (9)$$

where D is the number of dimensions of a vector, and Q is the population size. k is the generation counter, and i, α, β and γ denote the target vector, base vector, and two random vectors, respectively. F is a scaling factor in the range of (0,1), which controls the amount of perturbance to α by the difference of β and γ.

In the case of binary variables, the mutant $\bar{x}_j$ is obtained through some logic based on the {0,1} valued combinations of dimensions of the base and random vectors. Such logic is presented in Table 1, where $r_q^{(k)}$ ($q = 1, 2, \ldots, 8$) is a random number in the range of (0,1) and p_m is a user-defined low-valued mutation probability, which are considered for creating some randomness to the assumed logic.

3.3   Crossover Operator

In the crossover phase, a trial $\bar{\bar{x}}_j$ against x_j of the target vector is obtained as:

$$\bar{\bar{x}}_j^{(i,k)} = \begin{cases} \bar{x}_j^{(i,k)} & \text{if } r_j^{(k)} \leq p_c; \ j = 1,2,\ldots,D \\ x_j^{(i,k)} & \text{otherwise} \end{cases} \qquad (10)$$

where $r_j^{(k)}$ is a random number in the range of (0,1) and p_c is a user-defined crossover probability.

Table 1. Generation of mutants for binary variables of the binary-real-coded DE

$x_j^{(\alpha,k)}$	$x_j^{(\beta,k)}$	$x_j^{(\gamma,k)}$	$\bar{x}_j^{(i,k)}$
0	0	0	0 if $r_1^{(k)} \geq p_m$, 1 otherwise
0	1	1	0 if $r_2^{(k)} \geq p_m$, 1 otherwise
1	0	0	1 if $r_3^{(k)} \geq p_m$, 0 otherwise
1	1	1	1 if $r_4^{(k)} \geq p_m$, 0 otherwise
0	1	0	1 if $r_5^{(k)} \geq p_m$, 0 otherwise
0	0	1	0 if $r_6^{(k)} \geq p_m$, 1 otherwise
1	1	0	0 if $r_7^{(k)} \geq p_m$, 1 otherwise
1	0	1	1 if $r_8^{(k)} \geq p_m$, 0 otherwise

3.4   Acceptance Operator

Instead of taking any decision based on a pair of a target vector and its trial vector only, as done in the traditional DE, all the target and trial vectors of the binary-real-coded DE are first combined. Then the combined vectors are sorted according to their qualities (objective values). Finally, the first 50% of the best vectors of the combined population are extracted as the population for the next generation.

3.5   Diversity Generating Mechanism

One of the prime aims of a population-based technique is to work with a set of distinct solutions, so that the search space can be explored widely by generating diversified solutions. This directly helps a technique from not being trapped at a local optimum. However, due to the low value of the mutation probability p_m, the randomness imposed in Table 1 may not be able to maintain a good distance between the mutant and the base vectors. Hence, the vectors of the population may become indifferent after a certain number of generations. This may cause the binary-real-coded DE to fail in generating new potential vectors, i.e., to cause it to be trapped at a local optimum. Therefore, a mechanism is applied for generating additional diversity among the vectors. In this mechanism, if all the vectors converge to a single point during the execution, the value of a binary variable is altered from 0 to 1 or from 1 to 0 with a small probability (say, around 5%).

4   The Repairing Mechanisms for the UCP

Since the size of the discrete search space of the UCP increases exponentially with the increasing number of units to be scheduled, it becomes to be an NP-complete combinatorial problem. It is a tough job for any algorithm to regain the feasibility of the infeasible solutions of such problems, which suggests the use of some mechanisms for forcibly satisfying the constraints of a problem. In such

an attempt, the following three repairing mechanisms, used by many researchers
for the UCP [11, 18, 19, 28, 31, 32], are incorporated in the binary-real-coded DE
addressed in Section 3:

1. *Spinning reserve constraints repairing*: A heuristic algorithm is applied for
   repairing spinning reserve violation, in which uncommitted units are committed, in ascending order of their average full load cost, until spinning reserve
   is met.
2. *Minimum up and down time constraints repairing*: If the up/down time constraint of a unit is violated at any time instant, the unit is committed in the
   following time instants until such a constraint is satisfied.
3. *Decommitment of excess units*: Repairing the minimum up/down time constraints of a unit may lead to excessive spinning reserves, which is not desirable from the point of operating cost. Therefore, a heuristic algorithm is
   used to decommit some units, in descending order of their average full load
   cost, until the spinning reserve requirement is just met.

If the above three mechanisms are unable to repair an infeasible solution completely, the *penalty-parameter-less constraint handling approach*, proposed by
Deb [9], is applied for taking care of remaining constraints. In this approach, all
the infeasible solutions are first made inferior to any feasible solution through a
fitness function, and then all the solutions are treated as feasible solutions only.

5   Results and Discussion

The proposed DE-based technique is coded in C programming language and
it is executed in Fedora 8 Linux environment. For numerical experimentation,
a hypothetical 10-unit power system over 24-hour time horizon is taken from
literature, which has been studied by numerous researchers [3, 4, 7, 11, 13, 17, 19,
22, 21, 28, 29, 31, 32]. The unit related known data of the case study are given
in Table 2 with notations as per (1)–(8),except σ_i, which represents the initial
status of unit i. A positive value of σ_i means that unit i was 'on' for that
hours prior to the starting of the time horizon, while a negative value means
that the unit was off for that hours prior to the starting of the time horizon.

Table 2. Unit related known data of the considered 10-unit power system

Unit (i)	P_i^{max} (MW)	P_i^{min} (MW)	a_i ($/h)	b_i ($/MWh)	c_i ($/MW^{2}h)	d_i ($)	e_i ($)	f_i (h)	Γ_i^{up} (h)	Γ_i^{down} (h)	σ_i (h)
1	455	150	1000	16.19	0.00048	4500	9000	5	8	8	8
2	455	150	970	17.26	0.00031	5000	10000	5	8	8	8
3	130	20	700	16.60	0.00200	550	1100	4	5	5	-5
4	130	20	680	16.50	0.00211	560	1120	4	5	5	-5
5	162	25	450	19.70	0.00398	900	1800	4	6	6	-6
6	80	20	370	22.26	0.00712	170	340	2	3	3	-3
7	85	25	480	27.74	0.00079	260	520	2	3	3	-3
8	55	10	660	25.92	0.00413	30	60	0	1	1	-1
9	55	10	665	27.27	0.00222	30	60	0	1	1	-1
10	55	10	670	27.79	0.00173	30	60	0	1	1	-1

Table 3. Forecasted hourly power demand over the 24-hour time horizon

Hour	1	2	3	4	5	6	7	8	9	10	11	12
Demand (MW)	700	750	850	950	1000	1100	1150	1200	1300	1400	1450	1500
Hour	13	14	15	16	17	18	19	20	21	22	23	24
Demand (MW)	1400	1300	1200	1050	1000	1100	1200	1400	1300	1100	900	800

The forecasted hourly power demands in the case study over the 24-hour time horizon are given in Table 3. The minimum spinning reserve requirement at any time instant (R_t in (5)) is considered to be 10% of the forecasted power demand at that time instant.

In the computational experiment, 30 independent runs of the proposed binary-real-coded DE are performed with different initial solutions as well as different parameter settings. A population of 100 vectors is considered to be evolved over 1000 generations in each run. In different runs, the mutation probability (p_m) for binary variables is chosen randomly in the range of [10%,15%], while the perturbance factor (F) for real variables is taken in the range of [0.6,0.8]. A very low crossover probability (p_c) in the range of [3%,5%] is considered for binary variables, while the same for real variables is taken as ($1 - p_c$). In regard of constraints satisfaction, since it is nearly impossible for any numerical optimizer to exactly satisfy an equality constraint, the power balance constraint of the UCP, given by (4), must be relaxed by some small amount ϵ. Interestingly, no work could be found in the specialized literature addressing this issue. Hence, in order to study the effect of ϵ on the solutions of the UCP, three cases are considered here with $\epsilon = 1.0\%$, 0.5% and 0.1%.

From the computational experiment, it is observed that the binary-real-coded DE always leads to the same schedule of the units, irrespective of the values of ϵ. It is the production cost (objective value) only, which increases with decreasing values of ϵ. The plots of the generation-wise improvement of the objective function value, for the best out of 30 runs, against the three considered values of ϵ are shown in Fig. 1.It is seen in the plots that in all the three cases the objective function value is improved drastically in first few generations only, after which it is improved very slowly. The obtained best objective values against $\epsilon = 1.0\%$, 0.5% and 0.1% are 561170$, 562606$ and 563851$, respectively. The complete solution of the UCP against $\epsilon = 1.0\%$ is presented in Table 4,whose production cost comes out to be 561170$.

Finally, the best objective value given by the binary-real-coded DE, against $\epsilon = 1.0\%$, is compared with those obtained by various deterministic and meta-heuristics, as well as combination of such techniques. The comparison is presented in Table 5,where it is seen that the proposed binary-real-coded DE could successfully improve the previously known best objective value of the considered case study.

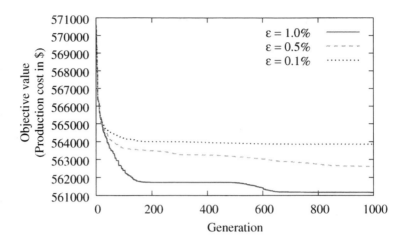

Fig. 1. Generation-wise improvement of the objective function value for different values of ϵ

Table 4. Complete solution of the considered case study for $\epsilon = 1.0\%$

Hour	Unit Schedule	Generated power (MW)										Spinning Reserve (MW)	Fuel Cost ($)	Start-up Cost ($)
1	1100000000	454	245	0	0	0	0	0	0	0	0	210	13672	0
2	1100000000	445	304	0	0	0	0	0	0	0	0	160	14550	0
3	1100100000	455	368	0	0	26	0	0	0	0	0	222	16800	900
4	1100100000	455	454	0	0	40	0	0	0	0	0	122	18581	0
5	1101100000	455	453	0	65	26	0	0	0	0	0	202	20045	560
6	1111100000	455	455	34	129	26	0	0	0	0	0	232	22429	1100
7	1111100000	455	455	85	130	25	0	0	0	0	0	182	23277	0
8	1111100000	455	455	128	130	31	0	0	0	0	0	132	24133	0
9	1111111000	455	455	130	130	83	21	25	0	0	0	197	27230	860
10	1111111100	455	455	130	130	161	34	25	10	0	0	152	30053	60
11	1111111110	455	455	130	130	161	71	27	10	10	0	157	31892	60
12	1111111111	455	455	130	130	162	76	37	32	11	10	162	33881	60
13	1111111100	455	455	130	130	162	33	25	10	0	0	152	30048	0
14	1111111000	455	455	130	130	85	20	25	0	0	0	197	27249	0
15	1111100000	455	455	128	130	31	0	0	0	0	0	132	24135	0
16	1111100000	452	325	122	124	25	0	0	0	0	0	282	21504	0
17	1111100000	455	372	68	78	26	0	0	0	0	0	332	20683	0
18	1111100000	455	455	36	129	25	0	0	0	0	0	232	22424	0
19	1111100000	455	455	128	129	32	0	0	0	0	0	132	24134	0
20	1111111100	455	455	130	130	161	33	25	10	0	0	152	30031	490
21	1111111100	455	455	130	130	84	20	25	0	0	0	197	27226	0
22	1100111000	455	455	0	0	142	21	25	0	0	0	137	22717	0
23	1100010000	455	425	0	0	0	20	0	0	0	0	90	17645	0
24	1100000000	451	349	0	0	0	0	0	0	0	0	110	15419	0

Table 5. Comparison of the objective values (production cost)

Method	Objective value ($)
Lagrangian relaxation method based memetic algorithm [29]	566686
Integer-coded genetic algorithm [7]	566404
Lagrangian relaxation based particle swarm optimization [3]	565869
Memetic algorithm [29]	565827
Genetic algorithm [13]	565825
Lagrangian relaxation method [17]	565825
Priority list method [22]	564950
Evolutionary programming [12]	564551
Binary-coded DE [11]	563997
Binary-coded DE [19]	563977
Enhanced DE [31]	563977
Characteristic classification based genetic algorithm [21]	563977
Enhanced particle swarm optimization [32]	563537
Improved DE [4]	562921
Optimized genetic algorithm [1]	561436
Proposed binary-real-coded DE	**561170**

6   Conclusions

The unit commitment problem (UCP) seeks the scheduling of power generating units, as well as the determination of the amounts of power to be generated by committed units, so as to meet the forecasted demand at minimum production cost over a time horizon. Due to its NP-complete nature, the UCP is known to be one of the most difficult problems in power systems. Various deterministic as well as metaheuristic techniques have been investigated for the UCP. However, differential evolution (DE), known as one of the powerful metaheuristics, is still immature for the UCP. This motivated the present work to investigate a binary-real-coded DE for the UCP. In the numerical experimentation with a hypothetical 10-unit power system over 24-hour time horizon, the proposed DE successfully improved the previously known best solution of the case study. In the future course of work, an attempt will be made to study different power systems involving higher number of units, such as the cases of 20, 40, 60, 80 and 100 units available in the literature.

Acknowledgement. The work is a part of the M.Tech. thesis of the first author, carried out, under the supervision of the second author, at National Institute of Technology - Silchar, Silchar - 788 010, India.

References

1. Abookazemi, K., Ahmad, H., Tavakolpour, A., Hassan, M.Y.: Unit commitment solution using an optimized genetic system. Electrical Power and Energy Systems 33(4), 969–975 (2011)

2. Abookazemi, K., Mustafa, M.W., Ahmad, H.: Structured genetic algorithm technique for unit commitment problem. Int. J. Recent Trends in Engineering 1(3), 135–139 (2009)
3. Balci, H.H., Valenzuela, J.F.: Scheduling electric power generations using particle swarm optimization combined with the Lagrangian relaxation method. Int. J. Applied Mathematics and Computer Science 14(3), 411–421 (2004)
4. Chang, C.S.: An improved differential evolution scheme for the solution of large-scale unit commitment problems. Informatica. 21(2), 175–190 (2010)
5. Cheng, C.P., Liu, C.W., Liu, C.C.: Unit commitment by Lagrangian relaxation and genetic algorithms. IEEE Transactions on Power Systems 15(2), 707–714 (2000)
6. Cohen, A.I., Yoshimura, M.: A branch-and-bound algorithm for unit commitment. IEEE Transactions on Power Apparatus and Systems PAS 102(2), 444–451 (1983)
7. Damousis, I.G., Bakirtzis, A.G., Dokopoulos, P.S.: A solution to the unit commitment problem using integer-coded genetic algorithm. IEEE Transactions on Power Systems 19(2), 1165–1172 (2004)
8. Datta, D., Figueira, J.R.: A real-integer-discrete-coded differential evolution algorithm: A preliminary study. In: Cowling, P., Merz, P. (eds.) EvoCOP 2010. LNCS, vol. 6022, pp. 35–46. Springer, Heidelberg (2010)
9. Deb, K.: An efficient constraint handling method for genetic algorithms. Computer Methods in Applied Mechanics and Engineering 186, 311–338 (2000)
10. Dieu, V.N., Ongsakul, W.: Enhanced augmented Lagrangian hopfield network for unit commitment. IEE Proc. on Generation, Transmission and Distribution 153, 624–632 (2006)
11. Jeong, Y.W., Lee, W.N., Kim, H.H., Park, J.B., Shin, J.R.: Thermal unit commitment using binary differential evolution. J. Electrical Engg. & Tech. 4(3), 323–329 (2009)
12. Juste, K.A., Kita, H., Tanaka, E., Hasegawa, J.: An evolutionary programming solution to the unit commitment problem. IEEE Transactions on Power Systems 14(4), 1452–1459 (1999)
13. Kazarlis, S.A., Bakirtzis, A.G., Petridis, V.: A genetic algorithm solution to the unit commitment problem. IEEE Transactions on Power Systems 11(1), 83–92 (1996)
14. Keleş, A.: Binary differential evolution for the unit commitment problem. In: Genetic and Evolutionary Computation Conference (GECCO 2007), London, UK, pp. 2765–2768 (2007)
15. Lee, T.Y., Chen, C.L.: Unit commitment with probabilistic reserve: An IPSO approach. Energy Conversion and Management 48(2), 486–493 (2007)
16. Mantawy, A.H., Abdel-Magid, Y.L., Selim, S.Z.: Unit commitment by tabu search. IEE Proc. on Generation, Transmission and Distribution. 145, 56–64 (1998)
17. Ongsakul, W., Petcharaks, N.: Unit commitment by enhanced adaptive Lagrangian relaxation. IEEE Transactions on Power Systems 19(1), 620–628 (2004)
18. Patra, S., Goswami, S.K., Goswami, B.: A binary differential evolution algorithm for transmission and voltage constrained unit commitment. In: Power System Technology and IEEE Power India Conference (POWERCON 2008), New Delhi, pp. 1–8 (2008)
19. Patra, S., Goswami, S.K., Goswami, B.: Differential evolution algorithm for solving unit commitment with ramp constraints. Electric Power Components and Systems 36(8), 771–787 (2008)
20. Pavez-Lazo, B., Soto-Cartes, J.: A deterministic annular crossover genetic algorithm optimisation for the unit commitment problem. Expert Systems with Applications 38(6), 6523–6529 (2011)

21. Senjyu, T., Yamashiro, H., Uezato, K., Funabashi, T.: A unit commitment problem by using genetic algorithm based on unit characteristic classification. In: IEEE Conf. on Power Engineering Society Winter Meeting, vol. 1, pp. 58–63 (2002)
22. Senjyua, T., Miyagia, T., Sabera, A.Y., Urasakia, N., Funabashib, T.: Emerging solution of large-scale unit commitment problem by stochastic priority list. Electric Power Systems Research 76(5), 283–292 (2006)
23. Storn, R., Price, K.: Differential evolution - A simple and efficient adaptive scheme for global optimization over continuous spaces. Tech. Rep. TR-95-012, International Computer Science Institute, Berkeley, CA (1995)
24. Storn, R., Price, K.: Differential evolution - A simple and efficient heuristic for global optimization over continuous spaces. Journal of Global Optimization 11, 341–354 (1997)
25. Su, C.C., Hsu, Y.Y.: Fuzzy dynamic programming: an application to unit commitment. IEEE Transactions on Power Systems 6(3), 1231–1237 (1991)
26. Takriti, S., Birge, J.: Using integer programming to refine Lagrangian-based unit commitment solutions. IEEE Transactions on Power Systems 15(1), 151–156 (2000)
27. Ting, T.O., Rao, M.V.C., Loo, C.K., Ngu, S.S.: Solving unit commitment problem using hybrid particle swarm optimization. J. Heuristics 9(6), 507–520 (2003)
28. Uyar, A.S., Türkay, B., Keleş, A.: A novel differential evolution application to short-term electrical power generation scheduling. Electrical Power and Energy Systems 33(6), 1236–1242 (2011)
29. Valenzuela, J., Smith, A.E.: A seeded memetic algorithm for large unit commitment problems. J. Heuristics 8(2), 173–195 (2002)
30. Wood, A.J., Wollenberg, B.: Power Generation Operation and Control. John Wiley, New York (1984)
31. Yuan, X., Su, A., Nie, H., Yuan, Y., Wang, L.: Application of enhanced discrete differential evolution approach to unit commitment problem. Energy Conversion & Management 50, 2449–2456 (2009)
32. Yuan, X., Su, A., Nie, H., Yuan, Y., Wang, L.: Unit commitment problem using enhanced particle swarm optimization algorithm. Soft Computing 15(1), 139–148 (2011)
33. Zhuang, F., Galiana, F.D.: Unit commitment by simulated annealing. IEEE Transactions on Power Systems 5(1), 311–318 (1990)

Gibbs Sampling with Deterministic Dependencies

Oliver Gries

Hamburg University of Technology, Hamburg, Germany

Abstract. There is a growing interest in the logical representation of both probabilistic and deterministic dependencies. While Gibbs sampling is a widely-used method for estimating probabilities, it is known to give poor results in the presence of determinism. In this paper, we consider acyclic Horn logic, a small, but significant fragment of first-order logic and show that Markov chains constructed with Gibbs sampling remain ergodic with deterministic dependencies specified in this fragment. Thus, there is a new subclass of Gibbs sampling procedures known to approximate the correct probabilities and expected to be useful for lots of applications.

Keywords: Probabilistic Inference, Gibbs Sampling, Deterministic Dependencies, Markov Networks.

1   Introduction

There is interest in both probabilistic and deterministic dependencies for many real-world problems. In applications with determinism only, exceptions and dependencies holding frequently can only hardly be considered (cf. e.g. [8]), and applications with only probabilistic dependencies do not use determinism that is present in many domains and is often required to be represented.

Gibbs sampling [4] is a widely-used Markov chain Monte Carlo (MCMC) method estimating conditional probabilities. For strictly positive distributions, Gibbs Markov chains are known to be ergodic, and estimates are known to approximate the correct probabilities in the long run. However, in the presence of determinism, the state graph usually is broken into disconnected regions such that Gibbs sampling returns incorrect answers. Similarly, in the presence of near-determinism, i.e., with very strong dependencies among the variables, Gibbs sampling involves state transitions with probabilities near zero, leading to unacceptably long convergence times (cf. [11]).

In this paper, we consider Horn logic, a fragment of first-order logic, and show that Markov chains constructed with Gibbs sampling remain ergodic with deterministic dependencies specified in this fragment, as long as there are no cycles with respect to logical implication. To the best of our knowledge, until now there has not been a language discovered that, in addition to determinism through given evidence, allows for global deterministic dependencies in Gibbs sampling.

C. Sombattheera et al. (Eds.): MIWAI 2011, LNAI 7080, pp. 418–427, 2011.

Acyclic Horn logic is a small fragment of first-order logic, but corresponding Horn clauses include significant and frequently-used deterministic dependencies such as inclusion for establishing taxonomies, disjointness of first-order predicates, implicit typing such as specifying the domain and range of a binary predicate, or functionality of a predicate, just to name a few. Acyclic Horn logic thus can be considered as a fundament for many applications using ontologies that are very often based on Description Logics [1], the Web Ontology Language (OWL)[1] or RDFS[2]. Depending on the application, the expressivity of acyclic Horn logic also allows for lots of dependencies that can be useful for more specific problems.

The incorporation of deterministic Horn clauses to Gibbs sampling is based on ideas presented in [6]. However, while [6] investigates a simple description logic for the representation of determinism that corresponds to an acyclic set of Horn clauses with exactly two literals and that therefore e.g. does not include unit clauses (i.e., evidence), our approach generalizes this deterministic fragment to arbitrary first-order Horn clauses (as long as there are no cycles).

Our approach is specified in the context of Markov networks, but it can also be applied to Bayesian networks.

The paper is organized as follows: In Section 2, we introduce notational conventions as well as the probabilistic formalism and the type of queries we will focus on. Then, in Section 3, we introduce to problems with Gibbs sampling and (near-)determinism in knowledge representation. In Section 4 the ergodicity of Gibbs Markov chains in the presence of the proposed deterministic fragment is proven. Finally, in Section 5, we summarize and discuss the results.

2 Preliminaries

2.1 Notation

Probabilistic Knowledge Representation. Let $\mathbf{X} = \{X_1, ..., X_n\}$ be a set of propositional variables with values from $\{1, 0\}$ resp. $\{true, false\}$ and let $\mathbf{x} = (x_1, ..., x_n)$ denote a *complete assignment* with $X_i = x_i$ for $i = 1, ..., n$, where the notation x_i is used to denote a fixed, but unknown value of X_i. A logical conjunction of assignments to specific variables $r_1 \wedge \quad \wedge r_t$ is also denoted with $x_1, ..., x_t$. If it is clear from the context, we write x_i also as an abbreviation for $X_i = true$ and $\neg x_i$ as an abbreviation for $X_i = false$.

A *(marginal) distribution* $\mathbf{P}(X_i)$ of a propositional variable X_i is a mapping from $\{1, 0\}$ to probability values p in $[0, 1]$ such that both values sum up to 1. A complete assignment can also be associated with a probability $P(\mathbf{X} = \mathbf{x}) = p$. Let $\Omega = \{\mathbf{x}_1, ..., \mathbf{x}_r\}$ be the set of all complete assignments. Given a *full joint distribution* $\mathbf{P}(\mathbf{X})$, probabilities for all complete assignments $P(\mathbf{X} = \mathbf{x}_i)$ are specified such that $\sum_{i=1}^{r} P(\mathbf{X} = \mathbf{x}_i) = 1$.

---

[1] http://www.w3.org/TR/owl-features/
[2] http://www.w3.org/TR/2004/REC-rdf-schema-20040210/

Let $\mathbf{e}$ be an abbreviation for a set of known assignments to variables. A *conditional probability distribution* of X_i given evidence $\mathbf{e}$ is defined with $\mathbf{P}(X_i \mid \mathbf{e}) = \frac{\mathbf{P}(X_i, \mathbf{e})}{P(\mathbf{e})} = \alpha\, \mathbf{P}(X_i, \mathbf{e}) = \alpha < P(x_i, \mathbf{e}), P(\neg x_i, \mathbf{e})>$, where α is a normalizing constant and $< ., . >$ is a notation for a vector. Note that $\mathbf{P}(X_i \mid \mathbf{e})$ is only defined, if $P(\mathbf{e}) > 0$.

Acyclic Horn Logic. We assume the reader to be familiar with propositional and first-order logic. Let $\mathbf{Cl} = \{Cl_1, ..., Cl_m\}$ be a set of propositional clauses over $\mathbf{X}$, where a clause is a disjunction of literals, and a literal corresponds to a variable X_i or its negation $\neg X_i$. A unit clause has exactly one literal. An assignment is said to satisfy a clause Cl_i, if it evaluates Cl_i to *true*, i.e., if there is at least one literal in Cl_i that is evaluated to 1 resp. *true*. Analogously, an assignment is said to falsify a clause Cl_i, if it evaluates Cl_i to *false*. Clauses of the form $\neg X \vee Y$ are also denoted with $X \rightarrow Y$ (implication). Further, $X \leftrightarrow Y$ (equivalence) and $X \oplus Y$ (exclusive or) are used as abbreviations for pairs of clauses $\neg X \vee Y, \neg Y \vee X$ resp. $X \vee Y, \neg X \vee \neg Y$.

A *Horn clause* is either of the form $\neg W_1 \vee ... \vee \neg W_p \vee Z$ (definite clause), including the case of a unit clause Z, or of the form $\neg W_1 \vee ... \vee \neg W_p$ (disjointness clause). It is also denoted with $W_1, ..., W_p \rightarrow Z$ or $W_1, ..., W_p \rightarrow$, respectively.

A set $\mathbf{Cl}$ of Horn clauses is said to be *acyclic with respect to logical implication* if for all variables $X_1, ..., X_n$ appearing in $\mathbf{Cl}$ there is an order $X_1 < ... < X_n$ such that for each definite Horn clause $W_1, ..., W_p \rightarrow Z$ in $\mathbf{Cl}$, no variable Z is lower in the order than variables $W_1, ..., W_p$.

In this paper, first-order logic is used to specify sets of dependencies between propositional variables in a very compact way. For example, in the limit of a finite domain, the first-order Horn clause $\forall x \forall y\, R(x, y) \rightarrow A(x)$ corresponds to a set of propositional Horn clauses (or ground clauses) of the form $R(c, d) \rightarrow A(c)$, where c, d are arbitrary constants representing individuals of the domain.

2.2   Markov Logic with Determinism

A *Markov network graph* is a tuple $\mathbf{G} = (\mathbf{X}, \mathbf{E})$, where $\mathbf{X}$ is a set of nodes corresponding to the variables of the domain and $\mathbf{E}$ is a set of undirected edges (X_i, X_j), $i \neq j$, between these nodes. A clique C is a subgraph of $\mathbf{G}$, whose nodes are all adjacent to each other. Let $\mathbf{X}_C$ be the set of nodes contained in C and $\mathbf{C} = \{C_1, ..., C_m\}$ be a set of cliques of $\mathbf{G}$ consisting of all nodes of $\mathbf{X}$, i.e., $\mathbf{X}_{C_1} \cup ... \cup \mathbf{X}_{C_m} = \mathbf{X}$.

A *Markov network* $\mathcal{M} = (\mathbf{G}, \mathbf{F})$ (cf. [9]) consists of a Markov network graph $\mathbf{G}$ and a set $\mathbf{F}$ which is comprised of non-negative real-valued functions f_i for each clique $C_i, i = 1, ..., m$ in $\mathbf{G}$. A full joint probability distribution of a Markov network is given by

$$P(\mathbf{X} = \mathbf{x}) = \frac{1}{Z} \prod_{i=1}^{m} f_i(\mathbf{x}_{C_i}) \tag{1}$$

where Z is a normalizing constant summing over the products in (1) for all assignments $\mathbf{x}$ ensuring that $\sum_{k=1}^{r} P(\mathbf{X} = \mathbf{x}_k) = 1$. Each f_i does only depend on the values of variables corresponding to its clique C_i.

For the representation of both probabilistic and deterministic knowledge, we prefer the formalism of Markov logic [3] including potentials with values 0 as follows:

We specify deterministic knowledge with a set $\mathbf{Cl}_{det}$ of propositional clauses and for the specification of probabilistic knowledge we use a set of weighted propositional clauses (Cl_i, w_i), i.e., clauses Cl_i that are assigned weights w_i, with $w_i \in \mathbb{R}$.

Markov logic [3] allows to apply the formalism of Markov networks to knowledge representation with logic: Given a set $\mathbf{Cl} = \{Cl_1, ..., Cl_m\}$ of both weighted and deterministic propositional clauses there is a corresponding Markov network, where the Markov network graph is $\mathbf{G} = (\mathbf{X}, \mathbf{E})$ with $\mathbf{E}$ being the set of pairs of variables (X_i, X_j) appearing together in at least one Cl_i, and where each clause Cl_i is associated to a clique C_i. As a consequence, for each Cl_i there is a function $f_i \in \mathbf{F}$. We use the notation Cl_i^w and Cl_i^{det} to indicate that clause Cl_i is weighted resp. deterministic. In the presence of determinism, the full joint distribution for Markov logic can be specified with (1), where

$$f_i(\mathbf{x}_{C_i}) = \begin{cases} e^{w_i}, & \text{if } \mathbf{x}_{C_i} \text{ satisfies } Cl_i^w \\ 0, & \text{if } \mathbf{x}_{C_i} \text{ does not satisfy } Cl_i^{det} \\ 1, & \text{otherwise .} \end{cases} \qquad (2)$$

In case of a finite domain, a finite set $\mathbf{Cl}$ of propositional clauses for example is given by first converting a Markov logic network [3] with soft and hard formulas to a set of (weighted) first-order clauses followed by grounding these clauses. Formulas with probabilities are equivalent (and can be converted) to weighted formulas, if maximum entropy is assumed [10] such that $\mathbf{Cl}$ is also implicitly given in the presence of formulas with probabilities, if there is an additional set of deterministic clauses $\mathbf{Cl}_{det}$. For Bayesian networks, the full joint distribution of this formalism incorporating determinism has to be applied.

2.3 Queries

Asking for the probability $P(x_1, ..., x_t \mid \mathbf{e})$ of a set of assignments to variables $x_1, ..., x_t$ conditioned on a set of assignments to variables (the evidence) is a frequent query type in practice. In this paper we use a more general type of queries of the form $P(x_1, ..., x_t \mid \mathbf{Cl}_{det})$ where a set of assignments to variables is conditioned on the set $\mathbf{Cl}_{det} \subseteq \mathbf{Cl}$ of deterministic propositional clauses. Note that the set of all deterministic unit clauses corresponds to given evidence such that the more general query type extends the former one with deterministic dependencies.

3 Gibbs Sampling in Knowledge Representation

Markov chain Monte Carlo (MCMC) is a class of approximate inference algorithms walking through the state space $\Omega = \{\mathbf{x}_1, ..., \mathbf{x}_r\}$ (a state corresponds to a complete assignment). These algorithms are often applied to answer conditional probability queries. *Gibbs sampling* [4] is a widely-used special case of MCMC. With respect to an arbitrary but fixed order, each non-evidence variable X_i is sampled from $\mathbf{P}(X_i \mid x_1, ..., x_{i-1}, x_{i+1}, ..., x_n)$. This process is repeated N-times and the fraction of the number of states visited satisfying a given query is taken as the estimated conditional probability. In graph-based formalisms such as Markov networks, Gibbs sampling can be optimized by sampling from $\mathbf{P}(X_i \mid mb(X_i)) = \alpha <P(x_i, mb(X_i)), P(\neg x_i, mb(X_i))>$, where $mb(X_i)$ are the values of the Markov blanket of X_i (the values of the neighbours of X_i in $\mathbf{G}$) such that only clauses containing X_i have to be considered.

In case of a finite state space Ω, probability estimates of Gibbs sampling are known to approximate the correct probabilities, if the constructed Markov chain is *ergodic*. This can be assured if the chain is *aperiodic* (it is sufficient that the state graph is reflexive) and if the chain is *irreducible*, i.e., if for all pairs of states $\mathbf{x}_i, \mathbf{x}_j$ there is a number v such that there is a strictly positive probability of getting from $\mathbf{x}_i$ to $\mathbf{x}_j$ in v steps. If the probability distribution is strictly positive, finite-state Markov chains constructed with Gibbs sampling are known to be ergodic and to converge to a unique *stationary distribution* $\pi(\mathbf{X})$.

However, in the presence of deterministic dependencies, Markov chains constructed with Gibbs sampling usually are not ergodic such that the state graph often is broken into disconnected regions:

Example 1. Consider propositional variables X_1, X_2 with the deterministic constraint $X_1 \leftrightarrow X_2$. The state graph for applying Gibbs sampling is depicted in Fig. 1. If the chain starts with $(0,0)$, it will never reach $(1,1)$. Consequently, $\pi((0,0)) = 1$ and $\pi((1,1)) = 0$, though there is no information of any preference.[3]

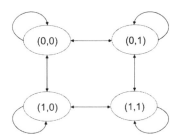

Fig. 1. Gibbs sampling state graph for two propositional variables

---

[3] Note that logical equivalence $X_1 \leftrightarrow X_2$ is an abbreviation for $X_1 \rightarrow X_2$ and $X_2 \rightarrow X_1$ such that it yields a cycle with respect to logical implication.

Similarly, in the presence of near-determinism (e.g. under consideration of very highly weighted clauses) Gibbs sampling involves transitions with probabilities near zero, leading to unacceptably long convergence times [11]. Thus, since (near-)determinism is required in many applications, Gibbs sampling in general is not sufficient for reasoning about knowledge.

4   Gibbs Sampling with Deterministic Horn Clauses

A simple Gibbs sampling procedure incorporating deterministic dependencies can be specified as in Algorithm 1.

Algorithm 1. Gibbs Sampling with Deterministic Dependencies

Input: Cl, $\mathbf{x}_0$, an assignment $x_1, ..., x_t$ of interest, N
Output: an estimate of $P(x_1, ..., x_t \mid \mathbf{Cl}_{det})$
begin
    counter $:= 0$;
    for j $:= 1$ to N **do**
        for all non-evidence variables X_i **do**
            sample x_i' from $\mathbf{P}(X_i \mid mb(X_i))$;
            if $(x_i \neq x_i')$ update $\mathbf{x}_0$;
            if $(x_1, ..., x_t$ is compatible with $\mathbf{x}_0)$ increase *counter*;
        end for
    end for
    return *counter*$/(N \times \#X_i)$;
end

Given a set of clauses **Cl**, the sampling procedure has to start with a state $\mathbf{x}_0$ satisfying $\mathbf{Cl}_{det}$. Such a state can e.g. be computed with the weighted MAX-SAT version of Walksat [7], a local search algorithm for the weighted satisfiability problem. All deterministic clauses are assigned with a weight greater than the sum l of all weights of weighted clauses. Then, a state violating clauses of total weight l or less satisfies $\mathbf{Cl}_{det}$ (cf. [7]). The algorithm will find a node that will be (near to) the mode of the distribution such that the Markov chain will approximate faster than initialized with an arbitrary solution.

In addition, a set of assignments and an integer N is required as input, and the Gibbs sampler computes an estimate for $P(x_1, ..., x_t \mid \mathbf{Cl}_{det})$. A complete sample is referred to as the result of sampling each non-evidence variable. The greater the number N of complete samples the more accurate the estimate for the probability will be. The procedure starts by initializing the counter for samples satisfying the query. Given **Cl**, $\mathbf{P}(X_i \mid mb(X_i))$ can be computed with (1) where functions f_i are only required if the corresponding clause contains X_i and are defined according to (2). If a bit-flip for X_i occurs, $\mathbf{x}_0$ is updated. If $\mathbf{x}_0$ satisfies the assignment of the query, *counter* is increased. Finally, the fraction of states satisfying the query is the estimate for $P(x_1, ..., x_t \mid \mathbf{Cl}_{det})$.

As can be seen from Example 1, the ergodicity of the Markov chain is not retained, if X_1 and X_2 are constrained to be equal. This is also the case if they are constrained to be different, i.e., by constraining $X_1 \oplus X_2$. In the following we show that Markov chains constructed with Gibbs sampling remain ergodic in the presence of determinism, if deterministic dependencies are specified with an acyclic set of Horn clauses $W_1, ..., W_p \rightarrow Z$ and $W_1, ..., W_p \rightarrow$.

Definition 1. *Let D be a set of deterministic dependencies. A Markov chain is irreducible with respect to D if for all pairs of states x_i, x_j both satisfying D, there is a number v such that there is a strictly positive probability of getting from x_i to x_j in v steps.*

If the initial state $\mathbf{x}_0$ satisfies D, i.e., $P(\mathbf{X} = \mathbf{x}_0) > 0$, the difference to irreducible Markov chains with strictly positive distributions is that there are states $\mathbf{x}_i$ with $P(\mathbf{X} = \mathbf{x}_i) = 0$ that are simply not stepped into.

Theorem 1. *A finite-state Markov chain constructed with Gibbs sampling is irreducible with respect to a set $\mathbf{Cl}_{det}$ of deterministic propositional Horn clauses that is acyclic with respect to logical implication.*

Proof. Definite Horn clauses $W_1, ..., W_p \rightarrow Z$ are falsified only if the variables $W_1,...,W_p$ are assigned 1 (*true*) and if Z is assigned 0 (*false*), and disjointness Horn clauses $W_1, ..., W_p \rightarrow$ only if the variables $W_1,...,W_p$ are assigned 1. If there are no cycles with respect to logical implication, an order $X_1 < ... < X_n$ can be defined for all variables such that for each definite Horn clause no variable Z is lower in the order than $W_1,...,W_p$. Variables only mentioned in disjointness clauses can then be added arbitrarily. Consider now two states $\mathbf{x} = (x_1, ..., x_n)$ and $\mathbf{y} = (y_1, ..., y_n)$ satisfying $\mathbf{Cl}_{det}$ and respecting the defined order. Then, variables corresponding to deterministic unit clauses Z resp. $\neg W_i$ are fixed to their known values. Let j be the leftmost position with $x_j \neq y_j$. If $X_j = 1$ and $Y_j = 0$, let $\mathbf{x}'$ be the state equal to $\mathbf{x}$ with the exception that $X_j = 0$ ($\mathbf{y}'$ is defined analogously, if $Y_j = 1$ and $X_j = 0$). Since $\mathbf{x}$ and $\mathbf{y}$ satisfy $\mathbf{Cl}_{det}$, $\mathbf{x}'$ (resp. $\mathbf{y}'$) is known to also satisfy $\mathbf{Cl}_{det}$: If the value of a variable is changed to 0, no additional disjointness Horn clause is falsified. A definite Horn clause in this case is only falsified, if the variable corresponds to Z and $W_1, ..., W_p$, known to be lower in the order than Z, are assigned with 1. This cannot be the case, since $\mathbf{y}$ (resp. $\mathbf{x}$) is known to satisfy $\mathbf{Cl}_{det}$, and $\mathbf{x}'$ and $\mathbf{y}$ (resp. $\mathbf{y}'$ and $\mathbf{x}$) are assigned the same values for $i = 1, ..., j$. The question of interest is now reduced to whether there is a path of states satisfying $\mathbf{Cl}_{det}$ from $\mathbf{x}'$ to $\mathbf{y}$ resp. from $\mathbf{y}'$ to $\mathbf{x}$. The process of changing the value of X_j resp. Y_j to 0 at the leftmost position j where $x_j \neq y_j$ can be continued until the two states are equal. $\square$

Further, by considering the process described in the proof, the minimal distance of a pair of states satisfying $\mathbf{Cl}_{det}$ in the state graph can be defined as the number of variables that are assigned with different values.

For every state $\mathbf{x}$ satisfying a set of deterministic Horn clauses there is a positive probability for a self-loop, i.e., for staying in $\mathbf{x}$ after sampling such that the Markov chain is aperiodic in the presence of these Horn clauses.

Corollary 1. *A finite-state Markov chain constructed with Gibbs sampling is ergodic with respect to a set of deterministic propositional Horn clauses that is acyclic with respect to logical implication.*

Finally, a finite-state Markov chain being ergodic with respect to a set of deterministic dependencies has a unique stationary distribution $\pi(\mathbf{X})$. Thus, a Gibbs sampling procedure such as Algorithm 1 is known to approximate the correct probabilities in the presence of deterministic Horn clauses as described above.

Example 2. Consider the deterministic inclusion axioms

$$\forall x\, Student(x)\ \ \rightarrow Person(x)$$
$$\forall x\, Professor(x) \rightarrow Person(x)$$

establishing a small taxonomy within the domain of a university. In acyclic Horn logic, *Student* and *Professor* can further be specified strictly disjoint,

$$\forall x\, Student(x), Professor(x) \rightarrow\ .$$

Also the domain and range of the binary predicate $Teaches(x, y)$ can be deterministically typed with

$$\forall x \forall y\, Teaches(x, y) \rightarrow Professor(x)$$
$$\forall x \forall y\, Teaches(x, y) \rightarrow Student(y)\ .$$

The set of all corresponding propositional deterministic Horn clauses is acyclic, since unary predicates are ordered according to a taxonomical structure (where it does not matter whether a variable $Student(s_1)$ or a variable $Professor(p_1)$ is higher in the order for arbitrary constants s_1 and p_1), and binary predicates only occur on the left side of definite clauses.

As usual in Gibbs sampling, but now in addition to the deterministic dependencies specified above, evidence can be specified as well as probabilistic dependencies with the expressivity of first-order logic (with the restriction of a finite set of associated complete assignments). An example for a probabilistic dependency within the university domain is the weighted clause

$$1.1\ \forall x \forall y\, Student(x), HasFriend(x, y) \rightarrow Student(y)\ .$$

Equivalence of Variables. In Example 1, it is shown that constraining equivalence does not preserve ergodicity. While this is generally the case, ergodicity can, however, be preserved in the special case of exactly two propositional variables X_1, X_2 involved in the equivalence, if all occurrences of one variable, e.g. X_2, are substituted with the other, X_1, until the last sample has been computed, followed by taking results for X_1 as results for X_2. This especially holds e.g. for groundings of symmetry $\forall x \forall y\, R(x, y) \leftrightarrow R(y, x)$ and inverse binary relations $\forall x \forall y\, R(x, y) \leftrightarrow S(y, x)$.

5 Conclusion

We have shown that Markov chains constructed with Gibbs sampling remain ergodic in the presence of deterministic Horn clauses that are acyclic with respect to logical implication. This is significantly different to previous results, where Gibbs sampling with (near-)determinism was considered to give poor results, regardless of the deterministic fragment.

Compared to [6], we extended the deterministic fragment to Horn clauses of arbitrary size including evidence. The approach is applicable to all domains in which the required expressivity for determinism does not extend acyclic Horn logic. Determinism extending this fragment still is not known to retain the ergodicity of Gibbs Markov chains and can be isolated in advance, if applicable.

Acyclic Horn logic includes fundamental dependencies used in most ontology-based applications. We have shown that the expressivity of Gibbs sampling can further be extended with deterministic symmetry, inverse binary relations and many other deterministic equivalences involving exactly two first-order atoms.

The mixing time of Gibbs sampling, i.e., the time in which the chain approximates its stationary distribution with an acceptable error, is known to be shorter the less strong the variables are correlated. Thus, the approach can be expected most appropriate for applications in which (near-)determinism and strong probabilistic dependencies are represented with acyclic Horn logic and probabilistic dependencies outside this fragment are rather weak (e.g. clauses are assigned only with weak or moderate weights).

It can be shown that acyclic dual Horn logic, the counterpart of acyclic Horn logic whose clauses contain at most one negative literal, does also preserve ergodicity of Gibbs Markov chains. However, it remains to explore possible opportunities for applications with this fragment.

Related work includes a framework incorporating determinism [2] as well as other sampling schemes introduced recently incorporating deterministic dependencies [11,5]. An open question is to what extent the approach can be incorporated to other MCMC algorithms.

References

1. Baader, F., Calvanese, D., McGuinness, D.L., Nardi, D., Patel-Schneider, P.F.: The Description Logic Handbook: Theory, Implementation and Applications. Cambridge University Press (January 2003)
2. Dechter, R., Mateescu, R.: Mixtures of Deterministic-Probabilistic Networks and their and/or Search Space. In: Proc. of the 20th Conference on Uncertainty in Artificial Intelligence (UAI), pp. 120–129 (2004)
3. Domingos, P., Richardson, M.: Markov Logic: A Unifying Framework for Statistical Relational Learning. In: Introduction to Statistical Relational Learning, pp. 339–371. MIT Press, Cambridge (2007)
4. Geman, S., Geman, D.: Stochastic Relaxation, Gibbs Distribution and Bayesian Restoration of Images. IEEE Transactions on Pattern Analysis and Machine Intelligence 6, 721–741 (1984)
5. Gogate, V., Domingos, P.: Formula-Based Probabilistic Inference. In: Proc. of the 26th Conference on Uncertainty in Artificial Intelligence (UAI), Catalina Island (2010)
6. Gries, O., Möller, R.: Gibbs Sampling in Probabilistic Description Logics with Deterministic Dependencies. In: Proc. of the 1st International Workshop on Uncertainty in Description Logics, Edinburgh (2010)

7. Jiang, Y., Kautz, H., Selman, B.: Solving Problems with Hard and Soft Constraints Using a Stochastic Algorithm for MAX-SAT. In: Proc. of the 1st Joint Workshop on Artificial Intelligence and Operations Research (1995)

8. McCarthy, J.: Applications of Circumscription in Formalizing Common Sense Knowledge. Artificial Intelligence 28, 89–116 (1986)

9. Pearl, J.: Probabilistic Reasoning in Intelligent Systems. Morgan Kaufmann, San Mateo (1988)

10. Pietra, S.D., Pietra, V.J.D., Lafferty, J.D.: Inducing Features of Random Fields. IEEE Transactions on Pattern Analysis and Machine Intelligence 19(4), 380–393 (1997)

11. Poon, H., Domingos, P.: Sound and Efficient Inference with Probabilistic and Deterministic Dependencies. In: Proc. of AAAI 2006, July 2006, Boston, Massachusetts (2006)

Author Index